Duygu Damar

Wilful Misconduct in International Transport Law

Springer

Dr. Duygu Damar
Max-Planck-Institut für ausländisches
und internationales Privatrecht
Mittelweg 187
20148 Hamburg
Germany
Damar@mpipriv.de
duygudamar@gmail.com

Dissertation zur Erlangung der Doktorwürde
an der Fakultät für Rechtswissenschaft der Universität Hamburg
Vorgelegt von: Duygu Damar
Erstgutachter: Prof. Dr. Dr. h.c. Jürgen Basedow, LL.M. (Harvard)
Zweitgutachter: Prof. Dr. Ulrich Magnus
Tag der mündlichen Prüfung: 26. Januar 2011

ISSN 1614-2462   e-ISSN 1867-9587
ISBN 978-3-642-21508-7   e-ISBN 978-3-642-21509-4
DOI 10.1007/978-3-642-21509-4
Springer Heidelberg Dordrecht London New York

Library of Congress Control Number: 2011933106

Cover design: WMXDesign GmbH, Heidelberg

Printed on acid-free paper

Springer is part of Springer Science+Business Media (www.springer.com)

To my family

Preface

For the preparatory work on the new Turkish Commercial Code of 2011, the question of how to translate the common law legal term "wilful misconduct" into Turkish should have been clarified. Dr. *iur.* F. Kerim Atamer, who was the member of the Commission in charge of the preparation of the Draft of the Code, attracted my attention to the problem, thus providing the starting point of this work. Upon having been accepted as a scholar at the International Max Planck Research School for Maritime Affairs (IMPRS), I conducted this study under the supervision of Prof. Dr. Dr. *h.c.* Jürgen Basedow, LL.M. (Harvard), Director of the Max Planck Institute for Comparative and International Private Law. I am most grateful for his support, encouragement and detailed advice, without which this work would not have been completed. I would also like to thank Prof. Dr. Ulrich Magnus, Director of the Seminar of Foreign and Private International Law of the Faculty of Law at the University of Hamburg and Judge at the Hanseatic Court of Appeal, for the timely submission of the second opinion on my thesis. I am also thankful to Prof. Dr. Dr. *h.c.* Peter Ehlers, former Director of the Federal Maritime and Hydrographic Agency of Germany, and to Prof. Dr. Rainer Lagoni, Managing Director of the Institute of Maritime Law and the Law of the Sea at the University of Hamburg, for their informative seminars on the law of the sea which helped me foster a wider view and a better understanding of how maritime law and the law of the sea interlink.

I wish to express my particular gratitude to two individuals. Firstly, I am grateful to Dr. *iur.* F. Kerim Atamer, Director of the Dr. Nüsret-Semahat Arsel Research Center for International Business Law and Associate Professor for Maritime, Insurance and Transport Law at the Koc University in Istanbul, who has always fully supported and encouraged me in my career, especially in becoming a scholar at the IMPRS, from whom I have learned a great deal and, who invested much time and effort into my personal development as a research fellow in maritime, insurance and transport law. Secondly, I am grateful to Dr. *iur.* Yeşim M. Atamer, Associate Professor for Civil Law and Comparative Civil Law at the Istanbul Bilgi University, for her support and encouragement in general and specifically as regards my application to the IMPRS.

I am most thankful to the IMPRS and its directors for granting me the scholarship which made my stay and my research in Hamburg and in Cambridge possible. For their help during my two-month research stay at the Squire Law Library at the University of Cambridge, I am deeply thankful to Professor Malcolm A. Clarke, Professor of Commercial Contract Law at the University of Cambridge, and to Dr. *iur.* Jens M. Scherpe. I am, further, deeply thankful to the staff members of the libraries of the Max Planck Institute for Comparative and International Private Law and the Squire Law Library at the University of Cambridge, who have been very patient with my endless book requests and inquiries on the where-abouts of various legal sources. I am also thankful to Michael Friedman for the speedy proof reading of the thesis.

I should not forget to thank all my close friends for supporting and encouraging me. However, I am above all deeply grateful to my family: to my father Dr. *med.* Hüseyin Damar, my mother Ayhan Damar, my sister Sevgi Damar and my brother H. Selim Damar, for their endless love, support, encouragement and understanding, without which no single achievement in my life would have been possible.

Duygu Damar
Hamburg, May 2011

Outline Table of Contents

Table of Contents

Abbreviations and Citations

A.C.	Appeal Cases
AcP	Archiv für die civilistische Praxis
AG	Amtsgericht
AL	Air Law
Air & SL	Air & Space Law
Air LR	Air Law Review
AJIL	American Journal of International Law
ALR	Archiv für Luftrecht
A.M.C.	American Maritime Cases
Am. J. Comp. L.	American Journal of Comparative Law
Anm.	Anmerkung
Annals Air & Space	Annals of Air and Space Law
Art.	Article / Artikel
Atl. 2d	Atlantic Reporter 2nd
Aufl.	Auflage
AS	Amtliche Sammlung der Bundesgesetze und Verordnungen
Batider	Banka ve Ticaret Hukuku Dergisi (Banking and Commercial Law Journal)
Bd.	Band
BGB	Bürgerliches Gesetzbuch
BGBl.	Bundesgesetzblatt
BGE	Entscheidungen des Schweizerischen Bundesgerichts
BGH	Bundesgerichtshof
BGHZ	Entscheidungen des Bundesgerichthofes in Zivilsachen
BIMCO	Baltic and International Maritime Council
BK (1926)	1926 tarihli Borçlar Kanunu (Turkish Code of Obligations of 1926)
BK (2011)	2011 tarihli Borçlar Kanunu (Turkish Code of Obligations of 2011)
Bus. LR	Business Law Review
c.	cilt
CA	Court of Appeal(s)
Ch.	Chapter
CITEJA	Comité international technique d'experts juridiques aériens

C.L.R.	Commonwealth Law Reports
CMI	Comité Maritime International
Com. Cas.	Commercial Cases
DC	District Court
DenizHD	Deniz Hukuku Dergisi (Maritime Law Journal)
DePaul Bus. L. J.	DePaul Business Law Journal
Dir. Mar.	Il Diritto Marittimo
Diss.	Dissertation
DLR	Dominion Law Reports
DVIS	Deutscher Verein für Internationales Seerecht
Ed.	Edition
EJCCL	European Journal of Commercial Contract Law
E.R.	The English Reports
ETL	European Transport Law
EWHC	High Court of England and Wales
Exch.	Exchequer Reports
F.2d	Federal Reporter 2nd
F.3d	Federal Reporter 3rd
Fed. Cas.	Federal Cases
fn.	footnote
FCR	Federal Court Reports (1982 - ...) (Australia)
F.R.D.	Federal Rules Decisions
F.Supp.	Federal Supplement
F.Supp.2d	Federal Supplement, Second Series
Hansa	Zeitschrift für Schiffahrt, Schiffbau, Häfen
HansOLG	Hanseatisches Oberlandesgericht
HmbSeeRep	Hamburger Seerechts-Report
HmbSchRZ	Hamburger Zeitschrift für Schifffahrtsrecht
HD	Hukuk Dairesi (Civil Law Division)
HGB	Handelsgesetzbuch
HGK	Hukuk Genel Kurulu (Turkish Court of Cassation, Appellate Division for Civil Law Matters)
HL	House of Lords
Hou. L. R.	Houston Law Review
Hrsg.	Herausgeber
ICLQ	International and Comparative Law Quarterly
IJIL	International Journal of Insurance Law
IJOSL	International Journal of Shipping Law
Int. I.L.R.	International Insurance Law Review
Int.M.L.	International Maritime Law
IPRax	Praxis des internationalen Privat- und Verfahrensrechts
İÜHFM	İstanbul Üniversitesi Hukuk Fakültesi Mecmuası (Istanbul University Faculty of Law Journal)
J. Air L.	Journal of Air Law
J. Air L. & Com.	Journal of Air Law and Commerce

J.B.L.	Journal of Business Law
J. Mar. L. & Com.	Journal of Maritime Law and Commerce
JIML	Journal of International Maritime Law
JPIL	Journal of Personal Injury Litigation
JuS	Juristische Schulung
JZ	Juristenzeitung
K.B.	Law Reports, King's Bench Division
KBD	King's Bench Division
LG	Landgericht
L.J. (N.S.)	Law Journal Reports, New Series
L.J. (Q.B.)	Law Journal Reports (Queen's Bench Division)
L.T.	Law Times Reports
Ll. L. Rep.	Lloyd's List Law Reports (1919-1950)
Lloyd's Rep.	Lloyd's Law Reports
LMCLQ	Lloyd's Maritime and Commercial Law Quarterly
Mar. Policy	Marine Policy
McGill L. J.	McGill Law Journal
MDR	Monatsschrift für deutsches Recht
MIA	Marine Insurance Act
MK	Türk Medeni Kanunu (Turkish Civil Code)
MLAANZ Journal	Maritime Law Association of Australia and New Zealand Journal
MLR	Modern Law Review
MSA	Merchant Shipping Act
NLJ	New Law Journal
NJW	Neue Juristische Wochenschrift
NJW-RR	NJW-Rechtsprechungs-Report Zivilrecht
NSWSC	Supreme Court of New South Wales Decisions
N.Y.S.2d	New York Supplement 2nd
NYU L. Rev.	New York University Law Review
N.Y.U.L.Q. Rev.	New York University Law Quarterly Review
OGH	Oberster Gerichtshof der Republik Österreich
OLG	Oberlandesgericht
Ox. J. Leg. Stud.	Oxford Journal of Legal Studies
para.	paragraph
PDAD	Probate, Divorce and Admiralty Division
Pol. Y.B. Int'l L.	Polish Yearbook of International Law
Q.B.D.	Law Reports, Queen's Bench Division
QBD	Queen's Bench Division
RabelsZ	Rabels Zeitschrift
RGBl.	Reichsgesetzblatt
RIW	Recht der internationalen Wirtschaft
Rn.	Randnummer
RRa	ReiseRecht aktuell
S.C.	Session Cases
S. Cal. L. Rev.	Southern California Law Review

S.Ct.	Supreme Court Reporter
SCULR	Southern Cross University Law Review
SDR	Special Drawing Right
So.2d	Southern Reporter, Second Series
SOLAS	International Convention for the Safety of life at Sea
Stan. L. Rev.	Stanford Law Review
Stat.	United States Statutes at Large
Tex. Int. L.J.	Texas International Law Journal
TranspR	Transportrecht
TTK (1956)	1956 tarihli Türk Ticaret Kanunu (Turkish Commercial Code of 1956)
TTK (2011)	2011 tarihli Türk Ticaret Kanunu (Turkish Commercial Code of 2011)
Tul. L. Rev.	Tulane Law Review
Tul. Mar. L. J.	Tulane Maritime Law Journal
UK	United Kingdom
ULR	Uniform Law Review
UNCITRAL	United Nations Commission on International Trade Law
US	United States
U.S.	United States Reports
U.S.F. Mar. L.J.	University of San Francisco Maritime Law Journal
USAvR	United States Aviation Reports
US&CAvR	United States and Canadian Aviation Reports
V.	Volume
Va. L. Rev.	Virginia Law Review
Vill. L. Rev.	Villanova Law Review
VersR	Versicherungsrecht
VVG	Versicherungsvertragsgesetz
WL	Westlaw Citations
W.L.R.	Weekly Law Reports
Yale LJ	Yale Law Journal
YD	Yargıtay Dergisi (Journal of Turkish Jurisprudence)
YKD	Yargıtay Kararları Dergisi (Journal of Turkish Court of Cassation Jurisprudence)
ZEuP	Zeitschrift für europäisches Privatrecht
ZHR	Zeitschrift für das gesamte Handelsrecht und Wirtschaftsrecht
ZIEV	Zeitschrift für den internationalen Eisenbahnverkehr (Bulletin des transports internationaux par chemins de fer)
ZLW	Zeitschrift für Luft- und Weltraumrecht
ZStW	Zeitschrift für die gesamte Strafrechtwissenschaft

§ 1 Introduction

A person liable is not entitled to limit his liability, "if it is proved that the damage resulted from an act or omission of [the person liable][1] done with intent to cause damage or recklessly and with knowledge that damage would probably result". This provision, though sometimes with small but important differences, is an invariable and indispensable part of almost every international regime with regard to the carriage of goods and passengers. It adopts the principle that liability cannot be limited in case of a certain type of faulty conduct, which is known as wilful misconduct.

Breaking the liability limits in case of wilful misconduct is almost as old as the concept of limitation of liability. Limitation of liability has been the most important privilege adopted for carriers and shipowners. The roots of, and policy behind, the limitation of liability can be found in its historical development, which will be explained briefly in chapter 2 of this work. It is essential to understand the policy behind the limitation of liability which has been harshly criticized in recent years and to understand why limitation of liability cannot be sustained in cases of wilful misconduct.

Naturally, under modern transport law regimes, wilful misconduct is not the only situation whereby the carrier or shipowner loses his right to limit. For example, Art. 4 (4) of the Warsaw Convention stipulates that an air carrier is not entitled to limit his liability if he does not issue a luggage ticket for every piece of luggage he accepts. Similarly, in carriage by sea, a carrier cannot avail himself of the provisions which limit his liability if he has issued an *ad valorem* bill of lading (Art. IV (5)(a) of the Hague/Visby Rules). There are also some doctrines where unlimited liability has been based on a substantial breach of the carriage contract. Nevertheless, this study will concentrate only on wilful misconduct, since examination of other provisions and doctrines where carrier cannot limit his liability would be beyond the scope of this work. However, where necessary, those provisions and doctrines will be mentioned briefly.

Wilful misconduct is a term of common law. The first appearance of the degree of fault with regard to admiralty law can be traced back to the UK's Merchant Shipping Act of 1894, but the first literal use of the term with regard to transport law was in the carriage by rail cases, again in the UK. The first act which mentions the term wilful misconduct literally is the UK's Marine Insurance Act of 1905. Chapter 3 is devoted to this historical development and the meaning of the term in English law. The explanation for causation and procedural law issues will be explored within the same chapter since they only involve the explanation of English law.

---

[1] Due to the complex legal relations in transport law, the variety of persons legally responsible can range from servants and agents to carriers or shipowners. Depending on the international regime applicable to legal dispute, a carrier might also be vicariously liable for his servants' and agents' conduct, which gives rise to unlimited liability.

The first adoption of the term wilful misconduct in an international convention was with the Warsaw Convention regarding carriage of goods and passengers by air in 1929. The Convention has been adopted officially in the French language (Art. 36), and in order to break the air carrier's liability, the carrier should have been guilty of *dol*, or an equivalent degree of fault (Art. 25). The term wilful misconduct is used in the provision's English translation. When the Convention was amended by the Hague Protocol in 1955, the provision regarding breaking the liability limits was also amended; and it was decided to define the degree of fault which gives rise to unlimited liability, instead of using national legal terms to refer to certain degrees of fault. Thereby, the definition adopted by almost every transport law convention came into existence.

In this study, chapter 4 is devoted to a detailed examination of the historical development of the definition adopted by the Hague Protocol and the examination of the requisites of the degree of fault adopted by that definition. Chapter 5 will provide a detailed study of unlimited liability within the international maritime conventions, which have invariably adopted the unlimited liability principle so long as the carrier or shipowner is personally at fault. Due to the fact that, today, almost every carrier or shipowner is a corporation, attribution of grave fault to a corporation and the effect of the ISM Code on the attribution of fault will also be examined in detail within the same chapter.

The situation in international regimes with regard to carriage by road, rail, inland waterways and multimodal transport will be discussed briefly in chapter 6. Thereafter, causation, together with the burden and standard of proof issues under relevant international conventions will be examined in chapter 7.

In discussing the problems which have arisen under the international transport law regimes, it is of great importance to find the correct meaning of legal provisions, which can be done by using the rules of interpretation. According to the Vienna Convention on the Law of Treaties 1969, "a treaty shall be interpreted in good faith in accordance with the ordinary meaning to be given to the terms of the treaty in their context and in the light of its object and purpose" (Art. 31). Nevertheless, preparatory work on the treaty and the circumstances of its conclusion may be used as supplementary means of interpretation in order to confirm the result gathered from the general rule of interpretation, or to determine exactly the meaning of the provision, if its meaning is ambiguous (Art. 32). Taking into consideration these universally accepted rules of interpretation, the *trevaux preparatoires* of the relevant international conventions constitute an important part of this study.

Most of the issues regarding wilful misconduct have been resolved in the course of the development of international transport law. For instance, it was previously disputed whether the term "the carrier" under the Hague/Visby Rules Art. IV (5)(e) refers only to the carrier himself, or includes servants and agents of the carrier as well. Art. 4 of the 1976 London Convention and Art. 61 (1) of the Rotterdam Rules put an end to the debate by referring explicitly to a "personal act or omission".

Nonetheless, there is still an unresolved issue with regard to wilful misconduct: To which degree of fault does the term wilful misconduct refer under civil law?

There are different answers to this question, which generally refer either to *dolus eventualis* or advertent gross negligence. Chapter 8 will try to ascertain the equivalent degree of fault to wilful misconduct under the continental law system, by defining the degrees of fault and comparing the prerequisites of wilful misconduct with prerequisites of different degrees of fault under civil law.

However, difficulty emerges with such a comparison as the degrees of fault have not been defined and studied in a detailed manner in private law, since it has been unnecessary. On the other hand, degrees of fault have been examined in a detailed manner under criminal law, when criminal liability is at stake. Thus, in trying to ascertain the equivalent degree of fault to wilful misconduct under civil law, the criminal law degrees of fault will also be taken into consideration.

The last point that is worth emphasizing is the spelling of the term "wilful". The term in its modern usage is "wilful"; however it used to be spelled also as "willful". In this work, the modern usage of the term is preferred. In direct quotations, however, the usage in the quoted text has not been changed.

Part I Historical Background

§ 2 Limitation of Liability and Wilful Misconduct

Although liability under general tort and contract law principles is not limited to a certain amount, liability arising under a carriage contract is limited by the majority of international transport conventions and national legislatures. Undoubtedly, limitation of liability is one of the most important elements of shipping law since, today, the carrier's liability insurance system is based exclusively upon it[1]. However, it is also said that the limitation of liability is like "smoking" for the legislators, "difficult to justify, but also difficult to quit"[2]. It is rightfully stated that the limitation of liability, which is nowadays considered to be a basic right rather than a privilege[3], is not a matter of justice, but merely a matter of public policy[4]. Nevertheless, there are certain reasons given to justify the "essential departure from the current rules of civil law"[5]; and this chapter will outline those reasons, together with their criticism and the reasons for breaking those limits.

---

[1] *Cleton*, p. 16; *Hodges/Hill*, pp. 152-153; *Mandaraka-Sheppard*, p. 863; *Buglass*, 1364; *Haak*, 163; see also *Place v. Norwich & New York Transp. Co.* 118 U.S. 468, 495 (Supreme Court of the US, 1886).

[2] *Røsæg*, 294.

[3] *Gaskell, Hamburg Rules*, p. 161.

[4] *The Bramley Moore* [1963] 2 Lloyd's Rep. 429, 437 (CA); *Caltex Singapore Pte. Ltd. and Others v. BP Shipping Ltd.* [1996] 1 Lloyd's Rep. 286, 299 (QBD); *Place v. Norwich & New York Transp. Co.* 118 U.S. 468, 495 (Supreme Court of the US, 1886); *Polish Steam Ship Co. v. Atlantic Maritime Co. (The Garden City (No. 2))* [1984] 2 Lloyd's Rep. 37, 44 (CA) *per* Justice Griffiths: "The right of shipowners to limit their liability is of long standing and generally accepted by the trading nations of the world. It is a right given to promote the general health of trade and is in truth no more than a way of distributing the insurance risk."; *Gold/Chircop/Kindred*, p. 718; *Mandaraka-Sheppard*, p. 863; *Killingbeck*, 2; *Makins*, 653-654.

[5] *Milde*, p. 42.

A. Unlimited Liability

I. General Principle

A party who commits a tort or who fails to properly perform a contract is liable for the damage he caused under tort or contract law principles. The person liable might be required to specifically perform the contract or to pay some designated amount in order to compensate for the damage he caused. Most broadly, the courts impose liability up to a specific amount of compensation. Under every legal regime, there are certain principles to determine the extent of this liability. The person liable can be required, *e.g.* to compensate the full amount of the object which was the subject of total loss, or to compensate the difference between the former and the present value of the goods which suffered damages, or even to compensate the pure economic loss in some cases. In the event of physical injury to or death of a person, again, there are certain principles for remunerating the injuries, disadvantages or losses sustained by the injured person or his relatives.

In all these cases, there is no cap on the amount of the compensation. The wrongdoer is obliged to pay the full amount of damages he caused, once those damages have been assessed[6]. The damages are to be assessed irrespective of whether the liability is a strict one or a fault-based liability. Similarly, it is also of no importance whether damages were caused by intentional wrongdoing or negligence. The wrongdoer should restore the aggrieved party to its former state, as if he had not broken the contract or committed a tort[7]. This principle is known as "*restitutio in integrum*".

II. Exceptions

There are some legal exceptions to the principle of unlimited liability. Limitation of liability for certain assets is the first example of such an exception. Under inheritance law principles, heirs inherit both rights and obligations of the deceased. However, under German law, their liability for these obligations is legally limited to the rights and assets they inherited if certain conditions are met. So, if the financial amount of obligations is higher than the rights and assets being inherited, heirs are not obliged to fulfil the obligations in the excessive amount[8]. Similarly, under Turkish law, the Turkish State is responsible for the obligations of the deceased only up to the amount of the totality of the rights and assets in the inheritance, should the Turkish State be the heir where the deceased has no other heirs at all[9].

---

[6]   *Griggs, Limitation,* 369; *Killingbeck,* 2.
[7]   *Palandt/Sprau,* Einf v § 823 Rn. 17; *Markesinis and Deakin,* p. 951; *Williams/ Hepple,* pp. 15, 28; *Winfield & Jolowicz,* para. 22-16; MünchKommBGB – *Oetker,* § 249 Rn. 98; *Larenz,* pp. 424-425.
[8]   § 1975 BGB.
[9]   MK Art. 501, 631.

It is also legally possible to limit the liability which may arise from a contractual relationship by way of contractual clauses. Such a limitation depends solely on the will of the parties to the contract. Parties can agree to limit the liability to certain assets or up to a certain financial amount. Nevertheless, such a limitation is not applicable if the liable party has broken the contract through grossly negligent, reckless or intentional conduct. There are also strict rules regarding consumer contracts and general terms and conditions[10].

Liability can also be limited up to a certain amount, which is the case under transport law. However, this was not the case at the beginning of the development of transport law principles. Thus, the historical development of the limited liability in transport law should be briefly considered.

B. Limited Liability in Transport Law

I. Historical Development

1. Carriage by sea

a) First appearance

Limitation of liability was first seen in maritime carriage[11], since carriage by sea was the first means of cargo carriage. Nevertheless, it is unknown when the limitation of liability was first applied in a maritime law case and what its origin is. Although it is possible to find principles regarding the vicarious liability of shipowners pertaining to contractual obligations and tort under Roman law, there is no clear principle as to the limitation of this liability[12]. Nonetheless, the inspiration might be the *noxae deditio* principle under Roman law, which is the first general principle of limitation of liability. Under this principle, the owner of property could satisfy a claim by surrendering the property which occasioned the loss[13]. The principle was generally applied in cases where an animal or a slave caused damage. Nevertheless, it is rightfully stressed that there is no apparent reason for the principle not to be applied to seagoing ships. Therefore, under the principle a shipowner was able to abandon his ship, or the ship and freight, or even the ship, freight and cargo on board; thus limiting his liability[14].

---

[10] See *e.g.* UK Unfair Contract Terms Act 1977; §§ 276, 277, 305 *et seqq* BGB; BK (1926) Art. 99 and BK (2011) Art. 20-25 (Turkish Code of Obligations of 2011 will enter into force on 1st July 2011), 115; Tüketicinin Korunması Hakkında Kanun (Turkish Consumer Protection Act of 1995).

[11] For a detailed examination of the development of shipping law see Edgar *Gold,* Maritime Transport: The Evolution of International Marine Policy and Shipping Law, Toronto 1981.

[12] See the references given in *The Rebecca* Fed. Cas. 20 (1895), 373, 376 (DC Maine, 1831).

[13] *Donovan,* 1000; *Kierr,* 639.

[14] *Grime, 1976 Limitation Convention,* p. 306. However see William *Lewis*/Emil *Boyens,* Das deutsche Seehandelsrecht, Leipzig 1897, pp. 183 *et seqq.*

A special type of contract, *contrat de commande*, developed before the twelfth century, can also be the source of the limitation of liability. Under this type of contract, it was possible for an investor to use his capital together with a merchant or a mariner, and be entitled to receive a proportion of the profits. However, the key point was that the investor was never to be held liable for more than the amount he invested into the venture[15]. This type of contract also developed close cooperation between investors and mariners; and the *societé en commandite*, a type of limited partnership, finds its roots in this cooperation[16].

Nonetheless, it is believed that the limitation of liability specifically for maritime carriage was first developed in Italy in the eleventh century. The commercial code adopted for the Republic of Amalphia in Italy, the Amalphitan Table, adopts a system of a common fund, which is the money contributed to the ship's voyage[17] and in certain cases orders respective claims to be made against this common fund[18]. Moreover, the Table has provisions regarding the limitation of part-owners' liability[19].

Similarly, the *Consolat de Mar* of Barcelona[20] had express provisions on limitation. Pursuant to these rules, shipowners' liability arising out of cargo damage or

---

[15] *Donovan*, 1001; *Jefferies*, 274-275; *Haddon-Cave*, p. 235; *Staring*, 322; *The Rebecca* Fed. Cas. 20 (1895), 373, 378-379 (DC Maine, 1831).

[16] *Kierr*, 639; *The Rebecca* Fed. Cas. 20 (1895), 373, 379 (DC Maine, 1831).

[17] See Amalphitan Table Art. 1 and the explanations in the Black Book of the Admiralty, V. 4, p. 3 fn. 3.

[18] *E.g.* Art. 45.

[19] Art. 8: "if any of the part-owners do not wish to risk their share which they have in the vessel, in any particular voyage, and the master of the vessel sails with his adventure, and the vessel suffers shipwreck or incurs some disaster, the aforesaid vessel ought to be sold, and together with what remains of the adventure ought to be divided in shares proportionate to their respective ventures amongst those persons who risked their property in the ship; and those part-owners, who did not wish to risk their shares in that voyage, ought to have recourse against the other property of the master, who has acted against their wishes, *and they have no action against the ship or the part-owners, who have shared in the common adventure*" (Emphasis added); Art. 62: "[...] and if the shares of the owners do not suffice to pay the aforesaid debts, [...]", for the original Italian text and the translation, see Black Book of the Admiralty, V. 4, pp. 8-9, 46-49.

[20] Reprinted in English in Stanley S. *Jados*, Consulate of the Sea and Related Documents, Alabama 1975. See especially ch. 34 (Which of the creditors has the legal priority to a claim when a vessel is sold after completing its first voyage): "[...] If the equity of the patron of the vessel who had arranged these loans is insufficient to satisfy the claims of the creditors, the difference will be met by the guarantors if they had guaranteed that the patron would repay these loans; otherwise they will not be held responsible for the repayment of these loans [...]", ch. 186 (Cargo damages aboard the vessel): "[...] The shareholders in the vessel are responsible to the degree of their investment in the vessel.", ch. 227 (Damage caused to a vessel due to lack of proper equipment aboard): "[...] The shareholders of the vessel shall not be required to share in the payment of these damages beyond the amount they had invested in the vessel.", ch. 239 (Purchase of essential provisions and equipment for the vessel): "[...] If no profit had been made, but rather a loss incurred,

the masters' transactions for ship supplies was limited to their shares in the ship in order to encourage investment in shipping[21].

Thereafter, the idea of the limitation of liability spread from Italy and Spain, throughout Europe through the Statutes of Hamburg of 1603, the Hanseatic Ordinances of 1614 and 1644, the maritime codes of Sweden dated 1667, the Marine Ordinance of Louis XIV dated 1681 and the 1721 Ordinance of Rotterdam. Under all these acts, it was possible for the shipowner to limit his liability up to the ship's full amount or to abandon his ship to satisfy the claims, so that his other property was exempt from respective claims unless the shipowner had agreed otherwise[22]. The incorporation of the French Ordinance of 1681 – which itself has been a model for regulations in countries such as the Netherlands, Spain and Prussia[23] – into the *Code Napoléon* (1807) played a vital role in spreading the limitation of liability throughout Europe and Latin America[24]. Finally, limitation of liability for maritime claims reached England in the eighteenth century[25] and the USA in the nineteenth century[26].

---

every shareholder is bound to reimburse the patron the amount due from him, dependent upon the amount of his investment in the vessel".

[21] *Donovan*, 1001-1002; *Özçayır*, p. 300; *Sprague*, 568-569; *Staring*, 323; *The Rebecca* Fed. Cas. 20 (1895), 373, 376 (DC Maine, 1831).

[22] *Özçayır*, p. 300; *Kierr*, 640; *Donovan*, 1003; *Griggs, Limitation*, 370; *Puttfarken*, Rn. 870; *Stachow*, p. 44; *Staring*, 323; *The Rebecca* Fed. Cas. 20 (1895), 373, 376-377 (DC Maine, 1831); *The 'Scotland'* 105 U.S. 24, 28 (Supreme Court of the US, 1882) *per* Justice Bradley. According to the 1681 Ordinance Title Fourth (II), "the owners of the ship shall be answerable for the deeds of the master; but shall be discharged, abandoning their ship and freight" (reprinted in English in Fed. Cas. 30 (1897), 1203), see also *Donovan*, 1004; *Seward*, p. 162; *Chen, Limitation*, p. xiv; *Sprague*, 569; *The Rebecca* Fed. Cas. 20 (1895), 373, 377 (DC Maine, 1831). It should also be remembered that persons contracting with the master for the ship's expenditure were provided with bottomry, see *Sprague*, 570; *The Rebecca* Fed. Cas. 20 (1895), 373, 376 (DC Maine, 1831).

[23] *Griggs, Limitation*, 370; *Killingbeck*, 2; *Sprague*, 570; *The Main v. Williams* 152 U.S. 122, 127 (Supreme Court of the US, 1894) *per* Justice Brown.

[24] *Donovan*, 1003-1004; *Özçayır*, p. 300.

[25] For more information see *infra* B I 1 b.

[26] Limitation of Liability Act, 1851, see *Angino*, 725. Before the federal statute, some states already passed acts regarding limited shipowners' liability modelled on the corresponding English provisions, see *Donovan*, 1009-1010; *Kierr*, 640-641; *Chen, Limitation*, p. xiv; *Jefferies*, 277; *Sprague*, 574-577. For more information on the historical background and the federal statute see *Donovan*, 1011 *et seqq.*; *Kierr*, 641-643; *Chen, Limitation*, p. xiv; *Buglass*, 1365-1367; *Jefferies*, 277 *et seqq.*; *Rein*, 1263-1264; *Sprague*, 577 *et seqq.*; Walter W. *Eyer*, Shipowners' Limitation of Liability – New Directions for an Old Doctrine, (1963-1964) 16 Stanford Law Review 370.

b) England

The Rules of Oleron, dated 1150, which are a source of English admiralty law, make no mention of limitation of shipowner's liability[27]. The enactment regarding limitation of liability in England is, in fact, the result of a theft. In a case where the master of the ship stole the Portuguese gold carried on board, the court ruled that the shipowner was personally liable for the full amount[28].

Shipowners, being very unhappy about the outcome of the judgement, subsequently addressed a petition to the English Parliament, stating that they did not expect to be exposed to such a risk, or to any greater liability than the amount of the ship and freight together, when they became shipowners. They complained that such a liability is insupportable and unreasonable and that no shipowner in other nations is subject to such a liability. Further, they stated that if they were to be held liable even if they are not personally at fault, this would discourage trade and navigation[29].

Thereupon, in 1734, the English Parliament passed an act to determine the extent to which shipowners shall be responsible for the acts of masters and crew. The Act is known shortly as the Responsibility of Shipowners Act, 1734[30]. By virtue of this Act, it was allowed for the shipowners to limit their liability to the value of the ship and freight in case of theft by master or crew. Clearly, the Act was adopted to promote the development of the merchant fleet and to encourage the investment in the shipping business despite the perils of the sea[31].

After another case[32], where it was discussed whether the wording of the Act was broad enough to also cover cases where the theft was not committed by master or crew, but the necessary intelligence for the robbery was given by a member of the crew, shipowners again petitioned the English Parliament. Subsequently, the extent of the Responsibility of Shipowners Act was broadened in 1786. It was adapted that shipowners are not liable provided that the act or omission by the master or crew occurred without the privity of the shipowner[33]. The "privity of the shipowner" principle was accepted gladly and therefore remained in the Act. Further legislation concerning the extent of the limited liability followed; *e.g.* in 1813 it was extended to cover collision cases[34]. Finally, by virtue of the Merchant Ship-

---

[27] *Donovan*, 1005; *Özçayır*, p. 305; *Jefferies*, 276; *Sprague*, 569. Reprinted in English in Fed. Cas. 30 (1897), 1171 and in the Black Book of the Admiralty, V. 1, pp. 88 *et seqq.*

[28] *Boucher v. Lawson* 95 E.R. 53 (KBD, 1733).

[29] *Donovan*, 1007; *Coghlin*, pp. 236-237; *Mustill*, 496; *Özçayır*, pp. 313-314; *Thomas, British Concepts*, 1205-1206; *Griggs, Limitation*, 370; *Haddon-Cave*, p. 235.

[30] 7 Geo. II, Ch. 15. The exact name of the act is "Act to settle how far Owners of Ships shall be answerable for the Acts of the Masters or Mariners".

[31] *Donovan*, 1007-1008; *Özçayır*, p. 299; *Thomas, British Concepts*, 1206; *CMA CGM S.A. v. Classica Shipping Co. Ltd.* [2003] 2 Lloyd's Rep. 50, 52 (QBD).

[32] *Sutton v. Mitchell* 99 E.R. 948 (KBD, 1785).

[33] 26 Geo. III, Ch. 86. *Griggs/Williams/Farr*, p. 5; *Brice*, pp. 18-19; *Özçayır*, p. 315; *Thomas, British Concepts*, 1207; *Griggs, Limitation*, 371.

[34] 53 Geo. III, Ch. 159.

ping Act 1894 § 503, earlier legislation regarding limitation of liability was consolidated.

2. Carriage by land

Limitation of liability in the carriage other than by sea first appeared with the carriage by rail in the 18th century. A declaration of the value of the goods by shippers was mandatory due to the variety of the goods carried. However, the increase in the amount of goods carried by rail resulted in the classification of the goods, which subsequently resulted in shippers' declaring merely the type of the goods. This, however, caused a lack of information on the value of the goods, and therefore, carriers were not able to assess the risk they have been taking. As a form of protection, they started to insert liability clauses into their general terms where they fixed the financial amount payable in case of damage or loss. Nevertheless, shippers had the option to declare the value of the goods in which case the carrier would be held liable for the full amount. Limited liability turned to be the general practice, and the option of declaring the value of the goods the exception. This system, afterwards, has been adopted by international conventions on the carriage of goods[35].

II. Motives behind the Limitation of Liability

Limitation of liability finds its roots in history. Together with its historical development, there have been several grounds to support it. With the technological development in recent centuries, new motives developed. Although most of the motives for limiting liability in shipping law are valid for every means of transportation, only some of them are peculiar to a certain type of carriage.

Nevertheless, it is highly controversial today whether limitation of liability is still necessary. Nowadays, it is considered by many to be an archaic and anachronistic institution[36]. Criticism against the limited liability system in transport law will also be addressed here next to the motives behind it.

1. General

a) Protection of an industry

As the historical background highlights, the first and most basic reason for accepting limited liability in certain matters was the need to support merchants in their investments. Carriage by sea, as the first means of transport where limited liability was accepted, was a risky, but also an important business. Generally, the perils and dangers of the sea are acknowledged. Shipowners, whether or not simultaneously acting as masters, were at risk of losing more than they had in-

---

[35] *Basedow, Transportvertrag*, pp. 408-410; *Kadletz*, pp. 106-107. See also *Basedow, Common Carriers*, 276-278.

[36] *Gauci, Limitation*, p. 68; *Puttfarken*, Rn. 873; *Chen, Limitation*, p. xv. For an overview see *Basedow, Transportvertrag*, p. 505.

vested, risking even bankruptcy, when, for example, they were held personally liable to cargo owners in case of a ship sinking[37]. Also, the possibility that a ship would be lost without any further trace, with the cargo on board becoming a total loss was far from minimal.

Moreover, shipowners did not have any control over their ships. No matter how careful they were in choosing the master and crew, not all seamen were trustworthy. It is a known fact that, due to its dangerous nature, seamanship was not a preferred profession, and, therefore, it was generally chosen by people who had no other choice[38]. It was also not possible to control the ship or the crew due to the lack of any means of communication. Consequently, when they left the shore, the destiny of the ship and cargo was in the hands of the master and the crew[39] who were by no means under the shipowners' control.

Despite these risks, shipping needed to be encouraged and supported. Carriage by sea was in some traffic relation the only means of transport, and in others a feasible alternative to the often impracticable carriage by land. Therefore, it was necessary to encourage and support shipping despite its risky, adventurous and dangerous nature (*navigare necesse est*)[40]. Today, the importance of the maritime industry lies in its economic capacity. Although the reasons for supporting the industry have changed, the policy considerations in favour of support have not. Consequently, the limitation of liability has, almost without exception, been accepted under every national and international regime in order to support the shipping industry and to encourage investment[41].

The risks involved in the aviation industry and the sector's economic importance is parallel to the maritime industry. When the Warsaw Convention was adopted in 1929, aviation industry was in its infancy: technically undeveloped and financially weak[42]. It was not possible for the industry to carry the entire financial

---

[37] *Seward*, pp. 161-162.

[38] *Cleton*, pp. 15-16.

[39] *Gold/Chircop/Kindred*, p. 718; *Mustill*, 492.

[40] *Rein*, 1259; *Hill*, p. 394; *Mustill*, 493; *Killingbeck*, 5; *McGilchrist, Limitation*, 259; *Steel*, 79; *Staring*, 326-327.

[41] *Davies/Dickey*, p. 452; *Mandaraka-Sheppard*, p. 863; *Schoenbaum*, V. II, p. 136; *Angino*, 722, 725; *Gaskell, Athens 1974*, 384; *Steel*, 80-81; *Lannan*, 903. See also the preamble of the Responsibility of Shipowners Act, 1734 (7 Geo. II, Ch. 15): "Whereas it is of the greatest consequence and importance to this kingdom, to promote the increase of the number of ships and vessels, and to prevent any discouragement to merchants and others from being interested and concerned therein: and whereas it has been held, that in many cases owners of ships or vessels are answerable for goods or merchandize shipped or put on board the same, although the said goods and merchandize, after the same have been so put on board, should be made away with by the masters or mariners of the said ships and vessels, without knowledge or privity of the owner or owners by means whereof merchants and others are greatly discouraged from adventuring their fortunes, as owners of ships or vessels, which will necessarily tend to the prejudice of the trade and navigation of this kingdom".

[42] *Basedow, Haftungshöchstsummen*, 353; *Clarke, Carriage by Air*, p. 24; *Strock*, 291; *Drion*, p. 15; *Basedow, Common Carriers*, 329. See also the facts given in the

burden of a catastrophic accident[43], namely the loss of the substantial amount of money invested as well as the compensation to be paid[44]. It was also considered that any person choosing travelling by air is familiar with the risks involved[45]. Therefore, protection was provided by means of limited liability in order to support the industry[46]. Although catastrophic aviation accidents have not ceased to exist, the liability regime in respect of the carriage of passengers has been changed radically. Today, there is no limitation cap on the compensation amounts to be paid to passengers[47].

The idea of promoting an industry through means of a limited liability system is highly challenged. It is said that a sea voyage is not as adventurous as it used to be due to the technological developments and advanced means of communication[48]. The same reasoning is rendered from the date of the argument of the uncontrollability of the crew on board[49]. Investment in shipping is also satisfactorily widespread so that the shipping industry does not require any special treatment[50]. Even if there is need for support, government subsidies are a better way to support an industry than the utilisation of the limitation system[51]; what might in other words be labelled "subsidies paid by injured persons"[52] or "at the expense of other interests"[53]. It is believed that, today, by means of limitation of liability, the shipping industry is escaping the consequences of its activities[54].

Report, Warsaw, 255-256; *McGilchrist, Limitation*, 259; *Kilbride*, p. 183. For a discussion see *Taylor*, 118-119.

[43] *Meyer*, pp. 148-149; *Matte*, p. 17. For the counterview see *Taylor*, 119; *Milde*, pp. 42-43; *Tobolewski*, pp. 86-88; for the discussion of the issue in light of surface damage caused by aircraft see *Drion*, pp. 17-20.

[44] *Report, Warsaw*, 256; *Taylor*, 115; *Kreindler*, p. 10-4.

[45] *Taylor*, 115; *Schobel*, p. 8. In fact, in the early stages of air carriage, passengers were left to obtain personal accident insurance themselves, see *Kilbride*, p. 183.

[46] *Ruhwedel, Montrealer Übereinkommen*, 189; *Taylor*, 116; *Kreindler*, p. 10-4; *Tobolewski*, pp. 80-85; *Vlacic*, 449; *Basedow, Transportvertrag*, p. 463; *Schobel*, pp. 8, 106-114; *Drion*, pp. 15-17; *Milde*, p. 42; *Georgiades*, p. 44 (last five writers do not accept this motive as a justification for limited liability in aviation law); *In re Korean Air Lines Disaster of September 1, 1983* (CA, 1991) 932 F.2d 1475, 1484; *In re Air Disaster at Lockerbie, Scotland on December 21, 1988 & In re Hijacking of Pan American World Airways, Inc. Aircraft at Karachi International Airport, Pakistan on September 5, 1986* (CA, 1991) 928 F.2d 1267, 1270-1271, 1287.

[47] For more information see *infra* § 4 C. For an analysis of the limited liability system in the carriage of passengers by air see Sven *Brise*, Some Thoughts on the Economic Significance of Limited Liability in Air Passenger Transport, in: Arnold Kean (Editor), Essays in Air Law, The Hague 1982, p. 19.

[48] *Gold / Chircop / Kindred*, p. 720; *Chen, Limitation*, p. xv; *Eyer*, 372.

[49] *Chen, Limitation*, p. xv. Strongly opposing to the idea that the nautical fault defence is an anachronism *Makins*, 659.

[50] *Gauci, Limitation*, p. 66; *Haddon-Cave*, p. 241.

[51] *Chen, Limitation*, p. xv.

[52] *Maryland Casualty Company and Others v. Gertrude Picard Cushing and Others* (Supreme Court of the US, 1954) 1954 A.M.C. 837, 858 *per* Justice Black.

[53] *Gauci, Limitation*, p. 66. See also *Eyer*, 389-390.

[54] *Røsæg*, 295.

It is also asserted that limitation of liability is not necessary anymore since it is a system which was created when the means of corporate law were still unknown. Today, the same result as the limitation of liability can be achieved through limited liability corporations[55]. Moreover, carriage by air, sea, rail and road are classified by some as public services. Accordingly, it has been said that a public service needs to serve the interests of the public. Thus, a public service provider should not be allowed to limit his liability if he does not perform the service in question properly or at all[56].

Not surprisingly, the arguments against the limitation of liability were objected to as well. It has been asserted that limitation of liability provides support not only to shipowners: it is the limitation of liability system which allows shipowners to have larger fleets, thus increasing the need for a larger workforce not only on ships, but also in the industries providing services to shipping, such as insurance. Hence, the limited liability system is not only advantageous to a commercial minority but also to the community at large[57]. Asserting that the limitation of liability serves in the advantage of the community at large is, clearly, too far reaching.

b) Joint adventure

Another idea lying behind the limitation of liability is that carriage was a joint adventure. Initially, this idea was born in maritime carriage as concerns the carriage of cargo. By sending his ship to the sea, the shipowner was risking his valuable asset, and by sending his cargo on board that ship, the cargo-owner was risking his cargo. They were, so to speak, "participants in a common adventure"[58]. If the ship reached her destination, this provided a common benefit for both parties; however, if the ship, for one reason or another, was not able to arrive at the port of discharge, the risk was placed solely on the shipowner which created an unreasonable burden on the shipowner. Thus, by means of limitation of liability, risk was distributed between all parties to the contract of carriage. This concept has its roots in the general average idea[59].

It is very doubtful whether carriage by any means of transport can be seen as an adventure today as it was hundreds of years ago. The idea of joint adventure has lost its justification from an economic point of view as well. When there was no means of insurance, the risk must have been shared between different parties to a maritime adventure, which serves as a micro economic solution. However, today,

---

[55] *Puttfarken*, Rn. 873; *Chen, Limitation*, p. xv; *Killingbeck*, 13; *Eyer*, 372; *Billah*, 312 *et seq*. For the counterview see *Staring*, 328-330.

[56] *Georgiades*, pp. 47-48.

[57] *Mandaraka-Sheppard*, p. 864; *Seward*, pp. 166-167. Similarly *Schobel*, pp. 8-9.

[58] *Mustill*, 492; *Grönfors*, 696.

[59] *Mustill*, 492; *Killingbeck*, 5.

by means of insurance, any risk can be spread on a macro economic scale[60] which renders the risk allocation on a micro economic scale unnecessary[61].

However, the joint adventure idea still stands behind the compensation regime set for the carriage of oil by sea. By virtue of relevant international conventions[62], damage and loss is compensated by two industries, namely the shipping industry and the oil industry. A similar scheme has been drawn for the carriage of dangerous goods by sea by virtue of the International Convention on Liability and Compensation for Damage in Connection with the Carriage of Hazardous and Noxious Substances by Sea, 1996; however, that Convention has not entered into force yet.

c) High value cargo

In ancient times, it was only sailing ships which carried the goods, and, except for relatively rare situations, goods carried on board were not of high financial value. Together with industrialization and parallel developments in the shipping industry, a large variety of goods of increasing size started to be carried on board ships. Most of those goods were generally delivered to the carrier in packed form. Even if they were not, it was not possible for the carrier to be familiar with each and every good and their exact financial value[63].

Against the danger of being held liable for amounts they could not financially support[64], carriers sought protection in contractual clauses, although subsequently the clauses served as protection against more than just liability for highly valuable cargo. Nevertheless, one of the basic reasons behind the limitation of carriers' liability in the carriage by sea was the protection against liability for goods of excessively high value[65].

Although the reason is explained in relation to carriage by sea, it is also valid for other means of transportation. Additionally, when carriage by containers is taken into account, it is not wrong to say that the logic behind this reasoning remains actual as it relates to the limitation of liability. Nonetheless, it is not the function and responsibility of private law to protect certain parties in a market against liability for high amounts. Every diligent businessman should agree only

---

[60] See *Richter-Hannes, Vereinheitlichung*, pp. 96-99; *Rodopoulos*, pp. 35-42.

[61] *Lopuski*, 182; *Haddon-Cave*, p. 242. For the counterview see *Makins*, 656-657 (The author defends that the joint adventure motive is still valid, since maritime casualties with burdensome economic consequences still occur; and, therefore, there is still need for the risk allocation based on the joint adventure criterion.).

[62] International Convention on Civil Liability for Oil Pollution Damage, 1992, and the International Convention on the Establishment of an International Fund for Compensation for Oil Pollution Damage, 1992, and the Protocol of 2003 to the International Convention on the Establishment of an International Fund for Compensation for Oil Pollution Damage, 1992.

[63] *Herber, Überblick*, 94-95.

[64] *Mustill*, 492.

[65] *Herber, Überblick*, 95; *Girvin*, para. 29.02; International Law Association, Report of the Thirtieth Conference (held at The Hague between 30th August – 3rd September 1921), V. II: Proceedings of the Maritime Law Committee, London 1922, pp. 178 *et seqq.* See also *Diplock*, 529; *Lannan*, 903 *et seq.*

to obligations which he can also fulfil financially. Furthermore, even the smallest transport companies can insure against a wide range of risks. Liability in excessive amounts can cause financial ruin only in case of a lack of the necessary insurance cover[66]. Nevertheless, if protection were desired against liability causing financial ruin, giving the opportunity for judges to limit the amount to be paid out, serves another solution for the protection[67].

d) Insurance

aa) Liability insurance

(1) Insurance premiums

Insurance premiums to be collected are determined according to the financial amount of the insured value and the risk. Liability insurance premiums, in this respect, are calculated according to the limitation amounts set by international and national law provisions since, independent from the insured risk, the limitation amounts reflect the maximum which can be paid by a carrier or shipowner. It was said that if a carrier or shipowner were to be held liable for the full amount of the financial damage, this would result in higher insurance premium rates due to the unknown value[68]. Consequently, fixed liability amounts mean ascertainable risk[69], and ascertainable risk means reasonable insurance premiums[70].

It is true that liability insurance is a common feature of the transportation market and serves everybody's interests. However, adopting rules only on the basis of insurable liability means to make the liability insurance an inevitable part of the liability and, therefore denies the compensatory function of the liability. Insurability of liability is not a juridical requirement and, therefore, should not serve as a basis in establishing legal regimes. The basic function of liability is to compensate for damage. It is not just and fair to sacrifice this function at the cost of the individuals by shifting the results of carriers' faulty conduct upon third parties, just to ease the job of the insurance market[71].

Moreover, it is possible to insure even unknown or financially unlimited risks, such as the personal injury claims in the USA, for reasonable premiums under the present competitive insurance market conditions[72]. Additionally, if the limits of liability in transport law would be abolished, this would create a new product for the insurance market, and insurers will accordingly supply insurance cover with adjusted premiums. Under the present market conditions, it is by no means accu-

---

[66] *Basedow, Transportvertrag*, pp. 466-467.

[67] *Kötz*, 39-40.

[68] *Seward*, pp. 164-165; *Rein*, 1272; *Vlacic*, 446-447, 450. It was said that liability insurance premiums might increase 25% to 30% if the limited liability system were to be abandoned, see *Buglass*, 1364. See also *McGilchrist, Limitation*, 261-263.

[69] *Gold/Chircop/Kindred*, p. 719; *Seward*, p. 163; *Milde*, p. 43.

[70] *Clarke, Carriage by Air*, pp. 24-25; *Özçayır*, pp. 377-378; *Dockray*, p. 348; *Coghlin*, pp. 239-240; *Mandaraka-Sheppard*, p. 863; *Steel*, 79-80, 82-83.

[71] *Basedow, Transportvertrag*, pp. 466, 478; *Puttfarken*, Rn. 875.

[72] *Basedow, Transportvertrag*, p. 464; *Taschner*, pp. 87-88; *Røsæg*, 295.

rate to speak of uninsurable risk[73]. Furthermore, besides the fact that not every change in the liability system causes change in the insurance premiums[74], there is no statistical data which shows that the abolishment of the limited liability system will cause a radical change in them[75].

Additionally, the amount of liability and the amount of insurance cover are two distinct legal issues. The extent of liability is to be calculated according to the contract or tort law principles, whereas the amount of the liability insurance premium is to be set by the insurer after an evaluation of the risks involved. An insurance contract does not have to cover the full risk to which the insured, in case of transportation the carrier is exposed[76].

It has already been mentioned that insurance premiums are determined according to the financial amount of the insured value and the risk. If the risk – in case of transportation the risk of an occurrence of damage – is high, a higher insurance premium is required. If the risk of an occurrence of damage is low, low insurance premiums are to be expected. Thus, the frequency of an occurrence of damage increases the premium to be charged[77] despite the limited liability system. Even if the limited liability system would be abolished, carriers can find insurance cover with reasonable premiums by being more diligent, such as improving safety precautions, and thereby decrease the risk, which, at the end, would decrease the insurance costs[78]. Unfortunately, carriers tend to be less careful if the potential damage is insured. The insurance market has its own preventive measures against this, such as higher premiums the following year, or cost sharing[79].

(2) Freight rates

It was also stated as a motive behind the limited liability system that a carrier who pays lower insurance premiums will charge lower freight rates. Thus, the limited liability system serves also the interests of cargo owners[80]. If, on the other hand, cargo owners wish to be compensated for the full amount in case of loss of or damage to goods, they can declare the exact value of the goods in exchange for a higher freight rate. Cargo interests who pay lower freight rates may charge lower

---

[73] *Basedow, Transportvertrag,* pp. 464-465; *Basedow, Haftungshöchstsummen,* 353; *Billah,* 310 *et seq.,* 314 *et seqq.*
[74] *Richter-Hannes, Vereinheitlichung,* p. 100.
[75] *Taschner,* p. 85.
[76] *Basedow, Transportvertrag,* pp. 465-466; *Gauci, Limitation,* p. 66; *Taschner,* p. 83; *Kötz,* 38; Hermann *Weitnauer,* Grundsätze der Haftung, in: Karlsruher Forum –Beiheft zu VersR- 1962, 3, 11-12.
[77] *Taschner,* pp. 83-84.
[78] *Kadletz,* p. 261.
[79] *Basedow, Transportvertrag,* pp. 490-491; *Rodopoulos,* pp. 42-46; *Lopuski,* 184, 188-189; *Kadletz,* pp. 322 *et seqq.; Billah,* 312. However, Nigel *Carden,* Non Technical Measures for the Promotion of Quality Shipping for Carriage of Goods by Sea, CMI Yearbook 2009, p. 329 stipulates that neither hull insurance nor P&I insurance has necessarily such a strong affect in encouraging an improvement in quality.
[80] *Wilson,* p. 195; *Mustill,* 493; *Killingbeck,* 6; *Haak,* 163; *Makins,* 652-653, 655.

prices for their goods and, at the end of the chain, consumers throughout the world pay lower prices[81].

It has been stated that the percentage of the liability and the liability insurance costs in overall transportation costs and in freight rates are very small. Therefore, even if there was a rise in insurance premiums, this cannot cause a drastic increase in freight rates, especially not in today's competitive international shipping market[82]. Even if the increase in insurance premiums would cause rise in the freight rates, why do the carriers insist on the limited liability system, when it is possible to cover the alleged costs with a certain increase in freight rates?[83] Last but not least, a proper legal analysis should concentrate on the amount of damages instead of transportation costs, since the frequency of occurrence of damage or loss adds to the insurance and claim adjustment costs[84].

The insignificant correlation between insurance and freight rates with product prices has no relevance in the carriage of passengers. It is of no importance for a passenger whether he pays more or less for a trip when his life or physical integrity is at stake. Furthermore, as a matter of practice, it has been correctly stated that a passenger must be satisfied with what he obtains from the limitation fund, whereas cargo owners, almost invariably, protect themselves with cargo insurance. Thus, limitation of liability does not affect the cargo owners personally, yet this is not the case in instances of physical injury to a passenger[85]. Moreover, limitation amounts can substantially vary depending on the mode of transport (carriage by rail, road, air or sea) and depending on the place of departure and arrival. Since not all of the states are parties to the same international instruments, illogical and often immoral outcomes result[86]. As such, an international regime should not put the interests of commerce before the right to physical integrity[87].

However, compulsory insurance together with the right of direct action against the insurer has been accepted by some as a valid argument in case of the passenger carriage[88]. It is asserted that it is the limited liability system which enables insurance cover. Especially the compulsory insurance regime in the carriage of passengers, oil, and dangerous goods has been considered as a "social necessity" by

---

[81] *Buglass*, 1364-1365; *Vlacic*, 450; Birch *Reynardson*, The Maritime Carrier's Liability under the Hamburg Rules – The P&I Insurance Aspect, in: Hans Peter Ipsen/Rolf Stödter (Editors), Recht über See: Festschrift zum Rolf Stödter zum 70. Geburtstag, Hamburg 1979, pp. 15-20.

[82] *Basedow, Transportvertrag*, pp. 467, 484-487; *Hellawell*, 366-367; *Lopuski*, 189; *Selvig*, 315-316; *Richter-Hannes, Vereinheitlichung*, pp. 100-101; *Kröger, Passengers*, p. 250: "the argument that the customer always pays in the end is only theoretically correct".

[83] *Richter-Hannes, Vereinheitlichung*, p. 101.

[84] *Basedow, Transportvertrag*, pp. 480-481; *Billah*, 317 *et seq*.

[85] *Angino*, 721-722. Similar *Davies/Dickey*, p. 452.

[86] *Mustill*, 500; *Taylor*, 126. See also Reinhard *Beine*, Kritische Betrachtung der gesetzlichen Entwicklung des Haftungsrechts der Personenbeförderung unter besonderer Berücksichtigung des Luftverkehrs, ZLW 1978, 3, 6-8.

[87] *Georgiades*, p. 48.

[88] *Drion*, pp. 20-21.

having taken into consideration of the liability insurance's function to protect the victims of the marine shipping activity[89]. Thus, victims of disastrous events are protected through the compulsory insurance which was made possible through limitation of liability[90]. Against this argument, a very simple solution has been suggested to meet the insurance market's concerns: unlimited liability with a limited amount of compulsory insurance[91].

bb) Cargo insurance or personal insurance

It is said that the limitation of liability does not put others in a financially disadvantageous position. In the case of the carriage of passengers, life and health insurance is available to individuals. If they or their relatives suffer any damages, the life insurer or health insurer will provide compensation. In case of the carriage of goods, no cargo owner will allow his goods to be carried without cargo insurance. Again, if he suffers damage, he can obtain the insurance benefit up to the full amount of the goods[92]. Although there is a cap on the limitation amount, only the insurers of passengers or cargo interests will bear the consequences, not the passenger or the cargo owner. There is a balance within the insurance market between different insurers[93]. Consequently, the limitation system enables relevant parties to the contract of carriage to obtain insurance for themselves[94], therefore causing no injustice to anyone.

Although it is the reality that goods are generally carried under cargo insurance cover, it is not necessarily always so. Especially in short routes, goods are generally not carried under a cargo insurance cover[95]. Moreover, the extent of the cargo insurance varies considerably. Cargo insurance does not always provide cover against all risks[96]. From this point of view, it is not possible to say that cargo interests do not bear the consequences of the limited liability system at all.

If the limited liability system in the case of carriage of goods were to be abolished, cargo owners would have the option of recovering the full amount of damages or loss, therefore, to save the cargo insurance. Undoubtedly, this would have a negative effect on cargo insurance market, since the demand for cargo insurance, and consequently the premium volume of the cargo insurance market would be reduced [97]. It should not be surprising for anyone, that cargo insurers oppose an increase in liability amounts or abolition of the limited liability system altogether. However, their case for the limited liability system is based on purely economic

---

[89] *Lopuski*, 183-184, 188.
[90] *Mandaraka-Sheppard*, p. 864; see also *Lopuski*, 187-188.
[91] *Taschner*, p. 85.
[92] *Seward*, p. 163.
[93] *Seward*, p. 163. In fact, it was even said that spreading the risk among cargo insurers is a cheaper way of insuring a risk instead of assuring the whole risk under a single P&I policy, see *Diplock*, 530; *Makins*, 650-651.
[94] *Clarke, Carriage by Air*, pp. 24-25; see also *Schobel*, pp. 122-124.
[95] *Basedow, Transportvertrag*, pp. 474-475; *Selvig*, 308.
[96] *Selvig*, 308-310.
[97] *Basedow, Transportvertrag*, p. 474; *Selvig*, 313.

concerns and cannot be accepted as a valid argument on which a legal regime should be based[98]. Nevertheless, cargo insurance will still be needed, since collecting the damage from the cargo insurer rather than the carrier means quicker settlements, which is commercially of substantial importance[99].

From the cargo interests' standpoint, what has been said thus far shows that means of cargo insurance do not serve as a justification for limitation of liability. In case of the carriage of passengers as well, limitation of liability must be justified on other grounds[100]. Otherwise, airlines, bus lines and ferry companies should print a warning on the ticket, urging the passenger to obtain life and health insurance, or at least travel insurance, before getting on board[101].

e) Liability regime

aa) Balance of different interests

Indubitably, the most important feature of the limitation of liability is the liability system adopted together with it. Since the limitation of liability puts shipowners and carriers in an advantageous position, another advantage in favour of the cargo interests or passengers should be adopted in order to balance these interests.

The historical background of the issue can be found in the Hague Rules. Before the Rules were adopted, it was the practice of carriers to impose contracts which exempted themselves from any kind of liability. In order to prevent such a practice, a certain liability regime has been adopted and exemption clauses have been no longer allowed[102].

The liability regimes adopted by international conventions are based on different principles. They can vary from strict liability to presumed fault based liability. In any event, cargo interests, passengers or persons suffering from damage are under no obligation to prove the shipowner's or carrier's fault provided that the shipowner or carrier is liable within the limits set by the relevant international convention[103]. As a result, cargo interests, passengers and persons suffering damage have abandoned their right to unlimited liability of shipowner or carrier; but in

---

[98] *Lopuski*, 180-181.

[99] *Hellawell*, 366; *Selvig*, 312; *Makins*, 650.

[100] See also *Report, Warsaw*, 258; *Taylor*, 120-121; *Kilbride*, pp. 191-192; *Tobolewski*, pp. 91-92.

[101] See also *Gaskell, Athens 1974*, 386; however also *Drion*, p. 27; *Milde*, p. 43. It has been suggested "in the interest of consumer protection" that carriers can assist passengers in finding such insurance, see *Kröger, Passengers*, p. 252.

[102] For more information see *infra* § 5 A 1 1 a. See also *Rabe*, Vor § 556 Rn. 2-3; *Puttfarken*, Rn. 137; *Nelson Pine Industries Ltd. v. Seatrans New Zealand Ltd. (The "Pembroke")* [1995] 2 Lloyd's Rep. 290, 294 (New Zealand High Court); *Rolls Royce Plc and Another v. Heavylift-Volga Dnepr Ltd. and Another* [2000] 1 Lloyd's Rep. 653, 657 (QBD).

[103] *Krause & Krause*, pp. 11-12 – 11-13; *Kilbride*, pp. 183-184; *Gaskell, Athens 1974*, 383-384; *Rolls Royce Plc and Another v. Heavylift-Volga Dnepr Ltd. and Another* [2000] 1 Lloyd's Rep. 653, 657 (QBD).

return, they have been put in a more advantageous position by means of an aggravated and expanded liability regime[104].

Whether there is a justifiable *quid pro quo* or, alternatively, a win-win situation must be analysed separately for different liability regimes. It was rightly stated that fault based liability regimes adopted by international conventions reflects the general principles of contract law. Under those principles, it is sufficient for the creditor to prove that the debtor did not fulfil or properly fulfil the contract. Therefore, the principle that the shippers do not need to prove the fault of the carriers is just a reflection of the pre-existing general principles, and consequently does not serve as an advantage in favour of cargo interests[105]. It was stated that a just legal regime should at least offer the option of choosing between price and liability alternatives. Unlimited liability can be adopted as the basic principle, and carriers and shippers can have the option of agreeing on limited liability in exchange for lower freight rates[106].

Counterbalancing the strict liability system with the limitation of liability in the carriage of oil and dangerous goods has also been criticised. It is contended that the imposition of a strict liability regime on such dangerous activities is supported by the nature of the issue and that there is no need to find an excuse for its imposition[107]. Furthermore, it is argued that, with limitation of liability for oil pollution claims, commerce has taken precedence over the environment[108]. However, it must be recalled here that the reason for having limited liability under the CLC and HNS is not subsidizing an industry: the aim is to share the compensation burden between two industries[109]. Under the CLC regime, every loss caused by the pollution is, in the end, compensated. Nevertheless, it has been found illogical to limit the tanker owner's liability against third parties, whereas the IOPC Fund can take recourse action against shipowners[110]. However, if the payment system in oil pollution cases is taken into consideration, it will be seen very clearly that the whole regime favours the pollution victims[111].

bb) Loss prevention

Due to its strong international character, economic considerations rank, unfortunately, well ahead of the social concerns in transport law. Following this incen-

---

[104] *Hickey*, 608; *Jefferies*, 307; *Hill*, p. 394; *Seward*, p. 165. For discussion and criticism with regard to the carriage by air see *Drion*, pp. 31-36; *Schobel*, pp. 124-135; *Milde*, p. 43; *Report, Warsaw*, 259, 262; *Taylor*, 121.

[105] *Basedow, Transportvertrag*, p. 506; *Abraham, Grade des Verschuldens*, p. 260, see also *Grönfors*, 701-702; *Hellawell*, 361-362.

[106] *Basedow, Transportvertrag*, pp. 506-507; *Basedow, Common Carriers*, 345.

[107] *Gauci, Limitation*, p. 69. See also *Kötz*, 38-39; *Taschner*, pp. 82-83. As regards to the carriage by air, see *Tobolewski*, pp. 94-101.

[108] *Killingbeck*, 14.

[109] See *supra* § 2 B II 1 b.

[110] *Røsæg*, 295.

[111] For more information see *Damar, Compulsory Insurance*, 155-156, 160-161, 165-166.

tive, international conferences called for the adoption or amendment of an international convention search for the cheapest solution for the allocation of risks in the shipping market[112]. It has been asserted that liability regimes for the carriage of goods are not concerned with the loss prevention, and their only concern is the allocation of the risks between market actors. Therefore, "equity" and "fairness" are irrelevant perceptions[113]. However, it is clear that an international convention should contribute not only to the risk allocation but also to loss prevention.

In this respect, the preventive function of compensation should be in the forefront. It is a known fact that one would do his best to omit a wrongful act if he knows that he will be held accountable for compensating the damage which occurred as a result of the wrongful act[114]. However, in transport law, a carrier does not take the necessary precautions for the loss prevention if they will cost him more than the freight, and the compensation to be paid is of insignificant amount[115]. As a result, accidents are considered as a damage factor in the present shipping market[116]. From this point of view, it is clear that the limited liability does not contribute to loss prevention[117]. However, it is also clear that the preventive function of the private law liability has no lobby within the shipping market[118].

In the field of carriage of passengers, on the other hand, the incentive to prevent accidents by means of an aggravated liability system is only of theoretical importance. Today, due to the high and constantly revised safety standards adopted by the international and national legal provisions, there is no need to pressurize the shipping market with the aggravated amounts of liability[119].

f)   Unification of law

Another feature of the limitation of liability is that the system unifies the law with respect to the amount of damages to be paid. As mentioned before[120], this unification has certain advantages regarding insurance. Whether this unification has any advantage from cargo interests' or passengers' point of view is highly questionable.

It is generally the case, especially in container transport, that there will be goods on board of different origins in international carriage. It is also highly likely that every good carried may be subject to a different liability regime due to the application of the private international law principles, and therefore, compensation

---

[112] *Lopuski*, 179-181.

[113] *Makins*, 655-656, 658, 662.

[114] *Basedow, Transportvertrag*, p. 487; *Lopuski*, 185; see also Eike *von Hippel*, Unfallrecht: Vorbeugen ist besser als heilen, JZ 1977, 706, 709.

[115] *Basedow, Transportvertrag*, pp. 496-497; *Billah*, 301 *et seq.*, 304, 306 *et seqq.*, 317 *et seqq.*

[116] *Basedow, Transportvertrag*, pp. 489-490.

[117] For an analysis see *Hellawell*, 363-365.

[118] *Basedow, Transportvertrag*, pp. 494-496; *Lopuski*, 185.

[119] *Basedow, Transportvertrag*, pp. 487-489; *Kröger, Passengers*, p. 251.

[120] See *supra* B II 1 d aa.

to be paid to cargo interests may differ. The situation might also be similar in case of the carriage of passengers where passengers with different nationalities and socio-economic background are on board. Therefore, it has been said, it is not just and fair that different persons on board are to be compensated in different amounts. Unification of compensation amounts in this respect is to be welcomed[121].

However, in either the carriage of goods or in the carriage of passengers, there are a high number of international conventions and several amendments to them. This inflation in the number of applicable international conventions may result in different applicable amounts to the same carriage. Therefore, a mention of unified compensation amounts in transport law cannot be made under the present legal fragmentation[122]. Furthermore, it has been rightly stated that the benefit realised by shipowners and carriers is greater than that by claimants; especially when the fluctuating amounts are taken into consideration. The SDR[123] was provided as a solution, but it provides no solution in practice[124].

g) Litigation

In addition to the other motives, it was asserted that limitation of liability makes the quickest settlements possible. Since international conventions or national law provisions determine the maximum amount of the recoverable damages beforehand, there would not be any argument for ascertaining the exact amount of damages. Limitation of liability, consequently, avoids litigation by facilitating quick settlements[125] and simplifying the claim handling procedure[126], thus providing a fast extrajudicial compensation system[127]. However, today, limitation of liability is one of the sources of increasing litigation. Especially in case of unrealistically low limitation amounts, claimants seek to break limits with different arguments[128]. The occurrence of quick settlements and simple claim handling procedure is not as often as it used to be[129].

---

[121] *Taylor*, 124. For the counterview see *Drion*, pp. 41-42; *Milde*, p. 44; *Schobel*, pp. 138-139.

[122] For the carriage by air see *Taylor*, 124-126; *Schobel*, pp. 139-141.

[123] The SDR has been created by the International Monetary Fund (IMF) in 1969. It is an international reserve asset, but not an international currency. Its value is determined by calculating certain proportions of key international currencies. For more information see <www.imf.org/external/np/exr/facts/sdr.HTM> (07.08.2010).

[124] *Røsæg*, 295. See also *Tobolewski*, pp. 186-204.

[125] *Drion*, p. 38; *Clarke, Carriage by Air*, p. 25; *Report, Warsaw*, 259; *In re Air Disaster at Lockerbie, Scotland on December 21, 1988 & In re Hijacking of Pan American World Airways, Inc. Aircraft at Karachi International Airport, Pakistan on September 5, 1986* (CA, 1991) 928 F.2d 1267, 1287.

[126] *Taylor*, 121; *Gaskell, Athens 1974*, 385.

[127] *Hickey*, 613; *Milde*, p. 44.

[128] *Taylor*, 121-122; *Gaskell, Athens 1974*, 385; see also *Schobel*, pp. 135-137; *Billah*, 316.

[129] *Haddon-Cave*, p. 242. See also *Tobolewski*, pp. 101-108.

2. Carriage by air

In addition to the general rationale valid for all means of transportation, another reason can be mentioned with regard exclusively to carriage by air. This reason is, however, more a statement of the factual situation than a justification of the limitation of liability.

Although first attempts were made in the 1910's, regular passenger carriage services did not begin until the twenties[130]. Starting from the twenties, a considerable number of airlines in Europe were able to offer scheduled flights. These airlines were, though small, mostly private entities. Nevertheless, due to the adventurous character of flying and due to the expenses of this new mode of transport, these private entities were, generally, heavily subsidized by states[131]. In the second half of the twenties, some of the air transport companies, with the financial support of states, merged. A good example is the Deutsche Lufthansa which was founded on 6 January of 1926 merging the two existing companies Deutscher Aero Lloyd and Junkers Luftverkehr. When the Deutsche Lufthansa was founded, 36 % of its initial capital was held by the German government[132]. Imperial Airways Ltd., one of the predecessors of the present British Airways, was incorporated in 1924 merging four existing companies. This company was also heavily subsidized[133]. Aeroflot, the Soviet state airline was founded in 1928 under the name Dobroflot and merged two former airlines Dobrolyot and Ukranian Airways[134]. The situation in France was also not too different. Several air transport companies have merged in 1929. After the Second World War ended, the new air transport company, Compagnie Nationale Air France, was incorporated in 1948. 70 % of the new company was owned by the French government[135]. An example of the unhappy fate of unsubsidized air transport companies is the Det Norske Luftfahrts Rederi. The Norwegian company was liquidated due to the lack of the necessary subsidy from its government[136].

As a result, it can be said that when the first convention regarding carriage by air was drafted, most of the airlines were either significantly subsidized or owned by states. Therefore, by means of an international convention and limited liability

---

[130] For more information see *Davies, World's Airlines*, pp. 3-20.

[131] For details see *Davies, World's Airlines*, pp. 21-38. See also *Encyclopaedia Britannica*, Flight, History of (2010), The First Airlines, retrieved from Encyclopaedia Britannica Online, <www.search.eb.com/eb/article-260583> (07.08.2010).

[132] *Davies, World's Airlines*, p. 56. See also *Die Zeit – Das Lexikon*, Bd. 3 (Char-Dur), Deutsche Lufthansa AG, Mannheim 2005; *Encyclopaedia Britannica*, Lufthansa (2010), retrieved from Encyclopaedia Britannica Online, <www.search.eb.com/eb/article-9049286> (07.08.2010).

[133] *Davies, World's Airlines*, pp. 33-34.

[134] See also *Encyclopaedia Britannica*, Aeroflot (2010), retrieved from Encyclopaedia Britannica Online, <www.search.eb.com/eb/article-9003874> (07.08.2010).

[135] See also *Encyclopaedia Britannica*, Air France (2010), retrieved from Encyclopaedia Britannica Online, <www.search.eb.com/eb/article-9005201> (07.08.2010).

[136] *Davies, World's Airlines*, p. 36.

system, states were not only providing advantages for private entities; but they were also lightening the burden on the government budgets[137].

C. Wilful Misconduct and Breaking the Limits

The motives for the limitation of liability lose their importance and justification when the shipowner or carrier causes damage intentionally. It is also not possible to support any policy consideration for putting a shipowner or carrier in an advantageous position in case of a malicious act or omission on their side. Therefore, it is evident that a shipowner or carrier cannot avail himself of the limits if he intended to cause the damage incurred. As a result, the idea of depriving the ship-owner or carrier of the limits of liability is as old as the limitation concept itself.

In this respect, the first provision as to fraud was adopted in the Amalphitan Table. Art. 32 of the Table stipulates that "if a master of a ship or any other merchant in making up his account shall in any manner or way defraud any person who has given him a commission, and the aforesaid principal can at any time afterwards prove the fraud, in that case the fraudulent master or merchants are bound without fail to pay for everything anew, and may levy an execution against the said merchant or master, notwithstanding the contract was so made as to be subject even to a prescription of time after the form of the new rule, and notwith-standing the contract was made in a case in which an execution does not take place"[138]. According to this provision, if a master or a merchant (who can be also owner or part-owner of the ship) commits fraud, the fraud can be proved any time and the master or merchant is bound to pay the whole amount of damage. Furthermore, judgement can be executed at any time irrespective of the time limi-tation and contractual provisions.

Nevertheless, the first clear provision, which is not limited to fraud cases, can be found in the Ordinance of Rotterdam of 1721. The Ordinance stated that the liability of the shipowner should be limited "unless the shipowner ordered the act which caused the loss or damage"[139]. In other words, the owner would not be entitled to rely on the limitation provisions if he, personally, is responsible for the act or omission which caused the actual loss or damage.

Undoubtedly, any justification for limitation of liability becomes worthless in case of an intentional wrongdoing[140]. Pursuant to the principles of ethics or general understanding of justice, it is unthinkable and immoral that an intentional wrongdoer can limit the liability resulting from his very own intentional

---

[137] *Drion*, p. 15; *In re Air Disaster at Lockerbie, Scotland on December 21, 1988 & In re Hijacking of Pan American World Airways, Inc. Aircraft at Karachi Interna-tional Airport, Pakistan on September 5, 1986* (CA, 1991) 928 F.2d 1267, 1271.

[138] For the original Italian text and the translation see Black Book of the Admiralty, V. 4, pp. 20-23.

[139] *Kierr*, 640.

[140] Entwurf eines Gesetzes zur Neuregelung des Fracht-, Speditions- und Lagerrechts (Transportrechtsreformgesetz – TRG), Begründung (zu den einzelnen Vorschrif-ten), zu § 435, BT 13/8445, p. 71.

conduct[141]. In addition to the ethical principles, protecting a shipowner or carrier by means of limited liability in case of intentional wrongdoing also offends public policy[142]. Because of this characteristic, provisions in international conventions regarding unlimited liability are mandatory and any alteration made in violation of these provisions is null and void[143].

Here, the liability regime argument should also be remembered. As mentioned before[144], it was alleged that one of the basic features of limited liability is the presumed fault based or strict liability regime accepted in exchange. The win-win situation created by this exchange fails when the damage is caused by the intentional wrongdoing of shipowner or carrier. If the limitation of liability was also accepted for cases where the damage incurred was caused by intentional or reckless conduct, the situation would turn into a win-lose situation in favour of the shipowner or carrier since although guilty of criminal conduct, he enjoys the benefit of the limited liability[145].

Nevertheless, it is not always his own conduct which deprives the carrier of the liability limits. For example, under the Warsaw Convention[146] or the CMR[147], the carrier loses his right to limit also in case of wilful misconduct by his servant or agent; in other words, he is not entitled to limit even where he is not personally guilty of the malicious conduct. The basic reason for such legislation is that, today, carriers cannot and do not perform the carriage personally: they employ servants and hire agents and use their services for the performance of the carriage contract. Therefore, reserving unlimited liability for the cases of personal conduct has not been accepted under some international regimes[148].

---

[141] *Drion*, p. 46; *Thume, CMR-Frachtführer*, 931; *Modjaz*, p. 8; *Hickey*, 608; *The Garden City* [1982] 2 Lloyd's Rep. 382, 398 (QBD), *per* Justice Staughton.
[142] Mr. Poulton (Austria), in: *Minutes, Hague*, p. 170; *Hickey*, 608.
[143] *Abraham*, Art. 25 Anm. 14; *Liesecke*, p. 97; *Müller-Rostin*, p. 126.
[144] See *supra* B II 1 e aa.
[145] *Hickey*, 608; *Koller, Aufklärung*, 554.
[146] See *infra* § 4.
[147] See *infra* § 6 B I 1.
[148] *Drion*, p. 47.

§ 3 Roots of Wilful Misconduct

Being a term of Anglo-Saxon law, wilful misconduct originates from English law. As is the case in all terms of British law, the term of wilful misconduct has also been developed through case law. Nonetheless, it would be beyond the scope of this thesis to search and explain the origin of the term in ancient cases.

The term "wilful misconduct" was, for the first time in an act, adopted in the Marine Insurance Act (MIA), 1906 § 55 (2)(a). Undoubtedly, the drafters of the MIA 1906 had been inspired by the case law regarding carriage by rail, since the term used to be a part of a contractual clause which leads to the unlimited liability of the railway.

However, prior to the adoption of the term "wilful misconduct" in the MIA, the appearance of the phrase "wilful fault" in the Merchant Shipping Act (MSA) 1894 is also worth mentioning. In application, the phrase "wilful fault" in MSA 1894 also referred to the same degree of fault as the term "wilful misconduct"[1]. However, the interpretation of "wilful fault" in the MSA 1894 was related to criminal liability, whereas the consequences of "wilful misconduct" within marine insurance or railway carriage were, naturally, borne within private law.

A. Criminal Liability under Admiralty Law

I. Merchant Shipping Act, 1894 § 419

The MSA 1894 was enacted for the purpose of consolidating the shipping legislation of the UK[2]. It covered almost all aspects of merchant shipping such as registration of ships, training of seamen, liability of shipowners, wrecks, legal proceedings etc[3]. Among these issues, the MSA also regulated safety at sea in Part V. The first section of Part V was on the "Prevention of Collisions", and § 419 of the Act was provided for the observance of collision regulations[4]. The first three paragraphs of the section stated:

> "(1) All owners and masters of ships shall obey the collision regulations, and shall not carry or exhibit any other lights, or use any other fog signals, than such as are required by those regulations.
>
> (2) If an infringement of the collision regulations is caused by the wilful fault of the master or owner of the ship, that master or owner shall, in respect of each offence, be guilty of a misdemeanour.

---

[1] *Clarke, Carriage by Air*, p. 160 fn. 967.

[2] 57&58 Vict., Ch. 60. The exact name of the Act is "An Act to Consolidate Enactments relating to Merchant Shipping".

[3] Today, all these aspects are covered by the MSA of 1995 which consolidates the UK shipping legislation since the MSA, 1894; for detailed information see Aengus Richard Martyn *Fogarty*, Merchant Shipping Legislation, 2nd Ed., London 2004.

[4] *Marsden*, p. 731 para. 20-22.

(3) If any damage to person or property arises from the non-observance by any ship of any of the collision regulations, the damage shall be deemed to have been occasioned by the wilful fault of the person in charge of the deck of the ship at that time, unless it is shown to the satisfaction of the court that the circumstances of the case made a departure from the regulation necessary."

Accordingly, owners and masters of ships were required to comply with the collision regulations and if they infringed the regulations by "wilful fault", they were held criminally accountable and punished[5]. Furthermore, if any damage arose from the non-observance of the regulations, damage was deemed to have been occasioned by the "wilful fault" of the person in charge of the deck of the ship at the time of the accident[6].

II. Cases and "Wilful Fault"

The interpretation of the term "wilful fault" by the courts is of core importance in showing the parallelism between "wilful fault" and "wilful misconduct". To this end, cases addressing § 419 of MSA 1894 should be examined.

1. Cases

a) *Bradshaw v. Ewart-James (The "N.F. Tiger")*

The master of the "N.F. Tiger" ordered a course in accordance with the collision regulations then in force. After a period of time he left the bridge and handed over the navigation of the ship to his chief officer. However, during the watch of the chief officer, the ship crossed the traffic lane, infringing the collision regulations. The Secretary of State for Trade claimed that the master of the ship was in contravention of the MSA 1894 § 419. The prosecutor further claimed that the master could not delegate his statutory duty of obeying collision regulations and this fact would support his being found guilty of an offence under MSA 1894 § 419 (2)[7].

The defendant contended "that it was not sufficient [...] to show merely a breach of duty or act of negligence because sub-section (2) of Section 419 of the Merchant Shipping Act, 1894 requires any infringement of the Collision Regulations to be caused by the wilful fault of the master before the master can be guilty of an offence and further that 'wilful' meant deliberately and 'fault' meant knowing and intending so that to succeed the appellant had to prove the master knew of

---

[5]   Part XIII – Legal Proceedings – Prosecution of offences, § 680: "(1) Subject to any special provisions of this Act and to the provisions hereinafter contained with respect to Scotland, (a) an offence under this Act declared to be a misdemeanour, shall be punishable by fine or by imprisonment not exceeding two years, with or without hard labour, but may, instead of being prosecuted as a misdemeanour, be prosecuted summarily in manner provided by the Summary Jurisdiction Acts, and if so prosecuted shall be punishable only with imprisonment for a term not exceeding six months, with or without hard labour, or with a fine not exceeding one hundred pounds, [...]".

[6]   *Marsden*, p. 731 para. 20-22.

[7]   [1982] 2 Lloyd's Rep. 564, 565 (QBD).

and intended or permitted the infringement or had been deliberately negligent in carrying out his statutory duty to obey the Regulations"[8].

After discussing whether the necessary *mens rea* element[9] was met in the delegation of his duties, the court rejected the submission of the prosecutor and decided that the master's behaviour did not amount to wilful fault.

b) *Taylor v. O'Keefe (The "Nordic Clansman")*

During the navigation of the vessel "Nordic Clansman" through the Strait of Hormuz, the master of the ship ordered a course to pass through the Strait which was in contravention of the collision regulations in force. However, the master considered that the course he ordered was fully lawful. Subsequently, the master was charged with the offence of infringement of the collision regulations. It was claimed that the master's conduct amounted to wilful fault because he knew what he was doing and intended to do it and that by no means was he acting lawfully[10].

The defendant asserted that "the words "wilful fault" required the court to find not only that the defendant consciously committed the act which constitutes the offence, but also that he knew and appreciated that the act was wrong. The word "wilful" was intended to qualify the word "fault". A fault could not properly be described as wilful if the defendant believed that his actions were lawful."[11].

The defendant also claimed that the principles in cases on the Warsaw Convention Art. 25[12] should apply in construing the meaning of the term "wilful fault". However, the court declined the application of a principle derived from the private law actions to criminal liability[13].

The court discussed the scope of the *mens rea* element of the offence and "wilful fault", and, observing the principle *ignorantia juris non excusat*, concluded that the master was criminally liable.

2. Meaning of the term

In *Bradshaw v. Ewart-James (The "N.F. Tiger")*, it was stated that "it was not established to the satisfaction of the Justices that the [master] had knowledge of the infringement or that he had been deliberately negligent", and that the "third stage in the argument is to construe the word "wilful" as being synonymous with the word "conscious" so that what is required is a conscious fault"[14].

In *Taylor v. O'Keefe (The "Nordic Clansman")*, it was stated that "the words "wilful fault" in this context appear to [the Court] to mean that the master must, by his act or omission, have brought about the state of affairs which constitutes an

---

8   [1982] 2 Lloyd's Rep. 564, 566 (QBD).
9   For further information regarding *mens rea* element in criminal law see *Card, Cross & Jones*, pp. 76 *et seqq.*; *Smith & Hogan*, pp. 94 *et seqq.*
10   [1984] 1 Lloyd's Rep. 31, 31-32 (QBD).
11   [1984] 1 Lloyd's Rep. 31, 33 (QBD).
12   See *infra* § 4 A II 2.
13   [1984] 1 Lloyd's Rep. 31, 37 (QBD).
14   [1982] 2 Lloyd's Rep. 564, 566-567 (QBD) *per* Lord Lane.

infringement of the Collision Regulations, and that either (1) his act or omission was deliberate and that it was a conscious act in the sense that he was aware of all relevant facts giving rise to the infringement, or (2) he did not care whether his act or omission would cause an infringement of the Collision Regulations or not."[15].

As a result, in order to be guilty of infringement of collision regulations by wilful fault, an owner or master must either commit an intentional act or omission; in other words consciously acting or failing to act and simultaneously appreciating the consequences of this behaviour; or a reckless act or omission, namely acting or failing to act without caring what the result might be. Accordingly, wilful fault, in the MSA 1894 sense, is an act or omission done with the intent to infringe the regulations or with reckless indifference whether an act or omission is going to cause an infringement of the regulations.

B. Private Law

I. Carriage by Rail

Before the MIA 1906, the term "wilful misconduct" was being used as a part of a contractual clause used in railway carriage. According to custom, which was also accepted as legally valid by the case law[16], railways were entitled to exempt themselves from every liability other than wilful misconduct when they carried goods at a reduced rate, provided that they offered an ordinary rate alongside the reduced rate[17]. When they carried the goods at the ordinary rate, they were liable as common carriers and were liable as insurers of the carried goods: they were strictly liable for any delay, as well as for any loss or damage[18].

1. Cases

a) *Glenister v. Great Western Railway Company*

The plaintiff was one of the ordinary customers of the Great Western Railway Company (GWR). It was customary between them for the GWR to carry goods at

---

[15]   [1984] 1 Lloyd's Rep. 31, 35 (QBD) *per* Lord Webster.

[16]   *Glenister v. Great Western Railway Company* (1873) 29 L.T. 423 (QBD); *Lewis v. Great Western Railway Company* (1878) 47 L.J. (N.S.) 131 (CA).

[17]   If railways did not offer any choice other than carriage at the owner's risk, such clauses were considered unjust and unreasonable; and, therefore, null and void by virtue of the Railway and Canal Traffic Act, 1854 § 7 (17&18 Vict., Ch. 31): "Every [...] company [...] shall be liable for the loss of or for any injury done to [...] any articles, goods or things, in the receiving, forwarding, or delivering thereof, occasioned by the neglect or fault of such company or its servants, notwithstanding any notice, condition, or declaration made and given by such company contrary thereto, [...] declared to be null and void". For more information on the "doctrine of fair alternative" see *Kahn-Freund*, pp. 223-227.

[18]   *Kahn-Freund*, pp. 193-202. For detailed information on the concept of common carriers see *Basedow, Common Carriers*, 256 *et seqq.*

the reduced rate, which was half of the ordinary rate, and exempted itself from ordinary common carrier liability. In the case which caused the conflict at hand, the plaintiff delivered chairs for transport. On the consignment note, the following clause was printed: "Receive and forward the [...] goods, to be carried at the reduced rate below the company's ordinary rate; in consideration whereof I undertake to relieve the Great Western Railway Company, and all other companies over whose lines the goods may pass, from all liability in case of damage or delay, except upon proof that such loss, detention or injury arose from wilful misconduct on the part of the company's servants."[19]. Consequently, at the reduced rate for carriage, the GWR was not liable except for its servants' wilful misconduct.

At the station where the goods were loaded on the train, other goods also being carried, cattle were unloaded. Servants of the railway took them into a yard; however, some strayed and caused loss of some and damage to the rest of the plaintiff's goods. The cargo owners contended that the servants of the railway were guilty of wilful misconduct due to inconsiderate and improper unloading of the cattle and due to lack of adequate and sufficient care.

The judge of the local court left the issue to the jury and instructed them that they need to solve the issue in the light of "whether the defendants by their servants had used *all reasonable care and precaution such as experienced and careful men ought to have adopted under the circumstances* [...] If the servants of the defendants had not done so, it would amount to wilful misconduct, within the meaning of the conditions in the consignment notes [...] – "wilful" not to be taken to mean from any desire to do damage, but wilful and culpable neglect to do what was proper and the neglect of which would be a wilful abandonment of a duty imposed upon them."[20]. The jury decided in favour of the cargo owners.

The GWR appealed and the issue came before the Queen's Bench Division. The court accepted the appeal and ruled that the circumstances of the case do not show a fault amounting to wilful misconduct, and that the judge was wrong in instructing the jury that culpable negligence is necessarily wilful misconduct. The court further stated that "there may have been some neglect by the company's servants, but [the Court] cannot see how they can possibly be said to have been guilty of wilful misconduct. There is nothing to show that what they wilfully did – that is, drive the cattle into the yard – was likely to cause injury to the plaintiff's goods"[21].

b) *Lewis v. GWR*

Cargo owners entered into an agreement for the carriage of cheese with the GWR. The consignment note signed by the cargo owners contained a clause stating that

---

[19] *Glenister v. Great Western Railway Company* (1873) 29 L.T. 423 (QBD).

[20] Emphasis added; *Glenister v. Great Western Railway Company* (1873) 29 L.T. 423, 425 (QBD).

[21] *Glenister v. Great Western Railway Company* (1873) 29 L.T. 423, 426 (QBD) *per* Justice Blackburn.

the cargo owners agreed to the carriage at the reduced rate and that they relieved the GWR of all liability for loss, damage or delay; in other words, the goods were sent at owner's risk. However, the goods arrived at their destination in a greatly damaged condition due to their faulty packing. On appeal, the Court of Appeal ruled in favour of the GWR stating that even if there was negligence, there was not wilful misconduct on the servants' side of the GWR, also taking into consideration that the servants were generally not familiar with cheese packing methods.

Furthermore, the Court stated that "[w]hat is meant by "wilful misconduct" is misconduct to which the will is a party, it is something opposed to accidental or negligent; the mis part of it, not the conduct must be wilful. If a person knows that mischief will result from his conduct, then he is guilty of wilful misconduct if he so conducts himself. Further, [the Court] think[s] it would be wilful misconduct if a man misconducted himself with an indifference to his duty to ascertain whether such conduct was mischievous or not."[22]; and that "[t]here cannot [...] be any doubt that wilful misconduct is something entirely different from negligence, something far beyond it, whether it is what is called culpable or gross or anything of the sort. There must be a doing of something which the person doing it knows will cause risk or injury, or the doing of an unusual thing with reference to the matter in hand, either in spite of warning or without care, regardless of whether or not it will cause injury."[23].

c) Haynes v. GWR

Goods in the form of horse rakes were delivered in sound condition to the GWR for carriage at owner's risk, but at a reduced freight rate. However, when they arrived at their destination, they were greatly damaged and broken because they had been placed on a truck which was shorter than the rakes and which lacked any cover for protection. Thus, the damage was caused due to insufficient packing. The Court ruled in favour of the GWR due to a lack of evidence and stated that "[wilful misconduct] is stronger than the phrase "wilful negligence", because it involves something in the nature of a wrong action – something that is not mere negligent omission, but wrong conduct on the servants of the company."[24].

d) Gordon v. GWR

Cargo owners delivered some cattle to the defendant GWR to be carried at the reduced rate in exchange for being relieved of liability except for wilful misconduct of the GWR's servants. Upon the arrival of the animals to the unloading station, the GWR refused to deliver the goods since its clerk at the loading station had omitted to write on the consignment note that the freight was prepaid. Until

---

[22] *Lewis v. Great Western Railway Company* (1878) 47 L.J. (N.S.) 131, 135 (CA) *per* Justice Bramwell.

[23] *Lewis v. Great Western Railway Company* (1878) 47 L.J. (N.S.) 131, 139 (CA) *per* Lord Justice Cotton.

[24] *Haynes v. Great Western Railway Company* (1879-1880) 41 L.T. 436, 438 (Common Pleas Division) *per* Justice Grove.

the mistake could be ascertained the next day, the animals were retained. Consequently, they were exposed to the weather and, as a result, damaged. The cargo owners sued the GWR for wrongfully withholding of the cargo and for negligence.

The Court decided that withholding of the cargo was not covered by the clause, and, therefore, relief for damage caused by such retention was not given; consequently, the railway was liable for the damage. Although the Court decided in favour of the cargo owners, it stated that "mere honest forgetfulness such as that of the clerk at [the loading station], if he had simply forgotten to write "carriage paid" on the note" is not wilful misconduct[25].

e) *Forder v. GWR*

Goods consisting of sheepskins were delivered to the GWR in good condition. The goods were, however, delivered in damaged condition, since they had been packed upon a bedding of wood chips which became entangled in the wool. The cargo owners complained to the railway and warned them not to pack their goods with wood chips in the future. GWR agreed, and, therefore, the cargo owners sent a second parcel of the sheepskins at the owner's risk. However, the second parcel arrived also in damaged condition owing to their having again been packed with wood chips although GWR's attention had been specifically called to the packing method. The cargo owners sued the GWR and alleged that the damage to the second parcel was caused by wilful misconduct of the GWR's servants.

The Court ruled in favour of the GWR, although it accepted that the case at hand is "one of those cases which come very near the line"[26]. The Court stated that the cargo owners warned the GWR not to use a certain packing method, but did not warn that this certain mode of packing causes damage to their goods. Furthermore, there is no evidence that the message was relayed to the persons at the loading station who were in charge of the control and management of the loading. The stationmaster's having omitted to pass on the message does not constitute wilful misconduct, but constitutes only negligence[27].

f) *Bastable v. North British Railway Company*

Cargo owners delivered a plant to the railway to be carried at the owner's risk. One of the railway's regulations clearly ordered that all goods must be measured if there was any reason to doubt that they were not within the dimensions specified for the route on which the goods have to travel. The stationmaster failed to measure the pieces of the plant; rather he judged their height visually and concluded that they were within the specified dimensions. He was, however, wrong and the pieces came into contact with a bridge and were damaged during the carriage.

---

[25]   *Gordon v. Great Western Railway Company* (1881-1882) 8 Q.B.D. 44, 47 (QBD)
per Justice Grove.

[26]   *Forder v. Great Western Railway Company* [1905] 2 K.B. 532, 535 (KBD) *per*
Justice Alverstone.

[27]   *Forder v. Great Western Railway Company* [1905] 2 K.B. 532 (KBD).

The cargo owners sued the railway and asserted that the stationmaster who failed to measure the goods was guilty of wilful misconduct. The Court ruled in favour of the cargo owners; however one of the judges dissented from the general opinion of the Court. In his opinion, he stated that "[i]n wilful misconduct [...] the will must be party to the misconduct. Negligence, even gross and culpable negligence, excludes the idea of will. Negligence done on purpose is a contradiction in terms. The moment that an act of omission or commission, which involves the neglect of a known duty, is done intentionally, or with the will, in disregard of that duty, it ceases to be negative negligence and becomes positive misconduct and that wilful, and in such wilful misconduct there is, [...] involved a recklessness of consequences."[28].

2. Meaning

The meaning given to the term wilful misconduct in the sense of the carriage by rail is clear. First of all, it should be stressed that wilful misconduct is wholly different from negligence and involves a different level of culpability, regardless of how gross the negligence may be[29]. Negligence, *e.g.* mere forgetfulness[30], is not sufficient for a finding of wilful misconduct[31].

In order to be guilty of wilful misconduct, a relevant person (in the case of carriage by rail, typically servants of the railway) must have acted or omitted to act with the intention to cause damage to the goods[32]. The act or omission must be wrong for a finding of "misconduct"[33], and the wrongdoer must be aware that he is committing misconduct[34]. In addition to misconduct, the wrongdoer should foresee and appreciate that damage will likely result[35]; and either with the motive to cause the foreseen damage or with indifference as to whether the damage would result, the wrongdoer should continue committing the misconduct[36].

---

[28] *William Bastable v. The North British Railway Company* 1912 S.C. 555, 562 (Court of Session) *per* Justice Johnston (dissenting).

[29] *Glenister v. Great Western Railway Company* (1873) 29 L.T. 423 (QBD); *Lewis v. Great Western Railway Company* (1878) 47 L.J. (N.S.) 131 (CA); *William Bastable v. The North British Railway Company* 1912 S.C. 555, 562 (Court of Session) *per* Justice Johnston (dissenting); *Kahn-Freund,* p. 257; *Clarke, CMR,* p. 317.

[30] *Gordon v. Great Western Railway Company* (1881-1882) 8 Q.B.D. 44 (QBD).

[31] *Glenister v. Great Western Railway Company* (1873) 29 L.T. 423 (QBD).

[32] *Glenister v. Great Western Railway Company* (1873) 29 L.T. 423 (QBD).

[33] *Lewis v. Great Western Railway Company* (1878) 47 L.J. (N.S.) 131 (CA).

[34] *Lewis v. Great Western Railway Company* (1878) 47 L.J. (N.S.) 131, 137 (CA) *per* Lord Justice Brett; *William Bastable v. The North British Railway Company* 1912 S.C. 555, 562 (Court of Session) *per* Justice Johnston (dissenting); *Kahn-Freund,* p. 257.

[35] *Forder v. Great Western Railway Company* [1905] 2 K.B. 532, 538 (KBD) *per* Justice Ridley; *Kahn-Freund,* p. 257.

[36] *Lewis v. Great Western Railway Company* (1878) 47 L.J. (N.S.) 131 (CA); *William Bastable v. The North British Railway Company* 1912 S.C. 555, 562 (Court of Session) *per* Justice Johnston (dissenting); *Kahn-Freund,* pp. 257-258.

II. Marine Insurance Act, 1906 § 55 (2)(a)

1. Basic principles

a) Provision

It is worth underlining that the MIA 1906 is the result of the effort to codify the existing British law of marine insurance. Provisions of the Act were taken from the Marine Insurance Bill, which was introduced in the House of Lords towards the end of the 19th century. The main aim of the Bill was to codify the existing law as exactly as possible without any amendment[37]. Thus, the issues to be discussed below had been the existing law also before the MIA 1906 was enacted.

According to § 55 (1) of the MIA 1906, subject to the provisions of the Act, and unless the policy otherwise provides, the insurer is liable for any loss proximately caused by a peril[38] insured against, whereas he is not liable for any loss which is not proximately caused by a peril that had been insured for.

§ 55 (1) of the MIA 1906 states the general rule. As to this general rule, parties of a marine insurance contract can specify the perils insured against (named perils insurance) or not insured against (all risks insurance)[39], and the insurer is only liable for the losses proximately caused by the perils insured against. However, § 55 (1) of the MIA 1906 has some exceptions which are stated under section (2) of the provision.

The first exception is wilful misconduct of the assured[40]. By virtue of § 55 (2)(a) "The insurer is not liable for any loss attributable to the wilful misconduct of the assured, but, unless the policy otherwise provides, he is liable for any loss proximately caused by a peril insured against, even though the loss would not have happened but for the misconduct or negligence of the master or crew". This provision is the first legislative instrument where the term "wilful misconduct" is literally used.

It has been emphasized[41] that the basis of § 55 (2)(a) during the codification work had been the case of *Trinder, Anderson & Co. v. Thames and Mersey Marine Insurance Co.* The case regarded the stranding of the ship *Gainsborough* by the negligence of the master, who was also co-owner. The co-owners sued the insurance company for the indemnity. The legal question was whether the loss was caused by the perils of the sea and whether the plaintiffs were entitled to recover. In his judgment, Lord Kennedy stated that the plaintiffs were entitled to recover and that the negligence of the assured was not an adequate defence for the

---

[37]   M. D. *Chalmers*/J. G. *Archibald*, The Marine Insurance Act, 1906, 3rd Ed., London 1922, p. vii.

[38]   According to § 3 (2) of the MIA 1906; 'Maritime perils' means the perils consequent on, or incidental to, the navigation of the sea, that is to say, perils of the seas, fire, war perils, pirates, rovers, thieves, captures, seizures, restraints and detainments of princes and peoples, jettisons, barratry, and any other perils, either of the like kind, or which may be designated by the policy.

[39]   *Clarke*, p. 493; *Rose*, pp. 267-269; *O'May*, pp. 164-168.

[40]   For other exceptions, see MIA 1906 § 55 (2)(b) and (c).

[41]   *Thomas*, p. 244 para. 7.3.

defendant insurance company. He also stated that if the conduct of the plaintiff amounted to wilful misconduct, the defendant underwriters would be entitled to succeed[42].

Both § 55 (2)(a) MIA and the underlying case clearly show that there is difference between negligence and wilful misconduct. However, in order to determine the meaning of wilful misconduct precisely, and to determine the difference between negligence and wilful misconduct under marine insurance law, some more basic rules have to be discussed.

b) Risk-related principles

Insurance contracts are made against risks. Whether it is a named perils or an all risks insurance policy, the function of every insurance contract is to transfer risk from the assured on to the insurer. Risk is an ambiguous event which might occur, and causes loss or harm if it occurs. Consequently, loss or harm should be caused by an accidental event and an accidental or fortuitous event should be "neither expected nor intended"[43], which leads to another general rule of insurance law that an insurer is not liable in cases where harm or loss is deliberately caused by the assured. This is clearly regulated in most countries in enactments regarding insurance contracts[44], but there is no such enactment under English law, which covers all insurance contracts.

According to English law, the loss or harm caused by the wilful misconduct of the assured is not covered, first of all, due to the contingency requirement of insurance (the principle of fortuity). Although there is a difference between the principle of fortuity and wilful misconduct in the sense that the principle of fortuity is assessed at the beginning of the insurance period whereas wilful misconduct of the assured can affect the insurance contract at any time[45], it is clear that if the damage or loss is caused by the assured's wilful misconduct, that damage or loss has not resulted from an accidental event[46]. Secondly, if the assured causes the damage or harm deliberately, it constitutes a breach of the duty of good faith, which is one of the essential conditions of an insurance contract and one which continues during the whole contractual relationship[47]. Furthermore, the law will not allow someone to take advantage of his own wrong, in other words cause

---

[42]   *Trinder, Anderson and Co. v. North Queensland Insurance Co.* (1897) 66 L.J. (Q.B.) 802, 803 (QBD); affirmed by *Trinder, Anderson & Co. v. Thames and Mersey Marine Insurance Company* (1898) 2 Q.B.D. 114 (CA).

[43]   *Clarke*, p. 804.

[44]   For German law see § 81 VVG and for Turkish law see TTK (1956) Art. 1278, 1380 and TTK (2011) Art. 1429, 1477. For American law see Russell M. *Pfeifer*, Navigating Through the Shoals of the Marine Hull Policy: A Chart for Insurers, (2004-2005) 17 U.S.F. Mar. L.J. 89, 93-99.

[45]   *Clarke*, p. 497.

[46]   *Merkin*, p. 76; *Colinvaux*, p. 123; *Rose*, pp. 347-348.

[47]   For more information see *Clarke*, pp. 879 *et seqq.*; *Colinvaux*, pp. 133 *et seqq.*

damage or loss deliberately and obtain indemnification for it. Clearly, such a result would be against public policy[48].

MIA 1906 § 55 (2)(a) reflects these general principles. The Marine Insurance Act also does not allow the assured to take advantage of his own fraudulent conduct. Accordingly, § 55 (2)(a) does not contain the expression "unless the policy otherwise provides."[49]. In *Trinder, Anderson & Co. v. Thames and Mersey Marine Insurance Company* it was stated that "the wilful fault of the owner inducing the loss will debar him from suing on the policy in respect of it on two grounds, either of which would suffice to defeat his right: first, because no one can take advantage of his own wrong, using the word in its true sense which does not embrace mere negligence; secondly, because the wilful act takes from the catastrophe the accidental character which is essential to constitute a peril of the sea"[50].

2. Case law and wilful misconduct

In order to precisely determine the meaning of wilful misconduct in British marine insurance law, its application in case law and the meaning given to the term by the courts should be stated. Alongside the cases from the first half of the 20th century, cases and insurance practice from recent times are equally helpful in analysing the application and interpretation of the term.

a) Cases

aa) Hull insurance

There are a considerable number of hull insurance cases with regard to the MIA 1906 § 55 (2)(a) and they almost always involve casting away of the ship by or with the privity of the assured. Scuttling of a ship is the clearest example of the loss caused by wilful misconduct of the assured[51].

It should be noted that most of the cases are the result of the economic crisis after World War I. It appears that, owing to the sharp fall in freight rates in the shipping market, most shipowners were not able to pay their debts, mortgage instalments, *etc.* Due to these reasons, they chose to cast away their ships and made fraudulent claims against insurers. Insurers asserted wilful misconduct of the assured. Consequently, courts awarded their decisions considering relevant factors such as over-insurance[52], the assured's financial position[53], financial loss due to

---

[48]   *Ivamy*, p. 232; E. R. *Ivamy*, General Principles of Insurance Law, 6th Ed., London 1993, pp. 288-290; *Clarke*, p. 498; *O'May*, p. 108; *Arnould*, p. 957.
[49]   *O'May*, p. 108; *Arnould*, p. 957; *Rose*, p. 347.
[50]   (1898) 2 Q.B.D. 114, 127 (CA) *per* Justice Smith.
[51]   *Merkin*, p. 75; *O'May*, p. 108; *Arnould*, p. 957; *Bennett*, p. 220.
[52]   Though the fact of over-insurance exists almost in every case, the most important cases are worth to note: *Visscherrij Maatschappij Nieuwe Onderneming v. Scottish Metropolitan Assurance Company* (1922) 10 Ll. L. Rep. 579 (CA); *Doriga Y Sanudo v. Royal Exchange Assurance Corporation, Ltd., Same v. Scottish Metropolitan Assurance Co., Ltd. (The "Marianela")* (1922) 13 Ll. L. Rep. 166 (KBD); *Anghelatos v. Northern Assurance Co. London Joint City & Midland Bank v. Same*

operating the ship[54], the nature of the casualty, the conduct of the assured[55] or the master and crew[56] following the casualty[57], explanations of the master and crew

---

(1924) 19 Ll. L. Rep. 255 (HL); *Banco de Barcelona v. Union Marine Insurance Co.* (1925) 22 Ll. L. Rep. 317 (KBD) (the court awarded a decision in favour of the defendant insurance company in spite of the fact that the captain went down with the ship).

[53] *Visscherrij Maatschappij Nieuwe Onderneming v. Scottish Metropolitan Assurance Company* (1922) 10 Ll. L. Rep. 579 (CA); *Anghelatos v. Northern Assurance Co. London Joint City & Midland Bank v. Same* (1924) 19 Ll. L. Rep. 255 (HL); *Continental Illinois National Bank & Trust Co. of Chicago and Xenofon Maritime S.A. v. Alliance Assurance Co. Ltd. (The "Captain Panagos D.P.")* [1986] 2 Lloyd's Rep. 470 (QBD); *Continental Illinois National Bank & Trust Co. of Chicago and Xenofon Maritime S.A. v. Alliance Assurance Co. Ltd. (The "Captain Panagos D.P.")* [1989] 1 Lloyd's Rep. 33 (CA).

[54] *Visscherrij Maatschappij Nieuwe Onderneming v. Scottish Metropolitan Assurance Company* (1922) 10 Ll. L. Rep. 579 (CA); *Anghelatos v. Northern Assurance Co. London Joint City & Midland Bank v. Same* (1924) 19 Ll. L. Rep. 255 (HL); *Domingo Mumbru Soc. Anon. and Others v. Laurie and Others (The "Ramon Mumbru")* (1924) 20 Ll. L. Rep. 189 (KBD); *Continental Illinois National Bank & Trust Co. of Chicago and Xenofon Maritime S.A. v. Alliance Assurance Co. Ltd. (The "Captain Panagos D.P.")* [1986] 2 Lloyd's Rep. 470 (QBD); *Continental Illinois National Bank & Trust Co. of Chicago and Xenofon Maritime S.A. v. Alliance Assurance Co. Ltd. (The "Captain Panagos D.P.")* [1989] 1 Lloyd's Rep. 33 (CA).

[55] Such as not asking nor receiving any information regarding the casualty from the master, see *Bank of Athens v. Royal Exchange Assurance (The "Eftychia")* (1937) 57 Ll. L. Rep. 37 (KBD); *Bank of Athens v. Royal Exchange Assurance (The "Eftychia")* (1937) 59 Ll. L. Rep. 67 (CA).

[56] Such as lack of effort to save the ship, see *Visscherrij Maatschappij Nieuwe Onderneming v. Scottish Metropolitan Assurance Company* (1922) 10 Ll. L. Rep. 579 (CA); *Domingo Mumbru Soc. Anon. and Others v. Laurie and Others (The "Ramon Mumbru")* (1924) 20 Ll. L. Rep. 189 (KBD); *Grauds v. Dearsley* (1935) 51 Ll. L. Rep. 203 (KBD); *Compania Naviera Santi, S.A. v. Indemnity Marine Assurance Company, Ltd. (The "Tropaioforos")* [1960] 2 Lloyd's Rep. 469 (QBD) (Captain of the ship was perfectly dressed and clean shaven); or rejection of the salvage offer, see *Astrovlanis Compania Naviera S.A. v. Linard (The "Gold Sky")* [1972] 2 Lloyd's Rep. 187 (QBD); *Continental Illinois National Bank & Trust Co. of Chicago and Xenofon Maritime S.A. v. Alliance Assurance Co. Ltd. (The "Captain Panagos D.P.")* [1986] 2 Lloyd's Rep. 470 (QBD); *Continental Illinois National Bank & Trust Co. of Chicago and Xenofon Maritime S.A. v. Alliance Assurance Co. Ltd. (The "Captain Panagos D.P.")* [1989] 1 Lloyd's Rep. 33 (CA).

[57] Such as lack of communication between the owner and the captain, see *Anghelatos v. Northern Assurance Co. London Joint City & Midland Bank v. Same* (1924) 19 Ll. L. Rep. 255 (HL); *Continental Illinois National Bank & Trust Co. of Chicago and Xenofon Maritime S.A. v. Alliance Assurance Co. Ltd. (The "Captain Panagos D.P.")* [1986] 2 Lloyd's Rep. 470 (QBD); *Continental Illinois National Bank & Trust Co. of Chicago and Xenofon Maritime S.A. v. Alliance Assurance Co. Ltd. (The "Captain Panagos D.P.")* [1989] 1 Lloyd's Rep. 33 (CA).

and the condition of the vessel[58]. And yet, these factors were not regarded as sufficient in every case to prove a scuttling claim[59], and in some cases, despite the good financial situation and high reputation of the assured, courts awarded a decision in favour of the defendant insurance companies[60].

It is beyond doubt that in cases of scuttling with a fraudulent claim against the insurer filed afterwards, culpable intent is clear. However, sometimes determination of wilful misconduct is not so simple for insurers. In the case *Papadimitriou v. Henderson*[61] a Greek flagged ship was captured by an insurgent Spanish ship, forced to proceed to a Spanish port and, subsequently confiscated there. Consequently, the ship became an actual and constructive total loss. At the time of the capture, the ship was proceeding upon her chartered voyage, and the port of discharge agreed by charterers and the shipowner was close to a dangerous area where some stoppages or searches were expected. War insurers claimed that the shipowner was warned about the danger, but he nevertheless ran his ship into danger. Therefore, the loss was not caused by an insured risk, but by wilful misconduct of the assured. The court ruled in favour of the assured shipowner and stated that "it would be a very dangerous doctrine to lay down [...] that the captain of a neutral ship or the owner of a neutral ship or the owner of a ship belonging to a country not at war, is guilty of wilful misconduct if he tries to proceed with his contract voyage, simply because there is a risk of capture, as there must always be a risk of capture during a war, which is the very reason why shipowners and merchants insure against war risks"[62]. However, the Court did not stop here and proceeded to state what would constitute wilful misconduct in a similar case: "Of course, if it was a case in which the shipowner got warning that a blockade had been established at a particular port or that a ship was lying waiting at a particular point, and the shipowner deliberately sent his ship forward to that point to run the blockade, it may be that there would be, in certain cases, an inference to be drawn that he was not endeavouring to carry out the voyage, but what he was endeav-

---

[58]   *Merkin*, p. 75; *Ivamy*, pp. 233-242; *O'May*, pp. 109-114; *Bennett*, pp. 221-223.

[59]   *Elfie A. Issaias v. Marine Insurance Co., Ltd.* (1923) 15 Ll. L. Rep. 186 (CA); *Lemos v. British & Foreign Marine Insurance Company, Ltd.* (1931) 39 Ll. L. Rep. 275 (KBD); *Maris and Another v. London Assurance* (1935) 52 Ll. L. Rep. 211 (CA); *Compania Naviera Vascongada v. British & Foreign Marine Insurance Co., Ltd. (The "Gloria")* (1936) 54 Ll. L. Rep. 35 (KBD); *Piermay Shipping Co. S.A. and Brandt's Ltd. V. Chester (The "Michael")* [1979] 1 Lloyd's Rep. 55 (QBD); *N. Michalos & Sons Maritime S.A. and Another v. Prudential Assurance Co. Ltd., Public Corporation for Sugar Trade v. N. Michalos & Sons Maritime Co. Ltd. (The "Zinovia")* [1984] 2 Lloyd's Rep. 264 (QBD); *Strive Shipping Corporation and Another v. Hellenic Mutual War Risks Association (The "Grecia Express")* [2002] 2 Lloyd's Rep. 88 (QBD).

[60]   *National Justice Compania S.A. v. Prudential Assurance Co. Ltd. (The "Ikarian Reefer")* [1993] 2 Lloyd's Rep. 68 (QBD); *National Justice Compania S.A. v. Prudential Assurance Co. Ltd. (The "Ikarian Reefer")* [1995] 1 Lloyd's Rep. 455 (CA).

[61]   (1939) 64 Ll. L. Rep. 345 (KBD).

[62]   *Papadimitriou v. Henderson* (1939) 64 Ll. L. Rep. 345, 348 (KBD).

ouring to do was to get his ship captured, and that, of course, would be wilful misconduct"[63]. As it is clearly stated in the decision, deliberately causing the insured risk is an essential element of wilful misconduct.

bb) P&I insurance

Although the range of the protection and indemnity (P&I) insurance cases regarding the MIA 1906 § 55 (2)(a) is not as wide as it is with the hull insurance cases, certain and specific issues which have arisen in the area of P&I insurance should be emphasised. MIA 1906 § 55 (2)(a) is also applicable to P&I insurance as expressly stated in the MIA § 85 (4) as "the provisions of this Act apply to a mutual insurance". Despite the express provision in the MIA 1906, Clubs nonetheless prefer to insert special clauses with regard to wilful misconduct into the membership agreements, for example:

> "There shall be no right of recovery of any claim from the Association if it arises out of wilful misconduct on the part of the Member (being an act intentionally done or a deliberate omission by the Member with knowledge that the performance or omission will probably result in injury or loss, or an act done or omitted in such a way as to allow an inference of a reckless disregard for the probable consequences)"[64].

Clear examples of wilful misconduct in the context of P&I insurance are, for instance, a deliberate collision with another ship and intentional injury inflicted on the passengers or crew[65]. These obvious examples are not specifically mentioned in the membership agreements. However, provisions in the said agreements expressly exclude some other instances, for example issuing a false bill of lading[66], so that the relevant Club does not need to satisfy the burden of proof regarding the mental element[67].

---

[63] *Papadimitriou v. Henderson* (1939) 64 Ll. L. Rep. 345, 349 (KBD).
[64] Shipowners' Mutual Protection & Indemnity Association Rules 2008, Part V, Rule 30: "Liabilities Excluded if as a Result of Wilful Misconduct".
[65] *Hazelwood*, p. 244.
[66] *E.g.* Shipowners' Mutual Protection & Indemnity Association Rules 2008, Part II, Rule 14 (E)(iv) "Certain Exclusions from Cover": Unless the Board in its discretion shall otherwise determine, there shall be no right of recovery from the Association in respect of any liabilities, costs and expenses arising from: (a) the issue of a bill of lading, way bill or other document containing or evidencing the contract of carriage, issued with the knowledge of the Member or his Master with an incorrect description of the cargo or its quantity or its condition; (b) the issue of a bill of lading, way bill or other document containing or evidencing the contract of carriage which contains any fraudulent misrepresentation, including but not limited to the issue of an antedated or postdated bill of lading; (c) delivery of cargo carried under a negotiable bill of lading without production of that bill of lading by the person to whom delivery is made; (d) delivery of cargo carried under a way bill or similar nonnegotiable document to a party other than the party nominated by the shipper as the person to whom delivery should be made.
[67] For more information see *Hazelwood*, pp. 178-180, 182 *et seqq.*, 245-246.

Although failing to clearly mention the term "wilful misconduct" and not being a case regarding insurance, *Standard Chartered Bank v. Pakistan National Shipping Corporation and Others (No. 2)*[68] is a clear example of the issuance of a false bill of lading with the intention to defraud another. In a shipment from Iran to Vietnam, the cargo should have been loaded on board the ship not later than 25 October 1993 as provided by the letter of credit agreement provisions. Although loading on board the ship *Lalazar* started on October 18th, it was not completed on the 25th. In order to fulfil the conditions of the letter of credit, the shipper asked the carrier to issue an antedated bill of lading and assured by a letter of indemnity that he would indemnify them in respect of any liability. The carriers issued the antedated clean bill of lading to the shipper on 8 November, although the loading was not completed until 5 December. Subsequently, the bank was deceived and suffered financial damage. The Court held that the carrier is "guilty of dishonest conduct approved at the highest level"[69].

b) Meaning

Despite the multiplicity of cases involving the assured's wilful misconduct[70], there is no discussion of the question of what constitutes wilful misconduct, owing to the fact that almost all cases are concerned with scuttling by or with the privity of the shipowner. Accordingly, courts have had no difficulty in deciding whether a shipowner's conduct amounts to the degree of fault stated in the MIA 1906 § 55 (2)(a)[71].

Since most of the cases are concerned with a deliberate casting away of the ship, the degree of fault in these cases regarding the MIA 1906 § 55 (2)(a) has always been equal to the degree of fault labelled *dolus* in continental law. Approvingly, wilful misconduct has been defined as wilful, deliberate or conscious performance of the misconduct by the assured with the intention to cause the loss actually occurred[72]. Furthermore, it was stated in *Trinder, Anderson & Co. v. Thames and Mersey Marine Insurance Company* that the Court is not discussing "a loss brought about by the wilful act of an assured. Negligent navigation has never been held to be equivalent to 'dolus'..."[73]. The Court stated that the wilful act of an assured together with the intention to cause a specific loss is *dolus*.

However, wilful misconduct in the context of marine insurance does not cover only wilful acts of the assured. As stated in *Trinder, Anderson & Co. v. Thames*

---

[68] [1998] 1 Lloyd's Rep. 684 (QBD).

[69] [1998] 1 Lloyd's Rep. 684, 710 (QBD).

[70] It should be noted that unseaworthiness has never been discussed as wilful misconduct in the context of the MIA 1906 owing to the special regulation under § 39 of the Act.

[71] *Arnould*, p. 958.

[72] *Ivamy*, p. 232; *Merkin*, p. 75; *Arnould*, p. 958; *Bennett*, p. 218; *Rose*, p. 348; *Hazelwood*, p. 245. See also the example given in *Papadimitriou v. Henderson* (1939) 64 Ll. L. Rep. 345, 349 (KBD).

[73] (1898) 2 Q.B.D. 114, 123 (CA) *per* Lord Smith.

and Mersey Marine Insurance Company[74], "acts which are done knowingly or wilfully, or, at least, with a reckless disregard of possible risk to the safety of the subject of the insurance" constitute wilful misconduct. Setting aside the part concerning intentional acts, it was stated that if the assured closes his eyes to the foreseen probable consequences with a reckless disregard, this fault also amounts to wilful misconduct in the field of marine insurance.

This approach has also been accepted by English doctrine. It is emphasised by many writers that wilful misconduct also covers acts done in reckless disregard of the probable consequences of them[75]. In such cases, the assured is either aware of the high probability of exposure to the loss or is indifferent to that probability[76].

It is also emphasised that the approach stated above should, owing to policy considerations, be strictly applied in cases of safety. According to this view, breaches of safety regulations and accepted safety standards should be considered as wilful misconduct if the basic elements of intention, knowledge and reckless-ness exist[77]. Undoubtedly, breaches of rules and regulations and breaches of basic safety standards constitute *mis*conduct.

Finally, it is emphasised that the meaning of wilful misconduct in the field of marine insurance should be reconsidered[78] in conjunction with the development of the term in transport law. However, this view has been opposed owing to the reason that the meaning of wilful misconduct is different in the context of carriage of goods and passengers. As the function of wilful misconduct in transport law is to break the limits of liability, it is important to ascertain the carrier's or ship-owner's actual intention. But with regard to wilful misconduct in the context of marine insurance law, it is also important whether the insurer intended to assume the risk of the assured's conduct[79]. However, in a case regarding property insur-ance, the term wilful misconduct was discussed together with its definition under carriage by rail cases as well as transport law cases. At the same time, the Court took into consideration the function of the term in insurance law and premised its decision upon this function[80]. There is no reason preventing courts from reconsidering the definition of the term and allowing a reconsidered definition to reflect the function of wilful misconduct within the insurance law.

3. Wilful misconduct v. negligence

MIA 1906 § 55 (2)(a) states that the insurer is not liable in cases where the loss is caused by wilful misconduct of the assured, whereas he is liable for losses caused by the misconduct or the negligence of the master or crew[81]. Accordingly, there is

---

[74]   (1897) 66 L.J. (Q.B.) 802, 804 (QBD) *per* Lord Kennedy.
[75]   *Merkin*, p. 75; *Arnould*, p. 958; *Bennett*, p. 218; *Rose*, p. 348.
[76]   *Arnould*, p. 958.
[77]   *Thomas*, p. 247.
[78]   *Thomas*, p. 252.
[79]   *Clarke*, p. 498.
[80]   *National Oilwell (UK) Ltd. v. Davy Offshore Ltd.* [1993] 2 Lloyd's Rep. 582, 619-623 (QBD).
[81]   *Merkin*, p. 76; *Chalmers*, p. 79.

a difference between ordinary misconduct and negligence as opposed to wilful misconduct as the negligence of the master or crew is one of the perils of the seas whereas wilful misconduct is not. Undoubtedly, it is possible to agree by means of an insurance contract that the insurer will not be liable for the negligence of the master or crew or of the assured himself[82].

As stated above[83], the MIA 1906 was enacted with the intent of reproducing the existing law. The difference between negligence and wilful misconduct in the sense of marine insurance law has been clearly explained in *Trinder, Anderson and Co. v. North Queensland Insurance Co.*: "It is settled law, in regard to questions of marine insurance, [...] that negligence on the part of the agents and servants of the assured in the navigation of the ship conducing to that loss, affords no defence to underwriters. It is also settled law that if the loss, although perils of the seas be the proximate cause, is occasioned by the wilful act of the assured himself, as, for example, by scuttling, or by intentional running of the ship upon a rock, the assured cannot recover in respect of the loss from the underwriters."[84].

Therefore, wilful misconduct is essentially different from negligence either of the shipowner himself or of the crew. However, it is not always so easy to draw the line between the lowest degree of wilful misconduct, *i.e.* reckless conduct despite foresight of the probable consequences, and the highest degree of negligence[85].

III. Causation

1. Carriage by rail

The clauses employed by contracts of carriage by rail stipulate that cargo owners relieve the railway from liability "except upon proof that such [damage or loss] *arose from* wilful misconduct on the part of the company's servants"[86]. In deciding the cases, courts have discussed whether the loss or damage was "caused by"[87]

---

[82] *O'May*, pp. 106-108; *Merkin*, pp. 76-77. The legal situation is the same in other types of insurance contracts, see *Clarke*, p. 592.

[83] See *supra* B II 1 a.

[84] (1897) 66 L.J. (Q.B.) 802, 803 (QBD) *per* Lord Kennedy.

[85] See *Clarke*, p. 498.

[86] See *Glenister v. Great Western Railway Company* (1873) 29 L.T. 423 (QBD); *Lewis v. Great Western Railway Company* (1878) 47 L.J. (N.S.) 131, 132 (CA); *Haynes v. Great Western Railway Company* (1879-1880) 41 L.T. 436, 437 (Common Pleas Division); *Gordon v. Great Western Railway Company* (1881-1882) 8 Q.B.D. 44 (QBD); *Forder v. Great Western Railway Company* [1905] 2 K.B. 532 (KBD); *William Bastable v. The North British Railway Company* 1912 S.C. 555, 556 (Court of Session).

[87] *Glenister v. Great Western Railway Company* (1873) 29 L.T. 423, 425 (QBD) *per* Justice Blackburn; *Lewis v. Great Western Railway Company* (1878) 47 L.J. (N.S.) 131, 135 (CA) *per* Justice Bramwell.

or "arose from"[88] the wilful misconduct of the railway's servants. These terms, clearly, necessitate a causal connection between the wilful misconduct and the loss or damage occurred, that is, the loss or damage must result from the wilful misconduct of the person in question. However, this does not necessitate that the loss or damage is a direct consequence of wilful misconduct. It is sufficient if wilful misconduct is the effective or, in other words, the proximate cause.

2. Marine insurance

MIA 1906 § 55 (2)(a) stipulates that "[t]he insurer is not liable for any loss attributable to the wilful misconduct of the assured". It is disputed whether the phrase "attributable to" refers to the proximate cause and whether the insurer is exonerated from liability regardless of whether or not the wilful misconduct of the assured is the proximate cause of the loss or damage.

It is acknowledged by a number of authors to be beyond any doubt that the phrase "attributable to" refers to the proximate cause rule[89], even though it is stated in *Trinder, Anderson & Co. v. Thames and Mersey Marine Insurance Company* that the proximate cause rule does not apply in cases of wilful misconduct[90].

Contrary to the previous opinion, it was decided by the HL that the proximate cause rule is applicable also in cases of wilful misconduct and that the proximate cause is the most *effective* cause: "the question is whether the proximate cause of her sinking was the act of letting the water into vessel, or the actual inrush of the water. Apart from authority, [there is] no doubt that the former is the true view. There appears [...] to be something absurd in saying that, when a ship is scuttled by her crew, her loss is not caused by the act of scuttling, but by the incursion of water which results from it. No doubt both are part of the chain of events which result in the loss of the ship, but the scuttling is the real and operative cause – the nearest antecedent which can be called a cause"[91]. So, there is no doubt that the

---

[88] *Haynes v. Great Western Railway Company* (1879-1880) 41 L.T. 436, 438 (Common Pleas Division) *per* Justice Grove; *Forder v. Great Western Railway Company* [1905] 2 K.B. 532, 536 (KBD) *per* Justice Kennedy.

[89] *O'May*, p. 316; *Thomas*, p. 246; *Chalmers*, p. 79.

[90] (1898) 2 Q.B.D. 114, 124 (CA) *per* Lord Smith: "in a marine policy sea perils are what are insured against. The risk undertaken by an underwriter upon a policy covering perils of the sea is that, if the subject-matter insured is lost or damaged immediately by a peril of the sea, he will be responsible, and, in my judgement, it matters not if the loss or damage is remotely caused by the negligent navigation of the captain or crew, or of the assured himself, always assuming that the loss is not occasioned by the wilful act of the assured. In this last case the maxim above referred to, "causa proxima non remota spectatur", does not apply [...], for there not only does the maxim contravene the principles of insurance law and the manifest intentions of the parties, but is qualified by another legal maxim, "Dolus circuitu non purgatur".

[91] *PUK Samuel and Company v. Dumas* [1924] A.C. 431, 446-447 (HL) *per* Viscount Cave.

loss or damage should be the result of the act or omission amounting to wilful misconduct of the assured[92].

However, according to the counterview, it is of no importance whether the loss or damage was caused by the wilful misconduct of the assured. If there is wilful misconduct and if the wilful misconduct is one of the effective causes, insurers are under no obligation to indemnify[93]. Moreover, it is stated that the wilful misconduct need not be one of the effective causes; rather, it is sufficient for the insurer to be exonerated from liability merely when there is wilful misconduct of the assured: "[I]t is normally helpful, when considering the effect of negligence or misconduct on the cover afforded by a policy of marine insurance, to ask whether or not the negligence or misconduct is the "proximate cause" of the loss. Negligence and misconduct are generic terms that apply to acts or omissions that are coupled with a particular mental element. Where such act or omission results in loss or damage to property insured, this will be because the act or omission causes or permits a more direct physical cause of loss or damage to occur. […] A policy of marine insurance can provide cover against "negligence" or "misconduct" (other than of the assured) or exclude cover for losses attributable to such causes. In either case the cover or exclusion will apply whether or not the negligence or misconduct is the proximate cause of the loss."[94].

IV. Burden and Standard of Proof

1. Burden of proof

a) Carriage by rail

If a railway is liable as a common carrier, the cargo owner is under no burden to prove that the damage or loss was caused by negligence on the railway's part since the railway is strictly liable as a common carrier. Cargo owners need only prove that they delivered the goods to the railway in good condition and that they were damaged or lost when they were under the railway's possession[95]. However, when the goods are carried at the owner's risk, the cargo owner relieves the railway from all liability "except *upon proof* that the damage or loss caused by wilful misconduct of the servants of the railway"[96]. Therefore, the onus of proof that the

---

[92]   *Thomas*, p. 246; *Chalmers*, p. 79; *Bennett*, pp. 219-220.

[93]   *Arnould*, p. 958.

[94]   *State of the Netherlands v. Youell and Hayward and Others* [1998] 1 Lloyd's Rep. 236, 241 (CA) *per* Lord Phillips.

[95]   *Kahn-Freund*, p. 200.

[96]   See *Glenister v. Great Western Railway Company* (1873) 29 L.T. 423 (QBD); *Lewis v. Great Western Railway Company* (1878) 47 L.J. (N.S.) 131, 132 (CA); *Haynes v. Great Western Railway Company* (1879-1880) 41 L.T. 436, 437 (Common Pleas Division); *Gordon v. Great Western Railway Company* (1881-1882) 8 Q.B.D. 44 (QBD); *Forder v. Great Western Railway Company* [1905] 2 K.B. 532 (KBD); *William Bastable v. The North British Railway Company* 1912 S.C. 555, 556 (Court of Session).

servants of the railway caused the damage or loss by wilful misconduct rests with cargo owners[97]. If cargo owners fail to discharge this burden, the case against the railway fails[98].

b) Marine insurance

As a general rule of law, if an allegation is made, the person who makes it must also prove it. Therefore, in a case where the assured claims fortuitous loss of the ship and demands compensation, he should prove that the loss was fortuitous. Moreover, he also should prove that the loss was caused by a peril insured against. However, if the insurer alleges wilful misconduct of the assured, the onus of proof shifts to the insurer as a result of the general rule[99].

When these general principles are discussed with regard to wilful misconduct under marine insurance law principles, it has been stated that "it is quite plain that in the first instance the onus of proof is upon the [shipowner], as indeed it is upon all plaintiffs, to prove their case, that means, [...] that the [shipowner] has to establish by recognised methods that he has suffered a loss from a peril insured against", and "the onus is upon the underwriters to prove that the ship was scuttled"[100].

What if neither party can prove their claims, *i.e.* the assured cannot prove that the loss was caused by the risk insured against, and the insurer cannot prove that the loss was the result of the assured's wilful misconduct? In such a case, the judgement would be against the assured since the primary burden of proof that the loss was fortuitous and caused by a peril insured against rests upon his shoulders[101].

---

[97] *Haynes v. Great Western Railway Company* (1879-1880) 41 L.T. 436, 437 (Common Pleas Division) *per* Justice Grove.

[98] *Forder v. Great Western Railway Company* [1905] 2 K.B. 532, 536 (KBD) *per* Justice Alverstone and Justice Kennedy.

[99] *O'May*, p. 108; *Bennett*, p. 220; *Rose*, p. 347.

[100] *Societe d'Avances Commerciales (Societe Anonyme Egyptienne) v. Merchants' Marine Insurance Co.* (1924) 20 Ll. L. Rep. 140, 152-153 (CA) *per* Lord Atkin; followed by *Continental Illinois National Bank & Trust Co. of Chicago and Xenofon Maritime S.A. v. Alliance Assurance Co. Ltd.* (*The "Captain Panagos D.P."*) [1986] 2 Lloyd's Rep. 470, 510 (QBD); *National Justice Compania Naviera S.A. v. Prudential Assurance Co. Ltd.* (*The "Ikarian Reefer"*) [1993] 2 Lloyd's Rep. 68, 71 (QBD); *Strive Shipping Corporation and Another v. Hellenic Mutual War Risks Association* (*The "Grecia Express"*) [2002] 2 Lloyd's Rep. 88, 97 (QBD).

[101] *Arnould*, pp. 960-961; *La Compania Martiartu v. The Corporation of the Royal Exchange Assurance* [1923] 1 K.B. 650, 657 (CA) *per* Lord Justice Scrutton; *Ansoleaga Y Cia v. Indemnity Mutual Marine Insurance Co. Ltd.* (*The "Leonita"*) (1922) 13 Ll. L. Rep. 231, 246 (CA) *per* Lord Justice Scrutton; *Bank of Athens v. Royal Exchange Assurance* (*The "Eftychia"*) (1937) 59 Ll. L. Rep. 67, 77 (CA) *per* Lord Justice Greer; *Palamisto General Enterprises S.A. v. Ocean Marine Insurance Co. Ltd.* (*The "Dias"*) (1972) 2 Q.B.D. 625, 647 (CA) *per* Lord Justice Cairns.

2. Standard of proof

When a cargo owner claims that the damage or loss resulted from the wilful misconduct of the railway's servants or the insurer raises a wilful misconduct defence, they should prove their case. The question here is which standard of proof is required to prove wilful misconduct.

In carriage by rail cases, it is accepted that proof beyond reasonable doubt is not required. It is sufficient if the cargo owner can show, on a balance of probabilities, that the cause of the damage or loss is wilful misconduct[102]. If, upon the evidence given by both parties, both possibilities are equally likely, *i.e.* if the wilful misconduct possibility is not more likely than the alternative, that means that the cargo owner has failed to prove his case[103]. It is sufficient that the cargo owner provides the court with enough evidence so that an inference of wilful misconduct can be justified[104].

However, since scuttling a ship was also a criminal offence according to the Malicious Damage Act 1861 § 43[105], and is presently a criminal offence pursuant to the Criminal Damage Act 1971 § 1, the standard of proof in cases regarding wilful misconduct under marine insurance law has been controversial. Thus, it is worth explaining briefly the discussions regarding the standard concerning whether the insurer should prove his case with the same certainty as required for proof of a crime.

First, however, the required standard of proof for the shipowner seeking to prove that the loss was accidental and caused by a peril insured against should be mentioned briefly. It has been stated that "the plaintiffs have the burden of proving [...] that there was an accidental loss by perils of the seas, although the degree of proof required is only to show a balance of probabilities in favour of an accidental loss by perils of the seas"[106]. Therefore, it is not required that the shipowner prove his case by excluding all possibilities of scuttling[107].

After the shipowner has proven his claim on a balance of probabilities, the insurer must show that the loss occurred by the shipowner's wilful misconduct. The question of whether the insurer should prove his claim beyond reasonable doubt or on a balance of probabilities has been answered differently in the case law. When the issue was first discussed, it was stated that cases regarding casting

---

[102] *Kahn-Freund*, p. 260.

[103] *Haynes v. Great Western Railway Company* (1879-1880) 41 L.T. 436, 437 (Common Pleas Division) *per* Justice Grove; *Kahn-Freund*, p. 260.

[104] *Forder v. Great Western Railway Company* [1905] 2 K.B. 532, 535 (KBD) *per* Justice Alverstone.

[105] Repealed by the Criminal Damage Act 1971.

[106] *Compania Naviera Santi, S.A. v. Indemnity Marine Assurance Company, Ltd.* (*The "Tropaioforos"*) [1960] 2 Lloyd's Rep. 469, 473 (QBD) *per* Lord Pearson; followed by *N. Michalos & Sons Maritime S.A. and Another v. Prudential Assurance Co. Ltd., Public Corporation for Sugar Trade v. N. Michalos & Sons Maritime Co. Ltd.* (*The "Zinovia"*) [1984] 2 Lloyd's Rep. 264, 271 (QBD) *per* Justice Bingham.

[107] *Compania Naviera Vascongada v. British & Foreign Marine Insurance Co. Ltd.* (*The "Gloria"*) (1936) 54 Ll. L. Rep. 35, 50 (KBD), *per* Lord Branson.

away a ship with the privity of the owner are to be decided on a balance of probabilities[108]. However, it was also stated that "[s]cuttling is a crime, and the Court will not find that it has been committed unless it is proved with the same degree of certainty as is required for the proof of a crime."[109]. In a later case, however, it was stressed that "[t]he [scuttling] issue arises in a civil case, and the standard of proof required is therefore less than in a criminal case. Generally speaking, issues of fact in civil cases are decided on a balance of probability, but the more serious the issue the higher will be the standard of proof required."[110].

Accordingly, it can be said that the case law favours proof on a balance of probabilities; therefore, an insurer does not have to prove his claim beyond reasonable doubt[111]. Naturally, every claim is to be considered according to the facts of the case. Furthermore, "[d]efinite, positive and non-circumstantial proof that the vessel was criminally scuttled"[112] and "direct evidence cannot be expected in such matters"[113] due to the reason that in scuttling cases, the shipowner has the best access to all the primary sources of evidence and can both influence and limit their availability.

---

[108] *La Compania Martiartu v. The Corporation of the Royal Exchange Assurance* [1923] 1 K.B. 650, 657 (CA) *per* Lord Scrutton.

[109] *Compania Naviera Vascongada v. British & Foreign Marine Insurance Co. Ltd. (The "Gloria")* (1936) 54 Ll. L. Rep. 35, 50-51 (KBD), *per* Lord Branson.

[110] *Piermay Shipping Co. S.A. and Brandt's Ltd. v. Chester (The "Michael")* [1979] 1 Lloyd's Rep. 55, 67 (QBD), *per* Justice Kerr; affirmed by *Piermay Shipping Co. S.A. and Brandt's Ltd. v. Chester (The "Michael")* [1979] 2 Lloyd's Rep. 1, 12-13 (CA).

[111] *Strive Shipping Corporation and Another v. Hellenic Mutual War Risks Association (The "Grecia Express")* [2002] 2 Lloyd's Rep. 88, 98 (QBD), *per* Justice Colman: "The balance of probability standard means that a court is satisfied an event occurred if the court considers that, on the evidence, the occurrence of the event was more likely than not. When assessing the probabilities the court will have in mind as a factor, to whatever extent is appropriate in the particular case, that the more serious the allegation the less likely it is that the event occurred and, hence, the stronger should be the evidence before the court concludes that the allegation is established on the balance of probability." See also *Arnould*, pp. 959-960 fn. 343; *Bennett*, p. 221; *Rose*, p. 347; *Ivamy*, p. 247 and *infra* § 7 B II 1.

[112] *Anghelatos v. Northern Assurance Co. London Joint City & Midland Bank v. Same* (1924) 19 Ll. L. Rep. 255, 257 (HL) *per* Earl of Birkenhead.

[113] *Elfie A. Issaias v. Marine Insurance Co. Ltd.* (1923) 15 Ll. L. Rep. 186, 187 (CA), *per* Lord Sterndale. See also *Arnould*, pp. 962-963.

Part II Wilful Misconduct in Transport Law

§ 4 First Time in an International Transport Convention: Convention for the Unification of Certain Rules relating to International Carriage by Air, 1929

The necessity of unifying the rules regarding air carriage has arisen due to the international character of carriage by air and due to the lack and/or insufficiency of national legislation at the beginning of the 20th century. This necessity triggered the initiative of France, and on this initiative the First Conference on International Private Air Law[1] ("First Conference") was held in Paris. It was agreed at this Conference to establish a specialist committee, CITEJA[2], whose assignment was to improve the draft convention relating to the international carriage by air established by the First Conference. Consonant with its establishment purpose, in May 1926 CITEJA started to work on the unification of international air transport law, basically on the rules of liability and elaboration of the documents of carriage. As a result, the draft convention was submitted to the International Conference in Warsaw ("Warsaw Conference") which took place between 4 and 12 October 1929 and after which the Convention for the Unification of Certain Rules relating to International Carriage by Air ("Warsaw Convention") was signed. The Warsaw Convention entered into force on 13 February 1933[3].

A. Article 25

I. Historical Background

Due to various reasons, but mostly owing to the infancy of the aviation industry, the liability of the air carrier has been limited up to a certain amount[4]. The pro-

---

[1] 26 October – 6 November 1925.

[2] For detailed information on CITEJA see Linus R. *Fike*, The CITEJA, (1939) 10 Air LR 169.

[3] *Matte*, p. 17; *Guldimann*, pp. 3-4; *Milde*, pp. 19-20, 22; *Meyer I*, pp. 97-98; *Çağa*, pp. 177-178; *Göknil*, p. 17; *Sözer, Kurallar*, pp. 373-374; *Koffka/Bodenstein*, p. 239; *Dettling-Ott*, p. 7; *Schobel*, pp. 7-8; *Orr*, pp. 423-425; *Shawcross and Beaumont*, VII 104; *Giemulla/Schmid*, WA Rn. 1-2; *Stachow*, pp. 65-66.

[4] See *supra* § 2 B II 1 a.

posal to break these limits was not made until the second session of CITEJA. The draft convention established by the First Conference did not include any provision with regard to the unlimited liability. At the second session of CITEJA, it was agreed that the carrier should not have the right to limit his liability in cases of intentional illicit acts (*actes illicites intentionelles*)[5]. The formula in the preliminary draft convention[6] which was submitted to the Warsaw Conference reads as follows:

> (Article 24 (2))
> "If the damage arises from an intentional illicit act for which the carrier is responsible, he will not have the right to avail himself of the provisions of this Convention, which exclude in all or in part his direct liability or that derived from the faults of his servants."[7].

After the discussions in the Third Session of the Warsaw Conference, the provision was sent to the drafting committee for further work. As a result, the wording of Article 24 (2) was changed to the following:

> (English translation)
> "The carrier shall not have the right to avail himself of the provisions of the present Convention which exclude or limit his liability, if the damage arises out of the wilful misconduct of the carrier or from a fault which, according to the law of the tribunal which has taken jurisdiction, is considered as the equivalent of wilful misconduct."[8].

During the discussions in the Seventh Session, it was decided that Art. 24 should be divided in two; accordingly Art. 24 (2) became Art. 25 (1)[9].

After the discussions and work of the drafting committee, the final version of Art. 25 reads as follows:

> (French version)
> "Le tranporteur n'aura pas le droit de se prévaloir des dispositions de la présente Convention qui excluent ou limitent sa responsabilité, si le dommage provient de son *dol* ou d'une faute qui, d'apres la loi du tribunal saisi, est considérée *comme équivalente au dol*.
>
> Ce droit lui sera également refusé si le dommage a été causé dans les méemes conditions par un de ses préposés agissant dans l'exercice de ses fonctions."[10].

> (English translation)
> "The carrier shall not be entitled to avail himself of the provisions of this Convention which exclude or limit his liability, if the damage is caused by his *willful misconduct* or

---

5   *Drion*, pp. 44, 197; *Guldimann, Auslegung*, p. 272.
6   Preliminary Draft of the Convention relating to documents of air carriage and the liability of the carrier in international carriage by aircraft, adopted by CITEJA during its Third Session in May 1928; see *Warsaw Conference Minutes*, pp. 257-268.
7   *Warsaw Conference Minutes*, pp. 265-266.
8   *Warsaw Conference Minutes*, pp. 211-212.
9   *Warsaw Conference Minutes*, p. 214.
10   Emphasis added.

by such fault on his part as, in accordance with the law of the Court seized of the case, is considered *to be equivalent to willful misconduct.*

Similarly the carrier shall not be entitled to avail himself of the said provisions, if the damage is caused as aforesaid by any agent of the carrier acting within the scope of his employment."[11].

Until Art. 25 had been finally formulated, there had been intense discussions during the Warsaw Conference. These discussions mostly concentrated on two issues: what degree of fault should break the air carrier's limited liability, and, since the French version of the Convention would be binding, what would be the proper translation of the relevant degree of fault into English.

1. Degree of fault

It was stated in the report presented in the name of CITEJA by Mr. Henri De Vos on the Draft Convention submitted to the Warsaw Conference that "[i]t was expressly provided that the carrier will not have the right to avail himself of the provisions limiting his liability if the damage arises out of an intentional illicit act for which he is liable."[12]. Obviously, the aim of CITEJA by including such a provision into the Draft was to eliminate the right to limit liability in cases where the air carrier had the intention to cause damage, harm or injury. According to the draft version, the air carrier had to have intended to cause the damage, harm or injury for him to be liable without limitation[13].

It should also be noted that the reason for CITEJA's using the term *actes illicites intentionnels* instead of *dol* in the draft version is the criticism, notably by the British Delegation, that it is impossible to translate the term *dol* into English, whereupon the drafting committee had decided to substitute the term *dol* with the words *actes illicites intentionnels*[14].

However, the drafter's intention was neither reflected by the phrase of "intentional illicit act for which the carrier is responsible", since there had been questions on the meaning of it. These questions arose after the proposal of the German delegate, Mr. Richter, recommending that also in cases of *faute lourde*, namely gross negligence, the air carrier's liability should be unlimited. This proposal had

---

[11]   Emphasis added.
[12]   *Warsaw Conference Minutes*, p. 254.
[13]   *Goedhuis*, p. 273.
[14]   Mr. Arendt (Luxembourg) during the Third Session (October 6th, Morning Session): "The question which is submitted at this time by Sir Alfred Dennis [the British Delegate] is not new; it was discussed already by CITEJA. The difficulty comes from trying to explain the word "dol" in certain languages. For us, steeped in Roman law, the thing would be resolved by the word "dol". But it is because the word "dol" has been criticized by certain delegations and, if my recollections are exact, notably by the British Delegation which said that it had no word which completely renders the word "dol", that we took the decision to explain the word "dol" by the words "intentional illicit act"; but if one wished to return to pure and simple law, one would replace this expression by the word "dol", see *Warsaw Conference Minutes*, p. 60.

been criticized as "dangerous" by different delegates[15]; but nevertheless the question was left to be solved by the drafting committee and just before the referral to the drafting committee, Mr. Pittard, the Swiss delegate and the member of the drafting committee[16], stated that they had been inclined to add *faute lourde* in *actes illicites intentionnels*, if they could have found a formula which satisfied the various judicial languages[17].

2. English version

Since the official version of the Warsaw Convention would be in French and the Convention would have to be applied by local courts, it had to be translated into other languages. This issue arose specifically on the translation of the degree of fault adopted by Art. 25 into English.

Discussions[18] regarding the meaning and the translation of the term which was used to describe the degree of fault started with the question by the Greek delegate. The delegate asked for an explanation on the meaning of *actes illicites intentionnels*. Subsequently, Sir Alfred Dennis, the British delegate, stated that it is very hard to understand for the English lawyers what the term means. As far as it can be understood by the Minutes of the Conference, the British delegate was confused about the meaning of the words. He exemplified an emergency situation where a pilot has to land in an area which is not designed for landings. According to the delegate, the landing is intentional and it is also illicit, yet it should not be a case where the limits of liability could be broken. The delegate further stated that the application of the provision should be restricted to the cases of the "act done deliberately for the purpose of injury"[19].

Obviously, the British delegate was confused whether the term *actes illicites intentionnels* covers the cases of necessity[20] or not. He asked for further explana-

---

[15]   Mr. De Vos (Reporter): "I esteem that it would be to enter upon a dangerous course to accept this proposal.", *Warsaw Conference Minutes*, p. 58; Mr. Ripert (France): "The German Delegation proposes to make the carrier liable anytime that he has committed a serious error. This proposal is extremely dangerous. If it is true that, in certain countries, as in France, the "faute lourde" is included in certain cases in "faute intentionnelle", it is because that when this formula is applied in a certain country, there can be no inconvenience in doing so; but if you introduce in an international convention an expression so broad, so imprecise as "faute lourde", it is to be feared that in other countries that have no aeronautical operations, the courts will declare, with regard to an accident, that a "faute lourde" was committed. I am not opposed to the idea, but I am suspicious of all general formulae which risk the destruction of the Convention. You understand that a court is always free to declare, in the case of an accident, that the carrier has committed a serious wrong.", *Warsaw Conference Minutes*, p. 61.

[16]   *Warsaw Conference Minutes*, p. 27.

[17]   *Warsaw Conference Minutes*, p. 62.

[18]   During the Third Session.

[19]   *Warsaw Conference Minutes*, p. 59.

[20]   Also termed as "choice of evils" or "duress of circumstances", which explains a situation in which the defendant's act was necessary to prevent greater damage to

tion in order to find the appropriate term for translation into English. However, before the explanation, he also stated that he believed that the term "willful misconduct" would cover both deliberate acts and also "careless acts done without regard for the consequences". As to the translation of *faute lourde*, the delegate stated that this term is unknown in English law and that it is impossible to properly translate it into English[21].

At the end of the discussion, the problem was left to be solved by the drafting committee.

3. Outcome

The outcome of the work by the drafting committee was announced[22] by the president of the committee. He announced that the drafting committee had succeeded in finding a formula which satisfied every delegation's and mostly the British delegate's concerns by adopting the expression *faute lourde et de dol*[23]. The phrase expressing the degree of fault adopted by the provision was changed to "*dol*, or such fault on his part as, (in accordance with the law of the Court seized of the case), is considered to be equivalent to *dol*".

However, the British delegate, again, stated that it is a question of terms used by law and that, since *dol* is a civil law concept and an equivalent term in common law for that concept does not exist[24], they would translate the term of *dol* into English as "willful misconduct", which is a well-known and well-defined term in English law[25].

4. Result

At a first reading, the Minutes of the Conference indicate that it was the intention of the drafters that the gross negligence of the carrier should result in unlimited liability as well. However, there are two points to be examined. First, the exact meaning of the terms used to define the degree(s) of fault should be assessed. Afterwards, the British delegate's insistence in using the term "wilful misconduct" as the equivalent of the term *dol* should be evaluated.

The Convention mentions in its official version the cases of *dol* and the fault which is considered as equivalent to *dol*. The problem to be solved is whether the phrase "fault which is considered as equivalent to *dol*" is a phrase formed in order to describe *faute lourde* or in order to meet the British delegate's concern about the translation.

---

the claimant or to a third party, see Black's Law Dictionary, 9th Ed. (by BRYN A. GARNER), Minnesota 2009; for further information see *Clerk & Lindsell*, para. 3-128 *et seqq.*; *Prosser and Keeton*, pp. 145-148.

[21] *Warsaw Conference Minutes*, pp. 59-60.
[22] During the Seventh Session.
[23] *Warsaw Conference Minutes*, p. 212.
[24] *Kreindler*, Ch. 10 p. 84; *Matte*, p. 60; *Goldhirsch*, p. 152.
[25] *Warsaw Conference Minutes*, p. 213.

For the purpose of finding a formula to be applied both by civil and common law jurisdictions, the drafting committee could have drafted the provision in different ways. When the British delegation expressed opposition to the term *dol*, CITEJA changed the term and used the expression *actes illicites intentionnels* instead[26]. When this expression was also opposed during the Conference, the drafting committee's preference was to use the original juridical term *dol*. Hence, attention should be focused on the preferences of the drafting committee in choosing the terms by forming the provision. Could the drafting committee have chosen to define the term *faute lourde* as "the fault which is considered as equivalent to *dol*" instead of using the juridical term of *faute lourde* itself, even though they have preferred using the civil law term in cases of acts done with the intent to cause damage? If the drafting committee desired to break the carrier's liability limits also in *faute lourde* cases, why did they not formulate a provision using both the original civil law terms of *dol* and *faute lourde* and explain both of the terms' meaning to the British delegate in order to meet his concerns? Given that they adopted the phrase "fault which is considered as equivalent to *dol*" in order to explain *faute lourde*, why did they not explain *dol* as well, since the British delegate's concern was mostly caused by this term?

Since the minutes of the meetings of the drafting committee are not published, the answers to the questions above remain unclear. However, it is assumed that the aim in adopting the phrase "the fault which is considered as equivalent to *dol*" was to meet the British delegate's concern regarding translation of the term *dol*, although it was announced that the drafting committee was successful in adopting the expression *faute lourde et de dol*. The main reason for this assumption is the language and method used to form the provision. The drafting committee did not show any doubt in adopting the civil law term *dol*; hence, they could have adopted the term *faute lourde* if they had intended to prevent the right to limit liability in cases of gross negligence[27].

Once the phrase "fault on his part as, [...], is considered to be equivalent to *dol*" was accepted, the drafting committee had succeeded in finding a formula for jurisdictions other than civil law to choose the terminology used to define the degree of fault. Consequently, *dol* would be used by civil law jurisdictions and the phrase "fault on his part as, [...], is considered to be equivalent to *dol*" would be used by other jurisdictions, in which the term *dol* was unknown, in order to find the appropriate terminology for the degree of fault adopted by Art. 25. As a result,

---

[26] See *supra* A I 1.

[27] In fact, just four years after the Warsaw Convention, it was preferred to use the terms *dol* and *faute lourde* to hold the operator liable without any financial limitation under the International Convention for the Unification of Certain Rules Relating to Damage Caused by Aircraft to Third Parties on the Surface, signed in Rome, 29 May, 1933. The first part of the first paragraph of Art. 14 reads: "The operator may not avail himself of the provisions of this Convention limiting his liability – (a) if it is proved that the damage results from the *faute lourde* or *dol* of the operator, or his servants or agents, [...]"; for information on the provision, see Ferdinand *Imbach*, Das Römer Lufthaftungsabkommen von 1933 und seine Revision von 1952, Beromünster 1955, pp. 142-149; *Drion*, pp. 44, 232; *Meyer*, p. 159; *Göknil*, pp. 256-258.

the British delegate's insistence on a formula covering the common law terminology and the main aim of the harmonisation of law have been met[28].

This assumption can be supported with the timing of the first mention of the common law term of wilful misconduct by the British delegate. As previously mentioned[29], the British delegate's concern was mostly to find the appropriate English term for *actes illicites intentionnels*. During the first sessions, he stated that the equivalent term would be "willful misconduct". After the drafting committee's work was completed and announced as a success in adopting the expression *faute lourde et de dol*, the delegate again stated that they intend to use the term "willful misconduct" as a translation. Thus, the delegate mentioned the same term again that he had mentioned for translation of *actes illicites intentionnels*. For this reason, it could be assumed that the delegates of the Conference believed that there had not been any change in the degree of fault adopted by the provision.

Furthermore, it is also believed that the British delegate's statement as to the impossibility of translating the term of *faute lourde* into English[30] was actually an objection to the extension of the scope of Art. 25. Although the concept of *dol* has no exact connotation in English legal terminology, *faute lourde* can be easily translated into English as "gross negligence" or "inadvertent negligence"[31]. Consequently, it is asserted that the British delegate's main concern in objecting to the term *faute lourde* was distinct from the translation issue[32], which is also consonant with the other delegates' objections[33].

Additionally, it is to be noted that the reference to local law[34] in the provision was adopted in order to allow judges to determine the term equivalent to *dol* in their own legal terminology. Consequently, this reference was adopted in the sense of terminology, not in the sense of substantive law[35]. What had to be done by local courts was finding the equivalent legal term to *dol*, rather than re-determining the degree of fault which would give rise to unlimited liability of the carrier[36].

Finally, it should also be kept in mind that the main purposes of the Warsaw Convention were the unification of law and providing support to an industry

---

[28]   *Guldimann, Auslegung,* p. 274; *Matte,* p. 60; *Beaumont, Revision,* p. 408.

[29]   See *supra* A I 2.

[30]   See *supra* A I 2.

[31]   *Knauth,* p. 323; *Shawcross and Beaumont,* VII 471.

[32]   *Drion,* pp. 199-200, 202, 207; *Goedhuis,* p. 275.

[33]   See *supra* A I 1.

[34]   "[...] in accordance with the law of the Court seized of the case [...]".

[35]   *Drion,* p. 200; MünchKommHGB 1997 – *Kronke,* WA 1955 Art. 25 Rn. 16; *Clarke, Carriage by Air,* p. 157; *Kuhn,* p. 201; *Philipson/et al.,* p. 147; *Clarke, CIM,* p. 28.

[36]   *Drion,* p. 203; *Piamba Cortes v. American Airlines* (CA, 1999) 177 F.3d 1272, 1290 *per* Judge Birch: "Ultimately, the delegates rejected the inclusion of "faute lourde" and retained the French word "dol", adding that a court may apply the legal equivalent of "dol" as defined by the law of the forum jurisdiction. [...] The drafting history thus reveals that conferees rejected an effort to define willful misconduct to encompass gross negligence".

which was in its infancy. If it is accepted that the reference to national laws must be understood in a sense of substantive law, it would not be consistent with the purpose of unifying the law[37] and it would, moreover, be dangerous because it would encourage forum-shopping[38]. Furthermore, if it were accepted that air carriers would be liable without any limitation every time they committed a serious error, the result would also not be consistent with the ideas of supporting a weak industry and limiting the air carrier's liability[39].

However, as it will be explained in the following passage[40], the phrase referring to local laws has not been generally understood in a sense of legal terminology, but has been understood in a sense of substantive law, both by some authorities[41] and by some common law[42] and nearly all civil law courts[43].

5. Inaccurate translation

The Warsaw Convention had to be enacted as British law in order to bring it into force in the UK. For this purpose, the Carriage by Air Act of 1932[44] was enacted. In another common law country, the USA, the Declaration of Adherence was stated by the president in 1934 and the official translation of the Warsaw Convention has been published[45]. In both translations, the term of wilful misconduct has

---

[37] *Berner v. British Commonwealth Pacific Airlines, Ltd.* (DC New York, 1963) 219 F.Supp. 289, 322: "If unity among the nations was the goal at Warsaw, it was not achieved."; also see Bezirksgericht Zürich, 15.12.1964, ZLW 1965, 338 (344).

[38] MünchKommHGB 1997 – *Kronke*, WA 1955 Art. 25 Rn. 16.

[39] *Goedhuis*, p. 275; *S.S. Pharmaceutical Co. Ltd. and Another v. Qantas Airways Ltd.* [1991] 1 Lloyd's Rep. 288, 294 (CA of the New South Wales), *per* Judge Kirby: "it is essential to approach the construction of the international instruments [...] keeping in mind their international character and the desirability [...] that they should be given a consistent construction by the Courts of the several contracting parties. [...] Were such an approach not taken, the result would be forum shopping or the unequal application of an international treaty in an unpredictable way according to the approach of the domestic Court".

[40] See *infra* II.

[41] *Goldhirsch*, p. 155; *Milde*, pp. 71-72; *Riese*, p. 466; *Miller*, pp. 79-80, 196, 199; *Giemulla/Schmid*, Art. 25 WA Rn. 16, 18-19; *Abraham*, p. 366; *Basedow, Transportvertrag*, p. 420 fn. 118; *Dettling-Ott*, p. 215; *Gerber*, p. 19; *Modjaz*, pp. 37-38; *Cheng*, p. 63; *Guldimann, Auslegung*, pp. 276-277; *Müller-Rostin*, p. 126; *Koffka/Bodenstein*, p. 334; *Sözer, Taşıyıcının Sorumluluğu*, pp. 794-795; *Kırman*, pp. 151-152; *Strock*, 291; *Müller-Rostin*, in: *Fremuth/Thume*, Art. 25 WA Rn. 5; *Koller*, WA 1929 Art. 25 Rn. 3; *Ruhwedel, Durchbrechung im Luftrecht*, 139. However, some of these scholars stressed that gross negligence shall result in unlimited liability only in cases of *"wirklich schweres Verschulden"*, namely grave fault, see *Riese*, p. 466; *Koffka/Bodenstein*, p. 334; *Goedhuis*, pp. 275-276. For the criticism of the equivalence of gross negligence and intentional misconduct see *Marsilius*, 303-304.

[42] See *infra* II 2.

[43] See *infra* II 1.

[44] 22&23 Geo. V, Ch. 36.

[45] 49 Stat. 3000.

been used in order to translate the term of *dol*. It has been accurately stated that wilful misconduct is not the appropriate term to translate *dol* into English[46].

As a result of this inaccurate translation, an anomaly has arisen. Since the phrase referring to the equivalent degree of fault as *dol* has been adopted to enable the jurisdictions to choose the equivalent legal term used by their own legal system, the phrase "fault on his part as, [...], is considered to be equivalent to willful misconduct" has become meaningless, since *dol* has been translated as wilful misconduct. Indeed, common law does not know such a type of fault, since an act or omission amounts either to wilful misconduct or not[47].

Overall, Art. 25 has been referred to as the "most unhappy phrase" of the Warsaw Convention[48].

II. Article 25 in Practice

Provisions of international conventions are always applied by local courts. Due to the legal diversity and miscellaneous interpretations of law, decisions of local courts on an issue can be different. Nevertheless, this fact has been an enriching factor in finding the right solution aimed at by the legislator or needed in light of present concerns in the area of unification of law on an international level. Further, it is also normal that if a legal instrument is new and there is not much case law, the decisions of local courts belonging to different legal systems will differ slightly. However, if the practice regarding an issue differs substantially from one jurisdiction to another, it causes legal uncertainties. Unfortunately, exactly that problem has arisen in the application of Art. 25.

---

[46] *Drion*, p. 195 fn. 168.2; *Report, Warsaw*, 260, 263; *Beaumont, Revision*, p. 408; *McGilchrist*, p. 542; *Berner v. British Commonwealth Pacific Airlines, Ltd.* (DC New York, 1963) 219 F.Supp. 289, 321. It is claimed before American courts that the accurate translation would be "fraud" or "malice", an argument which has not been accepted, see *American Airlines v. Ulen* (CA, 1949) 186 F.2d 529, 533. In fact in one case a court based its decision upon the original term of *dol*, see *Simo Noboa v. Iberia Lineas Aereas de España* (DC Puerto Rico, 2005) 383 F.Supp.2d 323.

[47] *Drion*, pp. 178-179; *Shawcross and Beaumont*, VII 474; *Mankiewicz*, p. 122; *Miller*, pp. 80-81, 199; *Basedow, Transportvertrag*, p. 420; *Cheng*, pp. 63-64; *Giemulla/Schmid*, Art. 25 WA Rn. 27; *Dettling-Ott*, p. 215; *Modjaz*, p. 48; *Kuhn*, p. 202; *Hickey*, 605; *Horabin v. British Overseas Airways Corporation*, [1952] 2 Lloyd's Rep. 450, 458 (QBD) *per* Justice Barry: (after quoting Art. 25(1)) "You need not trouble about the latter phrase, members of the jury, because in the law of this country a fault or an omission to do something can be just as much misconduct as the doing of something which is wrong".

[48] *Drion*, p. 197; *Riese*, p. 466; *Berner v. British Commonwealth Pacific Airlines, Ltd.* (DC New York, 1963) 219 F.Supp. 289, 322 *per* Judge Ritter: "It is this unhappy phrase in Article 25(1) which we must apply. It is by no means clear and certain. Unity among the delegates could not be reached on an obligatory text".

1. Approach by civil law

The phrase referring to local laws has been interpreted by civil law courts as a reference to substantive law, consequently *culpa lata dolo equiparatur* (Dig. 11, 6, 1, 1; Dig. 50, 16, 226)[49]. Thereby, civil law courts have been inclined to consider gross negligence as the equivalent of *dol* and hold the air carrier liable without any financial limit whenever his fault amounts to gross negligence[50]. This interpretation by civil law jurisdictions has favoured plaintiffs claiming unlimited liability of the carrier, since they do not face the problems they would face at a common law court in order to prove wilful misconduct[51].

The civil law courts have decided that gross negligence amounts to *dol*[52]. Basically[53], there is *dol* (*Vorsatz, dolo*) when the person causes the damage wilfully and in violation of law. The wilful performance of an act or omission needs to have been done in order to achieve the illicit result, namely the damage. Thus, the actor must have foreseen the damage and performed the act or omission to cause that damage[54]. Gross negligence (*faute lourde, grobe Fahrlässigkeit, culpa lata*) is one step backwards. When a person acts or makes an omission negligently in a grave manner and to such a degree that he is in violation of the duty of care which he had to show according to the facts of the case, his fault amounts to gross negligence[55].

Finally, it should be noted that the cases mentioned below are not always cases regarding international carriage. Some of them have been decided under national

---

[49] For the historical background of the maxim in Roman law see *Marsilius*, 299-300.

[50] Bezirksgericht Zürich, 15.12.1964, ZLW 1965, 338 (344); *Giemulla/Schmid*, Art. 25 WA Rn. 18; *Modjaz*, pp. 39-47, 63-64, 71-73; *Schobel*, pp. 78-79; *Risch*, pp. 56-58; *Abraham, Rechtsprechung*, pp. 85-86; *Döring*, p. 5 (however in a critical manner); *Mühlbauer*, 185; *Schmid, Zwei Motoren*, pp. 290-292; *Clarke, Carriage by Air*, p. 157 (refers to the issue as the "unintended effect"); *Abraham, Rechtsprechung 1952*, p. 71; for the subjective approach by Belgian courts, see *Modjaz*, pp. 69-70; *Stachow*, pp. 139-140. For the historical background of the Latin phrase see *Marsilius*, 299-300.

[51] *Matte*, p. 60; MünchKommHGB 1997 – *Kronke*, WA 1955 Art. 25 Rn. 14; *Clarke, Carriage by Air*, p. 157; the choice of jurisdiction is also referred to by *Abraham*, p. 368; *Abraham, Luftbeförderungsvertrag*, p. 58.

[52] LG Frankfurt, 08.03.1939, ALR 1939, 180; LG Köln, 09.04.1964, ZLW 1965, 88; Obergericht Zürich, 04.03.1966, ASDA-Bulletin 1966/2, 8, 14; BGH, 10.05.1974, VersR 1974, 766 = ETL 1974, 630 = BB 1974, 860; OGH, 10.10.1974, ZLW 1979, 287; OLG München, 01.04.1998, NJW-RR 1998, 898 = ZLW 1998, 564 = TranspR 1998, 473; OLG Frankfurt, 14.09.1999, TranspR 2000, 260; OLG München, 07.05.1999, ZLW 2000, 118; BGE 93 II 345 (14.11.1967).

[53] For more information see *infra* § 8.

[54] MünchKommHGB 1997 – *Kronke*, WA 1955 Art. 25 Rn. 14.

[55] *Giemulla/Schmid*, Art. 25 WA Rn. 19; *Abraham*, p. 366; *Hofmann/Grabherr*, § 48 Rn. 6; *Dettling-Ott*, p. 220; *Schmid, Zwei Motoren*, pp. 290-291; MünchKommHGB 1997 – *Kronke*, WA 1955 Art. 25 Rn. 17; BGH, 11.05.1953, BGHZ 10 (14); LG Köln, 09.04.1964, ZLW 1965, 88 (89); Bezirksgericht Zürich, 15.12.1964, ZLW 1965, 338 (343).

transport law regimes. The reason for mentioning those decisions here is their close relationship to the Warsaw Convention system. Most of the national laws with regard to the carriage of passengers and cargo by air have been inspired by the Warsaw Convention. For instance, carriage by air and liability provisions of the "*Luftverkehrsgesetz*" (1936)[56] is the adaptation of German law to the Warsaw Convention[57]. The purpose of adopting the "*Lufttransportreglement*"[58] (1952) in Switzerland was also the same[59].

Nevertheless, it should never be forgotten that they are local laws. However, they are important since those national aviation laws have been based on the interpretation of the Warsaw Convention by local legislators and therefore reflect their understanding of the international rules[60].

a) Carriage of passengers

The situations which have been considered as instances of gross negligence are various. They mostly appear as errors by pilots, owing to the reality that except for a person who is planning to commit a suicide, no pilot will crash a plane on purpose. Therefore, the piloting errors causing a crash have often been the result of gross negligence. In terms of the carriage of passengers by air, gross negligence is to be found when the pilots have violated the basic aeronautical and flight safety rules[61].

The first example dates back to 1939. In that case, a very experienced pilot also having experience in flying over the Alps had started the flight after obtaining necessary information from the weather forecast station. However, the flight encountered very bad weather and, rather than turning back, the pilot insisted on continuing to fly. Unfortunately the plane crashed and the claimant's husband and father passed away. The court decided that it is not clear whether the pilot could have done something else to prevent the crash and that gross negligence was not proved[62].

In accordance with previous decisions, the breach of valid flight rules has been accepted as fault equal to gross negligence. For instance, if a pilot starts a flight

---

[56] RGBl. I S. 653, as amended in 1943 (RGBl. I S. 69). § 29e of the Act was dealing with the unlimited liability of the carrier. *Luftverkehrsgesetz* 1959 (BGBl. I S. 9) § 48 involves the same principle.

[57] *Abraham*, p. 366.

[58] AS 1952, 1060 *et seq.*; Art. 10 of the Regulation deals with unlimited liability.

[59] *Dettling-Ott*, p. 53.

[60] The provision regulating the unlimited liability of the air carrier in the Swiss *Lufttransportreglement* was revised in 1962 (AS 1963, 679 *et seq*) due to the adoption of Art. 25 of the Warsaw Convention by the Hague Protocol, 1955 (see case note in TranspR 1985, 390). However, contrary to the adaptation in Swiss law, the unlimited liability provision of the German *Luftverkehrsgesetz* has not been adapted to the revision of Art. 25 by the Hague Protocol, 1955. This is, of course, the choice of the German legislator.

[61] BGH, 11.07.1967, VersR 1967, 909 = ZLW 1968, 85.

[62] LG Frankfurt, 08.03.1939, ALR 1939, 180.

without being provided with necessary information on the weather situation and violates the visual flight rules during the flight, his fault amounts to gross negligence[63]. Likewise, a pilot's conduct constitutes gross negligence when he decides to continue a visual flight through a bad weather area instead of looking for an alternative airport to land, or turning back[64]. Similarly, if a pilot omits changing from visual flight to instrumental flight when necessary, or if he does not observe the altimeter sufficiently and therefore drops below the minimum flight height, his fault amounts to gross negligence[65]. If a pilot starts a flight under visual flight rules and changes it to an instrumental flight although he does not have an instrumental flight licence, his conduct also amounts to gross negligence[66].

Gross negligence was not found in cases of attempting to land at an airport without proper facility and equipment[67]; inattention to the mariner's compass during an attempt to turn back in order to exit a cloud[68]; an accident due to the wrong approach tactic and the shortness of the runway[69].

In another case, the pilot lost too much altitude to gain visual contact with the runway, although ground control warned him that the plane is too low. When the pilot tried to right the plane, the plane crashed. The Swiss Federal Court did not consider whether the conduct of the pilot constituted gross negligence since the damages claimed did not exceed the limits of the Warsaw Convention[70]; but in light of the previous decisions, it was likely that such a ruling would have been in favour of unlimited liability owing to the grossly negligent conduct.

b) Carriage of cargo

While it is unlikely to identify a damage caused by *dol* in the carriage of passengers, the situation is different in the carriage of cargo by air since theft is a significant problem in airports. In fact, it is believed that the rationale in adopting Art. 25 of the Warsaw Convention was the prevention of theft which might possibly occur during the ground handling of the luggage and cargo by removing the air carrier's liability limits[71].

Nevertheless, the first case of theft of a cargo deals with the question of gross negligence. The court decided that the air carrier did not handle the valuable cargo of banknotes with gross negligence where the cargo was not visible through the sealed package, although the compartment in the cargo hold of the plane in which

---

[63] LG Oldenburg, 08.08.1975, VersR 1976, 456; OLG Köln, 24.04.1980, VersR 1982, 251; LG Ravensburg, 04.06.1981, VersR 1982, 389.
[64] OLG Stuttgart, 22.02.1978, VersR 1979, 1051.
[65] LG Braunschweig, 08.03.1979, VersR 1979, 931.
[66] LG Freiburg, 30.09.1986, ZLW 1988, 86.
[67] LG Köln, 09.04.1964, ZLW 1965, 88.
[68] OLG München, 11.02.1983, ZLW 1984, 171; affirmed by BGH, 20.12.1983, VersR 1984, 395.
[69] OLG Karlsruhe, 18.06.1986, ZLW 1987, 392.
[70] BG, 28.06.1960, ASDA-Bullettin 1960/3, 7.
[71] *Drion*, p. 211.

the banknotes were stored was opened during the stopovers[72]. However, in another case of theft of valuable cargo, a different decision was reached in favour of the plaintiff, although the facts were almost identical with the previously mentioned case. In this case, 4 of the 5 envelopes containing banknotes had been stolen and the identity of the thief or the location of the occurrence could not be determined. The court ruled in favour of the claimant due to the insufficient security measures. The court reasoned that the banknotes were visible due to the poor quality of the packaging, the fact that the cargo hold of the plane had to be opened on a stopover for another loading and the carrier had not taken any precautions against the possibility of theft. Thus, the lack of sufficient precautions for carriage of valuable cargo amounted to gross negligence[73]. Similarly, in another case of theft of valuable cargo, the court decided in favour of the plaintiff due to the lack of necessary security measures[74].

In another case, the court discussed whether the fault of the air carrier amounted to gross negligence where the employee of the carrier left the package unattended on an open transport vehicle in front of the cargo building instead of securing it inside, and where the package was subsequently stolen. The German Federal Court decided that this failure causing the damage was enough to enter into judgement in favour of the claimant and that the air carrier was liable due to his grossly negligent conduct[75].

Besides theft, loss of cargo sometimes resulted in the unlimited liability of an air carrier. In the first judgement discussing the issue, the court decided in favour of the defendant carrier, when the cargo got lost during the carriage and its location could not be designated. The plaintiff cargo owner alleged that the loss of cargo without a trace showed that the carrier acted in a grossly negligent manner and that the burden of explaining the precautions taken and the arrangements made to prevent such a loss fall on the defendant carrier. It was stated by the court that the loss of the cargo alone did not necessarily constitute gross negligence and that if it was decided that the carrier was under such an obligation as alleged by the plaintiff, it would mean shifting the burden of proof[76]. However, this allegation was accepted by another court as sufficient basis for gross negligence. According to the court, the fact that the carrier could not supply any information on the location of the cargo showed that he had not taken the necessary precautions in his operating procedure to avoid the loss. Thus, his fault equalled gross negligence unless he could prove that he took all appropriate organisational, managerial and operational measures[77]. However, the absence of a single check

[72] Bezirksgericht Zürich, 15.12.1964, ZLW 1965, 338; affirmed by Obergericht Zürich, 04.03.1966, ASDA-Bulettin 1966/2, 8.
[73] BGE 93 II 345 (14.11.1967).
[74] Bezirkgerich Zürich, 01.10.1968, ASDA-Bullettin 1969/2, 14.
[75] BGH, 10.05.1974, VersR 1974, 766 = ETL 1974, 630 = BB 1974, 860.
[76] LG Frankfurt, 27.01.1997, TranspR 1997, 236.
[77] OLG München, 01.04.1998, NJW-RR 1998, 898 = ZLW 1998, 564; OLG Frankfurt, 14.09.1999, TranspR 2000, 260.

point and a comparison between the cargo and the travel documents have not been considered as unsatisfactory and poor organisation[78].

2. Approach by common law

Most of the common law courts have dealt only with the term of wilful misconduct in solving the cases involving Art. 25 of the Warsaw Convention. In order to hold the air carrier liable without any financial limits, his wilful misconduct needs to be proved. So, in principle, the common law courts have not examined "fault on his part as, [...], is considered to be equivalent to wilful misconduct"[79].

However, the same misinterpretation as seen in the civil law courts regarding the reference to local law in Art. 25 has also evolved during some trials before common law courts. Although these cases are not numerous, they are important for showing that civil law courts are not the only ones interpreting the reference to local law in the sense of substantive law. Nevertheless, the reference to local law has not been interpreted by common law courts in a manner which broadens the scope of Art. 25 by attaching another degree of fault to it; rather it has been interpreted that the standard and/or the definition of wilful misconduct has to be determined by the local law[80].

The most important source regarding the cases concerning the unlimited liability of air carrier has been the USA, since it has not ratified the Hague Protocol[81] due to the insufficient increase in the limits of liability[82]. Therefore, cases arising

---

[78] OLG München, 07.05.1999, ZLW 2000, 118.

[79] See *supra* A I 5.

[80] *Berner v. British Commonwealth Pacific Airlines, Ltd.* (DC New York, 1963) 219 F.Supp. 289, 322; *Hill v. United Airlines* (DC Kansas, 1982) 550 F.Supp. 1048, 1055; *Brink's Limited v. South African Airways* (DC New York, 1995) 1995 WL 225602. However, the CA in the *Brink's* case rejected the interpretation of "a reference to local terminology", but nonetheless seemed to apply the standard accepted by the USA case law, see *Brink's Limited v. South African Airways* (CA, 1996) 93 F.3d 1022. In fact, the judgement of the DC of New York, later reversed by the CA, had applied the British legal standard as determined by the British case law since there had not been any South African case law regarding the issue, *Brink's Limited v. South African Airways* (DC New York, 1997) 1997 WL 323921; followed by *Insurance Company of North America v. Federal Express Corporation* (CA, 1999) 189 F.3d 914; *D'Alessandro v. American Airlines, Inc.* (DC New York, 2001) 139 F.Supp.2d 305; *Simo Noboa v. Iberia Lineas Aereas De España* (DC Puerto Rico, 2005) 383 F.Supp.2d 323.

[81] Protocol to Amend the Convention for the Unification of Certain Rules relating to International Carriage by Air, 1955.

[82] The USA was insisting on higher limits of liability and since this aim was not achieved by the Hague Protocol, the USA announced its denunciation of the Warsaw Convention. However, long discussions and negotiations within the international aviation community have resulted in an agreement between the USA and the air carriers who fly from and to the USA, where air carriers have waived their liability limits for international carriage to $75,000 per passenger in 1966. This agreement is referred to generally as the Montreal Agreement or Interim Agreement. After this agreement was been signed, the USA withdrew its notification of

out of the flights to or from the USA have continued to be covered by the unamended version of the Warsaw Convention[83].

Wilful misconduct is defined by common law courts, although the definition and terms could differ slightly, as "wilful performance of an act, or omission, with the knowledge that the act or omission will cause damage or harm; or wilful performance of an act, or omission, with reckless and wanton disregard of probable consequences of that act or omission"[84].

In order to explain this definition, different elements of the term have been examined. As a starting point, it should be stressed that there is a dual requirement of wilfulness and misconduct. Misconduct is the first element to be considered[85], since if there is no misconduct, wilfulness alone does not amount to any fault. Misconduct includes any unlawful conduct, any conduct violating law, including regulations and other rules such as internal company instructions (*e.g.* rules and procedures to be followed during cargo handling) and also any negligent conduct[86]. In this respect, violation of the rules and regulations regarding the safety of the aircraft and passengers has played a key role in constituting misconduct[87] in

---

denunciation. For the developments and more information, see *Basedow, Haftungshöchstsummen*, 353-354; *Kreindler*, Ch. 10 pp. 5-6; *Lacey*, pp. 387-390; *Silets*, pp. 339-343; *Jacobson*, 276-277.

[83] *Clarke, Carriage by Air*, pp. 157-158; *Schobel*, p. 81.

[84] *American Airlines v. Ulen* (CA, 1949) 186 F.2d 529, 533 *per* Judge Clark; *Ritts v. American Overseas Airlines, Inc.* (DC New York, 1949) 1949 USAvR 65, 68 *per* Judge Picard; *Pekelis v. Transcontinental & Western Air Inc* (CA, 1951) 187 F.2d 122, 124 *per* Judge Augustus N. Hand; *Froman, Ross, Markoff v. Pan American Airways, Inc.* (Supreme Court of New York, 1953) 1953 US&CavR, 1, 6 *per* Judge Steuer; followed by *Grey v. American Airlines Inc* (CA, 1955) 227 F.2d 282, 285; *Koninklijke Luchtvaart Maatschappij N. V. v. Tuller* (CA, 1961) 292 F.2d 775, 778; *Berner v. British Commonwealth Pacific Airlines, Ltd.* (CA, 1965) 346 F.2d 532, 537; *Cohen v. Varig Airlines (S.A. Empresa de Viacao Aerea Rio Grandense)* (Supreme Court of New York, 1978) 405 N.Y.S.2d 44, 47; *International Mining Corporation v. Aerovias Nacionales de Colombia* (Supreme Court of New York, 1977) 393 N.Y.S.2d 405, 407-408; *Butler v. Aeromexico* (CA, 1985) 774 F.2d 429, 430; *Royal Insurance v. Amerford Air Cargo* (DC New York, 1987) 645 F.Supp. 679, 684; *Delvag Luftfahrtversicherungsag v. United Air Lines, Inc.* (DC Illinois, 1987) 1987 WL 8623, 1; *In re Korean Air Lines Disaster of September 1, 1983* (DC Columbia, 1988) 704 F.Supp. 1135, 1136; *Victoria Sales Corporation v. Emery Air Freight, Inc.* (DC New York, 1989) 1989 WL 76227, 5; *Koirala v. Thai Airways International* (CA, 1997) 126 F.3d 1205, 1209-1210.

[85] *Froman, Ross, Markoff v. Pan American Airways, Inc.* (Supreme Court of New York, 1953) 1953 US&CavR, 1, 7.

[86] *Dettling-Ott*, p. 231; *Clarke, CIM*, p. 29.

[87] *Ritts v. American Overseas Airlines, Inc.* (DC New York, 1949) 1949 USAvR 65, 68-70; *American Airlines v. Ulen* (CA, 1949) 186 F.2d 529, 533-534; *Rashap v. American Airlines, Inc.* (DC New York, 1955) 1955 US&CAvR 593, 605 *per* Judge Dawson: "It is essential to remember that it is the misconduct, not the conduct, which, under the statute, must be wilful".

aviation case law. Another conclusion to be drawn as to the element of misconduct is that acts of necessity do not constitute misconduct[88].

Here, a parenthesis should be added. In *Horabin v. British Overseas Airways Corporation*[89], the importance of violations of safety rules in respect of misconduct was stressed. During the instructions to the jury, the court stated that: "the first problem that you have to consider is whether or not any act or acts on the part of this unfortunate pilot – who as you know was killed in the crash – or of any of the other servants of the defendants (such as the official responsible for the issue of maps, to take one example) in fact constituted something which amounted to misconduct. You may think that it would be misconduct for anyone employed by B.O.A.C. to break, without any justification, some regulation which was designed to ensure the safety of the aircraft and the safety of its passengers. Also you may think that it would be misconduct if the pilot departed from the generally accepted standards of safe aerial navigation.", and then continued with other examples of misconduct. This phrase is normally cited and assessed as an example of wilful misconduct. It was argued that violations of basic safety regulations almost always constitute wilful misconduct[90]. Here, it should be underlined that the court did not mention wilful misconduct, but misconduct. Thus, violation of safety regulations constituted misconduct, but not automatically wilful misconduct. Misconduct should be coupled with wilfulness[91].

The first characteristic of wilfulness is that the act or omission should be done intentionally or knowingly, namely "the will must be a party to the conduct" meaning that the person must be aware of the fact that he is committing misconduct and have the conscious intent of so doing[92]. Alternatively, the person in ques-

---

[88]   *Horabin v. British Overseas Airways Corporation*, [1952] 2 Lloyd's Rep. 450, 487 (QBD) *per* Justice Barry: "[...] I am bound to say to you [the jury] that the mere fact that an act was done contrary to a plan, or contrary to some instructions, or even contrary to the standards of safe flying – the mere fact that it was done in that way, contrary to some instructions and contrary to the plan to the knowledge of the person who did it – does not necessarily establish wilful misconduct on his part, because in the exigencies of the flight it is always possible that a pilot may consciously depart from instructions, taking the view that, in the best interests of the safety of his aircraft, it is wiser and safer for him to depart from that instruction than to adhere to it. The pilot, as you know, is solely responsible for the safety of the aircraft on its journey. And, again, a finding on your part that the pilot acted contrary to instructions, and knew that he acted contrary to instructions, will not involve him as a man who committed wilful misconduct merely because you now think that he was wrong in departing from those instructions".

[89]   *Horabin v. British Overseas Airways Corporation*, [1952] 2 Lloyd's Rep. 450, 459 (QBD) *per* Justice Barry.

[90]   *Sullivan*, p. 44.

[91]   *Drion*, pp. 221, 225-228; *Goedhuis*, pp. 273-274; *Müller-Rostin*, p. 126; *Guerreri, Wilful Misconduct*, 270; *Kreindler*, Ch. 10 p. 87.

[92]   *Ritts v. American Overseas Airlines, Inc.* (DC New York, 1949) 1949 USAvR 65, 68-69; *Goepp v. American Overseas Airlines, Inc.* (Supreme Court of New York, 1952) 117 N.Y.S.2d 276, 281; *Horabin v. British Overseas Airways Corporation* [1952] 2 Lloyd's Rep. 450, 459 (QBD); *Froman, Ross, Markoff v. Pan American*

tion should have acted in a reckless manner whereby he did "not car[e] whether he was doing the right or the wrong thing"[93].

Secondly, there must be an intention with regard to the result of the act or omission. The person who has performed the act or omitted to act has to have desired to cause the harm or damage as well. When the element of intending to act or omitting to act and the element of desire for the direct consequences are combined, this degree of fault is called criminal intent[94] or, simply, intention[95]. However, for the sake of preventing misunderstandings as to the gravest degree of fault and a person's desire or motive, it is preferable here to refer to the gravest degree of fault as "intentional wrongdoing"[96]. As a final point as to this gravest degree of fault in common law[97], it should be noted that it is referred to as *dol*, *Absicht* or *dolo* in civil law.

On the other hand, the person does not need to have criminal intent to be found guilty of wilful misconduct. It is also within the borders of wilful misconduct, if one has committed reckless misconduct[98]. In order to be guilty of reckless miscon-

---

Airways, Inc. (Supreme Court of New York, 1953) 1953 US&CavR, 1, 6; *Rashap v. American Airlines, Inc.* (DC New York, 1955) 1955 US&CAvR 593, 605; *In re Korean Air Lines Disaster of September 1, 1983* (DC Columbia, 1988) 704 F.Supp. 1135, 1136.

[93] *Horabin v. British Overseas Airways Corporation* [1952] 2 Lloyd's Rep. 450, 459 (QBD); see also *Rashap v. American Airlines, Inc.* (DC New York, 1955) 1955 US&CAvR 593, 605.

[94] *American Airlines v. Ulen* (CA, 1949) 186 F.2d 529, 533.

[95] *Williams/Hepple*, p. 91; *Smith & Hogan*, p. 97; *Card, Cross & Jones*, p. 77. The element of intent has also been expressed in words other than "intention", such as "with intent to" or "with the purpose of" or "wilfully", see *Report on the Mental Element*, p. 4-9. *Cunliffe v. Goodman* [1950] 2 K.B. 237, 253 (CA) *per* Lord Justice Asquith: "An "intention" to my mind connotes a state of affairs which the party "intending" – I will call him X – does more than merely contemplate: it connotes a state of affairs which, on the contrary, he decides, so far as in him lies, to bring about, and which, in point of possibility, he has a reasonable prospect of being able to bring about, by his own act of volition".

[96] The term was also used in *D'Alessandro v. American Airlines, Inc.* (DC New York, 2001) 139 F.Supp.2d 305, 309.

[97] Restatement (Second) of Torts, § 500 (Reckless Disregard of Safety Defined), Special Note: "The conduct described in this section is often called "wanton or wilful misconduct" both in statutes and judicial opinions. On the other hand, this phrase is sometimes used by courts to refer to conduct intended to cause harm to another."; intention as to the result of the misconduct is connoted as "expected consequences", see *Saba v. Compagnie Nationale Air France* (CA, 1996) 78 F.3d 664, 668 fn. 2.

[98] *Berner v. British Commonwealth Pacific Airlines, Ltd.* (DC New York, 1963) 219 F.Supp. 289, 324: "[...] recognizes the very important particular which distinguishes reckless misconduct from intentional wrongdoing, namely, the actor need not intend to cause the harm which results from the conduct. [...] In order to be 'wilful misconduct' he need not have intended to cause the harm which resulted."; see also *Rustenburg Platinum Mines Ltd v. South African Airways* [1977] 1 Lloyd's Rep. 564, 569 (QBD); Restatement (Second) of Torts, § 500 (intentional miscon-

duct, the person needs to have disregarded the consequences of his wilful act or omission, and he should have acted or omitted to act with reckless indifference as to the results[99]. In the *Horabin v. British Overseas Airways Corporation* case, Justice Barry provided an example which illustrates this characteristic and has been useful[100] in explaining wilful misconduct:

"Let us take the case of two men driving motor cars who pass traffic lights after they have changed from yellow to red. Now, the act in both cases is the same, the same traffic lights, the same cross-roads and both men driving motor cars. In the first case the man may have been driving a little too fast; he may not have been keeping a proper look-out, and he may not have seen these lights (*although he certainly ought to have seen them*) until he was much too close to them and was unable to stop and therefore crossed the cross-roads when the lights were against him. He was not intending to do anything wrong; he was not intending to disregard the provisions of the Road Traffic Act or endanger the lives of anyone using the road, but he was careless in not keeping a proper look-out and going too fast, and as a result, without intending to do anything wrong, he did commit an act which was clearly an act of misconduct.

Then we take the second driver. He is in a hurry. He knows all about the lights, and he sees in plenty of time that they are changing from yellow to red, but he says to himself: "Well, there is hardly any traffic ever coming out of this side road which I am crossing; I will go on; I am not going to bother to stop." He does not expect an accident to happen, but he knows that he is doing something wrong. He knows that he should stop, and he is able to stop, but he does not, and he goes on and commits exactly the same act as the other driver. But in that frame of mind no jury would have very much difficulty in coming to the conclusion that he had committed an act of wilful misconduct. Of course, he did not intend to kill anyone

---

duct and recklessness contrasted) and *Guerreri*, p. 9. It was clearly stated that "wilfulness" as a degree of fault covers also recklessness, see *Report on the Mental Element*, p. 5.

[99] *Dettling-Ott*, p. 231; *Philipson/et al.*, p. 154; *Ritts v. American Overseas Airlines, Inc.* (DC New York, 1949) 1949 USAvR 65, 68; *Goepp v. American Overseas Airlines, Inc.* (Supreme Court of New York, 1952) 117 N.Y.S.2d 276, 281; *Horabin v. British Overseas Airways Corporation* [1952] 2 Lloyd's Rep. 450, 459, 486 (QBD); *Rashap v. American Airlines, Inc.* (DC New York, 1955) 1955 US&CAvR 593, 605: "[...] such a line of conduct with knowledge of what the consequences would be and went ahead recklessly, despite his knowledge of these conditions."; *In re Korean Air Lines Disaster of September 1, 1983* (DC Columbia, 1988) 704 F.Supp. 1135, 1136. This is the kind of conduct meant by the British Delegate Sir Alfred Dennis during the Warsaw Conference, see *Warsaw Conference Minutes*, pp. 59-60 and see *supra* A 1 2.

[100] Cited by *Kahn-Freund*, p. 259; *Drion*, p. 218; *Clarke, Carriage by Air*, pp. 160-161; *Abraham, Rechtsprechung 1952*, p. 72; *Philipson/et al.*, pp. 154-155; *Clarke/Yates*, para. 1.172. For a similar example see Restatement (Second) of Torts, § 500 (perception of risk) ; *Froman, Ross, Markoff v. Pan American Airways, Inc.* (Supreme Court of New York, 1953) 1953 US&CavR, 1, 6 and *Rashap v. American Airlines, Inc.* (DC New York, 1955) 1955 US&CAvR 593, 605, 608-609.

or to injure anyone coming out of the side road; he thought that in all probability nobody would be coming out of the side road. None the less, he took a risk which he knew he ought not to take, and in those circumstances he could be rightly found to have committed an act of wilful misconduct."[101].

The example clearly shows the difference between the states of mind in two different situations. In the first example, the person ought to have seen the lights, viz. ought to have been careful enough not to violate any rules and cause damage or harm. In the second example, however, the person is aware of his misconduct and its probable consequences, which he disregards although he does not intend to cause them. It is stated by the Judge that the second driver commits wilful misconduct, whereas the first one does not. So, for the misconduct, the wrongdoer's state of mind at the time of the misconduct (*subjective test*) was taken into account, not the reasonable person's state of mind (*objective test*). The wrongdoer's actual intention must be inquired into[102].

For an objective test, the standard of a reasonable person is used. The state of mind of a reasonable person in the same circumstances as the wrongdoer will be assessed in order to determine whether the wrongdoer should have foreseen the consequences. However, for a subjective test the actual state of mind of the wrongdoer before and during the carriage will be considered, so the wrongdoer's state of mind will not be compared with that of the reasonable person[103].

Consequently, the test to be applied for a finding of wilful misconduct is a subjective one[104], although there have been some calls for an objective test[105]. As a

---

[101] Emphasis added; [1952] 2 Lloyd's Rep. 450, 460 (QBD).

[102] *Goldhirsch*, p. 154; *Krause & Krause*, Ch. 11, p. 75 fn. 7; *Miller*, pp. 216-217; *Jacobson*, 274.

[103] *Miller*, p. 205; *Kırman*, pp. 158-159; *Dettling-Ott*, p. 233; *Taylor*, 122.

[104] *Shawcross and Beaumont*, VII 478; *Clarke, Carriage by Air*, p. 158; *Strock*, 294-295; *Jacobson*, 289; *Koning*, 325; see also *Maschinenfabrik Kern v. Northwest Airlines* (DC Illinois, 1983) 562 F.Supp. 232, 240; *Saba v. Compagnie Nationale Air France* (CA, 1996) 78 F.3d 664, 667 *et seq.*; *Tokio Marine & Fire Insurance Co., Ltd. v. United Air Lines, Inc.* (DC California, 1996) 933 F.Supp. 1527, 1534.

[105] See *Berner v. British Commonwealth Pacific Airlines, Ltd.* (DC New York, 1963) 219 F.Supp. 289, 323, 325-326, 328; reversed by *Berner v. British Commonwealth Pacific Airlines, Ltd.* (CA, 1965) 346 F.2d 532, 536: "the court in its opinion was in error in concluding that the Second Circuit does not require knowledge that damage would probably result." (for an analysis of the case from an objective-subjective test point of view see *Lacey*, pp. 390-391). Also see *Saba v. Compagnie Nationale Air France* (DC Columbia, 1994) 866 F.Supp. 588; reversed by *Saba v. Compagnie Nationale Air France* (CA, 1996) 78 F.3d 664 stating that subjective knowledge of the risk shall be, at least, inferred; *In re Air Crash near Cali, Colombia on December 20, 1995* (DC Florida, 1997) 985 F.Supp. 1106, 1124-1129 is also in favour of an objective test; however, the objective interpretation of "reckless disregard" was rejected by *Piamba Cortes v. American Airlines* (CA, 1999) 177 F.3d 1272, 1280-1290. See also *Jacobson*, 297-306. It must be emphasised, however, that during the time between the DC and CA decisions, the USA adhered to the Montreal Protocol No. 4 which employs the same wording with the Hague Protocol. Nevertheless, the CA stated clearly that both of the Protocols do not

result of the basic element of subjective awareness, the principle which holds ignorance of the law to be inconsequential is not a factor in determining wilfulness, yet it does remain important in determining misconduct.

Another important point referred to by courts is that wilful misconduct is "wholly different in kind of mere negligence or carelessness, however gross that negligence or carelessness might be"[106]. This fact, actually, also has been stressed by the example given above of two drivers passing through traffic lights. In the first example, the driver has acted grossly negligent, since he ought to have realized the possibility of causing harm. However, in contrast to the first driver, the second one has realised the possibility but has done the act nonetheless.

As a brief summary of the definition given and the elements of wilful misconduct explained above, wilful misconduct covers both the intentional performance of the act or omission accompanied with intent to cause damage and the performance of an act or omission while recklessly disregarding the probable consequences of it[107]. Therefore, unlike the objective standard of *faute lourde* in wilful misconduct cases, the person in question must have foreseen but disregarded the probability of the damage. Consequently, wilful misconduct covers *dol* but does not cover *faute lourde*, namely gross negligence[108].

Finally, it must be emphasised that an error of judgement made in the best interest of others, including cases of necessity[109], does not constitute wilful misconduct[110]. In terms of aviation law, the person needs to have known that he is

---

change the substantive law, but rather clarify it; thus, the subjective approach has not been changed and remains applicable; followed by *Bayer Corporation v. British Airways, Plc.* (CA, 2000) 210 F.3d 236, 238.

[106] *Horabin v. British Overseas Airways Corporation* [1952] 2 Lloyd's Rep. 450, 459 (QBD) *per* Justice Barry; see also *Ritts v. American Overseas Airlines, Inc.* (DC New York, 1949) 1949 USAvR 65, 69 *per* Judge Picard; *Pekelis v. Transcontinental & Western Air Inc* (CA, 1951) 187 F.2d 122, 125 *per* Judge Augustus N. Hand; *Ospina v. Trans World Airlines, Inc. & Youssef v. Trans World Airlines, Inc.* (CA, 1992) 975 F.2d 35, 37 *per* Judge Meskill; *Rustenburg Platinum Mines Ltd v. South African Airways* [1977] 1 Lloyd's Rep. 564, 569 (QBD) *per* Justice Ackner: "It is common ground that "wilful misconduct" goes far beyond any negligence, even gross or culpable negligence"; Restatement (Second) of Torts, § 500 (negligence and recklessness contrasted); *Beaumont, Revision*, p. 408; *Philipson/et al.*, p. 156.

[107] *Matte*, p. 61; *Kırman*, p. 154. For further information see *infra* B I 2 c.

[108] *Abraham*, p. 367; *Abraham, Luftbeförderungsvertrag*, p. 58; *Abraham, Rechtsprechung*, p. 87; *Orr*, pp. 432-433; *Guerreri*, pp. 9-10; for the counterview see *Matte*, p. 61. It must be noted that sometimes also common law courts had disregarded the distinction between wilful misconduct and gross negligence, nevertheless stressed the necessity of the reckless disregard of the consequences for a finding of wilful misconduct, see *Tarar v. Pakistan International Airlines* (DC Texas, 1982) 554 F.Supp. 471, 475-476 *per* Judge Hannay.

[109] See *Shawcross and Beaumont*, VII 477; Restatement (Second) of Torts, § 500 (unreasonableness of risk).

[110] *Rashap v. American Airlines, Inc.* (DC New York, 1955) 1955 US&CAvR 593, 607.

involving others in a greater risk than the risk they would be exposed to if he took another course[111]. The element of unlawfulness, however, is a preliminary condition; hence, taking a greater risk would have to be in violation of relevant rules and regulations concerning safety with an indifference to the probable consequences[112].

It is quite obvious that the concept of wilful misconduct is not an easy one to apply to actual cases[113]; and yet the case law is full of examples regarding wilful misconduct involving carriage by air.

a) Carriage of passengers

aa) Passengers

Even though it is believed that Art. 25 was adopted for cases of theft, *viz.* for cases of carriage of cargo rather than the carriage of passengers, there has been considerable case law involving the death of or injury to passengers with plaintiffs claiming wilful misconduct of the carrier. The death or physical harm of a passenger could be caused by various reasons. Unfortunately, the main reason has been plane crashes. However, inappropriate behaviour by employees of the carrier could also cause physical or psychological harm to the passenger[114].

The first group of examples with regard to wilful misconduct involving carriage of passengers is the infringement of basic safety rules. If someone violates the basic safety rules embodied in the relevant laws and regulations, it has been decided that this fault amounts to wilful misconduct since it is assumed that the person or relevant people involved in the infringement have foreseen the probable consequences. The first example is the case of *Ulen v. American Airlines* where the court concluded that the planning and executing of a flight far below the minimum altitude which had given rise to a crash into a mountain constituted wilful misconduct[115]. Similarly, in another case, the court stated that violations of the duty to abort the landing approach when the airport was not visible at a certain altitude and the duty to activate the radar amounted to wilful misconduct, and the carrier was liable without any financial limitation for the death of the passengers resulting from the plane crash[116]. Additionally, where the crew did not abort the

---

[111] Restatement (Second) of Torts, § 500 (unreasonableness of risk).

[112] Restatement (Second) of Torts, § 500 (violation of statute); *Guerreri*, p. 10; *American Airlines v. Ulen* (CA, 1949) 186 F.2d 529, 533; *Horabin v. British Overseas Airways Corporation* [1952] 2 Lloyd's Rep. 450, 488 (QBD).

[113] *Horabin v. British Overseas Airways Corporation* [1952] 2 Lloyd's Rep. 450, 486 (QBD).

[114] *Drion*, pp. 212-213.

[115] *Ulen v. American Airlines* (DC Columbia, 1947) 7 F.R.D. 371, affirmed by *American Airlines v. Ulen* (CA, 1949) 186 F.2d 529 (also *Larsen/Sweeney/Gillick*, pp. 369-371); for the summary of the facts see *Drion*, p. 214; *Guerreri*, pp. 7-8; *Abraham, Rechtsprechung*, p. 87; (1950) 44 AJIL 412; *Guerreri, Wilful Misconduct*, 267-269; this case is referred to as one of the clearest examples of wilful misconduct by *Guerreri*, p. 8; *Guerreri, Wilful Misconduct*, 269.

[116] *Butler v. Aeromexico* (CA, 1985) 774 F.2d 429.

flight when they noticed that the inertia navigation system was not functioning or malfunctioning, and where, consequently, the flight deviated off-course invading a state's territory prohibited for flights and was, as a result of this invasion, shot down by that state's military aircraft, the airline is guilty of wilful misconduct[117]. However, incorrect interpretation of the rules and regulations has not amounted to misconduct[118].

The last point to be emphasised with regard to the violation of rules and regulations is that the requirement of subjective awareness is essential for a finding of wilful misconduct. Where the pilots were preparing to land the plane on an airport in a valley in the middle of mountainous terrain, the flight went significantly off course and yet the pilots continued to descend, violating the rules and regulations in a grave manner. Subsequently, the plane crashed into a mountain causing the death of everyone on board. It was decided that the crash was not attributable to the wilful misconduct of the pilots since subjective awareness of the danger was missing[119].

Another example of infringement of basic safety rules is the failure to properly instruct passengers on the location and usage of life vests. In one case, the airplane had crashed in the tidewaters of a river at the end of the airport runway; after the crash, whilst waiting to be rescued, the passenger, Mr. Tuller, lost his footing four hours after having succeeded to stand up on the tail of the aircraft. He consequently fell into the river and drowned, but he could have been rescued if he had been wearing a life vest. In this particular case, the failure to send a distress message, the failure to take necessary steps for the safety of Mr. Tuller after his peril was known and the failure of the airline's agents to be aware of the loss of the radio communication with the plane and to initiate prompt search and rescue operations were found to be other contributing causes to the death of Mr. Tuller[120].

---

[117] *In re Korean Air Lines Disaster of September 1, 1983* (DC Columbia, 1988) 704 F.Supp. 1135, overruled on different grounds by *In re Korean Air Lines Disaster of September 1, 1983* (CA, 1991) 932 F.2d 1475. In another case arising out of the same crash, a different court also decided that the death of 269 persons on board was attributable to wilful misconduct of the carrier, see *Zicherman v. Korean Air Lines Co., Ltd.* (DC New York, 1993) 814 F.Supp. 605.

[118] *Rashap v. American Airlines, Inc.* (DC New York, 1955) 1955 US&CAvR 593; *Goepp v. American Overseas Airlines, Inc.* (Supreme Court of New York, 1952) 117 N.Y.S.2d 276; *Ritts v. American Overseas Airlines, Inc.* (DC New York, 1949) 1949 USAvR 65. It should be noted that although the two cases arose from the same crash, the court decided to the limited liability in *Goepp*, whereas the court in *Ritts* ruled that the airline was exempt from liability under Art. 20 of the Warsaw Convention; see *Guerreri, Wilful Misconduct*, 270; *Modjaz*, pp. 61-62; *Abraham, Rechtsprechung 1952*, pp. 73-74.

[119] *Piamba Cortes v. American Airlines* (CA, 1999) 177 F.3d 1272 (also *Larsen/ Sweeney/Gillick*, pp. 388-403). For the district court decision, see *In re Air Crash near Cali, Colombia on December 20, 1995* (DC Florida, 1997) 985 F.Supp. 1106.

[120] *Koninklijke Luchtvaart Maatschappij N. V. v. Tuller* (CA, 1961) 292 F.2d 775 (also *Larsen/Sweeney/Gillick*, pp. 372-375). This decision has been criticised on the grounds that by using the "grave danger" argument, the court did not take into consideration the proof of state of mind, and that situation led to a finding of a degree

Dangerous conduct without violating any rules or regulations regarding the safety might also constitute wilful misconduct. In the *Horabin* case, the plaintiff alleged wilful misconduct of the pilot and, consequently, the wilful misconduct of the air carrier. In this case, during a flight from England to France, the pilot was directed to another airport with which he was not familiar. Thus, the pilot first decided to fly back to England but then diverted to France. Afterwards, he hesitated to land at the airport and diverted once again to England. However, the plane crashed owing to shortage in fuel. Before the case was decided by the court, the plaintiff and the claimant settled[121]. In another case, the crew had misled the controller as to their position, and the controller had therefore authorised the plane to descend. However, after only five minutes, the plane crashed into a mountain while it was descending. The plaintiff claimed that the crew falsely and deliberately reported their position. The court decided in favour of plaintiffs stating that the flight crew was guilty of wilful misconduct[122]. When a plane was approaching an airport which had been rated as one of the most difficult airports for landings due to the mountainous terrain surrounding the airport and the generally poor visibility conditions, the flight crew mistakenly made a 360 degree turn instead of 180 and descended to an altitude ordered by air traffic control. However, since they had incorrectly executed the turn, the plane headed towards the mountains; since the flight crew was busy programming a navigational flight system, they did not realise the severity of the situation until the first officer warned the pilot of the situation only 30 seconds before the plane was set to crash into the mountains. However, the pilot did not understand the warning and took no action. The court stated that the conscious inattention to flight duties amounted to wilful misconduct[123].

Conduct which endangers passengers' lives could result in a finding of wilful misconduct as well. In one case, a passenger with chronic respiratory problems who was consequently dependant on her bag containing a breathing device and relevant medicine was asked to relinquish her bag before boarding, although the passenger's relative informed the employees of the airline that the bag should be with the passenger at all times, including the flight. The employee who took the bag from the passenger guaranteed that the bag would be delivered at the destination point. However, all checked bags and also the bag in question were missing at the arrival. The airline was, again, informed that bags were missing and that the particular bag was extremely important since it contained critical medical products. The passenger was told that the bag would be on the next flight. However,

---

of fault below the required one, see (1962) 37 NYU L. Rev. 323 and *Modjaz*, pp. 53-54. It is true that the court did not examine the state of mind of relevant people in each case; however the court did stress the reckless disregard of the consequences of the act or omission every time, see *Koninklijke Luchtvaart Maatschappij N. V. v. Tuller* (CA, 1961) 292 F.2d 775, 779-782.

[121] *Horabin v. British Overseas Airways Corporation* [1952] 2 Lloyd's Rep. 450 (QBD).

[122] *LeRoy v. Sabena Belgian World Airlines* (CA, 1965) 344 F.2d 266.

[123] *Koirala v. Thai Airways International* (DC California, 1996) 1996 WL 40243; affirmed by *Koirala v. Thai Airways International* (CA, 1997) 126 F.3d 1205.

the bag was never delivered, even though the airline kept informing the passenger that "it will be on the next flight". After a week, the passenger was admitted to a hospital, where she died. The court entered into judgement in favour of the plaintiff stating that the airline's conduct amounted to wilful misconduct[124].

The delay of passengers and the consequent results arising out of the delay could also be caused by the wilful misconduct of the carrier. An example is intentional misrepresentation. Where the airline informed the passengers that the airport into which they were to fly was closed due to weather conditions, passengers informed the airline that they were scheduled to take a connecting flight from that airport. In response to their enquiry, the airline informed them that they would still catch their connecting flight since all the flights into and out of that airport were cancelled due to weather conditions. However, the passengers later learned that the airport was open at all times and that their flight into that airport had been cancelled because the necessary equipment, *i.e.* an airplane, was not ready. Consequently, the passengers in fact missed their connecting flight. The court ruled in favour of the plaintiffs stating that the airline was guilty of wilful misconduct[125].

Defamation by employees of the carrier could also amount to wilful misconduct. However, in order to be guilty of wilful misconduct, the employee must have been engaged in "misconduct". Where an employee's oral warning had a legal basis, even rude warnings would not constitute wilful misconduct[126]. Similarly, if the search and detention of a passenger and passenger's luggage was in conformity with the airline's security procedures, it did not constitute "misconduct"[127].

Finally, wilful misconduct has been claimed in case of terrorist attacks[128]. In the first case, the plaintiff claimed that the airline was guilty of wilful misconduct due to its failure to search the plane before the flight during which a hidden bomb under a seat exploded and caused the death and serious injury of some passengers. Whereas the jury found that the explosion was attributable to the airline's wilful misconduct[129], the decision of the court was reversed on appeal because of the airline's compliance with all safety procedures and regulations in force[130]. Nevertheless, the air carrier was guilty of wilful misconduct where it ignored a written warning from a federal office stating that a bomb would be placed on board the subject flight and where, subsequent to the explosion of a bomb, the plane was

---

[124] *Prescod v. Amr, Inc., American Airlines* (CA, 2004) 383 F.3d 861.

[125] *Hill v. United Airlines* (DC Kansas, 1982) 550 F.Supp. 1048.

[126] *Asher v. United Airlines* (DC Maryland, 1999), 70 F.Supp.2d 614.

[127] *Tseng v. El Al Israel Airlines, Ltd.* (DC New York, 1996) 919 F.Supp. 155 (further discussed in relation to the "accident" requirement of the Warsaw Convention in *Tseng v. El Al Israel Airlines, Ltd.* (CA, 1997) 122 F.3d 99 and *El Al Israel Airlines, Ltd. V. Tsui Yuan Tseng* (Supreme Court of the US, 1999) 119 S.Ct. 662).

[128] For an analysis of the correlation between terrorist attacks and wilful misconduct see *Silets*, pp. 367-374.

[129] *In re Inflight Explosion on Trans World Airlines, Inc. Aircraft Approaching Athens, Greece on April 2, 1986* (DC New York, 1991) 778 F.Supp. 625.

[130] *Ospina v. Trans World Airlines, Inc. & Youssef v. Trans World Airlines, Inc.* (CA, 1992) 975 F.2d 35.

destroyed[131]. However, the airline was not liable without financial limitation where the damages were not caused by the wilful misconduct of the carrier. In this respect, it was decided in a hijacking case that fraudulent misrepresentation[132] could amount to wilful misconduct; however, the carrier's liability was still limited owing to the fact that the damages were not caused by fraudulent misrepresentation of the carrier, but rather caused by terrorist activity. At a time when the terrorist activities within airports were widespread, the airline advertised that it had brought in an increased security system, whereas it had not; and several passengers were killed and injured during a hijack attempt[133].

bb) Luggage

There have been some cases regarding the carriage of luggage. Damage claims concerning the loss of luggage can arise from an accident, *e.g.* a plane crash, or out of a failure on the carrier's side in handling the luggage[134].

An American court ruled that the air carrier was guilty of wilful misconduct in a case where the employees of the air carrier refused to remove the baggage from the plane on to which the baggage was loaded by mistake, claiming that it would be too expensive and then asserting that the baggage had been lost[135]. Similarly, a court entered into judgement in favour of plaintiffs stating that the airline was guilty of wilful misconduct where the carrier incorrectly ticketed the baggage and, despite repeated requests by plaintiffs, refused to ticket it correctly[136]. However, in another case of loss of luggage, the court ruled that the attempt to cover-up the

---

[131] *In re Air Disaster at Lockerbie, Scotland on December 21, 1988* (DC New York, 1992) 811 F.Supp. 84, affirmed by *In re Air Disaster at Lockerbie Scotland on December 21, 1988: Pagnucco v. Pan American World Airways, Inc.* (CA, 1994) 37 F.3d 804 (also *Larsen/Sweeney/Gillick*, pp. 376-387).

[132] For the term, see Restatement of Torts, § 525 (liability for fraudulent misrepresentations), § 526 (conditions under which misrepresentation is fraudulent); *Dobbs*, pp. 1345-1349; *Street*, pp. 330-335; *Markesinis and Deakin*, pp. 565-570.

[133] *In re Hijacking of Pan American World Airways, Inc. Aircraft at Karachi International Airport, Pakistan on September 5, 1986* (DC New York, 1996) 920 F.Supp. 408; affirmed by *Shah v. Pan American World Services, Inc.* (CA, 1998) 148 F.3d 84. For a comparative analysis of the case, see Ruwantissa I. R. *Abeyratne*, Fraudulent Misrepresentations of the Carrier as Acts of Wilful Misconduct, (1999) 24 Air & SL 280, 281-285.

[134] *Drion*, pp. 213-214.

[135] *Cohen v. Varig Airlines, S.A. Empresa de Viacao Aerea Rio Grandense* (Civil Court New York, 1975) 380 N.Y.S.2d 450 affirmed by *Cohen v. Varig Airlines (S.A. Empresa de Viacao Aerea Rio Grandense)* (Supreme Court of New York, 1978) 405 N.Y.S.2d 44; for a comment on the case see Alona E. *Evans*, International air transport – carrier liability – lost luggage – Warsaw Convention of 1929, (1979) 73 AJIL 687.

[136] *Kupferman v. Pakistan International Airlines* (Civil Court New York, 1981) 438 N.Y.S.2d 189.

collusion between custom officers and agents of the carrier which resulted in the loss of luggage did not constitute wilful misconduct[137].

There are also some cases where the valuable cargo was carried as a checked baggage. In one such case, a bag containing two million dollars disappeared. The court's decision was in favour of the carrier since the acceptance of currency as checked baggage did not as such create a probability of loss. Further, failure to adopt procedures for handling high value baggage was also not considered as fault amounting to wilful misconduct[138].

b) Carriage of cargo

Similar to the field of carriage of passengers, there have been a considerable number of decisions involving carriage of cargo by air. When these cases are examined, the factual causes on which the claims of wilful misconduct were built mostly deal with theft, either by employees of the carrier, or by third parties.

An air carrier, having issued documents of title, delivered goods without checking whether the person claiming delivery was entitled to them; when it later turned out that he was not when the lawful consignee asked for them, the court decided that the air carrier was guilty of wilful misconduct[139]. On the other hand, in a similar case, the Supreme Court of New York decided to the contrary[140].

In some cases, armed robbery in airports was also a problem which plaintiffs alleged was caused by wilful misconduct. In one of those cases, the owner of the goods claimed wilful misconduct of the carrier since his goods were stolen during an armed robbery in the special valuable cargo area despite all the precautions which were taken. The plaintiff claimed that there had been another robbery in the previous year in the same area, and that the carrier should have taken stricter precautions than he had. The court concluded that the proximate cause of the loss of cargo was the armed robbery, not the carelessness of the carrier[141]. In an English case, banknotes in the amount of US $540,000.00 were stolen during an armed robbery from the valuable cargo storage. The plaintiff claimed that the air carrier's valuable cargo handling procedure and facilities were so weak that they constitute wilful misconduct. After examining the case carefully, Queen's Bench Division decided that there was not any misconduct on the part of the carrier and even if there had been, it was not wilful. Furthermore, since the carrier's valuable cargo procedure is based on immediate delivery of the cargo to the consignee and the contractor of the plaintiff failed to collect the banknotes from the side of the air-

---

[137] *Rymanowski v. Pan American World Airways, Inc.* (Supreme Court of New York, 1979) 416 N.Y.S.2d 1018.

[138] *Republic National Bank of New York v. Eastern Airlines, Inc.* (CA, 1987) 815 F.2d 232.

[139] *Outlook Store, Inc. v. Cardinal Air Services and Scandinavian Airlines System* (Civil Court of the City of New York, 1970) 317 N.Y.S.2d 37.

[140] *International Mining Corporation v. Aerovias Nacionales de Colombia* (Supreme Court of New York, 1977) 393 N.Y.S.2d 405.

[141] *Wing Hang Bank, Ltd. v. Japanese Air Lines Co., Ltd.* 357 F.Supp. 94.

craft, the plaintiff had failed to show any causation between the alleged wilful misconduct and the damage. Consequently, the carrier's liability was limited[142].

Another type of theft is the one occurring during intermediate stops or when the goods are in or in front of the warehouse. Where the air carrier used a normal plastic bag instead of using a valuable cargo bag and 13 kilos of gold bullion were lost, the court decided that the liability should be limited since the elements necessary for a finding of wilful misconduct were missing[143]. Likewise, another case where it was claimed that the loss of the goods resulting from the failure to follow high value cargo procedure was attributable to the wilful misconduct of the carrier was dismissed on the grounds of the difference between negligence and wilful misconduct[144]. Similarly, the court ruled in favour of the defendant stating that the unexplained loss of goods from the storage did not constitute wilful misconduct[145].

Theft by the carrier's employees raises not only questions of wilful misconduct, but also questions of the scope of employment. Distinct from the scope of employment issue[146], it has been concluded that the mere fact of theft is not enough to hold the carrier liable without any financial limits if the identity of the thief and the occurrence of the theft is unknown[147], such that the link between the theft and the carrier cannot be built. However, in a case where one of the carrier's employees stole the cargo, the court refrained from examining the issue on the ground that there was no admissible evidence[148]. In a similar case, where the goods were stolen by an employee of the carrier, the American court concluded that theft by the employee is an act serving only his interests, with the result that the carrier's liability was limited[149]. However, in one exceptional case, the Court of Appeal concluded that theft by an employee (or servant) constituted wilful misconduct and therefore the liability of the carrier was unlimited[150].

There are also some other cases involving cargo damage. One of those is the *Saba* case. In this case, the cargo packed in bales and consisting of 575 Persian hand-woven carpets was exposed to heavy rain owing to their outdoor-storage; it was damaged due to both insufficient packaging and the heavy rain. Contrary to

---

[142] *Thomas Cook Group Ltd. and Others v. Air Malta Co. Ltd.* [1997] 2 Lloyd's Rep. 399 (QBD).

[143] *Perera Co., Inc. v. Varig Brazilian Airlines, Inc.* (CA, 1985) 775 F.2d 21.

[144] *Delvag Luftfahrtversicherungsag v. United Air Lines, Inc.* (DC Illinois, 1987) 1987 WL 8623.

[145] *Royal Insurance v. Amerford Air Cargo* (DC New York, 1987) 645 F.Supp. 679.

[146] See *infra* D II.

[147] *Brink's Limited v. South African Airways* (DC New York, 1997) 1997 WL 323921, 7; affirmed by *Brink's Limited v. South African Airways* (CA, 1998) 149 F.3d 127.

[148] *Tokio Marine & Fire Insurance Co., Ltd. v. Unites Air Lines, Inc.* (DC California, 1996) 933 F.Supp 1527, 1534-1535.

[149] *Insurance Company of North America v. Federal Express Corporation* (CA, 1999) 189 F.3d 914.

[150] *Rustenburg Platinum Mines Ltd v. South African Airways and Pan American World Airways Inc.* [1977] 1 Lloyd's Rep. 564 (QBD); affirmed by *Rustenburg Platinum Mines Ltd v. South African Airways and Pan American World Airways Inc.* [1979] 1 Lloyd's Rep 19 (CA).

the District Court decision[151], the Court of Appeals decided that the air carrier's employees were not subjectively aware of the risk of damage, and, for this reason the carrier was not liable for the full amount of the cargo[152].

An exceptional case decided by an American court is the *Tarar* case. In this case, a casket bearing the remains of a famous Pakistani writer, who had made it known that he wanted to be buried in Pakistan, had been prevented from being loaded on to the plane at a transit point where it could readily have been done. This refusal by agents of the carrier caused delay in transportation of the casket and caused both financial loss and psychological harm. The court concluded that the wilful refusal done with reckless disregard of the consequence of unnecessary and avoidable delay in the delivery of the casket amounted to wilful misconduct[153]. In a similar case, where the airline lost the plaintiff's mother's ashes, the court ruled that the loss was not caused by wilful misconduct since special care was given to the transportation of the decedent's ashes by carrying them in the valuable items compartment, although notice was not given to the destination airport office[154].

3. Result

It is of great importance to keep in mind that Art. 25 was applicable both in the carriage of passengers and their luggage as well as the carriage of cargo. Although intentional wrongdoing in respect of the carriage of passengers is limited to the case of a pilot committing suicide, pilferage and the theft of baggage and cargo do not require such an unfortunate scenario[155]. However, since the degree of fault requirement by Art. 25 of the Warsaw Convention has been lowered through different methods of interpretation, wilful misconduct has been considered in the carriage of passengers as well as in the carriage of cargo in numerous cases.

Again, the difference in interpretation has led to diversity between common law and civil law[156]. Common law jurisdictions by dealing only with the term of wilful misconduct, considered the state of mind of the wrongdoer as a necessary element. However, decisions by civil law courts have clearly shown that the actor's state of mind is not the crucial point to be examined. Rather, the decisive point is whether the wrongdoer showed the necessary care which a reasonable person would apply.

The most important consequence of this result has been to realize the significance of the choice of jurisdiction[157]. For instance, the flight which was under-

---

[151] *Saba v. Compagnie Nationale Air France* (DC Columbia, 1994) 866 F.Supp. 588.
[152] *Saba v. Compagnie Nationale Air France* (CA, 1996) 78 F.3d 664.
[153] *Tarar v. Pakistan International Airlines* (DC Texas, 1982) 554 F.Supp. 471.
[154] *Simo Noboa v. Iberia Lineas Aereas de España* (DC Puerto Rico, 2005) 383 F.Supp.2d 232.
[155] *Drion*, pp. 211-212.
[156] For a summary of interpretation differences between different jurisdictions, see *Guldimann, Auslegung*, pp. 275-276.
[157] *Abraham, Luftbeförderungsvertrag*, p. 58.

taken and which gave rise to the *Goepp*[158] and *Ritts*[159] cases was intended to be done between New York (USA) and Frankfurt (Germany). Both cases were decided by the New York courts and in the *Goepp* case, the court ruled that the liability of the defendant air carrier was limited. However, it is not hard to assert that if the plaintiff had filed the suit before the Frankfurt courts[160], the result would have been different[161].

However, it is also true that sometimes judges held it to be unjust that relatives of victims of a plane crash should only receive compensation up to the limits adopted by the Convention. This led to the avoidance or breaking of the limits of the regime set by the Convention[162]. It is understandable from the first cases decided on the basis of the Warsaw Convention and especially those decided by juries, that judges did their best to explain the term of wilful misconduct and to stress the importance of the actual state of mind; however, juries decided in favour of plaintiffs since some members no doubt thought that holding the air carrier responsible but only up to certain limits, especially relatively low limits, was wrong[163]. Consequently, it has been stated that there were not any big differences as to the results reached by common and civil law courts[164].

On the other hand, it should be remembered that as the precedents started to take shape and after the limits were increased by the Montreal Agreement[165], decisions in favour of the defendant air carriers have been taken which were based on the element of actual knowledge[166].

---

[158] *Goepp v. American Overseas Airlines, Inc.* (Supreme Court of New York, 1952) 117 N.Y.S.2d 276.

[159] *Ritts v. American Overseas Airlines, Inc.* (DC New York, 1949) 1949 USAvR 65.

[160] According to Art. 28 of Warsaw Convention, the action could be brought before a court having jurisdiction at the place of destination.

[161] *Abraham, Luftbeförderungsvertrag,* p. 59; *Abraham, Rechtsprechung 1952,* pp. 74-75. Professor Abraham stated that also in the *Horabin* case, a civil law court would have ruled on gross negligence and entered into judgement in favour of the plaintiffs; see *Abraham, Luftbeförderungsvertrag,* pp. 59-60.

[162] *Schobel,* pp. 100-102.

[163] See also *Modjaz,* pp. 62-63.

[164] *Abraham, Rechtsprechung,* p. 88.

[165] See *supra* A II 2 fn. 82.

[166] E.g. *Rashap v. American Airlines, Inc.* (DC New York, 1955) 1955 US&CAvR 593; *Goepp v. American Overseas Airlines, Inc.* (Supreme Court of New York, 1952) 117 N.Y.S.2d 276; *Ritts v. American Overseas Airlines, Inc.* (DC New York, 1949) 1949 USAvR 65; *Piamba Cortes v. American Airlines* (CA, 1999) 177 F.3d 1272; *In re Hijacking of Pan American World Airways, Inc. Aircraft at Karachi International Airport, Pakistan on September 5, 1986* (DC New York, 1996) 920 F.Supp. 408; *Shah v. Pan American World Services, Inc.* (CA, 1998) 148 F.3d 84. Generally see *supra* A II 2 a aa.

B. The Hague Protocol, 1955

After the Warsaw Convention was signed and entered into force, aviation technology started to develop rapidly. The capacity to carry more passengers and the supply need in light of the growing demand resulted in an increase in the number of airline companies. So, the industry became stronger and stronger. Due to these developments, liability limits set out by the Warsaw Convention caused general dissatisfaction and needed to be changed[167].

Work on the revision of the Convention started in 1938; however it broke off by the start of Second World War. After the War, the work was restarted by CITEJA and, upon the dissolution of CITEJA in 1947, continued by the International Civil Aviation Organization (ICAO) which took over the assignments of CITEJA. The draft amendments were discussed during a diplomatic conference (International Conference on Private Air Law) held in The Hague ("Hague Conference") in September 1955. The result of this Conference was the Protocol to Amend the Convention for the Unification of Certain Rules relating to International Carriage by Air signed at Warsaw on 12 October 1929 ("Hague Protocol"), signed on 28 September 1955 and entering into force in 1 August 1963[168].

I. Modification of Article 25

1. Reason for modification

The wording of Art. 25, which makes a uniform interpretation almost impossible, led to uncertainties caused by the differences in interpretation as well as the case law developed by common and civil law countries[169]. It was also believed that the

---

[167] *Guldimann*, pp. 5-6; *Milde*, pp. 47-48; *Krause & Krause*, Ch. 11 p. 18; *Gerber*, pp. 25-30; *Silets*, pp. 336-337; *Stachow*, p. 77; for an analysis see Arnould W. *Knauth*, Some Notes on the Warsaw Convention of 1929, (1947) 14 J. Air L. & Com. 44.

[168] Report on Revision of the Warsaw Convention (adopted by the Legal Committee of ICAO), in: *Documents, Hague*, p. 93; *Minutes, Hague*, p. xv-xvi; *Matte*, p. 18; *Shawcross and Beaumont*, VII 122; *Guldimann*, pp. 4-5; *Schobel*, pp. 11-12; *Sözer, Kurallar*, pp. 375-376; *Modjaz*, pp. 28-30; *Stachow*, pp. 78-79. For an overview regarding the changes done, see Julian G. *Verplaetse*, Proposed Changes in the Law of Carriage by Air, 1956 Bus. LR 95.

[169] Generally see *supra* A I 5 and A II; Report on Revision of the Warsaw Convention (adopted by the Legal Committee of ICAO), in: *Documents, Hague*, p. 98; *Matte*, p. 62; *Guerreri*, p. 12; *Mankiewicz*, p. 200; *Giemulla/Schmid*, WA Art. 25 Rn. 3, 25; *Döring*, p. 4; *Dettling-Ott*, p. 222; *Gerber*, pp. 39-40; *Schobel*, pp. 77-78; *Calkins*, p. 265; *Çağa*, pp. 199-200; *Kırman*, p. 152; *Cheng*, pp. 82-83; *Kilbride*, p. 185; *Liesecke*, p. 96; *McGilchrist*, pp. 542-543; *Schmid, Zwei Motoren*, p. 290; *Sözer, Taşıyıcının Sorumluluğu*, p. 795; *Strock*, 293; *Guldimann, Auslegung*, pp. 275-277; *Clarke/Yates*, para. 3.150; *Müller-Rostin*, in: *Fremuth/Thume*, Art. 25 WA Rn. 6; the different interpretation was also referred by a civil law court, see Bezirksgericht Zürich, 15.12.1964, ZLW 1965, 338 (343-344).

phrase in Art. 25 referring to local law[170] had been interpreted very liberally by juries and courts in order to break the low liability limits[171]. Since the aim of uniformity could not be realized[172], it was strongly recommended that Art. 25 should be amended[173].

Different approaches were suggested by various scholars. Besides some suggestions[174], advice was offered encouraging that a method for describing the conduct giving rise to unlimited liability in the Convention on Damage Caused by Foreign Aircraft to Third Parties on the Surface ("Rome Convention, 1952") be adopted[175]. Others suggested that only intentional wrongdoing should give rise to unlimited liability[176].

In order to ensure the uniformity of rules regarding unlimited liability of the carrier in cases of a certain degree of fault, work on the amendment of Art. 25 was also done by the Legal Committee of the ICAO[177].

2. New wording

a) Legislative history

Similarly to proposals regarding other provisions to be amended, the proposal to amend Art. 25 was also drafted according to the remarks made by the contracting states, other interested governments and international organisations in their response to the questions asked by the ICAO Legal Committee[178]. It was reported that the general tendency as to the conduct for which the air carrier should be held liable without any limitation was that the carrier or one of his employees must be guilty of an act or omission done with the knowledge that it was wrong and with

---

[170] Which, actually, has been seen as the source of the divergent interpretation also by the states invited to the Hague Conference, see Comments and Proposals submitted to the Draft Protocol by Germany, Netherlands, Norway, in: *Documents, Hague*, pp. 159, 171, 174.

[171] *Mankiewicz*, p. 124; *Clarke/Yates*, para. 3.151; *Çağa*, p. 200; *Kilbride*, pp. 184-185; *Mankiewicz, Hague Protocol*, p. 80, 82; as to the tendency in courts to expand the wilful misconduct to negligence and gross negligence, see *Beaumont*, pp. 16-17.

[172] It was stated that "uniformity, one of the principal objectives of the Convention, is sacrificed" as to Art. 25, see *Sullivan*, p. 43.

[173] *Drion*, p. 44; *Goedhuis*, p. 278; *Döring*, p. 4.

[174] *E.g.* establishing a system similar to the one in CIV and CIM, where the carrier was held liable for an amount the double of the maximum liability limit in cases of intentional wrongdoing, see *Goedhuis*, p. 278; see also Report on Revision of the Warsaw Convention (adopted by the Legal Committee of ICAO), in: *Documents, Hague*, p. 98.

[175] *Goedhuis*, p. 278; *Beaumont, Revision*, p. 409: "It is no use explaining that green is a mixture of blue and yellow to a man who is colour blind".

[176] *Riese*, p. 479.

[177] ICAO News Release, 29 January 1952.

[178] Report on Revision of the Warsaw Convention (adopted by the Legal Committee of ICAO), in: *Documents, Hague*, p. 93; *Beaumont*, pp. 14, 17.

the intent to cause damage[179]. Consequently, Art. 25 was proposed to be changed in the following way:

> "The limits of liability specified in Article 22 of the Convention shall not apply if it is proved that the damage resulted from a deliberate act or omission of the carrier, his servants or agents, done with intent to cause damage; provided that, in the case of a deliberate act or omission of a servant or agent, it is also proved that he was acting in the course of his employment."[180].

There are two obvious conclusions to be drawn from this proposal. First, it is preferable to define the conduct which gives rise to unlimited liability instead of using legal terms. This preference is not too hard to understand since the wording of the Warsaw Convention referring to legal terms was the cause of the problems which made the amendment necessary. Secondly, the conduct giving rise to unlimited liability is, from a legal perspective, intentional wrongdoing (*Absicht, dol, dolo*)[181]. The person in question must have acted or omitted to act in a manner intended to cause the unlawful result. The proposal clearly excludes cases of gross negligence[182].

Prior to the Hague Conference, states which were invited to the Conference submitted their comments and proposals. The ones regarding Art. 25 clearly welcomed the improvement and stated their satisfaction with regard to the conduct being defined rather than relying on the use of legal terms[183]. It was further emphasised that the new formula would achieve unification and uniform application[184].

It was also specified that the proposed amendment had almost the same wording as Art. 12[185] of the Rome Convention, 1952[186]. However, this fact has been

---

[179] *Beaumont*, p. 17.

[180] Draft Protocol to Amend the Convention for the Unification of Certain Rules relating to International Carriage by Air signed at Warsaw on 12 October 1929 (formulated by the Legal Committee of ICAO in Rio de Janeiro in September 1953), in: *Documents, Hague*, p. 80. This Draft Protocol is known as the Rio de Janeiro Draft.

[181] See also ICAO News Release, 1 September 1955.

[182] *Gerber*, pp. 85-86; *Modjaz*, pp. 28-30; ICAO News Release, 29 September 1955; Comments and Proposals submitted to the Draft Protocol by Netherlands and Switzerland, in: *Documents, Hague*, pp. 171, 181. Furthermore, the adjective of "deliberate" was used instead of "wilful"; however the meaning is the same with the latter. For an example of usage of "deliberate" instead of "wilful" see *Bank of Athens v. Royal Exchange Assurance (The "Eftychia")* (1937) 57 Ll. L. Rep. 37, 57, 62. The reason the drafters of the Rio de Janeiro Draft used "deliberate" must be the intention to define the degree of fault in words other than its name.

[183] Comments of Australia, in: *Documents, Hague*, p. 150.

[184] Comments of Australia, in: *Documents, Hague*, p. 150.

[185] "If the person who suffers damage proves that it was caused by a deliberate act or omission of the operator, his servants or agents, done with intent to cause damage, the liability of the operator shall be unlimited; [...]"; for information on the provision, see Peter *Kistler*, Das Römer Haftungsabkommen von 1952, Winterthur 1959, pp. 59-62; *Drion*, pp. 44, 232-236; *Meyer*, pp. 159-160; *Milde*, pp. 120-121. Rome

criticised because the two conventions deal with different situations and their liability principles are different, especially as to the limits of liability. Therefore, Art. 12 of the Rome Convention was rejected as a model[187].

Nevertheless, the most harshly criticised point was the nature of conduct resulting in unlimited liability. Since the proposal provided unlimited liability only in cases of intentional wrongdoing, it was said that it would be very difficult, if not impossible, to prove such a high degree of fault and that practically no unlimited liability on the part of the carrier would exist[188]. On the other hand, the proposed degree of fault was assessed as a beneficial factor in developing international commercial aviation and, in the light of the increased financial limits of liability, it was considered to be acceptable[189].

The criticism also continued during the Conference. Some delegates stated that the proposal was against public policy, at least in a number of states, to such an extent that it would cause ratification problems[190]. Furthermore, some delegates stressed, again, the impossibility of proving such conduct and expected difficulties in the application of the provision[191].

Upon strong criticism, it was decided to form a working group to redraft Art. 25 on the basis of the proposal of Norway and Italy along with the amendments proposed by various delegations[192]. The proposal made by Norway and Italy was as follows:

> "The carrier shall be liable without limitation, if the claimant proves (a) that the damage is caused by an act or omission of the carrier or of a servant or an agent of the carrier, other than members of the crew, in the course of his employment, and (b) that such act

---

Convention of 1952 was adopted in order to amend the Rome Convention of 1933. Art. 14 of the Rome Convention of 1933 which provided for the carrier's unlimited liability in cases of *dol* and *faute lourde* was also changed and the final formula was reached during the Conference on Private International Air Law done in Rome; for the discussions see Conference on Private International Air Law, Rome, September-October 1952, V. I: Minutes, Montreal 1953, pp. 76-92.

[186] Report on Revision of the Warsaw Convention (adopted by the Legal Committee of ICAO), in: *Documents, Hague*, p. 99; Comments of Netherlands, in: *Documents, Hague*, p. 170.

[187] Comments of Norway, in: *Documents, Hague*, p. 174.

[188] Comments of Germany, Norway, Switzerland, in: *Documents, Hague*, pp. 159, 174, 181.

[189] Comments of Australia, Netherlands, Sweden, in: *Documents, Hague*, pp. 150, 171, 177.

[190] Mr. Meyer (International Chamber of Commerce), Mr. Ambrosini (Italy) and Mr. Stalder (Switzerland), in: *Minutes, Hague*, pp. 165, 167-168, 171 and Mr. Pedreira (Portugal), in: *Minutes, Hague*, pp. 184-185. For the counterview see Mr. Cooper's (International Air Transport Association) speech, in: *Minutes, Hague*, p. 183.

[191] Mr. Meyer (International Chamber of Commerce), Mr. Alten (Norway), Mr. Stalder (Switzerland), Mr. Riese (Germany) and Mr. Gómez Jara (Spain), in: *Minutes, Hague*, pp. 165-166, 171-172, 178.

[192] *Minutes, Hague*, p. 190.

or omission was committed either with the intention to cause damage or recklessly by not caring whether or not damage was likely to result."[193].

The result of the working group's effort provided for a formula that satisfied most of the delegations:

> "The limits of liability specified in Article 22 of the Convention shall not apply if it is proved that the damage resulted from an act or omission of the carrier, his servants or agents, done with intent to cause damage or recklessly and with knowledge that damage would probably result; provided that, in the case of such act or omission of a servant or agent, it is also proved that he was acting within the scope of his employment."[194].

After the redrafted proposal was presented, intense discussions started on the term "recklessness"[195]. Questions were posed in order to make the meaning of the term clear. It was asked whether the term recklessness covers the cases where the actor *should have known* that damage would probably result, in addition to cases where the actor *knows* that damage would probably result. It was stressed that if it also covers the cases where the actor *should have known* the probability of damage, the draft should be amended to read "where he should have had knowledge" instead of "with knowledge". The question was put to vote and the option of *"should have known"* was not accepted[196]. However, as to the final voting on the working group's proposal, it was decided that the unlimited liability issue was connected to the liability limits, so the final decision should be made later. The issue was later discussed intensively in connection with the financial limits. As a result, the proposal of the working group was accepted by a vote of 23 for and 16 against[197].

b) Comments on the new wording

Due to the complications caused by the wording of the original version of Art. 25, it was preferred to incorporate the degree of fault by defining it[198]. Undoubtedly, the main reason for preferring to state the precise conditions giving rise to unlimited liability instead of making reference to legal terminology was to avoid the contrasting interpretations reached by different jurisdictions[199]. By defining the conduct, determining the prerequisites of unlimited liability was made simpler and clearer, thus it was believed that a step forward was taken towards unification of law, albeit with language unfamiliar to continental law[200].

---

[193] *Documents, Hague*, p. 174.

[194] *Documents, Hague*, p. 121.

[195] See the discussions during the sixteenth and seventeenth meetings, *Minutes, Hague*, p. 192 *et seqq.*

[196] *Minutes, Hague*, pp. 205-206; see also *Giemulla/Schmid*, WA Art. 25 Rn. 36.

[197] *Minutes, Hague*, p. 286; see also the final version in the Hague Protocol, in: *Documents, Hague*, pp. 7-8. For an overview of the whole discussion regarding Art. 25 in The Hague, see *Dettling-Ott*, pp. 223-225.

[198] *Goldhirsch*, p. 151; *Giemulla/Schmid*, WA Art. 25 Rn. 3.

[199] *Guerreri*, p. 14; *Guerreri, Wilful Misconduct*, 275; *Miller*, p. 81; *Mankiewicz*, pp. 124, 200; *Schoner*, p. 98.

[200] *Schneider*, p. 115-116; *Schoner, Rechtsprechung 1974-1976*, p. 260.

It is, however, undoubtedly clear that the origin of the definition of the conduct adopted by the Hague Protocol is the common law term wilful misconduct[201]. When the adapted version of Art. 25 is read by a common law lawyer, its wording is simply a clearer version of the term. Correspondingly, for common lawyers, there was not any substantial change between the original and adapted version of Art. 25[202].

---

[201] Mr. Ambrosini (Italy), in: *Minutes, Hague*, p. 168; *Liesecke*, p. 96; *Mankiewicz, Hague Protocol*, p. 82 fn. 12; *Dettling-Ott*, pp. 227, 230-231; *Goldhirsch*, pp. 151, 153; *Miller*, pp. 200-201; *Matte*, *ETL*, p. 885; *Report, Warsaw*, 263-264; *Giemulla/Schmid*, WA Art. 25 Rn. 34; *Clarke/Yates*, para. 3.150; *Kuhn*, p. 202; *Philipson/et al.*, p. 166; *Lacey*, p. 386; *Silets*, p. 338; *Stachow*, p. 185; *Hickey*, 605; *Richter-Hannes*, p. 79; *Tekil*, p. 180; *Chen*, pp. 199-200; MünchKommHGB 1997 – *Basedow*, CMR Art. 29 Rn. 13; *Helm*, in: Großkomm. HGB Anh. VI nach § 452: CMR Art. 29 Rn. 7; *Beier*, p. 158; *Clarke, Transport in Europe*, 61; *Herber, Anmerkung*, 176; *Thume, Vergleich*, 3; Obergericht Zürich, 25.11.1969, ASDA-Bulletin 1970/2, 18 (20); BGE 98 II 231 (241) (11.07.1972); *In re Korean Air Lines Disaster of September 1, 1983* (CA, 1991) 932 F.2d 1475, 1489 *per* Judge Mikva; *Piamba Cortes v. American Airlines* (CA, 1999) 177 F.3d 1272, 1282-1284 *per* Judge Birch; *Bayer Corporation v. British Airways, Plc* (CA, 2000) 210 F.3d 236, 238 *per* Judge Wilkinson; *D'Alessandro v. American Airlines, Inc.* (DC New York, 2001) 139 F.Supp.2d 305, 310 *per* Judge Gershon; *Weiss v. American Airlines, Inc.* (DC Illinois, 2001) 147 F.Supp.2d 950, 952-953 *per* Judge Shadur; *G.D. Searle & Co. v. Federal Express Corporation* (DC California, 2003) 248 F.Supp.2d 905, 910 *per* Judge Armstrong; *Nipponkoa Insurance Company, Ltd. V. Globeground Services, Inc.* (DC Illinois, 2007) 2007 WL 2410292, *per* Judge Hart. However, it was also stressed that "some of the borderline cases of wilful misconduct" should be excluded when the original and amended texts are compared, see *S.S. Pharmaceutical Co. Ltd. and Another v. Qantas Airways Ltd.* [1991] 1 Lloyd's Rep. 288, 301 (CA of the New South Wales) *per* Justice Kirby; similar view in *Antwerp United Diamonds BVBA and the Excess Insurance Co. Ltd. v. Air Europe* [1993] 2 Lloyd's Rep. 413, 415 (QBD) *per* Justice Phillips: "Article 25 removes the limits of liability imposed by Art. 22 when damage has been caused by what can be described conveniently, if not wholly accurately, as wilful misconduct on the part of the carrier, his servants or agents"; however on p. 417: "[…] when damage is caused by wilful misconduct, *as defined by Art. 25* […]" (Emphasis added). In *Rolls Royce Plc and Another v. Heavylift-Volga Dnepr Ltd. and Another* [2000] 1 Lloyd's Rep. 653 (QBD) the conduct defined by Art. 25 and Art. 25A has been referred to "wilful misconduct or recklessness".

[202] *Clarke, Carriage by Air*, p. 159; *McNair*, p. 247; *Beaumont, Hague Protocol*, p. 418; *Giemulla/Schmid*, WA Art. 25 Rn. 11; *Calkins*, pp. 266-267; *Cheng*, p. 83; *Kilbride*, p. 185; *Mankiewicz*, p. 124; *Piamba Cortes v. American Airlines* (CA, 1999) 177 F.3d 1272, 1283-1287, the court also cites (pp. 1288-1290) a report prepared by the Senate Committee on Foreign Relations stating that the Protocol (meaning the Montreal Protocol No. 4 – Additional Protocol No. 4 to Amend Convention for the Unification of Certain Rules relating to International Carriage by Air signed at Warsaw on 12 October 1929, as amended by the Protocol done at The Hague on 28 September 1955 – which contains the same amendment with the Hague Protocol to Art. 25) replaces the term *wilful misconduct* with *the common law definition of wilful misconduct*. The conclusion to be drawn from the statement

c) Components

aa) Intent to cause damage

In every legal system, whether belonging to common law or civil law, the gravest degree of fault[203] is intentional wrongdoing (*Vorsatz, dolo, dol*). It is also common in every legal system that no one can escape the consequences of his intentional wrongdoing (*malitiis non indulgendum*). As a logical result, a carrier cannot rely on a limitation of liability when he caused the damage intentionally[204].

However, before starting to analyse this qualified degree of fault, the construction of the relevant phrase should be examined. If only the degree of fault defined by the amended article is read, the article defines it as "an act or omission [...] done with intent to cause damage *or* recklessly *and* with knowledge that damage would probably result"[205]. Consequently, there are two different degrees of fault in this phrase, namely "act or omission done with intent to cause damage" and "act or omission done recklessly and with knowledge that damage would probably result"[206]. Thus, the requirement of knowledge is connected to the reckless conduct, not to the acts or omissions done with intent to cause damage[207]. This finding could also be supported by the legislative history of the article. In the Rio de Janeiro Draft, the degree of fault defined only covered intentional wrongdoing. After strong objection, the second part of the phrase was added[208].

Nonetheless, this does not mean that knowledge of the wrongdoer as to the consequences is not a necessary element of intentional wrongdoing. On the contrary, this grave degree of fault necessitates intention and the desire to cause specific[209] damage. The person in question must have acted or omitted to act

---

of the court is that the precedents regarding the original version would have continued to be binding on common law courts.

[203] *Gerber*, p. 87.

[204] *Miller*, p. 73.

[205] Emphasis added.

[206] *S.S. Pharmaceutical Co. Ltd. and Another v. Qantas Airways Ltd.* [1991] 1 Lloyd's Rep. 288, 302 (CA of the New South Wales) *per* Judge Kirby: "The phrase 'recklessly and with knowledge that damage would probably result' [...] involves one composite concept".

[207] *Taylor*, 122; *Philipson/et al.*, pp. 168-169; *Gurtner v. Beaton* [1993] 2 Lloyd's Rep. 369, 387 (CA) *per* Lord Justice Neill (The court stated that they are "satisfied that [...] the pilot must do or omit to do something 'with knowledge that damage would probably result' from that act or omission". Here, the "act or omission" refers to the acts or omissions done recklessly.); for the counterview see *Clarke, Carriage by Air*, p. 157.

[208] See *supra* B I 2 a.

[209] It was proposed by the Swiss delegation and the International Union of Aviation Insurers that the phrase "with intent to cause damage" should be replaced by the phrase "with intent to cause *the* damage". The reason for this proposal was to distinguish the cases of necessity from the cases of intentional wrongdoing, see *Documents, Hague*, p. 180, 210; also see *Minutes, Hague*, p. 192. However, this proposal was not discussed. Nonetheless, this fact does not mean that the air carrier will also be liable in cases of necessity which would be a result contrary to the

intentionally and in order to cause the damage that he has foreseen and chosen to cause. Thus, intention should be apparent in two regards: firstly, there should be intention at the stage of the act or omission; secondly there should be intention as to the damage occurred[210]. The element of illegality of the act or omission is undoubtedly inherent. Otherwise, in cases where the damage resulted from an act or omission done to prevent loss of life or to prevent greater harm, an air carrier would be liable without limitation, which, in fact, cannot be accepted[211].

Although this fashion of gravest fault is almost unthinkable in the carriage of passengers cases, its requirements have never been controversial[212]. It has been said that intentional wrongdoing covers both direct intention (*Absicht, dolus directus*) and *dolus eventualis* (*Eventualvorsatz*)[213]. Theft is a typical example of intentional wrongdoing[214]. If one of the employers or agents of the carrier steals a

---

general principles of law. However, intention as to the specific damage occurred is not necessary according to *Calkins*, p. 266.

[210] *Clarke, Carriage by Air*, p. 159; *McNair*, p. 190; *Guldimann*, p. 147; *Giemulla/Schmid*, WA Art. 25 Rn. 30; *Shawcross and Beaumont*, VII 498; *Kirman*, pp. 155-157; MünchKommHGB 1997 – *Kronke* WA 1955 Art. 25 Rn. 14; *Dettling-Ott*, p. 229; *Cheng*, pp. 84-85; *Guerreri, Wilful Misconduct*, 275; *Koffka/Bodenstein*, p. 333; *Müller-Rostin*, in: *Fremuth/Thume*, Art. 25 WA Rn. 7; see also *Card, Cross & Jones*, pp. 78-79; *Smith & Hogan*, pp. 101-103.

[211] *McNair*, p. 191. Thus, the example given by the Australian delegate during the discussions (sixteenth meeting) is not one of intentional wrongdoing. The example speaks of a case of damage to the goods due to a delay caused instead by the carriage of a seriously ill passenger, see *Minutes, Hague*, p. 198. This example was also cited as an example of intentional wrongdoing by different scholars, see *Clarke, Carriage by Air*, p. 159; *Cheng*, pp. 84-85. Also some other scholars think that the carrier shall be liable without any limitation also in cases of necessity due to the wording of the provision, see *Gerber*, p. 104.

[212] *Dettling-Ott*, p. 229; *Schneider*, p. 116.

[213] *Milde*, p. 71; *Modjaz*, pp. 89-90; *Shawcross and Beaumont*, VII 498; *Philipson/et al.*, pp. 173-174; *Stachow*, pp. 172-173; *Kirman*, p. 157; for counterview see *Koller*, WA 1955 Art. 25 Rn. 3 and BGE 113 II 359 (365) (29.06.1987); for the term "oblique intention" see *Card, Cross & Jones*, pp. 79-81; *Smith & Hogan*, pp. 103-104; *Padfield*, p. 43; see also *Report on the Mental Element*, p. 27: "[...] a person should be regarded as intending a particular result of his conduct if, but only if, either he actually intends that result or he has no substantial doubt that the conduct will have that result"; it was proposed by the Law Commission a standard test of intention could be applied by answering the questions of "Did the person whose conduct is in issue either intend to produce the result or have no substantial doubt that his conduct would produce it?" (*Report on the Mental Element*, p. 56); intention was also described by another Law Commission as "a person acts 'intentionally' with respect to a result when (i) it is his purpose to cause it; or (ii) although it is not his purpose to cause that result, he knows that it would occur in the ordinary course of events if he were to succeed in his purpose of causing some other result." (*Report, Criminal Code*, pp. 8, 90); for detailed information see *infra* § 8.

[214] MünchKommHGB 1997 – *Kronke* WA 1955 Art. 25 Rn. 14; II *Wigmore, Evidence* § 242 (1) (Chadbourn rev. 1979) defines criminal intent as "[the] distinct element

piece of baggage or some property being carried in that baggage, the damage caused by the theft is intentional.

bb) Act or omission done recklessly and with knowledge that damage would probably result

The second part of the phrase employed by the Hague Protocol defines a degree of fault which is unfamiliar to civil law systems. This degree of fault requires both a reckless act or omission and knowledge of the probable consequences. All these elements contained in the phrase should be examined individually, which is hard to achieve, since the meaning of recklessness also contains a reference to the state of mind of the wrongdoer[215].

(1) Recklessness

(a) Degree of fault

Recklessness as a degree of fault refers to conduct of conscious and unreasonable risk taking. A wrongdoer who acts or omits to act recklessly, deliberately takes an unjustifiable risk[216]. In this sense, it has always been disputed whether reckless-ness has an objective or subjective meaning[217].

If recklessness is defined as an extreme departure from the standard of conduct of a reasonable person, *viz.* objectively, it is not necessary to examine the state of mind of the wrongdoer. It is sufficient to determine the objective standard of a reasonable person and the degree of the departure from that standard. Conse-quently, the wrongdoer would act or omit to act recklessly, if he took an unreason-able risk which a reasonable and prudent man would not have taken[218].

---

in criminal intent consists not alone in the voluntary movement of the muscles (i.e., in action), nor yet in a knowledge of the nature of an act, but in the combination of the two – *the specific will to act*, i.e., the violation exercised with conscious refer-ence to *whatever knowledge the actor has* on the subject of the act." (Emphasis added). For the examination of theft and its relation to the scope of employment see *infra* C II 2. For different examples regarding intentional wrongdoing, see *Milde*, p. 71; *Shawcross and Beaumont*, VII 498-499; *Philipson/et al.*, p. 174.

[215] *Cheng*, pp. 85-88.
[216] *Card, Cross & Jones*, p. 91; *Smith & Hogan*, p. 107; *Padfield*, p. 50.
[217] *Nugent and Killick v. Michael Goss Aviation Ltd. and Others* [2000] 2 Lloyd's Rep. 222, 227 (CA) *per* Lord Justice Auld: "Recklessness is notorious for its dif-ferent meanings in English law according to the subject matter." For an overview as to the meaning of recklessness, see *Shawcross and Beaumont*, VII 499-500; *Sta-chow*, pp. 168-169, 186-191.
[218] *Smith & Hogan*, pp. 110-114; *Card, Cross & Jones*, p. 92. E.g. in *Shawinigan, Ltd. v. Vokins & Co., Ltd.* [1961] 2 Lloyd's Rep. 153 (QBD), recklessness was consid-ered objectively, namely as gross negligence.

In opposition to the objective interpretation, recklessness could also be defined as unjustifiable risk taking including a realisation of the risk[219]. A person should be regarded as acting recklessly, when "(a) he foresees at the time of that conduct[220] that it might have that result and, (b) on the assumption that any judgement by him of the degree of that risk is correct, it is unreasonable for him to take the risk of that result occurring"[221]. In the case of realisation of the risk, it is essential to look into the wrongdoer's mind as to what he had foreseen[222]. In order to determine whether a course of conduct was reckless, questions such as "[d]id the person whose conduct is in issue foresee that his conduct might produce the result and, if so, was it unreasonable for him to take the risk producing it?" should be answered[223]. It is obvious that an answer to such a question "relates to the state of mind of that person and is to be decided on a subjective basis"[224].

(b) Aviation context

Apart from the dispute whether recklessness has an objective or subjective meaning as a degree of fault itself, the degree of fault adopted by the Hague Protocol should be read completely. In the Hague Protocol context, reckless conduct should be completed with the knowledge that damage will likely occur[225]. So, even if an objective meaning is given to recklessness[226], the phrase "with knowledge that damage would probably result" necessitates a subjective assessment[227]. As a result, in a transport law context, recklessness connotes the conduct of the wrongdoer, either as an act or an omission, which is in violation of his general duty of care[228]. From this point of view, recklessness correlates with the term "misconduct"[229].

---

[219] *Card, Cross & Jones*, pp. 91-92; *Report, Criminal Code*, pp. 11, 90-91; *Smith & Hogan*, pp. 108-110.

[220] Any act or omission was meant by conduct, see *Report on the Mental Element*, p. 26 fn. 154.

[221] Footnote added; *Report on the Mental Element*, p. 48.

[222] *Card, Cross & Jones*, pp. 93-94.

[223] Standard test proposed by the Law Commission, see *Report on the Mental Element*, p. 60.

[224] Explanatory notes for the standard test to be applied, *Report on the Mental Element*, p. 61.

[225] *Clarke, Carriage by Air*, p. 159; *Kırman*, p. 157; MünchKommHGB 1997 – *Kronke* WA 1955 Art. 25 Rn. 25; *Sözer, TSHK*, p. 55.

[226] The objective interpretation has been accepted by German courts, see OLG Stuttgart, 24.02.1993, TranspR 1995, 74 (75) (gross negligence); OLG Köln, 27.06.1995, TranspR 1996, 26 (conscious gross negligence).

[227] *Shawcross and Beaumont*, VII 500-510; *Kuhn*, pp. 203-204.

[228] In aviation context, this duty of care can be stated as "always to take due care of passengers and cargo", see explanations of Mr. Alten (Norway), in: *Minutes, Hague*, p. 196. See also *Koller*, WA 1955 Art. 25 Rn. 5; BGH, 16.02.1979, BGHZ 74, 162, 169. Especially the IATA regulations and the air carrier's own regulations play a vital role in determining reckless conduct, MünchKommHGB 1997 –

However, unlike the "misconduct" element[230], conduct which violates or disregards the relevant rules or regulations or, alternatively, a general duty of care must be extreme in order to constitute reckless conduct[231]; in other words, it should be conduct which creates, at a minimum, an undue risk[232]. Moreover, it is clear from the statements of some delegates of the Hague Conference[233] that the subjective meaning of the term of recklessness has been adopted. Thus, conscious risk taking notwithstanding, an appreciation of the probable consequences is necessary in order to break the air carrier's liability limits. In this sense, it is also necessary that the wrongdoer was aware that he was violating the law.

Here, the dangers of an objective interpretation, which was the most important discussion point during the Hague Conference and whose future avoidance was aimed at[234], should be addressed. Defining recklessness as an extreme violation or disregard of the relevant rules or regulations, or of a general duty of care, does not mean that the degree of fault employed by the Hague Protocol adopts an objective standard. On the contrary, when the phrase is read completely, it is obvious that there are two safety valves. The first one is the subjective meaning of reckless-

---

Kronke WA 1955 Art. 25 Rn. 34. As to the time period where the duty starts and ends for passenger luggage and cargo, see *Mühlbauer*, p. 186.

[229] *Clarke, Carriage by Air*, p. 160.

[230] See *supra* A II 2.

[231] Mr. Gómez Jara (Spain): "[...] there was the absence of the least amount of human diligence which the most careless person could have in acting. The inclusion of the word "recklessly" responded to this concept.", in: *Hague, Minutes*, p. 195; *Çağa*, p. 201; *Özdemir*, p. 113; *Giemulla/Schmid*, WA Art. 25 Rn. 33; *Schoner*, p. 98; MünchKommHGB 1997 – *Kronke* WA 1955 Art. 25 Rn. 28; *Modjaz*, p. 92; *Müller-Rostin*, in: *Fremuth/Thume*, Art. 25 WA Rn. 8; BGH, 16.02.1979, BGHZ 74, 162 (168); OLG Stuttgart, 24.02.1993, TranspR 1995, 74 (75); LG Hamburg, 03.12.1992, TranspR 1995, 76; AG Rüsselheim, 20.10.1997, TranspR 1998, 199; in this sense, the translation of the term into German as "leichtfertig" and into French as "témérairement" has been found somewhat weak, see *Guldimann*, p. 147; *Giemulla/Schmid*, WA Art. 25 Rn. 33; MünchKommHGB 1997 – *Kronke* WA 1955 Art. 25 Rn. 24; *Schoner, Rechtsprechung 1974-1976*, p. 260; *Kuhn*, p. 203; *Stachow*, pp. 168, 181-182; *Puttfarken*, Rn. 260; *Rabe, Vortrag*, p. 18; *Koller*, WA 1955 Art. 25 Rn. 5; OLG Frankfurt, 22.10.1980, VersR 1981, 164 (165); BGH, 12.01.1982, TranspR 1982, 100 (101); Handelsgericht Zürich, 10. Juli 1987, ZLW 1988, 102 (104); for an overview of the discussions on the translation issue during the Hague Conference, see *Modjaz*, pp. 91-93; *Calkins*, p. 266.

[232] *Drion*, p. 221; *Dettling-Ott*, pp. 233-234.

[233] Mr. Drion (Netherlands): "There was no desire to have a certain act, because it was a grave error, considered as reckless, quite apart from the state of mind of the person performing that act.", in: *Hague, Minutes*, p. 198; Mr. Alten (Norway): "[...] it was supposed that the carrier and his servants or agents foresaw that there might be some danger of damage, but that they had taken the decision to act as they did without regard to whether damage would be caused or not. This was the same as what would be implied by consciousness. Possibly, the word 'recklessly' could be replaced by the word 'conscious'.", in: *Hague, Minutes*, p. 204; *Stachow*, p. 194.

[234] For an overview of the discussion, see *Cheng*, pp. 86-88; also see the explanations by Mr. Wilberforce (UK), Mr. Alten (Norway), in: *Hague, Minutes*, p. 196.

ness; and the second one is the phrase "with knowledge that damage would probably result"[235].

After having made clear that the subjective meaning of recklessness was employed by the Hague Protocol and that the recklessness needs to be coupled with a conscious risk taking, the last point requiring emphasis is the composition of reckless conduct. As it is already clearly stated in the amended article, reckless conduct can be either an act or an omission. Additionally, reckless conduct may consist of a single act or omission, but a single act or omission is not a necessity. Rather, a series of acts or omissions can also constitute recklessness[236] although the jury was instructed to the contrary in the *Horabin* case[237]. Nonetheless, the warning contained in the instruction to the jury by Justice Barr is also important: Small acts of carelessness should not be considered in the assessment. They can be disregarded in this sense, unless they "reflect an overall frame of mind or course of conduct which led to them."[238]. However, a final decision whether the aggregation of relevant acts or omissions amounts to recklessness should be undertaken by the judge (or the fact-finder) taking into consideration the complete chain of events leading to the harmful result[239].

---

[235] Mr. Gómez Jara (Spain), after his explanation why recklessness was included in the text: "[…] But, besides, there was a second element which, according to the Spanish Delegation, was the really important one among the category of acts. This was a reference to the fact that the servant or agent knew the probability that damage would result.", in: *Hague, Minutes*, p. 195 and Mr. Drion (Netherlands): "There was even a danger that the courts might apply certain objective standards to the question whether certain acts were reckless or not, without looking into the state of mind of the carrier or his servant or agent, and that was exactly the thing which it was sought to prevent.", in: *Hague, Minutes*, p. 198; *Stachow*, pp. 192-193; *S.S. Pharmaceutical Co. Ltd. and Another v. Qantas Airways Ltd.* [1991] 1 Lloyd's Rep. 288, 301 (CA of the New South Wales) *per* Judge Kirby: "Having regard to the history and context in which the word 'recklessly' appears in Art. 25 of the Warsaw-Hague Convention, the occasional modern use of 'reckless' to connote 'mere carelessness' can be entirely excluded".

[236] *Clarke, Carriage by Air*, p. 160; *Goldhirsch*, p. 153; *Shawcross and Beaumont*, VII 490-491; *Philipson/et al.*, pp. 157-158; *In re Air Disaster at Lockerbie Scotland on December 21, 1988: Pagnucco v. Pan American World Airways, Inc.* (CA, 1994) 37 F.3d 804, 823-824 *per* Judge Cardamone; *In re Air Crash Disaster, Polec v. Northwest Airlines, Inc.* (CA, 1996) 86 F.3d 498, 544-546 *per* Judge Boggs; LG Hamburg, 03.12.1992, TranspR 1995, 76.

[237] *Horabin v. British Overseas Airways Corporation* [1952] 2 Lloyd's Rep. 450, 486-487 (QBD).

[238] *In re Air Crash Disaster, Polec v. Northwest Airlines, Inc.* (CA, 1996) 86 F.3d 498, 545 *per* Judge Boggs.

[239] E.g. *Koninklijke Luchtvaart Maatschappij N. V. v. Tuller* (CA, 1961) 292 F.2d 775, 778-779 *per* Judge Burger; *Butler v. Aeromexico* (CA, 1985) 774 F.2d 429, 431-432 *per* Judge Dumbauld; *In re Air Disaster at Lockerbie, Scotland on December 21, 1988* (DC New York, 1992) 811 F.Supp. 84, 87-89 *per* Judge Platt, affirmed by *In re Air Disaster at Lockerbie Scotland on December 21, 1988: Pagnucco v. Pan American World Airways, Inc.* (CA, 1994) 37 F.3d 804.

(2) Knowledge

The second element of the degree of fault is the "knowledge that damage would probably result". Knowledge in this context means the actual knowledge. If the wrongdoer believes that certain facts or circumstances exist, he should be regarded as knowing[240]. Finally, if the wrongdoer is sure about certain facts or circumstances, but deliberately shuts his eyes to the obvious or refrains from making enquiries which might confirm the facts and circumstances (wilful blindness[241]), he should also be considered as knowing[242].

It seems quite clear from the wording that knowledge as to the consequences of the act or omission should be present and, moreover, that subjective awareness is necessary. In order to be guilty of wilful misconduct, awareness as to the consequences, probability[243] and damage should coexist in addition to the reckless behaviour[244].

(a) Knowledge as to the consequences

Recklessness must be coupled with the foresight of the consequences of the wrongful conduct. This foresight, however, does not include the desire to cause specific damage. If the wrongdoer deliberately desires to cause damage and acts or omits acting in order to cause that specific damage, he is guilty of intentional wrongdoing[245]. Here, in reckless behaviour, the state of mind of the wrongdoer is different from intentional wrongdoing.

The person, being aware that his conduct is wrong, must foresee the consequences of his act or omission, but still insist on continuing. However, he does not desire the probable consequences. He is quite indifferent as to whether they will ensue[246]. Here, the person should understand and foresee that there is a probability of damage (*culpa in concreto*).

---

[240] *Report on the Mental Element*, pp. 28, 58; *Stachow*, p. 174.

[241] This is also called "blind eye" knowledge; "after Admiral Lord Nelson at the Battle of Copenhagen (1803) was informed of a flag signal by a superior officer which he choose to ignore by putting his telescope to his blind eye and declaring that he saw nothing" (*Gaskell, Breaking Limits*, p. 5).

[242] *Smith & Hogan*, pp. 119-120; *Card, Cross & Jones*, p. 97-98; *Padfield*, p. 49; *Gaskell, Breaking Limits*, p. 5.

[243] BGH, 16.02.1979, BGHZ 74, 162 (171).

[244] *Goldhirsch*, p. 163; *Basedow, Transportvertrag*, p. 421; *Clarke, Carriage by Air*, pp. 160-161; *Özdemir*, p. 113; *Stachow*, pp. 169-170; OLG Stuttgart, 24.02.1993, TranspR 1995, 74 (75); OLG München, 10.08.1994, TranspR 1995, 118 (120); AG Rüsselheim, 20.10.1997, TranspR 1998, 199; BGH, 21.09.2000, ETL 2001, 248 (264); OLG München, 13.12.2001, TranspR 2004, 35 (36); BGE 128 III 390 (395) (06.06.2002).

[245] See *supra* B I 2 c aa.

[246] Mr. Alten (Norway): "As to the second condition, that is, 'recklessly without caring that damage would probably result' [...] The second condition meant that the person in question understood that there might be damage caused by his act or omission, but, nevertheless, he took the position of saying: 'I am quite indifferent

It must be noted that just before the final voting on the Art. 25 amendment during the Hague Conference, it was proposed to insert the word "actual" before the word "knowledge"; however, the proposal was not accepted because the "actuality" was implicit in the French and Spanish versions of the amendment[247]. As a result, this refusal does not effect the requirement of subjective knowledge in light of both the wording of the amendment[248] and the reason for the refusal[249].

Acts of unawareness, to wit, situations where the wrongdoer should have foreseen the probable consequences but has not (*culpa in abstracto*), are not included[250]. This clear result derives not only from the precise language but also from the legislative history of the provision[251]. Both the subjective meaning of recklessness[252] and the phrase "knowledge that damage would probably result" stress the subjective awareness. Further, the version of *"should have known* the probability of damage" was proposed but not accepted by the Hague Conference[253].

Consequently, it is necessary for a finding of wilful misconduct that the wrongdoer has the actual "conscious knowledge" of the consequences. "Background knowledge" and "imputed knowledge" are not sufficient to meet the requirements of Art. 25. In the *Nugent* case, plaintiffs claimed that actual knowledge also includes background knowledge, which was defined as the "knowledge which

---

as to whether damage will occur or not.' [...]", in: *Minutes, Hague,* p. 196; the wording "recklessly without caring that damage would probably result" has been changed after the warnings by Mr. Drion (Netherlands) and Mr Garnault (France) that this wording could cause some misunderstandings and that the subjective knowledge must be stressed in the wording, see *Minutes, Hague,* pp. 198-199. *Rustenburg Platinum Mines Ltd v. South African Airways* [1977] 1 Lloyd's Rep. 564, 569 (QBD); *McNair,* p. 190; *Clarke, Carriage by Air,* p. 161; *Drion,* p. 224; *Özdemir,* p. 114; *Kahn-Freund,* p. 257: "At its worst negligence may be defined as an "it will be all right" attitude. Wilful misconduct is an "I don't care" attitude".

[247] Proposal by Mr. Poulton (Australia), Mr. Diaeddine Saleh (Egypt) and Mr. Heller (New Zealand); explanations by Mr. Garnault (France) and Mr. Loaeza (Mexico), see *Hague, Minutes,* pp. 284-285.

[248] *Ruhwedel,* p. 328.

[249] *Guldimann,* p. 147; *Cheng,* pp. 89-91.

[250] *McNair,* p. 190; *Özdemir,* pp. 114-115; BGE 113 II 359 (365-366) (29.06.1987); BGE 128 III 390 (395) (06.06.2002).

[251] Same conclusion was drawn in *S.S. Pharmaceutical Co. Ltd. and Another v. Qantas Airways Ltd.* [1991] 1 Lloyd's Rep. 288, 299-301 (CA of the New South Wales) *per* Judge Kirby.

[252] See *supra* B I 2 c bb (1) (a).

[253] See *supra* B I 2 a. See also *Goldman v. Thai International Ltd.* [1983] 1 W.L.R. 1186, 1194 (CA) *per* Judge Eveleigh: "[...] I cannot believe that lawyers who intended to convey the meaning of the well-known phrase 'when he knew or ought to have known' would have adopted 'with knowledge'".

would be present to the mind of the person if he or she thought about it"[254]. The argument was, however, rejected by the court[255].

However, although there are various grounds contradicting the objective interpretation, it is still claimed by plaintiffs[256]; but more importantly it is still referred to by courts. Under the objective test, some courts still rule in favour of unlimited liability if the wrongdoer should have foreseen probable consequences according to the reasonable person criterion[257].

The last point to be emphasised is the timing of the subjective knowledge. Actual knowledge as to the consequences must exist at the moment of the reckless conduct[258]. In case of a series of acts or omissions, actual knowledge at the moment of one of those acts or omissions in the series is sufficient to meet the requirement.

Knowledge as to the consequences does not deal with the degree of risk, or in other words, a degree of awareness[259]. This degree of awareness is stated as "probable" in the Hague Protocol.

(b) Knowledge as to the probability

Knowledge as to the results of the wrongful conduct also includes the knowledge as to the likelihood of the occurrence of the consequences. Therefore, it is not enough to foresee the consequences; it is also necessary that this foresight includes the degree of likelihood.

The degree of likelihood can be stated in three categories: certainty (*Gewissheit*), probability (*Wahrscheinlichkeit*) and possibility (*Möglichkeit*). The term

---

[254] *Nugent and Killick v. Michael Goss Aviation Ltd. and Others* [2000] 2 Lloyd's Rep. 222, 232 (CA) *per* Judge Dyson.

[255] *Nugent and Killick v. Michael Goss Aviation Ltd. and Others* [2000] 2 Lloyd's Rep. 222 (CA). A similar argument as to the knowledge was declined in *Gurtner v. Beaton* [1993] 2 Lloyd's Rep. 369, 387 (CA) as well.

[256] *E.g.* it was claimed by the plaintiffs in BGE 113 II 359 (29.06.1987); however rejected by the Swiss Federal Court on the grounds that it is clear from the minutes of the Hague Conference that subjective knowledge is necessary, see BGE 113 II 359 (363-364, 365-367) (29.06.1987).

[257] It was explained by various authorities that especially French case law is in favour of an objective interpretation, see *Miller*, p. 205; *Özdemir*, pp. 114-115; Münch-KommHGB 1997 – *Kronke* WA 1955 Art. 25 Rn. 26-27; *Sözer, TSHK*, p. 56; *Risch*, pp. 59-60; *Philipson/et al.*, p. 172; for the French case law see *Miller*, pp. 206-213; *Shawcross and Beaumont*, VII 514; *Giemulla/Schmid*, WA Art. 25 Rn. 41; *Schoner, Rechtsprechung 1974-1976*, pp. 261-262; *Stachow*, pp. 133-139; *Rabe, Vortrag*, pp. 12-13. For the difference between the French and common law approach, see *Miller*, pp. 219-223; and for the view that this difference encourages forum shopping, see *Taylor*, 123.

[258] *S.S. Pharmaceutical Co. Ltd. and Another v. Qantas Airways Ltd.* [1991] 1 Lloyd's Rep. 288, 301 (CA of the New South Wales) *per* Justice Kirby; *Nugent and Killick v. Michael Goss Aviation Ltd. and Others* [2000] 2 Lloyd's Rep. 222, 225 (CA) *per* Lord Justice Auld.

[259] *Report on the Mental Element*, p. 10.

"certainty" in this context means the "inevitableness" of the result of a given conduct, which states the situation of being unavoidable or unalterable[260]. If the wrongdoer foresees that the consequence will arise certainly as a result of his wrongful conduct, in other words, if foresight of certainty is present, and still insists on his conduct, he is guilty of intentional wrongdoing[261]. This highest degree of foresight is not, however, to be argued here, since the Hague Protocol refers to "probability".

Both probability and possibility state a degree of likelihood which is less than certainty. However, they do not involve the same degree of plausibility. Possibility can be defined as the "capability of being happening or existing; something that may exist or happen"[262]. On the other hand, probability is defined as "likely to occur"[263]. As it is clear from these definitions, probability represents a higher degree of likelihood than possibility[264]. In fact, probable consequence was defined as an "effect or result that is more likely to follow its supposed cause than not to follow it"[265]. Therefore, the difference between the two terms arises out of the situation of closeness to the occurrence. In possibility, the result can exist; whereas in probability, the result is likely to happen. In other words, it can be stated that with possibility, the likelihood is less than 50 %; whereas with probability, the likelihood is more than 50 %[266].

It is disputed whether the term "probable" in the Hague Protocol was used in the sense of stating the degree of likelihood. According to some scholars, realisation of any likelihood of the occurrence of damage is sufficient to be guilty of wilful misconduct, unless they are normal risks involved in the industry[267]. However, according to the majority view, likelihood more than 50 % is required[268]. Therefore, it is necessary for a finding of probability, that the likelihood of the

---

[260] The Shorter Oxford English Dictionary; <http://dictionary.reference.com/browse/ certain> (07.08.2010).

[261] See *supra* B I 2 c aa.

[262] Black's Law Dictionary, 9th Ed. (by BRYN A. GARNER), Minnesota 2009; The Shorter Oxford English Dictionary; <http://dictionary.reference.com/browse/ possible> (07.08.2010).

[263] The Shorter Oxford English Dictionary; <http://dictionary.reference.com/browse/ probable> (07.08.2010). Attention should be given also to *Saba v. Compagnie Nationale Air France* (CA, 1996) 78 F.3d 664, 669 *per* Judge Silberman: "reckless disregard, in the Warsaw Convention context, requires a showing that the defendant engaged in an act that is known to cause or to be likely to cause an injury".

[264] *Goldman v. Thai International Ltd.* [1983] 1 W.L.R. 1186, 1195-1196 (CA) *per* Judge Eveleigh: "Article 25 however refers not to possibility, but to the probability of the resulting damage. Thus something more than a possibility is required. The word 'probable' is a common enough word. I understand it to mean that something is likely to happen".

[265] Black's Law Dictionary, 9th Ed. (by BRYN A. GARNER), Minnesota 2009.

[266] *Drion*, p. 223; *Kuhn*, p. 203; *Stachow*, p. 171; *Beier*, p. 159; *Neumann*, 416.

[267] *Drion*, pp. 223-224.

[268] *Guldimann*, p. 147; *Özdemir*, p. 113; *Giemulla/Schmid*, WA Art. 25 Rn. 45; *Çağa*, p. 202 fn. 43; *Stachow*, pp. 171, 179-181; *Fremuth, Haftungsbegrenzungen*, 101; *Thume, Vergleich*, 3; OLG Frankfurt, 22.10.1980, VersR 1981, 164 (165).

occurrence of the risk should be more than the likelihood of not happening[269]. Just plain foreseeability is not enough for a finding of probability[270]. In this respect, also recalling the given definition of probability, the more untypical a situation the lesser would be the degree of awareness[271]. The assessment is also related to the graveness of the damage which will probably result as a consequence[272].

(c) Damage

Up to this point, it has been explained, that the wrongdoer has to be subjectively aware of the consequences and his degree of awareness must be one of probability. However, the kind of consequences the wrongdoer should foresee should also be explored. The distinction should be made between the damage that actually occurred and probable damages which could have been expected to occur.

The relevant part of Art. 25 specifies "damage", not "the damage". Therefore, it is enough for the wrongdoer to foresee the probability of any kind of damage. It is said that foresight of a specific type of damage or the damage that occurred is not necessary[273] in recklessness cases[274]. In fact, the provision itself makes a distinction between the damage occurred and probable damages. It reads as: "[...] if it is proved that *the damage* resulted from an act or omission [...] done with intent to cause *damage* or recklessly and with knowledge that *damage* would probably

---

[269] *Ruhwedel*, p. 328; MünchKommHGB 1997 – *Kronke* WA 1955 Art. 25 Rn. 30; *Özdemir*, p. 113; *Giemulla/Schmid*, WA Art. 25 Rn. 45; *Fremuth, Haftungsbegrenzungen*, 101; BGH, 16.02.1979, BGHZ 74, 162 (166).

[270] *Clarke, Carriage by Air*, p. 167; *Stachow*, p. 171.

[271] *Basedow, Transportvertrag*, pp. 421-422; MünchKommHGB 1997 – *Kronke* WA 1955 Art. 25 Rn. 30; *Koller*, WA 1955 Art. 25 Rn. 6.

[272] *Miller*, p. 219; *Giemulla/Schmid*, WA Art. 25 Rn. 44-45; *Schoner*, p. 98; BGH, 16.02.1979, BGHZ 74, 162 (168-169); *Nugent and Killick v. Michael Goss Aviation Ltd. and Others* [2000] 2 Lloyd's Rep. 222, 227 (CA) *per* Lord Justice Auld: "The greater the obviousness of the risk the more likely the tribunal is to infer recklessness and that the defendant, in so doing, knew that he would probably cause damage"; *Sellers Fabrics Pty. Ltd. v. Hapag-Lloyd AG* [1998] NSWSC 646 (Supreme Court of New South Wales) *per* Judge Rolf on 'recklessness': "It would be fanciful to suggest that an officer of his experience would not appreciate that the collapse of a stack of containers on a vessel would not cause probable damage".

[273] *Shawcross and Beaumont*, VII 497; *Dettling-Ott*, pp. 237-238; MünchKommHGB 1997 – *Kronke* WA 1955 Art. 25 Rn. 36; *Müller-Rostin*, in: *Fremuth/Thume*, Art. 25 WA Rn. 9.

[274] However, it should be emphasised that the foresight of the specific damage is necessary in intentional wrongdoing due to the nature of the concept itself, see *supra* B I 2 c aa.

result [...]"[275]. Here, "the damage" was intended to mean the damage occurred, with "damage" meaning probable damage[276].

Case law on the issue is also controversial. In a case where the passenger was seriously injured, the court stated that foresight of the probability of damage does not necessarily require the foresight of the actual damage which occurred; it is sufficient to meet the requirement of the provision that the wrongdoer has foreseen that "any sort of damage" would probably occur[277]. However, the Court of Appeal took a different view and concluded that at least the "kind of damage" should be known to the wrongdoer as the probable result, with the reservation, however, that the kind of damage should be understood as referring to the distinction between personal injury and damage to property[278]. This decision was also followed by the *Nugent* court[279]. On the other hand, in other cases, it has been stated that it is sufficient for a finding of wilful misconduct if the wrongdoer was aware that his conduct is likely to cause an injury or damage. It is not necessary to show that the wrongdoer was aware that his conduct would cause the actual damage occurred[280].

This problem is related not only to the wording of the provision, but also to the foreseeability criterion. It is clear that foresight of *any* damage is sufficient to fulfil the criteria set by the provision[281]. However, a person cannot be guilty of wilful misconduct if he has not foreseen the probable consequences. Therefore, the wrongdoer has to have foreseen at least the *kind* or *type* of damage which has occurred as a probable consequence. For example, it is within the normal scope of life experience that a pilot will foresee that there will be either physical injury or damage to property if he does not warn the passengers before entering a severe turbulence area. However, in another illustration, the result might be different. For example, if a box of medical supplies is stolen due to reckless conduct of an employee coupled with knowledge as to the probable consequences, the air carrier would be liable up to the full amount of the cargo. However, if there is a warning on the box saying that it contains scarce painkilling medicine for cancer patients, should the air carrier be held liable without any financial limits for the damage caused by the pain suffered by cancer patients for whom the painkilling medicine was intended?. The answer to this question is primarily related to the "remoteness

---

[275] Emphasis added. Attention was called to this point by Mr. Goodfellow (International Union of Aviation Insurers) during the negotiations, in: *Minutes, Hague*, p. 192.

[276] *Dettling-Ott*, pp. 237-238; same conclusion was drawn by *Stachow*, pp. 177-179 by comparing the wordings of maritime conventions and the modified version of Art. 25.

[277] *Goldman v. Thai Airways International Ltd.* (1981) 6 AL 187 (QBD).

[278] *Goldman v. Thai International Ltd.* [1983] 1 W.L.R. 1186, 1194, 1196 (CA) *per* Lord Justice Eveleigh.

[279] *Nugent and Killick v. Michael Goss Aviation Ltd. and Others* [2000] 2 Lloyd's Rep. 222, 225 (CA), *per* Lord Justice Auld: "[...] the omission [...] does involve probable damage of the *sort* contemplated in the article." (Emphasis added).

[280] *Husain v. Olympic Airways* (DC California, 2000) 116 F.Supp.2d 1121, 1140 *per* Judge Breyer; OLG Frankfurt, 21.04.1998, TranspR 1999, 24, 27.

[281] *Yetiş Şamlı*, p. 98.

of the damage" rather than the foreseeability of the resulting damage. Therefore, it is likely that local courts might differ in opinion.

The reference to damage includes any damage that the carrier is responsible for. Under the Warsaw Convention system, the carrier is liable for the damage suffered from an event of death or personal injury[282], as well for the damage to baggage or cargo[283]. Moreover, the damage should have arisen from an accident or delay[284] or issuance of an air consignment note[285].

cc) Result

There are two possibilities in order to break the liability limits under Art. 25 of the Warsaw Convention. These two possibilities correspond to two different degrees of fault. The first one is intentional wrongdoing. To be guilty of intentional wrongdoing, the person needs to have intended to cause specific damage. Moreover, the wrongdoer's act or omission must be unlawful, so cases of necessity are not covered by Art. 25.

The second degree of fault "recklessly and with knowledge that damage would probably result" necessitates a reckless act or omission coupled with awareness of the probable results of this act or omission. The main and most important difference of this conduct from intention is the results of the conduct. The wrongdoer, although having foreseen probable results, does not have the desire to cause them.

In order to examine whether one of these degrees of fault is present in a case before court, the court must determine first whether the act or omission was done intentionally. If so, the wrongdoer's intention as to the foreseeable results must be determined. If the wrongdoer had the intention to cause the damage incurred, he is guilty of intentional wrongdoing.

If the act or omission is reckless, then the court must examine the state of mind of the wrongdoer. First, the wrongdoer must have foreseen the results of his act or omission. However, every manner of foresight is not enough to be guilty of this kind of fault. The wrongdoer must have foreseen that the occurrence of the result is more likely than its non-occurrence.

---

[282] Art. 17 of the Warsaw Convention, for more information see *Clarke, Carriage by Air*, pp. 80-90; *Giemulla/Schmid*, WA Art. 17 Rn. 3-5b.

[283] Art. 18 of the Warsaw Convention, for more information see *Clarke, Carriage by Air*, pp. 104-119; *Giemulla/Schmid*, WA Art. 18 Rn. 1-15; MünchKommHGB 1997 – *Kronke* WA 1955 Art. 18 Rn. 3-31; *Müller-Rostin*, in: *Fremuth/Thume*, Art. 18 WA.

[284] Art. 17 and 19 of the Warsaw Convention, for more information see *Clarke, Carriage by Air*, pp. 91-98, 119-124; *Giemulla/Schmid*, WA Art. 17 Rn. 6-15; WA Art. 18 Rn. 1-18a; *Shawcross and Beaumont*, VII 630-682, 941-961; MünchKommHGB 1997 – *Kronke* WA 1955 Art. 19 Rn. 4-17; *Müller-Rostin*, in: *Fremuth/Thume*, Art. 19 WA.

[285] Art. 12 (3) of the Warsaw Convention, for more information see *Giemulla/Schmid*, WA Art. 12 Rn. 13-16; the German Federal Court ruled in favour of the claimant in a case where the air carrier issued an airway bill without receiving the goods and stressed that if the conditions of Art. 25 have been met, the carrier's liability is unlimited, see BGH, 19.03.1976, ZLW 1977, 79 = NJW 1976, 1583.

II. Cases on Article 25 as amended by the Hague Protocol

Although it was asserted that the aim in tightening the conditions for unlimited liability was to make it almost impossible to exceed the liability limits[286], case law has developed since the adoption of the provision.

Intentional wrongdoing has always been identified with a suicide case[287] and is therefore regarded as almost unthinkable[288]. Moreover, establishing a person's intention both as to an act or omission and to the result is harder than proving recklessness with knowledge that damage would probably result. Consequently, cases regarding Art. 25 amended by the Hague Protocol mostly involve allegations of reckless conduct.

1. Civil law

Whereas the case law concerning the original version of the provision covered gross negligence cases, the case law concerning the amended version has stated clearly that a finding of actual knowledge is necessary[289]. Gross negligence is no longer sufficient for unlimited liability[290].

---

[286] *Calkins*, p. 258.

[287] *Dettling-Ott*, p. 234.

[288] As just mentioned, it is "almost" unthinkable. An interesting example is the crash of the Egypt Air plane into the Atlantic Ocean on south of Massachusetts, USA. After approx. 20 minutes after the take off, when both the captain and the command first officer were not in the cockpit, the relief first officer had manually disconnected the autopilot and made the plane fly nose-down, which resulted in a sudden dive. After the captain returned to the cockpit and was trying to control the plane, the relief first officer was still commanding the plane to fly nose-down, whereas the captain was commanding nose-up. The plane climbed again towards its normal altitude before it started a second dive. Soon after the second dive started, the plane impacted the ocean. During this period, the relief first officer was very calm and said 11 times "I rely on God". Lack of significant meteorological conditions and technical deficiencies indicates that the cause of the crash was the manual commands given by the relief first officer. For detailed information see the accident investigation report of the U.S. National Transportation Safety Board accessible at <www.ntsb.gov/Publictn/2002/AAB0201.pdf> (07.05.2010). Egypt, on the other hand, reached another conclusion after its own investigation; see the report of the investigation of the Egyptian Civil Aviation Authority accessible at <www.ntsb.gov/events/ea990/docket/ecaa_report.pdf> (06.05.2010).

[289] MünchKommHGB 1997 – *Kronke* WA 1955 Art. 25 Rn. 32; French case law is excepted; for cases where a French court rules in favour of an objective test see *Dettling-Ott*, pp. 243-245.

[290] BGH, 16.02.1979, BGHZ 74, 162 (165); OLG Frankfurt, 22.10.1980, VersR 1981, 164 (165); BGE 128 III 390 (395) (06.06.2002).

a) Carriage of passengers

aa) Passengers

On 18 January 1971, a plane flying to Zurich – Kloten airport crashed during the landing approach. Only one of the passengers and the captain survived. The investigation report stated that the crash was caused by a violation of the minimum flight altitude under instrumental flight rules and the late restarting of the flight. Both the Court of Appeal (Frankfurt a.M.)[291] and the German Federal Court[292] ruled that the conduct of the captain did not constitute recklessness because he did not violate the rules in a grave manner. The courts, further, did not accept that the captain had foresight of the probable result, namely the crash. If he would have foreseen that the crash was probable, he would have cancelled the landing, since his own life was at stake.

The case arising from a plane crash in Ankara in 1983 was decided in favour of the plaintiff. The plane which crashed at the beginning of the runway was carrying passengers from Paris to Ankara. The plane approached the airport in heavy weather conditions, namely in dense fog and under heavy snow fall. However, instead of concentrating on the landing approach, the pilots were trying to figure out why one of the windshield wipers was malfunctioning, even as late as at 300 feet of altitude. Moreover, despite this fact and the heavy weather conditions, they tried to make a landing approach by visual flight rules. In this case, Turkish Court of Cassation stated that the conduct of the pilots amounted to recklessness. However, the necessary knowledge requirement was not discussed[293].

On a flight from Paris to Madrid, the pilots changed the route with the permission of the approach control in Madrid. During the checklist control for landing, the co-pilot made a serious reading mistake and indicated the altitude of the plane as 2382 instead of 3282 feet. After the flight received landing permission, the pilots started to descend. After a short period of time, the ground proximity warning system (GPWS) began to warn the pilots that the plane was too close to the ground. Although the GPWS continued to sound, the captain said calmly "yes, yes, all right", and "yes, yes" again after 5 seconds. The plane still continued descending, while the co-pilot was also asking some questions calmly. 14 seconds after the first warning signals, the plane crashed into a mountain. The Swiss Federal Court ruled in favour of the defendants, since the necessary knowledge was

---

[291] OLG Frankfurt, 22.10.1980, VersR 1981, 164 = ZLW 1981, 87.

[292] BGH, 12.01.1982, TranspR 1982, 100 = VersR 1982, 369.

[293] 11. HD, 28.11.1984, 84/5161, 84/5886 (YKD 1985/3, pp. 381-386). The Turkish Court of Cassation did not maintain its decision in favour of the plaintiffs after the defendant air carrier applied for a revision of the former decision, see 11. HD, 22.03.1985, 85/1624, 85/1626 (YKD 1985/6, pp. 840-844). However, when the local court insisted on its decision on unlimited liability, the issue was discussed and decided by the Appellate Division of the Turkish Court of Cassation for Civil Law Matters. The Appellate Division's decision was in favour of unlimited liability, see HGK, 25.03.1987, 86/11-154, 87/235. For the case and the decisions see Çağa, pp. 206-211, Kırman, pp. 160-162.

lacking due to the calm state of the pilots even though the GPWS was warning them[294].

bb) Luggage

The first case in this area is not a loss of or damage to baggage, but a loss of the personal items of a passenger. After the emergency landing decision by the pilot due to a problem encountered in the hydraulic system of the plane, the flight personnel collected all personal items of passengers and locked them into the toilet-rooms after placing them into plastic bags. After the emergency landing, the flight personnel returned the personal items to passengers; however, one passenger's watch and sunglasses were lost. The passenger claimed that the flight personnel acted recklessly and with knowledge that damage would probably result because they did not mark the plastic bags with the names of the passengers. The German Federal Court ruled that in an emergency landing situation, it cannot be expected that the personnel consider marking the plastic bags. So, a finding of subjective knowledge was rejected[295].

Where the delayed baggage is lost, because it was left unattended by the carrier in a public area where many people have access, courts have considered this loss to be caused by reckless conduct with knowledge of probable consequences. The first case decided in this respect arose from a lost baggage during a flight from Houston to Düsseldorf. Two out of three bags of the passenger were delayed; the carrier delivered one of them afterwards; however, the other one was left in the customs area, although the carrier had an office in the same airport which is big enough to store a luggage. The luggage was left unattended in the customs area, and subsequently got lost. The court ruled that the carrier's conduct was grossly negligent and reckless, because the customs area where the baggage was left is an area open to all passengers arriving at the Düsseldorf airport, and therefore the danger of theft was fairly high. After taking into account the circumstances of the case, the court also ruled that the employees of the air carrier were subjectively aware of the probable result[296].

However, if baggage is lost and the carrier cannot explain exactly when and where the loss occurred, this fact does not necessarily lead to unlimited liability. In several cases arising from lost luggage, the plaintiffs asserted that the loss of bags indicates an inadequate organisational structure, and therefore, it must be accepted that the loss is a result of the conduct defined in Art. 25 of the Warsaw Convention, unless the carrier explains when and under which circumstances the bags got lost[297]. The courts ruled that the sole fact of an unexplained baggage loss does not fulfil the requirements of reckless conduct coupled with foresight of the

---

[294] BGE 113 II 359 (29.06.1987) = ETL 1988, 498 = ZLW 1988, 96.

[295] BGH, 28.11.1978, VersR 1979, 188 = NJW 1979, 496.

[296] AG Düsseldorf, 31.07.1986, TranspR 1988, 285 = VersR 1988, 640.

[297] The carrier is under the burden to share the information known to him and his operational procedure under German procedural law, For more information see § 7 B II 2 a.

probable consequences[298]. Similarly, the sole fact of loss of baggage during a strike by ground personnel is also not sufficient for a finding of recklessness, if the carrier had taken special precautions during the strike[299]. Furthermore, delivery only after confirming that the number on the luggage receipt corresponds with the number on the air ticket of the passenger is impracticable, and almost impossible in the present state of air travel. Therefore, a claim of inadequate organisational structure based on the lack of such a confirmation procedure was also dismissed[300].

b) Carriage of cargo

Cases with regard to the carriage of cargo can be classified in two groups: valuable and non-valuable cargo. Firstly, it should be mentioned that in cases involving the loss of valuable cargo, the outline and sequence of the events should be clear. If it is unknown where and when the cargo was lost, it cannot be determined whose knowledge needs to be considered[301].

The case arising from the loss of two parcels of banknotes in a carriage performed from Las Palmas to Stockholm with stopovers in Madrid and Frankfurt was ruled against the carrier. The parcels were not deposited in the cargo hold, but were handed over to the chief stewardess by the station manager. The chief stewardess placed them, without informing the captain, in a cabinet which could not be locked. Furthermore, the shift manager in Madrid did not take any further precautions in relation to the valuable cargo although he was informed. After the carriage to Stockholm was completed, the packages could not be found. The court ruled that the conduct of the stewardess, shift manager and station manager was reckless since they were in serious violation of their duties. The court, after taking into account of the circumstances of the case, presumed that knowledge of the probable consequences also existed[302].

Carriage of valuable cargo always needs special attention. If there is any recklessness during the handling of the valuable cargo, this conduct can cause the unlimited liability of the air carrier. In a case decided by a Swiss court, four sealed packages of valuable cargo should have been carried from Zurich to Montevideo. When the plane arrived at its final destination, one of the packages was missing. The court entered into judgement in favour of the plaintiff, considering the transparent wrapping of the sealed packages which left their content visible, the storage of the valuable cargo with the general cargo and the lack of supervision during loading and stopovers which are notorious for thievery, to be reckless conduct

---

[298]   AG Hannover, 25.06.1996, RRa 1996, 207; LG Hannover, 10.04.1997, RRa 1997, 204; AG Düsseldorf, 20.03.1998, TranspR 1998, 473; OLG Köln, 11.08.1998, ZLW 1999, 163; LG Köln, 11.12.2002, TranspR 2003, 204.

[299]   LG Berlin, 22.03.2002, ZLW 2002, 466.

[300]   LG Frankfurt, 16.01.2003, TranspR 2003, 203; 11. HD, 19.04.2001, 2001/2983, 2001/3333 (YKD 2002/1, pp. 58-60).

[301]   Handelsgericht Zürich, 10.06.1987, ZLW 1988, 102.

[302]   BGH, 16.02.1979, BGHZ 74, 162 = VersR 1979, 641 = ETL 1980, 229 = NJW 1979, 2474 = ZLW 1980, 55.

since they raised the danger of theft. However, the court did not consider the knowledge criterion, and simply stated that all requirements of the wilful misconduct have been fulfilled[303]. In another case where the carrier was held liable in excess of the limits, the valuable cargo consisting of banknotes was carried successfully to the destination but could not, however, be delivered to the consignee; on its return transport it was lost under unclear circumstances. The Swiss Federal Court found recklessness on the part of the carrier since the cargo was not identified as valuable cargo in the cargo manifest, no pre-advice was given to the stopover airport, the cargo was loaded in the general cargo hold and special precautions were not taken. The court, furthermore, emphasised that the knowledge element was proved during the hearing held by the lower courts, and that the Federal Court was not entitled to question the lower courts' finding on that issue[304].

However, in a case before the Swiss Federal Court, it was ruled that the necessary subjective elements of the described degree of fault had not been met. The valuable cargo consisting of 5 packages of banknotes was shipped from Zurich to Nicaragua via New York and Mexico. The banknotes were received in New York; however the cargo was never found in Mexico and it was unclear on which flight from New York to Mexico it was loaded. The transport documents were later found in New York. The court dismissed the allegation of wilful misconduct of the carrier since it was not proven that damage was caused with knowledge that damage would probably result, although the lack of information on the flight onto which the cargo was loaded did constitute recklessness. The court, furthermore, stated that the failure to send the transport documents constitutes recklessness. Nevertheless, foresight of probable damages failed to be proven[305].

If valuable cargo is lost, as a result of its being left unattended, this loss may also lead to the carrier's unlimited liability. In a case where two packages of valuable cargo consisting of "bonding wire made of gold" were lost due to their being left unattended, the court ruled in favour of the plaintiffs even though the packages were left unattended only for a short time. The court stated that it was known by the employees of the carrier that the type of cargo necessitated special security measures and that the employees did not even perform ordinary care let alone the special measures. The court also stated that the employees would have foreseen the probability of damage[306].

However, the case law is different when the cargo is not valuable. The court ruled in favour of the air carrier when one of the employees left the cargo unattended in order to join a warning strike. It was stated that recklessness necessitates a grave violation of the due diligence duty, and that the conduct of the employee did not amount to recklessness since during the strike the area where the cargo was stored was closed to all access. The court, moreover, stressed that not every instance of reckless conduct is coupled with the knowledge of probable conse-

---

[303] Obergericht Zürich, 25.11.1969, ASDA-Bulletin 1970/2, 18.
[304] BGE 128 III 390 (06.06.2002).
[305] BGE 98 II 231 (11.07.1972) = ZLW 1973, 129.
[306] OLG Frankfurt, 15.10.1991, TranspR 1993, 61 = ZLW 1993, 208.

quences, which was also the situation in the case[307]. In another case, two packages of ship components were to be carried from London to Manila via Frankfurt a.M. After the goods arrived in Frankfurt they were loaded on to the Manila plane. When the plane has arrived in Manila, only one package was on it. Despite the detailed search of the air carrier, it was not possible to clarify how, when and under which circumstances the package got lost. The court stated that in order to hold the air carrier liable without any financial limits, the plaintiff must prove recklessness coupled with knowledge of probable consequences. The court, further, stressed that "mistakes" during the air carriage of large amount of goods can happen, and that the sole fact that the goods got lost is not sufficient for a finding of recklessness coupled with knowledge of probable consequences. If it would be sufficient, then every case of unexplained loss of the goods would result in the unlimited liability of the air carrier which has, clearly, not been foreseen by the Warsaw Convention[308].

Loss of or damage to cargo can also be the result of an inadequate organisational structure, and if this inadequacy is coupled with the foresight of the probable consequences, it can result in the unlimited liability of the air carrier. In a case where the air carrier agreed to carry two precision models from Abu Dhabi to Munich, the goods were damaged. The plaintiff cargo insurer asserted that the damage occurred was result of the inadequate organisation of operating and cargo handling procedures of the carrier. The court stated that unlimited liability can be considered, if inadequate organisation leads to insufficient protection and a violation of the safety interests of the contracting party. However, in the case at hand, the plaintiff based his claim on the sole fact that the damage occurred. This is not sufficient for a finding of recklessness based on inadequate organisation. It is also not sufficient for satisfying the subjective prerequisites set by Art. 25 of the Warsaw Convention[309].

Undoubtedly, recklessness is one of the prerequisites for a judgement of unlimited liability. In a case decided by the Basel City Court, live tropical fishes were to be transported; however, some of them died since they had not been kept in a warm place notwithstanding the warnings provided on the transport document by the sender. The court ruled in favour of the defendant air carrier, since the IATA regulations provided that fish must be packed by the sender in such a way that they can live forty-eight hours unattended. Consequently, reckless conduct on the part of the carrier was not found[310]. Similarly, reckless conduct was not found in a case arising from the carriage of 115 packages of medical wares. In order to transport the goods from the airplane to the warehouse, an open transport vehicle, instead of a closed one, was used, and the driver did not cover the goods with a net to prohibit any of them to fall off. A package fell from the vehicle, and the driver did not notice it. It was evening time, therefore the package was not visible to other vehicles, and subsequently it was run over from another vehicle, and was

---

[307] OLG Stuttgart, 24.02.1993, TranspR 1995, 74.
[308] AG Rüsselheim, 20.10.1997, TranspR 1998, 199.
[309] OLG München, 13.12.2001, TranspR 2004, 35.
[310] Zivilgericht Basel-Stadt, 22.03.1985, TranspR 1985, 388.

totally destroyed. The court took into account the fact that only one package out of 115 has fallen off the vehicle, and that this fact does not justify a finding of reckless conduct[311].

Moreover, the carrier is again liable without any financial limitation if cargo is left in the open air and consequently damaged. In a carriage from Cologne to Warsaw, the employees left the cargo packed in carton boxes in the open air on the airport ground after discharge. As a result, the cargo was exposed to rain and damaged. The court held that the carrier is liable without any limits and stated that the conduct of the carrier was reckless since the cargo was left unprotected and, moreover, because as a result of the reckless conduct the search for the cargo was not successful for a long period of time. The court concluded that the employees *should* have known of the probable wetness damage if they leave the carton boxes in the open air, even during the summer season[312].

Theft is, again, one of the reasons for unlimited liability. Generally, theft by the carrier's employees is regarded as damage caused by intentional wrongdoing and therefore a reason for unlimited liability. In one case, the air carrier agreed to carry two second hand laptops and its electronic devices from Frankfurt a.M. to St. Petersburg. The goods were loaded on to the plane, however got lost after the plane has arrived at its destination. The court was convinced that the goods were stolen by the employees of the air carrier, since some peaces of the wrapping of the goods were found near to the airport[313]. Similarly, if the plaintiff and the defendant air carrier are sure, and so is the court, on which leg the theft has occurred, unlimited liability has been ruled without hesitation. In a carriage of 600 mobile phones and their accessories from Düsseldorf to Hong Kong, the goods were packed in three equally big cartons. After the goods were delivered to the consignee, it has been reported that just one carton was its original size, other two cartons are smaller than they should be, and there were considerable amounts of mobile phones missing. The plaintiff and the air carrier were sure that the theft occurred when the goods were in the warehouse – a high security structure in the secure area of the airport. The court ruled that the air carrier was liable for the total amount of the loss, since some employees of the warehouse stole the missing goods and there was intentional misconduct[314]. However, it is not necessary to exactly determine the time period and the place where the theft occurred. In another case, the carrier agreed to transport six diamond rings from Germany to the USA. When the jewellery boxes were delivered to the consignee, they were empty. The court was convinced that the rings were stolen by employees or agents of the air carrier, since no one else had access to the goods. Due to the intentional misconduct, the air carrier was held liable for the total amount[315].

---

[311] OLG Frankfurt, 30.06.1999, TranspR 1999, 399.
[312] LG Hamburg, 03.12.1992, TranspR 1995, 76.
[313] BGH, 21.09.2000, ETL 2001, 248.
[314] LG Frankfurt, 16.01.1996, TranspR 1996, 424.
[315] LG Darmstadt, 24.09.2002, TranspR 2003, 114.

c) Assessment

As seen from the cited examples, the civil law courts regarded recklessness generally as the grave violation of flight rules and of the duties with respect to the carriage of passengers and cargo. This interpretation of recklessness by civil law courts basically corresponds with the gross negligence notion, and therefore, the courts did not have any difficulties in assessing it.

Decisions of the civil law courts have generally been based on the existence or absence of the subjective knowledge requirement. In the carriage of passengers, such knowledge has been declined due to the fact that the pilot's own life is also at stake. With regard to the loss of the checked in baggage, the courts generally ruled that inadequate organisational structure alone is not sufficient to fulfil the subjective knowledge requirement.

With regard to the carriage of valuable cargo, failure to take necessary precautions to protect the cargo has been considered as recklessness, and in such a situation, subjective knowledge has been generally presumed. It is well known that the danger of thievery is very high for valuable cargo, and the courts seem to consider this general fact as foreseeable by anyone. On the other hand, the courts were hesitant in ruling for unlimited liability in carriage of non-valuable cargo. Some unexplained losses were just considered as "mistakes of the air carriage". If, on the other hand, the violation of the due diligence duty was too grave, the courts tend to presume subjective awareness of probable consequences as they did in the valuable cargo cases. Finally, in theft cases, the courts did not hesitate to rule in favour of the cargo interests if they were convinced that the goods were stolen by servants or agents of the air carrier, since theft is the clearest example of wilful misconduct.

2. Common law

Before proceeding with the cases decided by common law courts, it should be noted that the USA is not a party to the Hague Protocol. However, it became a contracting party to the Montreal Protocol No. 4[316], in 1998. Montreal Protocol No. 4, which has been in force since 1999 for the USA[317], also replaces the original wording of Art. 25 with the version adopted by the Hague Protocol. Thus, the cases from the USA referred to below were decided under the regime set by the Montreal Protocol No. 4, which, however, does not differ from the Hague Protocol for purposes of unlimited liability.

---

[316] Additional Protocol No. 4 to Amend Convention for the Unification of Certain Rules Relating to International Carriage by Air signed at Warsaw on 12 October 1929, as amended by the Protocol done at The Hague on 28 September 1955, signed at Montreal on 25 September 1975.

[317] *Carey v. United Airlines* (CA, 2001) 255 F.3d 1044, 1047.

a) Carriage of passengers

The first case reported from a common law court regarding the carriage of passengers under the amended version of the Warsaw Convention Art. 25 arose from a flight from London to Bangkok. When the plane was close to Istanbul air space, it encountered severe clear air turbulence. Moderate clear air turbulence had been forecast for the area. Despite this forecast and clear instructions, the cockpit crew omitted to switch on the "fasten seat belt" sign. Consequently, some of the plaintiffs and cabin crew were seriously injured. Queen's Bench Division concluded that the cockpit crew's omission was reckless and that even in the case of moderate clear air turbulence some sort of damage would almost inevitably result. Hence, the airline's liability was unlimited[318]. However, this decision was reversed on appeal. The Court of Appeal stated that neither the severity of the turbulence nor the kind of injury suffered by the plaintiff has been foreseen by the pilot as a probable result[319].

The second case as to the carriage of passengers arose from a helicopter crash. The passenger was travelling from Bolton to London in a helicopter which crashed as a result of the pilot's fault. The claimants asserted that the pilot of the helicopter was reckless, since his flying skills were not updated, he did not use the navigational aids with which the helicopter was equipped, did not plan the flight properly, and flew when he was tired. The claimants, further, argued that the background knowledge, namely the knowledge he generally has with regard to the death or serious injury in case of a crash, fulfils the subjective knowledge requirement. Although such knowledge was not present in his mind at the material time, he would have foreseen the probable result had he addressed his mind to the issue. The members of the court discussed only the knowledge issue, and concluded unanimously that the pilot did not have the necessary actual knowledge, because background knowledge cannot be considered as actual knowledge. Further, the court found no basis for a conclusion that the drafters of the amended Art. 25 of the Warsaw Convention intended to include background knowledge. As a result, the liability of the carrier was limited[320].

Although warnings by crew do not constitute misconduct as long as they have a legal basis[321], the oral defamation of a passenger could cause a finding of wilful misconduct. During a flight from Costa Rica and Los Angeles, the plaintiff bought two tickets for the first class and three tickets in the economy class for his children. During the flight, two of the children started to have pain in their ear, and came to the first class area to see their father and to seek help. A crew member warned the plaintiff that his children are not allowed to come to the first class cabin. When the plaintiff tried to explain the situation, same crew member told him that he can get arrested because of his behaviour. A heated discussion contin-

---

[318] *Goldman v. Thai Airways International Ltd.* (1981) 6 AL 187 (QBD).
[319] *Goldman v. Thai International Ltd.* [1983] 1 W.L.R. 1186 (CA).
[320] *Nugent and Killick v. Michael Goss Aviation Ltd. and Others* [2000] 2 Lloyd's Rep. 222 (CA).
[321] See *supra* A II 2 a aa.

ued, and the crew member insulted and humiliated the plaintiff in front of other people. The court accepted that such an attitude by the crew member can be considered as an accident within the scope of the Warsaw Convention, and that oral defamation goes beyond the limits of a rightful warning and constitutes intentional misconduct. However, since the court concluded that the emotional distress is not recoverable under the Warsaw Convention regime, the case was dismissed[322].

Another case where the court ruled that the airline was guilty of wilful misconduct was the death of a passenger during a flight from Athens to New York. The passenger, who suffered from asthma, was seated in the airplane's non-smoking section but, nonetheless, extremely close to the smoking section which was only three rows away. After take-off, smoking began and the place where the passenger was seated was inundated with smoke. With increasing urgency, the passenger's wife asked a flight attendant to move her husband away from the smoking section three times, each time explaining her husband's health condition. However, her requests were ignored or refused on the ground that the plane was totally full, which in fact it was not. After the third request, the flight attendant permitted the passenger's wife to ask other passengers to switch seats with her husband, which was in fact the flight attendant's duty. The passenger's wife was not able to find someone who agreed to switch seats. After a while, the passenger moved towards the front of the cabin to breathe fresh air; however, on his way he started to have a severe asthma attack and unfortunately died, despite all attempts to save him. The court held that the flight attendant, and consequently the airline, was guilty of wilful misconduct and that the airline's liability was unlimited. The court stated that, despite the warnings of the passenger's wife regarding the seriousness of the medical condition of her husband, the flight attendant's failure to provide assistance constitutes recklessness. The fact that the flight attendant allowed the passenger's wife to contact other passengers indicated that she understood the seriousness of the passenger's medical condition and "that by refusing to perform her duties, [she] deliberately closed her eyes to the probable consequences of her acts" which constitutes wilful misconduct[323].

b) Carriage of cargo

A case arising from a carriage from Sydney to Tokyo was the first case decided by a common law court under the amended version of Art. 25. In this case, cargo containing pharmaceutical products which should not be exposed to water was damaged due to outdoor storage when rain showers with occasional thunderstorms had already been forecast. Stencilled umbrella marks were to be found on each package, and, thus, it was known to everyone that the cargo was vulnerable. The court ruled in favour of the plaintiff cargo owners, stating that the conduct by the

---

[322] *Carey v. United Airlines* (DC Oregon, 1999) 77 F.Supp.2d 1165; *Carey v. United Airlines* (CA, 2001) 255 F.3d 1044.

[323] *Husain v. Olympic Airways* (DC California, 2000) 116 F.Supp.2d 1121; affirmed by *Husain v. Olympic Airways* (CA, 2002) 316 F.3d 829 and by *Husain v. Olympic Airways* (Supreme Court of the US, 2003) 124 S.Ct. 1221 (discussed on the "accident" requirement of the Warsaw Convention).

airline constituted recklessness with knowledge that damage would probably result[324]. In a similar case, the cartons containing more than 5 tonnes of pharmaceutical dangerous goods were carried from Frankfurt a.M. to California. However, it was determined, when the cartons arrived in California, that they were wet, crushed, contained holes, torn and dirty, which shows clearly that they were not stored inside. It was clear that they were not stored properly and consequently suffered water damage during the thunderstorm in Frankfurt a.M. The court stated that the facts of the case are sufficient to conclude that the damage was caused by the wilful misconduct of the carrier[325].

In another case, aircraft engines produced by Rolls Royce were damaged while being unloaded from a lorry. One of the five engines fell from the fork-lift, because the driver of the fork-lift had tried to unload it in an inappropriate manner. The cargo owners contended that allowing an employee to drive such a fork-lift truck without training as to its proper use and to commence loading and unloading operations constituted the fault defined in Art. 25 of the Warsaw Convention. The court, rightfully, stated that the content only constituted negligence, perhaps even gross negligence, but not recklessness with knowledge that damage would probably result[326].

If a cargo owner does not give an air carrier specific information regarding the cargo, this fact can lead to a finding that the air carrier did not have the necessary subjective knowledge as to the probable consequences. For instance, in a case arising from the carriage of fragile medical products, the cargo was packed in wet ice and should have been stored between 2-8 degrees. However, the cargo owner did not inform the air carrier about how long the cargo would be safe without refrigeration even though he was well-informed that the carrier was incapable of providing refrigeration. The court rejected the unlimited liability and the decision was affirmed by the Court of Appeal[327].

Theft occurring as a result of releasing valuable cargo without properly checking the documents could result in a finding of wilful misconduct[328]. However, in a case where laptops were delivered to a person without checking the papers purporting to authorise that person as the consignee, the court ruled in favour of the air carrier stating that mere failure to follow the applicable or appropriate procedure in delivery does amount to negligence, but not to wilful misconduct. The court stressed that recklessness with subjective awareness of the probable consequences necessitates foresight of the serious potential risks which are likely to

---

[324] *S.S. Pharmaceutical Co. Ltd. and Another v. Qantas Airways Ltd.* [1989] 1 Lloyd's Rep. 319, Supreme Court of New South Wales; affirmed by *S.S. Pharmaceutical Co. Ltd. and Another v. Qantas Airways Ltd.* [1991] 1 Lloyd's Rep. 288 (CA of the New South Wales).

[325] *G.D. Searle & Co. v. Federal Express Corporation* (DC California, 2003) 248 F.Supp.2d 905.

[326] *Rolls Royce Plc and Another v. Heavylift-Volga Dnepr Ltd. and Another* [2000] 1 Lloyd's Rep. 653 (QBD).

[327] *Bayer Corporation v. British Airways, Plc.* (CA, 2000) 210 F.3d 236.

[328] See *supra* A II 2 b.

occur, and that such a foresight is missing in the case at hand[329]. Theft by the employees of the carrier, on the other hand, was considered as one of the clearest examples of damage committed with the intent to cause damage. In the case before the Canadian court, a parcel containing banknotes were handed over to the pilot for the carriage from Zurich to Montreal, who delivered them to the person who was in charge of taking it from the pilot to the storage. This person then handed the parcel over to the person in charge with the storage of the valuable cargo. Thereafter, the parcel was never found. The court concluded that it is clear from the facts of the case that the parcel was stolen by one of the employees of the carrier, and therefore, the air carrier is liable without any financial limit[330].

c) Assessment

The redrafting of the wilful misconduct provision did not cause substantial material changes in the decisions of the common law courts. Most of the decisions have been given after an analysis of the subjective awareness of the probable results. The argument of background knowledge has been, rightfully, refused. Wilful blindness, on the other hand, has been considered as sufficient in fulfilling the requirement of subjective awareness.

Nevertheless, in the cases arisen from the carriage of cargo, most of the cases were decided on whether the air carrier acted recklessly. In this respect, acts of negligence or gross negligence failed to be sufficient to constitute recklessness. Cases of theft by the employees of the air carrier, of course, were ruled in the disadvantage of the carrier, although the person who stole the goods could not be ascertained.

3. Result

The most important result of the amended provision has been the elimination of gross negligence cases for the purposes of unlimited liability. Consequently, the decline in the number of cases based on Art. 25 in civil law jurisdictions is not surprising[331].

As can be seen from the cited examples, case law under common law and civil law has been unified up to a certain degree in respect of the unlimited liability resulting from the wilful misconduct of the carrier or his servants and agents. Undoubtedly, the method of defining the necessary degree of fault to break the carrier's liability limits has been proved as successful. Both common and civil law courts have reached decisions based on the criteria given by modified Art. 25. Thus, divergence in the case law between common and civil law has been elimi-

---

[329] *Nipponkoa Insurance Company, Ltd. V. Globeground Services, Inc.* (DC Illinois, 2007) 2007 WL 2410292.

[330] *Air Canada v. Swiss Bank Corporation et al.* (1988) 44 DLR (4th) 680 (Federal CA).

[331] *Dettling-Ott*, p. 248-249.

nated and the aim of unifying the application, and, hence, the law, has been achieved[332].

However, it is also clear from the above mentioned examples, that there are still some misunderstandings on the requirements of the defined degree of fault. Thus uncertainty has been sometimes caused by the disagreement whether "reckless-ness" should be considered as objective or subjective[333] or whether the actual damage needs to have been foreseen. However, it has been mostly caused by the civil law application of the defined degree of fault since the definition has been constructed from a common law term signifying a certain degree of fault[334].

C. The Present Regime

After the Hague Protocol, a significant number of amendments have been made to the Warsaw Convention[335]. As a result, there was not a single unified regime regarding carriage by air, since the Warsaw Convention was in force in different versions in different parts of the world. This was obviously an obstacle from the unification perspective[336]. Additionally, the strong criticism of the Warsaw Convention regime made the revision of the whole system necessary[337]. For the sake of proper unification work[338], the Convention for the Unification of Certain Rules for International Carriage by Air was adopted in 1999 ("Montreal Convention")[339]. It has been in force since 4 November 2003 and a substantial number of states are party to the Convention[340].

---

[332] *Schobel*, pp. 86-87.

[333] *Dettling-Ott*, p. 228.

[334] *Dettling-Ott*, p. 250; on this point, specific reference should be made to the French case law, see references in fn. 257 and 289.

[335] Protocol to Amend the Convention for the Unification of Certain Rules relating to International Carriage by Air signed at Warsaw on 12 October 1929, done at The Hague on 28 September 1955; the Convention, Supplementary to the Warsaw Convention, for the Unification of Certain Rules relating to International Carriage by Air Performed by a Person Other than the Contracting Carrier, signed at Guadalajara on 18 September 1961; the Protocol to Amend the Convention for the Unification of Certain Rules relating to International Carriage by Air signed at Warsaw on 12 October 1929 as Amended by the Protocol done at The Hague on 28 September 1955, signed at Guatemala City on 8 March 1971, Additional Protocol Nos. 1 to 3 and Montreal Protocol No. 4 to Amend the Warsaw Convention as Amended by the Hague Protocol or the Warsaw Convention as Amended by both the Hague Protocol and the Guatemala City Protocol, signed at Montreal on 25 September 1975.

[336] *Koning*, 319; *Brinkmann, Vergleich*, 146; *Krause & Krause*, p. 11-51; *Yetiş Şamlı*, p. 51.

[337] *Jacobson*, 279-280; MünchKommHGB 2009 – *Ruhwedel*, MÜ Einl. Rn. 14.

[338] *Brinkmann, Vergleich*, 146.

[339] For the historical background see *Giemulla/Schmid, Montrealer Übereinkommen*, MÜ Rn. 17-35.

[340] <www.icao.int/icao/en/leb/mtl99.pdf> (07.08.2010).

I. Liability and the Limitation of Liability

The liability of the carrier under the Montreal Convention regime is based on different liability regimes for different types of damage. The air carrier is strictly liable for the death or injury of passengers up to 113.100 SDRs (Art. 17, 21 (1))[341]. In the case of damages exceeding the specified amount and delay his liability is based on presumed fault, and he can be relieved of liability by proving that he and his servants and agents did not contribute to the damage. If he fails to prove the lack of fault, the carrier will be liable for the full amount of damages suffered by the passenger or his relatives (Art. 17, 19, 21 (2))[342].

For the carriage of cargo, the carrier's liability is based on presumed fault in case of delay (Art. 19)[343]. However, the carrier's liability for damage to or loss of the goods is a strict one (Art. 18)[344]. The extent of compensation and limitation amounts in case of cargo carriage are specified under Art. 22 of the Convention[345]. The air carrier will be wholly or partly exonerated from liability when he can prove that the damage was caused or contributed to by the negligence or other wrongful act or omission of the passenger or cargo interests (Art. 20).

II. Loss of the Right to Limit

Pursuant to Art. 22 (5) of the Montreal Convention, limitation amounts specified for delay in the carriage of passengers and their baggage and limitation amounts for damage to or loss of baggage are not applicable, if the damage results from an act or omission of the carrier, its servants or agents, done with the intent to cause damage or recklessly and with knowledge that damage would probably result provided that, in the case of such act or omission of a servant or agent, it is also proved that such servant or agent was acting within the scope of its employment.

By virtue of Art. 22 (5) of the Montreal Convention, liability for the carriage of cargo is, in any case, limited since the provision refers only to limitation amounts specified for the carriage of passengers and their baggage. Thus, under the Montreal Convention regime, the limits for carriage of cargo have been made unbreak-

---

[341] The previous limit of 100.000 SDRs has been increased and became effective on 30th December 2009, for more information see Alex *Losy*/Nicholas *Grief*, The Montreal Convention 1999: An Increase in the Limits of Liability, [2010] J.B.L. 529.

[342] *Ruhwedel, Montrealer Übereinkommen*, 194; *Giemulla/Schmid, Montrealer Übereinkommen*, Art. 21 MÜ Rn. 1; *Krause & Krause*, p. 11-61 *et seqq.*

[343] *Koller*, Art. 19 MÜ Rn. 3; *Müller-Rostin, Montrealer Übereinkommen*, 237; *Müller-Rostin, Unverbrüchlichkeit*, pp. 228-229; Ebenroth/Boujong/Joost/Strohn/ *Pokrant*, MÜ Art. 19 Rn. 1.

[344] *Koller*, Art. 18 MÜ Rn. 1; *Brinkmann, Vergleich*, 147; *Müller-Rostin, Montrealer Übereinkommen*, 237; *Ruhwedel, Montrealer Übereinkommen*, 192, 196; *Giemulla/ Schmid, Montrealer Übereinkommen*, Vorbemerkungen Art. 18 MÜ Rn. 2; *Müller-Rostin, Unverbrüchlichkeit*, p. 229; *Yetiş Şamlı*, p. 75; Ebenroth/ Boujong/Joost/ Strohn/*Pokrant*, MÜ Art. 18 Rn. 1.

[345] For more information see *Koller*, Art. 22 MÜ; *Giemulla/Schmid, Montrealer Übereinkommen*, Art. 22 MÜ.

able[346] in exchange for strict liability[347]. This has been criticised due to the violation of the *ordre public*[348]. Nonetheless, unbreakable limits have also found some support since they, it has been alleged, facilitate quick settlements, save time and money otherwise spent on lengthy proceedings and reduce insurance costs[349].

Accordingly, only the amounts specified for delay and loss of or damage to baggage can be broken. Limitation amounts specified for the death or injury of passengers cannot be broken either. However, it should be kept in mind that the air carrier is, nonetheless, liable for death or injury to passengers almost without any limitation[350].

D. Servants and Agents

I. Liability

1. Vicarious liability

According to Art. 20 of the Warsaw Convention, the carrier is not liable if he proves that he and his servants and agents have taken all necessary measures to avoid the damage. If formulated differently, the provision states that the carrier is liable if he and his servants and agents have not taken all necessary measures to avoid the damage. Therefore, the air carrier is liable for the acts of omissions of his servants and agents[351]. Another provision clearly establishing the liability of the carrier for his servants and agents is Art. 25 (2). This provision states that

---

[346] Nevertheless, the shipper can make a special declaration as to the full value of the cargo in exchange for a supplementary payment (Art. 22 (3)) or a special agreement as to higher or no limits of liability (Art. 25). However, it is also a known fact that the supplementary sum is generally higher than the cargo insurance premiums; therefore, the special declaration has nearly no practical significance at all, see *Koller, Unbeschränkte Haftung*, 178; see also *Müller-Rostin, Unverbrüchlichkeit*, pp. 237-241.

[347] *Müller-Rostin, Montrealer Übereinkommen*, 238; *Ruhwedel, Montrealer Übereinkommen*, 197; *Giemulla/Schmid, Montrealer Übereinkommen*, Art. 22 MÜ Rn. 57-58; *Müller-Rostin, Unverbrüchlichkeit*, pp. 229-231; *Ebenroth/Boujong/Joost/Strohn/Pokrant*, MÜ Art. 22 Rn. 9; for the historical background see *Koning*, 326-330; *Müller-Rostin, Unverbrüchlichkeit*, pp. 231-232.

[348] *Müller-Rostin, Montrealer Übereinkommen*, 238; *Ruhwedel, Montrealer Übereinkommen*, 196-197; *Ruhwedel, Durchbrechung im Luftrecht*, 137-139; *Koller, Unbeschränkte Haftung*, 178. See also *Yetiş Şamlı*, p. 101.

[349] *Brinkmann, Vergleich*, 149; *Ruhwedel, Montrealer Übereinkommen*, 196-197; *Ruhwedel, Durchbrechung im Luftrecht*, 141; *Müller-Rostin, Unverbrüchlichkeit*, p. 230.

[350] *Haak*, 163.

[351] *Giemulla/Schmid*, WA Art. 20 Rn. 2; *Clarke, Carriage by Air*, p. 125; *Abraham*, p. 355; *Koffka/Bodenstein*, p. 323; *Kaner*, pp. 426-427; *Knöfel*, pp. 241-242; *Stachow*, p. 73; *Müller-Rostin*, in: *Fremuth/Thume*, Art. 20 WA Rn. 1; for the general principles as to the carrier's liability for his servants and agents see *Meyer*, pp. 148-150.

limits of liability are also broken when the damage is caused by the wilful misconduct of servants or agents. The natural result of this provision is that the air
carrier is liable for the conduct of his servants and agents.

Analysis of the Montreal Convention provisions leads to the same conclusion.
Art. 21 (2)(a) of the Convention stipulates that, in case of death or injury of passenger, the carrier will not be liable for damages exceeding 100.000 SDRs if he
can prove that such damage was not due to the negligence or other wrongful act or
omission of the carrier or his servants and agents. In other words, the carrier is
vicariously liable if the damage resulted from wrongful act or omission of his
servants and agents. A similar provision has been adopted for the delay in the
carriage of passengers. Art. 19 of the Convention states that the carrier is not liable
for damage resulted from delay if he and his servants and agents took all necessary
measures to prevent the damage, or it was, for him and his servants and agents,
impossible to take such measures. In other words, the carrier is vicariously liable,
if his servants and agents did not take the necessary measures. Due to the strict
liability rules adopted for the carriage of the cargo, there is no need to explain in
detail that the carrier is liable for wrongful acts and omissions of his servants and
agents. The few instances where the carrier is not liable for damage to cargo is
listed in Art. 18 (2) of the Convention.

2. Criterion

A servant or agent is every person to whom the carrier delegates an obligation
which arises from the carriage contract[352]. For the purposes of breaking the liability limits, it makes no difference whether these persons are under the command of
the carrier or whether they are subject to his instructions[353]. The main criterion is
whether they fulfil a function in the performance of the carriage contract undertaken by the carrier. In other words, if they perform services on behalf of the
carrier, they should be considered as servants or agents[354].

---

[352] For the scope of the term "carrier" *McNair*, pp. 227-229; *Mankiewicz*, pp. 94-95;
Schmid, p. 14; *Milde*, p. 86-91; *Ülgen*, pp. 61-68; *Drion*, pp. 133-135; *Gie-
mulla/Schmid*, WA Art. 25 Rn. 6; *Kuhn*, pp. 75-92; *Ruhwedel*, pp. 410-411, 417 *et
seq.*; *Notes*, pp. 1012-1016; *Sözer, Kurallar*, pp. 385-393; *Müller-Rostin*, in:
Fremuth/Thume, Art. 20 WA Rn. 8; *Royal Insurance v. Amerford Air Cargo* (DC
New York, 1987) 645 F.Supp. 679; AG Frankfurt, 07.02.1997, TranspR 1997, 346.

[353] For the counterview see *Kaner*, p. 427.

[354] *Goedhuis*, pp. 224-226; *Koffka/Bodenstein*, pp. 323-324; *Abraham*, pp. 355-356;
Schmid, pp. 14-21; 130-131; *Abraham, Luftbeförderungsvertrag*, p. 49; *Riese*,
p. 454; *Liesecke*, p. 97; *Abraham, Grade des Verschuldens*, 260; *Ruhwedel, Flugzeugkommandanten*, p. 191 f. 61; *Ülgen*, p. 206; *Kırman*, p. 109; *Giemulla/Schmid*,
WA Art. 20 Rn. 26, Art. 25 Rn. 7; *Shawcross and Beaumont*, VII 980-990; *Clarke,
Carriage by Air*, pp. 125-127; *Ruhwedel*, pp. 407-408; J.W.E. *Strom van's Grave-
sande*, The Employee in Air Law, ETL 1982, 149, 151-153; *Hofmann/Grabherr*,
§ 48 Rn. 4; *Dettling-Ott*, pp. 111-113; *Özdemir*, pp. 90-91; *Schmid*, pp. 89-90;
Knöfel, pp. 247-249; *Stachow*, pp. 73, 222-223; *Giemulla*, p. 126; *Müller-Rostin*,
in: *Fremuth/Thume*, Art. 20 WA Rn. 8; *Koller*, WA 1955 Art. 20 Rn. 18-19; BGH,

In this respect, both flight and ground personnel of the carrier are within the scope of "servants and agents". Moreover, ground handling agencies, actual carriers[355] and employees of the owner of the chartered[356] aircraft, security check point personnel hired by the carrier, fuel and water providers, catering services, airport operators[357], airport warehouses and cargo handling agents belong to the class of "servants and agents"[358]. However, since they do not perform any part of the carriage contract, aircraft manufacturers, aircraft component manufacturers (*e.g.* engine producers)[359] and repair, maintenance and overhaul service providers[360] are not within the scope of the definition of servant and agent. This group of persons are called independent contractors since they perform services on their own account[361], in other words, not on behalf of the carrier.

It is, however, disputed whether the air carrier is liable also for monopoly[362] service providers, such as weathercast information providers and air traffic controllers. Some of the ground services can also be legal monopolies. The question has been analysed on the basis of the option to choose with whom to enter into contract. From this point of view, an air carrier should not be liable for monopoly service providers since he is under a legal obligation to enter into a contract with them in order to procure those services[363]. However, from a passenger interest

---

14.02.1989, TranspR 1989, 275; *Brink's Limited v. South African Airways* (DC New York, 1997) 1997 WL 323921, 6.

[355] *Ruhwedel*, p. 408; *Özdemir*, p. 91; *Dettling-Ott*, p. 115; MünchKommHGB 1997 – *Kronke* WA 1955 Art. 20 Rn. 34; OLG Düsseldorf, 12.01.1978; VersR 1978, 964; LG Frankfurt, 20.09.1985, TranspR 1985, 432; LG Stuttgart, 21.02.1992, TranspR 1993, 141.

[356] Except the hull charter, which is termed as "lease" (*Notes*, p. 1014), since this kind of charter does not place an obligation upon the owner of the aircraft to provide crew, see *Abraham*, p. 356; for general information see *Schmid*, pp. 237-240.

[357] However, on the contrary OLG Köln, 09.01.1997, ZLW 1998, 117.

[358] *Abraham*, p. 356; *Ruhwedel*, pp. 407-410; *Ülgen*, p. 206; *Kırman*, p. 109; *Report, Warsaw*, 261; *Özdemir*, p. 91; *Giemulla/Schmid*, WA Art. 20 Rn. 26-26a; Münch-KommHGB 1997 – *Kronke* WA 1955 Art. 20 Rn. 34; *Schmid*, pp. 171-176, 182-185, 196-199, 203-209, 231-236, 241-245; *Drion*, pp. 243.

[359] *Abraham*, p. 356; *Giemulla/Schmid*, WA Art. 20 Rn. 26; *Drion*, pp. 239-242; *Schmid*, pp. 223-226; for the counterview see *Report, Warsaw*, 260-261.

[360] *Schmid*, pp. 227-230; *Drion*, pp. 242-243 (depending on the condition that the repair was not made for a specific flight).

[361] *Philipson/et al.*, p. 174; *Knöfel*, p. 268.

[362] Here the term monopoly refers to legal monopolies, not monopolies resulting from market conditions; the second category of monopolies is also considered as "servants or agents" of the air carrier, see *Giemulla/Schmid*, WA Art. 20 Rn. 29-30; *Schmid*, pp. 126-129; *Müller-Rostin*, in: *Fremuth/Thume*, Art. 20 WA Rn. 9; *Clarke/Yates*, para. 3.166.

[363] *Giemulla/Schmid*, WA Art. 20 Rn. 29; *Schmid*, pp. 125-126; from the scope of employment point of view see *Knöfel*, p. 267.

point of view, the air carrier should also be liable for monopoly service providers; having an option of choosing a contracting party is irrelevant[364].

The issue can be solved where legal monopolies are, at the same time, governmental authorities. It is clear that governmental authorities are outside the class of servants and agents. The air carrier is, for instance, not vicariously liable for wrongful acts or omissions of customs authorities, and of weathercast information providers and air traffic controllers if they are governmental authorities[365]. It might, at first, be awkward to link the air carrier's liability for the same group of persons whether they are governmental authorities or not. The reason for such a differentiation is that the liability of the governmental authorities is subject to the administrative law principles. Under those principles, states are, generally, under the burden of proving that the damage is not caused by the wrongful act of the state, which puts plaintiffs in an advantageous position. If legal monopolies, on the other hand, are not governmental authorities, and if they are not counted as servants and agents of the air carrier, passengers might need to sue them under the tort law principles which necessitates passengers to prove that their wrongful conduct caused the damage occurred, which is a heavy burden and puts passengers in a very disadvantageous position. Therefore, for the interests of passengers, legal monopolies are to be grouped as servants and agents of the air carrier, if they are not governmental authorities.

3. Limitation of liability and breaking the limits

Besides the vicarious liability of the carrier, servants and agents remain liable to third parties under tort law rules. Therefore, there is always the possibility of addressing a claim against servants and agents. Moreover, since they are not "carriers", their liability is also not limited[366].

This fact presents a danger of subverting the whole limited liability system set by the international conventions since claimants could sue servants or agents with the expectation that carriers will stand behind them. This expectation could be based upon the legal necessity arising out of employment law or out of contracts between carriers and agents or servants. As a result, carriers would pay the compensation determined under general tort law rules[367]. Consequently, plaintiffs

---

[364] OLG Nürnberg, 09.04.1992, TranspR 1992, 276; OLG Frankfurt, 21.04.1998, TranspR 1999, 24 affirmed by BGH, 21.09.2000, ETL 2001, 248 = ZLW 2001, 254.

[365] *Giemulla/Schmid*, WA Art. 20 Rn. 26; *Drion*, pp. 243-244; *Schmid*, pp. 210-211; *Ülgen*, p. 207, *Kırman*, p. 110; *Abraham*, pp. 356-357; *Müller-Rostin*, in: *Fremuth/Thume*, Art. 20 WA Rn. 9.

[366] Alex *Meyer*, Internationale Luftfahrtabkommen, Bd. III, Köln & Berlin 1957, pp. 143-144; *Müller-Rostin*, in: *Fremuth/Thume*, Art. 25a WA Rn. 1.

[367] *Liesecke*, p. 97; MünchKommHGB 1997 – *Kronke* WA 1955 Art. 25 A Rn. 1; *Calkins*, pp. 268-269; *Mankiewicz*, *Hague Protocol*, pp. 82-83; *Report, Warsaw,* 264; *Guldimann*, pp. 150-151; *Müller-Rostin*, in: *Fremuth/Thume*, Art. 25a WA Rn. 1.

would break the limits by a so called "short-circuit"[368] which results in the defeat of the uniformity provided[369].

The second danger as to the tort liability of the servants and agents is that once a court enters into judgement against them, they would face an economic downturn since they cannot afford to pay such high damages when the carrier for whom they work does not support them. This possibility also aptly leads to an unjust and unfair conclusion: The carrier who is capable of paying even the full amount of damages has the right to limit his liability, whereas his servants and agents who possess minimal assets cannot avail themselves of this financial limitation.

The question whether servants and agents of the carrier are entitled to take advantage of the limitation of liability set by the Warsaw Convention in its original version has produced opposing views both in doctrine[370] and case law[371]. Hence, it has been necessary to solve the problem by a legal regulation.

Therefore, in order to protect carriers against this kind of litigation[372] and in order to prevent the financial ruin of servants and agents, a provision also limiting servants' and agents' liability was proposed[373], and this proposal was widely supported[374]. After discussions during the Hague Conference, the following text was adopted as Art. 25A of the Convention:

"1. If an action is brought against a servant or agent of the carrier arising out of damage to which this Convention relates, such servant or agent, if he proves that he acted within the scope of his employment, shall be entitled to avail himself of the limits of liability which that carrier is entitled to invoke under Article 22.

2. The aggregate of the amounts recoverable from the carrier, his servants and agents, in that case, shall not exceed the said limits.

---

[368] *Calkins*, p. 258.

[369] *Philipson/et al.*, p. 163.

[370] Only *Drion*, pp. 157-158 and later *Dettling-Ott*, pp. 261-262 have argued that servants and agents should be entitled to limit their liability; the majority view contends the contrary, see *Kreindler*, Ch. 10 p. 27; *Meyer I*, p. 110; *Abraham*, p. 357; *Gerber*, p. 69; *Koffka/Bodenstein*, p. 269; *Riese*, pp. 440-441; *Sözer*, *Taşıyıcının Sorumluluğu*, pp. 791-792; *Stachow*, p. 73.

[371] *E.g.* in *Reed v. Wiser* (CA, 1977) 555 F.2d 1079, it was decided that an employee (servant) or an agent of the carrier is only liable to the same extent as the carrier himself. Similar decisions were held in *Chutter v. KLM Royal Dutch Airlines* (DC New York, 1955) 132 F.Supp. 611; *Julius Young Jewelry Manufacturing Co., Inc. v. Delta Air Lines* (Supreme Court of New York, 1979) 414 N.Y.S.2d 528; *Baker v. Lansdell Protective Agency, Inc.* (DC New York, 1984) 590 F.Supp. 165; however there have been decisions contrary to the previous ones as well, *e.g. Pierre v. Eastern Air Lines* (DC New Jersey, 1957) 152 F.Supp. 486; *Alleyn v. Delta Airlines* (DC New York, 1999) 58 F.Supp.2d 15.

[372] *Guldimann*, p. 151; *Ruhwedel, Flugzeugkommandanten*, pp. 188-191; *Beaumont, Hague Protocol*, p. 419.

[373] Report on Revision of the Warsaw Convention (adopted by the Legal Committee of ICAO), in: *Documents, Hague*, p. 99.

[374] See comments during the eighteenth meeting, in: *Minutes, Hague*, pp. 214 *et seqq.*

3. The provisions of paragraph 1 and 2 of this article shall not apply if it is proved that the damage resulted from an act or omission of the servant or agent done with intent to cause damage or recklessly and with knowledge that damage would probably result."

Basically, servants and agents are also entitled to limit their liability[375] unless the damage resulted from their wilful misconduct. Art. 25A (3) sets forth the same principle as to the conduct which gives rise to unlimited liability. When the unlimited liability of the servant of the carrier was also claimed, the court applied the same interpretation given to Art. 25 for the interpretation of the conduct specified by Art. 25A (3)[376].

The same principles have been adopted by the Montreal Convention for the right to limit of the servants and agents of the carrier (Art. 30) and of the actual or contracting carrier (Art. 43). Pursuant to Art. 30 (3) of the Montreal Convention, servants and agents are not entitled to limit if the damage results from their intentional or reckless conduct coupled with knowledge of the probable consequences. However, the provision brings a very important exception to the unlimited liability of servants and agents. Since the liability is limited in any case in the carriage of cargo, the liability limits will not be broken simply by suing servants or agents. Therefore, Art. 30 (3) of the Montreal Convention regulates breaking the liability limits except "in respect of the carriage of cargo". The same rule is applicable for the servants and agents of the actual or contracting carrier by virtue of Art. 43 of the Convention.

II. Scope of Employment

1. Term

Both the original and modified versions of Art. 25 of the Warsaw Convention and Art. 22 (5) of the Montreal Convention provide that the carrier cannot avail himself of the limitation of liability if his servants or agents committed said conduct. However, in case of servants' or agents' wilful misconduct, it is provided that the servant or agent must have acted "within the scope of employment". Moreover, Art. 25A of the Warsaw Convention and Art. 30 (1) of the Montreal Convention also provide that the servant or agent can avail himself of the financial limitation if he acted "within the scope of employment".

The scope of employment necessitates a functional connection between the damage incurred and the fulfilment of the servants' or agents' duties. The activities of the servant or agent should have an effect on the passengers or cargo during the fulfilment of duties which have arisen from the explicit or implicit instructions of the carrier or a service agreement[377]. In other words, conduct giving rise to

---

[375] For more information see *Guldimann*, pp. 150-152; *Ruhwedel*, pp. 413-415; *Ruhwedel, Flugzeugkommandanten*, pp. 194-196.

[376] *Gurtner v. Beaton* [1993] 2 Lloyd's Rep. 369 (CA); *Müller-Rostin*, in: *Fremuth/Thume*, Art. 25a WA Rn. 6.

[377] *Ruhwedel, Flugzeugkommandanten*, p. 193; MünchKommHGB 1997 – *Kronke* WA 1955 Art. 20 Rn. 38, Art. 25 Rn. 8; *Shawcross and Beaumont*, I 288; *Dettling-Ott*,

physical or financial damage needs to be connected to the duties of the servant or agent. In this respect, if a cabin crew attacks a passenger due to personal problems, this act would not be within his scope of employment[378]. Finally, it is of no importance whether the servant or agent was fulfilling duties which arose from the specific carriage contract entered into with the claimant passenger or cargo owner[379].

2. Theft

Theft of cargo or luggage of the passenger constitutes one of the clearest examples of wilful misconduct. Therefore, the carrier is liable if cargo or luggage was stolen by his servants and agents. However, according to Art. 25 of the Warsaw convention and Art. 22 (5) of the Montreal Convention, the claimant must prove that the act or omission giving rise to theft is within the scope of the servant's or agent's employment.

It has been disputed whether theft could be considered to be within the scope of the employment or not. In an early case decided by the Swiss Federal Court, it was ruled that the air carrier is liable for theft committed by the pilot since the pilot is under the duty to protect the owner's interests in the object which was placed into his custody[380]. In another case, a German court ruled in favour of the cargo owners where the cargo was stolen by an agent of the air carrier who, in fact, was in charge of dispatch[381].

Decisions of the common law courts on the issue are, however, divergent. In the *Rustenburg* case, theft by the servant who is in charge of the loading was considered as being within the scope of employment since his duty was not only to load the goods, but also to take reasonable care of the goods[382]. Similarly, theft was also considered within the scope of employment by the Federal Court of Appeal of Canada[383]. However in the *Rymanowski* case, the American court stated that theft was foreign to the interests of the air carrier. Thus the agent was not acting within his scope of employment and the air carrier could not be held liable[384]. This decision and reasoning has been followed by all American courts[385].

---

p. 261; *Özdemir*, p. 94; *Kaner*, p. 427; *Koffka/Bodenstein*, p. 334; *Drion*, pp. 246-254; *Sözer, Taşıyıcının Sorumluluğu*, p. 792; *Clarke, Carriage by Air*, p. 169; *Ülgen*, p. 207; *Kırman*, pp. 110-111; *Ruhwedel*, p. 412; *Schmid*, pp. 120-121; *Knöfel*, pp. 266-267; *Stachow*, p. 223; *Müller-Rostin*, in: *Fremuth/Thume*, Art. 20 Rn. 10, Art. 25 WA Rn. 14.

[378] *Shawcross and Beaumont*, VII 520-521.

[379] *Drion*, pp. 238-239; for the counterview see *Schmid*, pp. 99-119.

[380] BG, 15.06.1955, ASDA-Bulletin 1956/11, 9-10 (as quoted by *Dettling-Ott*, p. 260).

[381] LG Frankfurt, 16.01.1996, TranspR 1996, 424.

[382] *Rustenburg Platinum Mines Ltd v. South African Airways* [1977] 1 Lloyd's Rep. 564, 574-576 (QBD); affirmed by *Rustenburg Platinum Mines Ltd v. South African Airways and Pan American World Airways Inc.* [1979] 1 Lloyd's Rep 19 (CA).

[383] *Air Canada v. Swiss Bank Corporation et al.* (1988) 44 DLR (4th) 680.

[384] *Rymanowski v. Pan American World Airways, Inc.* (Supreme Court of New York, 1979) 416 N.Y.S.2d 1018, 1020.

Notwithstanding the approach of the US courts, it would not be wrong to say that theft has otherwise generally been considered to be within the scope of employment. If the servant or agent has access to the goods or luggage during and within the sphere of the fulfilment of his duty, theft by him should be regarded within the scope of employment[386]. From this point of view, it is not important whether the servant or agent committed theft during his working hours or not[387].

However, by virtue of Art. 30 (3) of the Montreal Convention, the liability of servants and agents will be limited in any case of the carriage of goods. Therefore, a servant or agent will be liable only up to the limits set out in the Convention, even if he steals the goods carried by air. It was suggested that for the sake of punishing theft by servants and agents in case of carriage of cargo by air, it might be asserted that the servants and agents were not acting within the scope of their employment if they commit theft, so that they are not allowed to avail themselves of the limits of liability[388]. However, this is exactly the opposite suggestion of the case law up to the present and it is very doubtful whether such an interpretation will be accepted by the courts.

---

[385] *Denby v. Seaboard World Airlines, Inc.* (DC New York, 1983) 575 F.Supp. 1134, 1148; *Baker v. Lansdell Protective Agency, Inc.* (DC New York, 1985) 1985 WL 3964, 3; *Brink's Limited v. South African Airways* (DC New York, 1995) 1995 WL 225602, 3; *Tokio Marine & Fire Insurance Co. v. United Air Lines, Inc.* (DC California, 1996) 933 F.Supp. 1527; *Insurance Company of North America v. Federal Express Corporation* (CA, 1999) 189 F.3d 914, 921-923.

[386] MünchKommHGB 1997 – *Kronke* WA 1955 Art. 20 Rn. 46, Art. 25 Rn. 8; *Drion*, pp. 246, 251; *Stachow*, p. 223; *Clarke/Yates*, para. 3.167.

[387] MünchKommHGB 1997 – *Kronke* WA 1955 Art. 25 Rn. 8; for the counterview see *Clarke, Carriage by Air*, p. 169; *Drion*, p. 252; *Giemulla/Schmid*, WA Art. 20 Rn. 27.

[388] *Koller, Unbeschränkte Haftung*, 179.

§ 5 Carriage by Sea

After being adopted by the Hague Protocol in the context of carriage by air, the description of the term "wilful misconduct" spread to other areas of transport law. In maritime law conventions, limitation was broken in case of "acts or faults of the shipowner". This principle has been later replaced with "actual fault or privity". Nevertheless, today, almost every maritime convention employs the description adopted by the Hague Protocol. However, during the drafting and adoption procedure, some small changes have been made. However, although small, these changes generate substantial differences in terms of application. In this chapter, breaking the liability limits under the international maritime conventions will be discussed in detail.

A. Carriage of Goods and Passengers

I. Carriage of Goods

1. Hague Rules as amended by the Visby Protocol

a) Hague Rules and limitation of liability

In the 19th century, carriers were exempting themselves generally from cargo liability by inserting clauses into bills of lading and carriage contracts, since they had the dominant position in the market[1]. The first regulation as to carriage by sea contracts in this respect, was adopted in the USA, namely the Harter Act in 1893[2] followed by legislation in New Zealand (in 1903), Australia (in 1904) and Canada (in 1910)[3] or example. However, a lack of international legislation and differing rules caused legal confusion. Furthermore, the British Empire was under pressure to pass legislation similar to the Harter Act. The Empire decided not to put its carriers in a disadvantaged position and therefore applied to the International Law Association ("ILA") to solve the problem on an international level[4].

In September 1921, the conference held in the Hague by the ILA agreed upon a number of principles which are known as the Hague Rules of 1921[5]. However,

---

[1] *Schoenbaum,* V. I, p. 636; *Puttfarken,* Rn. 135; *Rabe,* Vor § 556 Rn. 2; *Hill,* p. 269; *Rabe, TranspR,* 142-143; *Bonelli,* pp. 157-159; *Eilenberger-Czwalinna,* pp. 7-8; *Richter-Hannes,* p. 14; *Yazıcıoğlu,* p. 1; *Stachow,* p. 4; *Sturley,* 5; *Diamond,* 227: "The only freedom of the shipper was to take the bill of lading or leave it [...] even the latter freedom was often illusory".

[2] See *Basedow, Common Carriers,* 312.

[3] *Sturley,* 11-18; *Gold/Chircop/Kindred,* p. 433; *Rabe,* Vor § 556 Rn. 3; *Diamond,* 227; *Richter-Hannes,* p. 14; *Stachow,* p. 5.

[4] *Sturley,* 18-19; *Diamond,* 227; *Çağa, Batider,* pp. 314-315; *Carver,* para. 9-062 *et seq.*; *Richter-Hannes,* pp. 14-15; *Eilenberger-Czwalinna,* pp. 10-11.

[5] *Sturley,* 20-22; *Schoenbaum,* V. I, p. 636; *Aikens/Lord/Bools,* para. 1.51; *Çağa, Batider,* p. 315; *Girvin,* para. 15.06. For the work of the ILA on bills of lading up to the Hague Rules of 1921 see *Sturley,* 6-8.

these rules were suggested as being incorporated into the contracts of carriage on a voluntary basis and were, therefore without any binding effect short of the incorporation option[6].

However, those rules have not been incorporated into bills of lading other than in a few instances. So, CMI decided to adopt those rules as an international convention. The work of CMI resulted in the International Convention for the Unification of Certain Rules of Law relating to Bills of Lading signed on 25 August 1924 in Brussels. Since the principles embodied in this Convention were first formulated in The Hague, they are known as the "Hague Rules"[7].

The Hague Rules only cover liability rising out of a carriage covered by a bill of lading or any similar document of title. Written in common law style, the rules specify one by one the obligations of the carrier, such as the duty to provide a seaworthy ship (Art. III). Further, the Rules contain a long list of exemptions where the carrier is not liable at all (Art. IV (2)). Moreover, some provisions relieve the carrier from liability if certain conditions are fulfilled (Art. IV (1), (4)).

According to Art. IV (5) of the Hague Rules, the carrier shall not "in any event" be or become liable for any loss of or damage to or in connection with goods exceeding the amount stated in the Rules or fixed by the parties of the carriage contract[8]. The same article also contains the principle that the carrier would be liable for the total amount if the nature and value of such goods have been declared by the shipper and inserted into the bill of lading.

The wording of Art. IV (5) clearly stipulates that except in cases of declaration by the shipper, the carrier's liability is limited. The phrase "in any event" indicates that there is no restriction on the right to limit under the Hague Rules[9], although this literal interpretation has not been accepted by all writers[10]. According to the dissenting view, the historical reasons which led to the adoption of the Hague Rules justify the limitation of liability only in cases of the carrier's negligence. Therefore, in cases of fault which goes beyond negligence, the carrier should not be able to limit his liability[11]. Furthermore, it is also stressed that the words "in any event" shall be read as "in any event, unless there is a fundamental breach of the carriage contract", since when there is a fundamental breach, there is no longer a contract of carriage[12]. Therefore, and due to the lack of any express provisions in

---

[6]   *Sturley*, 22-23; *Rabe*, Vor § 556 Rn. 4; *Basedow, Hamburger Regeln*, p. 102; *Çağa, Batider*, p. 315; *Carver*, para. 9-063; *Yazıcıoğlu*, p. 2; *Girvin*, para. 15.06.

[7]   *Sturley*, 25-32; *Rabe*, Vor § 556 Rn. 4; *Eilenberger-Czwalinna*, pp. 11-12; *Stachow*, p. 5; *Clarke, Transport in Europe*, 38.

[8]   However, according to the same provision, the amount agreed upon by the parties cannot be less than the figure stated in the Rules.

[9]   *Scrutton*, p. 407; *Cooke/et al.*, para. 85.365; *Griggs/Williams/Farr*, p. 151; *Pingfat*, p. 144; *Yetiş Şamlı*, p. 143. See also *Atlantic Mutual Insurance Company v. Poseidon Schiffahrt* (DC Illinois, 1962) 206 F.Supp. 15, 18-19; BGH, 17.01.1983, TranspR 1983, 100.

[10]   *Bonelli*, p. 173; *Tetley*, pp. 260-261; *Ilse*, pp. 163-164; *Basedow, Transportvertrag*, pp. 422-423.

[11]   *Bonelli*, p. 173.

[12]   *Tetley*, pp. 255-257, 260-261.

the Hague Rules, doctrines of "fundamental breach" and of "unreasonable deviation" from the carriage contract have been used in order to deprive the carrier of the limits of liability in the course of the application of the Rules[13].

b) Visby Protocol and breaking the limits

Due to the developments in the field of carriage of goods by sea, the necessity of amending the Hague Rules arose[14]. That necessity was met by the Protocol to Amend the International Convention for the Unification of Certain Rules of Law Relating to Bills of Lading done at Brussels on 23rd of February 1968 ("Visby Protocol").

aa) Historical background

After the amendment decision, a CMI commission started its work. The idea of removing the limitation in case of wilful misconduct had been accepted already, before the Stockholm Conference of CMI, although there were some worries about the interpretation of the term "reckless" by national courts[15].

Although the draft text adopted by the Stockholm Conference does not contain any provisions on breaking liability limits[16], the draft text submitted to the 1968 Conference and the final text of the new Art. IV (5)(e) adopted by the same Conference[17] reads as follows:

> "Neither the carrier nor the ship shall be entitled to the benefit of the limitation of liability provided for in this paragraph if it is proved that the damage resulted from an act or omission of the carrier done with intent to cause damage, or recklessly and with knowledge that damage would probably result."

Clearly, the source of this definition is the Warsaw Convention as amended by the Hague Protocol[18].

---

[13] For more information see *Tetley*, pp. 223 *et seqq.*; *Dockray*, pp. 63 *et seqq.*; *Puttfarken*, Rn. 282-283; *von Ziegler*, pp. 186 *et seqq.*; *Stachow*, pp. 109-124; *Ilse*, pp. 171-175; *Aikens/Lord/Bools*, para. 10.264 *et seqq.*; *Carver*, para. 9-056; *Pingfat*, p. 127-128; *Yetiş Şamlı*, p.143-145.

[14] For more information see *Diamond*, 228-231; *Carver*, para. 9-065; *Ilse*, pp. 195-196.

[15] *Burchard-Motz*, p. 10.

[16] For the text see *CMI*, Conférence de Stockholm, 1963, pp. 546-551, or *Travaux Préparatoires, Hague-Visby Rules*, pp. 843-845.

[17] Discussions on the new Art. IV (5) were focused on the basis of the limitation of liability issue; for the discussions see *Travaux Préparatoires, Hague-Visby Rules*, pp. 511 *et seqq.*

[18] *Rabe*, § 607a Rn. 18; *Tetley*, p. 286; *Basedow, Transportvertrag*, p. 424; *Gaskell/ Asariotis/Baatz*, para. 16.52; *Eilenberger-Czwalinna*, p. 115; *Stachow*, p. 21 fn. 3; *Ilse*, p. 200; *Yetiş Şamlı*, p. 147; *Neumann*, 415.

bb) Similarities and differences in the wording

Although the wording of "in any event" has not been changed, it has been clarified with the new Art. IV (5)(e) that the carrier is liable without any financial limits in cases of wilful misconduct. Furthermore, the doctrines of fundamental breach and unreasonable deviation have also been referred to, since no changes were made in the provisions, which are the legal basis for those doctrines[19]. However, it is generally accepted that those doctrines are not to be applied anymore[20].

The requisites as to the degree of fault under the Warsaw Convention are applicable to Art. IV (5)(e) of the Hague/Visby Rules in the exact manner[21], *i.e.* intentional wrongdoing or recklessness coupled with an actual awareness of the probable consequences is necessary for a finding of wilful misconduct under the Hague/Visby Rules[22]. Deceit and fraud are the best examples of intentional wrongdoing. Unfortunately, deceit can be encountered in maritime practice from time to time. It frequently occurs as the intentionally wrongful issue of a bill of lading. On the request of shippers, carriers might issue wrong, *e.g.* antedated[23] bills of lading in order to defraud banks in letter of credit transactions or to defraud consignees.

As to the reckless conduct coupled with actual knowledge of the probable consequences, the case of the *Titan Scan* is a good example[24]. The case arose from a carriage of 198 containers which were loaded on board the *Titan Scan*, and a bill of lading was issued which fell under the Hague/Visby Rules. At an intermediate stop for discharge operations and in order to load new cargo below deck, some of the containers were re-stowed with a lashing and binding method which differed from the one used at the beginning. During the voyage to the port of discharge, some containers were lost overboard and some damaged. Itel, the owners of the containers, claimed that the different method of lashing and binding caused the loss of and damage to the cargo and that the crew was guilty of wilful misconduct and that, therefore, the carrier was not entitled to the limitation. The court dis-

---

[19] *von Ziegler*, pp. 201-202; *Stachow*, pp. 124-126; *Wilson*, p. 202.

[20] *Herber*, p. 334; *Scrutton*, p. 408; *Diamond*, 247.

[21] For explanations see *Cooke/et al.*, para. 85.417 *et seq.*; *Baughen*, p. 139; *Puttfarken*, Rn. 261; *Rabe*, § 607a Rn. 20-23; *Diamond*, 244-246; *Chen*, pp. 198-199.

[22] For detailed information see *supra* § 4 B I 2 c. However, it seems that the French courts continue to apply the objective interpretation also to carriage of goods by sea cases. For summaries of some French cases with regard to the Hague/Visby Rules see <www.comitemaritime.org/jurisp/ju_billading.html#Anchor-Loss-39463> (03.06.2010), see also *Puttfarken*, Rn. 258; *Stachow*, pp. 158-159.

[23] See *e.g. Standard Chartered Bank v. Pakistan National Shipping Corporation and Others (No. 2)* [1998] 1 Lloyd's Rep. 684 (QBD).

[24] *Itel Container Corporation v. M/V Titan Scan, et al.* (DC Georgia, 1996) 1997 A.M.C. 1568.

missed the allegation of wilful misconduct and stated that the crew acted only negligently since the foresight of the probable consequences was missing[25].

The carrier was also not found reckless in a case arising from a stolen container. Eleven containers containing electronic devices were transported from Shanghai to Rotterdam. After the carriage has been completed, the containers were unloaded and placed in the terminal. When they were collected for further carriage by inland waterways, it was understood that one of the containers was missing. It was discovered that a truck driver collected the container after he had delivered the necessary document. It was not possible to clarify how the truck driver obtained the original document which was issued for the cargo interests. The container was never found. The court held that the carrier is liable, but since he did not act or omit to act recklessly, he was entitled to limit. The court stated that the carrier was not reckless, because he used extra security measures for this carriage due to the high value of the cargo. That the container nevertheless got stolen does not justify a finding of recklessness[26].

The claim for reckless conduct and unlimited liability also failed in the *Trade Harvest* case which arose from the carriage of machinery in two shipments. The shipper, also the seller of the goods, endorsed the bills of lading for the first shipment to the claimant and to a company called Woodware. The claimant informed the shipper, *i.e.* the seller that the containers can be delivered to Woodware. Subsequently, the carrier delivered the first shipment to Woodware upon the surrender of the original bills of lading. After the bills of lading were issued for the second shipment, the seller sent them to the claimant with courier service. The bills of lading were endorsed as blank. The carrier, after the arrival of the ship into the port of discharge asked the seller whether he is allowed to deliver the goods without the surrender of the original bills of lading, since he was informed that they got lost. The seller agreed to the delivery, and the carrier delivered the second shipment to Woodware as well. However, after a while, the claimant contacted the carrier and claimed delivery upon the surrender of the original bills of lading. After considering the issue, the court ruled that the carrier was liable, since he did not deliver the goods to the rightful holder of the bills of lading. However, the court rejected the unlimited liability, since Woodware was authorized to deliver the first shipment, and that the second shipment should be delivered to the same person to whom the first shipment was delivered cannot be considered as unusual. Under these circumstances, it is not possible to hold that the carrier acted recklessly and with actual knowledge that such loss would probably occur[27].

---

[25] *Itel Container Corporation v. M/V Titan Scan, et al.* (DC Georgia, 1996) 1997 A.M.C. 1568, 1584; reversed in part on other grounds *Itel Container Corporation v. M/V Titan Scan, et al.* (CA, 1998) 1998 A.M.C. 1965.

[26] LG Hamburg, 13.03.2009, HmbSchRZ 2009, 129.

[27] LG Stuttgart, 21.07.2000, TranspR 2001, 41 ("*Trade Harvest*").

(1) The carrier

Yet a difference occurs in the application sphere of the Warsaw Convention and the Hague/Visby Rules. Under the Warsaw Convention regime, the carrier is also liable for the wilful misconduct of his servants and agents. However, Art. IV (5)(e) of the Hague/Visby Rules refer only to the carrier himself[28]. Therefore, only the conduct of the carrier himself would be relevant for the application of the provision. Accordingly, wilful misconduct of a servant or agent is not sufficient to break the limits of liability of the carrier[29], unless the servants' or agents' conduct can be attributed to the carrier[30].

The first reason for such an interpretation is the lack of a clear provision in the Hague/Visby Rules stating that the carrier is also liable for his servants' and agents' wilful misconduct, whereas such a provision can be found in the Warsaw Convention[31]. Clearly, the drafters of the Visby Protocol deleted the terms "his servants and agents" so that only the term "carrier" remains. This, of course, clearly shows the intention of the drafters of the Visby Protocol[32]. The historical background of the provision also supports such a conclusion. During the drafting period, breaking the limits in cases of wilful misconduct was first discussed with regard to the limited liability of servants and agents of the carrier[33]. The provision for the carrier's wilful misconduct was not adopted during the Stockholm Conference in 1963[34]. During the diplomatic conference in 1967 held in Brussels, it was decided to place the carrier in the same position as his servants and agents. There-

---

[28] *Baughen*, p. 139; *Griggs/Williams/Farr*, p. 34; *Mandaraka-Sheppard*, p. 891; *Rabe*, § 607a Rn. 16, § 660 Rn. 26; *Wilson*, p. 204; *Beier*, p. 256; *Rabe, TranspR*, 144; *Asariotis*, 149; *Yetiş Şamlı*, p. 148; *Gaskell/Asariotis/Baatz*, para. 16.53. However, it is reported that a German court ruled to the contrary, see *Rabe*, § 660 Rn. 26; *Ilse*, pp. 207-208. In two recently decided cases, a German court and the German Federal Court, after the comparison with the wording of the Warsaw Convention and CMR, ruled that due to the lack of clear reference to the servants and agents in the Hague/Visby Rules, it is only the carrier's conduct which can result in his unlimited liability, see HansOLG, 02.10.2008, HbgSchRZ 2009, 52 (58) (*"Caribia Express"*) and BGH, 18.06.2009, TranspR 2009, 327 (330).

[29] *Cooke/et al.*, para. 85.415; *Ping-fat*, p. 140; *Rabe*, § 607a Rn. 16, § 660 Rn. 26; *Carver*, para. 9-270; *Aikens/Lord/Bools*, para. 10.313; *Herber, Haftungsrecht*, p. 216; *Yazıcıoğlu*, p. 174; *Herber*, p. 332; *Eilenberger-Czwalinna*, pp. 118-120; *de la Motte*, pp. 294-295; *Häußer*, pp. 25, 50; *Herber, Überblick*, 98; *Ramming*, 302.

[30] *Scrutton*, p. 408; *Griggs/Williams/Farr*, p. 153; *Carver*, para. 9-270; *von Ziegler*, pp. 203-204; *Chen*, pp. 200-201. For more information see *infra* E.

[31] For information see *supra* § 4 D.

[32] *Diamond*, 244; *Richter-Hannes/Trotz*, p. 21; *Rabe, Vortrag*, p. 19; *Gaskell, Hamburg Rules*, p. 169; *Rabe, TranspR*, 144; *Browner International Ltd. v. Monarch Shipping Co. Ltd. (The "European Enterprise")* [1989] 2 Lloyd's Rep. 185, 192 (QBD) *per* Justice Steyn.

[33] For more information see *infra* D VI 3.

[34] For the draft adopted during the Stockholm Conference see Die Stockholmer Konferenz des Comité Maritime International (vom 9. bis 15. Juni 1963) (zusammengestellt vom DVIS), Hamburg 1964, pp. 29-30.

fore, it is clear that the drafters dealt with servants' and agents' wilful misconduct on one side, and carrier's wilful misconduct on the other[35].

Another point in this respect was stressed by the court in the *Encounter Bay* case. The slot charterer, being at the same time the carrier, was held liable to the cargo owners for the damage which arose when a container stack being carried under the Hague/Visby Rules fell. The cause of the collapse was improper lashing, and during the trial it was determined that the first officer knew that the lashing was improper. In fact, he foresaw the probable damage and, moreover, the timing of it. The court ruled that the first officer acted recklessly and was guilty of wilful misconduct. However, since under the Hague/Visby Rules the carrier is liable only for his own reckless conduct, the court entered into judgement for limited liability[36]. The court stressed that the drafters of the Hague/Visby Rules made a clear distinction by referring either to "carrier, master or agent" (Art. III (3)) or "carrier or his agent" (Art. III (6)) or only to "carrier" (Art. IV). The distinction shows that when the drafters wanted to refer to the carrier together with his servants and agents, they did it clearly.

The second reason derives from the historical and commercial development of maritime practice. It is clearly stated in the *European Enterprise* case. In a carriage where the parties incorporated the Hague/Visby Rules into the consignment note, the goods were delivered to the plaintiff in a damaged condition. The plaintiff contended that the carrier could not limit his liability. After discussing the issue whether the term "carrier" means only the carrier himself, or is broad enough to cover his servants and agents as well, the court decided in favour of the defendants. In its decision, the court stressed the historical and commercial reasons why the term "carrier" refers only to "the carrier himself". First of all, during a carriage, a carrier has limited control over the acts or omissions of his servants and agents. The crucial importance of the limitation provisions in the shipping industry was stated by the court as the commercial reason. Limitation of liability serves a commercial purpose by allowing the carrier to find insurance on reasonable premiums, and here, a narrow interpretation of the term "carrier" rather than a wide one serves this commercial purpose[37].

Therefore, the carrier will still be liable within the limits set by the Convention in cases of wilful misconduct of his servants and agents. This was also accepted by a German court in a case involving the transport of some meat products in a reefer container. After the container was loaded on board the ship and after the ship set sailed, it was understood that the custom's seal on the container was broken, its door was open and a case of meat products was missing. The seal was immediately renewed; however, at an intermediate stop where the container should have been loaded onto another ship, the public authorities did not allow further shipment of the container due to the lack of an intact seal. The container

---

[35] *Rabe, Vortrag,* p. 20.
[36] *Sellers Fabrics Pty. Ltd. v. Hapag-Lloyd AG* [1998] NSWSC 646 (Supreme Court of New South Wales).
[37] *Browner International Ltd. v. Monarch Shipping Co. Ltd. (The "European Enterprise")* [1989] 2 Lloyd's Rep. 185 (QBD).

was carried back, however since the shelf life of the goods had almost expired, it was not possible to put them on the market. In conclusion, the goods became a total loss. The court ruled that the carrier was liable; however, he was entitled to limit. The court stated that it is clear that the thief broke the seal, opened the door of the container, and stole the goods intentionally. Nevertheless, the wilful misconduct of the thief cannot be attributed to the carrier, and since the personal fault of the carrier is necessary to break his liability limits, wilful misconduct of his servants and agents, the crew or the stevedores do not deprive him of the limits of liability[38].

Nonetheless, according to the counterview, breaking the limits only in case of the carrier's wilful misconduct is erroneous. Such an interpretation will only cause lack of care and an increase in the reckless conduct on the part of masters and other servants. Furthermore, it is contrary to common sense[39] and is not consistent with today's shipping practice and company structure[40]. In order to support the interpretation in favour of cargo interests, the following lines from *the Pembroke*[41] case were also cited:

"[Attorney for the carrier] submitted that the recklessness and knowledge must be on the part of the carrier's management. I reject that. The recklessness and knowledge on the part of the master is what is in issue"[42].

However, those lines must be read together with the previous and following ones:

"It is plain that the master and the charterers took a calculated risk with full appreciation of the dangers and probable consequences [...] The evidence shows that [the charterers] and the master were in touch by fax while cargo was being loaded. I conclude that the carrier, and in particular the master, its agent, knew that damage to [the cargo] was probable and recklessly proceeded to stow the open top containers, [...] on deck.

[Attorney for the carrier] submitted that the recklessness and knowledge must be on the part of the carrier's management. I reject that. The recklessness and knowledge on the part of the master is what is in issue. However as I have said, [the charterers] in London were it seems kept fully informed and must have approved"[43].

So, here, the court reaches the conclusion that the carrier, himself, is also guilty of wilful misconduct. However, in doing so, the court first considers the conduct of the master and then afterwards proceeds to the contact between the master and the charterers. However, it is also true that the decision can be interpreted in both

---

[38] LG Hamburg, 16.01.2009, HmbSchRZ 2009, 88. See also OLG Hamburg, 07.09.2000, HmbSeeRep 2000, 185 ("*Hua Yin*" & "*Koyo Express*"); HansOLG Hamburg, 02.11.2000, TranspR 2001, 87 ("*New York Express*").

[39] *Bonelli*, pp. 185 *et seqq.*; *Tetley*, pp. 291-293, 1611-1612; *Puttfarken*, Rn. 262-263.

[40] *Basedow, Transportvertrag*, pp. 424-425; *Puttfarken*, Rn. 262.

[41] For more information about the case see *infra* A 1 1 c bb.

[42] *Nelson Pine Industries Ltd. v. Seatrans New Zealand Ltd.* (*The "Pembroke"*) [1995] 2 Lloyd's Rep. 290, 297 (New Zealand High Court) *per* Justice Ellis.

[43] *Nelson Pine Industries Ltd. v. Seatrans New Zealand Ltd.* (*The "Pembroke"*) [1995] 2 Lloyd's Rep. 290, 297 (New Zealand High Court) *per* Justice Ellis.

ways and can be understood as the court also holding the carrier responsible for the masters' conduct. If, in fact, the court decided so, this decision is not to be considered as consistent with the Hague/Visby Rules[44].

(2) Damage

The Hague/Visby Rules stipulate that the carrier will be deprived of the limits of liability if "... *the damage* resulted from an act or omission of the carrier done with intent to cause *damage*, or recklessly and with knowledge that *damage* would probably result"[45]. Clearly, the provision makes a clear distinction between the damage which has occurred and probable damages. Accordingly, liability limits will be lifted when the carrier was reckless and subjectively aware that damage would probably result. It is not necessary to show that the carrier was aware of the probability that the very damage was likely to occur[46].

However, under the Warsaw Convention, a distinction was made between physical injury to passengers and damage to property[47]. It was said that, due to the foresight criterion, foresight of the type or kind of damage is necessary for breaking the air carrier's liability limits[48]. Unlike the Warsaw Convention, the Hague/Visby Rules only cover loss or damage to cargo, not physical injury to persons. Therefore, the distinction found under the Warsaw Convention regime as to the type or kind of damage is not necessary under the Hague/Visby Rules. Thus, the carrier will lose his right to limit when he was reckless and subjectively aware that damage to cargo was likely to occur.

The second point to be emphasised is the exclusive reference to *damage* in Art. IV (5)(e), although the Hague/Visby Rules always mention *loss or damage* in various provisions[49]. Special attention should be drawn to Art. IV (5)(a) which establishes the limits of the carrier's liability. Like other provisions, this provision also speaks of "any *loss or damage* to or in connection with the goods"[50]. Accordingly, it is asserted that the carrier is liable up to the full amount only in cases of damage to cargo; in other words, his liability limits are unbreakable in cases of loss of cargo since Art. IV (5)(e) restricts the general application of Art. IV (5)(a) only to cases of damage. Notably, also the term *in any event* is taken into account; the provision does not deprive the carrier of the right to limit in cases of loss of cargo since damage under the Hague/Visby Rules only refers to physical damage to goods and does not cover loss[51]. A similar question arises in cases of monetary

---

44   *Gaskell/Asariotis/Baatz*, para. 16.53; *Sellers Fabrics Pty. Ltd. v. Hapag-Lloyd AG* [1998] NSWSC 646 (Supreme Court of New South Wales); *The "Tasman Pioneer"* [2003] 2 Lloyd's Rep. 713, 722 (New Zealand High Court) *per* Justice Williams.
45   Emphasis added.
46   *Griggs/Williams/Farr*, p. 154; *Gaskell/Asariotis/Baatz*, para. 16.53; see also *Tetley*, p. 906.
47   Art. 17-18 of the Warsaw Convention.
48   See *supra* § 4 B I 2 c bb (2) (c).
49   *E.g.* Art. III (5), III (6), III (8), IV, IV *bis* (1), VII.
50   Emphasis added.
51   *Griggs/Williams/Farr*, pp. 153-154; *Cooke/et al.*, para. 85.419.

loss. Assume that due to the insolvency of the carrier goods on board were sold under judicial sale; and, further, that the carrier knew that the ship was to be arrested and that everything on board was to be sold[52]. If other prerequisites are also present, will the carrier lose his right to limit? According to the view which restricts the application of Art. IV (5)(e) to damage cases alone, this question must be answered in the negative.

Such a literal interpretation is not consistent with the system of the Rules. First of all, there are no historical or commercial grounds to make a distinction between the damage to and loss of cargo cases. Second, the exclusive usage of the term "damage" can be explained from the historical background of the provision. As is known, the provision was taken from the Warsaw Convention Art. 25, which equally only referred to *damage*. It is unanimously accepted that the term "damage" under the Warsaw Convention Art. 25 refers both to personal injury and physical loss[53]; therefore, no interpretation problem occurred. It would not be wrong to say that the term "damage" under the Hague/Visby Rules should also be interpreted in such a way that it covers every type and kind of damage which can occur during the carriage of goods by sea and which is, at the same time, covered by the Hague/Visby Rules, *i.e.* loss of or damage to cargo and delay. In fact, if the literature is read carefully, it can be seen that most of the writers mention both of the terms, *i.e.* "loss or damage" with regard to the unlimited liability under the Hague/Visby Rules[54]. Moreover, in the *Titan Scan* case, while discussing whether the crew foresaw the probable result, the court did not have any doubts whether the total loss of the cargo (the cargo was thrown overboard) was covered by Art. IV (5)(e) of the Hague/Visby Rules[55].

c) Particulars

The function of the provision regarding wilful misconduct of the carrier is only to increase the amount of the compensation to be paid by the carrier. Therefore, it does not have any effect on the applicability of the Rules. However, there are some cases where the Hague/Visby Rules are not applicable and, consequently, the carrier cannot rely on the rules and therefore cannot limit his liability. Furthermore, there are some cases where the carrier is held presumably liable or where he is not held liable at all. Each of these situations is potentially confusing,

---

[52] John *Kooyman*, Cargo Claims Recoveries, in: The Hague-Visby Rules and the Carriage of Goods by Sea Act, 1971 (Seminar held on 8 December, 1977), London 1977, pp. 4-5.

[53] See *supra* § 4 B I 2 c bb (2) (c).

[54] *Chen*, p. 201; *Richter-Hannes/Trotz*, p. 19. *Carver*, para. 9-270 states clearly his doubt: "It is not clear why only the word "damage" is used and *what effect, if any, this has*." [Emphasis added]. In German version of the Convention, the term "Schaden" or "Schädigung" are used, which covers both loss of and damage to cargo. See *Puttfarken*, Rn. 256-257; *Rabe*, § 607a, Rn. 20-22; *Basedow, Transportvertrag*, p. 424.

[55] *Itel Container Corporation v. M/V Titan Scan, et al.* (DC Georgia, 1996) 1997 A.M.C. 1568, 1584 *per* Justice Edenfield.

and can also be coupled with the wilful misconduct provision, and is therefore worth to analysing.

aa) Geographical deviation

Art. IV (4) of the Hague/Visby Rules reads "any deviation in saving or attempting to save life or property at sea or any reasonable deviation shall not be deemed to be an infringement or breach of this Convention or of the contract of carriage, and the carrier shall not be liable for any loss or damage resulting therefrom". Therefore, any unreasonable deviation makes the carrier liable for the damage caused by the deviation.

Any voluntary departure from the usual route constitutes deviation. If the parties did not agree on the precise route to be followed, it is the usual and customary route[56]. The ship can deviate only if there is a reasonable ground for it, such as to save or attempt to save life or property at sea as clearly stated in the provision, so that the carrier is not liable for the damages arising from this deviation. A reasonable ground is, for example, avoiding imminent peril[57]. Nevertheless, it falls in the courts' discretion to analyse the particular circumstances of each case and decide whether the deviation was reasonable or not[58]. Weighing the reasonableness of a deviation was a task to be done with great care since, traditionally, any deviation rendered cargo insurance null and void and, thus, left the cargo uninsured[59]. However, cargo owners today can obtain insurance cover also in cases of deviation[60].

Although unreasonable deviation constitutes infringement or breach of the Hague/Visby Rules, the sanction to be applied to this infringement has generated opposing views. Some allege that infringement or breach of contract deprives the carrier of reliance on the provisions of the carriage contract. Therefore, the carrier cannot rely on the defences and limits of liability provided in the Rules[61]. However, the counterview asserts that the carrier is entitled to limit his liability "in any

---

[56] *Dockray*, pp. 64-65; *Carver*, para. 9-036; *Cooke/et al.*, para. 12.2; *Aikens/Lord/Bools*, para. 10.265; *Tetley*, pp. 1811-1812; *Schoenbaum*, V. I, p. 711; *Wilson*, p. 16; *von Ziegler*, p. 189; *Çağa/Kender*, p. 55. See also *Cunard Steamship Co. Ltd. v. Buerger* [1927] A.C. 1 = (1926) 25 Ll. L. Rep. 215 (HL); *Reardon Smith Line v. Black Sea and Baltic General Insurance Company* [1939] A.C. 562 = (1939) 64 Ll. L. Rep. 229 (HL).

[57] *Dockray*, p. 67; *Ping-fat*, p. 108; *von Ziegler*, p. 198.

[58] *Carver*, para. 9-041 *et seq.*; *Hill*, pp. 273-274; *Tetley*, pp. 1813 *et seqq.*; *Stachow*, p. 115; *Stag Line Ltd. v. Foscolo, Mango & Co. Ltd.* [1932] A.C. 328 = (1931) 41 Ll. L. Rep. 165 (HL). For some examples see *Cooke/et al.*, para. 12.4 *et seqq.*

[59] *Ping-fat*, p. 109; *Carver*, para. 9-037; *Stachow*, p. 109.

[60] See Institute Cargo clauses (A) – The "All Risks" Form (1/1/82), Clause 8.3: "The insurance shall remain in force [...] during delay beyond the control of the Assured, *any deviation*, forced discharge, reshipment or transhipment and during any variation of the adventure arising from the exercise of a liberty granted to shipowners or charterers under the contract of affreightment." [Emphasis added].

[61] *Puttfarken*, Rn. 239, 282; *Tetley*, pp. 253-257, 1830-1832; *Schoenbaum*, V. I, p. 713.

event". Therefore he still can rely on the limits even if he is in breach of the contract of carriage[62]. The first view must be accepted since there is a substantial breach of the carriage contract. When the carrier is in breach of the carriage contract which is governed by the Rules, he cannot rely on the defences and limits of liability provided in the Rules. The "in any event" provision is applicable, when the provision regarding limitation of liability could be applied[63]. Therefore the carrier loses his right to limit in cases of unauthorised deviation, just as he does in the wilful misconduct cases.

A voluntary deviation, although being a fundamental breach of contract, does not necessarily amount to wilful misconduct since the intention as to the deviation does not necessarily equal an intention to cause damage[64] although the deviation would constitute misconduct. However, if the carrier orders the ship to deviate from its usual route and if he is subjectively aware that the deviation will probably cause cargo damage, then he is guilty of wilful misconduct as well[65]. Suppose that there is food cargo on board which would become stale if it is not delivered within a certain period. Further, assume that the carrier orders a change in the usual route to load another cargo and that the deviation causes damage to the food cargo. The carrier would be liable without any financial limits if he is aware of the existence of the food cargo on board and the necessity to deliver it within a certain time period and is aware of the results of late delivery.

bb) Carriage on deck

It is common knowledge that if cargo is carried on deck, it is exposed to the sea and weather conditions. This makes carriage on deck a substantial risk for the cargo owners[66]. Therefore, Art. I (c) of the Hague/Visby Rules clearly states that the Convention is not applicable to the goods carried on deck if the shipper authorises the carrier for such a carriage. As it is generally accepted, the carrier cannot rely on the Hague/Visby Rules, if he loads goods on deck without the consent of shipper or cargo owner[67]. Undoubtedly, carriage on deck without the consent of shipper or cargo owner constitutes "misconduct"[68].

---

[62]   *Scrutton*, p. 406; *Diamond*, 246-247; *Carver*, para. 9-248; *Aikens/Lord/Bools*, para. 10.284, 10.307; *Cooke/et al.*, para. 85.361.
[63]   *Tetley*, p. 1834.
[64]   *Chen*, p. 203.
[65]   *Diamond*, 246; *Yetiş Şamlı*, p. 147.
[66]   *Ping-fat*, p. 127; *Rabe*, § 566 Rn. 1; *Hill*, p. 188.
[67]   Generally based on the "unreasonable deviation" or "fundamental breach" doctrine, see *Tetley*, pp. 258-259, 268, 275-276, 1578, 1581-1583; *Schoenbaum*, V. I, p. 661; *Puttfarken*, Rn. 239; *Rabe*, § 566 Rn. 19; *Stachow*, pp. 112-115; *Wibau Maschinenfabric Hartman S.A. and Another v. Mackinnon Mackenzie & Co. (The Chanda)* [1989] 2 Lloyd's Rep. 494 (QBD). However see also *Cooke/et al.*, para. 85.71; *Aikens/Lord/Bools*, para. 10.76; *Asariotis*, 150-151; *Daewoo Heavy Industries Ltd. and Another v. Klipriver Shipping Ltd. and Another (The "Kapitan Petko Voivoda")* [2003] 2 Lloyd's Rep. 1 (CA).
[68]   *Rabe*, § 607a Rn. 24.

An interesting example with regard to carriage on deck and wilful misconduct is the *Pembroke* case. On a carriage from Germany to New Zealand, the cargo of roller chains packed in open top containers were loaded on the vessel Pembroke and stowed under deck. However, contrary to the shipper's instructions, the Pembroke called into a port in Brazil which was not on her route to New Zealand. And at that port, a cargo of paper, which had to be stowed below deck, was loaded on the Pembroke. In order to stow the paper cargo below deck, some of the open top containers were displaced and stowed on deck. Stowage on deck was ordered by the master; however, the carrier and the master were in touch during the loading in Brazil. Due to the heavy weather conditions on the voyage, roller chains in one of the containers, which were stowed on deck became corroded. Plaintiffs claimed the full amount of their loss due to the corrosion damage.

New Zealand High Court decided in favour of the plaintiffs and stated that the Hague/Visby Rules were not applicable due to the carriage on deck. Therefore, the carrier could not avail himself of the provisions of the Hague/Visby Rules. However, the court further stated that even if the Rules were applicable, the carrier's liability would be unlimited due to reckless conduct with knowledge that such damage would probably result. Since the carrier was at all times in touch with the master and the master ordered the loading on deck after the carrier's approval, the carrier was aware of the misconduct. Furthermore, since heavy weather was expected, the carrier was also aware that the actual damage incurred, *i.e.* the corrosion damage, was probable[69].

cc) Unseaworthiness

Art. III (1) of the Hague/Visby Rules provides that the carrier shall exercise due diligence to (a) make the ship seaworthy, (b) properly man[70], equip and supply the ship, and (c) make the holds and all other parts of the ship in which goods are carried fit and safe for the reception, carriage and preservation. In other words, the carrier is required to provide a ship which is fit for the intended voyage. This duty of the carrier is known as the "duty to provide a seaworthy ship"[71].

As the provision clearly stipulates, the carrier's duty is to exercise due diligence. Therefore, the carrier is not liable for defects which were not reasonably

---

[69] *Nelson Pine Industries Ltd. v. Seatrans New Zealand Ltd. (The "Pembroke")* [1995] 2 Lloyd's Rep. 290 (New Zealand High Court).

[70] See Roger *White*, The Human Factor in Unseaworthiness Claims, [1995] LMCLQ 221.

[71] For the examples of unseaworthiness see *Carver*, para. 9-015; *Schoenbaum*, V. I, p. 685; *Tetley*, pp. 907 *et seqq.*; The necessities set by Art. III (1)(a)-(b) of the Hague Rules are called "seaworthiness" and the necessity set by Art. III (1)(c) is called "cargoworthiness" under German (HGB § 559) and Turkish law (TTK (1956) Art. 817, TTK (2011) Art. 932). For more information see *Puttfarken*, Rn. 155, 162; *Rabe*, § 559; *Herber*, pp. 313-314; *Çağa/Kender*, pp. 18-19; *Tekil*, pp. 275-277. Under common law, seaworthiness covers both terms, see *Cooke/et al.*, para. 85.94; *Carver*, para. 9-016, 9-139; *Aikens/Lord/Bools*, para. 10.91; *Schoenbaum*, V. I, pp. 681-682; *Davies/Dickey*, p. 333.

discoverable and to whose presence he has not contributed[72]. However, if the defects were to be discovered and remedied under the "reasonable/prudent carrier" criterion[73], the carrier is in breach of his duty. Nonetheless, the breach of the duty to provide a seaworthy ship leads only to the liability of the carrier and is not related to the amounts for which he is liable[74].

An example is the *Eurasian Dream* case. The Eurasian Dream was a pure car carrier on which a fire broke out during the discharging operations. The fire caused the total loss of the vessel and damage to her cargo. Cargo interests sued the carrier alleging that the vessel was unseaworthy due to her unfitness and the incompetency of her master and crew. The court decided in favour of the claimants stating that "a reasonably prudent" carrier would not have put her to sea with such an incompetent master and crew. Nevertheless, the court did not discuss whether the carrier should be liable beyond the financial limits[75].

However, the conduct of the carrier which renders the ship unseaworthy may have results as to the limitation of liability. Following the example of the *Eurasian Dream*, if the carrier had foreseen that a fire was likely to break out due to the unseaworthy condition of the vessel and that her master and crew were not capable of handling the fire properly, the carrier's subjective awareness and unlimited liability could have been at issue.

Another example for the unseaworthiness of a ship and unlimited liability of carrier would be the *Nicholas H*. The Nicholas H set sail from America to Europe with a cargo of lead and zinc. 14 days after the beginning of the voyage, a crack was found in her hull. The vessel immediately entered the nearest port. While she was anchored, further cracks developed. The owners contacted the vessel's classification society. The surveyor from the classification society examined the vessel and reported that the cargo on board should be discharged and permanent repairs done in drydock. Instead, however, the owners indicated a preference for temporary repairs and, somehow, the surveyor agreed that the vessel could continue the intended voyage but should be further examined after discharging her cargo. On 2 March 1986 the vessel sailed. As early as the next day, the welding of the repairs cracked. Further repairs were attempted at sea but the Nicholas H sank with all her cargo on 9 March. Cargo was carried under the Hague Rules which lack the provision for unlimited liability due to wilful misconduct; thus, the cargo owners sued the owners of the vessel and her classification society[76]. This case is

---

[72] *Ping-fat*, p. 47; *Baughen*, pp. 119-122; *Aikens/Lord/Bools*, para. 10.117 *et seqq.*; *Çağa/Kender*, pp. 177-178.

[73] A carrier who shows genuine, competent and reasonable effort to prevent casualty, see *Scrutton*, p. 388; *Ping-fat*, pp. 52-53; *Carver*, para. 9-014.

[74] *Tetley*, pp. 903-904; *Puttfarken*, Rn. 156, 239; *Asariotis*, 150.

[75] *Papera Traders Co. Ltd. v. Hyundai Merchant Marine Co. Ltd.* (*The "Eurasian Dream"*) [2002] 1 Lloyd's Rep. 719 (QBD). For a similar decision involving the relationship between seaworthiness and an incompetent crew see *Sanko Steamship Co Ltd v. Sumitomo Australia Ltd* 63 FCR 227 (Federal Court of Australia, 1995).

[76] For decisions see *Marc Rich & Co. A.G. and Others v. Bishop Rock Marine Co. Ltd., Bethmarine Co. Ltd. and Nippon Kaiji Kyokai* (*The "Nicholas H"*) [1992] 2 Lloyd's Rep. 481 (QBD); *Marc Rich & Co. A.G. and Others v. Bishop Rock*

basically related to the liability of a classification society[77], but its facts can be assessed as concerns wilful misconduct and the unlimited liability of a carrier under the Hague/Visby Rules.

It is clear that the Nicholas H was unseaworthy. It is also clear that the owner knew of her unseaworthy condition. So, there was misconduct in putting an unseaworthy vessel onto the sea and subjective awareness as to this misconduct was also present. The second stage would be the examination of whether the owners would have known that the Nicholas H would *probably* sink. It can be said from the facts of the case that the owners were aware that the vessel's sinking was more likely than not if the temporary repairs did not prove sufficient. If the carriage had been conducted under the Hague/Visby Rules and if the subjective awareness element were established, the court could have ruled against the shipowners for unlimited liability.

Another important point to be discussed with regard to the unseaworthiness is the *prima facie* inference of unseaworthiness. It is accepted that the cause of a ship's sinking is her unseaworthy condition when she sinks without an apparent reason[78]. Furthermore, it is also accepted that cargo interests can rely on the unseaworthiness being inferred as the cause of the loss or damage[79]. However, this inference should be carefully distinguished from wilful misconduct with regard to unseaworthiness. As will be discussed later[80], wilful misconduct cannot be presumed. So, if a ship sinks without a clear reason, inference of her unseaworthiness results in the limited liability of the carrier under the Hague/Visby Rules if the carrier did not fulfil his due diligence duty. Nevertheless, if the ship's unseawor-

---

Marine Co. Ltd., Bethmarine Co. Ltd. and Nippon Kaiji Kyokai (The "Nicholas H") [1994] 1 Lloyd's Rep. 492 (CA); Marc Rich & Co. A.G. and Others v. Bishop Rock Marine Co. Ltd., Bethmarine Co. Ltd. And Nippon Kaiji Kyokai (The "Nicholas H") [1995] 2 Lloyd's Rep. 299 (HL).

[77] For further information about and discussion of the case see Jürgen *Basedow*/ Wolfgang *Wurmnest*, Third-Party Liability of Classification Societies, Berlin 2005, pp. 17-20; Nicolai *Lagoni*, The Liability of Classification Societies, Berlin 2007, pp. 113-125; *Hodges/Hill*, pp. 44-45; *Mandaraka-Sheppard*, pp. 525-528; Coleen E. *Feehan*, Liability of Classification Societies from British Perspective: The Nicholas H, (1997) 22 Tul. Mar. L. J. 163; Tim *Howard*/Brian *Devenport*, English Maritime Law Update 1994/95, (1996) 27 J. Mar. L. & Com. 427, 448-449; Michael *Wood*/David H. *Reissner*, No Duty of Care Owed by Classification Societies, Int. I.L.R. 1996, 30; Maria *Oats*, Cargo Insurance – Liability for Negligence, Int. I.L.R. 1995, G209; Michael *Wood*/David *Reissner*, Duty of Care in English Law: The Tort of Negligence v The Doctrine of Binding Precedent, Int. I.L.R. 1994, 351; Peter *Cane*, Classification Societies, Cargo Owners and the Basis of Tort Liability, [1995] LMCLQ 433; Peter *Holtappels*, "Haftung von Klassifikationsgesellschaften", Hansa 2002 (9), 67, 70; Russell *Harling*, The Liability of Classification Societies to Cargo Owners: The Nicholas H, [1993] LMCLQ 1.

[78] *Tetley*, pp. 900-901; *Carver*, para. 9-023; *Aikens/Lord/Bools*, para. 10.88.

[79] *Davies/Dickey*, p. 334; *Dockray*, p. 47; *Rabe*, § 559 Rn. 40; *Aikens/Lord/Bools*, para. 10.88; *Wilson*, pp. 191.

[80] See *infra* § 7 B II.

thy condition can be shown and if, additionally, there is actual knowledge on the part of the carrier regarding the unseaworthy condition of a ship and the probability of sinking, the carrier cannot avail himself of the limitation of liability provisions of the Hague/Visby Rules.

The *Tuxpan* case is a clear example of joinder of unseaworthiness and wilful misconduct. The Tuxpan, a container ship, was suffering from cracks in several parts which had began on the 3rd day following her delivery and had increased both by width and number year by year. Additional to the cracking problem she was also suffering from engine problems which necessitated that the engine be stopped, for at least an hour, and restarted while at sea. Both the crack and engine problems had never been reported to the ship's classification society Germanischer Lloyd; on the contrary, the shipowner made his best effort to conceal necessary information regarding the unseaworthy condition from the classification society. The Tuxpan, unfortunately, sunk without a trace with all her crew and cargo on her voyage through the North Atlantic during wintertime after encountering heavy weather and sea conditions. The court concluded that the unexplainable sinking of the Tuxpan was caused by unseaworthiness and that the shipowner did not fulfil his duty to make his ship seaworthy and was, therefore, liable to the cargo owners. Moreover, the court stated that the shipowner's conduct was a clear example of a continuous course of recklessness and that he was well aware of the likelihood of damage, namely sinking, to a ship crossing the North Atlantic during winter. Therefore, the court held the shipowner, being the carrier at the same time, liable up to the full value of the cargo which was on board the ship on her last voyage[81].

Another example of unseaworthiness and wilful misconduct is the *Clan Gordon*. Although the case was discussed mostly on the unseaworthiness issue, the facts serve as a good illustration. The Clan Gordon was unusually constructed. For her to be stable, two of her 6 ballast tanks needed to be full. This necessity was brought to the knowledge of the owners when the vessel was delivered. However, the owners took no steps to inform her master on this point. The vessel set sail as two of her ballast tanks were full. However, after two days the master, being unaware of the special circumstances regarding the stability, ordered the two ballast tanks to be pumped empty. Not surprisingly, the vessel sank[82]. It is clear that the failure to inform the master would result in such an outcome. Therefore, the owners were guilty of wilful misconduct.

d)   Actual fault or privity

Art. IV (2)(q) of the Hague/Visby Rules provides that the carrier shall not be liable for loss or damage arising or resulting from any cause arising without the actual fault or privity of the carrier or the fault or neglect of his servants and agents. Accordingly, the carrier will be responsible for loss or damage caused with

---

[81]   *In re Tecomar S.A.* (DC New York, 1991) 765 F.Supp. 1150.
[82]   *Standard Oil Company of New York v. Clan Line Steamers Limited* 17 Ll. L. Rep. 120 (HL).

his or his servants' and agents' actual fault or privity. However, this provision, like the provision regarding seaworthiness, is not related to the amount of the limitation of the carrier's liability; rather it only states that the carrier will be liable. A similar approach has been taken for damage and loss caused by fire. According to Art. IV (2)(b) of the Hague/Visby Rules, the carrier is not responsible for the damage or loss caused by fire unless the fire was caused by the actual fault or privity of the owner.

Some writers assert that the terms "actual fault or privity" and "wilful misconduct" are equal to each other and, therefore, if damage or loss is caused by a reason within the carrier's actual fault or privity, the carrier must be automatically deprived of the limitation of liability[83]. However, as generally accepted, the carrier will be liable under Art. IV (2)(b) and (q) if he is grossly negligent, *i.e.* if he violates his duty of care in a grave manner. Subjective knowledge is not necessary for a finding of "actual fault or privity" of the carrier. It is enough to show that the carrier *ought to have* acted like a reasonable carrier, but failed to do so[84]. Therefore, even if the carrier is liable for loss or damage as a result of his actual fault or privity, this does not necessarily mean that he is not entitled to rely on the limitation provisions.

e) Inadequate organisational structure (*Organisationsverschulden*)

An important principle developed by German case law needs to be mentioned here. According to Art. III (2) of the Hague/Visby Rules, the carrier is under the obligation of properly and carefully loading, handling, stowing, carrying, keeping, caring for, and discharging the goods carried. German courts ruled that, in order to fulfil this fundamental obligation, every carrier must have a properly organised operational structure. If there are any shortcomings in the operational structure, this can result in the liability of the carrier. How the carriage needs to be organised, and what precautions need to be taken in order to ensure the carriage of goods without any damage, will depend on the facts of each case. Necessary precautions are not the same in cases of, for instance, high value and non-valuable cargo[85].

The selection of the crew, and other agents and servants plays an important role in the operational organisation. A carrier, at the same time a shipowner, cannot rely on the navigational fault exemption, if he has hired a master who is well

---

[83]   *Carver*, para. 9-212, 9-230 (however, still accepting that wilful misconduct requires more culpable conduct at para. 9-270); *Ping-fat*, p. 142 fn. 257.

[84]   *Hill*, p. 272; *Aikens/Lord/Bools*, para. 10.210; *Cooke/et al.*, para. 85.347; *Rabe*, § 607 Rn. 28-29; *Hodges, ISM Code*, 58: "… whilst there is a sea between privity and recklessness, there is a whole ocean between privity and wilful misconduct". For more information see *infra* C II 1. For a comparison of the phrases "actual fault or privity" and "wilful misconduct" in the marine insurance context see *Compania Maritime San Basilio S.A. v. The Oceanus Mutual Underwriting Association (Bermuda) Ltd. (The "Eurysthenes")* [1976] 2 Lloyd's Rep. 171.

[85]   *Ramming*, 305.

known for his alcohol addiction, and is not capable of controlling a ship[86]. Similarly, instruction and supervision of the agents and servants are also important in determining whether the organisational structure functions properly[87].

If a certain type of damage or loss occurs repeatedly, and the carrier does not take any precautions to prevent similar damage or loss, this leads also to the conclusion that the carrier's organisational structure is inadequate. It, further, shows that the carrier had, at least, blind eye knowledge[88] as to the repeating loss or damage. In other words, the supervision and improvement measures are also important legs of a proper organisational structure in the carriage of goods[89].

Inadequate organisational structure is considered as the carrier's personal fault; in other words, it is distinct from his vicarious liability for his servants and agents. It is, further, distinct from the issue of determining whose fault in a corporate structure can be attributed to the corporation itself[90]. Nevertheless, the sole fact of an inadequate organisational structure is not sufficient for a finding of recklessness coupled with the actual knowledge. Recklessness and subjective knowledge as to the probable damage or loss needs to be proven as well. The ground of inadequate organisational structure is of general character for the personal fault of the carrier, and therefore, is applicable not only to the carriage of goods, but also to the carriage of passengers and also in cases of the global limitation. Nevertheless, case law has mostly developed in the field of the carriage of goods.

In the *Trade Harvest* case, the facts of which were mentioned earlier[91], the claimants alleged that the carrier has an inadequate organisational structure, since he delivered the goods to a person other than the rightful holders of the bill of lading. The court ruled that there is no inadequacy on the side of the carrier's organisation, since the carrier had rightfully presumed that the third person is entitled to accept the delivery the goods[92].

In the *Caribia Express* case, the German court also ruled in favour of the carrier. The dispute has arisen from the carriage of three military trucks equipped with radar systems from Sweden to Venezuela. The carrier and the shipper had expressly decided on the carriage under deck. After the trucks were delivered, it was found out that the radar equipment on them was not functioning due to the corrosion damage. After further investigation, it was understood that the trucks had been carried not under deck, but on deck, although the bill of lading was issued that the trucks were "shipped under deck". The loading and stowage of the ship was done by the stevedores. The stevedores, during the stowage operation, noticed that the trucks were oversize and had excess width, of which they were not informed. Without asking the carrier or the shipper, they changed the stowage plan and loaded the trucks on deck. The claimant alleged that loading on deck without

[86] *Atamer, 1976 ve 1992 Sözleşmeleri*, p. 898.
[87] *Ramming*, 305.
[88] For the term see *supra* § 4 B I 2 c bb (2).
[89] *Ramming*, 305.
[90] See *infra* E I.
[91] See *supra* A I 1 b bb.
[92] LG Stuttgart, 21.07.2000, TranspR 2001, 41 (44-45) (*"Trade Harvest"*).

consulting them shows that the carrier's organisational structure was inadequate to fulfil his obligations. The court took into account that the carrier is a big company which has more than 4000 employees and operates more than 170 ships. In such a big company, transport operations will be managed based on the instructions given by the higher management level. The company, indeed, had clear instructions that the demands of the customers are to be followed strictly, and if it is not possible, how to solve the problem needs to be decided after the consultation with them. The company, after giving such clear instructions, can rightfully expect that they will be followed by all his employees or independent contractors. Nonetheless, it would be possible to find an inadequate organisational structure, if the instruction would be to the contrary, *i.e.* to ignore the demands of the customers if it is possible to reach a bigger transport capacity. Furthermore, the delegation of the stowage does constitute neither inadequacy in the organisation nor personal fault of the carrier. Even if the stowage were done by the carrier, it would not be done by the higher management of the company, but by the servants of the carrier whose reckless acts or omission is insufficient for the unlimited liability of the carrier[93].

Similarly, in a recently decided case by the German Federal Court, the freight forwarder was not held liable without any financial limits for the damage occurred during the carriage by sea. A second hand car has been transported from Germany to Luanda, Angola. According to the contract for carriage, the car should have been transported in a container during the maritime carriage leg. The car was loaded onto a ship in Antwerp, and in Dakar it was transhipped to another one sailing to Luanda. However, when the car was unloaded in Luanda it was heavily damaged, since it was not carried in a container during the voyage from Antwerp to Dakar, and although it was carried in a container during the voyage from Dakar to Luanda, extra measures to fix the car in the container have not been taken. Though the German Federal Court did not mention inadequate organisational structure, it ruled that the freight forwarder gave necessary instructions to the maritime carrier, and that he can rightfully expect that these instructions will be followed. Moreover, the freight forwarder assigned agents at the port of loading and transhipment with the duty to observe and supervise the relevant operations. Due to the lack of the fundamental breach of any duties, it is not possible to rule that the freight forwarder acted recklessly[94]. Based on this decision, it is possible to say that if necessary instructions are given and necessary precautions are taken to supervise the operational procedure, allegation of inadequate organisational structure cannot be made.

The most recent case where the court held the carrier liable without any financial limits due to the inadequate organisational structure has arisen from the carriage of the gondola of a wind turbine from Denmark to Australia and back from Australia to Denmark. The carriage from Denmark to Portland, Australia was completed without any problems. However, during the carriage by land to the place of delivery, the gondola was damaged due to an accident, and therefore needed to be transported back to Denmark and be repaired. The cargo interests

---

[93]   HansOLG, 02.10.2008, HbgSchRZ 2009, 52 (59) ("*Caribia Express*").
[94]   BGH, 18.06.2009, TranspR 2009, 327.

made a separate contract for the carriage from Australia to Denmark. The damaged gondola was loaded onto a ship, and when the ship arrived in Hamburg, Germany (from where it should have been carried by road to Denmark), it was seen that the gondola was severely damaged. The gondola had fallen over together with the flat rack on which it was carried due to the insufficient lashing. The lashing was insufficient, because the weight of the gondola – almost 49 tonnes – was incorrectly given as 15 tonnes in the loading and stowage plans. The district court ruled that the carrier is entitled to limit his liability, since he was not personally at fault[95]. However, the Hanseatic Court of Appeal of Bremen reversed this decision. The Court of Appeal stated that the circumstances under which the weight of the gondola was incorrectly given in the loading and stowage plans cannot be explained by the carrier. The carrier, further, did not explain what kind of instructions he had given to prevent damages, if he has given any, and what kind of measures he has taken for supervising whether his instructions are followed. Since the carrier cannot provide any explanation, it leads to the conclusion that the damage is the result of the inadequate organisational structure[96]. Since this inadequacy is the personal fault of the carrier, he cannot limit his liability[97]. This decision has been affirmed by the German Federal Court without any material remark as to the Court of Appeal's conclusions[98]. It is correct, that the organisational structure of the carrier was inadequate, and that this inadequacy creates also a personal fault. However, unfortunately, the courts did not feel the need to discuss whether the carrier was subjectively aware of any probable damage to cargo.

2. Hamburg Rules

The disadvantageous position of the developing countries as shippers under the Hague/Visby regime and the developments in shipping, construction and navigation techniques triggered a revision of the existing system. However, the revision was made by UNCITRAL since CMI wished to maintain the legal principles set by the Hague/Visby Rules and the unification achieved by it. The draft prepared by UNCITRAL was submitted to the United Nations Conference on the Carriage of Goods by Sea held in Hamburg in 1978. The result was the United Nations Convention on the Carriage of Goods by Sea 1978, which is known as the Hamburg Rules[99].

Since the Hamburg Rules are more in favour of the shippers[100], the major maritime countries have not ratified them. Nor are the Rules incorporated into the

---

[95] LG Bremen, 30.11.2005, HmbSchRZ 2009, 326.

[96] For more information on the explanation duty under the procedural cooperation duty in German law see *infra* B II 2 a.

[97] HansOLG Bremen, 02.11.2006, HmbSchRZ 2009, 323.

[98] BGH, 29.07.2009, HmbSchRZ 2009, 316 = TranspR 2009, 331 = NJW-RR 2009, 1482.

[99] *Rabe*, Vor § 556 Rn. 6; *Ilse*, pp. 228-230.

[100] For a general comparison see Jane *Martineau*, Hague, Hague-Visby and Hamburg Rules, (1996) 1 IJOSL 12; Francis *Reynolds*, the Hague Rules, the Hague-Visby

contracts of carriage, *e.g.* as it has occurred with the incorporation of the Hague/Visby Rules by clauses paramount[101], because P&I clubs do not cover the liability arising out of the Hamburg Rules unless the application of the Rules is mandatory under the applicable law[102].

Although they have not yet been ratified by major maritime countries, the Rules are definitely a model for national laws as can be seen, for example in changes in the national maritime laws of Denmark, Finland, Norway and Sweden[103], and the maritime law section of the Turkish Commercial Code of 2011[104].

a) Liability and limitation of liability

As distinct from the Hague/Visby Rules' common law approach, the Hamburg Rules are drafted in a more civilian method[105]. The most important differences are in the period and basis of liability. Basically, the carrier is liable for loss of or damage to goods and also for delay in delivery if the cause of the damage, loss or delay occurred when the goods were in his charge at the port of loading, during the carriage and at the port of discharge (Art. 4-5)[106]. The burden of proving that he and his servants and agents took all necessary measures rests with the carrier (Art. 5). Some of the exemption cases in the Hague/Visby Rules, *i.e.* fire, live animals and carriage on deck, are specifically regulated (Art. 5 (4)-(5), 9)[107].

Art. 6 of the Rules sets out in detail the limits of liability[108]. Unlike the corresponding provision in the Hague/Visby Rules, Art. 6 does not state that the carrier

---

Rules, and the Hamburg Rules, (1990) 7 MLAANZ Journal 16. See also *Waldron*, 318-319.

[101] For more information see *Cooke/et al.*, para. 85.1-85.8; *Carver*, para. 9-083, 9-090; *Aikens/Lord/Bools*, para. 10.33-10.35; *Tetley*, pp. 9-10, 13-14, 79-82; *Wilson*, p. 210; *Mankowski, Transportverträge*, Rn. 2899 *et seqq.*

[102] *Rabe*, Vor § 556 Rn. 7.

[103] *Rabe*, Vor § 556 Rn. 7; *Yazıcıoğlu*, p. 12.

[104] Türk Ticaret Kanunu Tasarısı (Draft Turkish Commercial Code – together with the explanatory memorandum and with the report of the Judiciary Committee of the Turkish Parliament), accessible at <www.tbmm.gov.tr/sirasayi/donem23/yil01/ss96.pdf> (08.06.2010). For more information on the provisions of the Turkish Commercial Code of 2011 regarding transport law see Kerim *Atamer*, Reform des türkischen Transport- und Seefrachtrechts, TranspR 2010, 50 and Kerim *Atamer*, Reform des Seehandelsrechts im Entwurf des Türkischen Handelsgesetzbuchs, in: Yeşim *Atamer*/Klaus *Hopt* (Hrsg.), Kompatibilität des türkischen und europäischen Wirtschaftsrechts, Tübingen 2009, p. 91.

[105] *Yazıcıoğlu*, p. 66.

[106] For more information see *Lüddeke/Johnson*, pp. 8 *et seqq.*; *Richter-Hannes*, pp. 31 *et seqq.*; *Kienzle*, pp. 121 *et seqq.*; *Yazıcıoğlu*, pp. 74 *et seqq.*; *von Ziegler*, Rn. 333 *et seqq.*; *Basedow, Hamburger Regeln*, pp. 107-111; *Waldron*, 309-310.

[107] For more information *Lüddeke/Johnson*, pp. 13-14, 21-22; *Richter-Hannes*, pp. 61 *et seqq.*; *Yazıcıoğlu*, pp. 102 *et seqq.*; *Basedow, Hamburger Regeln*, pp. 108-109; *Waldron*, 310-313.

[108] For more information see *Lüddeke/Johnson*, pp. 15-18; *Richter-Hannes*, pp. 71 *et seqq.*; *Kienzle*, pp. 196 *et seqq.*

can limit his liability "in any event". Consequently, the interpretation problems posed by the term "in any event" have been prevented.

b) Loss of the right to limit

Art. 8 of the Hamburg Rules sets the conditions when a carrier loses his right to limit his liability. Pursuant to the provision "the carrier is not entitled to the benefit of the limitation of liability provided for in article 6 if it is proved that the loss, damage or delay in delivery resulted from an act or omission of the carrier done with the intent to cause such loss, damage or delay, or recklessly and with knowledge that such loss, damage or delay would probably result".

aa) Historical background

The Hamburg Rules revised the system set by the Hague/Visby Rules and made substantial changes to them. In this context, the provision regarding the breaking of the limits was also revised and a substantial change in the provision was suggested. However, after years of discussion, Art. 8 of the Rules ultimately employed the same principles as the Hague/Visby Rules.

UNCITRAL adopted a resolution and created a working group in 1969. The Working Group on International Shipping Legislation ("Working Group") was appointed to survey the international shipping legislation. The Working Group decided to first consider the issues arising from the carriage by sea under bills of lading[109]. During its work, the Working Group authored detailed reports, which provide necessary information on the historical background of the provision regarding the breaking of the limits.

The first report of the Working Group which mentions the breaking of the limits dates back to 1973. During its fifth session, the Working Group discussed the issue and a draft provision was prepared, together with the draft provisions regarding the limitation of liability[110]. The draft provision prepared by the Working Group reads as follows:

> "The carrier shall not be entitled to the benefit of the limitation of liability provided for in paragraph 1 of article A if it is proved that the damage was caused by *wilful misconduct*[111] of the carrier, or *of any of his servants or agents acting within the scope of their employment*. Nor shall any of the servants or agents of the carrier be entitled to the benefit of such limitation of liability with respect to damage caused by wilful misconduct on his part"[112].

---

[109] For more information see Working Group on International Legislation on Shipping; report on the work of the first session, 22-26 March 1971 (A/CN.9/55), UNCITRAL Yearbook 1971, pp. 133-137.

[110] For information on the discussion see *Sweeney*, 336-340 (Part II).

[111] The term "wilful misconduct" was found more favourable than its definition "intent to cause damage or recklessly and with knowledge that damage would probably cause" since it was asserted that the definition would cause more ambiguities and uncertainties, see *Bonelli*, p. 211.

[112] Emphasis and footnote added.

This text is the result of the idea that the carrier shall be fully responsible for the wilful misconduct of his servants and agents since the modern carriage is performed mostly by servants and agents, but not directly by the carrier himself[113]. Furthermore, it was pointed out that in transport conventions regarding carriage by air, rail and road, it is the carrier who is liable for wilful misconduct of his servants and agents, and that the ocean carrier's liability should be brought in conformity with the other transport conventions[114]. Nevertheless, the proposal encountered strong objections[115].

Further discussion on the provision was made during the subsequent sessions of the Working Group. During its eighth session, the Working Group decided to replace the term "wilful misconduct" with its definition. The same session witnessed much discussion on the issue of whether the limits of the carrier's liability should be broken in case of wilful misconduct of his servants and agents. According to the report, the Working Group was almost equally divided on the issue[116]. Nevertheless, the wording was changed to the following:

> "The carrier shall not be entitled to the benefit of the limitation of liability provided for in article 6 if it is proved that the damage resulted from an act or omission of the carrier, done with the intent to cause such damage, or recklessly and with knowledge that such damage would probably result. Nor shall any of the servants or agents of the carrier be entitled to the benefit of such limitation of liability with respect to damage resulting from an act or omission of such servants or agents, done with the intent to cause such damage, or recklessly and with knowledge that such damage would probably result"[117].

The text which was submitted to the Conference was finally adopted by UNCITRAL in its ninth session. The Commission, after considering the proposals[118], decided to change the draft provision due to the fact that modern carriers are corporate institutions, and adopted the following text:

> "1. The carrier shall not be entitled to the benefit of the limitation of liability provided for in the article 6 if it is proved that the loss, damage or delay resulted from an act or omission done with the intent to cause such loss, damage or delay, or recklessly and

---

[113] Report of the Working Group on International Legislation on Shipping on the work of its fifth session (New York, 5-16 February 1973) (A/CN.9/76), UNCITRAL Yearbook 1973, pp. 203-205.

[114] Report of the Secretary-General, second report on responsibility of ocean carriers for cargo: bills of lading (21 March 1973) (A/CN.9/76/Add.1), UNCITRAL Yearbook 1973, p. 170.

[115] Report of the Working Group on International Legislation on Shipping on the work of its fifth session (New York, 5-16 February 1973) (A/CN.9/76), UNCITRAL Yearbook 1973, p. 206.

[116] Report of the Working Group on International Legislation on Shipping on the work of its eighth session (New York, 10-21 February 1975) (A/CN.9/105), UNCITRAL Yearbook 1975, p. 237.

[117] See the Draft convention on the carriage of goods by sea (A/CN.9/105, Annex), UNCITRAL Yearbook 1975, pp. 246-252.

[118] See also *Sweeney*, 187-188 (Part V).

with knowledge that such loss, damage or delay would probably result, which was an act or omission of:

(a) The carrier himself, or

(b) An employee of the carrier other than the master and members of the crew, while exercising, within the scope of his employment, supervisory authority in respect of that part of the carriage during which such act or omission occurred, or

(c) An employee of the carrier, including the master or any member of the crew, while handling or caring for the goods within the scope of his employment.

2. Notwithstanding the provisions of paragraph 2 of article 7, a servant or agent of the carrier shall not be entitled to the benefit of the limitation of liability provided for in article 6 if it is proved that the loss, damage or delay resulted from an act or omission of such servant or agent, done with the intent to cause such loss, damage or delay or recklessly and with knowledge that such loss, damage or delay would probably result"[119].

This text is the one which was submitted to the Conference and on which the discussions were based. During the Conference held in Hamburg from the 6th to 31st of March 1978, draft article 8 led to heated debates. The issue was forwarded to a consultative group and was to be discussed together with liability and limitation of liability issues. Ultimately, the text which provides for breaking the liability limits only in case of the carrier's personal conduct was adopted by 64 votes to 3, with 9 abstentions[120].

bb) Differences in the wording

(1) Carrier and actual carrier

Art. 8 of the Hamburg Rules clearly refers only to the "carrier" himself. Together with the drafting history of the provision, this clear reference indicates that the carrier loses his right to limit only if he is personally guilty of wilful misconduct. Acts and omissions of his servants and agents do not suffice to deprive the carrier of the right to limit[121]. This is reflected also in the clear distinction between the Hamburg Rules provisions. Art. 8 only refers to the carrier, whereas the Rules

---

[119] Emphasis added; Report of the United Nations Commission on International Trade Law on the work of its ninth session (New York, 12 April – 7 May 1976) (A/31/17), UNCITRAL Yearbook 1976, pp. 43-44.

[120] Official Records of the United Nations Conference on the Carriage of Goods by Sea (Hamburg, 6-31 March 1978), New York 1981, 12th and 34th meetings of the First Committee, pp. 246-251, 348-352.

[121] *Scrutton*, p. 508; *Griggs/Williams/Farr*, p. 154; *Lüddeke/Johnson*, p. 20; *Richter-Hannes*, pp. 79-80; *Yazıcıoğlu*, p. 174; *Gaskell, Hamburg Rules*, p. 169; *Kienzle*, pp. 216-217; *von Ziegler*, pp. 216-217; *Stachow*, pp. 225-226; *Häußer*, p. 183; *CMI Colloquium, Hamburg Rules*, p. 49; *Yetiş Şamlı*, p. 150; however see notes as to the French version of the Hamburg Rules Art. 8 in *Gaskell, Hamburg Rules*, pp. 170-171. *Basedow, Hamburger Regeln*, p. 113 suggests that at least the fault of the senior executives, *e.g.* the master and ship officers, should be considered as the carrier's fault.

invariably refer to his servants and agents together with the carrier in cases where he is vicariously liable for their acts and omissions (Art. 5, 10)[122].

However, the Hamburg Rules also make a clear distinction between the carrier and the actual carrier. Both of the terms are defined separately under Art. 1 of the Hamburg Rules. Consequently, the question arises whether the term carrier in Art. 8 also covers the actual carrier. If the answer is the affirmative, the actual carrier also loses the right to limit in case of wilful misconduct. However, if the answer is negative, the carrier would not be able to limit his liability when he is guilty of wilful misconduct, whereas the actual carrier would be entitled to limit his liability in any case. Fortunately, Art. 10 (2) of the Rules states that all provisions regarding the responsibility of the carrier apply to the responsibility of the actual carrier for the carriage performed by him. Therefore, Art. 8 is applicable also to the actual carrier if he is guilty of wilful misconduct[123].

The last point to be discussed is whether the actual carrier's wilful misconduct will deprive the carrier of the right to limit. According to the drafting history of Art. 8, servants and agents of the carrier are clearly exempted for the purposes of breaking the carrier's liability limits. However, the actual carrier is neither servant nor agent. Moreover, Art. 10 (1) of the Hamburg Rules states that the carrier is responsible, in relation to the carriage performed by the actual carrier, for the acts and omissions of the actual carrier and of his servants and agents acting within the scope of their employment. So, is it possible to say that the wilful misconduct of the actual carrier is sufficient to deprive the carrier of the right to limit? On this point, the same method of interpretation as to servants and agents answers the question in the negative. According to the historical background and the drafting method of the Hamburg Rules, the intention of the drafters is clear: only his personal conduct will result in the carrier's unlimited liability. Furthermore, Art. 10 (1) also adopts the vicarious liability of the carrier for the actual carrier's servants and agents. If the vicarious liability were extended to wilful misconduct, the carrier would be liable without any limits where the actual carrier's servants and agents are guilty of wilful misconduct; yet he will not lose his right to limit when his servants and agents are guilty of wilful misconduct. Clearly, this result could not have been intended. Consequently, the wilful misconduct of the actual carrier will not deprive the carrier of the right to limit[124].

(2) Loss, damage or delay

Art. 8 of the Hamburg Rules stipulates that the carrier will be deprived of the limits when he is subjectively aware that "such loss, damage or delay would probably result". Since the wording of the provision is clear, there is no need to examine in detail whether foresight of any loss, damage or delay is sufficient to

---

[122] *Kienzle*, pp. 216-217.

[123] *Lüddeke/Johnson*, p. 20.

[124] *Scrutton*, p. 508; *Kienzle*, pp. 218-219; *Stachow*, pp. 238-239; for the counterview see *Richter-Hannes*, p. 87; *Ilse*, p. 244; *Yetiş Şamlı*, pp. 152-153.

deprive the carrier of the right to limit. The right to limit will be lost if the actual loss, damage or delay occurred has been foreseen by the carrier[125].

During the preparatory work of the Conference, the provision was drafted to read if "such damage" had been foreseen. Afterwards, it was suggested that the term "damage" should be replaced with "loss, damage and delay" in order to bring the unlimited liability provision into harmony with the carrier's liability provision[126], UNCITRAL changed the wording before submitting the draft Convention to the conference[127]. Therefore, the provision shall be read as "*such* loss, *such* damage or *such* delay", since the adjective "such" is used for all terms.

However, the term "such delay" can pose some problems in wilful misconduct cases. If there is delay caused by the carrier intentionally in order to protect cargo, *e.g.* to avoid a zone famous for piracy and armed robbery against ships, is the carrier guilty of wilful misconduct[128]? It is clear that the carrier cannot be held liable for intentional wrongdoing if he did not intend to cause the actual loss or damage occurred. Furthermore, delay itself is not a loss or damage. According to Art. 5 (1) of the Hamburg Rules, the carrier is liable for loss "resulting from loss of or damage to the goods, as well as from delay in delivery". Therefore, the carrier would lose his right to limit if the loss within the meaning of Art. 5 (1) resulted from an act or omission of the carrier done with the intent to cause *such loss caused by delay*, or recklessly and with knowledge that *such loss caused by delay* would probably result[129].

(3) Carriage on deck

Carriage on deck is specifically regulated under the Hamburg Rules. According to Art. 9 of the Rules, the carrier is entitled to carry the goods on deck if carrying such goods on deck is the custom of a particular trade (*e.g.* containers except open-top containers) or is necessary under the statutory rules or regulations. Moreover, the carrier and shipper can enter into an agreement with regard to carriage on deck (Art. 9 (1)). The agreement need not be express or in writing[130]; however, if there is no written agreement as to the carriage on deck, the carrier should prove the authorisation for the carriage on deck (Art. 9 (2)). It is generally accepted that the liberty clauses in bills of lading or contracts of carriage even if

---

[125] *Griggs/Williams/Farr*, p. 155; *Gaskell, Hamburg Rules*, p. 166; *Wilson*, p. 222; *CMI Colloquium, Hamburg Rules*, p. 49.

[126] Report of the Secretary-General: analysis of comments by Governments and international organisations on the draft Convention on the Carriage of Goods by Sea (A/CN.9/110), UNCITRAL Yearbook 1976, p. 282.

[127] Report of the United Nations Commission on International Trade Law on the work of its ninth session (New York, 12 April – 7 May 1976) (A/31/17), UNCITRAL Yearbook 1976, p. 44.

[128] *Gaskell, Hamburg Rules*, p. 167.

[129] *Scrutton*, p. 508; *Gaskell, Hamburg Rules*, p. 167.

[130] *Ping-fat*, p. 133; *Yazıcıoğlu*, p. 106.

they are in fine print, will have that effect as a result of Art. 15 (1)(m)[131] of the Rules and the difference between the terms "agreement" and "express agreement" in Art. 9[132].

As distinct from the Hague/Visby Rules, goods to be carried on deck are not exempted from the scope of the Hamburg Rules. If the carriage on deck is in accordance with Art. 9 (1)-(2) conditions, the carrier is not liable for the damage, loss or delay only to the extent that such damage, loss or delay was caused solely by the carriage on deck[133]. Consequently, the carrier will be liable for all other damages, loss or delay under Art. 5 (1) which was not caused by the carriage on deck, but caused by the breach of the duty arising from Art. 5 (1)[134]. If the carriage on deck is not in accordance with Art. 9 (1)-(2), then the carrier is liable for the loss, damage or delay caused by the carriage on deck as well. However, his liability is to be determined pursuant to the financial limitation provisions[135].

Furthermore, if the carriage on deck is contrary to Art. 9 (1)-(2), the cargo interests have the opportunity to prove that the damage, loss or delay was the result of the wilful misconduct of the carrier (Art. 9 (3)). However, in this case, the claimants need to prove the intentional or reckless conduct as stated in Art. 8 of the Hamburg Rules[136].

The result of carriage on deck contrary to an *express* agreement requiring carriage below deck is, however, different. Pursuant to Art. 9 (4) of the Hamburg Rules, if loss of or damage to the goods is caused by the carriage on deck contrary to an *express* agreement, the loss or damage is deemed to be caused by an act or omission done with the intent to cause such loss or damage, or recklessly and with the knowledge that such loss or damage would probably result. The core issue here would be whether there was an express agreement between the shipper and the carrier[137]. If there was an express agreement, the carrier's liability would be unlimited in case of a loss caused by carriage on deck, whereas his liability would be limited if the carrier could not prove that there was an agreement as to the carriage on deck – unless the cargo owners can prove that he is guilty of wilful misconduct.

3. Rotterdam Rules

Due to the wish to standardise and update the existing rules regarding the carriage of goods by sea under a single international instrument and to solve the problems caused by the issues which were not regulated either by international conventions

---

[131] "1. The bill of lading must include, *inter alia*, the following particulars: [...] (*m*) the statement, if applicable, that the goods shall or may be carried on deck".

[132] *Scrutton*, p. 509; *Tetley*, p. 1615; *Ping-fat*, p. 133; *Yazıcıoğlu*, pp. 106-107.

[133] *Richter-Hannes*, p. 66; *Yazıcıoğlu*, pp. 110-111, for the counterview see *Lüddeke/Johnson*, p. 23.

[134] *Richter-Hannes*, p. 66; *Yazıcıoğlu*, p. 111.

[135] *Lüddeke/Johnson*, p. 22-23; *Richter-Hannes*, p. 67; *Yazıcıoğlu*, pp. 111-112; *Waldron*, 313; for the counterview see *Yetiş Şamlı*, pp. 151-152.

[136] *Lüddeke/Johnson*, p. 23.

[137] *Richter-Hannes*, p. 67; *Yetiş Şamlı*, p. 151.

or national laws, the UNCITRAL Working Group on Transport Law[138] ("Working Group") started its work based on a preliminary draft submitted by CMI on a new convention on the carriage of goods by sea[139]. However, after taking into consideration that most of the transport today is done on a door-to-door basis, rather than a port-to-port basis, the Working Group decided to concentrate the work on door-to-door operations[140] and formed the "Draft Instrument on the Carriage of Goods [wholly or partly][by sea]"[141]. The draft convention was adopted by UNCITRAL on 7 July 2008 at its 42nd session[142] and it was thereafter presented to the UN General Assembly. Pursuant to the resolution of the UN General Assembly, a signature ceremony was held from 21 to 23 September 2009 in Rotterdam, the Netherlands, and the Convention will be known as the "Rotterdam Rules"[143].

a) General remarks on the liability regime

Although formed for door-to-door operations, the core of the Rotterdam Rules is still carriage by sea[144]. Further, it can also be said that the liability regime set by the Rules is a mixture of the Hague/Visby and the Hamburg Rules[145], although on

---

[138] Working Group III. Between 1970 and 1975, its name was the Working Group on the International Legislation on Shipping, which drafted the Hamburg Rules. From 2002 to present, the work concentrated on transport law such that the Working Group III can be referred to as the Working Group on Transport Law. All reports and documents regarding the work of the Working Group and which are mentioned hereinafter are available at <www.uncitral.org/uncitral/en/commission/working_groups/3Transport.html> (07.08.2010).

[139] <www.comitemaritime.org/draft/draft.html> (07.08.2010). For the draft submitted by CMI see the document A/CN.9/WG.III/WP.21.

[140] Report of the Working Group III (Transport Law) on the work of its eleventh session (New York, 24 March to 4 April 2003), pp. 5-7.

[141] The draft instrument was formed during the twelfth session (Vienna, 6-17 October 2003) of the Working Group: A/CN.9/WG.III/WP.32.

[142] In Vienna on 29 June – 17 July 2008, see <www.unis.unvienna.org/unis/pressrels/2008/unisl121.html> (07.08.2010).

[143] 63rd General Assembly, Press Release of 11 December 2008, p. 3, available on <www.uncitral.org/pdf/english/workinggroups/wg_3/ga-10798.pdf> (07.08.2010). For the historical background see also Michael *Sturley*, Transport Law for the Twenty-First Century: an Introduction to the Preparation, Philosophy, and Potential Impact of the Rotterdam Rules, (2008) 14 JIML 461; Jose Angelo Estrella *Faris*, Uniform Law for International Transport at UNCITRAL: New Times, New Players, and New Rules, (2009) 44 Tex. Int. L.J. 277. For a general overview of the Convention see Anthony *Diamond*, The Rotterdam Rules, [2009] LMCLQ 445.

[144] See Rotterdam Rules Art. 26 (Carriage preceding or subsequent to sea carriage). See also Christopher *Hancock*, Multimodal Transport and the New UN Convention on the Carriage of Goods, (2008) 14 JIML 484; Tomotaka *Fujita*, The Comprehensive Coverage of the New Convention: Performing Parties and the Multimodal Implications, (2009) 44 Tex. Int. L.J. 349.

[145] *Sturley, UNCITRAL*, p. 255.

some points it differs substantially[146]. The period of responsibility (Art. 12), for instance, was regulated differently by the two previous regimes[147]. However, specific obligations (Art. 13 (1)), the duty to provide a seaworthy ship (Art. 14) and exonerations from liability (Art. 17 (3)), have been taken from the Hague/Visby Rules with some important changes[148]. In contrast, deck carriage and jurisdiction and arbitration provisions have principally been kept as they are found in the Hamburg Rules[149]. The fault-based liability framework has not undergone any changes[150].

b) Loss of the right to limit

In the Draft Instrument, the loss of the right to limit was drafted as follows:

> "Neither the carrier nor any of the persons mentioned in article ... shall be entitled to limit their liability as provided in articles ... of this instrument, [or as provided in the contract of carriage,] if the claimant proves that [the delay in delivery of,] the loss of, or the damage to or in connection with the goods resulted from a [personal] act or omission of the person claiming a right to limit done with the intent to cause such loss or damage, or recklessly and with knowledge that such loss or damage would probably result"[151].

After heated debates during the thirteenth session, it was decided to retain the word "personal"[152], such that the acts or omissions of servants and agents are not

---

[146] *Sturley, UNCITRAL*, p. 255: "proposed changes to existing law are not earth shattering. The new convention is deliberately evolutionary, not revolutionary". For an overview see *Baughen*, pp. 143 *et seqq*. See also D. Rhidian *Thomas*, An Appraisal of the Liability Regime Established under the New UN Convention, (2008) 14 JIML 496; Alexander *von Ziegler*, The Liability of the Contracting Carrier, (2009) 44 Tex. Int. L.J. 329.

[147] For more information see *Berlingieri, Comparative Analysis*, pp. 5-6; *Berlingieri, UNCITRAL*, p. 279; *Sturley, UNCITRAL*, pp. 256-257; *Baatz/et al.*, pp. 33 *et seqq*.

[148] For more information see *Berlingieri, UNCITRAL*, pp. 280-281; *Mbiah*, pp. 293-294; *Baatz/et al.*, pp. 35 *et seqq*. See also Theodora *Nikaki*, The Fundamental Duties of the Carrier under the Rotterdam Rules, (2008) 14 JIML 512; Stephen *Girvin*, Exclusions and Limitation of Liability, (2008) 14 JIML 524.

[149] For more information see *Berlingieri, Comparative Analysis*, pp. 43 *et seqq*.; *Berlingieri, UNCITRAL*, pp. 283-284; *Sturley, UNCITRAL*, p. 258; *Mbiah*, p. 296. See also Yvonne *Baatz*, Jurisdiction and Arbitration under the Rotterdam Rules, (2008) 14 JIML 608; Chester D. *Hooper*, Forum Selection and Arbitration in the Draft Convention on Contracts for the International Carriage of Goods Wholly or Partly by Sea, (2009) 44 Tex. Int. L.J. 417.

[150] *Berlingieri, UNCITRAL*, p. 281; *Mbiah*, pp. 289-291.

[151] Ellipsis in original. At the beginning, the provision with regard to the loss of the right to limit was drafted as Art. 19. During the provisional redraft, the provision has been numbered first as 66, thereafter 64.

[152] Report of the Working Group III (Transport Law) on the work of its thirteenth session (New York, 3-14 May 2004), Document A/CN.9/552, pp. 15-16. See also the Report of the Working Group III (Transport Law) on the work of its eighteenth session (Vienna, 6-17 November 2006), Document A/CN.9/616, p. 45.

sufficient to deprive the carrier of the limits of liability. Further, it was decided that the difference between intentional delay and intentional harm by delay should be reflected in the wording of the provision[153]. Later, it was decided to deal with intentional loss caused by delay in a separate paragraph[154]. In its final version, the provision reads:

"Article 61. Loss of the benefit of limitation of liability

1. Neither the carrier nor any of the persons referred to in article 18[155] is entitled to the benefit of the limitation of liability as provided in article 59, or as provided in the contract of carriage, if the claimant proves that the loss resulting from the breach of the carrier's obligation under this Convention was attributable to a personal act or omission of the person claiming a right to limit done with the intent to cause such loss or recklessly and with knowledge that such loss would probably result.

2. Neither the carrier nor any of the persons mentioned in article 18 is entitled to the benefit of the limitation of liability as provided in article 60 if the claimant proves that the delay in delivery resulted from a personal act or omission of the person claiming a right to limit done with the intent to cause the loss due to delay or recklessly and with knowledge that such loss would probably result."[156].

It is clear that this provision adopts the same subjective principle of interpretation and therefore allows breaking the limits only in exceptional circumstances[157]. The addition of the term "personal" puts an end to the discussions as to whether the carrier is also deprived of the right to limit in cases of wilful misconduct by his servants or agents or the actual carrier[158]. The specific regulation on intentional loss caused by delay must also be welcomed for the sake of clarity.

An important difference between the text in the Draft Instrument and the final text of the Convention must be addressed. According to the Draft Instrument, the carrier will lose the benefit of limitation if it is proved "that [...] *the loss of, or the damage to or in connection with the goods*" resulted from an act or omission "done with the intent to cause *such loss or damage*, or recklessly and with knowl-

---

[153] Report of the Working Group III (Transport Law) on the work of its thirteenth session (New York, 3-14 May 2004), Document A/CN.9/552, pp. 14, 16.

[154] See the document A/CN.9/WG.III/WP.56.

[155] *Article 18. Liability of the carrier for other persons*: "The carrier is liable for the breach of its obligations under this Convention caused by the acts or omissions of: (a) Any performing party; (b) The master or crew of the ship; (c) Employees of the carrier or a performing party; or (d) Any other person that performs or undertakes to perform any of the carrier's obligations under the contract of carriage, to the extent that the person acts, either directly or indirectly, at the carrier's request or under the carrier's supervision or control.", for more information on the provision see *Berlingieri, UNCITRAL*, p. 285.

[156] Footnote added. See the document A/CN.9/WG.III/WP.101. For a general comparison of Rotterdam Rules Art. 61 with other maritime carriage and unimodal carriage conventions see *Lannan*, 926 *et seq.*

[157] *Sturley, UNCITRAL*, p. 260; *Huybrechts*, pp. 376-377.

[158] *Berlingieri, Comparative Analysis*, p. 34; *Huybrechts*, p. 376; *Baatz/et al.*, p. 190; *Sturley/Fujita/van der Ziel*, para. 5.252.

edge that *such loss or damage*"[159] would probably result. According to the final text, however, the carrier will not be entitled to limit if it is proved that *"the loss resulting from the breach of the carrier's obligation under this Convention* was attributable to [an] act or omission [...] done with the intent to cause *such loss* or recklessly and with knowledge that *such loss* would probably result"[160]. The change in the wording from "the loss of, or the damage to or in connection with the goods" to "the loss resulting from the breach of the carrier's obligation under this Convention" is a result of the discussions on the scope of the compensation. The Working Group changed the wording in order to hold the carrier liable for misdelivery and misinformation as well[161]. Therefore, "the loss resulting from the breach of the carrier's obligations under this Convention" refers to the financial loss resulting from the loss of, damage to or misdelivery of the goods, and from the misinformation with regard to the transport documents and the qualification of the information contained therein[162].

After the change in the first part to "the loss resulting from the breach of the carrier's obligations under this Convention", maintaining the latter part of Art. 61 (1) as in its Draft Instrument version (such loss or damage) would result in inconsistency within the same provision. The UNCTAD Secretariat addressed the problem[163], and the necessary drafting adjustment was made by the Secretariat upon the delegation of the duty by the Working Group[164]. As a result, the phrase "such loss" in Art. 61 (1) of the Rotterdam Rules refers to the financial loss resulting from the breach of the carrier's obligations under the Rules[165], covering also the loss of or damage to the goods[166].

In the light of this conclusion, the carrier will be deprived of the limits of liability if he has foreseen "such loss", *i.e.* the financial loss has occurred[167]. It is, however, not possible to foresee the actual amount of a financial loss[168]. Therefore, it is sufficient for the carrier to have had actual knowledge of a possible financial loss which will be caused by the loss of, damage to or misdelivery of the

---

[159] Emphasis added.

[160] Emphasis added.

[161] Report of the Working Group III (Transport Law) on the work of its thirteenth session (New York, 3-14 May 2004), Document A/CN.9/552, pp. 11-12; Notes by the United Nations Conference on Trade and Development (UNCTAD) Secretariat, Document A/CN.9/WG.III/WP.56, p. 54 fn. 233; Report of Working Group III (Transport Law) on the work of its twentieth session (Vienna, 15-25 October 2007), Document A/CN.9/642, p. 36.

[162] *Berlingieri, Comparative Analysis*, p. 32.

[163] Notes by the UNCTAD Secretariat, Document A/CN.9/WG.III/WP.72, p. 7.

[164] Report of Working Group III (Transport Law) on the work of its eighteenth session (Vienna, 6-17 November 2006), Document A/CN.9/616, p. 46; Notes by the Secretariat, Document A/CN.9/WG.III/WP.81, p. 47.

[165] *Berlingieri, Comparative Analysis*, p. 33; Francesco *Berlingieri*, The Rotterdam Rules: The 'The Maritime Plus' Approach to Uniformity, EJCCL 2009, 58.

[166] *Mbiah*, pp. 298-299.

[167] The same interpretation is to be given also in case of delay, see *Sturley/Fujita/van der Ziel*, para. 5.256.

[168] *Berlingieri, Comparative Analysis*, p. 33.

goods, and from the misinformation with regard to the transport documents and the qualification of the information contained therein.

Finally, Art. 25 (5) of the Rotterdam Rules contains a similar provision to that found in the Hamburg Rules regarding deck carriage. According to this provision, if the goods have been carried on deck contrary to an express agreement for carriage under deck, the carrier is not entitled to limit his liability for loss, damage or delay which resulted from the deck carriage.

II. Carriage of Passengers – Athens Convention

The international regime covering the carriage of passengers by sea is basically regulated by the Athens Convention relating to the Carriage of Passengers and their Luggage by Sea, 1974[169]. The Convention entered into force on 28 April 1987, and 32 states representing 40% of the world's tonnage are party to it[170]. The Convention has been reviewed by the Protocols of 1976, 1990 and 2002. Unlike the others, the Protocol of 2002 brought substantial changes to the regime set by the Athens Convention 1974, and so the new system set by the Protocol of 2002 is to be referred to as the Athens Convention 2002[171].

Unfortunately, the Athens Convention 2002 has not entered into force yet. The basic reason for this is the problem encountered on the compulsory insurance issue. The problem has been overcome with the "Guidelines for the Implementation of the Athens Convention relating to the Carriage of Passengers and their Luggage by Sea 2002"[172]. Since discussions within the EU with regard to the liability of shipowners for carriage of passengers by sea and inland waterways have been completed[173], further ratifications of the Athens Convention 2002 are expected.

---

[169] For the historical background of the conventions adopted up to the seventies and the reasons for their failure and not entering into force see *Schubert*, pp. 51-53; *Kender, Atina Konvansiyonu*, pp. 105-110.

[170] See Summary of Status of Conventions as of 3 May 2011 on the IMO web site <www.imo.org> (07.05.2011).

[171] Protocol of 2002 Art. 17 (5).

[172] The text of the guidelines can be found at <http://folk.uio.no/erikro/WWW/corrgr/13.pdf> (07.08.2010). For the background see Erik *Røsæg*, The Athens Convention on Passenger Liability and the EU, in: Jürgen Basedow/et al. (Editors), The Hamburg Lectures on Maritime Affairs 2007 & 2008, Hamburg 2009, pp. 57-58. For more information on the compulsory insurance see *Soyer, Athens Convention*, 526-531; *Damar, Compulsory Insurance*, 163. See also Patrick *Griggs*, Making Maritime Law – Do Conventions Work?, in: Scritti in Onore di Francesco Berlingieri, V. I, Genova 2010, p. 540.

[173] By virtue of the Regulation (EC) No 392/2009 of 23 April 2009 on the liability of carriers of passengers by sea in the event of accidents (OJ L 131, 28.05.2009, pp. 24-46), the Athens Convention 2002 became a part of the Community legislation.

1. Liability and limitation

The Athens Convention 1974 stops short of generally presuming the liability of the carrier. By virtue of Art. 3 of the Convention, the fault of the carrier or his servants and agents needs to be proved by the claimant in order to hold them liable. Only if the physical injury or damage has arisen "from or in connexion with the shipwreck, collision, stranding, explosion or fire, or defect in the ship" is the fault or neglect of the shipowner or his servants and agents presumed. Art. 7 and 8 set the limits of liability which the Protocol of 1990 unsuccessfully attempted to revise[174].

The Athens Convention 2002 changes this liability regime fundamentally. The basis of liability of the carrier is set by Art. 3 – 6 of the Convention. Up to the amount of 250.000 SDRs per passenger per occasion, the carrier is strictly liable if the physical injury or damage is caused by a "shipping incident" (Art. 3 (1))[175]. Up to the amount of 400.000 SDRs per passenger per occasion, fault or neglect of the carrier or his servants and agents is presumed in case of a shipping incident (Art. 3 (1) and 7). If the physical injury or damage is not the result of a shipping incident, the carrier is only liable if it is proved by the claimant that the physical injury or damage is caused by the fault or neglect of the carrier or his servants and agents acting within the scope of their employment (Art. 3 (2) and (5))[176].

2. Loss of the right to limit

The conditions under which the carrier is deprived of his right to limit are set by Art. 13 of the Athens Convention 1974 and the provision has not been re-drafted by the Protocol of 2002. Art. 13 (1) stipulates that "the carrier shall not be entitled to the benefit of the limits of liability prescribed in Articles 7 and 8 and paragraph 1 of Article 10, if it is proved that the damage resulted from an act or omission of the carrier done with the intent to cause such damage, or recklessly and with knowledge that such damage would probably result".

a) Link between Art. 3 and Art. 13

As previously mentioned[177], the basis of the liability in the Athens Convention 1974 has been changed by the Protocol of 2002. Under the Athens Convention

---

[174] For more information on the liability regime and limits of the Athens Convention 1974 see *Griggs/Williams/Farr*, pp. 102-104; *Hill*, pp. 450-453; *Tsimplis, Passenger Claims*, 128-137; *Can*, pp. 126 *et seqq.*; *Schubert*, pp. 61 *et seqq.*; *Stachow*, pp. 35-40; *Basedow, Passagier*, pp. 248 *et seqq.*; *Gaskell, Athens 1974*, 286-287; *Herber, Athener Übereinkommen*, 2-7; *Kender, Atina Konvansiyonu*, pp. 113-118; *Soyer, Athens Convention*, 521.

[175] "Shipping incident" is defined in Art. 3 (5)(a) of the Convention as any "shipwreck, capsizing, collision or stranding of the ship, explosion or fire in the ship, or defect in the ship".

[176] For more information see *Atamer, Yolcu Taşıma*, pp. 172-175; *Soyer, Athens Convention*, 523-526; *Czerwenka, Athener Übereinkommen*, 158-160.

[177] See *supra* A II 1.

1974 regime, Art. 3 set the basis of liability and Art. 7 and 8 set the limits of liability. Furthermore, Art. 10 (1) allowed parties to the carriage contract to agree on higher limits than the limits set by the Convention. However, the Protocol of 2002 has adopted strict liability *up to the limitation amount set by Art. 3*. The limitation amounts for the liability of the carrier based on presumed fault are set by Art. 7 and 8. Again, agreement between the passenger and the carrier on higher limits of liability is allowed by Art. 10 (1) of the Athens Convention 2002.

Due to the change in the liability regime, it seems likely that the limitation amounts are set by Art. 3, 7 and 8 of the Athens Convention 2002. However, Art. 13 of the Convention has not been re-drafted. Leaving aside the circumstances as to the degree of fault which deprives the carrier of his right to limit, the provision reads that "the carrier shall not be entitled to the benefit of the *limits of liability prescribed in Articles 7 and 8 and paragraph 1 of Article 10*, if it is proved..."[178]. A clear reference to Art. 3 is, unfortunately, missing in Art. 13. This can lead to various interpretations, such as that the carrier is in no case liable for an amount exceeding the one mentioned in Art. 3. Such an interpretation would, however, be completely incorrect.

Firstly, Art. 3 is not a provision where any limitation amounts are set. Art. 3 sets the basis of liability of the carrier in case of shipping accidents and other events. Since the provision provides two liability systems in cases of shipping incidents, namely strict liability and liability based on presumed fault, it needs to draw a distinction between the two liability systems. In order to draw that line, the provision mentions the monetary amount of 250.000 SDRs. It is not a limitation amount in the sense of limitation of liability. Limitation of liability amounts are set by Art. 7 and 8. This is probably also the reason why the Conference which adopted the Protocol of 2002 did not perceive any need to revise Art. 13 in this respect[179].

Furthermore, even if the previous interpretation is not accepted, Art. 7 clearly specifies that "[t]he liability of the carrier for the death of or personal injury to a passenger *under Article 3* shall in no case exceed ..."[180] 400.000 SDRs. So, there is a clear reference to Art. 3 in Art. 7. Therefore, in case of wilful misconduct, the carrier loses his right to limit. For these reasons, it is not possible to draw a conclusion that the carrier will in any given case only be liable up to 250.000 SDRs.

Another interpretation in this respect is that the strict liability limits are breakable merely by fault. This means that the carrier is strictly liable up to 250.000 SDRs, and in case of the carrier's or his servants' and agents' fault where a shipping incident occurred, the carrier's fault would be presumed and he will be liable up to 400.000 SDRs. So, presumed fault is enough to raise the strict liability

---

[178] Emphasis added.
[179] See IMO documents LEG/CONF.13/3 and LEG/CONF.13/CW/RD/4. The author is much obliged to the IMO Maritime Knowledge Centre for providing the Conference documents.
[180] Emphasis added.

limits; therefore, there is no need to analyse whether the strict liability limits would be broken by wilful misconduct[181].

b) Carrier and performing carrier

The term "carrier" in Art. 13 refers to the carrier himself. This is a clear result of the comparison between the preliminary draft of the 1974 text and the adopted text of the Convention, and of the comparison between the Convention's provisions. In the preliminary draft of the Convention, the provision for the unlimited liability of the carrier and his servants and agents read as "[t]he carrier and his servants and agents shall not be entitled to the benefit of the limitation of liability provided for in Articles 7, 8 and 11 if it is proved that the prejudice, loss or damage resulted from an act or omission of the responsible party done with the intent to cause damage or recklessly and with knowledge that damage would probably result"[182]. However, in the final text the provision for the carrier and for the servants and agents are drafted separately, which shows that the carrier's unlimited liability is independent from his servants' and agents' acts or omissions. Furthermore, in the 1974 text, where the carrier is also liable for his servants' and agents' act or omissions, this is stated clearly, *e.g.* Art. 3 reads "[t]he carrier shall be liable for the damage [...] due to the fault or neglect of the carrier or of his servants or agents [...]". The 2002 text goes a step further and explicitly states when the fault or neglect of the carrier also includes the fault and neglect of the servants. Art. 3 (5)(b) stipulates that "[f]or the purposes of this article: "fault or neglect of the carrier" includes the fault or neglect of the servants [*and agents*][183] of the carrier, acting within the scope of their employment". Further, during the negotiations of the provision, proposals holding the carrier liable without limitation in cases if his servants' and agents' wilful misconduct were rejected[184]. Finally, a provision to break the carriers' liability limits in the carriage of passengers was first introduced by the International Convention for the Unification of Certain Rules relating to the Carriage of Passengers by Sea signed in Brussels in 1961. Art. 7 of this Convention is literally identical to that of the Athens Convention. It has been stressed that in 1961, only 6 years after the Hague Protocol of 1955 to the Warsaw Convention, the provision was worded deliberately in a different way than the one in the Hague Protocol in order to achieve a different result[185].

Consequently, both under the 1974 or the 2002 regime, the term carrier in Art. 13 refers to the carrier himself. Therefore, in order to break the liability limits, the carrier's personal intention or reckless conduct coupled with subjective knowledge will be taken into account. A servant's or agent's conduct is not relevant for breaking the carrier's liability limits[186], unless that servant or agent is the *alter ego*

---

[181] *Gaskell, New Limits*, 333-334.
[182] CMI Yearbook 1969, V. II: Documentation, p. 102.
[183] Emphasis added. As to the term "agents" see *Atamer, Yolcu Taşıma*, p. 135.
[184] *Hill*, p. 453; *Herber, Athener Übereinkommen*, 8.
[185] *Gaskell, Athens 1974*, 323.
[186] *Griggs/Williams/Farr*, p. 106; *Tsimplis, Passenger Claims*, 138; *Gold/Chircop/ Kindred*, p. 488; *Mandaraka-Sheppard*, p. 891; *Hill*, p. 453; *Schubert*, p. 80;

of the carrier[187]. This interpretation has also been accepted by case law. In *The Lion*[188], the plaintiff's coach, which was parked on the car deck of the defendant's ferry, was badly damaged since it was not secured despite the heavy weather conditions, and, after setting sail the ferry rolled onto the starboard side heavily. The plaintiff claimed that the damage resulted from the wilful misconduct of the defendant's servants and agents and, therefore, that the defendant was not entitled to limit his liability. In its decision, the Queen's Bench Division referred to the separate provisions for the wilful misconduct of the carrier and of his servants and agents and to the definition of the term "carrier" under the Convention. The court further referred to the Hague/Visby Rules provision and the similarity between the Athens Convention and the Hague/Visby Rules provisions regarding the wilful misconduct of the carrier. The court stressed that there is a consistent policy that has been followed by the latest maritime conventions whereby the term carrier refers to the carrier himself and not to his servants and agents unless they are the *alter ego* of the carrier. Thus, the defendant carrier was entitled to limit[189].

Since the term "carrier" refers only to the carrier himself, it does not cover the "performing carrier" in addition to servants and agents. Although there is a clear provision as to the wilful misconduct of the servants and agents, a similar provision cannot be found with regard to the performing carrier. Does the absence of a clear provision regarding the performing carrier's wilful misconduct result in limited liability of the performing carrier even if he is guilty of wilful misconduct? This question must be answered in the negative since such a result cannot have been the intention of the drafters[190]. Furthermore, Art. 4 (1) of both 1974 and 2002 texts states that "the performing carrier shall be *subject* and entitled *to the provisions of this Convention* for the part of the carriage performed by him"[191]. Thus, the performing carrier will be liable without any financial limits when he is personally at fault as required by Art. 13[192].

Finally, the carrier will not lose his right to limit when the performing carrier is guilty of wilful misconduct. Art. 4 (2) of the Convention clearly states that the carrier shall, in relation to the carriage performed by the performing carrier, be liable for the acts and omissions of the performing carrier and of his servants and agents. However, this vicarious liability does not cover the wilful misconduct of the performing carrier since only the personal conduct of the carrier deprives him of his right to limit. This result can be supported also by the wording of the provi-

---

Atamer, Yolcu Taşıma, p. 196; *Gaskell, Athens 1974*, 323; *Gaskell, New Limits*, 325; *de la Motte*, p. 295; *Herber*, p. 371. This is considered as a weakness of the Convention, see *Basedow, Passagier*, p. 249.

[187] See *infra* E I 2.

[188] R.G. *Mayor (T/A Granville Coaches) v. P & O Ferries Ltd. and Others (The "Lion")* [1990] 2 Lloyd's Rep. 144 (QBD).

[189] R.G. *Mayor (T/A Granville Coaches) v. P & O Ferries Ltd. and Others (The "Lion")* [1990] 2 Lloyd's Rep. 144, 149-150.

[190] *Griggs/Williams/Farr*, p. 106; *Grime, Athens Convention*, p. 270 fn. 1.

[191] Emphasis added. For more information on the provision see *Atamer, Yolcu Taşıma*, pp. 169-170.

[192] *Atamer, Yolcu Taşıma*, p. 195; *Rabe*, Anl § 664 Art. 10 Rn. 5.

sion on vicarious liability. Pursuant to Art. 4 (2), the carrier is liable for the acts and omissions of a performing carrier's servants and agents. If it is accepted that Art. 4 (2) results in the attribution of the performing carrier's wilful misconduct to the carrier, then wilful misconduct by the performing carrier's servants and agents should also be attributed to the carrier. Clearly, it is unacceptable that the carrier will not be entitled to limit when the performing carrier's servants and agents are guilty of wilful misconduct but that he will be entitled to limit when his servants and agents are guilty of reckless conduct coupled with subjective knowledge[193].

c) Damage

There are two points to be clarified with regard to the term "damage" in Art. 13. Under the Athens Convention regime, unlike the regimes for carriage of goods by sea, both physical injury to a passenger and damage to property are regulated. Art. 13 mentions only "damage", not "physical injury"; however, this does not mean that the carrier will lose his right to limit only in case of damage to property. Art. 13 clearly refers to the limits prescribed in Art. 7, which sets limits for personal injury, and Art. 8, which sets limits for damage to property. Therefore, the term "damage" refers both to personal injury and damage to property[194].

Secondly, Art. 13 of the Athens Convention stipulates that the carrier should have been aware that *such* damage" would probably occur. This wording is similar to the one in the Hamburg Rules, it differs however from the one in the Hague/Visby Rules. Referring also to the remarks made before[195], it should be emphasised that the carrier loses his right to limit if he had subjective awareness of the *very* damage incurred[196].

B. Pollution Conventions

Compensating damages caused by marine pollution arising from oil carriage under the general carriage of goods by sea regime proved to be ineffective. Therefore, and especially after the *Torrey Canyon* disaster[197], the international community decided to regulate the issue under a specific regime, and the International Convention on Civil Liability for Oil Pollution Damage was adopted in 1969. This convention is known generally as CLC'69 and has been revised by several protocols, *i.e.* in 1976, 1984[198] and 1992. Since the 1992 Protocol amends the system under the CLC'69 significantly, the system set by the 1992 Protocol is referred to

---

[193] *Stachow*, p. 239.

[194] *Griggs/Williams/Farr*, p. 106.

[195] See *supra* A I 1 b bb (2) and A I 2 b bb (2).

[196] *Griggs/Williams/Farr*, p. 106; *Gaskell, Athens 1974*, 323; *Shaw/Tsimplis*, p. 214; *Tsimplis, Passenger Claims*, 142.

[197] The M/T "Torrey Canyon" laden with a full cargo of crude oil struck a reef off the Scilly Isles on 18 March 1967 and caused a major oil pollution disaster due to the spilling of 119,000 tonnes of crude oil.

[198] For brief information see *Özçayır*, p. 223 *et seqq*.

as CLC'92[199]; it entered into force on 30 May 1996. The CLC'92 is only the first tier of the three tier system for compensating the damage caused by oil pollution. The second tier is the IOPC Fund established by the International Convention on the Establishment of an International Fund for Compensation for Oil Pollution Damage, 1992 ("Fund'92"). The third tier is the Supplementary Fund, which was formed on a voluntary basis in 2003 and entered into force in 2005.

A similar approach was taken to regulate the compensation system as to hazardous and noxious substances. The International Convention on Liability and Compensation for Damage in Connection with the Carriage of Hazardous and Noxious Substances by Sea, 1996 ("HNS") is largely modelled on the CLC'92 and its complementary component, the IOPC Fund[200]. Unfortunately, HNS has not entered into force yet[201]. Nonetheless, due to the considerable effort put into revising the Convention and finding solutions to the key issues preventing its entry into force, the Protocol of 2010 to the HNS Convention has been adopted by the diplomatic conference called by the IMO[202]. It is expected that the amended version will find more acceptance and support[203].

Although there were conventions regarding pollution caused by carriage of oil and dangerous goods, an unacceptable gap still existed as to the pollution caused by bunker spills. CLC'92 covers only pollution caused by discharge or escape of bunkers from tankers[204]. HNS also does not mention any spills of bunker oil. Therefore, civil liability for the pollution damage caused by bunker discharge or escape from ships remained uncovered by any international regime. In order to fill the gap, the International Convention on Civil Liability for Bunker Oil Pollution Damage, 2001 ("Bunker Convention") was adopted and entered into force on 21 November 2008.

I. Strict Liability

According to the CLC'92 Art. III, HNS Art. 7 (1) and the Bunker Convention Art. 3, the owner of the ship at the time of the incident shall be liable for any pollution

---

[199] Protocol of 1992 to Amend the International Convention on Civil Liability for Oil Pollution Damage, 1969 (signed on 27 November 1992) Art. 11.

[200] *Mandaraka-Sheppard*, p. 980; *Puttfarken*, Rn. 792; *Gauci, Oil Pollution*, p. 23.

[201] For the reasons for not entering into force see *Tsimplis, Marine Pollution*, pp. 277, 287-290.

[202] See   <www.imo.org/Newsroom/mainframe.asp?topic_id=1859&doc_id=12832> (07.08.2010); the preliminary version of the Protocol can be found on <http://folk. uio.no/erikro/WWW/HNS/2010Protocol.pdf> (07.08.2010).

[203] For more information see Måns *Jacobsson*, The HNS Convention – Prospects for its Entry into Force, CMI Yearbook 2009, p. 418; Erik *Røsæg*, The Rebirth of the HNS Convention, in: Scritti in Onore di Francesco Berlingieri, V. II, Genova 2010, p. 852; Richard *Shaw*, The 1996 HNS Convention – an Impossible Dream?, in: Scritti in Onore di Francesco Berlingieri, V. II, Genova 2010, p. 906.

[204] See the definition of the ship in CLC'92 Art. I (1).

damage[205]. No claim shall be made against any person other than the owner, *i.e.* against persons listed in relevant provisions of the Conventions[206], or otherwise[207]. Although there is no mention of "strict liability" or "strictly liable" in the pollution conventions, the lack of an opportunity to sue any person other than the owner, and the emphasis that the owner "shall be liable" indicates that the pollution conventions creates strict liability for shipowners. Moreover, the fact that the owner can escape liability only in a few exceptional circumstances listed in the relevant provisions[208] of the conventions also supports the idea of a strict liability regime[209].

II. Right to Limit Liability

The owner is strictly liable under the pollution conventions regime; however, he is entitled to limit his liability up to the limit specified in the CLC'92 (Art. V) and HNS (Art. 9)[210]. Nonetheless, the shipowner's right to limit does not mean that the damage caused by oil pollution would not be compensated. The damage above the shipowner's liability limits will be compensated by the IOPC Fund and the HNS Fund. The main rationale of this system is that the damage is compensated by different industries benefiting from the carriage of oil by sea. Up to a certain limit, the shipowner, *i.e.* the shipping industry, is compensating for the damage. The remaining damage is to be compensated by the IOPC or HNS Fund, *i.e.* the oil industry or the chemical industry[211].

---

[205] Here, however, an important difference between the CLC'92 and HNS on one side and the Bunker Convention on the other should be emphasised. Under the CLC'92 and HNS regimes, the liability is channelled to the registered shipowner, since the term "owner" covers primarily only the registered shipowner (CLC'92 Art. I (3); HNS Art. 1 (3)). However, the Bunker Convention differs from the two Conventions on this point. Pursuant to Art. 1 (3) of the Bunker Convention, the term "shipowner" means the owner, including the registered owner, bareboat charterer, manager and operator of the ship. This is considered as a "complex channelling arrangement", see *Tsimplis, Bunker Pollution*, 88.

[206] CLC'92 Art. III (4); HNS Art. 7 (5). However, naturally, the owner acquires subrogated rights up to the amount he has paid (CLC'92 Art. V (5)-(6); HNS Art. 9 (5)-(6)). Since such provisions and a list of relevant persons is not adopted in the Bunker Convention, *i.e.* the protection given by the CLC'92 and HNS is not provided under the Bunker Convention, it is said that all those persons listed in the CLC'92 and HNS are exposed to the danger of being sued according to national laws when there is a bunker oil pollution, see *Tsimplis, Bunker Pollution*, 89-90.

[207] *Hodges/Hill*, p. 152; for the counterview, namely that the CLC "does not preclude victims from claiming compensation outside the Convention from persons other than the registered owner", see *Mandaraka-Sheppard*, p. 963.

[208] CLC'92 Art. III (2); HNS Art. 7 (2)-(3); Bunker Convention Art. 3 (3)-(4).

[209] *Hodges/Hill*, pp. 150, 165; *Rabe*, § 485 Rn. 87, 90; *Tsimplis, Marine Pollution*, pp. 255, 280; *Tsimplis, Bunker Pollution*, 88-89; *Herber*, p. 193.

[210] For detailed information see *Hodges/Hill*, pp. 153-155. The limits under the HNS Convention have been raised by the 2010 Protocol.

[211] *Hodges/Hill*, p. 160.

However, the limitation system of the Bunker Conventions differs from the CLC'92 and HNS. As to the limits, the Bunker Convention refers to "any applicable national or international regime", such as the 1976 London Convention, as amended. Consequently, the Bunker Convention does not have a "built in" or "stand-alone" limitation system[212]. When bunker oil pollution occurs, limits of liability are to be determined according to the limitation regime of the applicable law.

III. Loss of the Right to Limit

1. CLC and HNS

Starting in the chronological order, the CLC'69 Art. V (2) reads "[i]f the incident occurred as a result of the actual fault or privity of the owner, he shall not be entitled to avail himself of the limitation". Pursuant to this provision, the fault or privity must be "actual", *i.e.* the shipowner must be personally at fault[213]. Unless they can be considered as the *alter ego* of the company, the servants' and agents' fault or privity is not sufficient to deprive the shipowner of the right to limit[214]. Moreover, it was not possible to direct any claim against servants and agents under the CLC'69 regime (Art. III (4)); therefore, the shipowner, being the only person to be sued, was entitled to limit his liability in case of actual fault or privity of his servants and agents, due as well to the lack of any provision regarding servants' and agents' actual fault.

Although the phrase "actual fault or privity" stipulates personal conduct of the shipowner, it does not necessarily stipulate subjective awareness. If the shipowner does not meet the "prudent shipowner" criterion, he can be found personally at fault. Therefore, the provision adopted a different type of degree of fault other than the previously analysed conventions with regard to the carriage of goods and passengers by sea, in order to deprive the shipowner of his right to limit.

The wording of Art. V (2) has been, for the first time, modified by the Protocol of 1984, which has, however, never come into force. However, during the revision preparations which led to the CLC'92, the modified version of the Protocol of 1984 has been adopted without any change. The reasons for modification in the actual fault or privity criterion were several: divergent court decisions with regard to the "actual fault or privity", the need to align the provision with other provisions of the carriage by sea conventions and to settle the burden of proof issue[215].

---

[212] *Hodges/Hill*, p. 166; *Mandaraka-Sheppard*, p. 979; *Hill*, p. 440; *Tsimplis, Marine Pollution*, p. 255; *Tsimplis, Bunker Pollution*, 91-92.

[213] *Hodges/Hill*, p. 142.

[214] For the analysis of the phrase "actual fault or privity" see *infra* C II 1, and information on the attribution of the fault of the servants and agents to the shipowning company see *infra* E I.

[215] Official Records of the International Conference on Liability and Compensation for Damage in connexion with the Carriage of Certain Substances by Sea, 1984 and the International Conference on the Revision of the 1969 Civil Liability Convention and the 1971 Fund Convention, 1992, London 1993, V. 1, pp. 149-150, 159.

All these demands have been met by the amended Art. V (2). Pursuant to the provision "[t]he owner shall not be entitled to limit his liability under this Convention if it is proved that the pollution damage resulted from his personal act or omission, committed with the intent to cause such damage, or recklessly and with knowledge that such damage would probably result". HNS Art. 9 (2) employs the same wording with the CLC'92 as to the loss of the right to limit.

There is no doubt that breaking the limits of liability under the CLC'92 regime is more difficult than under the CLC'69 regime[216] since the degree of fault adopted by the CLC'92 refers to a more serious fault than the actual fault or privity.

It is also clear from the wording of the CLC'92 and HNS that only the personal acts or omissions of the shipowner will deprive him of the right to limit; acts of his servants and agents are not sufficient to break the liability limits unless those servants or agents can be regarded as the *alter ego* of the owner[217].

Both conventions also clearly state that *such* damage shall have been foreseen. Such damage is clearly the pollution damage. However, if both of the conventions are analysed in this respect, it can be seen that both personal injury and loss of or damage to property are covered by the term "damage". Pollution damage under the CLC'92 regime basically means the "loss or damage caused outside the ship by contamination resulting from the escape or discharge of oil from the ship". This definition does not limit the term "damage" only to loss of or damage to property; it also covers personal injury[218]. HNS Art. 1 (6) clearly defines the term damage and states that personal injury is also within the term "damage". Since both conventions cover personal injury and loss of or damage to property, the phrase "such damage" refer to the actual damage that occurred.

The last point to be emphasised is that the compensation for pollution damage does not only depend upon the shipowner. Therefore, if the owner cannot meet his financial obligations when he loses his right to limit, the amount which could not have been paid by the shipowner will be compensated by the IOPC or the HNS Fund[219].

2. Bunker Convention

As previously mentioned[220], the Bunker Convention does not have a specific limitation regime. As to the limitation, it simply refers to the applicable national or international regime, *e.g.* the 1976 London Convention. Clearly, the Bunker Convention refers to the whole regime as to the limitation, not only to specific limitation of liability provisions. Therefore, it depends on the applicable limitation

---

[216] *Gauci, Oil Pollution*, p. 169.
[217] *Tsimplis, Marine Pollution*, pp. 262, 282.
[218] *Gauci, Oil Pollution*, pp. 53-54.
[219] Fund'92 Art. 4 (1) – (2); HNS Art. 14 (1)(b).
[220] See *supra* B II.

regime whether the shipowner would be entitled to limit and, if yes, which degree of fault would be applicable as to breaking the limits[221].

C. Global Limitation

The parties, as stated in the relevant conventions, are entitled to limit their liability for claims arising from the carriage of goods or passengers by sea. However, those limits are sometimes considered very high. Therefore, shipowners or carriers are entitled to further reduce those limits by way of constituting a fund under one of the limitation conventions. Consequently, there is a second cap of limitation set by the limitation conventions, and the financial amount to be paid by a shipowner or carrier will not exceed the limits set by the global limitation conventions in any case[222].

Today, there are two conventions primarily applicable in cases of limitation of liability. States representing almost 50% of the world's tonnage are parties to the Convention on Limitation of Liability for Maritime Claims, 1976 ("1976 London Convention"), and almost 45% of the world's tonnage are parties to the Protocol of 1996 to Amend the Convention on Limitation of Liability for Maritime Claims, 1976 ("Protocol of 1996"), which raised the limitation amounts significantly[223]. However, a considerable number of states are still party to the International Convention relating to Limitation of Liability of Owners of Seagoing Ships, 1957 ("1957 Brussels Convention")[224].

I. Main Features

Both of the conventions are related only to the limitation issue; in other words, they do not set the basis of liability. Pursuant to the 1957 Brussels Convention Art. 1 and the 1976 London Convention Art. 2[225], they only set the limits when liability has arisen[226]. However, they do not cover all kinds of claims which can be brought

---

[221] For more information on the 1957 Brussels Convention and the 1976 London Convention see *infra* C.

[222] Relevant provisions are: Athens Convention Art. 19; Hague – Hague Visby Rules Art. VIII; Hamburg Rules Art. 25 (1); Rotterdam Rules Art. 86. However, claims must be fall under the 1976 London Convention Art. 2-3. For more information see *Griggs/Williams/Farr*, pp. 52-55, 134; *Puttfarken*, Rn. 500; *Atamer, Yolcu Taşıma*, pp. 122-123, 176-177; *Gaskell, Athens 1974*, 287; *Grime, 1976 Limitation Convention*, p. 310; *Herber, Athener Übereinkommen*, 10-12.

[223] See Summary of Status of Conventions as of 3 May 2011 on the IMO web site <www.imo.org> (07.05.2011).

[224] See CMI Yearbook 2009, pp. 467-468.

[225] 1976 London Convention Art. 2 (1): "... the following claims, *whatever the basis of liability may be*, shall be subject to limitation of liability: ..." (Emphasis added). The issue was not stated so clearly under the 1957 Brussels Convention; but it also does not set any basis of liability.

[226] *Seward*, p. 182; *Grime, 1976 Limitation Convention*, p. 309.

against the persons who are under the conventions' cover. Claims subject to limitation are listed in Art. 1 of the 1957 Brussels Convention and Art. 2 of the 1976 London Convention[227]. Both conventions provide limitation of liability for claims arising from loss of life or personal injury or loss of or damage to property on board, claims based on tort liability, and removal, destruction or the rendering harmless of wrecks. Compared to the 1957 Brussels Convention, 1976 London Convention covers a wider range of claims, such as claims arising from the operation of the ship or the salvage operations, claims in respect of loss resulting from delay, claims arisen from the removal, destruction or the rendering harmless of the cargo of the ship. The act of invoking limitation of liability is not an admission of liability. Claims for salvage or contribution in general average, and claims arisen from labour contracts are exempted from the application of the conventions (1957 Brussels Convention Art. 1 (4), 1976 London Convention Art. 3). Furthermore, civil liability arising from the carriage of oil, nuclear material and hazardous and noxious substances is excluded from the global limitation under the 1976 London Convention regime[228].

1957 Brussels Convention Art. 3 and 1976 London Convention Art. 6 and 7 provide the limits of liability which have been raised quite substantially by 1976 London Convention compared to the 1957 Brussels Convention. The limits are to be calculated according to the ship's size[229]. The limits provided under both conventions are applicable to the aggregate of all claims which have arisen from each distinct occasion (1957 Brussels Convention Art. 2 (1), 1976 London Convention Art. 9).

In order to invoke the right to limit liability, a limitation fund may be constituted by depositing the limitation amount or by producing a guarantee. The fund thus constituted is available only for the payment of claims for which the liability may be limited. The constitution of the fund bars the persons having made a claim against the fund from exercising any right regarding the claim against any other assets of the person liable. The fund is then to be distributed among the claimants in proportion to the amounts of their established claims (1957 Brussels Convention Art. 2-3, 1976 London Convention Art. 10-13).

Both of the conventions also adopt the principle that under certain conditions the person liable is not entitled to limit liability. Under the 1957 Brussels Conven-

---

[227] For more information see *Griggs/Williams/Farr*, p. 17 *et seqq.*; *Davies/Dickey*, pp. 461-467; *Gold/Chircop/Kindred*, pp. 725-731; *Brice*, pp. 22-28; *Richter*, pp. 12-15; *Williams, 1976 Limitation Convention*, 121-124; for a comparative study see *Watson*, 262-266; *Chen, Limitation*, pp. 30 *et seqq.*

[228] 1976 London Convention Art. 3 (b) clearly excludes the claims for oil pollution damage. Protocol of 1996 to the 1976 London Convention Art. 7 allows states to make a reservation to exclude the application of the Convention to the HNS claims. This provision has been adopted, because it was foreseen that the Protocol of 1996 will enter into force before the HNS. So, if a state is party to both of the conventions, it will decide whether the global limitation will be applicable to the HNS claims, see *Gaskell, New Limits*, 316.

[229] For more information with respect to 1976 London Convention see *Griggs/Williams/Farr*, pp. 47 *et seqq.*

tion regime, "actual fault or privity" has been adopted as the condition for unlimited liability; whereas under the 1976 London Convention regime, the definition of wilful misconduct has been adopted with some additional changes.

II. Breaking the Limits

1. 1957 Brussels Convention

Initially, the 1957 Brussels Convention has been adopted to replace the International Convention for the Unification of Certain Rules relating to the Limitation of the Liability of Owners of Seagoing Vessels, 1924 ("1924 Limitation Convention"). It was only the shipowner who was entitled to limit his liability under the 1924 Limitation Convention. However, limitation of liability was not applicable if the liability arose, basically, from "acts or faults of the owner of the vessel"[230]. It can be said that the owner of the ship was entitled to limit unless he himself caused any damage.

Besides the shipowner, the class of persons entitled to limit their liability against a maritime claim has been widened with Art. 6 (2) of the 1957 Brussels Convention. Pursuant to this provision the charterer, manager and operator of the ship, master, members of the crew and other servants of the owner are entitled to limit their liability under the convention regime. The class of persons entitled to limit liability was extended by the 1957 Brussels Convention in order to overcome the *Himalaya*[231] problem. With the extension, it was not possible for a claimant to circumvent the limitation system by simply suing a servant or agent of the owner[232].

The person liable under the 1957 Brussels Convention was entitled to limit "unless the occurrence giving rise to the claim resulted from the actual fault or privity of the owner" (Art. 1 (1)). The criterion for unlimited liability was set as "actual fault or privity"[233], the absence of which should be proved by the person liable[234].

---

[230] 1924 Limitation Convention Art. 2: "(*para. 1*) The limitation of liability laid down in the foregoing article does not apply: (1) To obligations arising out of acts or faults of the owner of the vessel; (2) To any of the obligations referred to in No. 8 of article 1, when the owner has expressly authorized or ratified such obligation; (3) To obligations on the owner arising out of the engagement of the crew and other persons in the service of the vessel. (*para. 2*) Where the owner or a part owner of the vessel is at the same time master, he cannot claim limitation of liability for his faults, other than his faults of navigation and the faults of persons in the service of the vessel".

[231] See *infra* D VI 2 a.

[232] *Griggs/Williams/Farr*, p. 8; *Grime, 1976 Limitation Convention*, p. 311.

[233] The American correspondent of the conduct barring imitation is the "privity or knowledge". Although expressed by different terms, both phrases refer to the same degree of fault, see *Chen, Limitation*, pp. 60-61, see also *Buglass*, 1386-1387.

[234] *Gold/Chircop/Kindred*, p. 732; *Chen, Limitation*, p. 79. *Northern Fishing Company (Hull), Ltd. v. Eddom and Others* (*The Norman*) [1960] 1 Lloyd's Rep. 1, 10 (HL) *per* Lord Keith of Avonholm: "The appellants have been unable [...] to prove that

The meaning of the phrase can be explained by referring to the *Lennard's* case: "The words "actual fault or privity" [...] infer something personal to the owner, something blameworthy in him, as distinguished from constructive fault or privity such as the fault or privity of his servants or agents. But the words "actual fault" are not confined to affirmative or positive acts by way of fault. If the owner be guilty of an act of omission to do something which he ought to have done, he is no less guilty of an "actual fault" than if the act had been one of commission. To avail himself of the statutory defence, he must shew that he himself is not blameworthy for having either done or omitted to do something or been privy to something. It is not necessary to shew knowledge. If he has means *of knowledge which he ought to have used* and does not avail himself of them, his omission so to do may be a fault, and, if so, it is an actual fault and he cannot claim the protection"[235].

Consequently, there should be a distinction made between the two points: the actuality of fault and the degree of conduct. As to the actuality of fault, it is clear from what was stated is that the "fault or privity" must be "actual", *i.e.* the shipowner must be personally at fault[236]. Therefore, acts or omission of his servants and agents (constructive fault) cannot be considered in determining whether the shipowner should be deprived of the limits, unless those acts or omissions can be attributed to the shipowner.

Although the fault or privity should be "actual", the courts did not have difficulty in finding the shipowners personally at fault. For instance, in the *Lady Gwendolen* case the shipowners were found at fault because they did not exercise proper control over the master. The owners were the famous brewers Guinness. The Lady Gwendolen was navigating at full speed in dense fog, in breach of collision regulations. Therefore, she collided with the Freshfield lying at anchor. Setting aside the attribution issue[237], the court entered into judgement that the owners were at fault, since they turned a blind eye to the fact that the master was navigating in breach of law. The court examined the log book and found out that he was navigating at full speed all times, even in dense fog[238].

---

the loss of the ship and its crew was not due to their fault or privity"; *"The Lady Gwendolen"* [1965] 1 Lloyd's Rep. 335, 348 (CA) *per* Lord Willmer: "the plaintiff company never succeeded in discharging the burden of proving that this collision happened without their actual fault or privity"; *The "Marion"* [1984] 2 Lloyd's Rep. 1, 9 (HL) *per* Lord Brandon of Oakbrook: "it is impossible for the appellants to establish that the two actual faults of the appellants [...] did not contribute to the damage".

[235] Emphasis added; *Asiatic Petroleum Company, Limited v. Lennard's Carrying Company, Limited* [1914] 1 K.B. 419, 432 (CA) *per* Justice Buckley.

[236] See also *James Patrick and Company Limited v. the Union Steamship Company of New Zealand Limited* 1938 (60) C.L.R. 650, 670 (High Court of Australia) *per* Justice Dixon.

[237] See *infra* E I 2 c.

[238] *"The Lady Gwendolen"* [1964] 2 Lloyd's Rep. 99 (QBD); *"The Lady Gwendolen"* [1965] 1 Lloyd's Rep. 335 (CA).

As to the degree of conduct, it is again clear from the judgement that subjective awareness of the fault or of the probable consequences[239] is not necessary for being guilty of actual fault or privity. It is to be determined according to an objective standard: "if he has means of knowledge which he ought to have used and does not avail himself of them"[240], i.e. if he does not attain the standard of a reasonable, prudent shipowner in the management and control of his ship[241], known to lawyers with a civil law background as "gross negligence"[242], he has been actually at fault and privy and, thus, cannot avail himself of the limits[243].

The test to be applied with regard to the degree of conduct has been an objective one, where courts have compared "the conduct of the defendant with that of the "reasonable man" without attempting to assess what went on in the particular case"[244]. In this respect, *The Norman* is a good example. The fishing vessel of the shipowning company struck a rock in fog at night in Greenland territorial waters and sunk with the loss of 19 of 20 crew members. The information relating to the rock reached the owners after the ship set sail but they did not consider it necessary to transmit the information to the skipper since the rock was already in an area which was known by the skipper as unsafe due to the presence of uncharted rocks. Queen's Bench Division decided in favour of owners by stating that the failure to transmit the information did not contribute to the casualty[245]. However, the Court of Appeal and the House of Lords entered into judgement in favour of the claimants, who were the relatives of the deceased crew members. The House

---

[239] *Grime, Loss of the Right*, p. 104.

[240] *Asiatic Petroleum Company, Limited v. Lennard's Carrying Company, Limited* [1914] 1 K.B. 419, 432 (CA) per Justice Buckley.

[241] *Özçayır*, p. 330; *Thomas, British Concepts*, 1222; *Seward*, p. 169; *Cheka*, 488; *Chen, Limitation*, pp. 61-62.

[242] *Hazelwood*, pp. 282-283.

[243] *Northern Fishing Company (Hull), Ltd. v. Eddom and Others (The Norman)* [1960] 1 Lloyd's Rep. 1, 11 (HL) per Lord Radcliffe: "What, if any, action should have been taken [...] by a reasonably prudent and conscientious owner"; *F. T. Everard & Sons, ltd. v. London and Thames Haven Oil Wharves, Ltd. and Others (The "Anonity")* [1961] 2 Lloyd's Rep. 117, 124 (CA) per Lord Justice Holroyd Pearce: "[the chairman of the company] *should have foreseen* and enforced as *a reasonable shipowner*" (Emphasis added); *The "Dayspring"* [1968] 2 Lloyd's Rep. 204, 213 (QBD) per Justice Cairns: "the fault, [...], would be one of negligence, failure to exercise care to do something which *ought to be done* or in doing something which *ought not to be done*. The standard of care required is not that of perfection but the standard of what would be done, or left undone, by *a reasonable shipowner* in all existing circumstances. This can be tested by asking whether any precautionary measure is one which is commonly taken by shipowners, and if not, whether it was a precaution which was obviously necessary in the circumstances." (Emphasis added).

[244] *Cheka*, 488.

[245] *Northern Fishing Company (Hull), Ltd. v. Eddom (The Norman)* [1958] 1 Lloyd's Rep. 141 (QBD).

of Lords held that the owners were personally at fault because they failed to provide necessary and adequate navigational information[246].

Meeting the requirement of a reasonable shipowner has been a heavy burden. It has not been enough for shipowning companies to delegate their duties to managing companies or subordinates, or leave certain issues, especially regarding navigation, solely to the master's discretion in order to prove that they have been reasonable, prudent shipowners. In order to be considered as a reasonable and prudent shipowner, one needs to instruct, assist, detect, supervise and inspect subordinates and masters. Otherwise, a shipowner is guilty of actual fault or privity[247].

The tendency towards unlimited liability grew in the mid 70's mostly because the funds were considered by courts as insufficient for satisfying damages[248]. In fact, "actual fault or privity" was interpreted so broadly that limitation of liability became an exception[249]. Even slight negligence was considered sufficient for breaking the limitation, as long as it is the shipowner's personal fault[250].

2. 1976 London Convention

a) Preliminary

Unrealistically low limitation amounts due to the depreciation in monetary values, increase in the size of ships, dissatisfaction with the "actual privity or knowledge" standard and various other issues arising out of the 1957 Convention (*e.g.* its application to salvors) created the need for revision of the 1957 Brussels Conven-

---

[246] *Northern Fishing Company (Hull), Ltd. v. Eddom (The Norman)* [1959] 1 Lloyd's Rep. 1 (CA); *Northern Fishing Company (Hull), Ltd. v. Eddom and Others (The Norman)* [1960] 1 Lloyd's Rep. 1 (HL). However, it was said that the CA and HL favoured the relatives of the crew members because if they would have entered judgement in favour of the shipowners, the relatives would have received a very low compensation figure due to the low limitation amounts. So, the basic reason for the final decision was not the proper application of law; rather, it was "a deep sense of justice", see *Sheen*, 479-480.

[247] For different examples see *Yuille v. B.&B. Fisheries, Ltd. and Bates (The "Radiant")* [1958] 2 Lloyd's Rep. 596 (QBD); *F. T. Everard & Sons, ltd. v. London and Thames Haven Oil Wharves, Ltd. and Others (The "Anonity")* [1961] 2 Lloyd's Rep. 117 (CA); *The "Dayspring"* [1968] 2 Lloyd's Rep. 204 (QBD); *Rederij Erven H. Groen v. The "England" (Owners) and Others* [1973] 1 Lloyd's Rep. 373 (CA); *The "Garden City"* [1982] 2 Lloyd's Rep. 382 (QBD); *The "Marion"* [1983] 2 Lloyd's Rep. 156 (CA) affirmed by *The "Marion"* [1984] 2 Lloyd's Rep. 1 (HL). See also *Cheka*, 489-493; *Thomas, British Concepts*, 1224; *Heerey*, p. 7.

[248] *Gold/Chircop/Kindred*, p. 720; *Coghlin*, p. 248; *Çağa, Batider*, p. 298; *Heerey*, p. 5. For an overview of different cases see *Sheen*, 481-482.

[249] *Gold/Chircop/Kindred*, p. 732; *Grime, Loss of the Right*, p. 104; *Rabe*, London-HBÜ 1976 Art. 4 Rn. 1; *Ataol*, pp. 77-78.

[250] *Richter*, p. 6.

tion regime[251]. In 1972, CMI decided to initiate preparations for the revision of the Convention, and submitted a questionnaire to its members[252]. In the light of the replies, two alternative documents, namely a draft protocol to amend the 1957 Convention (the so-called mini draft) and a draft international convention (the so-called maxi draft) were prepared and submitted to the IMO[253]. The IMO decided to submit the draft international convention text prepared by CMI, with some small modifications[254], to the International Conference for Limitation of Liability in 1976 in London. The result of the Conference was the 1976 London Convention.

b) Loss of the right to limit

Under the 1976 London Convention regime, contrary to the 1957 Brussels Convention system, it is not for the shipowner to show that he had no actual fault or privity in order to limit his liability. Conduct giving rise to unlimited liability is regulated in Art. 4 of the Convention. Pursuant to Art. 4 "[a] person liable shall not be entitled to limit his liability if it is proved that the loss resulted from his personal act or omission, committed with the intent to cause such loss, or recklessly and with knowledge that such loss would probably result."

aa) Historical background

A historical background analysis should begin with the first draft prepared by CMI. The draft provision submitted by CMI to the IMO Conference reads as follows:

"Article 4 – Conduct barring limitation

A person liable shall not be entitled to limit his liability if it is proved that the loss resulted from his personal act or omission, committed with the intent to cause such loss, or recklessly and with knowledge that such loss would probably result"[255].

The Chairman of the CMI Committee which prepared the alternative documents, Mr. Alex Rein, drafted a report and explained the reasons for particular changes. With regard to the change in the provision on the conduct barring limitation, he emphasised that the "actual fault or privity" rule gives rise to unlimited liability even in simple negligence cases, as well as divergent court opinions. Therefore,

---

[251] *Özçayır*, p. 352; *Herber, Haftungsrecht*, pp. 10-12; *Mandaraka-Sheppard*, p. 865; *Cleton*, pp. 20-22; *Coghlin*, pp. 234-235; *Richter*, p. 4; *Stachow*, pp. 54-55; *Çağa, Batider*, p. 293.

[252] For the text of the questionnaire see CMI Yearbook 1972, pp. 14-35 and for the replies pp. 36 *et seqq.*

[253] For the texts see CMI Yearbook 1974, pp. 34-51.

[254] For the modifications see Sergio M. *Carbone*, Limitation of Liability for Maritime Claims: An Analysis of the CMI Draft Convention as amended by IMCO, in: CMI Yearbook 1976, pp. 166 *et seqq.* For the historical background why the IMO has chosen the draft international convention see *Richter*, pp. 8-9.

[255] CMI Yearbook 1974, p. 44.

the Committee changed the wording defining the conduct and, consequently, also the degree of fault which is required to deprive the person liable of limits of liability[256].

It was decided to submit the draft international convention to the Conference. In the provision with regard to the conduct barring limitation, there was a small addendum: in the light of some observations and proposals, the IMO decided to add "[or from his own gross negligence]" at the end of the provision, so the delegations could discuss it[257]. However, before and during the Conference, this phrase was strongly opposed[258].

During the Conference, the French delegation proposed a change in Art. 4 regarding vicarious liability in cases of wilful misconduct. It was suggested that the person liable should lose the benefit of limitation of liability also when the loss resulted from the act or omission of his servants acting in the exercise of their duties[259]. However, this proposal did not gain any support during the Conference[260].

Thereafter, the French delegation proposed to treat the tortious claims for personal injury separately. Pursuant to this proposal, the person liable shall not be entitled to limit his liability if the personal injury was caused by a "personal act or gross omission, though not from any fault"[261]. This proposal was rejected by the Conference as well[262].

Finally, the provision was adopted without any change, *i.e.* in accord with the version submitted by CMI to the IMO Conference[263].

bb) "Almost" unbreakable limits

The requisites of the degree of fault as described in the Warsaw Convention are applicable *mutatis mutandis*, since Art. 4 of the 1976 London Convention is modelled on the provision adopted by the Hague Protocol[264]. Therefore, subjective awareness of the probable consequences is necessary for unlimited liability. Consequently, objective awareness, namely violation of the general duty of care in a grave manner is not sufficient for unlimited liability under the 1976 London Con-

---

[256] Alex *Rein*, Second Report by the Chairman of the International Subcommittee on the Revision of the International Convention relating to the Limitation of the Liability of Sea-Going Ships, in: CMI Yearbook 1974, pp. 24-26.

[257] *Official Records, London Conference*, p. 32.

[258] *Official Records, London Conference*, pp. 72 (Sweden), 73 (UK), 108 (New Zealand), 113-114 (International Chamber of Shipping), 119 (BIMCO), 147 (Spain); for the discussions on "gross negligence" see pp. 264, 269-270, 272-274, 277-278.

[259] *Official Records, London Conference*, p. 152.

[260] See *Official Records, London Conference*, pp. 272, 277, 292.

[261] *Official Records, London Conference*, pp. 184-186, 190.

[262] *Official Records, London Conference*, p. 384.

[263] *Official Records, London Conference*, p. 410. For the final text of the convention adopted by the Conference see *Official Records, London Conference*, pp. 506-517.

[264] *Dockray*, p. 348; *Griggs/Williams/Farr*, pp. 37-38; *Mandaraka-Sheppard*, pp. 897-901; *Özçayır*, pp. 359-360; *Williams, 1976 Limitation Convention*, 124. For more information on the criteria set by the Hague Protocol see *supra* § 4 B I 2 c.

vention regime[265]. This was also stressed by the Court of Appeal in *The Leerort* case. When the vessel Leerort, laden with cargo, was lying peacefully in berth, another vessel, the Zim Pireaus, collided with her and caused a breach in one of the holds and subsequently cargo loss and damage. The reason for the collision was the excessive speed of the Zim Pireaus and a failure in her engine, which did not respond to the astern mode, then stopped, and finally worked in an emergency manoeuvring mode but did not start again in the astern mode. The Court of Appeal concluded that an engine shutdown at a critical moment is nothing more than a coincidence "that is almost incredible", and that it is "totally absurd" to attribute a 50 second engine failure to the personal act or omission of the owners done with the intent to cause a collision or recklessly and with knowledge that such a collision would probably occur[266].

As can be seen from the comparison of the prerequisites for breaking the limitation under the 1957 and 1976 regimes, it is clear that breaking the limits under the 1976 London Convention regime is more difficult than under the 1957 Brussels Convention[267]. By adopting a higher degree of culpability for breaking the limitation, the 1976 London Convention definitely eliminates the uncertainty caused by "actual fault or privity"[268]. Clearly, shipowners agreed to higher limits in exchange for an almost unbreakable right to limit[269].

---

[265] *Davies/Dickey*, p. 468; *Dockray*, p. 348; *Hazelwood*, pp. 282-283; *Hodges/Hill*, pp. 592-593; *Mandaraka-Sheppard*, p. 896; *MSC Mediterranean Shipping Co. S.A. v. Delumar BVBA and Others* (*The "MSC Rosa M"*) [2000] 2 Lloyd's Rep. 399, 401-405 (QBD) *per* Justice David Steel; *Margolle and Another v. Delta Maritime Co. Ltd. and Others* (*the "Saint Jacques II" and "Gudermes"*) [2003] 1 Lloyd's Rep. 203, 207-208 (QBD) *per* Justice Gross. However, it seems that the French courts continue to apply the objective interpretation also to the limitation of liability in the maritime law context. For summaries of some French cases with regard to the 1976 London Convention Art. 4, see <www.comitemaritime.org/jurisp/ju_llmc. html#8> (07.08.2010).

[266] *Schiffahrtsgesellschaft MS "Merkur Sky" M.B.H. & Co. K.G. v. MS Leerort Nth Schiffahrts G.M.B.H. & Co. K.G.* (*The "Leerort"*) [2001] 2 Lloyd's Rep. 291 (CA).

[267] *Davies/Dickey*, p. 468; *Özçayır*, p. 358; *Shaw, ISM Code*, 171.

[268] *Dockray*, p. 348; *The "Marion"* [1982] 2 Lloyd's Rep. 52, 55 (QBD) *per* Justice Sheen: "During the last 20 years there has been a trend towards trying to find ways of circumventing the provisions of [limitation of liability], frequently with success. It does not surprise me, therefore, that in 1976 a Convention was agreed by which the shipowners of the world have agreed to higher limits of liability in exchange for certainty as to their right to limit".

[269] *Davies/Dickey*, p. 468; *Mandaraka-Sheppard*, p. 865; *Rabe*, LondonHBÜ 1976 Art. 4 Rn. 1; *Herber, Haftungsrecht*, pp. 13-14, 28; *Coghlin*, p. 248; *Grime, 1976 Limitation Convention*, p. 313; *Heerey*, p. 3; *Baughen*, pp. 425-426; *Wilson*, p. 288; *Rabe, TranspR*, 146; *Ogg*, 149: "By design, this is a very difficult nut to crack"; *The "Bowbelle"* [1990] 1 Lloyd's Rep. 532, 535 (QBD) *per* Justice Sheen; *The Breydon Merchant* [1992] 1 Lloyd's Rep. 373, 376 (QBD) *per* Justice Sheen; *MSC Mediterranean Shipping Co. S.A. v. Delumar BVBA and Others* (*The "MSC Rosa M"*) [2000] 2 Lloyd's Rep. 399, 401 (QBD) *per* Justice David Steel; *Schiffahrtsgesellschaft MS "Merkur Sky" M.B.H. & Co. K.G. v. MS Leerort Nth Schif-*

Consequently, under the 1976 London Convention only extraordinary circumstances give rise to a loss of the right to limit[270]. Undoubtedly, it is more in favour and protective of shipowners and the right to limit[271]. This situation also reflects the change in philosophy: limitation has become "a right rather than a privilege"[272]. Ensuring almost an indisputable right to limit for shipowners was, basically, a result of concerns regarding insurance[273]. It was aimed to bring the criteria of two important institutions in line with each other: the loss of the right to limit and the loss of insurance cover[274].

It is plain from the wording and the prerequisites of the 1976 London Convention Art. 4 that the owner will be deprived of the right to limit only in exceptional cases. Such an exceptional case is the *Saint Jacques II and Gudermes*[275]. The Saint Jacques II was navigating against the traffic flow in the English Channel in order to arrive at the fishing grounds before other vessels. She was therefore violating the 1972 Collision Convention provisions. Subsequently, she collided with the Gudermes. The skipper of the Saint Jacques II, who was at the same time one of the owners, had made a practice of navigating against the flow of the traffic. Therefore, the owners asserted in the trial that since the skipper was used to navigating in such a manner there was no actual knowledge as to the probability of a collision. Furthermore, they also asserted that the skipper did not have actual knowledge since at the time of the collision he was not in the wheelhouse, but below and sleeping. In addition to that, the skipper, before leaving the wheelhouse, warned all watch personnel to wake him up in case of the slightest doubt. Apart from the other issues, the court rejected these arguments by stating that navigating against the flow of the traffic constituted recklessness, and that the risk or probability of a collision did not decline with repeated reckless navigation. They concluded that a risk of collision and the probable consequences of such a risk were obvious when navigating in such a fashion. The court, further, stated that the warning of the skipper to all watch personnel clearly shows that he was actually aware of the collision risk and probable consequences. Therefore, the owners

---

fahrts G.M.B.H. & Co. K.G. (The "Leerort") [2001] 2 Lloyd's Rep. 291, 294 (CA) per Lord Phillips; *Margolle and Another v. Delta Maritime Co. Ltd. and Others (the "Saint Jacques II" and "Gudermes")* [2003] 1 Lloyd's Rep. 203, 207 (QBD) per Justice Gross; *The "Tasman Pioneer"* [2003] 2 Lloyd's Rep. 713, 719 (New Zealand High Court) per Justice Williams.

[270] *Dockray*, p. 338.
[271] *Dockray*, p. 348; *Özçayır*, pp. 358, 360.
[272] *Seward*, p. 182.
[273] *Richter*, p. 31; *Stachow*, p. 61.
[274] *Official Records, London Conference*, p. 264, Lord Diplock (UK): "the limits should be made as unbreakable as possible on the principle that breakability should begin where insurability ended"; *Coghlin*, pp. 249-250. See also *supra* § 3 B II.
[275] *Margolle and Another v. Delta Maritime Co. Ltd. and Others (the "Saint Jacques II" and "Gudermes")* [2003] 1 Lloyd's Rep. 203 (QBD).

of the Saint Jacques II were found guilty of wilful misconduct and therefore deprived of the right to limit their liability[276].

Notably, although the wording of the amended Warsaw Convention and the 1976 London Convention are almost identical, there are two important differences between the two conventions. The first one of these differences as found in the 1976 London Convention relates to the "personal act or omission" and the second one to the damage.

(1) Personal fault

Art. 4 stresses the necessity of the act or omission being the "personal act or omission" of the person liable[277]. Thus, the person liable, a term which refers to the persons entitled to limit liability as defined in Art. 1 of the Convention[278], must have intended to cause the damage or acted or omitted recklessly and with knowledge that the damage would probably result.

The qualification of the phrase "act or omission" by the attribute "personal" strongly indicates that the shipowner or salvor would not be accountable for acts or omissions of his servants and agents in wilful misconduct cases unless acts or omissions of those servants and agents can be attributed to the person liable[279]. The wording of the provision clearly indicates that every person liable would be accountable only for his own acts and omissions. Therefore, in a case against him, a shipowner would not be liable for wilful misconduct of the master[280], whereas in a case against him, the master would lose his right to limit if he is guilty of wilful misconduct himself[281].

---

[276] *Margolle and Another v. Delta Maritime Co. Ltd. and Others (the "Saint Jacques II" and "Gudermes")* [2003] 1 Lloyd's Rep. 203, 210 (QBD) *per* Justice Gross.

[277] The term "person liable" refers to the persons entitled to limit their liability under Art. 1 of the Convention.

[278] *Griggs/Williams/Farr*, p. 34; *Hodges/Hill*, p. 563; *Mandaraka-Sheppard*, p. 889; *Hill*, p. 406.

[279] *Davies/Dickey*, p. 468; *Gold/Chircop/Kindred*, p. 732; *Hodges/Hill*, p. 565; *Mandaraka-Sheppard*, p. 334; *Özçayır*, p. 358; *Puttfarken*, Rn. 832, 837; *Hill*, p. 407; *Herber, Haftungsrecht*, p. 71; *Grime, Loss of the Right*, p. 105; *Jefferies*, 305; *Wilson*, p. 288; *Williams, 1976 Limitation Convention*, 124; *de la Motte*, p. 293; *Watson*, 270; *Chen, Limitation*, pp. 73-74; *MSC Mediterranean Shipping Co. S.A. v. Delumar BVBA and Others (The "MSC Rosa M")* [2000] 2 Lloyd's Rep. 399, 401 (QBD) *per* Justice David Steel; *Schiffahrtsgesellschaft MS "Merkur Sky" M.B.H. & Co. K.G. v. MS Leerort Nth Schiffahrts G.M.B.H. & Co. K.G. (The "Leerort")* [2001] 2 Lloyd's Rep. 291, 294 (CA) *per* Lord Phillips; *Margolle and Another v. Delta Maritime Co. Ltd. and Others (the "Saint Jacques II" and "Gudermes")* [2003] 1 Lloyd's Rep. 203, 208 (QBD) *per* Justice Gross.

[280] See, for instance, the Maralunga case reported by Byung-Suk *Chung* and T.H. *Kim* in (1995) 7 Int.M.L. 176.

[281] *Griggs/Williams/Farr*, p. 35; *Gold/Chircop/Kindred*, p. 732; *Hodges/Hill*, p. 532; *Mandaraka-Sheppard*, p. 891; *Rabe*, LondonHBÜ 1976 Art. 4 Rn. 2; *Hill*, p. 407.

An important case as to the personal act or omission requirement along with the other basic requirements of the degree of fault in the 1976 London Convention is the German *"Heidberg"* case[282]. The vessel Heidberg flying the German flag came into collision with an oil pier. There was a pilot on board for the outgoing operations. During the operations, the master of the vessel left the wheelhouse in order to go to the engine room. Before leaving the wheelhouse, he did not put someone else from the crew in charge of the watch. When he was in the engine room, the collision occurred. The owner of the oil pier sued the shipowner, and the French court ruled for unlimited liability. The French court stated that the master was not able to put a member of the crew in charge in the wheelhouse when he was leaving since there were not enough crew members on board. The shipowners were held personally liable since they had to properly man the ship[283]. During the claim filed in Germany for the execution of the judgement, the shipowners asserted that the French court's judgement infringed the German *ordre public* since the vessel Heidberg was manned pursuant to the German manning regulations. In other words, they claimed there were enough crew members on board in accordance with German law in force at the time of the collision. The German court rejected such an application by stating that a decision for unlimited liability of a shipowner would also be obtained under German law[284].

Leaving aside the issue of the master's and pilot's negligence for which the shipowner is liable (which, however, results only in the limited liability of the shipowner), two important issue as to the unlimited liability should be addressed with regard to the *Heidberg* case. The first basic requirement of the unlimited liability under the 1976 London Convention is that there should be misconduct by the person liable, and shipowners in the *Heidberg* case asserted that they have manned the ship according to the flag state rules in force at the time of the collision[285]. Nevertheless, the German court stated that public law regulations set minimum standards, and meeting these minimum standards does not always mean fulfilling the duty to properly man a ship. The court stressed that if another officer would be on the bridge to keep the watch when the master was in the engine room, the collision could have been prevented. The general requirement of having two watch officers on board does not fulfil the duty to properly man the ship, since one of these officers can always be absent for one reason or another. The ignorance of

---

[282] OLG Hamburg, 15.09.1994, TranspR 1994, 451 = RIW 1995, 680. The facts of the case can be found also in *Partenreederei M/S "Heidberg" and Another v. Grosvenor Grain and Feed Co. Ltd. and Others (The "Heidberg")* [1993] 2 Lloyd's Rep. 324 (QBD).

[283] OLG Hamburg, 15.09.1994, TranspR 1994, 451 (452-453). See also *Griggs/Williams/Farr*, p. 40 fn. 121; *Puttfarken*, Rn. 836.

[284] OLG Hamburg, 15.09.1994, TranspR 1994, 451 (453).

[285] In a similar case, in fact, the German Federal Court emphasised that reference to unseaworthiness of the ship and, consequently, to personal fault of the shipowners cannot be made if the ship is properly manned according to the flag state's rules and regulations which comply with international standards, see BGH, 26.10.2006, TranspR 2007, 36 (*MS "CITA"*).

this risk together with the failure to properly man the ship constitutes personal grave fault on the side of the shipowner[286].

The second point to be addressed with regard to the case is that the personal fault needs to be coupled with the subjective knowledge as to the actual damage occurred. The misconduct and the foresight of the master and the pilot in the case cannot be attributed to the shipowners. Whether the shipowners, on the other hand, had foreseen the collision damage due to the insufficient number of crew on board, had not been discussed in the decision. Another basic requirement, *i.e.* the subjective knowledge as to the actual damage occurred seems to be missing.

However, if the master and one of the owners are the same person, it naturally becomes easier to fulfil the personal fault requirement. An example of such a situation is the *Saint Jacques II and the Gudermes* case, the facts of which were mentioned earlier[287]. There, the skipper of the vessel was at the same time one of the owners. Therefore, it was not hard to find the owners personally at fault[288].

Another case to be mentioned in respect of personal fault is *The Tasman Pioneer*. In that case, the vessel Tasman Pioneer was grounded due to the inappropriate selection of the sailing course by the master. As a result of the grounding, much of the cargo was damaged. At the time of the incident, the vessel was time chartered. The time charterers applied for an order of limitation of their liability, against which the cargo interests filed a claim of wilful misconduct and unlimited liability. The court concluded that the incident was the result of the master's negligence. However, even if the master were guilty of reckless conduct as defined in the 1976 London Convention Art. 4, the time charterers would still be entitled to limit their liability since unlimited liability can be imposed only if the person liable is personally at fault, and the time charterers of the vessel were not personally guilty of wilful misconduct[289].

(2) Such loss

Pursuant to Art. 4, a person liable would not be entitled to benefit from the liability limits if the loss resulted from his act or omission "committed with the intent to cause *such* loss, or recklessly and with knowledge that *such* loss would probably result"[290].

To start with, the term "loss" covers all types of loss referred to in Art. 2 of the Convention, *e.g.* loss of life, personal injury, loss of or damage to property, loss resulting from delay[291]. If, on the contrary, the term "loss" only referred to losses

---

[286] OLG Hamburg, 15.09.1994, TranspR 1994, 451 (453).

[287] See *supra* C II 2 b bb.

[288] *Margolle and Another v. Delta Maritime Co. Ltd. and Others (the "Saint Jacques II" and "Gudermes")* [2003] 1 Lloyd's Rep. 203 (QBD).

[289] *The "Tasman Pioneer"* [2003] 2 Lloyd's Rep. 713, 723 (New Zealand High Court).

[290] Emphasis added.

[291] *Griggs/Williams/Farr*, p. 35; parallel *Schiffahrtsgesellschaft MS "Merkur Sky" M.B.H. & Co. K.G. v. MS Leerort Nth Schiffahrts G.M.B.H. & Co. K.G. (The "Leerort")* [2001] 2 Lloyd's Rep. 291, 295 (CA) *per* Lord Phillips.

and not to damages, namely only to the paragraphs of Art. 2 where loss was clearly mentioned, breaking the limits of liability of the person liable would not be possible for claims where the term "loss" is not specifically mentioned. Naturally, such a result cannot be assumed to have been intended by the drafters of the Convention[292].

Does the term "such loss" refer to the *kind* or *type* of loss or the actual loss which occurred? On this point, one must refer to the discussion on the amended version of Art. 25 of the Warsaw Convention. There it was said that together with the foresight criterion, the wrongdoer must have foreseen at least the type or kind of damage incurred when the wording only refers to "damage" not "the damage"[293]. Here, Art. 4 of the 1976 London Convention clearly stipulates that only foresight of "*such* loss" would deprive the person liable of the limits. Therefore, under the 1976 London Convention regime the wrongdoer has to have foreseen the *very* actual damage, or in other words the *same* damage, which has occurred[294].

A good example in this respect is the *MSC Rosa M* case. There were some defects within the fuel and ballast systems of the MSC Rosa M. She nearly capsized and, therefore, substantial salvage and cargo claims were made. The cargo claimants alleged wilful misconduct. The court concluded that the demise charterers were grossly negligent, but not guilty of wilful misconduct. Furthermore, even if they had been guilty of wilful misconduct, "the nature of the risks associated with these defects was that of contamination and pollution and not that of capsize"[295]. So, the court stressed that foresight of the very actual damage is necessary.

However, the reference to the actual damage does not mean, for example, that the person liable in a collision case knew that his ship would collide with *the* ship; it is sufficient to show that the person liable knew that his ship would collide with *a* ship. And since the loss or damage which might result from a collision is known to everyone in the shipping industry, it is not wrong to say that if a collision was foreseen, the subsequent losses or damages were foreseen as well. *The Leerort* case can be cited in this regard: "where the loss in respect of which a claim is made resulted from a collision between ship A and ship B, the owners of ship A, or cargo in ship A, will only defeat the right to limit liability on the owner of ship B if they can prove that the owner of ship B intended that it should collide *with ship A,* or acted recklessly with the knowledge that it was likely to do so. The alternative, which is perhaps arguable, is that the claimant merely has to prove that the owner of ship B intended that his ship should collide *with another ship,* or

---

[292] *Griggs/Williams/Farr*, p. 154; *Mandaraka-Sheppard*, p. 903.

[293] See *supra* § 4 B I 2 c bb (2) (c).

[294] *Griggs/Williams/Farr*, p. 36; *Hodges/Hill*, pp. 593-594; *Mandaraka-Sheppard*, p. 334; *Dockray*, p. 349; *Grime, Loss of the Right*, p. 111; *Schiffahrtsgesellschaft MS "Merkur Sky" M.B.H. & Co. K.G. v. MS Leerort Nth Schiffahrts G.M.B.H. & Co. K.G.* (*The "Leerort"*) [2001] 2 Lloyd's Rep. 291, 294-295 (CA) *per* Lord Phillips.

[295] *MSC Mediterranean Shipping Co. S.A. v. Delumar BVBA and Others* (*The "MSC Rosa M"*) [2000] 2 Lloyd's Rep. 399, 405 (QBD).

acted recklessly with knowledge that it was likely to do so"[296]. This approach was also adopted by the *Saint Jacques II and the Gudermes* case. It was stated that the "knowledge of the probability of a collision, whether with *Gudermes* or with some other vessel would suffice for Art. 4 [of the 1976 London Convention]"[297].

A very good example in this respect is the *Maria* case. The defendant, producer of several chemical materials, has chartered the vessel Maria for a voyage from Norway to Germany for the carriage of packed chemical material. The material was not listed in the International Maritime Dangerous Goods (IMDG) Code[298], and hence the charterer of the vessel informed neither the master nor the ship-owner as to the natural character of the goods. On the bill of lading as well, the goods were described as non dangerous cargo. However, due to the nature of the goods, an explosive gas mixture came out if they came into contact with water, which necessitated that the holds of the vessel be ventilated regularly. The need for the ventilation was stated in the bill of lading. It was rainy during the loading operations, and after the loading was completed, there was considerable free space in the holds. Due to the heavy weather conditions on the voyage to Germany, the ventilators and hatches were kept closed in order to prevent the entry of the sea water to the holds. At the intermediate stop where the vessel needed to undergo minor repair work, a strong explosion occurred on the Maria which caused loss of life and severe injuries to the crew on board. Moreover, the Maria, some yachts around and the berth were all heavily damaged. The defendant alleged that it was not liable, and even if it was liable, it was entitled to limit its liability to the amounts specified in the 1976 London Convention. The court ruled that the defendant was liable since it did not provide the necessary information as to the nature of the goods which it had as the producer of chemical materials. The court, further, held that the defendant would not be entitled to limit its liability under the 1976 London Convention regime. The defendant was familiar with the carriage conditions, and therefore was in a position to foresee that, due to the rough seas, the ventilators and hatches would be closed. Furthermore, the defendant was involved in two previous explosions which occurred on other ships during the carriage of the same kind of cargo, with the difference that the goods were not packed but were carried as bulk. As a result, the defendant had actual knowledge that such loss, *i.e.* an explosion would probably occur[299].

The last point to be emphasised is the difference between the wordings of the Hague/Visby Rules (*damage*) and the Hamburg Rules, Athens Convention and the 1976 London Convention (*such loss or damage*). The difference between the Hague/Visby Rules and the Hamburg Rules on one side and the Athens Conven-

---

[296] Emphasis added; *Schiffahrtsgesellschaft MS "Merkur Sky" M.B.H. & Co. K.G. v. MS Leerort Nth Schiffahrts G.M.B.H. & Co. K.G. (The "Leerort")* [2001] 2 Lloyd's Rep. 291, 295 (CA) *per* Lord Phillips.

[297] *Margolle and Another v. Delta Maritime Co. Ltd. and Others (the "Saint Jacques II" and "Gudermes")* [2003] 1 Lloyd's Rep. 203, 210 (QBD) *per* Justice Gross.

[298] For more information about the carriage of dangerous goods by sea see Meltem Deniz *Güner-Özbek*, The Carriage of Dangerous Goods by Sea, Berlin 2008.

[299] LG Hamburg, 23.04 2003, HmbSchRZ 2009, 252.

tion on the other does not need any particular attention since they are not concurrently applicable. However, the Hague/Visby Rules and the 1976 London Convention can be applied to the same conflict. Hypothetically, a carrier can lose his right to limit under the Hague/Visby Rules (*damage*), since he had foreseen the type or kind of the damage occurred but still be able to limit his liability under the London Convention, since he had not foreseen the actual damage which occurred (*such loss*).

D. Persons

I. Owner

1. Registered owner

Art. 1 (2) of the 1976 London Convention states that the term "shipowner" means the "owner [...] of a seagoing ship". Bunker Convention Art. 1 (3) also contains a wide definition of the term "shipowner", including the registered owner of the ship. Specific reference to the registered shipowner can be found in the CLC'92 Art. I (3) and HNS Art. 1 (3). According to these provisions "owner" means the person or persons registered as the owner of the ship or, in the absence of registration, the person or persons owning the ship.

Consequently, as to the term "owner", a distinction can be made between the registered owner (or as is sometimes stated: the "legal owner") and the beneficial owner of a ship[300]. Fairly self-evidently and straightforwardly, the term "registered owner" can be defined as being the person who is registered as the owner in a ship registry or the person who has the legal title to the ship.

2. Disponent owner

The term beneficial owner can cause more problems, but they are not hard to overcome. If a person other than the registered owner has the full possession of the ship, meaning the responsibility for its navigation, management and commercial exploitation, either by a lease agreement or by a charter by demise (also called "bareboat charter"[301]) – in other words, if that person runs the ship through the master and crew he has appointed (or demised) on his own behalf – this person is

---

[300] *Griggs/Williams/Farr*, p. 7; *Hodges/Hill*, p. 528.

[301] For more information see Mark *Davis*, Bareboat Charters, 2nd Ed., London 2005; *Atamer, Cebrî İcra*, p. 155; *Gold/Chircop/Kindred*, pp. 380-381; *Özçayır*, p. 74; *Puttfarken*, Rn. 369 et seqq.; *Rabe*, § 510 Rn. 13-14; *Hill*, p. 168; *Scrutton*, pp. 55 et seqq.; *Athanassopoulou*, pp. 106 et seqq. Yet, there is still a slight difference between the bare-boat charter and charter by demise, see *Tetley*, pp. 578-579; *Scrutton*, p. 55 fn. 2; *Puttfarken*, Rn. 333; *Tetley, IoC*, p. 509; *Ülgener, DenizHD*, p. 19.

called as the "beneficial" or "disponent" owner or "owner *pro hac vice*"[302]. A disponent owner's responsibility to third parties is equal to a registered ship-owner's liability[303]; whereas the relationship between the registered and disponent shipowners remains subject to the lease or charter by demise[304].

However, an exception should be made here in relation to the CLC'92 and HNS. Both conventions channel liability to the "registered owner". Bareboat charterers, although being owner *pro hac vice*, may or may not be considered the registered owner. National laws should be addressed on the issue whether bareboat charterers need to be considered as the registered owner under the CLC'92 and the HNS regime[305].

II. Manager or Operator

Pursuant to Art. 1 (3) of the Bunker Convention, the term "shipowner" also means the manager or operator of the ship. The same provision can be found in the 1976 London Convention Art. 1 (2). It must be emphasised that although their definitions are not identical, these two terms are used interchangeably.

A ship manager, also known as a "shipbroker" or "agent", is a natural or legal person who is appointed to manage the ship (or ships) for its owners. As almost all of the shipowners are companies, ship managers are also (almost without exception) companies and are generally formed as the sister company of the shipowning company[306].

Although their tasks are various, it can be said that generally, managers enter into contracts on behalf of the owners. If the whole of management is delegated to a ship manager, he is obliged to, for example, supply all necessary services on board, employ the crew and arrange charterparties. Thus, a manager deals with the marketing, technical operation and manning of the ship on behalf of the ship-owner[307]. It is also worth mentioning that the crewing agent is not a manager in the sense of the 1976 London Convention. He is an independent contractor of the

---

[302] *Tetley*, pp. 578-579; *Schoenbaum*, V. II, p. 7; *Özçayır*, p. 78; *Chen, Limitation*, p. 4; *CMA CGM S.A. v. Classica Shipping Co. Ltd.* [2003] 2 Lloyd's Rep. 50, 54 (QBD).

[303] HGB § 510 (for more information see *Puttfarken*, Rn. 332; *Rabe*, § 510; *Herber*, pp. 131-135; *Athanassopoulou*, pp. 73 *et seqq*), TTK (1956) Art. 946, TTK (2011) Art. 1061. For English law see *Özçayır*, pp. 78-79; for American law see *Schoenbaum*, V. II, pp. 8, 43.

[304] *Athanassopoulou*, p. 96.

[305] See *e.g. Gauci, Oil Pollution*, pp. 92-93.

[306] *Mandaraka-Sheppard*, p. 299; *Ülgener, DenizHD*, p. 14; *Athanassopoulou*, pp. 209-210.

[307] *Mandaraka-Sheppard*, p. 300; *Rabe*, Vor § 556 Rn. 18, 28; *Atamer, Cebrî İcra*, pp. 157-158; *Ülgener, DenizHD*, p. 16. For the ship and crew management agreement forms visit the BIMCO web site: <www.bimco.org> and for general information on these agreements see *Mandaraka-Sheppard*, pp. 300-302; *Athanassopoulou*, pp. 214 *et seqq*. For detailed information see Malcolm *Willingale*, Ship Management, 3rd Ed., London 1998.

owner or manager or operator of the ship whose main obligation is to find a crew for the ship[308].

The term "operator" seems to cover the persons who are officially engaged in the operation of the ship but cannot be classified as owner, charterer or manager[309]. For instance, when a mortgagee of a ship takes the ship into his possession (if he is entitled to do so under national law[310]), he becomes "operator" of a ship and also entitled to limit his liability[311]. It has been said that the same legal situation arises when the stevedore takes over the complete control of the ship during loading or unloading operations[312].

The last point to be emphasised is that under the 1976 London Convention regime, only the limitation and loss of the right to limit with regard to third parties are regulated. The legal relationship between the operator or manager and the shipowner is covered solely by the provisions applicable to the particular case[313]. For example, if there is a management contract between the owner and the manager, provisions of that contract are to be applied. However, if the mortgagee of a ship takes over the operation, the terms of the legal relationship giving rise to the assumption of the operation will be determinative as to whether the operator is entitled to limit against the shipowner.

III. Charterer

The charterer is listed as one of the persons who is entitled to limit his liability under the 1976 London Convention regime. According to the Convention, the term "shipowner" also covers the charterer. Moreover, if he issues bills of lading or enters into contracts for the carriage of goods, the charterer is responsible towards the shippers in the capacity as "carrier"[314] and is entitled to limit his liability both under the relevant conventions regarding the carriage of goods and under the 1976 London Convention. In the case of carriage of passengers, the same legal situation exists towards the passengers as under the Athens Convention and the 1976 London Convention regimes.

Charterer is a broad term and needs to be specified for the purposes of the 1976 London Convention. There are different types of charter agreements, but the most common ones are demise charters, time charters, voyage charters and slot charters.

---

[308] *Griggs/Williams/Farr*, p. 9; *Mandaraka-Sheppard*, p. 868.
[309] *Rabe*, LondonHBÜ 1976 Art. 1 Rn. 10; *Atamer, Cebrî İcra*, pp. 158-159. However, the term is wide enough to cover managers and charterers as well, see *Griggs/Williams/Farr*, p. 9; *Hodges/Hill*, p. 529; see also the example given by *Brice*, p. 29.
[310] See *e.g.* Samim *Ünan*, Gemi İpoteğinde „Lex Commissoria" Yasağı, Marmara Üniversitesi Hukuk Fakültesi Hukuk Araştırmaları Dergisi X/1-3 (1996), p. 443.
[311] *Hodges/Hill*, p. 529; *Mandaraka-Sheppard*, p. 868; *Shaw/Tsimplis*, p. 203; *Griggs/Williams/Farr*, p. 8; whereby they generally appoint a manager since they are not involved in the day-to-day shipping business, see *Ülgener, DenizHD*, p. 15.
[312] *Chen, Limitation*, p. 8.
[313] *Mandaraka-Sheppard*, p. 309.
[314] For more information see *Puttfarken*, Rn. 388 *et seqq.*; see also *infra* D IV.

As stated above[315], a demise charterer is to be deemed a disponent owner, since he acts in the capacity of a shipowner. However, other charter types are still to be examined.

However, before proceeding with this examination, it should be mentioned that the range of persons against whom the charterers can limit their liability is highly disputed. Towards third persons, there is no doubt that charterers are entitled to limit their liability. However, whether a charterer has the right to limit his liability against a shipowner under the 1976 London Convention regime is hotly contested[316]. It is said that charterers are entitled to limit their liability "when acting in the capacity of shipowner"[317]. Acting in the capacity of shipowner, in other words acting *qua* owner[318], means for example "issuing bills of lading"[319] or "undertaking an activity usually associated with ownership"[320] [such as operating or managing the vessel]. Nevertheless, the case law on this point is developing in the advantage of the charterers[321].

---

[315] See *supra* D I 2.

[316] *Griggs/Williams/Farr*, pp. 9-10; *Mandaraka-Sheppard*, pp. 868-871; *Girvin*, para. 29.43; Patrick *Griggs*, Charterer's Right to Limit Liability, CMI Yearbook 2009, p. 364; Nicholas *Gaskell*, Charterers' Liability to Shipowner, in: Johan *Schelin* (Editor), Modern Law of Charterparties, Stockholm 2003, pp. 19 *et seqq*. For the situation under some national laws, see CMI Documents, Charterers' Right to Limit Liability, available on <www.comitemaritime.org/cmidocs/pdf/Synopsis. pdf> (09.08.2010).

[317] *Griggs/Williams/Farr*, p. 9; *Chen, Limitation*, p. 7; *Ataol*, p. 65.

[318] *CMA CGM S.A. v. Classica Shipping Co. Ltd.* [2003] 2 Lloyd's Rep. 50, 54 (QBD) *per* Justice David Steel; *Watson*, 253; *Chen, Limitation*, p. 7 (the two writers use the term "*qua* carrier").

[319] *Griggs/Williams/Farr*, p. 10; *Baughen*, p. 423.

[320] *CMA CGM S.A. v. Classica Shipping Co. Ltd.* [2003] 2 Lloyd's Rep. 50, 54 (QBD) *per* Justice David Steel; affirmed by *CMA CGM S.A. v. Classica Shipping Co. Ltd.* [2004] 1 Lloyd's Rep. 460 (CA).

[321] In the *Aegean Sea Traders Corporation v. Repsol Petroleo S.A. and Another, (The "Aegean Sea")* [1998] 2 Lloyd's Rep. 39, the Queen's Bench Division ruled that the charterer has the right to limit only when he is acting in the capacity of a shipowner (for a discussion of the case, see Cüneyt *Süzel*, 1976 LLMC Konvansiyonu Uyarınca Gemi Malikinin Talepleri Karşısında Çartererin Sorumluluğunu Sınırlama İmkanı, DenizHD 2003/1-4, p. 145); in the *CMA CGM S.A. v. Classica Shipping Co. Ltd.* [2003] 2 Lloyd's Rep. 50 the Queen's Bench Division followed the *Aegean Sea*; however its decision was dismissed by the Court of Appeal with regard to the charterer's right to limit, see *CMA CGM S.A. v. Classica Shipping Co. Ltd.* [2004] 1 Lloyd's Rep. 460. The Court of Appeal held that the charterer's right to limit is a natural result of the application of the Convention. Nonetheless, the claim brought against the charterer should fall within the sphere of Art. 2 of the 1976 London Convention. In the *Maria* case, the German court left the question unanswered whether a charterer can principally limit its liability against shipowner. However, the analysis of the court suggests a negative answer, see LG Hamburg, 23.04.2003, HmbSchRZ 2009, 252 (263).

1. Voyage charterer

A voyage charter is known as one of the oldest forms of contract of affreight-ment[322]. Voyage charter can be defined as a contract whereby a shipowner, registered or disponent, lets the use of his ship to the voyage charterer. The characteristic of a voyage charter is that the shipowner undertakes the carriage of a specified cargo for a particular voyage between two named ports[323].

2. Time charterer

A time charter is a contract whereby a shipowner lets the use of the whole carrying capacity of his ship to the time charterer. However, unlike the voyage charter, the shipowner undertakes the carriage of cargo as the charterer desires within a specified time. The nautical management, or in other words, the navigation of the ship through the master and crew is under the shipowner's authority, whereas the charterer has the right to give orders and instructions as to the economic utilisation of the ship[324].

The term "time charterer" also covers sub-time charterers for the purposes of the 1976 London Convention since there is no distinction under the Convention's regime on this point[325]. Time charterers are specifically important for the Bunker Convention since, under the time charter agreement, the time charterer is responsible for supplying the bunker[326].

3. Slot charterer

A slot charterer is the person who has the right to use a specified part of the ship, generally a hold or a portion of it, which is named as a slot. This person does not use the whole of the ship. This type of charter is used generally for container shipping[327]. Slot charterers can enter into contracts of carriage and issue a bill of lading in their name. In such a case, they will be liable in the capacity of a carrier and

---

[322] *Özçayır*, p. 75.
[323] *Gold/Chircop/Kindred*, pp. 378-379; *Özçayır*, p. 75; *Puttfarken*, Rn. 333; *Rabe*, § 556 Rn. 4. For more information see *Gold/Chircop/Kindred*, p. 381 *et seqq.*; *Özçayır*, p. 75-76; *Puttfarken*, Rn. 337 *et seqq.*; *Rabe*, § 556 Rn. 4-6; *Schoenbaum*, V. II, pp. 8-11; *Wilson*, pp. 49 *et seqq.*
[324] For more information see *Coghlin/et al.*, para. 19.1 *et seqq.*; *Scrutton*, p. 311 *et seqq.*; *Schoenbaum*, V. II, pp. 11-12; *Gold/Chircop/Kindred*, p. 399 *et seqq.*; *Atamer, Cebrî İcra*, p. 156; *Özçayır*, p. 76 *et seqq.*; *Puttfarken*, Rn. 333, 361 *et seqq.*; *Hill*, p. 171; *Wilson*, pp. 85 *et seqq.*; *Athanassopoulou*, pp. 150 *et seqq.*
[325] *The "Tasman Pioneer"* [2003] 2 Lloyd's Rep. 713, 718-719 (New Zealand High Court).
[326] *Hodges/Hill*, p. 166, for more information on the bunker issue, see *Coghlin/et al.*, para. 13.1-13.10.
[327] *Griggs/Williams/Farr*, p. 11; *Gold/Chircop/Kindred*, pp. 379-380; *Rabe*, London-HBÜ 1976 Art. 1 Rn. 8; *Hill*, p. 171.

will be entitled to limit their liability[328] under relevant international regimes. It is debated whether the slot charterers are entitled to limit as "charterers" under the 1976 London Convention regime. Such a discussion arises since all other persons mentioned in Art. 1 of the 1976 London Convention have an interest in the whole of the ship and their liability limit is calculated on the basis of the tonnage of the ship. If the question of whether a slot charterer is entitled to limit as a "charterer" is answered in the negative, a slot charterer will not be able to limit his liability under the 1976 London Convention regime[329]. However, though they are not using the whole of the ship, it is generally accepted that slot charterers are within the term "charterer" due to the general underlying policy for limitation and clear wording of the Convention and that they are entitled to limit their liability under the 1976 London Convention regime[330].

With regard to the question on which basis a slot charterer can limit his liability, there are two possibilities to be considered. Firstly, a slot charterer can limit his liability proportionately to the space which he has chartered. However, with this possibility, difficulty arises from the lack of any provision in the 1976 London Convention allowing such calculation. Secondly, a slot charterer can limit his liability according to the full tonnage of the ship, although he is using only a part of it[331]. It is generally accepted that slot charterers cannot limit their liability by reference to the space they are using due to the lack of relevant provisions. Therefore, they can only limit their liability according to the full tonnage of the ship[332].

IV. Carrier

1. Contractual carrier

According to the international conventions on the carriage of goods or passengers by sea, the "carrier" is entitled to limit his liability[333]. In this respect, all of the relevant conventions define the term "carrier". According to the Hague/Visby Rules Art. I (a) "carrier includes the owner or the charterer who enters into a contract of carriage with a shipper". According to the Hamburg Rules Art. 1 (1) "carrier means any person by whom or in whose name a contract of carriage of

---

[328] *Williams, 1976 Limitation Convention*, 118-119. Sometimes the multimodal transport operator is also the slot charterer, see *Rabe*, LondonHBÜ 1976 Art. 1 Rn. 11.

[329] *Griggs/Williams/Farr*, p. 11.

[330] *Griggs/Williams/Farr*, p. 11; *Rabe*, LondonHBÜ 1976 Art. 1 Rn. 8; *Shaw/Tsimplis*, p. 203; *Williams, 1976 Limitation Convention*, 119-120. See also *The "Tychy"* [1999] 2 Lloyd's Rep. 11 (CA); *Metvale Ltd v. Monsanto International Sarl (The "MSC Napoli")* [2009] 1 Lloyd's Rep. 246 (QBD).

[331] *Griggs/Williams/Farr*, p. 11.

[332] *Griggs/Williams/Farr*, p. 11; *Williams, 1976 Limitation Convention*, 120-121; *Metvale Ltd v. Monsanto International Sarl (The "MSC Napoli")* [2009] 1 Lloyd's Rep. 246, 249 (QBD) *per* Justice Teare; for the counterview see *Rabe*, LondonHBÜ 1976 Art. 1 Rn. 8.

[333] Hague/Visby Rules Art. IV (5); Hamburg Rules Art. 6 (1); Athens Convention 2002 Art. 3.

goods by sea has been concluded with a shipper". Pursuant to the Rotterdam Rules Art. 1 (5) "carrier means a person that enters into a contract of carriage with a shipper". Finally, carrier is defined in the Athens Convention 2002 Art. 1 (1) as "a person by or on behalf of whom a contract of carriage has been concluded, whether the carriage is actually performed by that person or by a performing carrier"[334].

If all these definitions are considered, for the purposes of the international maritime conventions for the carriage of goods and passengers by sea, a carrier is the person who enters into a contract of carriage[335] with the shipper (or the passenger) directly or through a representative and being either the owner or the charterer of the ship on which the goods or passengers are carried[336].

An important point here is that the contract entered into should be a "contract *of* carriage", but not a "contract *for* carriage"[337]. In this respect, a freight forwarder (or a forwarding agent), for example, who enters into a "contract *of* carriage" with the shipper (and issues a bill of lading) in his own name, will be ranked as a carrier. However, freight forwarders generally sign contracts as agent of the carrier, and, even if they sign the contract in their own name, they do not issue bills of lading. Their general duty is to "organise" the carriage ("contract *for* carriage"). Therefore, they cannot be classified as a "contractual carrier"[338].

2. Actual or performing carrier

a) Definitions

A contractual carrier is under no obligation to perform the carriage personally. The contract of carriage can be performed by someone else, which is, in fact, often the case in maritime practice. In light of this fact, the international conventions on maritime carriage either define the "actual" or "performing" carrier, or define the carrier in such a way that the definition also covers the actual carrier.

---

[334] It is said that the definition is intentionally designed so broadly in order to cover tour operators, ferry companies, cruise companies and the like as well, see *Griggs/ Williams/Farr*, p. 97; *Gold/Chircop/Kindred*, p. 483; *Herber, Haftungsrecht*, p. 160; *Schubert*, p. 56; *Atamer, Yolcu Taşıma*, p. 130.

[335] Hague and Hague/Visby Rules Art. I (b): "'Contract of carriage' applies only to contracts of carriage covered by a bill of lading or any similar document of title"; Hamburg Rules Art. 1 (6): "'Contract of carriage by sea' means any contract whereby the carrier undertakes against payment of freight to carry goods by sea from one port to another"; Rotterdam Rules Art. 1 (1): "'Contract of carriage' means a contract in which a carrier, against the payment of freight, undertakes to carry goods from one place to another."; Athens Convention Art. 1 (2): "'contract of carriage' means a contract made by or on behalf of a carrier for the carriage by sea of a passenger or of a passenger and his luggage, as the case may be".

[336] *Rabe*, Vor § 556 Rn. 9; *Ilse*, p. 11; *Tetley, IoC*, p. 508; *Cooke/et al.*, para. 85.59-85.62.

[337] *Aikens/Lord/Bools*, para. 10.66. However, the phrase "contract for carriage" is also used as a synonym of "contract of affreightment", see *Scrutton*, p. 1.

[338] *Rabe*, Vor § 556 Rn. 10; *Kienzle*, pp. 29-30; *Scrutton*, pp. 51-54.

Art. I (a) of the Hague/Visby Rules provides that the carrier includes the owner or the charterer who enters into a contract of carriage with a shipper. Although the provision only defines the term "carrier", it clearly states that the term "carrier" *includes* owner or charterer of the ship. Moreover, this definition is not exhaustive; on the contrary it only specifies owner and charterer. Nonetheless, it also covers the actual carrier[339].

Unlike the Hague/Visby Rules, the Hamburg Rules clearly define the actual carrier. According to the Hamburg Rules Art. 1 (2) "actual carrier" means any person to whom the performance of the carriage of the goods, or of part of the carriage, has been entrusted by the carrier, and includes any other person to whom such performance has been entrusted. Here, the person who is charged by the contractual carrier with the performance of the carriage or a part of it is the actual carrier. As for the purposes of the Hamburg Rules, it is not important whether this person actually performs the carriage or not[340]. The actual carrier can also entrust the performance of his carriage duty to another person. Since the Hamburg Rules state that "any other person to whom such performance is entrusted" is to be classified as the actual carrier, any person who has been entrusted the performance of a part or the whole of the carriage will be an actual carrier[341].

The Rotterdam Rules adopt the definition of "performing party" as "a person other than the carrier that performs or undertakes to perform any of the carrier's obligations under a contract of carriage with respect to the receipt, loading, handling, stowage, carriage, care, unloading or delivery of the goods, to the extent that such person acts, either directly or indirectly, at the carrier's request or under the carrier's supervision or control" (Art. 1 (6)(a)). It is clear that this wide definition also covers the actual or performing carrier since the definition also includes any "person other than the carrier that performs or undertakes to perform any of the carrier's obligations under a contract of carriage with respect to the [...] carriage". Nevertheless, the Rotterdam Rules adopt another provision defining the "maritime performing party" which covers specifically the performing carrier. According to Art. 1 (7) of the Rules, a maritime performing party "means a performing party to the extent that it performs or undertakes to perform any of the carrier's obligations during the period between the arrival of the goods at the port of loading of a ship and their departure from the port of discharge of a ship".

The Athens Convention 2002 also defines the performing carrier. According to Art. 1 (1) (b), "performing carrier" means a person other than the carrier, being the owner, charterer or operator of a ship, who actually performs the whole or a part of the carriage. Under this definition, if a person, either being the owner, charterer or operator of a ship, actually performs the carriage, that person would be liable as the performing carrier. However, here, different from the Hamburg Rules, a performing carrier can be only "a person" who "actually" performs the carriage; thus, the determining criterion is whether the person has "actually", *i.e.* through having the possession of the ship, performed the carriage. Therefore, a person who has

---

[339] *Tetley*, p. 566.
[340] *Kienzle*, p. 90; *Yazıcıoğlu*, p. 46.
[341] *Kienzle*, pp. 98; 108-110.

been entrusted, but has not actually performed the carriage, is not the performing carrier under the Athens Convention[342].

Although the focus is placed on the party who actually discharges the carriage under the Hamburg Rules, Rotterdam Rules and the Athens Convention 2002, it is clear that the Hamburg Rules and Rotterdam Rules definitions cover a wider sphere than the Athens Convention 2002[343]. Nevertheless, the important point as to the actual or performing carrier is that he is jointly and severally liable for the part of the carriage he has performed together with the contractual carrier (Art. 10 (2) of the Hamburg Rules, Art. 19-20 of the Rotterdam Rules, and Art. 4 (1) of the Athens Convention 2002).

b) Bill of lading contract?

Due to the complex contractual relationships in maritime law, there are generally many parties involved in the same carriage. The simplest example is that a shipowner lets his ship by means of a time charter to a time charterer, and the time charterer enters into contracts of carriage with third parties. In such cases where the shipowner and the contractual carrier are not identical persons, the bill of lading is issued by the time charterer on his own behalf, which is known as a "charterer's bill", and does not pose any problems since the contractual carrier and the carrier shown on the bill of lading are the same persons. In other words, the contractual carrier under the carriage contract and the person who is under the carriage obligation by virtue of the bill of lading are the same[344]. However, in shipping practice, it is rare that a time charterer issues bills of lading[345].

However, if the bill of lading is issued by the master, or if it is issued by the time charterer on behalf or as an agent of the master[346], and, additionally, if the name of the carrier is not shown clearly on the bill of lading (the so-called "owner's bill")[347], the question is whether the (registered or disponent)[348] ship-

---

[342] *Atamer, Yolcu Taşıma*, p. 133; *Herber, Haftungsrecht*, p. 160; *Kröger*, p. 10.

[343] *Lüddeke/Johnson*, pp. 2-3.

[344] *Wilson*, p. 246; *Hill*, pp. 193-194; *Tetley*, p. 580; *Rabe*, § 644 Rn. 3; *Coghlin/et al.*, para. 21.2-21.10.

[345] *Hill*, p. 198. However, the Hamburg Rules Art. 14 (2) provides that "A bill of lading signed by the master of the ship carrying the goods is deemed to have been signed on behalf of the carrier". Therefore, under the Hamburg Rules, a bill of lading issued is always a "charterer's bill". See also *Tetley*, p. 600.

[346] Which is the customary practice, see *Schmidt*, p. 51. See also BIMCO NYPE 93 Form, Clause 30 (Bills of Lading): "(a) [...] the Charterers may sign bills of lading or waybills on behalf of the Master, with the Owner's prior written authority".

[347] *Hill*, pp. 193-194; *Schoenbaum*, V. II, p. 18; *Wilson*, pp. 244-245; *Cooke/et al.*, para. 85.62; *Coghlin/et al.*, para. 21.11-21.13; see also *Schoenbaum*, V. I, p. 617 fn. 2. In German (§ 644 HGB) and Turkish (TTK (1956) Art. 1099, TTK (2011) Art. 1238) law, if the bill of lading issued by the master or by another agent of the shipowner does not contain the name of the carrier, the shipowner is to be deemed as the carrier. For more information see *Rabe*, § 644; *Puttfarken*, Rn. 116; *Schmidt*, pp. 30 *et seqq.*

owner is to be deemed at the same time the contractual carrier. In order to answer this question, it should first be determined whether a bill of lading constitutes a separate contract of carriage[349].

A bill of lading is a document of title (negotiable instrument), which should include certain entries. It is transferable, so it can be legally transferred by way of endorsement, and the endorsee becomes the owner of the goods since the bill of lading transfers the title to the goods[350]. This function of the bill of lading necessitates that the entries on it should be correct, especially the ones regarding the quantity and the conditions of the goods laden. The carrier is under the obligation to deliver the goods to the consignee (endorsee) as they are stated in the bill of lading. If he is in breach of this obligation, he is also in breach of the contract of carriage. By virtue of the transfer of the title to the goods by endorsement of a bill of lading, the endorser also transfers at least all rights of suit under the contract of carriage[351].

Since it is not a contract, the bill of lading is not a separate contract of carriage[352]. However, it performs a contractual function: it is written and *prima facie* evidence of the contract of carriage between the carrier and the shipper[353]. The bill of lading is a separate document in relation to the contract of carriage and that is also why the terms of the charter party prevail between the shipowner and the charterer[354]. However, when the bill of lading reaches the hands of a third party, it becomes conclusive evidence as to the contract of carriage and *reflects* the terms of the contract of carriage[355].

---

[348] In each case the master will not be employed by the time charterer; he will be employed either by the registered shipowner, or by the demise (or bare-boat) charterer. In this manner the master will be an employee of the registered or disponent shipowner. See *Tetley, IoC*, p. 504; *Cooke/et al.*, para. 18.66; *Hill*, p. 249; *Tetley*, pp. 578-579.

[349] *Schoenbaum*, V. II, p. 17.

[350] For the historical background see *Aikens/Lord/Bools*, para. 1.7 *et seqq.*

[351] See the Carriage of Goods by Sea Act 1992 Sec. 2 (1): "A person who becomes: (a) the lawful holder of a bill of lading; [...] shall (by virtue of becoming the holder of the bill, or as the case may be, to whom delivery is to be made) have transferred to and vested in him all rights of suit under the contract of carriage as if he had been a party to that contract". Under German law, it is accepted that the whole contract of carriage is transferred, see *Puttfarken*, Rn. 106.

[352] *Cooke/et al.*, para. 18.45; *Wilson*, p. 129; *Hill*, p. 168; *Rabe*, § 644 Rn. 13; *Gaskell/Asariotis/Baatz*, para. 2.15.

[353] *Cooke/et al.*, para. 18.45; *Hill*, p. 168; *Wilson*, p. 247; *Davies/Dickey*, p. 253; *Schmidt*, p. 45; *Girvin*, para. 7.05.

[354] *Aikens/Lord/Bools*, para. 7.20; *Wilson*, p. 243; *Carver*, para. 3-009; *Girvin*, para. 7.08 *et seq.*; *Çağa/Kender*, p. 84.

[355] *Cooke/et al.*, para. 18.46; *Aikens/Lord/Bools*, para. 7.4 *et seqq.*; *Carver*, para. 3-007 (the writers conclude that there is a separate bill of lading contract); *Schmidt*, p. 45; *Girvin*, para. 7.12; especially by way of incorporation of charter parties into the bills of lading, see *Hill*, p. 168; *Wilson*, pp. 129-132; also *Aikens/Lord/Bools*, para. 7.82 *et seqq.* When there is no charter party, but merely a contract of carriage

As a result, a bill of lading is never a separate contract of carriage, though it has a contractual function. Therefore, a person other than the carrier and on whose behalf a bill of lading was issued does not become a contractual carrier. Rather, he is the actual carrier as the person who actually performs the carriage.

c) Identity of carrier and demise clauses

Cargo interests, as holders of a bill of lading need to know or determine whom to sue as soon as possible because of the generally short time limits under international instruments or national laws regarding carriage of goods by sea. However, identifying the contractual counterparty is not always so easy due to the complex contractual relations within the maritime market[356]. Consequently, there are certain clauses in the bills of lading, known as the "identity of the carrier" or "demise" clauses, providing information as to who the carrier is, and consequently, whom to sue if anything goes wrong.

The "Identity of Carrier" (IoC) clause appears generally on the reverse side of almost every bill of lading where the carrier is not the shipowner. By way of an IoC clause, the shipowner is identified as the carrier[357], so all claims are to be directed to the shipowner. Even if someone other than the shipowner is held liable, that other person would be able to avail himself of the limitation of liability provisions which are available to the shipowner[358].

Besides other legal issues that the IoC clause creates[359], for the purposes of this work the clause needs to be analysed regarding the personal fault issue. If there is an IoC clause in the contract of carriage, whom should the cargo interests sue and whose personal conduct should be under scrutiny with regard to wilful misconduct? In order to answer these questions, it should be determined whether the IoC clause creates an alternative or an exclusive source for the direction of a claim.

(*e.g.* an oral agreement to carry the goods), the bill of lading *contains* the terms of the carriage contract, see *Carver*, para. 3-003.

[356] For some illustrations see *Özçayır*, p. 79 *et seqq.*

[357] "The contract evidenced by the bill of lading is between the merchant and the owner of the vessel named herein (or substitute) and it is therefore agreed that said shipowner only shall be liable for any damage or loss due to any breach of non-performance of any obligation arising out of the contract of carriage, whether or not relating to the vessel's seaworthiness. If, despite the foregoing, it is adjudged that any other is the carrier and or bailee of the goods shipped hereunder, all limitations of, and exonerations from liability provided for by law or by this bill of lading shall be available to such other. It is further understood and agreed that as the line, company or agent who has executed this bill of lading for and on behalf of the master is not a principal in the transaction, said line, company or agent shall not be under any liability arising out of the contract of carriage nor as carrier nor bailee of the goods." For the text of the clause see *Tetley, IoC*, p. 525.

[358] For more information see *Ülgener*, pp. 99-109; *Tekil*, pp. 170-171.

[359] See *Tetley*, pp. 601 *et seqq.*; *Ülgener*, pp. 109-113; *Tekil*, pp. 171-172. For an analysis from private international law point see *Mankowski, Transportverträge*, Rn. 2893-2896 and Peter *Mankowski*, Internationalprivatrechtliche Aspekte der IoC-Problematik, TranspR 1991, 253.

The main aim of the clause is to avail the carrier of the limitation of liability provisions available to the shipowner[360]. Therefore, it is accepted that the clause does not relieve the carrier of liability[361]. Furthermore, Art. III (8) of the Hague/Visby Rules, Art. 23 (1) of the Hamburg Rules and Art. 79 (1) of the Rotterdam Rules prohibit any provisions which lessen or exclude the carrier's liability under the conventions' regime. Consequently, the carrier would not be able to opt out of his responsibility by way of inserting an IoC clause into the bill of lading. Thus, the carrier remains liable alongside the shipowner[362].

However, the Rotterdam Rules contain a special provision regarding identity of carrier clauses. Art. 37 (1) stipulates that "[i]f a carrier is identified by name in the contract particulars, any other information in the transport document or electronic transport record relating to the identity of the carrier shall have no effect to the extent that it is inconsistent with that identification". So, if the carrier's name is shown in one of the documents mentioned in the provision, the IoC will have no effect, and only the carrier will be liable. However, according to Art. 37 (2) of the Rules, if no person is identified as the carrier, the registered owner of the ship is presumed to be the carrier, and if the ship is under bareboat charter, the bareboat charterer is presumed to be the carrier[363]. However, the shipowner or bareboat charterer always has the opportunity to identify the carrier and its address and thereby rebut the presumption.

However, as distinct from the identity of the carrier clause, the demise clause[364] addresses someone other than the carrier to be sued. A demise clause seeks to avoid the liability of the carrier by saying that either the owner or the demise charterer of the ship is the carrier. The clause is not even clear on the issue of whether the shipowner or the demise charterer is the carrier. By virtue of a demise clause a carrier seeks to relieve himself of liability whereas, by virtue of an IoC clause, he seeks to avail himself of the limitation of liability available to the shipowner. Therefore, a demise clause is a non-responsibility clause and, consequently, is in direct contravention of Art. III (8) of the Hague/Visby Rules, Art. 23 (1) of the Hamburg Rules and Art. 79 (1) of the Rotterdam Rules. It is invalid and has no legal effect under the Hague/Visby and Hamburg Rules regimes[365].

---

[360] *Hill*, p. 249; *Puttfarken*, Rn. 117; for the historical background see *Kienzle*, pp. 259-260; *Schmidt*, pp. 68-70.

[361] *Tekil*, p. 171; *Kienzle*, pp. 264-265; for the counterview see *Richter-Hannes*, p. 88.

[362] *Tetley*, p. 567; *Lüddeke/Johnson*, p. 3; *Kienzle*, pp. 265-267; *Schmidt*, p. 106. For the counterview see *Tetley, IoC*, p. 525.

[363] The situation should be the same also in case of a demise charter.

[364] "If the ship is not owned or chartered by demise to the company or line by whom this bill of lading is issued (as may be the case notwithstanding anything that appears to the contrary), the bill of lading shall take effect as a contract with the owner or demise charterer as the case may be as principal made through the agency of the said company or line who acts as agents only and shall be under no responsibility whatsoever under respect thereof." For the text of the clause see *Tetley, IoC*, p. 516; *Kienzle*, p. 260.

[365] *Tetley*, pp. 601 *et seqq.*; *Kienzle*, p. 260; *Tetley, IoC*, p. 518; for the counterview see *Wilson*, pp. 246-247; *Girvin*, para. 12.12; *Gaskell/Asariotis/Baatz*, para. 3.69 *et*

Consequently, if there is a demise clause in the bill of lading, it has no legal effect upon the cargo interests, whereas the IoC clause has legal effect and creates a direct connection for sueing the shipowner as the actual or performing carrier. Therefore, cargo interests can direct their claims either to the shipowner as the actual or performing carrier or to the contractual carrier. The IoC clause functions in favour of the cargo interests where they have to prove "personal" fault. If the shipowner is personally at fault, they can direct their claim to him due to the IoC clause; whereas if the contractual carrier is personally at fault, they can direct their claims to him based on the carriage contract. However, such an option is not possible under the Rotterdam Rules regime, since either the carrier or the shipowner (or bareboat charterer) will be subject to claims under the Rotterdam Rules (Art. 37).

V. Salvor

Extension of the right to limit to salvors is probably the most significant innovation introduced by the 1976 London Convention[366]. Pursuant to Art. 1 (3) of the Convention, a salvor is any person rendering services in direct connection with salvage operations.

Salvors were entitled to limit their liability as shipowners, managers or operators of a ship under the 1957 Brussels Convention. Thus, it might seem unnecessary to include salvors expressly in the group of persons entitled to limit. Why was such an extension necessary?

The reason for this extension was the aim of altering the legal situation set in the *Tojo Maru* case[367], where the salvors provided salvage services to the *Tojo Maru* under the Lloyd's standard form of salvage (LOF). During the salvage operations, a diver of the salvor acted negligently while trying to repair a crack at the bottom of the ship and caused an explosion which resulted in substantial damage to the tanker. The salvors claimed that they were entitled to limit their liability under English legal provisions regarding the limitation of liability, which derived from the 1957 Brussels Convention. The HL, in rejecting the salvors' limitation claim, stated that "a court must go by the provisions which have been agreed and enacted. If the special position of salvors was unforeseen, then we must await alteration of those provisions if those concerned see fit to make some alteration"[368]. Though the salvors were not given the right to benefit from the limitation of liability under the 1957 Brussels Convention where they do not provide services from a ship, they are expressly stated within the groups of persons entitled to

---

seqq. See also *Leo J. Epstein v. United States of America (War Shipping), United Fruit Company, J.H. Winchester* 1949 A.M.C. 1598 (DC New York, 1949); *Canadian Klockner Ltd. v. D/S A/S Flint, Willy Kubon and Federal Commerce & Navigation Co. Ltd. (The Mica)* [1973] 2 Lloyd's Rep. 478 (Canada Federal Court).

[366] *Griggs/Williams/Farr*, p. 12, *Hodges/Hill*, p. 530; *Özçayır*, p. 354; *Hill*, pp. 401-402; *Herber, Haftungsrecht*, p. 25.

[367] *The Tojo Maru* [1972] A.C. 242 (HL).

[368] *The Tojo Maru* [1972] A.C. 242, 270 (HL) *per* Lord Reid.

limit under Art. 1 of the 1976 London Convention[369]. Thus, salvors are entitled to limit their liability under the 1976 London Convention regime regardless of whether they provide salvage service from a salvage boat, from the salvaged ship, or in another way, *e.g.* through a diver[370].

The last point to be emphasised is that under the 1976 London Convention, Art. 3 (a), claims *for* salvage are exempted from the limitation of liability. That means that the claims brought by salvors against the shipowners are exempted; in other words, a shipowner cannot limit his liability against a salvor. However, naturally, claims against salvors are not exempted. That is to say, that salvors, in cases brought against them, are entitled to limit under the 1976 London Convention[371].

VI. Servant and Agent

A servant is every person who works for the carrier or the shipowner in an employment relationship and who is subject to the instructions of the carrier or shipowner and who is a part of the ship and board service organisation[372]. The crew is the classic example. The contractual relationship in the context of employment law need not be directly between the crew member and the ship-owner or the carrier; rather, the main criterion is whether the servant is under the command of the carrier or shipowner[373]. The term agent refers to persons who are not servants but are delegated an obligation which should otherwise be fulfilled by the carrier or the shipowner under the carriage contract[374]. In this respect, a steve-dore is an agent if the carrier is obliged to load and unload cargo[375]; however, a stevedore should be referred to as independent contractor if the carrier is under no obligation to load or unload cargo. Taking into account the definition of both terms, it can be said that a servant or agent is any person who is delegated an obli-gation which arises from a carriage contract entered into by the carrier[376], who can at the same time be the shipowner.

---

[369] *Mandaraka-Sheppard*, p. 873.

[370] *Richter*, p. 10; *Herber*, p. 215; *Chen, Limitation*, p. 14. It should be also noted that a clause entitling salvors to a limitation of liability was put in the LOF 1980 before the entry into force of the 1976 London Convention despite the fact that all salvage operations are not held under the LOF, see *Özçayır*, p. 354; *Chen, Limitation*, p. 15.

[371] *Baughen*, p. 423.

[372] *Carver*, para. 9-231; *Rabe*, § 607a Rn. 8; *Yazıcıoğlu*, p. 117; *Kienzle*, p. 170; *Ilse*, p. 59.

[373] For details see *Ilse*, p. 77.

[374] *Carver*, para. 9-231; *Ilse*, pp. 60-61, 82-87.

[375] *Carver*, para. 9-231.

[376] *Richter-Hannes*, p. 68.

1. Vicarious liability

Under all international maritime conventions, the vicarious liability of the ship-owner or the carrier for his servants and agents is either explicitly or implicitly regulated.

As the first unification work regarding carriage of goods by sea at an international level, the Hague/Visby Rules do not explicitly regulate the vicarious liability of the carrier for acts of his servants and agents. However, some of the exemptions listed in Art. IV of the Rules necessitate that neither the carrier nor his servants or agents shall have contributed to the loss or damage. Consequently, if his servants or agents are at fault or negligent, the carrier is vicariously liable[377]. The principle of vicarious liability is stated more clearly in the Hamburg Rules. According to Art. 5 (1) of the Rules, the carrier is liable unless he, his servants and agents took all necessary and reasonable measures to avoid the occurrence of the damage, loss or delay in delivery. Further, pursuant to Art. 10 (1) of the Rules, the carrier is liable even for the acts and omissions of the actual carrier and for the acts or omissions of the actual carrier's servants and agents acting within the scope of their employment. Art. 18 of the Rotterdam Rules clearly states that the carrier is liable for his servants and agents. Under the Athens Convention, the carrier is liable for his servants' and agents' acts or omissions[378] by virtue of Art. 3 (1) and (5)(b).

Pursuant to the CLC'92 Art. III (2) and (3), HNS Art. 7 (2) and the Bunker Convention Art. 3 (3) and (4), no liability can attach to the owner, if the pollution was the result of, *inter alia*, an act of God, a war or warlike operation, intentional conduct of a third party or negligence of the governmental authorities. Additional to these exceptions, failure of the shipper to advise the owner as to the nature of the cargo is another cause for the owner not to be held liable under the HNS regime, provided that neither the owner nor its servants or agents knew or ought reasonably to have known of the hazardous and noxious nature of the substances shipped (Art. 7 (2)). Except these few cases, the owner is strictly liable. Therefore, the owner is vicariously liable for the faults of his servants and agents.

2. Personal liability and limitation

a) Hague Rules

It is always possible to sue servants and agents of the carrier under general tort law principles, and when a servant or agent is sued, he cannot rely on the limits of liability under the Hague Rules since there is nothing to indicate that a servant or agent is also entitled to benefit from the limits set by the Rules[379]. Therefore, a cargo owner can always obtain a remedy up to the full amount of his damage from a servant or agent under the Hague Rules system with the hope that the carrier will

---

[377] *Yazıcıoğlu*, p. 114.
[378] *Griggs/Williams/Farr*, p. 97; *Gold/Chircop/Kindred*, pp. 484-485; *Mandaraka-Sheppard*, p. 928; *Kröger*, pp. 9-10.
[379] *Griggs/Williams/Farr*, p. 156; *Carver*, para. 9-286.

stand behind his servants or agents, sometimes because he is obliged to[380]. This, undoubtedly leads to the circumvention of the whole system, or in cases where the carrier does not support the servant or agent, financial ruin of the sued person[381]. In addition to servants and agents, independent contractors of the carrier or the shipowner, such as stevedores, terminal operators and cargo handling services also face claims based on tort law principles[382].

The solution to the problem has been found within commercial practice after a difficulty which was encountered for the first time in the *Himalaya* case. A passenger was injured while boarding the steamship Himalaya, and she could not have sued the shipowner-carrier due to the extremely wide exemption clause in the carriage contract which exempted the carrier from all liability. Therefore, the passenger sued the master and the boatswain in tort. On the preliminary issue, the court held that the servants cannot profit from the exemption clauses which exempt only the carrier from liability unless there is a specific clause for the servants[383]. After this preliminary issue had been solved, the master was held personally liable in tort[384]. Consequently, after this case the so-called "Himalaya clause" started to appear in bills of ladings and carriage contracts. A Himalaya clause[385] either extends all defences and limitations available to the carrier to the servants, agents and independent contractors of the carrier or obliges a cargo owner to

---

[380] It is said that under such a possibility, the system would not be "waterproof", see *Cleton*, p. 24.

[381] *Carver*, para. 9-294; *Diamond*, 250; *Puttfarken*, Rn. 264-265; *Chen, Limitation*, pp. 10-11.

[382] *Gold/Chircop/Kindred*, p. 438.

[383] *Adler v. Dickson* [1954] 2 Lloyd's Rep. 122 (QBD); affirmed by *Adler v. Dickson* [1954] 2 Lloyd's Rep. 267 (CA).

[384] *Adler v. Dickson* [1955] 1 Lloyd's Rep. 315 (QBD).

[385] "It is hereby expressly agreed that no servant or agent of the carrier (including every independent contractor from time to time employed by the carrier) shall in any circumstances whatsoever be under any liability whatsoever to the shipper, consignee or owner of the goods or to any holder of this Bill of Lading for any loss, damage or delay of whatsoever kind arising or resulting directly or indirectly from any act, neglect or fault on his part while acting in the course of or in connection with his employment and, without prejudice to the generality of the foregoing provisions of this clause, every exemption, limitation, condition and liberty herein contained and every right, exemption from liability, defence and immunity of whatsoever nature applicable to the carrier or to which the carrier is entitled hereunder shall also be available and shall extend to protect every such servant or agent of the carrier acting as aforesaid and for the purpose of all the foregoing provisions of this clause the carrier is or shall be deemed to be acting as agent or trustee on behalf of and for the benefit of all persons who are or might be his servants or agents from time to time (including independent contractors as aforesaid) and all such persons shall to this extent be or be deemed to be parties to the contract in or evidenced by this Bill of Lading." (*Tetley*, p. 1854).

direct his claim to the carrier, not to the servants, agents or independent contractors[386].

b) Other conventions

Art. IV *bis* (2) of the Hague/Visby Rules states that servants and agents are entitled to invoke the defences and limits provided for in the Rules for the carrier in a
case against them. However, as clearly stated in the Rules, independent contractors do not have the same right. Therefore, an important class of persons in carriage by sea is excluded from the limitation of liability sphere[387]. The most important ones among them are stevedores, ship's agents and managers, terminal
operators[388]. Nevertheless, they are again under the protection umbrella by way of
a Himalaya clause, although its justification is highly questionable[389].

Art. 7 (2) of the Hamburg Rules contains a similar provision to that of the
Hague/Visby Rules in respect of the defences and limits available to a servant or
agent of the carrier or actual carrier. However, there are two important points
which differ from the Hague/Visby Rules. First, in order to avail himself of the
limits set by the Hamburg Rules, a servant or agent must prove that he was acting
within the scope of his employment. Secondly, the Hamburg Rules do not make
any distinction between servants, agents and independent contractors, whereas the
Hague/Visby Rules clearly state that defences and limits of liability are not available to an independent contractor[390].

Rotterdam Rules Art. 4 (1) equally adopts the principle that the defences and
limits available to the carrier are also available to the maritime performing party
and to the ship personnel of the carrier and of the maritime performing party[391]. If

---

[386] *Griggs/Williams/Farr*, p. 156; *Gold/Chircop/Kindred*, p. 438; *Rabe*, § 607a Rn. 10.
For an analysis from the private international law point see Peter *Mankowski*,
Himalaya Clause, Independent Contractor und Internationales Privatrecht, TranspR
1996, 10.

[387] Although shipowners have been held liable for their acts or omissions occasion-
ally, see *e.g. Riverstone Meat Company v. Lancashire Shipping Company (The
"Muncaster Castle")* [1961] 1 Lloyd's Rep. 57 (HL). For the reason for such
exclusion see *Eilenberger-Czwalinna*, pp. 69-70.

[388] *Griggs/Williams/Farr*, p. 157; *Diamond*, 251; *Scrutton*, p. 411; stevedores are
regarded as servants or agents of the carrier under Australian law, see *Ping-fat*,
p. 88.

[389] *Tetley*, pp. 1864 *et seqq.*; *Puttfarken*, Rn. 270; *Rabe*, § 607a Rn. 11; in fact the
reason to exclude the independent contractors was that the mere fact of supplying
some services to the carrier does not justify the benefit of limitation of liability,
see *Rabe*, § 607a Rn. 7.

[390] *Griggs/Williams/Farr*, p. 158; *Lüddeke/Johnson*, p. 18.

[391] Rotterdam Rules Art. 4 (1): "Any provision of this Convention that may provide a
defence for, or limit the liability of, the carrier applies in any judicial or arbitral
proceeding, whether founded in contract, in tort, or otherwise, that is instituted in
respect of loss of, damage to, or delay in delivery of goods covered by a contract of
carriage or for the breach of any other obligation under this Convention against: (a)
The carrier or a maritime performing party; (b) The master, crew or any other per-

the provision is examined from the perspective of the servants' and agents' right to limit and invoke the defence, it is clear that the scope of the provision is even narrower than the corresponding provisions in the Hague/Visby and Hamburg Rules: agents and sub-contractors are not entitled to invoke the defences and limits of the Rules. Moreover, as distinct from the Hamburg Rules, servants who are entitled to limit do not have to prove that they were acting within the scope of their employment in order to avail themselves of the limits of liability.

However, here, an inconsistency should be addressed. Although Art. 4 (1) of the Rotterdam Rules narrows the group of persons who enjoys the right to limit, the wording of Art. 61 leads to a different result. As seen before[392], Art. 61 breaks the liability limits. It stipulates that neither the carrier nor *any of the persons referred to in article 18* is entitled to limit when they are guilty of wilful misconduct. Art. 18 of the Rules covers a wide range of persons, including also sub-contractors. Given that this large group of persons is mentioned in Art. 61, it must be implicitly accepted that they are also entitled to limit, since a person's liability limits cannot be broken if he is not entitled to limit in the first instance[393]. However, Art. 4 (1) clearly states that a smaller group of persons can enjoy the right to limit. Undoubtedly, this inconsistency will result in competing interpretations.

Athens Convention Art. 11 also provides that a servant or agent can limit his liability and avail himself of the defences which the carrier or performing carrier is entitled to invoke, subject to the condition that the servant or agent must prove that he was acting within the scope of his employment[394].

The 1976 London Convention Art. 1 (4) specifies that for "any person for whose act, neglect, or fault the shipowner or salvor is responsible, such person shall be entitled to avail himself of the limitation of liability provided for in this Convention". If he can show that the shipowner is responsible for his actions under the applicable national law, even a stevedore or a pilot can limit his liability[395]. However, cases where the shipowner is responsible for the acts or omissions of an independent contractor are rare, *e.g.* when the act or omission of the independent contractor renders the ship unseaworthy[396]. Except for these few cases, those independent contractors will not be entitled to limit their liability[397]. An example of an independent contractor for whose act or neglect the shipowner is

---

son that performs services on board the ship; or (c) Employees of the carrier or a maritime performing party".

[392] See *supra* A I 3 b.

[393] See also *Baatz/et al.*, pp. 13-14.

[394] For explanation of the term "scope of employment", see *supra* § 4 D II, and also *Rabe*, Anl § 664 Art. 2 Rn. 6.

[395] *Official Records, London Conference*, pp. 227-229; *Hill*, p. 402; *Shaw/Tsimplis*, pp. 203-204; *Herber, Haftungsrecht*, p. 50; *Cleton*, p. 25; *Richter*, p. 11; *Herber*, p. 215.

[396] See *e.g. Riverstone Meat Company Pty. Ltd. v. Lancashire Shipping Company Ltd. (The "Muncaster Castle")* [1958] 2 Lloyd's Rep. 255 (QBD), [1959] 2 Lloyd's Rep. 553 (CA), [1961] 1 Lloyd's Rep. 57 (HL).

[397] *Griggs/Williams/Farr*, p. 13; *Mandaraka-Sheppard*, p. 872; *Rabe*, LondonHBÜ 1976 Art. 1 Rn. 13; *Puttfarken*, Rn. 829.

not responsible is the freight forwarder. Therefore, freight forwarders are not entitled to limit their liability under the 1976 London Convention[398].

There are no specific provisions as to the right to limit under the pollution conventions since the liability is channelled to the shipowner, and by virtue of CLC'92 Art. III (4) and HNS Art. 7 (5) the servants and agents cannot be sued directly except where they are guilty of wilful misconduct. However, such a specific provision has not been adopted in the Bunker Convention, and, therefore, servants and agents of the shipowner under the Convention are not protected against the claims which can be brought under national provisions[399]. In such a case, servants and agents will not be entitled to limit under national or international limitation regimes, since Art. 6 of the Bunker Convention clearly stipulates that only the shipowner and liability insurer are entitled to limit. Since claims regarding bunker pollution are based on tort, it is also not possible to protect the servants or agents against claims under the Bunker Convention by way of a Himalaya clause.

3. Loss of the right to limit

a) Principle

According to the Hague/Visby Rules Art. IV *bis* (4), a servant or agent of the carrier shall not be entitled to invoke the defences and limits provided for in the Rules for the carrier if it is proved that the damage resulted from an act or omission of the servant or agent done with intent to cause damage or recklessly and with knowledge that damage would probably result. Here, the servant or agent's unlimited liability is independent from that of the carrier. If the servant or agent is personally at fault as defined in the Article, he will lose his right to limit[400].

This provision is particularly important in nautical fault cases. The carrier is not liable for the act, neglect or fault of the master and of his servants and agents in the navigation of the ship under Art. IV (2)(a) of the Hague/Visby Rules[401]. Since the servant or agent is entitled to avail himself of the provisions which provide defences and limits for the carrier, it is said that the servant or agent will also be exempted from liability in nautical faults[402]. However, this literal interpretation of the provisions led to the result that no one is liable for nautical fault, which cannot have been the intention of the drafters. Indeed, a report on the Stockholm Conference of CMI clarifies this point. During the discussions of the draft Visby Protocol, it was argued that nautical fault should be exempted from the application sphere of wilful misconduct. With the exception of one member of the drafting commission, all drafters were unanimous that wilful misconduct breaks the limits in all cases, including nautical fault[403]. In conclusion, a servant or agent should be

---

[398] *Griggs/Williams/Farr*, p. 156.
[399] *Tsimplis, Bunker Pollution*, 89-90.
[400] *Puttfarken*, Rn. 266; *Rabe*, § 607a Rn. 17.
[401] For detailed information see *Ping-fat*, pp. 90-95; *Rabe*, § 607 Rn. 11-18.
[402] *Diamond*, 252; *Puttfarken*, Rn. 268.
[403] *Burchard-Motz*, pp. 10-11.

held personally liable in nautical fault cases and will be entitled to limit[404]; how-ever, if his fault in the navigation amounts to wilful misconduct, he will not be entitled to limit his liability[405].

Furthermore, if guilty of wilful misconduct, a servant or agent is also deprived of the benefit of the time limitation provision, namely Art. VI of the Hague/Visby Rules. This result follows from the clear provisions of Art. IV *bis* of the Rules. According to Art. IV *bis* (2), a servant or agent is entitled to avail himself of the defences and limits of liability available for the carrier. Pursuant to Art. IV *bis* (4), a servant or agent of the carrier shall not be entitled to invoke the defences and limits provided for in the Rules for the carrier. Therefore, a servant or agent would not be able to invoke the time bar defence if he is guilty of wilful misconduct, since a time bar is one of the defences available to the carrier under the Rules[406].

In a case which arose from the carriage of goods by inland waterways, the rules of the German Commercial Code regarding the carriage of goods by sea were to be applied. The vessel *Thomas* was navigating in the inland waterway during the drawdown, with a pilot on her. According to the regulations, the authority in charge with the control of the navigation on the waterway was responsible to keep the ships deeper than 2,20 metres in the waiting line and not let them to continue their navigation during a drawdown phase. The depth of the *Thomas* was 2,50 metres. Before navigating in the inland waterway, the master needed to read the regulations and instructions given by the relevant authority, which the master failed to do. However, the pilot on the vessel did not warn the master, nor did he inform him that the *Thomas* is deeper than the allowed amount. On the contrary, although the master had concerns after the vessel came into contact with the river floor for the second time, the pilot ensured him that the water would get deeper and there was nothing to worry about. The cargo interests sued both the pilot and the master of the vessel for damages which occurred as a result of the accident. They also claimed that the master was guilty of wilful misconduct. The German court applied the provisions of the German Commercial Code regarding carriage of the goods by sea, which reflect the Hague/Visby Rules. According to § 607a HGB, the master was also entitled to limit his liability with the exception of the case of reckless conduct done with subjective knowledge that damage would probably occur. The court considered the master's conduct only as negligent. In its decision, the court stated that the failure of the master to read the regulations and instructions constitutes gross negligence, rather than recklessness. Moreover, the conduct of the master during the navigation constitutes only slight negligence, since the master can rightfully expect that the pilot is familiar with the waterway, and therefore the information he gave was reliable. Consequently, it cannot also be said that the master could have foreseen that damage to cargo would probably occur[407].

---

[404] *Rabe*, § 607a Rn. 9; *Eilenberger-Czwalinna*, p. 71; for the counterview see *Diamond*, 252.

[405] *Puttfarken*, Rn. 268; *Rabe, Vortrag*, p. 22; *Eilenberger-Czwalinna*, p. 71.

[406] *Diamond*, 252 fn. 74.

[407] OLG Hamburg, 22.06.1995, TranspR 1996, 33 ("*Thomas*").

The facts of another case serve also as a good illustration as to the wilful misconduct of the crew[408]. The ship *Excelsior* was carrying containers from Stuttgart to Rotterdam. When the ship was near Cologne, she was navigating in distress. Some of the containers fell into the river Rhine due to her heavy listing. In two cases brought by different cargo interests to the German courts, the courts found that the master of the vessel was reckless and has foreseen the probable damage which occurred. According to the expert reports, the vessel set sail with negative stability. Negative stability creates a situation called upsetting arms which tend to capsize the ship. In the case at hand, the heavy listing and the heeling of the vessel were the result of the negative stability. Due to the heavy wind coming from the portside, a manoeuvre to the starboard had to be made which increased the listing to the starboard and the heeling of the vessel causing the loss of cargo. The expert reports also stated that calculations as to the stability of a ship must be made before the commencement of every voyage. This was not done, which according to the courts, shows that the crew accepted the risk of negative stability and approved the possible harmful results. Moreover, it was ascertained later that the vessel heavily listed to the starboard side already during the loading operations, and at the commencement of the voyage, she sloped heavily to starboard and to portside. During the voyage the problem became more severe. The helmsman informed the master several times. He was actually so concerned that he was wearing a life vest. However, the master just ignored the warnings and said to the helmsman that he should not act like a coward. In order to balance the vessel, the master pumped water to the ballast tanks which is not allowed during navigation. Nevertheless, instead of solving it, the water in the ballast tanks aggravated the stability problem. After considering all these facts, the courts came to the conclusion that the failure to make the necessary calculations as to the stability of the vessel constituted recklessness, and that the master must have foreseen but ignored the probable damages[409]. If the case were brought against the master, he would not be able to limit his liability.

Similar to the Hague/Visby Rules, a servant or agent loses his right to limit under the Hamburg Rules if it is proved that the loss, damage or delay in delivery resulted from an act or omission of such servant or agent, done with the intent to cause such loss, damage or delay, or recklessly and with knowledge that such loss, damage or delay would probably result (Art. 8 (2)). A similar approach has also been taken in the Rotterdam Rules (Art. 61).

Regarding the carriage of passengers, the Athens Convention employs a similar principle. Pursuant to Art. 13 (2) of the Convention, the servant or agent of the

---

[408] The case was decided under the multimodal transport regime adopted by the German Commercial Code. § 435 HGB provides that the freight forwarder cannot rely on the provisions which exclude or limit his liability provided in the Code or in the contract for carriage if the damage is caused by an act or omission of the freight forwarder or his servants and agents done with the intent to cause damage or recklessly and with knowledge that damage would probably occur.

[409] OLG Stuttgart, 01.07.2009, HmbSchRZ 2009, 283 ("*Excelsior*"); LG Hamburg, 07.01.2010, HmbSchRZ 2010, 77 ("*Excelsior*").

carrier or of the performing carrier shall not be entitled to the benefit of those limits if it is proven that the damage resulted from an act or omission of that servant or agent done with the intent to cause such damage, or recklessly and with knowledge that such damage would probably result. Thus, the servant or agent will be deprived of the right to limit if he is personally at fault[410].

Under the 1976 London Convention, servants and agents are within the group of persons entitled to limit (Art. 1 (4)). Therefore, they will also lose their right to limit when they are guilty of wilful misconduct pursuant to Art. 4 of the Convention. Their unlimited liability is independent from their being owner, co-owner, charterer, manager or operator of the ship. During the negotiations for Art. 4 of the Convention, a proposal was made by the Australian delegation to add a paragraph such as the following:

"2. The master or a member of the crew of a ship shall be entitled to limit his liability in all cases unless it is found that:
(a) he is at the same time the owner, co-owner, charterer, manager or operator of the ship; and
(b) the loss resulted from his personal act or omission, committed in his capacity as the owner, co-owner, charterer, manager or operator and with the intent to cause such loss, or recklessly and with knowledge that such loss would probably result"[411].

The proposal was rejected by the Conference, since it provided the right to limit liability to the master and members of the crew in all cases, even in cases of wilful misconduct, unless they are at the same time owners or one of the other persons mentioned in the proposal[412]. In fact, the denial of the proposal has resulted in a substantial change in the servants' and agents' limitation right when compared to the 1957 Brussels Convention[413].

b) Theft and scope of employment

Unlike the Warsaw Convention, under the international maritime conventions the wilful misconduct of the servant or agent is not sufficient to break the carrier's limits of liability. Therefore, a claimant cannot claim unlimited liability of the carrier due to his servant's or agent's conduct. Consequently, there is no need to

---

[410] *Griggs/Williams/Farr*, p. 106; *Gold/Chircop/Kindred*, p. 488; *Grime, Athens Convention*, p. 270 fn. 2.

[411] *Official Records, London Conference*, p. 153.

[412] *Official Records, London Conference*, pp. 388-389.

[413] Pursuant to 1957 Brussels Convention Art. 6 (3) the master and the members of the crew were entitled to limit their liability even if the occurrence which gave rise to the claims resulted from their actual fault or privity. If, however, the master or member of the crew was at the same time owner, co-owner, charterer, manager or operator of the ship, his actual fault or privity in the capacity as the owner, co-owner, charterer, manager or operator would deprive him of the right to limit. The Australian proposal to the 1976 Conference was, obviously, based on the 1957 Brussels Convention provision.

prove that the act or omission of the servant or agent was within the scope of his employment[414].

As stated in the previous section[415], a servant or agent is accountable for his own wilful misconduct. Accordingly, if a servant or agent steals part of the cargo on board, or during loading or unloading operations, or if the servant or agent steals a passenger's personal belongings, he will be liable without any financial limits since theft is a very clear example of *dolus directus*. In order to hold the servant or agent liable without limit, the claimant consequently need not be concerned with the scope of employment issue.

c) Breaking the channelling

Personal conduct of the servant or agent results in the breaking of his liability limits under the carriage of goods and passenger regimes. Additionally, it breaks the channelling under the pollution conventions with the exception of the Bunker Convention. As previously stated[416], liability under the CLC'92 and HNS regimes is channelled to the shipowner. However, if the servant or agent is guilty of wilful misconduct, the channelling of liability will be broken by virtue of CLC'92 Art. III (4) and HNS Art. 7 (5), and he will be exposed to claims brought directly against him.

VII. Liability Insurer

Practically, no shipowner, manager, operator, charterer or carrier will be engaged in the shipping business without liability insurance. However, maintaining insurance or other financial security to cover the liability in respect of the carriage of goods or passengers was made compulsory under certain national or international liability regimes. In both cases, whether maintaining liability insurance is compulsory or not, both the amount of compensation which the liability insurer is obliged to pay and whether the wilful misconduct of the assured has any effect on that amount can be determined according to the applicable national or international regime.

Specific regulations in international transport conventions[417] and some national laws[418] making the liability insurance compulsory, also allow for direct claims

---

[414] For more information on the Warsaw Convention regime and the scope of employment see *supra* § 4 D II.

[415] See *supra* D VI 3 a.

[416] See *supra* B I.

[417] Athens Convention 2002 Art. 4 *bis*; CLC'92 Art. VII (8); HNS Art. 12 (8); Bunker Convention Art. 7; Nairobi International Convention on the Removal of Wrecks, 2007 ("Nairobi Convention") Art. 12.

[418] For more information on English law see *Hodges/Hill*, pp. 533-534; *Mandaraka-Sheppard*, pp. 874-875; on German law see *Rabe*, LondonHBÜ 1976 Art. 1 Rn. 15; on the new Turkish law see *Atamer, Cebrî İcra*, pp. 159-160.

against the liability insurer[419]. Thus, the amount up to which the liability insurer will be liable and the effect of the wilful misconduct of the assured must be determined in two different cases: (i) where the claim is brought by the assured, (ii) where the claim is brought directly against the insurer by a third party. The legal relation between the insurer and the assured is entirely subject to the insurance contract and to the legal principles to which the insurance contract is subject. Therefore, the insurer is under no obligation to compensate the assured beyond the amount agreed in the insurance contract. The insurer is entitled to invoke all defences arising from the insurance contract and the national legal provisions to which the insurance contract is subject[420].

When the claim is brought by a third party directly against the insurer, he always has the right to raise the defence that the assured would be entitled to limit his liability if a direct claim had been brought against him[421] provided that the assured had the right to limit. The insurer is furthermore entitled to limit liability by virtue of specific provisions, even if the assured has lost his right to limit and in cases where the assured is guilty of wilful misconduct[422]. Providing the insurer with the wilful misconduct defence in direct actions arising in the compulsory insurance cases has been considered as unfair and not consistent with the objective of making the insurance mandatory in specific cases. It was hotly debated before and during the Athens Convention 2002 negotiations. It was felt that passengers would not be adequately protected if the insurer was allowed to invoke the defence of wilful misconduct. It was also said that the insurers are in a better position to evaluate the shipowner and the ships. Thus, whereas they can refuse to provide insurance cover, passengers boarding those ships are not in such a position[423]. However, since insuring the wilful misconduct of the assured is held as being contrary to the public policy, and since the P&I clubs have strongly opposed to the removal of this defence, the wilful misconduct defence was also preserved in the Athens Convention 2002[424]. In conclusion, even in direct claim cases, the insurer has been granted the opportunity of being under no obligation to indemnify beyond the limits of liability set by the international regulations.

This conclusion, in fact, can also be reached through Art. 1 (6) of the 1976 London Convention. The provision states that the liability insurer of a person liable is entitled to limit his liability to the same extent as the assured himself. As

---

[419] Athens Convention 2002 Art. 4 *bis* (10) CLC'92 Art. VII (8); HNS Art. 12 (8); Bunker Convention Art. 7 (10); Nairobi Convention Art. 12 (10).

[420] In this respect see *e.g.* MIA § 55; § 2.4 Allgemeine Deutsche Seeversicherungsbedingungen; TTK (1956) Art. 1278, 1380, TTK (2011) Art. 1429, 1477.

[421] *Hodges/Hill*, pp. 537-538; *Özçayır*, p. 380; *Hill*, pp. 402-403.

[422] Athens Convention 2002 Art. 4 *bis* (10) CLC'92 Art. VII (8); HNS Art. 12 (8); Bunker Convention Art. 7 (10); Nairobi Convention Art. 12 (10).

[423] *Mandaraka-Sheppard*, p. 940; Erik Røsæg, *Compulsory Maritime Insurance*, <http://folk.uio.no/erikro/WWW/corrgr/insurance/simply.pdf> (09.08.2010), p. 10.

[424] *Griggs/Williams/Farr*, p. 119; *Mandaraka-Sheppard*, p. 940; *Soyer, Athens Convention*, 529-530. The proposal to remove the defence of wilful misconduct was made by Norway, and supported by China, Germany, France, The Netherlands and Spain, see *Czerwenka, Athener Übereinkommen*, 160.

mentioned before[425], the 1976 Convention does not set any basis for liability. Therefore, Art. 1 (6) of the Convention covers all cases whether liability insurance is compulsory or not.

Where the insurance is not compulsory, the legal situation between the insurer, the assured and the third parties as to the limitation of liability and the effect of wilful misconduct of the assured depends mostly upon the insurance contract and the national regulations.

In principle, there is no right of a direct claim against an insurer and therefore the assured will indemnify the third party and thereafter claim from his liability insurer the amount he has paid. The legal situation between the insurer and the assured in this case is, again, entirely dependent upon the insurance contract[426] and the national legal provisions to which the insurance contract is subject. The insurer will be under no obligation to compensate the assured beyond the amount specified in the insurance contract[427] irrespective of whether the assured has been denied the right to limit his liability or whether he has chosen not to enjoy the right to limit[428].

Nevertheless, the drafters of the 1976 London Convention apparently wished to stress this point and regulate it specifically in order to prevent any misapplication or misinterpretation. Consequently, Art. 1 (6) of the Convention is, in this respect, a statement of legal status rather than a declaration of a right[429]. However, due to national legislation, there might be cases where the third party enjoys the right to directly sue the liability insurer, even when the assured is under no obligation to maintain insurance. If, in such a case, the assured is not entitled to limit, is it possible to break the insurer's right to limit as well? According to the 1976 London Convention, the insurer would be liable "to the same extent as the assured himself"[430], and in case of wilful misconduct the assured will lose his right to limit. The answer will doubtless depend on the national legislation. However, it must be remembered that under most national regimes, the insurers enjoy the right to the defence that the damage resulted from the assured's wilful misconduct. For

---

[425] See *supra* C I.

[426] Compare *Hodges/Hill*, p. 536.

[427] *Hodges/Hill*, pp. 535-536.

[428] The liability insurer provides coverage for the legal liability of the assured, not more, see *Hazelwood*, pp. 278-281; *Hodges/Hill*, p. 537; *Özçayır*, pp. 378-379; *Seward*, p. 179. See also *e.g.* Shipowners' Mutual Protection & Indemnity Association Rules 2008, Part V, Rule 22 (1): "Other Limitations of the Association's Liability – General Limitation": "Subject to these Rules the Association insures the liability of a Member in respect of an insured vessel as his liability may ultimately be determined and fixed by law, including laws pertaining to limitation of vessel owners' liability. The Association shall in no circumstances be liable for any sum in excess of such legal liability. If less than the full gross tonnage of a vessel is entered in the Association, the Member concerned shall be entitled only to recover such proportion of his claim as the entered tonnage bears to the full gross tonnage".

[429] *Hodges/Hill*, p. 538. For a criticism see *Ataol*, pp. 67-69.

[430] *Hill*, pp. 402-403; *Griggs/Williams/Farr*, p. 35.

instance, pursuant to the UK Third Parties (Rights against Insurers) Act 2010[431] § 1 (2), the insurer is liable to the third party just as it would have been to the assured. Since, according to the MIA 1906 § 55 (2)(a), the insurer is not liable for any loss attributable to the wilful misconduct of the assured, the insurer will not be liable to the third party as well. German Act on Insurance Contracts (VVG) § 115 (1) adopts the same principle with regard to the direct action by third parties against the liability insurer. By virtue of § 81 of the VVG, the insurer is not liable for any loss attributable to the intentional wrongdoing (*Vorsatz*) of the assured. In conclusion, it can be without hesitation said that wilful misconduct of the assured does not result in the unlimited liability of the insurer[432], unless the national legislation provides another solution. Finally, it is unthinkable that the insurer himself would be guilty of wilful misconduct and held liable under general tort law principles[433].

E. Corporate Liability and Attribution

If the person liable is a natural person, attribution of an act or omission to that person does not pose any problems. Clearly, only that person's conduct will be under scrutiny for the purposes of the conduct barring limitation[434]. However, since suing a shipowner serves the best economic interests of claimants, natural persons such as the master of a ship would not be the likely targets of a lawsuit, rather shipowners who fall within the context of the 1976 London Convention and have liability insurance and enough property to pay the compensation would be subject to claims. However, if the claimant would like to break the shipowner's liability limits, he would face the problem of attribution, since the shipowner would almost invariably be a legal entity, a *persona ficta*, namely a corporation[435].

How can a corporation "personally" intend to cause a specific loss or act or fail to act recklessly and with knowledge that a specific loss would probably occur? Naturally, it is the corporation's bodies whose acts or decisions will bind that corporation. However, it is almost unthinkable that a body of a corporation, *e.g.* the board of directors, would take a decision to intentionally cause harm. It is generally natural persons within the corporate structure whose acts or omissions cause harm to third parties. Therefore, it should be determined whose acts or

---

[431] The Third Parties (Rights against Insurers) Act 1930 has been repealed by the Act dated 2010. The text of the latest Act can be found on the Office of Public Sector Information web site: <www.opsi.gov.uk/acts/acts2010/pdf/ukpga_20100010_en. pdf> (09.08.2010).

[432] *Griggs/Williams/Farr*, pp. 15-16, *Mandaraka-Sheppard*, p. 876; *Seward*, pp. 180-182; *Coghlin*, pp. 249-250; for the counterview see *Özçayır*, p. 379; for more information see *Damar, Compulsory Insurance*, 154-155, 164; see also *Kröger*, pp. 218-224.

[433] *Hodges/Hill*, p. 535.

[434] *Hodges/Hill*, p. 564; *Özçayır*, p. 333.

[435] It is thus even not correct to refer to a shipowner as "he" anymore; the phrase "it" must replace "he". However, as a traditional concept, "he" is still in use.

omissions can be attributed to a corporation and cause the corporation to be held liable without any financial limits.

What will be attributed to a legal entity is another question. *Attribution of liability* is based on vicarious liability. A legal entity is responsible towards the third parties as the *respondeat superior*, and knowledge as to a specific point is not required under the vicarious liability concept. Shipowners, carriers, and other persons involved in the shipping business are vicariously liable for the acts or omissions of their servants and agents[436]. However, their vicarious liability is not related to the liability limits. Although being vicariously liable, their liability will, nevertheless, be limited. In order to break the limits of liability, international regimes as to the carriage by sea require subjective knowledge and the personal conduct of the shipowner, carrier *etc.* So, for the purposes of unlimited liability, *attribution of knowledge* is the key issue, not the attribution of liability. As for the attribution of knowledge, vicarious liability does not provide an adequate solution[437].

The attribution of a person's acts and knowledge to a company with regard to breaking the liability limits can be regulated by specific provisions. Such provisions have been adopted in the German Commercial Code and the Turkish Commercial Code of 2011. However, both the provisions under the HGB and TTK (2011) clarify the attribution issue only under German and new Turkish law[438]. Furthermore, both provisions specify on the issue only in respect of the 1976 London Convention and CLC'92. Nevertheless, it is accepted that they are applicable by analogy to other conventions regarding carriage by sea as well where personal fault is necessary to break limits of liability[439].

§ 487d HGB stipulates that if the person liable or the shipowner is a legal entity, with respect to breaking the liability limits, only the acts or omissions of the organ or of a partner who is authorised to represent the legal entity will be under scrutiny. Joint shipowners cannot limit their liability when the personal act or omission (as defined in the two Conventions) of any joint shipowner caused the damage.

TTK (2011) Art. 1343 (1) covers a wider category of persons. According to that provision, with respect to the breaking the liability limits, the fault of the following persons shall be considered: (a) the natural person for his personal fault, (b)

---

[436] See *supra* D VI 1.

[437] *Hodges/Hill*, pp. 568-569; *Leigh*, 584; *Hodges, ISM Code*, 44; *Gower & Davies*, p. 183; *Mayson, French & Ryan*, p. 631.

[438] *Rabe*, § 487d Rn. 2; *Atamer, 1976 ve 1992 Sözleşmeleri*, p. 897. Turkish Commercial Code of 2011 will enter into force on 1st July 2012.

[439] *Herber, Haftungsrecht*, p. 216; *Rabe*, § 660 Rn. 26; *Eilenberger-Czwalinna*, p. 121; *Stachow*, p. 231; BGH, 29.07.2009, HmbSchRZ 2009, 316 (320) affirming HansOLG Bremen, 02.11.2006, HmbSchRZ 2009, 323 (326); BGH, 18.06.2009, TranspR 2009, 327 (331); OLG Hamburg, 07.09.2000, HmbSeeRep 2000, 185 (187) ("*Hua Yin*" & "*Koyo Express*"); HansOLG, 02.10.2008, HbgSchRZ 2009, 52 (59) ("*Caribia Express*"); for criticism and the view that § 487d HGB should not be applied to the cases arisen from a specific carriage contract see *Ramming*, 302-303.

the organs which are authorised to bind the legal entity according to the civil law provisions and the members of those organs for the legal entity, (c) every partner for an ordinary partnership, (d) every joint shipowner and the ship's husband for joint shipowners, (e) the representatives either generally or specifically authorised by the persons mentioned above.

Contrary to German and Turkish law, the rules of attribution[440] are not specifically regulated under English law. However, it can be said that the identification doctrine (also known as the *alter ego* concept) helps to determine the persons whose fault and knowledge can be attributed to the legal entity. Considering the specific provisions under German and Turkish law and the development under the common law, the attribution issue should be considered first with respect to organs and the *alter ego* of the legal entities. The effect of the ISM Code should also be analysed, since its requirements will have an impact on the "knowledge" element and on the attribution of certain information to the legal entities' organs and *alter ego*.

I. Attribution

1. Company's bodies

Legal entities function through their organs, which in turn consist of natural persons. Although named according to the type of the corporation[441], every corporation has a decisive and a managing organ, *e.g.* shareholders' board, board of directors, board of managers *etc.* As a juridical person, a corporation is legally bound by the decisions and acts of its organs[442]. It can be said that acts and knowledge of the organs are the acts and knowledge of a corporation.

Undoubtedly, wilful misconduct of one of the decisive and managing organs of a corporation is the wilful misconduct of that corporation. If one of the decisive or

---

[440] *Meridian Global Funds Management Asia Ltd. v. Securities Commission* [1995] 2 A.C. 500, 506 (Privy Council) *per* Lord Hoffmann: "Any proposition about a company necessarily involves a reference to a set of rules. A company exists because there is a rule (usually in a statute) which says that a persona ficta shall be deemed to exist and to have certain of the powers, rights and duties of a natural person. But there would be little sense in deeming such a persona ficta to exist unless there were also rules to tell one what acts were to count as acts of the company. It is therefore a necessary part of corporate personality that there should be rules by which acts are attributed to the company. These may be called 'the rules of attribution'".

[441] For English company law see *Mayson, French & Ryan*, pp. 424 *et seqq.*; *Gower & Davies*, pp. 365 *et seqq.*; for German company law see Adolf *Baumbach*/Klaus J. *Hopt*, Handelsgesetzbuch, 34. Aufl., München 2010; Ulrich *Eisenhardt*, Gesellschaftsrecht, 13. Aufl., München 2007; for Turkish company law see Reha *Poroy*/ Ünal *Tekinalp*/Ersin *Çamoğlu*, Ortaklıklar ve Kooperatif Hukuku, 12. bası, İstanbul 2010.

[442] § 31 BGB; MK Art. 50; *H. L. Bolton (Engineering) Co. Ltd. v. T. J. Graham & Sons Ltd.* [1957] 1 Q.B. 159, 172 (CA); *Tesco Supermarkets Ltd. v. Nattrass* [1972] A.C. 153, 170, 199 (HL).

managing organs acts or makes an omission with the intent to cause damage or does so recklessly and with knowledge that damage will probably result, that shipowning corporation will be deprived of the right to limit[443]. The *Tyne Bridge* case illustrates this general rule. The vessel Tyne Bridge called at the Hamburg port. According to the contract, the defendant was obliged to provide towage service to the vessel. However, during the towage manoeuvres, the vessel came into collision with one of the tugs due to the negligent navigation of the same tug's master. The court stated that the requisite fault must be at the level of an organ, which is authorised to represent the legal entity. Here, the owners were not personally at fault, since there was no fault by the representing organ of the company; and were, therefore, entitled to limit[444]. However, in another case which arose from the carriage of the gondola of a wind turbine, and whose facts were mentioned earlier[445], the organ of the carriage company was found at fault. The carrier was a limited liability company. The Hanseatic Court of Appeal of Bremen stated that the manager is the organ authorised to represent the company under German law, and therefore, his fault is the fault of the limited liability company. The manager was found to be reckless, and so was the company. As a result, the carrier was not entitled to limit[446].

The issue of whether members of the managing organ of a corporation can bind the corporation by their acts should also be addressed, since generally they (as opposed to the general decisive organ of the corporation) are involved in the day-to-day business. Under German and Turkish law, the issue can be solved by general and specific provisions. Pursuant to § 31 BGB, a corporation is also liable towards third parties for the acts of any member of the organ. § 487d HGB specifies this general rule for the organs and members of the organs[447]. The application of the provision can be found in the *Caribia Express* case, the facts of which were mentioned earlier[448]. The carrier was a limited partnership. In order to find out whose fault should be attributed to the carrier, the court applied § 487d HGB. Under German law, the organ which is authorized to represent the limited partnership is the personally liable partner. In this case the personally liable partner was

---

[443] *Gaskell, Hamburg Rules*, p. 172; *Puttfarken*, Rn. 833; *Richter-Hannes/Trotz*, p. 21. See also *Smitton v. The Orient Steam Navigation Company (Limited)* (1907) 12 Com. Cas. 270, 277: "It might be said that there never could be [fault] of the entity that is called corporation, but I think that in the case of a corporation the words mean the fault of the managing authority. [...] that would be the board of directors, the persons who have the general management of the affairs of the company. Fault on the part of such persons would, [...], be the fault of the company [...]; but it is otherwise in the case of fault on the part of an agent or servant who has not the general management of the concerns of the company".

[444] OLG Hamburg, 26.05.1988, TranspR 1988, 433.

[445] See *supra* A I 1 e.

[446] HansOLG Bremen, 02.11.2006, HmbSchRZ 2009, 323 (326), affirmed by BGH, 29.07.2009, HmbSchRZ 2009, 316 = TranspR 2009, 331 = NJW-RR 2009, 1482.

[447] *Herber, Haftungsrecht*, p. 71; *Puttfarken*, Rn. 832; *Rabe*, LondonHBÜ 1976 Art. 4 Rn. 7.

[448] See *supra* A I 1 e.

another limited partnership whose personally liable partner was, again, another limited partnership. The last limited partnership was represented by two natural persons being the personally liable partners in the partnership, and the court stated that these two partners' personal fault is to be attributed to the first limited partnership, *i.e.* the carrier[449].

The situation has not been clearly regulated under Turkish civil law: MK Art. 50 is silent on the issue whether any member of the organ is capable of legally binding the corporation. In this respect, the representative authority of the member is decisive[450]. However, TTK (2011) Art. 1343 (1)(b) clearly states that wilful misconduct of a member of a representative organ will deprive the shipowning corporation of the limits of liability.

Under English law, it is also accepted that wilful misconduct of any member of the managing organ is sufficient to break the liability limits[451]. It was stated in the *Ert Stefanie* that "[it is contended] that, if the fault is laid at the door of a member of the board of directors, it must inevitably involve [the fault] of the company. [...] [It is doubtful] whether [the court] would be prepared to go so far. It seems at least theoretically possible for a situation to exist where a particular director has been formally excluded from participation in the company's business and where, if nevertheless he did trespass upon that territory, his acts in so doing would not be attributed to the company."[452]. As a result, the *Ert Stefanie* clearly affirms that if a director has not been formally excluded from the company's business, his acts will be the acts of the company[453].

---

[449] HansOLG, 02.10.2008, HbgSchRZ 2009, 52 (59) (*"Caribia Express"*).

[450] M. Kemal *Oğuzman*/Özer *Seliçi*/Saibe *Oktay-Özdemir*, Kişiler Hukuku, 9. baskı, İstanbul 2009, pp. 217-220.

[451] *Gaskell, Hamburg Rules*, p. 172; *Cooke/et al.*, para. 11.53; see also *Tsimplis, Passenger Claims*, 138.

[452] *Societe Anonyme des Minerais v. Grant Trading Inc.* (*The "Ert Stefanie"*) [1989] 1 Lloyd's Rep. 349, 351 (CA) *per* Lord Mustill.

[453] See *Albert E. Reed & Co. Ltd. v. London & Rochester Trading Company Ltd.* [1954] 2 Lloyd's Rep. 463 (QBD); *Yuille v. B.&B. Fisheries, Ltd. and Bates* (*The "Radiant"*) [1958] 2 Lloyd's Rep. 596 (QBD) and *F. T. Everard & Sons, ltd. v. London and Thames Haven Oil Wharves, Ltd. and Others* (*The "Anonity"*) [1961] 2 Lloyd's Rep. 117, 124 (CA); *BHP Trading Asia Ltd. and Others v. Oceaname Shipping Ltd. and Another* 67 FCR 211 (Federal Court of Australia, 1996) where the acts and knowledge of the managing director and of the chairman were considered as the acts and knowledge of the shipowning companies. In the *Lady Gwendolen*, the fault of the assistant managing director who was at the same time a member of the board of directors was considered as the fault of the company despite the fact that the assistant managing director was not specifically entrusted with the operation of ships by the company's articles of association, see *"The Lady Gwendolen"* [1964] 2 Lloyd's Rep. 99 (QBD); [1965] 1 Lloyd's Rep. 335 (CA); for the discussion of the case from the attribution point of view see *Hodges/Hill*, pp. 572-574; *Mandaraka-Sheppard*, pp. 892-893; *Thomas, British Concepts*, 1227-1228; *Grime, Loss of the Right*, p. 106; *Özçayır*, p. 335; *Leigh*, 585-587. It must be, however, emphasised that the decisions were made on the footing of the *alter ego* concept.

As a result, it can be clearly said that, in essence, the wilful misconduct of a corporation's managing organ and/or members of that organ will be considered for the purposes of breaking the limits. The acts of subordinates, *i.e.* the servants and agents for whom the company is liable as the *respondeat superior*, do not bind the company for the purposes of unlimited liability[454]. However, what if a subordinate has the sole discretion, or in other words, what if he was delegated with the sole managing power? Is it still possible to say that his acts are not binding for the corporation and that his knowledge is not the knowledge of the corporation?

2. The identification doctrine

a) The doctrine

A corporate structure needs more than shareholders and directors in order to conduct business. To this end, servants and agents are employed and delegated with some rights and duties. Depending on their position in the corporate structure, it is possible to attribute their acts and knowledge to the corporation. If a servant or agent is identified as one of the senior managers, his acts and knowledge can be identified as the acts and knowledge of the corporation, in other words, as the *alter ego*[455] of the corporation.

The identification doctrine was established by the House of Lords in the *Lennard's* case[456]. In this case, the ship sank due to her unseaworthy condition which also resulted in the total loss of the cargo on board. The dispute centred on the issue of whether the shipowning company was personally aware of the conditions which led to the unseaworthiness of the ship, which was owned by the limited company Lennard's Carrying and managed by another limited company, the John M. Lennard & Sons Limited. The managing director of the managing company Lennard & Sons was John M. Lennard, who at the same time was a director in the shipowning company Lennard's Carrying. Furthermore, John M. Lennard was also registered as the manager of the ship in the ship's registry. It was stated that "a corporation is an abstraction. It has no mind of its own any more than it has a body of its own; its active and directing will must consequently be sought in the person of somebody who for some purposes may be called an agent, but *who is really the directing mind and will of the corporation* [...] the fault or privity is the fault or privity of somebody who is not merely a servant or agent for whom the company is liable upon the footing respondeat superior, but somebody for whom the company is liable because *his action is the very action of the company*

---

[454] *Sheen*, 476.

[455] *Tesco Supermarkets Ltd. v. Nattrass* [1972] A.C. 153, 171-172 (HL) *per* Lord Reid: "In some cases the phrase alter ego has been used. [...] it is misleading. When dealing with a company the word alter is [...] misleading. The person who speaks and acts as the company is not alter. He is identified with the company, and when dealing with an individual no other individual can be his alter ego. The other individual can be a servant, agent, delegate or representative [...]".

[456] *Lennard's Carrying Company, Limited v. Asiatic Petroleum Company, Limited* [1915] A.C. 705 (HL).

itself."[457]. Based on this reasoning, the court identified John M. Lennard as the *alter ego* of the shipowning company and held that the shipowning company was actually at fault.

The principles set by the HL in the *Lennard's* case were later expressed as the identification doctrine, since the doctrine identifies persons in the corporate structure who are the *alter ego* of a company[458]. The acts and knowledge of the *alter ego* are equal to that of the managing organs of the company, *i.e.* acts and knowledge of the *alter ego* are equal to that of the company[459].

The doctrine was further developed in *H. L. Bolton (Engineering) Co. Ltd. v. T. J. Graham & Sons Ltd.*[460]. It was stated that "[a] company may in many ways be likened to a human body. It has a *brain and nerve centre* which controls what it does. It also has hands which hold the tools and act in accordance with directions from the centre. Some of the people in the company are mere servants and agents who are nothing more than hands to do the work and cannot be said to represent the mind or will. Others are directors and managers who represent the *directing mind and will of the company*, and control what it does. The state of mind of these managers is the state of mind of the company and is treated by the law as such. So you will find that in cases where the law requires personal fault as a condition of liability in tort, the fault of the manager will be the personal fault of the company. [...] So also in the criminal law, in cases where the law requires a guilty mind as a condition of a criminal offence, the guilty mind of the directors or the managers will render the company itself guilty. [...] So here, the intention of the company can be derived from the intention of its officers and agents. Whether their intention is the company's intention depends on the nature of the matter under consideration, the relative position of the officer or agent and the other relevant facts and circumstances of the case."[461].

Therefore, in this case, it is stated that the person identified as the *alter ego* must be someone who is the brain and nerve centre of the corporate structure and who is the directing mind and will of the company. There is no standing rule as to identifying a person as the *alter ego* or not; the conditions of each case must be carefully considered. However, it cannot be someone who is a mere servant. In any case, the *alter ego* must be someone in the upper management structure[462].

---

[457] Emphasis added; *Lennard's Carrying Company, Limited v. Asiatic Petroleum Company, Limited* [1915] A.C. 705, 713-714 (HL) *per* Lord Viscount Haldane.

[458] *Mandaraka-Sheppard*, p. 905.

[459] *Richter-Hannes/Trotz*, p. 21.

[460] [1957] 1 Q.B. 159 (CA).

[461] Emphasis added; *H. L. Bolton (Engineering) Co. Ltd. v. T. J. Graham & Sons Ltd.* [1957] 1 Q.B. 159, 172-173 (CA) *per* Lord Denning.

[462] *Diamond*, 244-245; for discussions of the identification doctrine in criminal cases see *R. v. P & O European Ferries (Dover) Ltd.* (1991) 93 Criminal Appeal Reports 72 (Central Criminal Court) where the shipowning company was accused of manslaughter with respect to the *Herald of Free Enterprise* catastrophe; and see *Seaboard Offshore Ltd. v. Secretary of State for Transport (The "Safe Carrier")* [1994] 1 Lloyd's Rep. 589 (HL) where the management company was accused of

In the *Tesco Supermarkets Ltd. v. Nattrass* case, it was, again, emphasised that only someone from the upper management level can speak and act as the company. Subordinates, even if they are given some measure of discretion, do not act as the company. However, if the management delegates some of its functions to a subordinate and gives him full discretion and the right to act independently of instructions, then that subordinate, within the scope of the delegation, acts and speaks as the company[463]. Similar remarks were made by the Canadian Supreme Court in a maritime case: "The key factor which distinguishes directing minds from normal employees is the capacity to exercise decision-making authority on matters of corporate policy, rather than merely to give effect to such policy on an operational basis, whether at the head office or across the sea. While [the master] no doubt has certain decision-making authority on navigational matters as an incident of his role as master of [the tug] and was given important operational duties, governing authority over the management and operation of [the company's] tugs lay elsewhere."[464].

The approach to the issue of the persons to be identified with the company is similar under German law. Although § 487d HGB does not mention clearly any principle similar to the identification doctrine, it bears emphasis that the provision should not be interpreted from a mere company law perspective. The functions of organs or persons in the company should also be considered. If the provision is interpreted from a mere company law perspective, this would lead to unfair results since in small limited companies almost every person's act or knowledge will be attributed to the company, whereas in big corporations the person whose act or knowledge is to be attributed needs to be found in the most upper management of the corporation[465].

One of the basic provisions in the German Civil Code provides the solution. § 31 BGB regulates the liability of an association for its organs and states that "[t]he association is liable for the damage to a third party that the board, a member of the board or another constitutionally appointed representative causes through an act committed by it or him in carrying out the business with which it or he is entrusted, where the act gives rise to a liability in damages". If interpreted literally, the provision is applicable only to the board, members of the board and constitutionally appointed representatives of the association. However, the teleological interpretation by the German Federal Court has widened the application sphere of the provision. If an employee or a subordinate has been empowered with full and autonomous discretion in order to fulfil one or some of the operational or managerial functions of the association, this person is to be considered as a "*de facto* organ" whether or not he has been constitutionally appointed; in other

---

the offence of breaching the duty to secure that the ship is operated in a safe manner. See also *Christodoulou*, pp. 29-36.

[463] [1972] A.C. 153, 171 (HL) *per* Lord Reid.

[464] *The Rhône* [1993] 1 Supreme Court Reports 497, 526 (Canada).

[465] *Puttfarken*, Rn. 833.

words, he "is" the association within the scope of the delegation[466]. If this person intentionally causes damage in the course and within the scope of the performance of this function, the association is liable not based on the vicarious liability, but on the § 31 BGB principles[467].

This basic provision is applicable not only to associations, but to all private law entities including corporations[468]. Therefore, under German law as well, it can be said that not only the knowledge of the organs or the representatives of those organs are to be considered, but also the knowledge of the persons who are empowered with a function of the corporation and who can be identified with the company needs to be considered for the purposes of unlimited liability[469]. However, distinct from the common law identification doctrine, the "*de facto* organ" under German law does not have to take part in the decision making process. This is a very substantial and important difference and would cause different results in comparison with the common law as regards to the personal liability of a corporation. In the *Caribia Express* case, the facts of which were mentioned earlier[470] the court, unfortunately, did not further pursue the issue (since the issue was not raised by the claimant), of whether the fault of the members of the executive board should be considered as the partnership's personal fault when they have comprehensive authorization to manage the company. The court, however, stated that the fault of an "executive employee" (*leitende Angestellte*), who is the employee with the authority to act independently within the limits of his responsibilities, is not the fault of the partnership[471].

By virtue of TTK (2011) Art. 1343 (1)(e), the principle has been adopted under new Turkish law that the knowledge of company representatives either generally or specifically authorised by the company will be considered for the purposes of unlimited liability. It is clearly stated that the provision has been adopted in order to clarify who can be classified as the *alter ego* of a company[472]. Therefore, for the purposes of this provision, general or specific authorisation needs to be interpreted from the principles and perspective of the identification doctrine. Therefore, general or specific authorisation must be on the level of a delegation of a function of the legal entity. Otherwise, it is not the principles of attribution but the principles of vicarious liability which apply in rendering the personal conduct condition meaningless.

---

[466] *Palandt/Ellenberger*, § 31 Rn. 6, 8; Erman/*Westermann*, § 31 Rn. 3; MünchKomm BGB – *Reuter*, § 31 Rn. 20-21; Staudinger/*Weick* (1994), § 31 Rn. 26 *et seq.*

[467] *Palandt/Ellenberger*, § 31 Rn. 10; Erman/*Westermann*, § 31 Rn. 5; Münch-KommBGB – *Reuter*, § 31 Rn. 33 *et seq.*; Staudinger/*Weick* (1994), § 31 Rn. 39.

[468] *Palandt/Ellenberger*, § 31 Rn. 3; MünchKommBGB – *Reuter*, § 31 Rn. 11; Staudinger/*Weick* (1994), § 31 Rn. 51 *et seq.*

[469] *Rabe*, LondonHBÜ 1976 Art. 4 Rn. 7, § 487d Rn. 2; *Stachow*, pp. 235-237; *de la Motte*, p. 296. However, according to *Herber, Haftungsrecht*, p. 71, § 487d HGB should be applied exclusively.

[470] See *supra* A I 1 e.

[471] HansOLG, 02.10.2008, HbgSchRZ 2009, 52 (59) ("*Caribia Express*").

[472] *Atamer, 1976 ve 1992 Sözleşmeleri*, pp. 897-898.

b) The Meridian rule

The so-called Meridian rule of attribution or the Meridian doctrine clarifies and explains the attribution issue further. It summarises and states generally the rules of attribution; and, after analysing them, states a "special rule of attribution". The Privy Council has set a three tier application[473]: (1) the primary rules of attribution, (2) general rules of attribution, and (3) a special rule of attribution.

The primary rules of attribution can be found in company law rules and in companies' articles of associations, and they clearly show who is authorised to act on behalf of the company or, or in other words, as the company itself[474]. For instance, the resolutions of the board of directors count as the acts of the company[475]. However, in order "to go out into the world and do business", a company needs to use the primary rules of attribution, namely the principles of agency and vicarious liability[476]. The Privy Council further states that in some cases the primary and general rules of attribution do not bring an answer. One of these exceptional cases is where "a rule of law, either expressly or by implication, excludes attribution on the basis of general principles of agency or vicarious liability"[477]. As an example, the Council points to the cases where "some act or state of mind on the part of that person 'himself', as opposed to his servants or agents" is required[478]. There is no doubt that the "personal conduct" requirement of the international maritime conventions is one of the exceptional cases which the Privy Council mentioned. In such a case, special rules of attribution are to be applied.

"In such a case, the court must fashion a special rule of attribution for the particular substantive rule. This is always a matter of interpretation: given that it was intended to apply to a company, how was it intended to apply? Whose act (or knowledge, or state of mind) was *for this purpose* intended to count as the act etc. of the company? One finds the answer to this question by applying the usual canons of interpretation, taking into account the language of the rule (if it is a statute), its content and policy."[479]. Subsequently, the Council stated that what was said in the *Lennard's* case was later misinterpreted; instead of focusing on the formula "directing mind and will", one needs to concentrate on the purpose of the particular substantive rule[480].

---

[473] *Hodges/Hill*, p. 568.
[474] *Meridian Global Funds Management Asia Ltd. v. Securities Commission* [1995] 2 A.C. 500, 506 (Privy Council) *per* Lord Hoffmann.
[475] For more information see *supra* E I 1.
[476] *Meridian Global Funds Management Asia Ltd. v. Securities Commission* [1995] 2 A.C. 500, 506 (Privy Council) *per* Lord Hoffmann.
[477] *Meridian Global Funds Management Asia Ltd. v. Securities Commission* [1995] 2 A.C. 500, 507 (Privy Council) *per* Lord Hoffmann.
[478] *Meridian Global Funds Management Asia Ltd. v. Securities Commission* [1995] 2 A.C. 500, 507 (Privy Council) *per* Lord Hoffmann.
[479] Ellipsis in original; *Meridian Global Funds Management Asia Ltd. v. Securities Commission* [1995] 2 A.C. 500, 507 (Privy Council) *per* Lord Hoffmann.
[480] *Meridian Global Funds Management Asia Ltd. v. Securities Commission* [1995] 2 A.C. 500, 508-510 (Privy Council) *per* Lord Hoffmann.

Thus, the Council stated that the person whose act or knowledge or state of mind will be attributed to the company should be determined by considering the particular substantive rule. By means of usual interpretation methods, it should be determined whom the particular substantive rule considers as the company itself, even if this person cannot be considered as the *alter ego* of the company. The policy behind that substantive rule plays a vital role in such a determination[481].

However, the Council also felt the need to make a warning: "But their Lordships would wish to guard themselves against being understood to mean that whenever a servant of a company has authority to do an act on its behalf, knowledge of that act will for all purposes be attributed to the company."[482].

c) Examples from carriage by sea[483]

It was in the *Lady Gwendolen* case where it was argued for the first time whether the fault of a manager who is situated in the lower management structure can be attributed to a shipowning company[484]. The Court of Appeal, while affirming the Queen's Bench Division decision, found that one of the board members was actually at fault. However, the Court of Appeal did not stop here and stated that even the fault of the traffic manager could be attributed to the company. In the company structure, the traffic manager was situated under the board member who was found personally at fault. The reasoning for the traffic manager being found the company's *alter ego* in this case was that he was in charge of the shipping operations and was registered as the ship's manager[485].

In *The Garden City*, the court considered whether the inspectors' and marine superintendent's fault and knowledge could be attributed to the shipowning company. The vessels Garden City and Zaglebie Dabrowski collided, with the Garden City and the Zaglebie Dabrowski being found, respectively, 40% and 60% responsible for the collision occurring due to the excessive speed in fog and a bad radar lookout. As a result of the collision the Garden City sunk, and she and her cargo became a total loss. In the case against the owners of the Zaglebie Dabrowski, the court found that the inspectors and the marine superintendent were personally at fault since they failed in checking the log books for faulty navigation and in taking proper measures to prevent such navigation. The inspectors were responsible to

---

[481] *Mandaraka-Sheppard*, pp. 322-323, 912; *Shaw/Tsimplis*, p. 212; criticized by *Gower & Davies*, pp. 187-188 on the ground that the policy rule will result in nothing but uncertainty.

[482] *Meridian Global Funds Management Asia Ltd. v. Securities Commission* [1995] 2 A.C. 500, 511 (Privy Council) *per* Lord Hoffmann.

[483] An important point should here be highlighted: Most of the cases mentioned under this section are decided according to the "actual fault or privity" standard of fault. As mentioned before, "actual fault or privity" and "wilful misconduct" refer to different degrees of fault (see *supra* C II). However, since the phrase "actual fault or privity" necessitates a "personal" fault of the shipowner or carrier, the cases can be appropriately considered on the attribution issue.

[484] For the facts of the case see *supra* C II 1.

[485] *"The Lady Gwendolen"* [1965] 1 Lloyd's Rep. 335, 345 (CA).

the marine superintendent, and the marine superintendent was directly answerable to the deputy director, who was the head of technical and investment affairs. The deputy director (who was one of the seven deputies) was directly responsible to the director general. The court concluded that only the director and the deputies could be considered as the *alter ego* of the shipowning company. The inspectors and the marine superintendent were nothing more than subordinates[486].

Similarly in *The Smjeli*, the court stated that a shipowning company is not personally at fault in case of delegation of some duties to a proper subordinate. When the vessel Transporter III was towed by the tug Smjeli, the towing hawser parted and the tow took to the ground, causing substantial damage to the cargo on board. The tug and tow, stowage of the cargo and the towing hawser had been approved by an inspecting company which was delegated with those tasks by the director of the salvage and towing department of the shipowning company. The court concluded that the inspecting company is not the *alter ego* of the shipowning company; on the contrary, for the purposes of the case only the fault and knowledge of the director of the salvage and towing department can be attributed to the shipowning company[487].

It was in the *Charlotte* case that fault of a management company was for the first time attributed to the shipowning company[488]. The dispute arose from a collision between the Charlotte and another ship. The Charlotte was owned by a company and managed by a firm of two partners. The court stated that the fault of one of the two partners of the management firm was the fault of the shipowning company[489]. This decision was followed in *The Marion*. The vessel Marion was owned by a limited company and was managed by another limited company. She caused damage to a pipeline when her anchor came too close to it. The reason for the incident was that the master used an obsolete chart, although the updated chart was also on board. The obsolete chart was not removed, which was the task of the marine superintendent of the managing company, even though there had been a flag state inspection before the incident occurred and the report of that inspection included a warning and required immediate action on the correction of navigational charts. The court ruled that if the ship is owned by a limited company and managed by another limited company, the fault of the managing company will be taken into account in order to determine whether the owner is personally at fault[490]. The court, further stated that the master and the marine superintendent were negligent, but the negligence was not of the managing company, since the marine superintendent was not the *alter ego* of the company[491]. The Court of Appeal stated that the lack of action by the management company despite the flag state inspection report was the management company's personal fault; since the

---

[486] *The "Garden City"* [1982] 2 Lloyd's Rep. 382, 398-399 (QBD).
[487] *The "Smjeli"* [1982] 2 Lloyd's Rep. 74 (QBD).
[488] *"Charlotte" v. "Theory and Others"* (1921) 9 Ll. L. Rep. 341 (PDAD).
[489] *"Charlotte" v. "Theory and Others"* (1921) 9 Ll. L. Rep. 341, 342 (PDAD).
[490] *The "Marion"* [1982] 2 Lloyd's Rep. 52, 54 (QBD).
[491] *The "Marion"* [1982] 2 Lloyd's Rep. 52, 70-71 (QBD).

management company was the *alter ego* of the shipowning company, the ship-owning company was personally at fault[492].

In *The Star Sea*, the vessel became a constructive total loss after a fire broke out due to her unseaworthiness. The insurers claimed that the assured was privy to her unseaworthy condition[493]. The vessel was owned by one company; however, she was managed by another company. Additionally, another company was registered as the manager in the ship's registry. In its decision, the Court of Appeal stated that the question was "who was involved in the decision making process required for sending the *Star Sea* to sea?" and decided that all the directors of the two management companies were involved and, therefore, could be considered as the *alter ego*[494].

As an exception to the cases mentioned above[495], in *The Ert Stefanie*, it was stated that even when not a member of the board of directors, the fault and knowledge of any director can be attributed to the company, if that director is one of the senior managers[496]. In *The MSC Rosa M*, the technical director of the company was identified as the *alter ego* of the company[497].

---

[492] *The "Marion"* [1983] 2 Lloyd's Rep. 156 (CA); affirmed by *The "Marion"* [1984] 1 Lloyd's Rep. 1 (HL). For a consideration of the case under the ISM Code requirements see *Anderson*, pp. 258-262.

[493] MIA, 1906 § 39 (5): "In a time policy there is no implied warranty that the ship shall be seaworthy at any stage of the adventure, but where, with the privity of the assured, the ship is sent to sea in an unseaworthy state, the insurer is not liable for any loss attributable to unseaworthiness".

[494] *Manifest Shipping & Co. Ltd. v. Uni-Polaris Insurance Co. Ltd. and la Réunion Européene (The "Star Sea")* [1997] 1 Lloyd's Rep. 360, 375 (CA). Although they were considered as the *alter ego*, they have not been found privy to the unseaworthy condition, see *Manifest Shipping & Co. Ltd. v. Uni-Polaris Insurance Co. Ltd. and la Réunion Européene (The "Star Sea")* [2001] 1 Lloyd's Rep. 389 (HL). For a consideration of the case under the ISM Code requirements see *Anderson*, pp. 243-251.

[495] Similar decisions can be found also in the American case law; for more information see John D. Kimball, Country Analysis: U.S.A., in: *Griggs/Williams/Farr*, p. 452. For instance, in the *Tecomar* case it was the technical department which was responsible for the maintenance and repair of the vessel. The department was headed by a technical director who had complete authority over the maintenance. The director was also in charge of reporting regularly to the vice presidents. The Court stated that "the knowledge [...] of a corporate shipowner includes the corporation's managing agents, officers, or supervising employees. [...] A managing officer is anyone to whom the corporation has delegated general management or general superintendence of the whole or a particular part of the business". The court concluded that the ship's unseaworthy condition was actually known to the corporation since it was known to the director of the technical department, see *In re Tecomar S.A.* (DC New York, 1991) 765 F.Supp. 1150, 1153-1154, 1181.

[496] *Societe Anonyme des Minerais v. Grant Trading Inc. (The "Ert Stefanie")* [1989] 1 Lloyd's Rep. 349 (CA).

[497] *MSC Mediterranean Shipping Co. S.A. v. Delumar BVBA and Others (The "MSC Rosa M")* [2000] 2 Lloyd's Rep. 399, 404 (QBD).

Until now, the cases mentioned involved relatively small companies. The attribution issue becomes more complex when there is a group of companies. A good example is the *Sanko Harvest* case[498]. The vessel Sanko Harvest and her cargo became a total loss after her grounding due to the gross negligence of the crew and the master. The cargo owners sued the carrier alleging, notwithstanding other issues, that the carrier was personally at fault. However, the structure behind the carrier was a complex one. The vessel was owned by a corporation, which passed her possession by way of a bareboat charter to the company Grandslam. Grandslam entered into a time charter with Sanko. Together with Eastern, Sanko and Grandslam constituted a group of companies, where Sanko owned all the shares of both Grandslam and Eastern. Grandslam and Eastern entered into a management agreement where manning duties were also delegated to Eastern. However, after some time, Sanko and its subsidiaries encountered financial difficulties and, after an order of bankruptcy, became subject to control by trustees appointed according to the insolvency legislation. While under the administration of trustees, Sanko entered into a voyage charter with the cargo owners. The court ruled that, as the parent company, Sanko was closely involved in the subsidiary companies' management. Therefore, their fault could be attributed to Sanko.

d) Result

As a result of the relevant provisions under German and Turkish law and the identification doctrine under English law, it is clear that the issue of attribution is not a simple one. First of all, the issue here should be considered in the perspective of breaking liability limits[499]. To this end, the underlying policy and the substantive content of the rules[500] must be remembered. As seen before[501], the policy behind the present provisions under the carriage by sea conventions is to create almost unbreakable limits. This policy has also been established by the content of the provisions: it is either the intentional or the reckless conduct coupled with subjective knowledge as to the probable consequences which deprives one of the right to limit. Undoubtedly, this sets a very high degree of culpability, and the situation becomes more difficult when there is a corporation under scrutiny.

However, it is still possible to identify some natural persons who are at fault and consider their fault and knowledge as the fault and knowledge of the company. The identified person, or the *alter ego*, must be someone to whom a function of the legal entity is delegated. For the purposes of sea carriage, it must be someone who is entrusted with a function regarding shipping operations. However, just being in charge of the shipping operations is not sufficient to identify someone as the *alter ego* of the company. Additionally, that person should have the right to act

---

[498] *Sanko Steamship Co. Ltd. v. Sumitomo Australia Ltd. (No. 2)* 63 FCR 227 (Federal Court of Australia, 1995).

[499] *Gaskell, Hamburg Rules*, pp. 172-173.

[500] *Meridian Global Funds Management Asia Ltd. v. Securities Commission* [1995] 2 A.C. 500, 508-510 (Privy Council) *per* Lord Hoffmann.

[501] See *supra* C II 2 b.

independently of instructions[502] and have full discretion with regard to the function delegated to him. In other words, the person identified should not be someone who simply fulfils orders and complies with the corporate policy; rather, he should have the right to exercise decision-making authority in respect of corporate policy[503].

It is clear that such a person will be found generally in the upper management of a company. Mere employees, *e.g.* master, heads of departments in charge of navigational or operational matters, have, in most cases, not been regarded to be the *alter ego*[504]. Nevertheless, being in a senior managerial position or, contrarily, being in the lower positions in the company structure is not decisive. The important point is the responsibility of the person to be identified with the company[505]. It is possible that even persons on the directorial and managerial level can be regarded as mere employees, whereas persons who seem no more than employees can have enough responsibility to be regarded as the *alter ego*[506]. It will depend upon each case's facts and circumstances[507].

Consequently, if the shipowner delegates all of his functions to someone else, *i.e.* to another company as is done generally by management agreements in the shipping business, the delegate, *i.e.* the management company, will be the *alter ego* of the shipowner[508]. Accordingly, it is the fault and knowledge of the *alter ego* which will be under scrutiny for the purposes of unlimited liability. It has been argued that this principle cannot be applied under the 1976 London Convention, since managers can also limit their liabilities and every person is liable for his own fault under the Convention[509].

This interpretation cannot be accepted on several grounds. If the whole management of the ship is delegated to a manager and if, in this case, the manager's

---

[502] *Tesco Supermarkets Ltd. v. Nattrass* [1972] A.C. 153, 171 (HL) *per* Lord Reid.

[503] *The Rhône* [1993] 1 Supreme Court Reports 497, 526 (Canada) *per* Justice Iacobucci; *Christodoulou*, p. 46. *Manifest Shipping & Co. Ltd. v. Uni-Polaris Insurance Co. Ltd. and la Réunion Européene (The "Star Sea")* [1997] 1 Lloyd's Rep. 360, 375 (CA) *per* Lord Justice Leggatt: "If the assured were one corporation and if that one corporation alone were responsible for putting ships to sea, the search would be to draw the circle round the natural persons which fairly reflected the equivalent position to that which would prevail where a natural person was the assured.". The criterion of decision-making authority also facilitates the treatment of the issue in groups of companies. In a group of companies, a subsidiary company can be vested with the authority to act on behalf of the shipowning company or a parent company can take decisions in the name of a shipowning company. In such cases, the subsidiary or parent company should be considered as the *alter ego*, see *Puttfarken*, Rn. 834.

[504] *Hodges/Hill*, p. 577.

[505] *Societe Anonyme des Minerais v. Grant Trading Inc. (The "Ert Stefanie")* [1989] 1 Lloyd's Rep. 349, 352 (CA) *per* Lord Justice Mustill.

[506] It must be noted that the result reached by the case law in the USA are, as well, not different from the conclusions drawn here, see *Chen, Limitation*, pp. 63-65.

[507] *Hodges/Hill*, p. 577.

[508] *Aikens/Lord/Bools*, para. 10.313; *Grime, Loss of the Right*, p. 107.

[509] *Grime, Loss of the Right*, p. 108; *Shaw, ISM Code*, 171; *Anderson*, p. 117.

fault cannot be attributed to the shipowner, every shipowner can circumvent the law by simply delegating his functions to a third party[510]. This result is unacceptable. Further, if it is accepted that in case of a third party manager the manager's fault and knowledge cannot be attributed to the shipowner, the natural result from this standpoint would be that a person can be considered *alter ego* of the company if he has the competence and powers with regard to shipping within the company structure; however, if the authority and powers are delegated to a third party, he cannot be considered as the *alter ego*. This result is inconsistent with the rules of interpretation.

Here, the issue is determining the person to be identified with the company: either someone within the company structure or a third party. Therefore, if the management is delegated to a third party, *i.e.* to a management company, that third party is to be considered the *alter ego* of the shipowner. Since it will be necessary to identify the *alter ego* of the management company as well, it can be said that the *alter ego* of the management company is the *alter ego* of the shipowner[511].

II. ISM Code

1. The code

The International Safety Management Code for the Safe Operation of Ships and Pollution Prevention 1994 has been adopted by the IMO Resolution A.741(18) of 4 November 1993. The International Safety Management Code, known as the ISM Code, has been adopted in order to provide an international standard for the safe management and operation of ships and pollution prevention[512]. It became mandatory for a certain class of ships on 1 July 1998 and for other ships on 1 July 2002 under the SOLAS.

The ISM Code requires every company[513] to develop a "Safety Management System" (SMS) defined as a structured and documented system enabling company personnel, both on and off shore, to implement effectively the company safety and environmental protection policy[514]. The Code sets up a system of verification, reporting and auditing, all of which must be documented[515]. Clearly the main objective of the whole system created by the ISM Code is to verify and ensure compliance with the international safety and pollution prevention regimes and to

---

[510] *Hodges, ISM Code*, 48; *Grime, Loss of the Right*, p. 108; *Anderson*, pp. 118-119.

[511] *Hodges/Hill*, p. 587; *Hodges, ISM Code*, 48.

[512] ISM Code Preamble.

[513] For the purposes of the ISM Code, the term "company" refers to the owner of the ship or any other organisation or person such as the manager, or the bareboat charterer, who has assumed the responsibility for operation of the ship from the shipowner and who, on assuming such responsibility, has agreed to take over all duties and responsibility imposed by the Code (Art. 1.1.2).

[514] ISM Code Art. 1.1.4.

[515] For general information see *Pamborides*, 56-57; *Griggs/Williams/Farr*, p. 34; *Gold/Chircop/Kindred*, p. 227; *Looks/Kraft*, 222-223; for more information see *de la Motte*, pp. 24 *et seqq.*; *Gürses*, pp. 13 *et seqq.*

minimize human error causing casualties[516]; this has, in fact, been pointed out by courts on multiple occasions[517].

2. Impacts

a) Generally

The ISM Code has affected almost all aspects of ship operations[518]. Consequently, it has also had some impact on legal aspects, specifically on liability issues. Among them, the most important are the liability arising out of the duty to provide a seaworthy ship under contracts of carriage[519] and the insurance requirements with regard to the seaworthiness of the ship[520].

In addition to the impact on seaworthiness issues, the ISM Code has also had an effect on wilful misconduct and insurance cover. As previously stated, in cases of wilful misconduct the insurer is not liable against the assured[521]. "Misconduct" has been defined as "any unlawful conduct, namely any conduct violating law, including regulations, and other rules, and also including any negligent conduct"[522]. Consequently, there is no doubt that any violation of the ISM Code constitutes misconduct, and if other prerequisites of wilfulness are also present, the assured will lose his insurance cover due to wilful misconduct[523].

b) On the attribution

Art. 4 of the ISM Code provides that every company must appoint a designated person ashore having direct access to the highest level of management in order to

---

[516] *Gold/Chircop/Kindred*, p. 227; *Honka*, pp. 106-107; *Soyer, ISM Code*, 279; *Looks/Kraft*, 222. *Ogg*, 144: "The ISM Code has a mission and that is to squeeze human error out of ship operations".

[517] E.g. *"The Lady Gwendolen"* [1965] 1 Lloyd's Rep. 335, 346 (CA) *per* Lord Justice Wilmer: "any company which embarks on the business of shipowning must accept the obligation to ensure efficient management of its ships"; *The "Garden City"* [1982] 2 Lloyd's Rep. 382, 389 (QBD) *per* Justice Staughton: "the top management of every shipowning corporation ought to institute a system of supervision of navigation and detection of faults"; see also *The "Marion"* [1984] 2 Lloyd's Rep. 1 (HL).

[518] *Gold/Chircop/Kindred*, p. 227.

[519] For more information see *de la Motte*, pp. 103-110, 132-139; *Gürses*, pp. 51-62; *Mandaraka-Sheppard*, pp. 325-328; *Tetley*, pp. 941-945; *Honka*, pp. 112-117; *Ogg*, 145-147; *Looks/Kraft*, 224-225; *Pamborides*, 58-60; *Looks*, p. 6; *Pilley/Lorenzon*, p. 230; M. Deniz *Güner*, Uluslararası Güvenli Yönetim Kodu'nun Taşıyanın Sorumluluğuna Etkileri, DenizHD 1999/3-4, pp. 93 *et seqq.*

[520] For more information see Susan *Hodges*, Seaworthiness and Safe Ship Management, (1998) 5 IJIL 162; *Anderson*, pp. 164 *et seqq.*; *de la Motte*, p. 320-336; *Soyer, ISM Code*, 281 *et seqq.*; *Mandaraka-Sheppard*, pp. 328-333; *Hodges, ISM Code*, 51-54; *Looks*, pp. 18-19; *Pilley/Lorenzon*, p. 231; *Pamborides*, 61.

[521] See *supra* D VII.

[522] See *supra* § 4 A II 2.

[523] *Thomas*, p. 247 para. 7.10; *Chen*, p. 203; *Soyer, ISM Code*, 283-284.

ensure the safe operation of each ship, and to provide a link between the company and those on board. The designated person is also responsible and authorised for monitoring the safety and pollution-prevention aspects of the operation of each ship and for ensuring that adequate resources and shore-based support are applied, as required[524].

First of all, a designated person is entitled to limit his liability under the 1976 London Convention regime either as the manager of the ship or as a person for whose act, neglect or fault the shipowner is responsible. However, it should also be kept in mind that, as with any other person liable under the London Convention system, a designated person is also subject to unlimited liability if he is guilty of the conduct specified in Art. 4 of the Convention[525].

The position of the designated person assumes special importance in the field of corporate liability for the purposes of unlimited liability. The ISM Code mentions "a designated person ashore having direct access to the highest level of management". Under this provision, a designated person can be (a) a mere servant or employee, (b) a person having a directorial or managerial position, or (c) a member of the directing organs of the company, *i.e.* the board of directors[526]. If a member of the board of directors is appointed as the designated person, which is highly unlikely[527], his fault and knowledge will be considered as the fault and knowledge of the company[528].

If, alternatively, the designated person has a directorial or managerial position, his knowledge can be attributed to the company under the *alter ego* concept provided that the facts or the circumstances can lead to such a result. In order to determine whether the designated person can be identified with the corporation itself, the duties and responsibilities of the designated person should be taken into account. Pursuant to Art. 4 of the ISM Code "the responsibility and authority of the designated person [...] should include monitoring the safety and pollution-prevention aspects of the operation of each ship and ensuring that adequate resources and shore-based support are applied". By virtue of this provision, the designated person is basically to have the responsibility of "monitoring" and "ensuring" the shore-based support. The provision does not necessitate that the designated person be involved in the decision-making procedure of the corporation. Therefore, the designated person cannot be said to be the *alter ego* of the company if he only has responsibilities meeting the minimum requirements of the

---

[524] For more information see *Anderson*, pp. 77 *et seqq.*

[525] *Mandaraka-Sheppard*, p. 913.

[526] *Hodges/Hill*, p. 578; *Hodges, ISM Code*, 48. Due to the ISM Code requirements, the designated person cannot be someone who is not within the company structure, *Looks*, p. 10.

[527] *Looks*, p. 11; *Hodges, ISM Code*, 49; *Gürses*, pp. 34-35. The wording of the ISM Code ("having direct access to the highest level of management") also suggests that designated person is not a member of the upper management, see *Hodges, ISM Code*, 48-49; *Gaskell, Breaking Limits*, p. 7. However, this wording does not prevent someone in the upper management level being appointed as the designated person.

[528] See *supra* E I 1.

Code[529]. In order to determine whether the designated person is the *alter ego* or not, the criteria of the identification doctrine[530] needs to be applied[531].

The last alternative is that the designated person is a mere servant or employee. Here it would not be fair to consider his knowledge as the company's knowledge since he will not have any impact on the corporate policy. As a result, if the designated person does not have a high position in the management structure of the company, his knowledge would not be sufficient to challenge the liability limits[532].

Nonetheless, appointing a mere servant or agent as the designated person might result in the violation of the ISM Code requirements. The Code requires that the designated person needs to have the power for ensuring that adequate resources and shore-based support are applied (Art. 4). Such an assurance can be supplied only if the designated person has managerial power. That the designated person has such authority is actually one of the company's responsibilities under the Code. Art. 3.3 of the ISM Code states that "[t]he Company is responsible for ensuring that adequate resources and shore-based support are provided to enable the designated person or persons to carry out their functions". However, the question is whether a violation of the ISM Code by appointing a mere servant or agent as the designated person constitutes wilful misconduct on the part of the company. Does such a violation fulfil the knowledge requirement that the damage or loss would probably result? The answer to this question could be found in the assessment of another ISM Code requirement[533].

According to the ISM Code, the master of the ship is required to implement and to observe the safety and pollution prevention policy of the company as well[534]. All non-conformities, including all deficiencies, accidents and hazardous occurrences determined by the master or the designated person, are to be reported in writing to the company[535]. The non-conformities are to be determined according to Art. 10.1 of the ISM Code which states that "the Company should establish procedures to ensure that the ship is maintained in conformity with the provisions of the relevant rules and regulations and with any additional requirements which may be established by the Company". The term "relevant rules and regulations" cover all national and international crew, design, equipment, safety and management rules and regulations.

The duties of observing and reporting in writing will, without any doubt, give great opportunities to the claimants whilst trying to prove the company's personal

---

[529] *Rabe*, LondonHBÜ 1976 Art. 4 Rn. 7; for the counterview see *Ogg*, 148; *Looks/ Kraft*, 225; *Pamborides*, 61.

[530] See *supra* E I 2.

[531] *Shaw/Tsimplis*, pp. 212-213.

[532] *Hodges/Hill*, p. 578; *Mandaraka-Sheppard*, p. 334; *Pilley/Lorenzon*, pp. 230-231.

[533] In the *Caribia Express* case, the German court stated that the supervision and prevention measures with regard to the carriage of goods are not necessarily to be taken on the high management level. It is sufficient, if the responsibility of taking such measures is given to an executive employee. See HansOLG, 02.10.2008, HbgSchRZ 2009, 52 (59) ("*Caribia Express*").

[534] ISM Code Art. 5.1.

[535] ISM Code Art. 9.1.

act or omission. If a fact constituting a violation of the relevant rules and regulations is reported by the master or the designated person to the highest level of management with which he has direct contact, and if that fact is subsequently ignored, then the inaction by the management of the Company will constitute strong evidence of recklessness[536]. Furthermore, depending on the seriousness of the fact and the obviousness of its probable consequences, the reports in writing will be *prima facie* evidence that the management (or the *alter ego*) of a company was aware of the deficiencies and their probable consequences[537]. However, every violation of the ISM Code does not result in unlimited liability. A presumption of wilful misconduct must be avoided[538].

---

[536] *Mandaraka-Sheppard*, p. 334; *de la Motte*, pp. 303-304; *Christodoulou*, pp. 41-42; *Ogg*, 149; *Gürses*, p. 96; *Pamborides*, 60.

[537] *Griggs/Williams/Farr*, p. 34; *Anderson*, p. 118; *de la Motte*, pp. 304-305; *Gürses*, p. 96; *Looks/Kraft*, 225.

[538] *de la Motte*, pp. 307-308.

§ 6 Conventions on Other Means of Transportation

It is common for the liability of the carrier to be limited under the international regimes regarding means of transportation other than the carriage by air or sea. Therefore, conventions regarding other means of transportation also employ provisions for breaking the limits. However, mostly depending on the time when the conventions have been adopted, the wording employed by the conventions differs: some adopt the unamended Warsaw Convention version, some the definition adopted by the Hague Protocol of 1955 (sometimes with slight changes), and some refer only to specific terms for the necessary degree of fault for breaking the liability limits. In this chapter, after giving an overview of the conventions, solutions adopted by the conventions in order to deprive the carrier of the liability limits will be briefly addressed.

A. Conventions

I. Carriage by Road

Due to the need for a standardisation of the conditions to be applied to international carriage by road[1], the Convention on the Contract for the International Carriage of Goods by Road ("CMR") was signed in 1956 and entered into force on 2 July 1961[2]. Besides the unification achieved between almost all European states and additionally some Asian and African states, most of the states also brought their national law into conformity with the CMR[3].

The Convention unifies the rules applicable to carriage completed between two different countries of which at least one is a contracting party. Under the CMR, the carrier is liable for the loss of or damage to goods occurring during carriage and for delay in delivery. However, if the carrier can prove that the loss, damage or delay resulted from a cause which he was not able to prevent although he showed the utmost care, or from the fault or neglect of the claimant, he will be relieved of liability (Art. 17-18)[4]. Therefore, the liability of the carrier under the

---

[1] Preamble to the CMR.

[2] For the list of the contracting parties see <www.unece.org/trans/conventn/ legalinst_25_OLIRT_CMR.html> (09.08.2010). For the historical background of the Convention see *de la Motte/Thume*, in: *Thume, CMR-Kommentar*, Vor Art. 1 Rn. 2-3; *Koller*, CMR vor Art. 1 Rn. 1; *Clarke, CMR*, pp. 3-4; *Herber/Piper*, Einf Rn. 1-5; *Loewe*, 312-313; *Stachow*, pp. 91-92.

[3] In Germany by virtue of Transportrechtsreformgesetz (BGBl. I S.1588), in the UK by virtue of a Schedule to the Carriage of Goods by Road Act 1965 (see *Clarke, CMR*, p. 3); in Turkish legislation by virtue of TTK (2011) Art. 850 *et seqq.* For more information see *Thume*, in: *Fremuth/Thume*, Vor Art. 1 CMR Rn. 1-2.

[4] For more information see MünchKommHGB 1997 – *Basedow*, CMR Art. 17, CMR Art. 18; MünchKommHGB 2009 – *Jesser-Huß*, CMR Art. 17, CMR Art. 18; *Helm*, in: Großkomm. HGB Anh. VI nach § 452: CMR Art. 17, Art. 18; *Thume*, in: *Fremuth/Thume*, Art. 17 CMR, Art. 18 CMR; *Thume*, in: *Thume, CMR-Kommentar*,

CMR is based on the presumed fault of the carrier, coupled however with the duty of utmost care[5]. If the carrier is found liable for the damage to or loss of the cargo, or delay in delivery, he will be liable for compensating for the damage sustained by the cargo interests. The Convention regulates the calculation and the extent of the compensation and the limitation amounts under Art. 23 and 25 in detail[6].

The unification effort for the carriage of passengers and their luggage by road came later than for the carriage of goods. The Convention on the Contract for the International Carriage of Passengers and Luggage by Road ("CVR") was signed in 1973 and entered into force on 12 April 1994[7]. The Convention is applicable, irrespective of the place of residence and the nationality of the parties to the contract of carriage, when the carriage takes place in the territory of at least two different contracting states (Art. 1). The carrier is liable for the loss or damage resulting from physical injury to or death of passengers during the carriage or total or partial loss of or damage to their luggage (Art. 11, 14), unless he can prove that the loss or damage was caused by circumstances that the carrier could not have avoided and the consequences of which he was unable to prevent by showing "the diligence which the particular facts of the case called for" (Art. 11 (2), 14 (2)). It is clear that the liability of the road carrier for the carriage of passengers under the CVR is also based on presumed fault. The extent of compensation and the limitation of liability for personal injuries and for loss of or damage to luggage are regulated under Art. 12, 13 and 16.

Vor Art. 17, Art. 17, Art. 18; *Koller*, CMR Art. 17-Art. 18; *Clarke, CMR*, Ch. 5-7; *Clarke/Yates*, para. 1.78 *et seqq.*; *Carriage of Goods*, para. 3.1.2.17.1 *et seqq.*; *Erdil*, pp. 146 *et seqq.*; *Akıncı*, pp. 87 *et seqq.*; *Aydın*, pp. 29 *et seqq.*; *Loewe*, 360-370.

[5] MünchKommHGB 1997 – *Basedow*, CMR Art. 17 Rn. 3; MünchKommHGB 2009 – *Jesser-Huß*, CMR Art. 17 Rn. 3; *Clarke, CMR*, pp. 184-185; *Helm*, in: Großkomm. HGB Anh. VI nach § 452: CMR Art. 17 Rn. 24-34; *Thume*, in: *Fremuth/Thume*, Art. 17 CMR Rn. 20; *Aydın*, p. 34; *Özdemir, Eşya Taşıma*, p. 127; OGH Wien, 10.07.1991, TranspR 1991, 422; OGH Wien 19.01.1994, TranspR 1994, 282; OGH Wien, 12.11.1996, TranspR 1997, 104. According to the counterview, the liability regime set by the CMR is either a strict liability regime (Ebenroth/Boujong/Joost/Strohn/*Boesche*, CMR Vor Art. 17 Rn. 3; *Koller*, CMR Art. 17 Rn. 21; *Glöckner*, Vor Art. 17 CMR Rn. 2; *Brinkmann, Vergleich*, 147; *Loewe*, 361; *Erdil*, p. 148; *Gençtürk*, pp. 111-112; *Yetiş Şamlı*, pp. 16-17; BGH, 21.12.1966, VersR 1967, 153) or a presumed fault liability regime (*Akıncı*, p. 87). For information on the discussions within the German doctrine see *Thume*, in: *Thume, CMR-Kommentar*, Art. 17 Rn. 4-14.

[6] For more information see MünchKommHGB 1997 – *Basedow*, CMR Art. 23, CMR Art. 25; *Carriage of Goods*, para. 3.1.2.23.1 *et seqq* and 3.1.2.25.1; *Thume*, in: *Fremuth/Thume*, Art. 23 CMR, Art. 25 CMR; *Clarke, CMR*, pp. 295 *et seqq.*; *Clarke/Yates*, para. 1.144 *et seqq.*

[7] For the list of the contracting parties see <www.unece.org/trans/conventn/legalinst _28_OLIRT_CVR.html> (09.08.2010).

II. Carriage by Rail

As it was one of the earliest modes of modern transport, the unification of the rules regarding the carriage of goods by rail was done in the 19th century. The first convention regarding the international carriage of goods by rail was signed on 14 November 1890[8], whereas a convention regarding the international carriage of passengers was agreed upon in 1923[9]. Both of the conventions adopted a system for periodic revision of the uniform rules[10]. However, in 1980, it was decided that substantial changes to the convention's regime were necessary[11] and the Convention concerning International Carriage by Rail ("COTIF") was adopted on 9 May 1980, entering into force on 1 May 1985. The rules concerning the carriage of goods and passengers were regulated in the annexes of the Convention. Appendix A to COTIF adopted the Uniform Rules concerning the Contract for International Carriage of Passengers and Luggage by Rail ("CIV"), whereas appendix B adopted the Uniform Rules concerning the Contract for International Carriage of Goods by Rail ("CIM").

Although the Intergovernmental Organization for International Carriage by Rail ("OTIF") (COTIF Art. 1) was empowered to amend certain provisions of CIV and CIM (COTIF Art. 19)[12], the need to make some substantial changes in the uniform rules resulted in the Protocol of 3 June 1999, in which the uniform rules as to the carriage of goods and passengers were essentially changed. COTIF 1999 entered into force on 1 July 2006[13].

CIV and CIM are applicable to contracts of international carriage. In terms of carriage of passengers, international carriage means any carriage where the place of departure and place of destination are situated in two different contracting states[14]. Similarly, international carriage of goods is any carriage where the place of taking over the goods and the place designated for delivery are situated in two different contracting states[15]. Thus, both the starting and ending points of the car-

---

[8] *Haenni*, p. 12; *Carriage of Goods*, para. 4.1.1.3; *Koller*, CIM vor Art. 1 Rn. 1; MünchKommHGB 1997 – *Mutz*, Intern. Eisenbahntransportrecht Vorbem. Rn. 1; MünchKommHGB 2009 – *Freise*, Int. EisenbahntranspR Einl. Rn. 1; *Arkan, Sempozyum*, p. 48; *Clarke, Transport in Europe*, 37; for the historical background see *Becker*, pp. 28-29; *Arkan*, pp. 5-6.

[9] *Haenni*, p. 12; *Becker*, p. 31; *Pohar*, p. 272; for more information on the historical background see *Mutz*, pp. 45-46.

[10] For more information see *Haenni*, pp. 17-18; for more information on the revision conferences see *Arkan*, pp. 6-9.

[11] MünchKommHGB 1997 – *Mutz*, Intern. Eisenbahntransportrecht Vorbem. Rn. 1; *Arkan, Sempozyum*, p. 49; *Arkan*, p. 10; for more information on the changes see *Arkan*, pp. 16-24.

[12] For more information about the revision procedure see MünchKommHGB 1997 – *Mutz*, Intern. Eisenbahntransportrecht Vorbem. Rn. 13-17; MünchKommHGB 2009 – *Freise*, Int. EisenbahntranspR Einl. Rn. 29-35.

[13] <www.otif.org/en/about-otif/conventions-cotif.html> (09.08.2010). For the essential changes made on the CIM 1980 regime see *Clarke/Yates*, para. 2.477 *et seqq.*

[14] CIV 1999 Art. 1 (1).

[15] CIM 1999 Art. 1 (1).

riage must be in contracting states, which is different from the CMR in terms of the carriage of goods[16].

CIV 1999 Art. 26 sets the basis of liability in cases of physical injury or death of passengers. Pursuant to that provision, the carrier is presumably at fault if there is death of or personal injury to passengers. However, if the carrier can prove, despite "having taken the care required in the particular circumstances of the case", that he was unable to prevent the accident, he will be relieved of liability. Moreover, if the accident was caused by the neglect of a third party or the passenger, the carrier will not be liable for the consequences arising therefrom[17]. In case of delay, the carrier is liable, again, on the basis of presumed fault (Art. 32). The carrier's liability for registered baggage is, pursuant to Art. 36 of the Rules, based on presumed fault with the utmost duty of care. The extent of compensation and the limitation of liability are regulated under Art. 27-30 for the death of or physical injury to passengers and under Art. 41-43 for the loss of or damage to registered baggage.

CIM 1999 establishes a liability system based on presumed fault coupled with the utmost duty of care[18]. If, according to CIM, the goods are damaged or lost when they were under the possession of the carrier, or the delivery of the goods was delayed, the carrier is liable for such loss, damage or delay (Art. 23 (1)). If the carrier wishes to be relieved of such liability, he should prove that the loss, damage or delay was caused by circumstances which he could not avoid and the consequences of which he was unable to prevent (Art. 23 (2)) or by one of the reasons specified in Art. 23 (3). The extent of compensation and limitation amounts are regulated under Art. 30-35.

III. Carriage by Inland Waterways

There are three conventions with respect to the carriage of goods or passengers and the limitation of liability regarding carriage by inland waterways. The first convention is the Convention on the Contract for the International Carriage of Passengers and Luggage by Inland Waterway, signed in 1976 ("CVN") which has

---

[16] *Clarke, Transport in Europe*, 37.

[17] For the discussion of the basis of liability see *Mutz*, pp. 78-82 (the writer concludes that the liability of the carrier under CIV is strict liability). For detailed information see Rüdiger *Schmidt-Bendun*, Haftung der Eisenbahnverkehrsunternehmen, Jena 2007.

[18] For more information see *Koller*, CIM Art. 23; *Clarke/Yates*, para. 2.533 *et seqq.*; *Özdemir, Eşya Taşıma*, p. 127; *Haenni*, pp. 111-112. Since railways were state-owned and operated exclusively without alternatives at the beginning of the railway era, their liability was based on strict liability system until the mid fifties (*Arkan, Sempozyum*, p. 66; *Gençtürk*, p. 113; for more information see *Haenni*, p. 111). However, later, due to the developments in the road carriage, the liability regime of the CIM was changed. For the counterview, that the liability system has not been changed and that rail carrier's liability remains based on strict liability regime see *Gençtürk*, p. 114; *Beier*, pp. 94-95, 119, 123; *Arkan, Sempozyum*, pp. 66-67; *Spera*, Art. 36 Rn. 2.

not entered into force yet and seems unlikely to in the near future[19]. Since it is highly unlikely that this convention will contribute to unification at an international level, it will not constitute a part of this chapter.

On the other hand, the Strasbourg Convention on the Limitation of Liability of Owners of Inland Navigation Vessels ("CLNI") was signed on 4 November 1988 and has been in force since 1 November 1997. With the CLNI, the rules and principles of the 1976 London Convention have been adopted for inland navigation[20]. Vessel owners, a term which includes the owner, hirer, charterer, manager and operator of an inland navigation vessel, and salvors, are entitled to limit their liability for the claims set out in the Convention Art. 2, whatever the basis of liability may be. The Convention, similar to the 1976 London Convention, allows for the limitation of liability by way of constituting a fund (Art. 11-14). However, the right to limit does not depend on the constitution of a fund (Art. 10)[21].

The Budapest Convention on the Contract for the Carriage of Goods by Inland Waterways was signed in 2001 ("CMNI") and has been in force since 1 April 2005[22]. The Convention is applicable to international carriages between at least two states of which at least one is a contracting party (Art. 2 (1))[23]. Pursuant to Art. 16 of the Convention, the carrier is liable for loss of or damage to goods when the goods were in his possession, or delay in delivery, unless he proves that he showed the necessary due diligence and was not able to prevent the consequences causing loss, damage or delay[24]. If the performance of carriage is entrusted to an actual carrier[25], the contracting carrier, nevertheless remains liable for the entire carriage, whereas the actual carrier is also liable for the part of the carriage he has performed (Art. 4)[26]. If there are any of the special circumstances or risks listed in Art. 18, the carrier will be exonerated from liability unless the cargo interests can prove that the loss suffered did not result from one of the circumstances or risks (Art. 18)[27]. It can be said that the liability system of the Convention is based on the presumed fault of the carrier[28]. If the carrier is found liable, the compensation

---

[19] See <www.unece.org/trans/conventn/legalinst_36_IWT_CVN.html> (09.08 2010).

[20] *Müller, Inland Navigation*, p. 15.

[21] For an overview see *Müller, Inland Navigation*, pp. 57-59.

[22] <www.unece.org/trans/main/sc3/sc3_cmni_legalinst.html> (09.08.2010). For the historical background see *Czerwenka, CMNI*, 277-278. For more information on the implementation of the Convention in contracting parties see *Hacksteiner*, 147-149.

[23] It is said that CMNI is applicable to port-to-port carriages, see *Czerwenka, CMNI*, 278. However, according to Art. 3 (2) of the Convention, taking over and delivery of goods, unless otherwise agreed, take place on board the vessel, which refers to tackle-to-tackle carriage.

[24] For more information see *Koller*, CMNI Art. 16.

[25] Pursuant to Art. 1 (3) of the Convention, "actual carrier" means any person, other than a servant or an agent of the carrier, to whom the performance of the carriage or a part of such carriage has been entrusted by the carrier.

[26] For more information see *Koller*, CMNI Art. 4.

[27] For more information see *Koller*, CMNI Art. 18; *Korioth*, pp. 295-296.

[28] *Koller*, CMNI Art. 16 Rn. 2; *Czerwenka, CMNI*, 281; *Korioth*, p. 295.

payable by him is calculated according to Art. 19. Nevertheless, the amount payable may not exceed the limitation amounts specified in Art. 20[29].

IV. Multimodal Transport

An important unification work on the rules applicable to the multimodal transport of goods is the United Nations Convention on International Multimodal Transport of Goods signed in 1980 ("Multimodal Transport Convention"). The Convention is the result of the work conducted by the United Nations Conference on Trade and Development ("UNCTAD"). UNCTAD, which takes into account the fact that liner shipping is generally done via a combination of several means of transport and also takes into account the concerns of developing countries, initiated the work on a new convention[30]. The work was done simultaneously with the Hamburg Rules and, consequently, the principles adopted under the Multimodal Transport Convention are similar to those of the Hamburg Rules[31]. Unfortunately, unlike the Hamburg Rules, the Multimodal Transport Convention is not in force due to the requirement of a high number of contracting states[32].

According to the Convention, international multimodal transport covers any international carriage by at least two different modes of transport on the basis of a multimodal transport contract (Art. 1 (1)). Multimodal transport is organised by a multimodal transport operator ("MTO") who is not an agent of either the carriers participating in the multimodal transport or the consignor (Art. 1 (2)). Once the goods are taken over by the MTO, they are in his possession until the delivery to the consignee. The MTO is liable for any loss or damage when the goods are in his possession and for any delay in delivery (Art. 14 and 16). In order to be relieved of liability, the MTO has to prove that he and his servants and agents took all reasonable measures. Therefore, the liability of the MTO is based on presumed fault[33]. When the MTO is liable under the Convention's regime, his liability is

---

[29] For an overview see *Müller, Inland Navigation*, p. 42.

[30] *Carriage of Goods*, para. 6.5.1.1.2 *et seq.* For the historical background see Christoph *Birnbaum*, Vereinheitlichungsbestrebungen auf dem Gebiet des Rechts des kombinierten Verkehrs, Osnabrück 1985 (Diss. Osnabrück); *de Wit*, pp. 147-164; *Arkan, İnceleme*, pp. 27-29; *Driscoll/Larsen*, 195-198; *Herber, VN-Übereinkommen*, 38-41; *Richter-Hannes, Multimodale Güterbeförderung*, pp. 23-34; *Müller-Feldhammer*, pp. 59-95.

[31] *de Wit*, pp. 164-165; *Carriage of Goods*, para. 6.5.1.1.3; *Arkan, İnceleme*, p. 30.

[32] See <http://r0.unctad.org/ttl/docs-legal/unc-cml/status/UNConventionMTofGoods, 1980.pdf> (09.08.2010).

[33] *Carriage of Goods*, para. 6.5.1.4.2; *Gençtürk*, pp. 122-123; *Arkan, İnceleme*, p. 41; *Driscoll/Larsen*, 232; *Herber, VN-Übereinkommen*, 42; *Richter-Hannes, Multimodale Güterbeförderung*, p. 134; *Müller-Feldhammer*, pp. 201-202. This has been also clarified in the preamble of the Convention: "That the liability of the multimodal transport operator under this Convention should be based on the principle of presumed fault or neglect". For information on the drafting work of the provisions regarding the liability of the multimodal transport operator see *Arkan, İnceleme*, pp. 39-40.

limited as specified under Art. 18 and 19, and pursuant to two additional alternatives depending on whether carriage by sea was involved[34].

B. Loss of the Right to Limit

I. Carrier

1. Wilful misconduct or equivalent fault

The second convention after the Warsaw Convention which refers to wilful misconduct or equivalent fault is the CMR. Art. 29 of the Convention states that the carrier will not be entitled to limit his liability if the damage was caused by his wilful misconduct or by such fault on his part as, in accordance with the law of the court seized of the case, is considered as equivalent to wilful misconduct. The same provision is to be applied if the wilful misconduct or fault is committed by the agents or servants of the carrier or by any other persons whose services the carrier uses of for the performance of the carriage. Also, Art. 32 (1), which sets the time limits for the claims under the Convention stipulates that the one-year time limitation will be extended to three years in case of wilful misconduct or such fault, as in accordance with the law of the court or tribunal seized of the case, is considered as equivalent to wilful misconduct.

a) Scope of application

aa) General

It is clear that the wording of both articles was taken directly from the unamended version of the Warsaw Convention[35]. When the CMR was opened for signature in 1956, Art. 25 of the Warsaw Convention had however already been amended by the Hague Protocol of 1955, since the aim of unification was not achieved by the unamended version[36]. Therefore, the CMR was criticised for adopting the same principle which had already caused many problems from a unification point of view[37]. It was said that the aim of the drafters of the CMR was to leave space for

---

[34]   For more information see *Carriage of Goods*, para. 6.5.1.4.3 *et seqq.*; *Arkan, İnce-leme*, pp. 42-44; *Driscoll/Larsen*, 235-238; *Herber, VN-Übereinkommen*, 42-43; *Richter-Hannes, Multimodale Güterbeförderung*, pp. 147-152, 162-169.

[35]   MünchKommHGB 1997 – *Basedow*, CMR Art. 29 Rn. 1; MünchKommHGB 2009 – *Jesser-Huß*, CMR Art. 29 Rn. 1; *Thume*, in: *Fremuth/Thume*, Art. 29 CMR Rn. 2; *Harms*, in: *Thume, CMR-Kommentar*, Art. 29 Rn. 8; *Clarke, CMR*, p. 315; *Herber/Piper*, Art. 29 Rn. 5; *Loewe*, 383; *Akıncı*, p. 154; *Brinkmann, Vergleich*, 149; *Clarke, Transport in Europe*, 58; *Glöckner, TranspR*, 332; *Herber, Anmerkung*, 175-176; *Jesser*, 170; *Pöttinger*, 518; *Thume, CMR-Frachtführer*, 931; *Tuma, ETL*, 658; *Stachow*, pp. 99, 242; *Ruhwedel, Durchbrechung im Luftrecht*, 139.

[36]   For more information see *supra* § 4 B I 1.

[37]   *Marsilius*, 301, 305; MünchKommHGB 1997 – *Basedow*, CMR Art. 29 Rn. 6; MünchKommHGB 2009 – *Jesser-Huß*, CMR Art. 29 Rn. 6; *Harms*, in: *Thume*,

the imprecise interpretation in terms of unlimited liability; therefore, without attempting to define the degree of fault, they adopted the 1929 version of the Warsaw Convention[38]. Consequently, it would not be wrong to say that the drafters of the CMR intentionally referred to substantive law[39] by the phrase "by such fault on his part as, in accordance with the law of the court seized of the case, is considered as equivalent to wilful misconduct" whereas the drafters of the Warsaw Convention, in contrast, reformulated the same phrase to overcome the terminology problem[40]. Indeed, during the drafting work of the Convention it was suggested that the phrase should be replaced by the term "gross negligence", as was the case in the 1952 version of the CIM Art. 37[41]. However, the suggestion was objected to on the grounds that the common law system is not familiar with the term and that not all national systems make a distinction between different degrees of negligence. Therefore, the suggestion was rejected[42]. This explanation also shows that the drafters anticipated that the liability limits would be broken in cases of gross negligence as well[43].

Since the unamended version of Art. 25 Warsaw Convention has been the model for the CMR Art. 29, the inconsistency and problems encountered under the unamended Warsaw Convention have also been encountered under the CMR. Most of the civil law courts consider gross negligence as fault equivalent to wilful misconduct, whereas there is no such an equivalent degree of fault under common law[44]. This leads to the result that a carrier may be entitled to limit his liability before one court, yet he cannot limit his liability under the same conditions before another court since gross negligence is considered as the degree of fault equivalent

---

CMR-Kommentar, Art. 29 Rn. 8-9; Clarke, CMR, p. 315; Modjaz, pp. 32-33; Gençtürk, pp. 235-236; Hill & Messent, pp. 223-224; Clarke, Transport in Europe, 58; Jesser, 170; Stachow, p. 101. During the drafting work of the Convention, it was suggested by the UK delegation that the definition employed by the Hague Protocol should be employed also under the CMR. The official records of the drafting work are not published; therefore see Tuma, ETL, 656.

[38] Clarke, CMR, p. 315.

[39] Herber, Anmerkung, 175; Mankowski, Transportverträge, Rn. 2723; Jesser, 170, 172-173, 175; Pöttinger, 519; Stachow, pp. 100, 242.

[40] See supra § 4 A I 4.

[41] Thume, CMR-Frachtführer, 931; Zapp, 145.

[42] Loewe, 383; Modjaz, pp. 32-33; Hill & Messent, p. 223; Pöttinger, 519; Thume, CMR-Frachtführer, 931; Tuma, ETL, 657; Stachow, p. 242; Fremuth, Schwere Schuld, p. 161..

[43] It was, nevertheless, said that the intention of phrasing "by such fault on his part as, in accordance with the law of the court seized of the case, is considered as equivalent to wilful misconduct" was not "giving equal status to different degrees of culpability", but was overcoming the problem caused by different legal terms for the same degree of culpability, see Tuma, ETL, 669-680; Tuma, TranspR, 335-337; Otmar J. Tuma, Variations on the Theme: 'Wilful Misconduct' and 'grobe Fahrlässigkeit', in: K. F. Haak/E. C. Swart (Editors), Road Carrier's Liability in Europe, The Hague 1995, p. 17.

[44] Carriage of Goods, para. 3.1.2.29.3.

to wilful misconduct[45]. This situation results, without any doubt, in forum shopping. The fact that the English and French versions of the CMR are equally authentic[46] also supports such a result.

Nevertheless, under both civil and common law interpretations, the carrier will be liable without limitation if damage is caused by his intentional misconduct. Since it has been accepted by many scholars that the term intentional misconduct covers both *dolus directus* and *dolus eventualis*, the inconsistency appears only in the degree of fault which is considered as the equivalent of wilful misconduct[47].

Under CMR Art. 29 (2), it is explicitly stated that the carrier will not be entitled to limit his liability when his servants or agents are guilty of wilful misconduct or of the equivalent degree of fault. Thus, there is no room for the discussion whether the term carrier refers only to the carrier himself and whether wilful misconduct of his servants or agents is sufficient to break his liability limits. Nevertheless, in order to deprive the carrier of the liability limits, the servant or agent must have acted or made an omission within the scope of his employment[48]. In this respect, especially criminal activities by servants or agents, such as theft and smuggling, are to be considered as intentional misconduct within the scope of their employment[49].

---

[45] *Harms*, in: *Thume, CMR-Kommentar*, Art. 29 Rn. 10.

[46] CMR Art. 51 (3). Vienna Convention Art. 33: "(1) When a treaty has been authenticated in two or more languages, the text is equally authoritative in each language, unless the treaty provides or the parties agree that, in case of divergence, a particular text shall prevail. (2) A version of the treaty in a language other than one of those in which the text was authenticated shall be considered an authentic text only if the treaty so provides or the parties so agree. (3) The terms of the treaty are presumed to have the same meaning in each authentic text. (4) Except where a particular text prevails in accordance with paragraph 1, when a comparison of the authentic texts discloses a difference of meaning which the application of articles 31 and 32 does not remove, the meaning which best reconciles the texts, having regard to the object and purpose of the treaty, shall be adopted.", discussion of the issue of the equivalent degree of fault to wilful misconduct in the light of the Vienna Convention Art. 33 see *Jesser*, 173-174.

[47] *Thume*, in: *Fremuth/Thume*, Art. 29 CMR Rn. 3; *Harms*, in: *Thume, CMR-Kommentar*, Art. 29 Rn. 6; *Koller*, CMR Art. 29 Rn. 2; *Herber/Piper*, Art. 29 Rn. 2; MünchKommHGB 2009 – *Herber*, § 435 Rn. 8-9; *Thume, Vergleich*, 2; *Aydın*, p. 141; *Thume, CMR-Frachtführer*, 931; *Stachow*, p. 243; Ebenroth/Boujong/Joost/Strohn/*Schaffert*, § 435 Rn. 4. See also *supra* § 4 B I 2 c aa. However see *infra* § 8 B II.

[48] For the term see *supra* § 4 D II 1.

[49] *Harms*, in: *Thume, CMR-Kommentar*, Art. 29 Rn. 34; MünchKommHGB 2009 – *Jesser-Huß*, CMR Art. 3 Rn. 25. For other examples see MünchKommHGB 1997 – *Basedow*, CMR Art. 29 Rn. 25-26; *Clarke, Road Transport*, 429; *Thume, CMR-Frachtführer*, 933; OLG Hamburg, 14.05.1996, TranspR 1997, 100; BGH, 27.06.1985, TranspR 1985, 338; *Datec Electronic Holdings Ltd. v. United Parcels Service Ltd.* [2006] 1 Lloyd's Rep. 279 (CA) approved by *Datec Electronics Holdings Ltd v. United Parcels Service Ltd* [2007] 2 Lloyd's Rep. 114 (HL); for the counterview see *Glöckner*, TranspR, 327.

CMR Art. 29 holds the carrier liable without any financial limits if "the damage" is caused by his or his servants' or agents' wilful misconduct or equivalent fault. Firstly, foresight of the specific damage occurred is not necessary for the carrier to be deprived of the right to limit; it is sufficient if the carrier or his servants or agents have foreseen that damage to cargo will occur[50]. Nonetheless, "damage to cargo" is a restricted term compared to the "damage, loss or delay in delivery", since the carrier is liable for all these situations under the CMR. It has been argued whether the term "damage" as used in Art. 29 also covers loss and delay in delivery. It was asserted that the problem must be solved in the light of the *lex fori*[51] or the applicable law[52]. However, it is clear that the term damage under Art. 29 was used in broad sense and covers damage and loss, as well as delay in delivery[53].

bb) Time limitation

Another point to be emphasised is related to wilful misconduct and its effect on time limitation. Art. 32 (1) of the CMR stipulates that the one year time limitation should be extended to three years in case of wilful misconduct or equivalent fault. Here, two different interpretations can be considered: (1) the carrier's wilful misconduct relates, not to the carriage operation, but to the subsequent claims regulation; (2) the carrier's wilful misconduct only refers to the carriage. The question is whether the one year time limitation should be extended to three years in both cases.

It is said that in order to extend the time limitation, the carrier must have intentionally slowed down the commencement of the proceedings. For instance, if a carrier uses a company name on the consignment note which is very similar to the name of another company with the same registered address, this makes it difficult to lodge a claim within a one year time period. In this example, there is intentional deception and, therefore, the time limitation will be three years independent of whether the carrier was also guilty of wilful misconduct with regard to the carriage[54].

Undoubtedly, if the carrier deceives the cargo interest in order to slow down the commencement of a claim against him, there is wilful misconduct in terms of the time limitation; and, naturally, the time limitation will be extended to three years. However, extension of the time limitation should not be limited to cases where the carrier is guilty of wilful misconduct in delaying claims regulation. If the damage

---

[50] *Herber/Piper*, Art. 29 Rn. 14; BGH, 27.06.1985, TranspR 1985, 338 (340).

[51] *Thume*, in: *Fremuth/Thume*, Art. 29 CMR Rn. 24; MünchKommHGB 1997 – *Basedow*, CMR Einleitung Rn. 19; *Thume, CMR-Frachtführer*, 937; OLG Innsbruck, 26.01.1990, TranspR 1991, 12 (22).

[52] *Harms*, in: *Thume, CMR-Kommentar*, Art. 29 Rn. 82.

[53] *Koller*, CMR Art. 29 Rn. 5; *Clarke, CMR*, p. 319; *Helm*, in: Großkomm. HGB Anh. VI nach § 452: CMR Art. 29 Rn. 1, 4 Fn. 20; *Erdil*, p. 364; *Aydın*, pp. 141-142, 146.

[54] *Clarke, CMR*, p. 128; *Helm*, in: Großkomm. HGB Anh. VI nach § 452: CMR Art. 29 Rn. 4.

was caused by the carrier's wilful misconduct, the time limitation should also be extended to three years[55].

As a result, if the carrier intended to slow down the proceedings, the time limitation will be extended but since there is no wilful misconduct regarding the damage caused, the carrier will continue to be liable only within the liability limits specified under the CMR[56]. However, if there is wilful misconduct on the side of the carrier in terms of the damage which has occurred, both the time limitation will be extended and the liability limits will be broken.

The final point to clarify is the lack of any clear provision as to the wilful misconduct of the servants and agents of the carrier under Art. 32. Clear reference regarding the issue can be found in Art. 29. Thus, the question is whether acts and omissions of servants or agents are also relevant for the purposes of Art. 32. Considering the approach adopted by the CMR for breaking the liability limits, the question must be answered in the affirmative[57].

b) Approach by civil law

aa) Interpretation

As mentioned previously[58], the drafters of the CMR intentionally made a reference to the national law of the contracting parties so that every court can determine which degree of fault should be considered as equivalent to wilful misconduct. Courts have consequently considered the equivalent degree of fault according to their national law. Mainly, two different interpretations under civil law countries have appeared as a result of the reference to national law: (i) the interpretation which equates gross negligence to wilful misconduct, and (ii) the interpretation which refuses to accept gross negligence as an equivalent to wilful misconduct.

In Germany, the phrase "such fault on his part as, in accordance with the law of the court seized of the case, is considered as equivalent to wilful misconduct" is considered as a reference to the substantive law of *lex fori*. Therefore, it is accepted that the provisions of the HGB relating to the carriage by road should be applied in determining the equivalent degree of fault to wilful misconduct. The relevant provision of the HGB which regulates the unlimited liability of the road carrier due to his fault was amended in 1998[59]. Therefore, the degree of fault equivalent to wilful misconduct has been considered in different ways before and after 1998.

---

[55] MünchKommHGB 1997 – *Basedow*, CMR Art. 32 Rn. 11; *Thume, CMR-Frachtführer*, 936; OGH, 20.01.2004, ETL 2005, 122 (128); 11. HD, 21.10.2002, E. 2002/4923, K. 2002/9359 (YKD 2003/3, pp. 385-387).

[56] MünchKommHGB 1997 – *Basedow*, CMR Art. 32 Rn. 11.

[57] *Hill & Messent*, p. 256 fn. 136; MünchKommHGB 1997 – *Basedow*, CMR Art. 32 Rn. 11; MünchKommHGB 2009 – *Jesser-Huß*, CMR Art. 32 Rn. 11.

[58] See *supra* B I 1 a aa.

[59] For general information see Karl-Heinz *Thume*, Das neue Transportrecht, Betriebs-Berater 53 (1998), 2117.

The first decisions made by the German courts tend to interpret the provision primarily in favour of carriers since they stated that only *dolus eventualis* is the degree of fault equivalent to wilful misconduct[60]. The reasoning for such an interpretation was that the courts took the French version of the CMR into consideration and stated that "*dol*" means direct intention (*dolus directus*) and that only *dolus eventualis* can be considered as equivalent to *dolus directus*[61]. However, upon an appeal against such a decision taken by a lower court[62], the German Federal Court decided that, as under the unamended version of Warsaw Convention Art. 25, gross negligence should be considered the equivalent of wilful misconduct[63]. Afterwards, it has always been ruled that gross negligence is the equivalent of wilful misconduct under the CMR[64], although that interpretation has been strongly criticised by some writers[65].

In 1998, the provisions regarding carriage by road in the HGB were amended. Ever since then, in order to lose his right to limit, the carrier must be guilty of intentional misconduct or reckless conduct coupled with subjective knowledge as to the probable consequences (§ 435 HGB). Today, it is unanimously accepted that, according to the new German law, gross negligence can no longer be considered as the equivalent of wilful misconduct. Only reckless conduct with knowledge that damage will probably result is to be considered the degree of fault

---

[60]   LG Hamburg, 02.10.1972, VersR 1973, 28; OLG Hamburg, 19.02.1973, VersR 1974, 28; LG Frankfurt, 12.03.1981, TranspR 1982, 79; LG Frankfurt, 30.08.1982, TranspR 1983, 81; later also OLG Nürnberg 22.03.1995, TranspR 1996, 381 and BGH, 17.04.1997, TranspR 1998, 25.

[61]   *Glöckner*, Art. 29 CMR Rn. 2; *Glöckner, TranspR*, 332. During the drafting work, the French delegation, upon a question by the German delegation, had explained that the term "*dol*" under French law equates to the *dolus directus* under German law, and that the equivalent degree of fault to *dol* would be the degree of fault known as the *dolus eventualis* under German law, see *Thume, CMR-Frachtführer*, 931; *Tuma, ETL*, 656; *Zapp*, 145. For a discussion see *Stachow*, pp. 243-250.

[62]   OLG Bamberg, 27.04.1981, TranspR 1984, 184.

[63]   BGH, 14.07.1983, TranspR 1984, 68 = VersR 1984, 134; for discussion of the desicion see Klaus *Heuer*, Anmerkung zur Entscheidung des BGH vom 14.07.1983, TranspR 1984, 71; J. G. *Helm*, Welches Verschulden steht gem. Art. 29 CMR dem Vorsatz gleich?, IPRax 1985, 10.

[64]   OLG Frankfurt, 21.09.1983, TranspR 1984, 73; BGH, 16.02.1984, TranspR 1984, 182; BGH, 28.05.1998, TranspR 1998, 454; BGH, 16.07.1998, TranspR 1999, 19. For more information see MünchKommHGB 1997 – *Basedow*, CMR Art. 29 Rn. 9; *Harms*, in: *Thume, CMR-Kommentar*, Art. 29 Rn. 13-17; *Thume*, in: *Fremuth/ Thume*, Art. 29 CMR Rn. 4a; *Koller*, CMR Art. 29 Rn. 3; *Herber/Piper*, Art. 29 Rn. 4; *Tuma, ETL*, 665-666.

[65]   *Tuma, TranspR*, 338; *Zapp*, 145-146; *Marsilius*, 295-296 ("Fahrlässigkeit ist Nicht-Vorsatz"); Horst *Oeynhausen*, Art. 29 CMR: Grobe Fahrlässigkeit – dem Vorsatz gleichstehendes Verschulden?, TranspR 1984, 57. It is also said that only conscious gross negligence can be equal to wilful misconduct, see Klaus *Heuer*, Durchbrechung der Haftungsgrenzen (Art. 29 CMR), in: Aktuelle Fragen des deutschen und internationalen Landtransportrechts: Symposium der Deutschen Gesellschaft für Transportrecht (Nürnberg 1994), Luchterhand 1995, pp. 66-69.

equivalent to wilful misconduct[66], with the result that the unlimited liability of a road carrier becomes an exception[67].

The situation in other civil law countries as to what degree of fault should be considered as the equivalent of wilful misconduct is generally similar to that under German law prior to 1998. For the application of Art. 29 of the CMR, it is generally accepted in civil law countries, especially in France, that gross negligence is equal to wilful misconduct[68]. However, in Belgium, Portugal, Greece and Holland, it has not been accepted that gross negligence is equal to wilful misconduct[69].

The situation under Turkish law is parallel to that of German law. The Turkish Supreme Court also considers the degree of fault which was equivalent to wilful misconduct as "gross negligence". The reason for this interpretation was that Art. 29 refers to national law in respect of determining the equivalence of wilful misconduct, and according to TTK (1956) Art. 786, the road carrier loses his right to

---

[66]   *Thume*, in: *Fremuth/Thume*, Art. 29 CMR Rn. 19a; *Harms*, in: *Thume, CMR-Kommentar*, Art. 29 Rn. 13-14; *Helm*, in: Großkomm. HGB Anh. VI nach § 452: CMR Art. 29 Rn. 8-10; *Fremuth, Haftungsbegrenzungen*, 100; *Herber, Überblick*, 97; *Thume, Vergleich*, 2; *Starck*, pp. 133-134; Ebenroth/Boujong/Joost/Strohn/ *Bahnsen*, CMR Art. 29 Rn. 11; *Fremuth, Schwere Schuld*, pp. 162-165; OLG München, 27.07.2001, TranspR 2002, 161; OLG Düsseldorf, 14.11.2001, TranspR 2002, 73; BGH, 20.01.2005, TranspR 2005, 311; BGH, 21.03.2007, TranspR 2007, 361. Such an interpretation was suggested long before the amendment of the German national law, see *Herber, Anmerkung*, 177.

[67]   *Thume, Vergleich*, 7.

[68]   MünchKommHGB 2009 – *Jesser-Huß*, CMR Art. 29 Rn.10; *Helm*, in: Großkomm. HGB Anh. VI nach § 452: CMR Art. 29 Rn. 17; *Thume*, in: *Fremuth/Thume*, Art. 29 CMR Rn. 4a; *Koller*, CMR Art. 29 Rn. 4c-4f, 4h-4i; *Modjaz*, pp. 112-115; *Hill & Messent*, pp. 224-227; *Herber/Piper*, Art. 29 Rn. 6, 7; *Fremuth, Haftungsbegrenzungen*, 102; *Thume, CMR-Frachtführer*, 932; *Tuma, ETL*, 666-667; *Tuma, TranspR*, 338-339, 341-342; Helga *Jesser-Huß*, Haftungsbegrenzungen und deren Durchbrechung im allgemeinen Frachtrecht und nach der CMR in Österreich, TranspR 2004, 111; Helga *Jesser-Huß*, Aktuelle transportrechtliche Probleme in Österreich, TranspR 2009, 109; Johan *Schelin*, Haftungsbegrenzung und ihre Durchbrechung nach der CMR in den skandinavischen Staaten und Finnland, TranspR 2004, 107; Paul *Lutz*, Die Rechtsprechung der französischen Cour de Cassation zum Begriff des groben Verschuldens des Frachtführers nach Artikel 29 CMR, TranspR 1989, 139.

[69]   MünchKommHGB 1997 – *Basedow*, CMR Art. 29 Rn. 12; MünchKommHGB 2009 – *Jesser-Huß*, CMR Art. 29 Rn. 11-12; *Clarke, CMR*, pp. 323-324; *Helm*, in: Großkomm. HGB Anh. VI nach § 452: CMR Art. 29 Rn. 17; *Hill & Messent*, pp. 227, 232; *Herber/Piper*, Art. 29 Rn. 9; *Fremuth, Haftungsbegrenzungen*, 102; *Thume, CMR-Frachtführer*, 932-933; *Tuma, TranspR*, 339-343. For more information about Dutch case law see Jan P. *Eckoldt*, Die niederländische CMR-Rechtsprechung, TranspR 2009, 117; Krijn *Haak*, Haftungsbegrenzung und ihre Durchbrechung nach der CMR in den Niederlanden, TranspR 2004, 104; F.G.M. *Smeele*, Dutch Case Law on Art. 29 CMR, ETL 2000, 329; for the situation under Greek law Virginia *Murray*, Wilful Misconduct under the CMR: Hellenic Supreme Court (Areios Pagos) Case No. 18/1998, [1999] J.B.L. 180; for the summary of another Greek decision see TranspR 1992, 175.

limit in cases of intentional misconduct and gross negligence. Therefore, under Turkish law, the fault equivalent to wilful misconduct is gross negligence[70]. However, by virtue of TTK (2011) Art. 886, the principle which has been accepted globally has become one of the provisions of Turkish national law. The road carrier, under Turkish law, loses his right to limit only if he is guilty of intentional or reckless conduct coupled with knowledge of the probable consequences. Therefore, it can be said that gross negligence will no longer be accepted as the degree of fault equivalent to wilful misconduct.

bb) Examples

The most common situation where courts have decided that the carrier is grossly negligent has been theft cases. During carriage by road, it is not uncommon that either the vehicle or the goods in the vehicle are stolen. Courts have stressed that if the carrier and/or the driver did not take the necessary precautions against theft, which should be more stringent than usual in places where the theft ratio is extremely high, this fault amounts to gross negligence[71]. Other than theft by third parties, delivery to an unauthorised person or traffic accidents due to the negligent conduct of the driver have also been a basis for unlimited liability[72].

Nevertheless, one of the most common reasons for unlimited liability has been the inadequate organisational structure[73]. For instance, if the driver does not have enough money to buy the necessary amount of fuel for transportation[74] or if the

---

[70]   11. HD, 04.04.2005, 2004/6554, 2005/3212 (*Erdil*, pp. 368-371); 11. HD, 06.12. 2000, 2000/4546, 2000/5446 (*Erdil*, pp. 378-379; *Gençtürk*, p. 237 fn. 139); see also *Akıncı*, p. 156; *Aydın*, p. 142; *Gençtürk*, pp. 236-237; *Yetiş Şamlı*, pp. 39, 41-42.

[71]   MünchKommHGB 2009 – *Jesser-Huß*, CMR Art. 29 Rn. 17; *Thume*, in: *Fremuth/ Thume*, Art. 29 CMR Rn. 7, 12; *Harms*, in: *Thume, CMR-Kommentar*, Art. 29 Rn. 39-42; *Thume, CMR-Frachtführer*, 934; Ebenroth/Boujong/Joost/Strohn/ *Bahnsen*, CMR Art. 29 Rn. 22; *e.g.* BGH, 17.04.1997, TranspR 1998, 25; BGH, 28.05.1998, TranspR 1998, 454.

[72]   MünchKommHGB 1997 – *Basedow*, CMR Art. 29 Rn. 16-17, 19; *Thume*, in: *Fremuth/Thume*, Art. 29 CMR Rn. 9-19; *Harms*, in: *Thume, CMR-Kommentar*, Art. 29 Rn. 35-70; *Koller*, CMR Art. 29 Rn. 4-4a; *Clarke, CMR*, pp. 326-330; *Helm*, in: Großkomm. HGB Anh. VI nach § 452: CMR Art. 29 Rn. 20; *Erdil*, pp. 364-365; *Herber/Piper*, Art. 29 Rn. 10-13; *Koller, Leichtfertigkeit*, 1347-1349 (discussion from recklessness point of view); *Thume, CMR-Frachtführer*, 934-935; Ebenroth/Boujong/Joost/Strohn/*Schaffert*, § 435 Rn. 8-10.

[73]   For more information see also *Harms*, in: *Thume, CMR-Kommentar*, Art. 29 Rn. 88-94; MünchKommHGB 2009 – *Jesser-Huß*, CMR Art. 29 Rn. 17; *Koller, Leichtfertigkeit*, 1357; Ebenroth/Boujong/Joost/Strohn/*Bahnsen*, CMR Art. 29 Rn. 21; Karl-Heinz *Thume*, Grobes Verschulden und Fortsetzung der Vertragsbeziehungen, TranspR 1999, 85.

[74]   OLG Düsseldorf, 26.07.1984, TranspR 1985, 128. See also Carsten *Harms*, Vereinbarungen zur Qualität der Transportleistung und Art. 29 CMR, in: Vertrieb, Versicherung, Transport: Karl-Heinz Thume zum 70. Geburtstag, Frankfurt a.M. 2008, pp. 173-176.

goods are lost and it is impossible to designate the place of loss due to the lack of checkpoints during the redistribution and transportation of the goods[75], the courts have ruled that these are inadequacies in the organisational structure which can cause unlimited liability in terms of CMR Art. 29. However, in this respect, simply taking some precautions is not enough; they must be practically applicable and applied[76].

c) Approach by common law

It was accepted under the Warsaw Convention that there is no equivalent degree of fault to wilful misconduct under common law. The interpretation by common law writers and courts concerning the CMR is parallel to that of the Warsaw Convention: in terms of breaking the liability limits, there is no equivalent to wilful misconduct. Therefore, the phrase "or such fault as in accordance with the law of the court or tribunal seized of the case, is considered as equivalent to wilful misconduct" has no relevance under common law[77]. Nevertheless, it is stated that, in terms of its effect on the time limitation, the equivalent of wilful misconduct should be considered as fraud as under the UK Limitation Act 1980 § 32[78]. There should be no hesitation in concluding that intentionally deceiving someone is one of the clearest examples of wilful misconduct.

In contrast to the understanding in most of the civil law countries, wilful misconduct has been interpreted subjectively; thus the person must appreciate that he is acting or omitting to act unlawfully, foresee the probable consequences and nonetheless insist on so doing[79]. In this context, the carrier has been held guilty of wilful misconduct if the driver substantially exceeded the permissible driving time and fell asleep with the consequence that the vehicle went off the road causing substantial damage to the cargo. The court stated that the driver was well aware that he was exceeding the allowed driving period. The driver obviously knew that he was posing a great risk to safety to load or other road users by ignoring relevant regulations – the purpose of which (guard against fatigue) was known also to the driver. Therefore, persistence in acting wrongfully and being wholly indifferent to

---

[75] OLG Düsseldorf, 04.07.2001, TranspR 2002, 158; BGH, 04.03.2004, TranspR 2004, 460; BGH, 06.05.2004, TranspR 2004, 474; BGH, 11.11.2004, TranspR 2006, 161; BGH, 19.01.2006, ETL 2006, 668.

[76] OLG Düsseldorf, 04.07.2001, TranspR 2002, 158 (159).

[77] *Clarke, CMR*, p. 322; *Clarke/Yates*, para. 1.165; *Hill & Messent*, p. 233; MünchKommHGB 1997 – *Basedow*, CMR Art. 29 Rn. 11; MünchKommHGB 2009 – *Jesser-Huß*, CMR Art. 29 Rn. 11; *Helm*, in: Großkomm. HGB Anh. VI nach § 452: CMR Art. 29 Rn. 6; *Clarke, CIM*, p. 39; *Herber/Piper*, Art. 29 Rn. 7; *Fremuth, Haftungsbegrenzungen*, 102; *Aydın*, p. 142; *Herber, Anmerkung*, 176; *Jesser*, 174; *Clarke, Transport in Europe*, 59: "In English law, there is no such thing and these words are a collection of dead letters".

[78] *Clarke, CMR*, p. 128. § 32 of the Act provides the postponement of limitation period in case of fraud, concealment and mistake.

[79] *Clarke, Transport in Europe*, 58-59. See also Jan *Becher*, Die Anwendung der CMR in der englischen Rechtspraxis, TranspR 2007, 232.

the consequences constitutes wilful misconduct[80]. Nevertheless, if the driver did not exceed the driving hours, *i.e.* did not drive contrary to the regulations as to time and rest periods, there is no misconduct[81] and accordingly no room for a finding of wilful misconduct.

The carrier is also guilty of wilful misconduct if he instructs the driver to leave the transport vehicle unattended in a dangerous place, though the driver warned him about the probability of theft. In one case, the driver was instructed by the controlling director of the carriage company to leave the transport vehicle in a public car park. The driver warned him that it was unsafe to do so, since there were expensive electronic devices in the vehicle. The controlling director, after repeating his instruction, told the driver that someone else would be collecting the vehicle later, although the carriage company had the policy not to leave the transport vehicles unattended due to the high risk of theft,. Furthermore, at the time the driver was instructed to leave the vehicle, it was possible to take it to a secure place. The court, therefore, concluded that the controlling director was reckless, and he was well aware of the high risk. The carrier, in conclusion, has been found guilty of wilful misconduct[82].

In another case, on the other hand, the carrier was held liable due to the wilful misconduct of the driver. The driver was expressly instructed to deliver the goods only to the consignee's premises in London. The driver, who could not speak English, went to the street where the premises were, was met by two men, and told that the vehicle was too big to fit to the delivery door. He was subsequently instructed by gesture to drive somewhere else and transfer the goods to another vehicle which supposed to fit to the delivery door. In following these instructions, he let the two men transfer the goods to an unmarked vehicle, and delivered them the transport documents. He, thereafter, called his boss, and was told that the consignee was still waiting for the delivery. The court ruled that ignoring the clear instruction to deliver the goods to the consignee's premises, and the lack of any effort to identify two strangers constituted misconduct. Further, in allowing strangers to unload the goods into an unmarked vehicle, the experienced driver was well aware of the risk of theft. As a result, the carrier was guilty of wilful misconduct, and therefore could not limit his liability[83].

Wilful misconduct was rejected in a case where the claimants asserted that the plaintiff failed to properly inspect his vehicles, and that this persistent lack of inspection and maintenance caused the failure of the breaking system and subsequently a substantial traffic accident which resulted in the total loss of their cargo. The court rejected the claim, since the carrier provided a roadworthy vehicle, which was in a proper state for the work it was required to do[84].

---

[80] *Sidney G. Jones Ltd. v. Martin Bencher Ltd.* [1986] 1 Lloyd's Rep. 54 (QBD).
[81] *Denfleet International Ltd. v. TNT Global SPA* [2007] 2 Lloyd's Rep. 504 (CA).
[82] *Texas Instruments Ltd. v. Nason (Europe) Ltd.* [1991] 1 Lloyd's Rep. 146 (QBD).
[83] *Lacey's Footwear (Wholesale) Ltd. v. Bowler Int. Freight Ltd.* [1997] 2 Lloyd's Rep. 369 (CA).
[84] *Alena Limited v. Harlequin Transport Services* [2002] EWHC 2461 (QBD).

2. Wilful misconduct or gross negligence

In the carriage of passengers and their luggage by road, the carrier is deprived of the right to limit in both wilful misconduct and gross negligence cases. Pursuant to the first sentence of Art. 18 (2) of the CVR, if the loss or damage resulted from the wilful misconduct or gross negligence of the carrier or a person for whom he is responsible under the Convention, the carrier loses the right to limit his liability. The provision clearly states that the wilful misconduct or gross negligence of his servants, agents or independent contractors[85] will deprive the carrier of the liability limits. Consequently, there is no room for any debate.

Unlike the CMR, the CVR clearly stipulates that the carrier will be deprived of the liability limits when the damage or loss is caused by wilful misconduct or gross negligence. Therefore, it is sufficient for the claimant to show that the damage or loss would not have been caused if the carrier (or his servants or agents) had shown the necessary care, and that the carrier (or his servants or agents) violated the duty of care in a grave manner. The claimant is under no obligation to show that the negligent person has foreseen the probability of the loss or damage incurred.

Finally, the terms "loss or damage" should be understood in the context, as they are used in the provisions of the Convention which set the basis of carrier's liability. Consequently, loss or damage refers to either loss or damage resulting from the death or from any other physical or mental injury of the passenger (Art. 11) or loss or damage resulting from the total or partial loss of luggage and from damage to luggage (Art. 14).

3. Definition of wilful misconduct

a) COTIF 1999

Both CIV 1999 and CIM 1999 contain provisions as to the breaking of the carrier's liability limits. According to CIV 1999 Art. 48 and CIM 1999 Art. 36, the limits of liability are not applicable if it is proved that the loss or damage resulted from an act or omission, which the carrier has committed either with intent to cause such loss or damage, or recklessly and with knowledge that such loss or damage would probably result.

At a first glance, there is a substantial difference between the 1980 and 1999 texts. In their unamended version, CIV 1980 Art. 42 and CIM 1980 Art. 44 deprive the railway of the right to limit if the damage, loss or delay was caused by its wilful misconduct. However, if the loss, damage or delay is caused only by its gross negligence, instead of being broken, the amounts of the limits were to be doubled. These provisions have been amended in 1990 and new degrees of fault were adopted in conformity with the Hague Protocol of 1955. According to the amended provisions, limits of liability were not applicable if it is proved that the loss or damage resulted from an act or omission, on the part of the railway, done

---

[85]   CVR Art. 4.

with intent to cause such loss or damage, or recklessly and with knowledge that such loss or damage will probably result.

Before addressing the difference between the 1980 and 1999 texts, it must be stressed that, unlike the unamended Warsaw Convention and the CMR, CIV 1980 and CIM 1980 make a clear distinction between wilful misconduct and gross negligence. Since the provisions only provided for breaking the limits in case of wilful misconduct, there was no discussion as to the equivalent degree of fault. Therefore, the railway lost its right to limit only in case of wilful misconduct (*dol, Vorsatz*), but not in case of gross negligence. As also clearly stated in the provisions, in case of gross negligence (*faute lourde, grobe Fahrlässigkeit*), the amount of the compensation payable was doubled. Although decisions have varied from country to country, it has been decided that in cases of loss of the transport document, delivery to an unauthorized person or bad condition of the wagons, the railway is grossly negligent[86].

Nevertheless, both the original and amended versions of the 1980 text refer to the wilful misconduct "on the part of the railway". Thus, it was accepted that the term "on the part of the railway" refers also to the wilful misconduct of the servants, agents and independent contractors of the carrier and, therefore, that the railway also loses the right to limit when its servants, agents and independent contractors are guilty of wilful misconduct. However, CIV and CIM 1999 clearly refer to the fault of the "carrier". At a first reading, the lack of a clear or implicit reference to the fault of the servants, agents or independent contractors, and the reference to the acts or omission "which the carrier has committed" give the impression that, under the CIV and CIM 1999 regime, the act and omissions of the servants, agents and independent contractors of the carrier cannot deprive the carrier of the limits of liability. However, the change of the term "railway" to the "carrier" has another background. In the last 20 years, the trend has been towards the liberalization of the railway market in Europe. As a result, private companies started to be engaged in the carriage by rail. Existing railways and other infrastructure have been shared by different carriers. This development rendered the term "railway" in the 1980 text inconsistent with the existing factual and legal situation, and therefore the term has been changed throughout the whole text of CIV and CIM to the "carrier"[87]. The managers of the railway infrastructure are, nevertheless, to be considered as persons for whom the carrier is liable (CIM 1999 Art. 40, CIV 1999 Art. 51).

Furthermore, when the explanatory reports with regard to the 1999 reform are examined, it is clear that the drafters did not intend to change the existing legal situation under the 1980 text, which is that the acts or omissions of the servants or agents of the carrier can cause the unlimited liability of the carrier. In the reports with regard to CIV Art. 48 and CIM Art. 36, it was stated that the relevant provi-

---

[86] *Spera*, Art. 44 Rn. 8, 10; *Arkan*, p. 186.

[87] See the explanatory reports published in ZIEV 1999, 261 *et seqq* (in French and German), particularly the notes with regard to the historical background on 355-359. The reports in English are accessible at <www.otif.org/en/publications/conventions/explanatory-report.html> (09.08.2010).

sions have been taken from the corresponding provisions in the 1980 texts[88]. There is no other explanation. If the drafters would have intended to change the existing legal situation by only changing the terminology, they would have stated their intention in the explanatory reports, as they did with regard to other provisions. Therefore, the conclusion must be reached that, in the carriage of passengers and goods by rail, the acts or omission of the servants or agents of the carrier will deprive the carrier of its right to limit[89].

Another point to be clarified as to the term "carrier" is that, pursuant to Art. 3 (a) of the CIV and CIM 1999, "carrier" means the contractual carrier and pursuant to Art. 3 (b) of both of the texts, any carrier who is entrusted with the performance of the whole or a part of the carriage but who is not the contractual carrier is a "substitute carrier". The question is whether the term "carrier" under CIV 1999 Art. 48 and CIM 1999 Art. 36 also covers the substitute carrier.

CIV 1999 Art. 56 (6) and CIM 1999 Art. 45 (6) state that an action for liability may be brought against the substitute carrier to the extent that the provisions of the Rules are applicable to him. By virtue of CIV 1999 Art. 39 (2) and CIM Art. 27 (2), liability provisions are applicable to the substitute carrier. Therefore, for the part of the carriage performed by the substitute carrier, he will be subject to actions brought against him and, in this case, provisions governing liability will be applied. Provisions regarding loss of the right to limit are adopted in the chapter regarding liability under both instruments[90]. They are, therefore, applicable in a case brought against the substitute carrier. As a result, if an action is bought against the substitute carrier, he will lose his right to limit if it is guilty of wilful misconduct.

Moreover, the term "loss or damage" refers to the "loss or damage" as used in the provisions regarding liability, *i.e.* loss or damage resulting from death, physical injury, total or partial loss of or damage to the goods *etc*[91]. Furthermore, the provisions regarding the loss of the right to limit refer to "such" loss or damage, namely the very damage or loss that occurred.

Finally, in case of wilful misconduct as defined in the provisions CIV 1999 Art. 60 (2) and CIM 1999 Art. 48 (1), the time limitation will be extended to two years[92]. Undoubtedly, the time limitation will be extended if there is damage or loss caused by the carrier's wilful misconduct. The question is whether the time limitation should also be extended to two years if the carrier intentionally misleads the claimant regarding the commencement of the proceedings. Under the CMR, it was said that the time limitation should also be extended in cases where the carrier

---

[88] Explanatory reports in ZIEV 1999, 318 (CIV 1999 Art. 48), 401 (CIM 1999 Art. 36).

[89] See also MünchKommHGB 2009 – *Freise*, CIM Art. 36 Rn. 8.

[90] Under CIV 1999 in the Title IV and under CIM 1999 in the Title III.

[91] For detailed examination see *Pohar*, pp. 301-307. See also MünchKommHGB 2009 – *Freise*, CIM Art. 36 Rn. 5.

[92] Pursuant to Art. 55 of CIV 1980 and Art. 58 of CIM 1980, the period of limitation for an action against the railway was one year. However, if the railway was guilty of wilful misconduct, the period of limitation was to be extended to two years.

intentionally slows down the commencement of the proceedings[93]. However, in contrast to the CMR where only the term "wilful misconduct" is used, CIV and CIM use the terms "such loss or damage" in defining wilful misconduct; furthermore, it is stated that "loss or damage" should be understood as used in the liability provisions. However, in the context of time limitation, "such loss or damage" should be interpreted broadly, so that the terms also cover the loss or damage caused by the carrier's wilful misconduct intended to slow down the commencement of the proceedings.

b) CMNI

The definition which comes closest to the ones in the maritime conventions can be found in CMNI. According to Art. 21 (1) of the Convention, the carrier or the actual carrier is not entitled to the defences and limits of liability provided for in the Convention or in the contract of carriage if it is proved that he himself caused the damage by an act or omission, either with the intent to cause such damage, or recklessly and with knowledge that such damage would probably result.

First of all, the provision stipulates that the carrier or the actual carrier is only responsible for his own wilful misconduct *i.e.* the carrier will be entitled to limit if the actual carrier is guilty of wilful misconduct. Furthermore, it is also clear that the provision requires the personal conduct of the carrier or the actual carrier[94], so that the fault of the servants or agents is insufficient to break the carrier's or actual carrier's liability limits[95]. In this respect, the common practice of the carriage by inland waterways is in the advantage of the cargo interests. Although the master being at the same time as one of the shipowners is very exceptional in the carriage by sea, it is common practice in the carriage of inland waterways. Therefore, the cargo interests are in an advantageous position in proving the personal fault which is especially important in nautical fault cases[96].

Secondly, the carrier or actual carrier will lose the right to limit if "such damage", namely the very damage incurred was caused by wilful misconduct. Here, the inconsistency between the terms used in the liability provisions and the wilful misconduct provision should be addressed. Pursuant to Art. 16, the carrier is liable for "loss resulting from loss or damage to the goods". However, Art. 21 uses the term "damage" instead of "loss". The question arises whether Art. 21 is applicable only in the case of damage to goods. The question must be answered in the negative since there is only an inconsistency between the terms used in two provisions and it cannot have been the intention of the drafters of the Convention that the carrier loses his right to limit only in case of damage to goods, but not in case of the loss of the goods. Therefore, CMNI Art. 21 is applicable in case of total or partial loss of the goods, as well as in case of damage to the goods[97].

---

[93] See *supra* B I 1 a bb.
[94] *Koller*, CMNI Art. 21 Rn. 2; *Czerwenka, CMNI*, 282; *Korioth*, p. 300.
[95] *Koller*, CMNI Art. 21 Rn. 3; *Czerwenka, CMNI*, 282; *Hacksteiner*, 147.
[96] *Ramming*, 304.
[97] For a similar problem under the 1976 London Convention see *supra* § 5 C II 2 b bb (2).

c) CLNI

Since the rules and principles of the 1976 London Convention have been adopted for inland navigation by CLNI, the wording of the provision regulating the loss of the right to limit under CLNI is exactly the same as under the 1976 London Convention. CLNI Art. 4, under the title "conduct barring limitation", stipulates that a person liable is not entitled to limit his liability if it is proved that the loss resulted from his personal act or omission, committed with the intent to cause such loss, or recklessly and with knowledge that such loss would probably result.

The provision requires personal conduct of the person liable since the provision stipulates that the person liable will lose his right to limit if the loss resulted from his personal act or omission. The provision further stipulates that the person liable should have the knowledge that "such loss" would probably result. The term "such loss" refers to the very loss or damage incurred and includes all claims set out in Art. 2 of the Convention. As is the situation under the 1976 London Convention, CLNI also refers only to "such loss" but not to "such loss or damage". Nevertheless, the person liable will not be entitled to limit in cases of damage as well as in cases of loss if he is guilty of the conduct defined in the provision[98].

d) Multimodal Transport Convention

According to Art. 21 (1) of the Convention, the MTO is not entitled to the benefit of the limitation of liability if it is proved that the loss, damage or delay in delivery resulted from an act or omission of the MTO done with the intent to cause such loss, damage or delay or recklessly and with knowledge that such loss, damage or delay would probably result.

Since the provision clearly refers only to the MTO, the conduct of his servants and agents will not result in the unlimited liability of MTO[99]. In this respect, it should also be remembered that the Multimodal Convention reflects the system of the Hamburg Rules; under the Hamburg Rules regime, it is only the carrier's own conduct which deprives him of the limits of liability[100].

The provision, further, refers to "such loss, damage or delay in delivery", i.e. the actual loss, damage or delay occurred. The term "such delay in delivery" can pose problems. If the provision is interpreted literally, the MTO will be deprived of the liability limits if he intentionally or recklessly causes delay in delivery, even though he does not intend to cause any loss or damage occasioned by the delay in delivery. Clearly, this is not the case under this provision. The MTO will lose his right to limit only if "such loss or damage caused by delay in delivery" resulted from his intentional or reckless conduct in respect of loss or damage[101].

---

[98] For further explanation see *supra* § 5 C II 2 b bb (2).

[99] *Herber, VN-Übereinkommen,* 42; *de Wit,* p. 429; *Richter-Hannes, Multimodale Güterbeförderung,* pp. 159-160; *Müller-Feldhammer,* p. 224; for the counterview see *Arkan, İnceleme,* p. 45.

[100] See *supra* § 5 A I 2 b bb (1).

[101] For further explanation see *supra* § 5 A I 2 b bb (2).

II. Servant or Agent

1. Definition and vicarious liability

All the conventions mentioned above regulate the vicarious liability of the carrier explicitly under specific provisions. Pursuant to the relevant provisions[102] the carrier is responsible for the acts and omissions of his servants and agents; furthermore, he is also responsible for the acts and omissions of all other persons of whose services he makes use for the performance of the obligations arising out of the contract of carriage. It is clear that the vicarious liability of the carrier extends not only to his servants and agents but also to independent contractors provided that the independent contractor has been made employed for the performance of the contract of carriage[103]. When there are special provisions as to the actual or subsequent carriers, the carrier is also liable for the acts and omissions of the actual carrier and his servants and agents according to those special provisions[104].

However, there is one precondition for the carrier becoming vicariously liable for his servants, agents and independent contractors. The carrier is only liable if they were acting within the "scope of their employment"[105]. The carrier will not be vicariously liable for loss of or damage to goods which has occurred as a result of the acts or omissions of any servant, agent or independent contractor when they were not acting within their scope of employment.

2. Right to limit

The possibility for the servants and agents to be held personally liable under tort law principles for their acts and omissions poses a danger to these individuals' financial situation and to the limited liability system. A claimant can successfully circumvent the limited liability system created by the relevant convention by simply suing the servant or agent in tort. In order to prevent such a result, the conventions adopt specific provisions stating that servants and agents (and also

---

[102] CMR Art. 3; CVR Art. 4; CIV 1999 Art. 51; CIM 1999 Art. 40; CMNI Art. 17 (1); Multimodal Transport Convention Art. 14 (3) and 15. Under CLNI, such a provision is missing since it is not a convention which sets the basis of liability, see Art. 2 (1) of the Convention. A clear provision is also missing under the Montreal Convention since strict liability of the carrier is involved.

[103] For detailed information see MünchKommHGB 1997 – *Basedow*, CMR Art. 3 Rn. 13-20; *Koller*, CMR Art. 3 Rn. 3-4; *Helm*, in: Großkomm. HGB Anh. VI nach § 452: CMR Art. 3 Rn. 9; *Loewe*, 333; *Erdil*, pp. 40, 42; *Akıncı*, pp. 199-201; *Gençtürk*, pp. 189-196; *Özdemir, Eşya Taşıma*, pp. 189-192; *Beier*, pp. 34-35, 95; *Hill & Messent*, pp. 64-66; *Arkan, Sempozyum*, pp. 68-69.

[104] CMR Art. 34-36; CIV 1999 Art. 39; CIM 1999 Art. 27; CMNI Art. 17 (2).

[105] For the term see *supra* § 4 D II 1, and also MünchKommHGB 1997 – *Basedow*, CMR Art. 3 Rn. 21-24; *Schmid*, in: *Thume, CMR-Kommentar*, Art. 3 Rn. 32-38; *Koller*, CMR Art. 3 Rn. 5; *Helm*, in: Großkomm. HGB Anh. VI nach § 452: CMR Art. 3 Rn. 10; *Gençtürk*, pp. 196-198. The "scope of employment" criterion was adopted for the first time under the CIV 1999 and CIM 1999 for the international carriage of passengers and their luggage and of goods by rail.

independent contractors)[106] are also entitled to limit their liability[107]. However, under some conventions, it is provided that servant or agent must prove that he was acting within the scope of his employment[108].

3. Loss of the right to limit

Since they are subject to actions and since they have also the right to limit, servants and agents are also subject to provisions breaking the limits. Depending on the regime regarding the loss of the right to limit, the conditions required for breaking the servants' and agents' liability limits differ under relevant conventions.

Pursuant to CMR Art. 29 (2), agents, servants, and other persons for whom the carrier is liable are not entitled to avail themselves, with regard to their personal liability, of the liability limits if they are guilty of wilful misconduct or of such fault which, in accordance with the law of the court seized of the case, is considered as equivalent to wilful misconduct. Consequently, servants and agents will also be deprived of liability limits when the damage is caused by their gross negligence or reckless conduct coupled with knowledge of the probable consequences, whichever is considered as the equivalent to wilful misconduct by the court seized of the case. Clearly, the unlimited liability of the servants and agents solely depends on their own conduct[109].

The situation under the international regime for the carriage of passengers by road iss more clearly regulated than under the CMR. According to the second sentence of CVR Art. 18 (2), servants and agents of the carrier will lose their right to limit when the loss or damage results from their wilful misconduct or gross negligence. Therefore, the claimant does not need to prove the subjective knowledge of the servant or agent; a violation of the duty of care in a grave manner is sufficient to break the limits.

By virtue of CIV 1999 Art. 52 (2) and CIM 1999 Art. 41 (2), the conditions and limitations set by the Rules are applicable to servants and agents in an action brought against them. Thus, CIV 1999 Art. 48 and CIM 1999 Art. 36 are also applicable to the rail carrier's servants and agents; therefore, they will lose their right to limit if they are guilty of intentional or reckless conduct as defined in the provisions.

Under the regime regarding the carriage of goods by inland waterways, servants and agents of the carrier will be deprived of the liability limits by virtue of CMNI Art. 21 (2). The situation is the same under the global limitation regime.

---

[106] MünchKommHGB 1997 – *Basedow*, CMR Art. 28 Rn. 17; *Thume*, in: *Fremuth/Thume*, Art. 28 CMR Rn. 9; *Helm*, in: Großkomm. HGB Anh. VI nach § 452: CMR Art. 28 Rn. 12.

[107] CMR Art. 28 (2); CVR Art. 18; CIV 1999 Art. 52 (2); CIM 1999 Art. 41 (2); CMNI Art. 17 (3); CLNI Art. 1 (3); Multimodal Transport Convention Art. 20 (2).

[108] CMNI Art. 17 (3); Multimodal Transport Convention Art. 20 (2).

[109] *Thume*, in: *Fremuth/Thume*, Art. 29 CMR Rn. 25; *Harms*, in: *Thume, CMR-Kommentar*, Art. 29 Rn. 83; *Herber/Piper*, Art. 29 Rn. 24; *Thume, CMR-Frachtführer*, 937.

Servants and agents are named specifically under CLNI Art. 1 (3), which lists the persons entitled to limit. Consequently, they are also subject to Art. 4 of the Convention which sets the rules as to the breaking of liability limits.

Under the Multimodal Transport Convention regime, servants and agents will be deprived of the liability limits if they personally[110] are guilty of intentional or reckless conduct as defined in Art. 21 (2). Here, an important point should be emphasised: Art. 15 of the Multimodal Transport Convention which provides liability of the MTO for his servants, agents and other persons, also covers the actual or performing carriers. Consequently, actual or performing carriers will lose the right to limit if they are guilty of wilful or reckless conduct as defined in Art. 21 (2). However, it has been suggested that the actual or performing carriers might raise the defence that the contractual relationship between the MTO and the shipper prevents them from being subject to a tort claim under the Multimodal Transport Convention and that this point needs further clarification[111]. However, this point does not need any clarification due to Art. 20 (2) which clearly establishes that servants, agents and other persons can be sued under tort law principles; moreover, if they are sued, they can rely on the defences and limits of liability set by the Multimodal Transport Convention.

---

[110] *Driscoll/Larsen*, 231.
[111] *Driscoll/Larsen*, 231-232.

Part III Proof & Concept of Fault

§ 7 Causation and Proof

Apart from the problem of which prerequisites are necessary to break the limitation of liability, questions of causation and proof also play an important role. The answer to the question of which party carries the burden of proof generally determines the result of the whole process, since that party will suffer if it fails to meet this burden. The questions of what to prove and how to prove it also play an important role in convincing the court. Therefore, the standard of proof issues will also be addressed in this chapter.

A. Causal Connection

I. Connection

The relevant provisions in the conventions which were analysed in the previous chapters state that the damage must either be "caused by"[1] the wilful misconduct of the carrier (or his servants and agents) or the damage must have "resulted from"[2] the carrier's (or his agents and servants) act or omission as defined in the relevant provisions. Accordingly both the wordings "caused by" and "resulted from" necessitate a causal connection between wilful misconduct and the damage incurred[3].

---

[1] Warsaw Convention Art. 25; CMR Art. 29; CMNI Art. 21. It was argued in *Shah v. Pan American World Services, Inc.* (CA, 1998) 148 F.3d 84, that "caused by" is not the proper translation of the original French text of the Warsaw Convention. However, the court did not analyse the issue in detail and left it to "another day whether "provient de son" in Article 25 (1) is properly translated as "is caused by" or "arises from" (and if the latter, its significance)", see *Shah v. Pan American World Services, Inc.* (CA, 1998) 148 F.3d 84, 96-97 *per* Judge Walker.

[2] Warsaw Convention Art. 25 (as amended by the Hague Protocol); Hague/Visby Rules Art. IV (5)(e); Hamburg Rules Art. 8; Rotterdam Rules Art. 61; Athens Convention Art. 13; CLC'92 Art. V (2); HNS Art. 9 (2); 1976 London Convention Art. 4; CVR Art. 18 (2); CIV 1999 Art. 48; CIM 1999 Art. 36; CLNI Art. 4; Montreal Convention Art. 22 (5); Multimodal Transport Convention Art. 21.

[3] MünchKommHGB 2009 – *Jesser-Huß*, CMR Art. 29 Rn. 28; *Drion*, p. 230; *Goldhirsch*, p. 164; *Guldimann*, p. 146; *Shawcross and Beaumont*, VII 474; *Koffka/Bodenstein*, p. 333; MünchKommHGB 1997 – *Kronke* WA 1955 Art. 25 Rn. 5;

The causal connection, firstly, requires an identified cause. If the cause of the damage cannot be determined, the damage can not be linked to an act or omission[4]. An absence of this link between the damage and the act or omission leads to the outcome that the state of a certain person's actual knowledge cannot be questioned, which, in fact, results in the absence of one of the necessary criteria of wilful misconduct.

II. Condition sine qua non

When the cause of the damage is known, it should, as the first-step, be a "but for" cause (*haftungsbegründende Kausalität, conditio sine qua non*)[5]. Namely, the act or omission by the carrier (or his servants and agents) must be such an act or omission without which the damage would not have occurred. However, it need not be the sole cause of the damage. It is sufficient for a finding of wilful misconduct if the carrier (or his servants and agents) is involved as one of the concurrent causes which, self-evidently, must be a primary, in other words, a substantial or material one[6]. For instance, if goods are set on fire by a third person, this is the primary cause of the damage which occurred. However, if a servant of the carrier does not take the necessary steps to fight the fire after noticing it (for instance just watching the fire instead of calling for professional help as soon as possible), the

---

Modjaz, p. 35; *Philipson/ et al.*, pp. 165-166; *Berner v. British Commonwealth Pacific Airlines, Ltd.* (DC New York, 1963) 219 F.Supp. 289, 363 *per* Judge Ritter; OLG Frankfurt, 22.10.1980, VersR 1981, 164 (166), affirmed by BGH, 12.01. 1982, TranspR 1982, 100 = VersR 1982, 369; BGE 128 III 390 (398) (06.06.2002); for the view that the wording of the amended version of the Warsaw Convention is clearer on this point, see *Clarke, Carriage by Air*, p. 168.

4   *Goldhirsch*, p. 163; *Özdemir*, p. 118.
5   *Clarke, Carriage by Air*, p. 168; *Clarke, CMR*, pp. 216-217; *Clarke, CIM*, p. 43; *Thomas Cook Group Ltd. and Others v. Air Malta Co. Ltd.* [1997] 2 Lloyd's Rep. 399, 416 (QBD) *per* Justice Cresswell; *Shah v. Pan American World Services, Inc.* (CA, 1998) 148 F.3d 84, 95 *per* Judge Walker; *In re Air Crash near Cali, Colombia on December 20, 1995* (DC Florida, 1997) 985 F.Supp. 1106, 1146-1147 *per* Judge Marcus; BGE 128 III 390 (398-399) (06.06.2002).
6   *Clarke, Carriage by Air*, p. 168; *Philipson/et al.*, p. 149; *Ritts v. American Overseas Airlines, Inc.* (DC New York, 1949) 1949 USAvR 65, 69; *Grey v. American Airlines, Inc.* (CA, 1955) 227 F.2d 282, 285; *Horabin v. British Overseas Airways Corporation* [1952] 2 Lloyd's Rep. 450, 462 (QBD) *per* Justice Barry: "It need not be the sole cause, but it must be a cause which is still alive in active operation, and is still effective as a cause, at the time when the accident happens"; *Berner v. British Commonwealth Pacific Airlines, Ltd.* (DC New York, 1963) 219 F.Supp. 289, 363 *per* Judge Ritter: "[...] did not say it must be the sole substantial factor contributing to the death. In other words, if you find that wilful misconduct by the defendant or any of its employees was a substantial contributing factor to the death [...], that is sufficient [for a finding of wilful misconduct] even though you may find that there were also other substantial contributing factors."; *In re Air Crash near Cali, Colombia on December 20, 1995* (DC Florida, 1997) 985 F.Supp. 1106, 1147.

servant's indifference would amount to reckless conduct with the probable consequences being clearly foreseeable. In such a case, the servant's conduct is also one
of the primary, in other words "but for", causes[7].

Here, doubt may arise as to a "but for" cause, when more than one cause of the
injury or damage incurred exists, any of which is sufficient to bring the same
result. For instance, where a servant of the carrier in charge with the loading of the
cargo lights the goods on fire but, before it is noticed that the goods are on fire, a
third person enters the premises of the carrier and lights the same goods on fire,
both fire starting actions can be classified as sufficient causes. In such a case, it
could be argued that the fire starting action of the servant is not a "but for" cause
since even if he would not have set the goods on fire, they would have been
destroyed in any case due to the fire-setting action of the third person; therefore,
the act of the servant is not a *conditio sine qua non* and cannot be considered in a
wilful misconduct case. Naturally, such a result cannot be accepted since it is
absurd. In such a case, both causes are to be considered as "but for" causes[8].

III. Proximate Cause

It is said that the terms used in the conventions to stress the causative link do not
indicate what degree of causality should be looked for[9]. Moreover, it is emphasized that under the CMR regime, the degree of causal connection is to be determined either according to *lex fori*[10] or to the law applicable to the carriage contract
or to the national law[11]. However, in any case, a "but for" cause alone is not sufficient to establish the required causation[12]. Therefore, as the second-step, the act or
omission should be the proximate cause of the damage[13]. Even if the carrier's (or

---

[7] *Hart/Honoré*, pp. 127-128.
[8] *Hart/Honoré*, pp. 122-125; *Moore*, pp. 86-87; *Markesinis and Deakin*, p. 252;
    Prosser and Keeton, pp. 265-266; *Clerk & Lindsell*, para. 2-94; *Winfield &
    Jolowicz*, para. 6-7; *Street*, p. 152; *Dobbs*, pp. 414-416; *Tekinay/et al.*, p. 570;
    Karahasan, p. 516.
[9] *Beier*, pp. 107-108.
[10] MünchKommHGB 2009 – *Jesser-Huß*, CMR Art. 29 Rn. 28; *Thume*, in: *Fremuth/
    Thume*, Art. 29 CMR Rn. 19c; *Koller*, CMR Art. 29 Rn. 5.
[11] *Harms*, in: *Thume, CMR-Kommentar*, Art. 29 Rn. 31; MünchKommHGB 1997 –
    Basedow, CMR Art. 29 Rn. 26; *Helm*, in: Großkomm. HGB Anh. VI nach § 452:
    CMR Art. 29 Rn. 5; *Modjaz*, p. 107; Ebenroth/Boujong/Joost/Strohn/*Bahnsen*,
    CMR Art. 29 Rn. 47; *Beier*, p. 60; *Herber/Piper*, Art. 29 Rn. 14; *Clarke, CMR*,
    p. 322.
[12] *Shah v. Pan American World Services, Inc.* (CA, 1998) 148 F.3d 84, 95.
[13] *Chen*, pp. 201-202; *Goepp v. American Overseas Airlines, Inc.* (Supreme Court of
    New York, 1952) 117 N.Y.S.2d 276, 282 *per* Justice Cohn; *In re Air Crash near
    Cali, Colombia on December 20, 1995* (DC Florida, 1997) 985 F.Supp. 1106, 1147
    per Judge Marcus. The degree of causation is proximate cause under German and
    English law, where the CMR is applicable, see MünchKommHGB 1997 –
    Basedow, CMR Art. 29 Rn. 27; MünchKommHGB 2009 – *Jesser-Huß*, CMR Art.
    29 Rn. 29; *Helm*, in: Großkomm. HGB Anh. VI nach § 452: CMR Art. 29 Rn. 5,
    23; *Modjaz*, pp. 107-108; *Clarke, CMR*, p. 376.

his servants' and agents') conduct could be considered as wilful misconduct, if that conduct is not the proximate cause[14] (legal cause, *adäquate Kausalität*) of the damage, the claim would be denied by courts[15].

Since the consequences of an act or omission can be traced until the end of time, or, alternatively, "but for" causes can be traced back until the beginning of time (called also Adam-and-Eve causation[16]), there should be a limit drawn in determining the cause of an event. This limitation is known as the *proximate cause*[17]. The proximate cause is the efficient cause[18]. It should not be the exclusive cause[19], nor the nearest in time[20]. The proximate cause is the cause which is closely connected with the result and which is significant and important enough such that it is justified to impose liability based upon it[21].

IV. Intervening and Concurrent Causes

The chain of causation should not be broken by any operative intervening cause (*nova causa interveniens*)[22]. An intervening cause is also a proximate cause as well as a "but for" cause, and it is sufficiently causally significant that no other proximate cause can be traced back through it[23]. If, for instance, goods carried on deck contrary to an express agreement for the carriage under deck are damaged, the carrier could be found guilty of wilful misconduct. However, if the goods become total loss due to an explosion caused by dangerous goods loaded on board without the knowledge of the carrier, the total loss is the result of the explosion, not the result of the carriage on deck. The explosion is the later cause of independ-

---

[14] Some considers this term as unfortunate, since problems related to proximate cause were considered as questions of imposing liability rather than questions of causation, see *Prosser and Keeton*, pp. 264, 273; *Dobbs*, pp. 408, 448; Münch-KommBGB – *Oetker*, § 249 Rn. 111; *von Caemmerer*, p. 12.

[15] E.g. *Perera Co., Inc. v. Varig Brazilian Airlines, Inc.* (CA, 1985) 775 F.2d 21; *Johnson v. American Airlines, Inc.* (CA, 1987) 834 F.2d 721, 724.

[16] Glanville *Williams*, Causation in the Law, [1961] Cam. L. J. 62, 64.

[17] *Prosser and Keeton*, p. 264; MünchKommBGB – *Oetker*, § 249 Rn. 99; *Larenz*, pp. 434-436; *Dobbs*, p. 443; *von Caemmerer*, p. 10; *Oğuzman/Öz*, p. 519.

[18] MünchKommBGB – *Oetker*, § 249 Rn. 105; *Tekinay/et al.*, p. 573; *Kılıçoğlu*, p. 248; *Leyland Shipping Company, Limited v. Norwich Union Fire Insurance Society, Limited* [1918] A.C. 350, 369 (HL) *per* Lord Shaw of Dunfermline.

[19] *Reischer v. Borwick* [1894] 2 Q.B.D. 548, 551 (CA) *per* Lord Justice Lindley.

[20] *Markesinis and Deakin*, p. 245.

[21] *Prosser and Keeton*, pp. 264, 273; *Markesinis and Deakin*, pp. 244-245; *Clerk & Lindsell*, para. 2-92; MünchKommBGB – *Oetker*, § 249 Rn. 104. See also *Larenz*, pp. 435-440; *Atamer, Nedensellik Bağı*, pp. 42 *et seqq.*; *Karahasan*, pp. 510-511.

[22] OLG Frankfurt, 22.10.1980, VersR 1981, 164 (166), affirmed by BGH, 12.01. 1982, TranspR 1982, 100 = VersR 1982, 369; *In re Air Crash near Cali, Colombia on December 20, 1995* (DC Florida, 1997) 985 F.Supp. 1106, 1147.

[23] *Moore*, p. 234; *Clerk & Lindsell*, para. 2-101. See also *von Caemmerer*, p. 10; *Karahasan*, p. 512.

ent origin[24], in other words a superseding cause that breaks the causal link between the total loss of the goods and the carriage on deck.

Nevertheless, the natural consequences of the first cause do not break the direct relation between the cause and its effect[25]. For example, if a plane enters an area of severe turbulence, and if the pilot does not warn the cabin, it is normal that the cabin crew will continue serving passengers. If anyone is hit by the food or beverage trolley and suffers injury, the proximate cause of the injury is the lack of warning. It cannot be said that the last cause in the time sequence is the trolley impact and that it, therefore, should be considered as the cause of the injury. The continuing service and the trolley's presence in the aisle is a natural consequence of the lack of warning by the pilot. Consequently, the relation between the injury and the conduct of the pilot is not broken.

The proximate cause in unlimited liability cases is also related to the foreseeability criterion. If a new and independent factor arises *from the first act or omission*, and this independent factor causes the damage, it must be analysed whether the first act or omission remains the proximate cause. In such a determination, the foreseeability of the independent factor would be crucial. If the independent factor is reasonably foreseeable, in other words, if the independent factor was foreseen as *probable*, it cannot be said that the independent factor is an intervening cause. Therefore, the causal connection between the first act or omission and the damage incurred is not broken[26], and, consequently, the first act or omission remains as the proximate cause.

If an additional factor does not break the connection between the initial act or omission and the loss or damage incurred, but also contributes to the loss or damage that occurred, this additional factor is called a concurrent cause[27]. As it is clear from the definition of the concurrent (or contributory) cause, a concurrent cause does not break the causal connection with the initial act or omission and the result. Therefore, if the first act or omission is committed with wilful misconduct, a concurrent cause would not be considered with regards to the causal connection between wilful misconduct and the result[28]. The contributory cause might be

---

[24]   *Prosser and Keeton*, p. 301; *Moore*, p. 236; *Street*, p. 154.

[25]   *Leyland Shipping Company, Limited v. Norwich Union Fire Insurance Society, Limited* [1918] A.C. 350, 362 (HL) *per* Viscount Haldane. See also *von Caemmerer*, pp. 10-11.

[26]   *Clarke, Carriage by Air*, p. 168; *In re Air Crash near Cali, Colombia on December 20, 1995* (DC Florida, 1997) 985 F.Supp. 1106, 1147 *per* Judge Marcus. See also *Moore*, pp. 236-240; 251-253.

[27]   *Hart/Honoré*, p. 205; *Oğuzman/Öz*, p. 525.

[28]   An example of concurrent cause is the case *Grant v. Sun Shipping Company Limited* [1948] A.C. 549 (HL). Ship repairers working on the ship *Empire Impala* left a hatch uncovered. They also removed lights at the side of it, so it was not possible to see that the hatch was uncovered. A stevedore who was also working on the ship but had left for dinner, came back onto the board after the dinner interval, and not being able to see anything, fell down the hatch and sustained injuries. The HL found that the ship repairers were negligent, but the negligence of the shipowners

considered in determining the amount of the compensation if the law applicable allows such a consideration.

The situation is also no different if the contributory cause is generated as a result of plaintiff's negligence. This can be illustrated with two transport law cases considered earlier. In the *Saint Jacques II and Gudermes*[29] case[30], the vessel *Gudermes* was not negligent. Nevertheless, even if she had been negligent, *e.g.* navigating with excessive speed, this would not have nullified the causal connection between the wilful misconduct of the *Saint Jacques II* and the damage which occurred. Another example could be the *Husain v. Olympic Airways*[31] case[32]. In that case, the passenger was not negligent. Nevertheless, even if he had been negligent, *e.g.* he did not use his inhaler, this fact would not have broken the causal connection between the wilful misconduct of the airline and his death.

Thus, the contributory negligence of the plaintiff does not break the causal connection between the wilful misconduct and the loss or damage incurred. In other words, wilful misconduct or reckless conduct as defined in the international conventions nullifies the causal connection between the plaintiff's negligence, however gross that negligence may be, and the loss or damage incurred[33]. In an illustrative case, though not regarding transport law, the deceased was walking too closely alongside a streetcar route. He was hit from behind by a streetcar and died within minutes. During the trial, it was determined that, although he observed the deceased from a considerable distance, the motorist did not brake until the streetcar became too close to him. The court decided that the negligent behaviour of the deceased did not nullify the causal connection between the reckless conduct of the motorist and the death[34].

Even in cases where the subject matter is regulated under a specific provision as a special risk, the result would be the same. If there is wilful misconduct on the carrier's side, the plaintiff's negligence would not break the causal connection. For instance, CMR Art. 17 (4)(c) stipulates that the carrier is not liable for loss or damage resulting from the stowage of the goods by sender. If the sender demands a refrigerated lorry and the carrier provides such a lorry but knowingly provides one with a malfunctioning conditioning system with the result that the goods become a total loss, the carrier would be liable for his reckless or wilful conduct even if the goods were badly stowed and the bad stowage contributed to the loss. Bad stowage does not break the causal connection between the wilful misconduct of the carrier and the total loss[35].

---

in failing to provide a reasonably safe working place also contributed to the accident.

[29] *Margolle and Another v. Delta Maritime Co. Ltd. and Others (the "Saint Jacques II" and "Gudermes")* [2003] 1 Lloyd's Rep. 203 (QBD).

[30] For the facts of the case see *supra* § 5 C II 2 b bb.

[31] *Husain v. Olympic Airways* (DC California, 2000) 116 F.Supp.2d 1121.

[32] For the facts of the case see supra § 4 B II 2 a.

[33] *Hart/Honoré*, p. 214; *Dobbs*, p. 498. See also *Palandt/Grüneberg*, § 254 Rn. 65; BGH, 08.07.1986, NJW 1986, 2941; BGH, 05.03.2002, NJW 2002, 1643.

[34] *Kasanovich v. George* (Supreme Court of Pennsylvania, 1943) 34 Atl. 2d 523.

[35] For another example see OLG München, 23.09.2004, TranspR 2005, 254.

If both sides of an event are guilty of reckless conduct as defined in the relevant international conventions, which recklessness should be considered as the proximate cause of the event? For instance, during foggy weather, a ship stops in the middle of a channel without using necessary signals and lights without any proper reason. If another ship travelling at an excessive speed does not reduce her speed despite all warnings of the vessel traffic system and collides with the first ship, both ships are to be considered having acted recklessly with the recklessness of both ships concurrently causing the damage which occurs. In such a case, no causal connection is broken between the "two acts of recklessness" and the resultant damage. Both of the ships are jointly liable, but their mutually reckless conduct would bar a claim against one another for the damage to their respective ships[36].

B. Proof

I. Burden

The term "burden of proof" states the duty to meet the requirement as the law demands to prove a disputed fact (persuasive burden, *die objektive Beweislast*). This obligation also covers the evidentiary burden (*die subjektive Beweislast*), namely to produce sufficient and adequate evidence as to the existence (or non-existence) of the disputed fact, if called upon to do so. Normally, the evidentiary burden is on the same person who also bears the burden of proof[37].

1. Wording of the conventions

Conventions[38] which refer to wilful misconduct and the equivalent degree of fault do not include any statements as to the question of who carries the burden of proof. They simply state that the carrier will not be entitled to avail himself of the limitation of liability provisions in the case of wilful misconduct. However, this absence of any indication does not cause any difficulties due to the liability regimes set by those conventions.

Under the general tort law regime, anyone seeking a remedy for his damages has to prove that he has suffered damages and that those damages are the result of the defendant's delict. Moreover, he needs to prove that the defendant was at fault in his delict except in cases involving strict liability.

---

[36] *Hart/Honoré*, pp. 217-219.
[37] *Cross & Tapper*, pp. 139-142; *Schröder*, pp. 219-221; IX *Wigmore, Evidence* §§ 2485, 2487 (Chadbourn rev. 1981); *Speiser*, § 3:14; *Brinkmann*, pp. 18-21; Restatement (Second) of Torts, § 328 A (Proof of negligence – Burden of proof); *Zöller/Greger*, Vor § 284 Rn. 18; MünchKommZPO – *Prütting* § 286 Rn. 93, 97-103; *Stein/Jonas/Leipold*, § 286 Rn. 52; *Pekcanıtez/Atalay/Özekes*, pp. 424-426; *Seven*, 75-76.
[38] Warsaw Convention Art. 25; CMR Art. 29; CVR Art. 18 (2); CIV 1980 Art. 42; CIM 1980 Art. 44.

However, under the international transport convention regimes, the fault of the carrier is at least presumed, and, in some instances the carrier is strictly liable[39]. Therefore, the carrier generally faces liability irrespective of his fault; namely when injury or damage occurs, the claimant does not need to prove his fault[40]. Therefore, courts frequently do not need to consider any fault issue[41]. Thus, the basic rule is limited liability without the need to prove negligence on the side of the carrier. If anyone wishes to venture outside of this regime, that person will carry the onus of proof[42].

For instance, if the carrier wishes to be relieved of liability, he needs to prove that either he and his servants and agents took all necessary measures, or that the damage or injury was caused by circumstances which he was unable to prevent, or that the damage or injury was caused by the fault of the other party of the contract or a third party, or that the damage was caused by special risks listed in the relevant convention[43]. As a result, it is possible to say that if an exception to the limited liability is claimed, the person claiming that exceptional circumstance must carry the burden of proof[44].

Undoubtedly, provisions as to the breaking of the liability limits are the clearest exception to the limitation regime set by the relevant conventions. Appropriately, the claimant seeking compensation for the full amount of his damages carries the burden of proof even where there is no statement in the relevant provisions as to the burden. This has been widely accepted by legal commentators[45] and by the

---

[39] See *supra* § 4, 5 and 6.

[40] Which is an evidentiary presumption; for the term, see *Schröder*, p. 233; IX *Wigmore, Evidence* § 2489 (b) (Chadbourn rev. 1981).

[41] *Giemulla*, p. 119.

[42] MünchKommHGB 1997 – *Basedow*, CMR Art. 29 Rn. 30-31, 38; *Helm*, in: Großkomm. HGB Anh. VI nach § 452: CMR Art. 29 Rn. 2; *Herber/Piper*, Art. 29 Rn. 15; *Giefers*, pp. 203-205.

[43] Warsaw Convention Art. 20; CMR Art. 17-18; CVR Art. 11, 14; CIV 1980 Art. 26; CIM 1980 Art. 36.

[44] *Giemulla*, pp. 119-120; *Göknil*, p. 202; BGE 93 II 345 (349-350) (14.11.1967); *Herber/Schmuck*, 1211; *Koller, Aufklärung*, 553; *Thume, CMR-Frachtführer*, 937; Ebenroth/Boujong/Joost/Strohn/*Bahnsen*, CMR Art. 29 Rn. 16.

[45] *Giemulla*, pp. 119-120; *Abraham*, pp. 366, 369; *Matte*, p. 61; *Abraham, Luftbe-förderungsvertrag*, p. 55; *McNair*, p. 190; *Guldimann*, p. 149; *Guerreri*, p. 14; *Abraham, Grade des Verschuldens*, 263; *Riese*, p. 465; *Mankiewicz*, pp. 118, 126; *Miller*, p. 74; *Shawcross and Beaumont*, VII 479; *Gaskell, Breaking Limits*, p. 6; *Ramming*, 306; *Sturley/Fujita/van der Ziel*, para. 5.251; MünchKommHGB 1997 – *Kronke* WA 1955 Art. 25 Rn. 35; *Modjaz*, p. 34; *Gran*, pp. 848-849; *Kuhn*, p. 204; MünchKommHGB 1997 – *Basedow*, CMR Art. 29 Rn. 30-31, 38; Münch-KommHGB 2009 – *Jesser-Huß*, CMR Art. 29 Rn. 41; *Helm*, in: Großkomm. HGB Anh. VI nach § 452: CMR Art. 29 Rn. 2; *Herber/Piper*, Art. 29 Rn. 15; *Giefers*, pp. 203-205; *Müller-Rostin*, in: Fremuth/Thume, Art. 25 WA Rn. 10; *Thume*, in: Fremuth/Thume, Art. 29 CMR Rn. 26; *Harms*, in: Thume, CMR-Kommentar, Art. 29 Rn. 86; *Koller*, CMR Art. 29 Rn. 7; *Clarke, CMR*, p. 314; *Clarke/Yates*, para. 1.166; *Modjaz*, p. 122; *Helm*, in: Großkomm. HGB Anh. VI nach § 452: CMR Art. 29 Rn. 25; *Aydın*, p. 142; *Clarke, Road Transport*, 429; *Herber/Schmuck*, 1209;

case law[46]. If the claimant cannot prove that the carrier is guilty of wilful misconduct, the court will rule for limited liability[47].

The rule as to the burden of proof has also been clearly stated in the definition given for the first time by the Hague Protocol[48]. The amended version of Art. 25 of the Warsaw Convention states that the carrier will be liable without any financial limits "if it is proved" that the damage resulted from the conduct as defined in the provision. Consequently, intentional or reckless conduct must be proved. Since the claimant seeking unlimited liability will allege that the damage or injury was caused by intentional or reckless conduct, the burden of proof rests on him. Considering the fact that the wording of the Hague Protocol has been employed by almost all of the international transport conventions adopted after the Protocol, it is clear that the burden is on the claimant seeking the unlimited liability of the carrier under those regimes as well[49].

Clarke/Yates, para. 2.368; *Özdemir, Eşya Taşıma*, p. 176; *Gençtürk*, pp. 234, 248; *Thume, Vergleich*, 4; *Seven*, 67; *Arkan*, p. 186; *Becker*, p. 148; *Arkan, İnceleme*, p. 45; *Clarke, CIM*, p. 40; Ebenroth/Boujong/Joost/Strohn/*Bahnsen*, CMR Art. 29 Rn. 48; *Fremuth, Schwere Schuld*, p. 166.

[46] BGE 93 II 345 (349-350) (14.11.1967); BGE 98 II 231 (242) (11.07.1972); OLG Frankfurt, 22.10.1980, VersR 1981, 164 (166); *Grey v. American Airlines, Inc.* (CA, 1955) 227 F.2d 282, 285 *per* Judge Medina; *Rashap v. American Airlines, Inc.* (DC New York, 1955) 1955 US&CAvR 593, 612 *per* Judge Dawson; *Iyegha v. United Airlines, Inc.* (Supreme Court of Alabama, 1995) 659 So.2d 45, 49 *per* Justice Almon; for the counterview see OLG Frankfurt, 14.09.1999, TranspR 2000, 260 (261).

[47] 11. HD, 08.04.2002, E. 2001/10866, K. 2002/3205 (*Erdil*, pp. 375-376); 11. HD, 05.02.2002, E. 2001/8877, K. 2002/890 (*Erdil*, pp. 376-378).

[48] *Clarke, Carriage by Air*, p. 158; *Guldimann*, p. 149; *Özdemir*, p. 118; *Milde*, pp. 72-73; *Miller*, p. 203; *Giemulla/Schmid*, WA Art. 25 Rn. 47; *Ruhwedel*, p. 330; *Kırman*, p. 171; BGE 98 II 231 (242) (11.07.1972); 11. HD, 19.04.2001, 2001/2983, 2001/3333.

[49] *Herber, Haftungsrecht*, p. 215; *Eilenberger-Czwalinna*, p. 117; *Tetley*, pp. 284-285 (who thinks placing the burden of proof on the claimant goes too far); *Hill*, p. 277; *Chen*, p. 202; *Wilson*, p. 204; *Rabe*, § 660 Rn. 27; *Herber*, p. 333; *Lüddeke/Johnson*, p. 20; *Yazıcıoğlu*, p. 175; *Gaskell, Hamburg Rules*, p. 165; *Richter-Hannes*, p. 79; *Kienzle*, pp. 208-209; *Schubert*, p. 79 fn. 229 / *Gaskell, Athens 1974*, 322; *Mandaraka-Sheppard*, p. 889; *Hill*, p. 409; *Davies/Dickey*, p. 469; *Griggs/Williams/Farr*, pp. 39-40; *Gold/Chircop/Kindred*, p. 732; *Hodges/Hill*, pp. 594-596; *Özçayır*, p. 360; *Hill*, p. 407; *Shaw/Tsimplis*, p. 215; *Tsimplis, Marine Pollution*, p. 262; *Grime, Loss of the Right*, p. 111; *Seward*, p. 182; *Coghlin*, p. 250; *Cheka*, 498; *Grime, 1976 Limitation Convention*, p. 313; *Heerey*, pp. 12, 16; *Jefferies*, 304; *Baughen*, p. 426; *Wilson*, p. 288; *Gauci, Oil Pollution*, p. 166; *Seven*, 72; *Richter-Hannes, Multimodale Güterbeförderung*, p. 158; *Giemulla/Schmid, Montrealer Übereinkommen*, Art. 22 MÜ Rn. 39; *Chen, Limitation*, p. 80; *Yetiş Şamlı*, pp. 44, 91, 98, 147; *Neumann*, 418; *Gaskell/Asariotis/Baatz*, para. 16.53; *The "Capitan San Luis"* [1993] 2 Lloyd's Rep. 573, 578-579 (QBD) *per* Justice Clarke; *MSC Mediterranean Shipping Co. S.A. v. Delumar BVBA and Others (The "MSC Rosa M")* [2000] 2 Lloyd's Rep. 399, 401 (QBD) *per* Justice David Steel; *The "Tasman Pioneer"* [2003] 2 Lloyd's Rep. 713, 719 (New Zealand

2. Proof of criteria

What the claimant must prove is, in fact, self-evident in the wording of the relevant provisions. Generally, a claimant must show that the carrier or shipowner is guilty of wilful misconduct[50], in other words that he[51] or his servants and agents[52] acted or omitted to act recklessly and with knowledge that damage would probably result[53].

As a result, all criteria stated in the relevant provisions must be proven. In brief, reckless conduct[54] together with the actual awareness of probable consequences[55] and the causal link between this conduct and the suffered damages, namely the proximate cause[56], must be proven by the plaintiff. In addition to those criteria it must in most carriage cases[57] also be proven that the reckless conduct is attributable to the person liable and that the person liable has foreseen the very damage occurred. Finally, the burden of proving the amount of the suffered damages in excess of the limits specified in the conventions is also upon the plaintiff[58].

Nevertheless, if the claim is founded on the Hamburg Rules Art. 9 (4) or Rotterdam Rules Art. 25 (5), *i.e.* if the loss or damage is caused by carriage on deck contrary to express agreement for carriage under deck, the claimant must prove that there is an express agreement for carriage under deck, and that the goods were carried on deck contrary to this agreement, that the loss or damage was proximately caused by the carriage on deck. The claimant is under no burden to prove that the carrier was actually aware of the probable consequences since Art. 9 (4) of

---

High Court) *per* Justice Williams; *Margolle and Another v. Delta Maritime Co. Ltd. and Others* (*the "Saint Jacques II" and "Gudermes"*) [2003] 1 Lloyd's Rep. 203, 210 (QBD) *per* Justice Gross.

[50] CMR Art. 29; CVR Art. 18 (2).

[51] Hague/Visby Rules Art. IV (5)(e); Hamburg Rules Art. 8; Rotterdam Rules Art. 61; Athens Convention Art. 13; CLC'92 Art. V (2); HNS Art. 9 (2); 1976 London Convention Art. 4; CIV 1999 Art. 48; CIM 1999 Art. 36; CLNI Art. 4; CMNI Art. 21; Multimodal Transport Convention Art. 21.

[52] Warsaw Convention Art. 25; CMR Art. 29; CVR Art. 18 (2); Montreal Convention Art. 22 (5).

[53] *Drion*, p. 229-230; *Goldhirsch*, p. 162; *Giemulla*, p. 122; *Giemulla/Schmid*, WA Art. 25 Rn. 49; *Grey v. American Airlines, Inc.* (CA, 1955) 227 F.2d 282, 285 *per* Judge Medina; *Rashap v. American Airlines, Inc.* (DC New York, 1955) 1955 US&CAvR 593, 612 *per* Judge Dawson.

[54] *Özdemir*, p. 118; *Schobel*, pp. 80-81; MünchKommHGB 1997 – *Kronke* WA 1955 Art. 25 Rn. 35.

[55] *Goldhirsch*, p. 162; *Özdemir*, p. 118; *Shawcross and Beaumont*, VII 479; MünchKommHGB 1997 – *Kronke* WA 1955 Art. 25 Rn. 35; *Schobel*, pp. 80-81; *McGilchrist*, p. 542; *Clarke, Carriage by Air*, p. 158; OLG Düsseldorf, 21.01.1993, TranspR 1993, 246 = NJW-RR 1993, 811; *Alleyn v. Delta Airlines* (DC New York, 1999) 58 F.Supp.2d 15, 25 *per* Judge Trager.

[56] *Goldhirsch*, p. 162; *Grey v. American Airlines, Inc.* (CA, 1955) 227 F.2d 282, 285 *per* Judge Medina. See also *supra* A III.

[57] See *supra* note 51.

[58] *Goldhirsch*, p. 162.

the Hamburg Rules and Art. 25 (5) of the Rotterdam Rules adopt a clear presumption in this regard.

Furthermore, where the carrier is held responsible for his servants' and agents' misconduct[59], the burden to prove that this conduct is within the scope of his employment rests also with the claimant[60]. However, if the claimant directly sues the servant or agent who caused the damage, the burden of proving the scope of employment, if necessary, rests with the servant or agent[61]. Therefore, the claimant is under no obligation to prove the scope of employment issue in a claim brought directly against a servant or agent.

II. Standard

1. General rule

Although the burden of proof issue is regulated by the conventions, other aspects of proof are not. Therefore, as to the standard of proof general principles of law should be applied: questions of procedure are subject to the law of the court seized[62]. Consequently, the standard by which the criterion for breaking the limits needs to be proved is determined by the procedural law of the *lex fori*[63]. The question of the applicable standard arises especially on the actual knowledge element, since a reckless act or omission may be proven by indicating certain facts regarding violations of particular rules and regulations[64].

A fact shall be considered as proven when the judge (or the fact-finder) is convinced[65]. As to the degree of conviction with regard to the actual knowledge of the wrongdoer, there are two different standards (*Beweismaß*) in common law: proof beyond a reasonable doubt[66] and the balance of probabilities (expressed also as preponderance of probability). It is a well-settled rule that in civil law cases, there-

---

[59]   See supra note 52.

[60]   *Giemulla/Schmid*, WA Art. 25 Rn. 52; *Abraham, Grade des Verschuldens*, 263. There is no clear reference to the scope of employment criterion under CVR Art. 18 (2), but, nevertheless, the scope of employment criterion must be proved by virtue of CVR Art. 4.

[61]   Warsaw Convention Art. 25A (1); CMNI Art. 17 (3); Montreal Convention 1999 Art. 30; Multimodal Transport Convention Art. 20 (2).

[62]   This principle has been explicitly stated in the Warsaw Convention Art. 28 (2), see also BGE 98 II 231 (242) (11.07.1972).

[63]   *Mankiewicz*, p. 126; *Stachow*, p. 209; *Clarke, CIM*, p. 40.

[64]   *Giemulla/Schmid*, WA Art. 25 Rn. 49; In fact, several German courts ruled that the *prima facie* evidence method is not applicable for proof of recklessness, see OLG München, 10.08.1994, TranspR 1995, 118 (119); OLG Frankfurt, 21.04.1998, TranspR 1999, 24 (26), affirmed by BGH, 21.09.2000, ETL 2001, 248 (262).

[65]   *Schröder*, p. 222; *Brinkmann*, p. 31; MünchKommZPO – *Prütting* § 284 Rn. 8; *Baumbach/Lauterbach/Albers/Hartmann*, § 286 Rn. 16; *Pekcanitez/Atalay/Özekes*, pp. 396-397; BGE 98 II 231 (242) (11.07.1972).

[66]   The standard demanded in criminal cases, see *Cross & Tapper*, pp. 169-170; IX *Wigmore, Evidence* §§ 2497 *et seq.* (Chadbourn rev. 1981).

fore also in commercial transport law cases[67], the standard is the balance of probabilities[68]. After all proof has been submitted to the court, the court will consider whether disputed facts are more likely or not according to their evidentiary weight[69]. A claimant needs to adduce strong evidence in relation to the prerequisites of wilful misconduct[70]. If, at the end of the trial, the evidence submitted by both parties is equally balanced, this means that the plaintiff has failed to establish his claim[71].

The standard of proof in civil law, on the other hand, requires the plaintiff to actually persuade the court that the allegation is true. A fact cannot be deemed as proven just because its existence is more likely than its non-existence. This, however, does not mean that the plaintiff needs to prove an absolute certainty, but mere possibility is also not enough to fulfil this standard of proof[72].

In order to convince the court, a set of facts must be proven and evidence as to each of these facts must be submitted. If the consideration of a set of evidence or previously proven facts leads, according to human experience and typical course of events, to the conclusion of the occurrence (or absence) of a certain fact (although the contrary remains also possible[73]), then the fact in issue should be

---

[67] *Kahn-Freund*, p. 260; *Clarke, Carriage by Air*, p. 158; *Miller*, p. 218; *Philipson/et al.*, p. 177; *Clarke, CMR*, p. 314; *Clarke, Road Transport*, 430; *Clarke, Transport in Europe*, 60; *Grey v. American Airlines, Inc.* (CA, 1955) 227 F.2d 282, 285; *Datec Electronic Holdings Ltd. v. United Parcels Service Ltd.* [2006] 1 Lloyd's Rep. 279, 299 (CA) approved by *Datec Electronics Holdings Ltd v. United Parcels Service Ltd* [2007] 2 Lloyd's Rep. 114 (HL).

[68] *Cross & Tapper*, p. 174; *Schröder*, p. 222; IX *Wigmore, Evidence* § 2498 (Chadbourn rev. 1981); *Brinkmann*, pp. 27-29.

[69] *Brinkmann*, pp. 29-30, 38; *Horabin v. British Overseas Airways Corporation* [1952] 2 Lloyd's Rep. 450, 487 (QBD) *per* Justice Barry: "Looking at the evidence as a whole, it is more likely that some act was an act of wilful misconduct than that it was an act of mere negligence or carelessness"; *Rashap v. American Airlines, Inc.* (DC New York, 1955) 1955 US&CAvR 593, 612 *per* Judge Dawson: "[B]y a fair preponderance of evidence, which means that the evidence in support of its contentions outweighs, […], the evidence to the contrary".

[70] *Philipson/et al.*, pp. 177-178.

[71] *Horabin v. British Overseas Airways Corporation* [1952] 2 Lloyd's Rep. 450, 487 (QBD) *per* Justice Barry: "Looking at the evidence as a whole, it is more likely that some act was an act of wilful misconduct than that it was an act of mere negligence or carelessness. If it might be one or might be the other, and there is nothing to show you what the true inference to be drawn from that is, then, of course, wilful misconduct has not been established."; *Rashap v. American Airlines, Inc.* (DC New York, 1955) 1955 US&CAvR 593, 613 *per* Judge Dawson.

[72] *Zöller/Greger*, § 286 Rn. 17-20; MünchKommZPO – *Prütting* § 284 Rn. 8, 32-40; *Baumbach/Lauterbach/Albers/Hartmann*, § 286 Rn. 16-17; *Stein/Jonas/Leipold*, § 286 Rn. 5-9. For the Swiss law, see *Gerber*, pp. 87-88 and also BGE 98 II 231 (243) (11.07.1972).

[73] *Hoffmann*, p. 9; *Pekcanıtez/Atalay/Özekes*, p. 438.

considered as proven unless disproved or rebutted[74]. This method of proof (*Beweismethode*)[75] is known as *prima facie* evidence (*Anscheinsbeweis*)[76]. It is widely accepted, especially by the common law courts, that the method of *prima facie* evidence is sufficient in wilful misconduct cases[77]. However, the civil law courts have generally declined to accept the *prima facie* evidence as the mechanism of proof, on the grounds that the subjective interpretation could be circumvented by inferring subjective knowledge from objective facts[78]. The standard *prima facie* evidence has even been seen as a change in the burden of proof[79]. And yet, if the main current underlying these rulings is surveyed, it is clear that what

---

[74] *Cross & Tapper*, p. 166; *Schröder*, p. 222; *Hoffmann*, pp. 32, 42; MünchKomm-ZPO – *Prütting* § 286 Rn. 48; *Pekcanıtez/Atalay/Özekes*, p. 438; see also Heinz *Wassermeyer*, Der prima facie Beweis, Münster 1954, pp. 37-38.

[75] See *Schröder*, p. 13.

[76] For detailed information see IX *Wigmore, Evidence* § 2494 (I)(1) (Chadbourn rev. 1981); *Zöller/Greger*, Vor § 284 Rn. 29; MünchKommZPO – *Prütting* § 286 Rn. 48-55; *Hoffmann*, pp. 42-49; *Baumbach/Lauterbach/Albers/Hartmann*, Anh § 286 Rn. 15-17; *Stein/Jonas/Leipold*, § 286 Rn. 129; *Pekcanıtez/Atalay/Özekes*, pp. 437-439; *Keser Berber*, pp. 231-236; *Ritts v. American Overseas Airlines, Inc.* (DC New York, 1949) 1949 USAvR 65, 69 *per* Judge Picard: "You may find that the death of the decedent was caused by the wilful misconduct or by acts or omissions equivalent to wilful misconduct of the defendant not only from direct evidence but also by fair inference from the facts proved."; *Iyegha v. United Airlines, Inc.* (Supreme Court of Alabama, 1995) 659 So.2d 45, 49 *per* Justice Almon: "evidence of such weight and quality that fair-minded persons in the exercise of impartial judgement [could] reasonably infer".

[77] *Gran*, p. 849; *Clarke, Carriage by Air*, pp. 162 *et seq.*; *Goldhirsch*, p. 163; *Ruhwedel*, p. 331; *Kuhn*, pp. 204-205; *Herber, Haftungsrecht*, p. 215; *Eilenberger-Czwalinna*, p. 117; *Tetley*, pp. 284-285 (who thinks that this goes too far); *Hill*, pp. 277, 407; *Chen*, p. 202; *Rabe*, § 660 Rn. 27; *Herber*, p. 333; *Schubert*, p. 79 fn. 229; *Gaskell, Athens 1974*, 322; *Yazıcıoğlu*, p. 175; *Kienzle*, pp. 215-216; MünchKommHGB 1997 – *Basedow*, CMR Art. 29 Rn. 39; *Helm*, in: Großkomm. HGB Anh. VI nach § 452: CMR Art. 29 Rn. 25; *Herber/Piper*, Art. 29 Rn. 15; *Giefers*, p. 209; *Becker*, p. 148; *Marsilius*, 309; *Keser Berber*, p. 235 (generally for fault); *Hoffmann*, pp. 173-183 (as to the discussions on the proof of gross negligence and intentional wrongdoing by *prima facie* evidence); *Baumbach/Lauterbach/Albers/Hartmann*, Anh § 286 Rn. 24 (generally for fault); *Stein/Jonas/Leipold*, § 286 Rn. 174; *Koller*, WA 1955 Art. 25 Rn. 9; *Yetiş Şamlı*, p. 97; *Horabin v. British Overseas Airways Corporation* [1952] 2 Lloyd's Rep. 450, 476 (QBD) *per* Justice Barry; *In re Korean Air Lines Disaster of September 1, 1983* (DC Columbia, 1988) 704 F.Supp. 1135, 1136 *per* Judge Robinson; *Saba v. Compagnie Nationale Air France* (CA, 1996) 78 F.3d 664, 669 *per* Judge Silberman; *Koirala v. Thai Airways International* (CA, 1997) 126 F.3d 1205, 1211 *per* Judge Thomas; BGH, 21.09.2000, ETL 2001, 248 (264); LG Frankfurt, 22.08.2000, TranspR 2001, 174 (175). However, if the defendant proves a fact by another means of evidence, the plaintiff cannot continue with *prima facie* evidence, see LG Köln, 09.04.1964, ZLW 1965, 88 (91).

[78] BGH, 16.02.1979, BGHZ 74, 164 (169); OLG Frankfurt, 22.10.1980, VersR 1981, 164 (165); BGE 98 II 231 (242-243) (11.07.1972); BGE 128 III 390 (396) (06.06.2002); also in tort law cases, see *Stachow*, p. 216.

[79] BGE 98 II 231 (242-243) (11.07.1972).

the courts primarily rejected was actually the notion of a presumption of wilful misconduct[80]. Thus, while most of the civil law courts also applied the *prima facie* evidence, they always stressed the danger and the need to avoid an objective interpretation[81]. As a result, it is possible to say that the civil law courts also accepts the application of *prima facie* evidence as concerns the subjective awareness of the carrier or shipowner; they stress, however, the need to avoid any presumption of wilful misconduct.

In order to convince a judge of a fact, adequate material should be submitted. To this extent, direct evidence has the highest probative value; *e.g.* if a black box recording clearly shows what the pilot was thinking, the judge would not have any difficulties in reaching a conclusion. However, as such direct evidence cannot be gathered in most cases, the result would be the failure of the claim, if only direct evidence were required[82]. Therefore, every jurisdiction accepts proof by the type of evidence (mode of proof; *Beweismaterial*)[83] which is known as circumstantial evidence (*Indizienbeweis*)[84] in cases where the state of mind needs to be proven[85]. Wilful misconduct cases are no exception to this general rule. In fact, it has been stressed that circumstantial evidence is sufficient to prove the wrongdoer's actual state of mind[86].

The general proposition that no pilot will crash a plane intentionally, since his own life is also at stake, constituted an important *prima facie* evidence in the

---

[80]   See MünchKommHGB 1997 – *Kronke* WA 1955 Art. 25 Rn. 38; *Becker*, p. 148; *Giemulla/Schmid, Montrealer Übereinkommen*, Art. 22 MÜ Rn. 39-40.

[81]   OLG Frankfurt, 22.10.1980, VersR 1981, 164 (165); OLG München, 23.09.2004, TranspR 2005, 254 (255). For the conscious gross negligence cases, see BGH, 11.05.1953, BGHZ 10, 14 (17); BGH, 11.07.1967, VersR 1967, 909 (910); OLG Saarbrücken, 22.07.1983, VersR 1984, 880 (882). The danger of objective interpretation was also pointed by *Schoner*, p. 98.

[82]   *Cross & Tapper*, p. 31.

[83]   *Schröder*, pp. 13-14.

[84]   An evidentiary fact from which the judge could infer the existence of the fact at issue; for detailed information see *Cross & Tapper*, pp. 31 *et seqq.*, I *Wigmore, Evidence* § 25; *Zöller/Greger*, § 286 Rn. 9a; MünchKommZPO – *Prütting* § 284 Rn. 24-25; *Baumbach/Lauterbach/Albers/Hartmann*, Einf § 284 Rn. 16. For the difference between *prima facie* evidence and circumstantial evidence, see *Hoffmann*, pp. 77-78 und Enka *Pawlowski*, Der prima-facie-Beweis bei Schadenersatzansprüchen aus Delikt und Vertrag, Göttingen 1966, pp. 54-56.

[85]   *Cross & Tapper*, pp. 34-35; II *Wigmore, Evidence* § 371, §§ 190 *et seq.*, §§ 245 *et seq.*, §§ 300 *et seq.* (Chadbourn rev. 1979).

[86]   *Gran*, pp. 849-850; *Miller*, p. 217-218; *Ruhwedel*, p. 331; *Dettling-Ott*, p. 240; *Kuhn*, p. 205; *Stachow*, p. 218; *Müller-Rostin*, in: *Fremuth/Thume*, Art. 25 WA Rn. 13; *Rabe*, § 607a Rn. 23; *Neumann*, 420; *Berner v. British Commonwealth Pacific Airlines, Ltd.* (DC New York, 1963) 219 F.Supp. 289, 361 *per* Judge Ritter; *Saba v. Compagnie Nationale Air France* (CA, 1996) 78 F.3d 664, 669 *per* Judge Silberman; *Koirala v. Thai Airways International* (CA, 1997) 126 F.3d 1205, 1211 *per* Judge Thomas; BGE 98 II 231 (243) (11.07.1972); BGH, 16.02.1979, BGHZ 74, 162 (170-171); AG Rüsselheim, 20.10.1997, TranspR 1998, 199; BGE 128 III 390 (396) (06.06.2002).

advantage of the air carriers[87]. Another general proposition that a person facing a life threatening situation will react immediately constituted another *prima facie* evidence in the advantage of the air carriers. For instance, the calm state of the pilots despite the warnings of the navigation systems as to the impending crash risk constitutes evidence that the pilots were not aware that the plane would be crashing[88]. The court also did not consider the fact of a damaged cargo as sufficient for the inference of the subjective prerequisites of wilful misconduct[89]. Further, merely the fact that the checked baggage was lost, even in unexplained circumstances, was not found sufficient for an inference of wilful misconduct[90]. However, if the cargo, especially the valuable cargo gets lost under unknown circumstances, and the evidence shows that the possibility of theft by a third party is minor, this leads to the conclusion that it was stolen by the employees of the carrier[91].

Few detailed examples as to the application of the above mentioned principles by the courts would be helpful in understanding how these principles function. In the *Korean Air Lines Disaster* case, the crew of the flight were aware that the navigation system which shows the route of the flight was malfunctioning. Due to this fact, the flight deviated off-course, and since the crew knew that they should not fly without the relevant navigation system, they omitted to report their substantial deviation to the air traffic control centres along the route. Due to the substantial deviation the flight invaded the Soviet Union's territory prohibited for flights and was, as a result of this invasion, shot down by the Soviet military aircraft. The court took into account the facts of the duration and magnitude of the deviation, the malfunctioning navigation system and the persistent false reports as to the flight's position as circumstantial evidence, and stated that these facts lead, in a normal course of events, to the conclusion that the crew was, at all times, aware of the malfunctioning navigation system (*prima facie* evidence). The court, further, found that the crew was familiar with the route, and therefore knew that they were flying over Soviet territory prohibited for flights. The airlines' prior experience with Soviet interception procedures constituted another piece of circumstantial evidence for the court. In 1978, another plane of the same airline was forced down by Soviet military aircraft causing severe damage to the plane and the deaths of passengers. The court concluded that due to this experience, the crew had foreseen the probable consequences.

---

[87] *E.g.* BGH, 12.01.1982, TranspR 1982, 100 = VersR 1982, 369; OLG Frankfurt, 22.10.1980, VersR 1981, 164 = ZLW 1981, 87.

[88] BGE 113 II 359 (29.06.1987) = ETL 1988, 498 = ZLW 1988, 96.

[89] OLG München, 30.12.1994, TranspR 1995, 300 (302).

[90] *Iyegha v. United Airlines, Inc.* (Supreme Court of Alabama, 1995) 659 So.2d 45, 49 *per* Justice Almon; LG Hannover, 10.04.1997, RRa 1997, 204 (205); OLG München, 13.12.2001, TranspR 2004, 35; LG Köln, 11.12.2002, TranspR 2003, 204 (206).

[91] *Air Canada v. Swiss Bank Corporation et al.* (1988) 44 DLR (4th) 680 (Federal CA); BGH, 21.09.2000, ETL 2001, 248; LG Frankfurt, 16.01.1996, TranspR 1996, 424; LG Darmstadt, 24.09.2002, TranspR 2003, 114.

Another example is the *Pembroke* case. On a carriage from Germany to New Zealand, the cargo of roller chains packed in open top containers were loaded on the ship Pembroke and stowed under deck. However, at an intermediate port, some of the open top containers were displaced and stowed on deck. Stowage on deck was ordered by the master; however, the carrier and the master were in touch during the loading in Brazil. Due to the heavy weather conditions on the voyage, roller chains in one of the containers were rust damaged as a result of sea water taken on board in storms and heavy seas. The court took into account the circumstantial evidence of the master and the carrier being in touch at all times and concluded according to the human experience (*prima facie* evidence) that the carrier was kept fully informed and must have approved. The court, therefore, ruled that the carrier knew that the goods in the open top containers would probably be rust damaged since they were reloaded on deck, and since heavy weather conditions were expected; *i.e.* the carrier had subjective knowledge as to the probability of the damage occurred[92].

In another case, the court took a failure in the ship's engine as circumstantial evidence as to the absence of the subjective knowledge requirement. The ship Zim Pireaus, collided with the ship Leerort which was lying in berth. The collision caused damage in the Leerort's hull and subsequently cargo loss and damage. The reason for the collision was the excessive speed of the Zim Pireaus and a failure in her engine, which did not respond to the astern mode, then stopped, and finally worked in an emergency manoeuvring mode but did not start again in the astern mode. The court concluded according to the typical course of events (*prima facie* evidence) that an engine shutdown at a critical moment is just a coincidence and a 50 second engine failure cannot be attributed to the wilful misconduct of the shipowners[93].

2. Specific principles

Despite the standard of proof set by different jurisdictions in order to ease the burden on the claimant to prove subjective knowledge, it is still not a simple burden to discharge. However, there are some procedural principles applicable in certain jurisdictions which help claimants in discharging the burden. Two of these procedural principles are to be mentioned since they have played a special role in wilful misconduct cases and have caused uncertainty as to whether they result in a change in the burden of proof.

a) Procedural cooperation duty

The first principle is so-called procedural cooperation duty (*die prozessuale Mitwirkungspflicht*) under German procedural law. According to this principle, a

---

[92] *Nelson Pine Industries Ltd. v. Seatrans New Zealand Ltd. (The "Pembroke")* [1995] 2 Lloyd's Rep. 290 (New Zealand High Court).

[93] *Schiffahrtsgesellschaft MS "Merkur Sky" M.B.H. & Co. K.G. v. MS Leerort Nth Schiffahrts G.M.B.H. & Co. K.G. (The "Leerort")* [2001] 2 Lloyd's Rep. 291 (CA).

party in a civil law trial who is not carrying the burden of proof may be obliged to state and explain certain facts in order to support the procedure. Where a party under the onus of proof cannot explain some facts which have occurred entirely out of his field of influence and it is therefore impossible for him to provide the necessary information, the other party may be asked by the court for an explanation of the course of events which occurred in his field of influence, unless he also cannot explain them[94].

The same principle emerged from the good faith principle under Swiss and Austrian law[95]. Under Turkish law, it is accepted that under specific conditions the judge has the authority to rule that the party who is not carrying the burden of proof should carry the evidential burden. One of these specific circumstances is the case where the claimant carries the burden of proof yet the defendant has all the materials of proof[96]. Consequently, the procedural cooperation duty can be found in various civil law jurisdictions.

As a matter of course, this principle has been applied to transport law conflicts[97]. When all data is to be collected from the carrier's field of operation, the carrier is under the duty to elucidate at least the main outline of the course of events leading to the damage when it is possible for him to do so. If he does not meet this requirement, the allegations of the counter-party, mostly those of the claimant in carriage cases, will be deemed as proven[98]. The carrier is under the same duty even when he did not perform the carriage himself but through an agent; namely, the carrier must explain the chain of events which occurred in his agent's field as well[99].

---

[94]   *Zöller/Greger*, § 138 Rn. 8-8b; MünchKommZPO – *Wagner* § 138 Rn. 21-22; *Wieczorek/Schütze*, § 138 Rn. 107-109, 130; *Stachow*, pp. 210-211; *Koller*, CMR Art. 29 Rn. 7; *Herber/Piper*, Art. 29 Rn. 16; *Giefers*, pp. 206-207; *Koller, Aufklärung*, 559.

[95]   BGE 98 II 231 (243) (11.07.1972) and OGH, 29.11.2001, TranspR 2004, 36 = ETL 2002, 825; OGH, 14.07.1993, TranspR 1994, 189; *Herber/Schmuck*, 1212.

[96]   *Seven*, 77.

[97]   For an overview regarding the application of the principle to cases relating to passenger luggage by air carriage, see *Mühlbauer*, pp. 186-188. See also Nina Franziska *Marx*, Die Darlegungs- und Beweislast beim qualifizierten Verschulden im Transportrecht nach der aktuellen Rechtsprechung des Bundesgerichtshofs, TranspR 2010, 174.

[98]   MünchKommZPO – *Wagner* § 138 Rn. 21; *Wieczorek/Schütze*, § 110; *Stachow*, pp. 210-212; *Müller-Rostin*, in: *Fremuth/Thume*, Art. 25 WA Rn. 10; *Koller*, CMR Art. 29 Rn. 7; *Giefers*, p. 208; *Fremuth, Schwere Schuld*, pp. 166-167; *Seven*, 79; OLG Köln, 27.06.1995, TranspR 1996, 26 = ZLW 1997, 534 = NJW-RR 1997, 98; AG Frankfurt, 07.02.1997, TranspR 1997, 346; OLG Frankfurt, 14.09.1999, TranspR 2000, 260 (261-262); LG Frankfurt, 22.08.2000, TranspR 2001, 174 (175); OLG Köln, 26.03.2002, TranspR 2003, 111 (113); for the counterview see *Giemulla*, pp. 123-124.

[99]   *Gran*, p. 854; *Giemulla*, pp. 126-127 (only in cases that the carrier has control over the agent); *Koller*, CMR Art. 29 Rn. 7; *Koller, Aufklärung*, 559; OLG Hamburg, 07.02.1991, TranspR 1991, 294 (295); AG Frankfurt, 07.02.1997, TranspR 1997, 346 (348); OLG Frankfurt, 21.04.1998, TranspR 1999, 24; OGH, 20.01.2004, ETL

It has also been ruled by courts that the duty to explain does not violate the relevant conventions since it does not cause any change in the burden of proof[100]: once this secondary duty is met by the carrier, all necessary criteria are to be proven by the claimant[101]. In other words the risk of *non liquet* remains on the plaintiff[102]. The carrier is under the duty to explain and cooperate only for events leading to the damage, namely where and how the damage occurred. However, the duty does not require explicit details; a reproduction of events so far as the carrier or shipowner can explain is sufficient[103]. Accordingly, the duty does not create a presumption that the carrier is guilty of wilful misconduct[104], even when the carrier intentionally does not explain the chain of events. A result of the breach of the cooperation duty is that the objective facts claimed by the plaintiff are deemed to be proven, but not the wilful misconduct of the carrier. So the consequences to be suffered lie in the procedural law sphere, not in substantive law[105]. Moreover, one would be correct in saying that the procedural cooperation duty does not shift

---

2005, 122 (132); BGH, 04.03.2004, TranspR 2004, 460 (462). However see OLG Celle, 24.10.2002, TranspR 2003, 253 affirmed by BGH, 03.11.2005, NJW-RR 2006, 616.

[100] However, a German court ruled that the cooperation duty results in a change in the burden of proof since the good faith rule necessitates this change, see AG Frankfurt, 07.02.1997, TranspR 1997, 346 (348). This ruling has been criticised, see case comment by Dieter *Gran* in TranspR 1997, 349. The view that this principle causes a change in the burden of proof has been supported by some authors as well, together with the criticism and emphasis that it also violates the Warsaw Convention, see *Giemulla*, p. 121; *Giemulla/Schmid*, Art. 25 WA Rn. 51; for criticism from the CMR perspective see *Fremuth, Haftungsbegrenzungen*, 103-104.

[101] MünchKommZPO – *Wagner* § 138 Rn. 22; *Ruhwedel*, pp. 333, 385; *Herber/Piper*, Art. 29 Rn. 16; *Koller, Aufklärung*, 554; *Thume, CMR-Frachtführer*, 937; *Harms*, in: *Thume, CMR-Kommentar*, Art. 29 Rn. 95; *Fremuth, Schwere Schuld*, p. 169; *Giemulla/Schmid, Montrealer Übereinkommen*, Art. 22 MÜ Rn. 42; OLG Düsseldorf, 02.04.1992, TranspR 1992, 331 (332-333); OLG Köln, 27.06.1995, TranspR 1996, 26 (27); AG Rüsselheim, 20.10.1997, TranspR 1998, 199; BGH, 21.09.2000, ETL 2001, 248 (263-264); OLG Stuttgart, 11.06.2003, TranspR 2003, 308 (311). However see BGH, 04.03.2004, TranspR 2004, 460 (462); *Ruhwedel, Durchbrechung im Luftrecht*, 140.

[102] OLG Nürnberg, 10.12.1992, TranspR 1993, 138 (139). The case law in Germany has been ciriticized from this point, see *Fremuth, Schwere Schuld*, p. 170.

[103] *Giefers*, pp. 207-208; *Harms*, in: *Thume, CMR-Kommentar*, Art. 29 Rn. 91; *Koller, Aufklärung*, 557; *Thume, CMR-Frachtführer*, 937; *Seven*, 79-80; LG Hannover, 10.04.1997, RRa 1997, 204 (205); OLG Düsseldorf, 04.07.2001, TranspR 2002, 158 (159); LG Berlin, 04.02.2000, TranspR 2000, 181 (182); OLG Nürnberg, 10.12.1992, TranspR 1993, 138 (139).

[104] *Thume, CMR-Frachtführer*, 938; however see BGH, 04.03.2004, TranspR 2004, 460; 11. HD, 26.01.1999, E. 1998/5499, K. 1999/136 (YKD 1999/6, pp. 798-800); 11. HD, 06.12.2000, E. 2000/4546, K. 2000/5446 (*Erdil*, p. 378 (379)); 11. HD, 04.04.2005, E. 2004/6554, K. 2005/3212 (*Erdil*, p. 368 (370)). It was stressed that, under English law, the fact that the carrier refuses to give any explanation is not sufficient to raise a presumption of wilful misconduct, see *Kahn-Freund*, p. 260.

[105] *Gran*, p. 851.

the burden of proof; instead it merely shifts the evidentiary burden merely within a certain narrow scope[106].

As mentioned earlier[107], an inadequate organisational structure could cause the unlimited liability of the carrier if it is combined with subjective awareness[108]. The procedural cooperation duty is also applicable in organisational inadequacy cases. If the plaintiff claims that the damage resulted from the poor organisation on the carrier's side but cannot state exactly the organisational structure, then the carrier is obliged to explain his organisational structure, the events leading to the damage and the general organisational measures he has adopted in order to avoid similar damage. After the carrier's explanation, it is the claimant's burden to show recklessness and the subjective knowledge to be inferred from the facts before court[109]. However, if the carrier is charged with the duty to explain the "events from which his limited liability could emerge"[110], this effectively results in a presumption of wilful misconduct. This would be a change in the burden of proof[111] and a substantial violation of the regime set by various international conventions.

It is said that the procedural cooperation duty is not applicable where the personal conduct of the carrier or shipowner is necessary to break the limits of liability[112] and that the application of the duty will result in holding the carrier or shipowner liable for the wilful misconduct of his servants and agents which would like to be prevented by relevant international regimes[113]. This is not entirely correct. It is correct that an explanation of the chain of events leading to damage does not help the cargo owners if the fault is one of servants or agents. Nonetheless, the procedural cooperation duty is of great help in gathering the necessary documents

---

[106] *Stein/Jonas/Leipold*, § 138 Rn. 25-26, 37-38.

[107] See *supra* § 4 B II 1 b and § 4 B II 2 a; § 5 A I 1 e; § 6 B I 1 b bb. See also Jürgen *Basedow*/Christian *Jung*, Die Haftung der Paketdienste: Der Verlust von Sendungen als Problem der Betriebsorganisation und die Grenzen des groben Organisationsverschuldens, Heidelberg 1997, pp. 22-55.

[108] In a case arising out of a towage contract, the Hamburg Court of Appeal considered whether there was organisational inadequacy and personal fault, see OLG Hamburg, 26.05.1988, TranspR 1988, 433 (435).

[109] *Stachow*, pp. 212-214; *Koller*, CMR Art. 29 Rn. 7; *Ramming*, 307; BGH, 29.07.2009, HmbSchRZ 2009, 316 (320-321); OLG München, 07.05.1999, ZLW 2000, 118 (123); OLG München, 13.12.2001, TranspR 2004, 35; OLG Köln, 26.03.2002, TranspR 2003, 111 (113); LG Frankfurt, 27.01.1997, TranspR 1997, 236 (237); LG Köln, 11.12.2002, TranspR 2003, 204 (205-206); OGH, 29.11.2001, TranspR 2004, 36 (38).

[110] LG Hamburg, 25.02.1999, TranspR 1999, 401; OLG München, 07.05.1999, ZLW 2000, 118 (123).

[111] *Müller-Rostin*, in: *Fremuth/Thume*, Art. 25 WA Rn. 11; *Giefers*, p. 208; *Koller, Leichtfertigkeit*, 1358-1359.

[112] *Ilse*, p. 221.

[113] LG Bremen, 23.03.2005, HmbSeeRep 2005, 94 (95-96) ("*Canmar Pride*"); LG Bremen, 30.11.2005, HmbSchRZ 2009, 326 (330), however dismissed by HansOLG Bremen, 02.11.2006, HmbSchRZ 2009, 323 (326) and by BGH, 29.07.2009, HmbSchRZ 2009, 316 (320-321).

relating to the personal fault of the carrier or shipowner[114]. For instance, if a designated person pursuant to the ISM Code has a high position in the management structure and is involved in the decision making procedure of a shipowning company, this person's knowledge can be attributed to the company[115]. In such a case, documents produced in consequence of the observing and reporting duties under the ISM Code can be helpful to prove the designated person's state of mind. Undoubtedly, the procedural cooperation duty is the only way to oblige shipowning companies to submit those documents to the court.

A few examples will show how the procedural cooperation duty functions in practice. In one case, the air carrier had agreed to carry a carton of electronic devices by air. The electronic devices were, however, damaged. Allegedly, the carton was run over during the transport from the plane to the warehouse by one of the employees of the carrier. The court stated that the carton was relatively big, at least big enough that it is not possible to run it over and not notice it. Moreover, it was afterwards discovered that some of the electronic devices in the carton were missing, which permitted the court to come to the conclusion that they were stolen. The carrier refused to share the identity of the driver and the person who noticed and reported the damage, since, it was alleged, he was not able to identify them. The court ruled that the carrier did not provide the necessary information which would help to reveal further details and, therefore, did not fulfil his duty which indicates that there is intentional misconduct by the employees and that the carrier did not want to share this information. The court further stated that even if the carrier cannot, indeed, identify the relevant persons, this shows that there is inadequate organisational structure. This inadequacy allows the employees to act or omit recklessly, since they know that they would not be held accountable. As a result, the carrier was liable for the damages without any financial limit[116].

In another case arising from the air carriage of an electronic device from the USA to Düsseldorf via Amsterdam in 1998, the cargo has never been delivered to the consignee. According to the plaintiff's research, the cargo got lost after it was delivered to the cargo handling agency of the carrier in Düsseldorf which, in fact, was a subsidiary company of the air carrier. The plaintiff also provided information that there had been organised theft in this cargo handling agency since 1997 where lots of employees were involved. A criminal procedure had already been started. The plaintiff believed that his cargo was also stolen during this criminal activity. The air carrier responded that the plaintiff only guessed that the cargo got lost when it was in the cargo handling agency's custody and that the air carrier did not know where, when and under which circumstances the cargo got missing. The court stated that an explanation of the structure of the transportation process and the precautions taken by the carrier to prevent similar damage is necessary in order to fulfil the procedural cooperation duty. In the case, the air carrier failed to fulfil his duty which *prima facie* indicates that the loss occurred under the circum-

---

[114] See also *Ramming*, 307-308.
[115] For more information see *supra* § 5 E II 2 b, and more generally see supra § 5 E.
[116] OLG Köln, 27.06.1995, TranspR 1996, 26 = ZLW 1997, 534 = NJW-RR 1997, 98.

stances the plaintiff had explained. In conclusion, the loss was caused intentionally and, therefore, the carrier was not entitled to limit his liability.

Procedural cooperation duty has recently been used in a case involving the maritime carriage of cargo as well. In the case which was arisen from the carriage of the gondola of a wind turbine, and the facts of which were mentioned in detail earlier[117], the gondola had fallen over together with the flat rack on which it was carried due to the insufficient lashing which was caused by the incorrect information as to the gondola's weight in the loading and stowage plans. The carrier was asked to explain under which circumstances the weight of the gondola was incorrectly given in the loading and stowage plans. He was, further, asked to explain what kind of instructions he had given to prevent damages, if he had given any, and what kind of measures he had taken for supervising whether his instructions were followed. The carrier was not able to explain any of these facts, and therefore, both the Hanseatic Court of Appeal of Bremen and the German Federal Court ruled that the lack of explanation creates a rebuttable presumption of fact that there is inadequate organisational structure, and that the carrier was guilty of wilful misconduct[118]. It must be stressed here that both courts drew the conclusion as to the subjective awareness not from the facts, but from the failure to fulfil the procedural cooperation duty. The carrier's failure to explain the reasons for the incorrect records as to the weight of the gondola, the instructions he had given and the supervision measures created a rebuttable presumption of an inadequate organisational structure. It was also the carrier's personal fault[119]. However, the circumstances why the courts assumed that the carrier was subjectively aware that the damage would probably occur have not been explained in the decisions. As a result, this leads to the conclusion, that the courts presumed the wilful misconduct of the carrier.

b) *Res ipsa loquitur*

The doctrine of *res ipsa loquitur*, also known as *res ipsa*, means literally "the thing speaks for itself"[120]. The doctrine was conceived in order to support claimants and judges in cases where necessary evidence regarding circumstances leading to an unusual event, such as injury or accident, cannot be submitted[121]. Under this doctrine, it is possible to presume or infer negligence on the part of the opposing party in tort cases[122].

According to the *res ipsa* doctrine, if a factor which caused an unusual event was under the control or management of the opposing party and if the unusual

---

[117] See *supra* § 5 A I 1 e.

[118] HansOLG Bremen, 02.11.2006, HmbSchRZ 2009, 323 (326) affirmed by BGH, 29.07.2009, HmbSchRZ 2009, 316 (321).

[119] See *supra* § 5 A I 1 e.

[120] *Speiser*, § 1:1; Restatement (Second) of Torts, § 328 D (*a*) (*Res ipsa loquitur*); *Porat/Stein*, p. 84.

[121] *Speiser*, §§ 1:2, 1:3; *Porat/Stein*, p. 85.

[122] *Speiser*, § 1:5; however the procedural effect is still disputed, see Restatement (Second) of Torts, § 328 D (*m*) (*Res ipsa loquitur*).

event would not have occurred if this party would have used proper care in the ordinary course of control or management, then there is reasonable evidence that the unusual event was caused by the negligence of the opposing party[123]. However, the circumstances surrounding the unusual event should be of such a character that, in light of general knowledge and past experience, they justify a presumption of negligence[124]. Once the presumption of negligence has arisen, it is the opposing party's burden to explain, in other words his burden to offer necessary evidence, that the unusual event was not the result of his negligence[125]. It is said that the *res ipsa* doctrine does not shift the burden of proof; rather, it shifts the evidentiary burden[126].

The *res ipsa* doctrine is applicable in transportation cases as well[127]. However, if the general structure of the relevant international conventions is taken into consideration, it is clear there is no need for the *res ipsa* doctrine under those regimes since their liability system is based, at the least, on presumed fault. Moreover, the *res ipsa* doctrine creates a presumption of ordinary negligence. Therefore, it is not applicable where the claimant needs to prove more than ordinary negligence. Namely, the doctrine of *res ipsa* is inapplicable in wilful misconduct cases[128]. Furthermore, if the application of the doctrine were accepted for wilful misconduct cases, this would result in a change in the burden of proof since the carrier would be under the obligation of proving that he has not committed wilful misconduct. Clearly, this would be a violation of the regime set by the relevant international conventions.

III. Result

The burden of proof placed on the claimant is not an easy one. Due to this difficulty, the burden of proving wilful misconduct of the carrier or his agents and servants is a *probatio diabolica* (devil's proof)[129], if not impossible[130]. Naturally,

---

[123] Restatement (Second) of Torts, § 328 D (*a*) (*g*) (*Res ipsa loquitur*); *Speiser*, § 1:1; IX *Wigmore, Evidence* § 2509 (Chadbourn rev. 1981); *Prosser and Keeton*, pp. 248-251 (criticising the "control" test); *Hoffmann*, pp. 41, 82-108; *Porat/Stein*, p. 84; *Johnson v. American Airlines, Inc.* (CA, 1987) 834 F.2d 721, 724.

[124] Restatement (Second) of Torts, § 328 D (*c*) (*d*) (*Res ipsa loquitur*); *Prosser and Keeton*, pp. 244-248.

[125] *Speiser*, § 1:1; *Porat/Stein*, p. 85.

[126] *Speiser*, § 3:14, *Porat/Stein*, p. 89; see also Restatement (Second) of Torts, § 328 D (*n*) (*Res ipsa loquitur*). However, it is also pointed out that in cases where the strong presumptive effect has been accepted, the doctrine shifts the burden of proof, namely the persuasive burden, see *Porat/Stein*, p. 92 *et seq.*

[127] Restatement (Second) of Torts, § 328 D (*b*) (*Res ipsa loquitur*) and see generally *Speiser*, §§ 10, 12.

[128] *Speiser*, § 3:2; Restatement (Second) of Torts, § 328 D (*j*) (*Res ipsa loquitur*); *Johnson v. American Airlines, Inc.* (CA, 1987) 834 F.2d 721, 724 *per* Judge Farris; *Onyeanusi v. Pan American World Airways, Inc.* (DC Pennsylvania, 1990) 1990 WL 84774, 3 *per* Judge Ludwig.

[129] *Guerreri*, p. 14.

this heavy burden has resulted in a limited number of cases where the unlimited liability of the carrier or shipowner has been claimed[131]. In order to ease the *probatio diabolica*, case law has eased the burden of proof by ruling that *prima facie* evidence and circumstantial evidence is sufficient for a finding of wilful misconduct. Moreover, the procedural cooperation duty under the procedural law regime of several countries further assists the claimants in balancing the procedural disadvantage[132] or hopelessness[133].

Although it is just and reasonable to assist the claimants with such a heavy burden, the manner of assistance has resulted in some small divergences in practice, variations which are inevitable since the procedural matters are solely subject to *lex fori*[134]. However, as important as the result of the divergences caused by the standard of proof is, it is also important to ask whether the standard set by different jurisdictions results in equivalence between the objective and subjective interpretations. This poses a significant problem, especially when the language of the provision is vague, such as "wilful misconduct and equivalent fault". The answer to this question will determine whether all the efforts to improve the unification of law have come to nothing or not.

The discussion arising out of this criticism claims that there is no differentiation between the objective and subjective interpretations of the degree of fault set by the international conventions as long as the subjective awareness can be proven by *prima facie* and circumstantial evidence[135] – so-called "relaxed evidentiary requirements"[136]. The discussion is worth analysing, but first it should be emphasised that there is certainly some validity to the criticism since judges are sometimes careless on this point and draw conclusions, *i.e.* make inferences, too easily[137].

Turning to the criticism, firstly, substantive law and procedural law requirements should be handled separately. The biggest difference between the objective and subjective tests arises on the point of the wrongdoer's actual state of mind. Knowledge of the possible consequences of the misconduct is necessary for a finding of wilful misconduct; however, since a breach of the average duty of care in a grave manner is sufficient under an objective interpretation the effect is that the degree of fault is reduced to gross negligence. Actual knowledge is not a necessary element for a finding of gross negligence; it is sufficient that the actor failed to show necessary care.

---

[130] *Georgiades*, p. 45; *Matte, ETL*, p. 885; *Ruhwedel*, pp. 330-331; *Chen, Limitation*, p. 75; Regula *Dettling-Ott*, Internationales und nationales Lufttransportrecht im Widerstreit, ASDA Bulletin 1989/1-2, pp. 29-32.

[131] *Matte, ETL*, p. 885.

[132] *Mühlbauer*, p. 185.

[133] *Ruhwedel*, pp. 330-331.

[134] *Clarke, Carriage by Air*, p. 158; *Risch*, pp. 60-61.

[135] *Goldhirsch*, p. 154; *Miller*, pp. 214-215; *Schoner, Rechtsprechung 1974-1976*, pp. 262-263; *Schobel*, p. 81; Frederick P. *Alimonti*, Recent Developments in Aviation Liability Law, (1998-1999) 64 J. Air L. & Com. 29, 77.

[136] *Miller*, p. 214.

[137] *E.g.* see *McGilchrist*, pp. 540-541.

Secondly, implication of the actual state of mind from circumstantial evidence is a matter of procedural law and it does not change the necessary elements to be proved[138]. Thus, the result that it has been easier for courts to make a finding of gross negligence compared to a finding of wilful misconduct is still valid[139]. The difference was articulated clearly in the *Cortes* case[140]:

"The difference, when the tests are put into practice, is a fine one. The objective test is satisfied if a grave risk is sufficiently obvious, because the person "should have" been aware of the risk regardless of whether he actually recognized it. [...]. The subjective test, on the other hand, precludes a finding of liability if the fact-finder concludes that, even though a grave risk is obvious, no inference can be made that the actor actually became aware of the risk. [...] ("That a trier of fact may infer knowledge from the obvious ... does not mean that it must do so."). In this way, a plaintiff may rely solely upon circumstantial evidence related to the obviousness of a grave risk to satisfy both tests, but the subjective test is satisfied only if the circumstances also permit an inference that the actor "must have known" about the risk. [...]. "It is not enough merely to find that a reasonable person would have known, or that the defendant should have known," of the risk. [...]. Thus, while an objective test asks whether an actor "should have known" of an obvious risk, the subjective test requires, at a minimum, a showing that the actor "must have known" of the risk."

Although this concludes the issue, it can be emphasised that an important difference exists between subjective and objective interpretations, though a subtle one. Although both tests may be satisfied with the same circumstantial evidence, the objective test will only require an inference as to what the defendant should have been aware of while the subjective test requires the more substantial inference as to what the defendant was actually aware of. Moreover, an inference must not be made solely from the obviousness of the risk, but other factors surrounding the occurrence must show that the wrongdoer was aware of the probable consequences.

---

[138] *Stachow*, p. 131 fn. 3; *Gaskell, Hamburg Rules*, p. 166 fn. 164.

[139] *Saba v. Compagnie Nationale Air France* (CA, 1996) 78 F.3d 664, 669 *per* Judge Silberman: "Intent can, of course, always be proved through circumstantial evidence. That is by no means the same thing as saying the defendant *should* have known about the danger." (Emphasis in original).

[140] *Piamba Cortes v. American Airlines* (CA, 1999) 177 F.3d 1272, 1291 *per* Judge Birch.

§ 8 Degrees of Fault and Wilful Misconduct

Amongst other topics, one of the most controversial issues with regard to wilful misconduct or its definition is its equivalent under civil law. If one looks at the literature, it is very clear that wilful misconduct initially covers the gravest fault degree, *i.e.* intentional wrongdoing. However, there are several views as to the equivalent fault degree of recklessness coupled with the foresight of the probable consequences. It is possible to say that the question to exactly which degree of fault the phrase "recklessly and with knowledge that damage would probably occur" exactly refers has remained unanswered so far.

For the sake of international unification, definitions given by the international conventions should not be classified in national terms, since the main aim by defining the degree of fault instead of referring to national terms is to achieve the uniform application of the provisions regarding the breaking the limits[1]. However, there have been attempts to designate the degree of fault that is equivalent to wilful misconduct, or to its definition, under civil law. To this end, first the fault defined by the relevant international conventions should be compared with the common law fault concepts so that the prerequisites of the degree of fault are clarified. Subsequently, the definitions and prerequisites of the civil law fault concepts should be analysed and, thereafter, compared with the prerequisites of wilful misconduct so that the equivalent degree of fault under civil law can be determined. For the purpose of the analysis, not only the degrees of fault as referred to in private law but also those used in criminal law will be taken into consideration, since fault concepts are examined in a more detailed manner under criminal law and since there are no great differences between the definition of fault under criminal and private law[2].

A. Wilful Misconduct under Common Law

The fault element of a tort or crime is divided into several categories. The categories are almost the same under criminal and tort law, albeit with some small differences in their naming and grouping. Under criminal law, the fault element is analysed basically under three forms: intention, recklessness and negligence. It is analysed under three forms under tort law as well: malice, intention and negligence. Malice, as will be seen, is a type of intention[3]. Intention, under tort law, covers also recklessness[4]. Consequently, the degrees of fault under tort law are classified in a more compact manner. Therefore, degrees of fault, here, will be analysed according to the detailed classification under criminal law.

---

[1] *Fremuth, Haftungsbegrenzungen*, 101; *Jesser*, 172; *Starck*, p. 132; *Clarke, CMR*, pp. 4-5; *Gaskell, Breaking Limits*, p. 5; *Gençtürk*, p. 248; *Yetiş Şamlı*, p. 96.
[2] *Goldschmidt*, p. 12.
[3] See *infra* A I 1.
[4] *Markesinis and Deakin*, pp. 30-31; *Winfield & Jolowicz*, para. 3-3.

I. Intention

First of all, an important distinction should be emphasized between the two possibilities of what the term intention can signify. Intention can cover, above all, both the act or omission and the results of that act or omission. Nevertheless, intention can also be related only to the act, but not to the results of that act[5]. Intention as to the act alone is sufficient for committing some torts under English tort law[6], *e.g.* in trespass to land.

Nonetheless, intention signifies the guilty state of mind of a wrongdoer who foresees and desires a particular consequence[7]. However, for the purposes of English tort law, intention still lacks an exact definition. There are several reasons behind this situation. Firstly, cases of intentional torts are not frequent. Secondly, it is easier to sue a wrongdoer under the tort of negligence, which covers a wide area, than under an intentional tort. Finally, although intention must cover all elements of a crime, that is not the case under tort law as intention or foresight might not be necessary regarding the consequences of an act or omission[8]. Therefore, the definition of intention given for criminal matters is of great help in ascertaining the elements of intention.

When does a person act intentionally? The answer to this question provides the definition and elements of intention. "A person acts "intentionally" with respect to a result when he or she acts either: (1) in order to bring it about, or (2) knowing that it will be virtually certain to occur; or (3) knowing that it would be virtually certain to occur if he or she were to succeed in his or her purpose of causing some other result"[9]. In the light of this definition, intention is subdivided into two categories: direct intention and oblique intention.

1. Direct (purposive) intention

There is no controversy as to what direct intention is. If a person acts or makes an omission in order to produce a particular result, which has been his purpose and which is a consequence of his act or omission, he acts or makes an omission with direct intention[10]. For instance, if A throws a stone at a window for the purpose of breaking that window, A has direct intention in breaking that window. This gravest degree of fault, which requires both the motive of causing harm and unlawful

---

[5]   *Street*, p. 236.

[6]   It must be remembered that, during the drafting period of the Warsaw Convention, the difference between intention as to the act and the intention as to the act and the results of the act caused the confusion as to the term *dol*, see *supra* § 4 A I 1.

[7]   *Markesinis and Deakin*, p. 31; *Williams/Hepple*, pp. 91, 94.

[8]   *Winfield & Jolowicz*, para. 3-2.

[9]   Law Commission Consultation Paper No. 177 (2005), para. 4.3. For a similar definition *Report, Criminal Code*, p. 8.

[10] *Smith & Hogan*, pp. 97-98; *Card, Cross & Jones*, pp. 77-78; *Padfield*, p. 41; *Prosser and Keeton*, p. 34; *Report, Criminal Code*, p. 9.

conduct, is called malice under English tort law[11]. There is no doubt that direct intention is the gravest degree of fault and is covered by the definition of wilful misconduct, as direct intention necessitates a harmful result and the intention to create that result, *i.e.* "an act or omission done with intent to cause damage".

2. Oblique intention

If a person's purpose is not to cause a specific result, but if he actually knows that his act or omission will result in a virtually certain (inevitable, inseparable) consequence in the ordinary course of events, it is accepted that he acts or makes an omission with intention as well, even though he does not intend to cause the specific result in question. This type of intention is called oblique intention[12].

For instance, A wants to hit B with a stone. B is standing behind a window. A throws the stone and hits B. Naturally, before hitting B, the stone breaks the window. A had no intention to break the window, but he actually knew that by throwing the stone the window would be certainly (necessarily)[13] be broken. Accordingly, the act of breaking the window has been committed with oblique intention[14].

Oblique intention also covers the results known to be almost certain to accompany achievement of an illicit purpose, *i.e.* side effects. The classical example of this type of oblique intention is that A puts a bomb on a plane to collect cargo insurance compensation. Although he has no purpose of killing the crew, the virtually certain result of a bomb explosion on a plane is that everyone on board will be killed. Therefore, intention here covers also the death of the crew[15].

Thus, the motive behind the act or omission is not important in determining the oblique intention. It was stated that "[a] man who at London Airport, boards a plane which he knows to be bound for Manchester, clearly intends to travel to Manchester, even though Manchester is the last place he wants to be and his motive for boarding the plane is simply to escape pursuit. The possibility that the plane may have engine trouble and be diverted to Luton does not affect the matter. By boarding the Manchester plane, the man conclusively demonstrates his intention to go there, because it is a moral certainty that that is where he will arrive."[16]. Analogously, it was said that if a carrier allows perishable goods to perish when he brings a passenger to hospital, he intends the damage to goods since the result-

---

[11] *Clerk & Lindsell*, para. 1-57 *et seq.*; *Winfield & Jolowicz*, para. 3-8; *Markesinis and Deakin*, pp. 30-31.

[12] *Report, Criminal Code*, pp. 9-10; *Smith & Hogan*, pp. 98-99; *Card, Cross & Jones*, pp. 77, 83-85; *Padfield*, p. 43. *Report, Criminal Code*, p. 10: "the definition of "intention" should treat a person as intending a result that he knows to be, in the ordinary course of events, a necessary concomitant of achieving his main purpose *if* that purpose is achieved".

[13] *Report, Criminal Code*, p. 10.

[14] *Report, Criminal Code*, p. 9; *Smith & Hogan*, p. 102.

[15] *Report, Criminal Code*, p. 9; *Smith & Hogan*, p. 103; *Card, Cross & Jones*, pp. 79-80.

[16] *Regina v. Moloney* [1985] A.C. 905, 926 (HL) *per* Lord Bridge.

ing damage is virtually certain, and it plays no role whether the carrier's purpose is to damage the goods[17].

All the facts of a case should be considered in order to determine whether the carrier has acted or failed to act with oblique intention. If a carrier agrees to carry a sick passenger to a hospital although he has concluded another agreement to ship perishable goods, and he knows that the goods will perish in the course of transporting the passenger to the hospital, reference can be made to oblique intention. However, if a passenger's health status during a flight creates an emergency requiring that the passenger be immediately taken to a hospital, and, in so doing, the goods perish, it cannot be said that the carrier caused the damage to the goods with oblique intention since the health situation of the passenger constituted a necessity and the carrier had no other choice. Therefore, reference cannot be made to misconduct.

It is also clear that the definition "act or omission done with intent to cause damage" covers oblique intention, since oblique intention entails both misconduct and wilfulness.

II. Recklessness

If a person does not intend to cause any harm, but nevertheless accepts an unjustifiable risk of causing it, he is reckless[18]. Thus, recklessness can be defined broadly as taking an unjustifiable risk[19]. More broadly, a person is reckless if he is aware that a specific risk will probably occur under the circumstances known to him, yet he, nevertheless, takes this unreasonable and unjustified risk[20]. In the case of both oblique intention and recklessness, the wrongdoer foresees the risk. However, under recklessness, the results of the risk are not regarded by the wrongdoer as inevitable and virtually certain[21]. Nonetheless, recklessness is called "quasi-intent"[22], signifying a classification with intention[23].

Recklessness involves knowledge of the unjustifiable risk. Knowledge can refer to the actual state of mind of the wrongdoer, or it can be constructed according to a certain standard. From this point of view, recklessness can be divided into the two sub-classifications of subjective and objective recklessness.

1. Subjective (advertent) recklessness

If a person is actually aware, *i.e.* conscious of the existence of the unjustifiable risk, his recklessness is subjective, or in other words, his conduct is classified as

---

[17] *Clarke, CIM*, p. 31.
[18] *Report, Criminal Code*, p. 11; *Smith & Hogan*, p. 107. In American law, recklessness is also called wanton or wilful misconduct.
[19] *Padfield*, p. 50.
[20] *Card, Cross & Jones*, p. 91; *Williams/Hepple*, p. 92; *Dobbs*, p. 51.
[21] *Report, Criminal Code*, p. 10; *Card, Cross & Jones*, pp. 91-92; *Markesinis and Deakin*, p. 31; *Prosser and Keeton*, p. 36; *Dobbs*, p. 52.
[22] *Prosser and Keeton*, p. 212.
[23] *Williams/Hepple*, p. 92; *Dobbs*, p. 52.

advertent recklessness. It is subjective, because it focuses on the wrongdoer's own perceptions as to the existence of the unjustifiable risk[24]. It is very important to note that the foresight of a risk alone is not sufficient to constitute recklessness. The risk known or foreseen must be an unreasonable risk, *i.e.* an unjustifiable one[25].

It is generally accepted that the knowledge requirement of wilful misconduct necessitates actual knowledge of the wrongdoer. The actual knowledge must cover the probable consequences of the act or omission (unjustifiable risk)[26]. Therefore, the conduct described as "recklessly and with knowledge that damage would probably result" necessitates a subjective interpretation.

2. Objective (inadvertent) recklessness

Unlike subjective recklessness, the wrongdoer need not be actually aware of the unjustifiable risk under objective recklessness. It is sufficient for a finding of objective recklessness that a reasonable person would have seen the risk, even if the wrongdoer did not see it[27]. Therefore, a person is objectively reckless when he should have seen the unjustifiable risk. It should be noted that the objective definition of recklessness overlaps with negligence[28].

Objective recklessness no longer plays a role in English criminal law[29]. Similarly, it should also not be taken into consideration in transport law cases since it does not fulfil the "actual knowledge" prerequisite which attaches to the degree of fault of wilful misconduct.

III. Negligence

1. Definition

Negligence is defined simply as the inadvertent taking of an unjustifiable risk[30]. Accordingly, a person is negligent if he does not realise a risk where he ought to have been aware of it[31]. However, a person is also negligent if he has foreseen the risk, but unreasonably considered that either there was no risk or that the risk was minor such that taking it was justifiable[32]. Negligence can be in the form of the commission or omission of an act. If a person does not take any precautions to

---

[24] *Smith & Hogan*, p. 108; *Clerk & Lindsell*, para. 1-59.
[25] *Card, Cross & Jones*, pp. 91-92.
[26] See *supra* § 4 B 1 2 c bb (2).
[27] *Smith & Hogan*, p. 111.
[28] See *infra* III. See also *Dobbs*, p. 52.
[29] *Smith & Hogan*, p. 114.
[30] *Smith & Hogan*, p. 116; *Winfield & Jolowicz*, para. 3-4; *Dobbs*, p. 50.
[31] *Card, Cross & Jones*, pp. 100-102; *Smith & Hogan*, p. 116; *Markesinis and Deakin*, p. 31; *Williams/Hepple*, p. 92.
[32] *Smith & Hogan*, p. 116; *Markesinis and Deakin*, p. 31.

avoid a risk, or if the precautions he took were inadequate, his conduct falls below the required standard and, consequently, he is negligent[33].

Consequently, "[n]egligence is the omission to do something which a reasonable man, guided upon those considerations which ordinarily regulate the conduct of human affairs, would do, or doing something which a prudent and reasonable man would not do."[34]. Thus, the standard in determining negligence is the standard of reasonable person[35].

2. Degrees of negligence

In English law, it is generally said that there are no degrees of negligence[36]. The reasoning behind this statement is that, under English tort law, if someone acts below the necessary standard and causes physical injury to a person or damage to goods, he is liable under tort of negligence. It is of no importance how far below the objective standard he fell. However, a new approach states that there are in fact degrees of negligence. Since negligence is a failure to comply with an objective standard, "[o]ne person may fall just short of the required standard of conduct, another may fall far short."[37]. Therefore, a higher degree of negligence is called gross negligence[38].

In American law, there are two different approaches: degrees of negligence and degrees of care. American courts mostly adopt the degrees of care approach. However, under some torts, statutes and judicial opinions, the idea of gross negligence has been adopted[39]. Accordingly, slight negligence is defined as the "failure to exercise great care, which persons of extraordinary prudence and foresight are accustomed to use"; and gross negligence is defined as the "failure to exercise care which a careless person would use"[40]. So, slight and gross negligence are different from each other only in degree, not in kind[41].

---

[33] *Card, Cross & Jones*, p. 100; *Markesinis and Deakin*, p. 223; *Williams/Hepple*, p. 94.

[34] *Blyth v. Birmingham Waterworks Co.* (1856) 11 Exch. 781, 784 *per* Justice Alderson.

[35] For more information *Markesinis and Deakin*, pp. 223-224, 227, 232-235; *Winfield & Jolowicz*, para. 3-6; *Prosser and Keeton*, pp. 173-175; *Williams/Hepple*, p. 114; *Smith & Hogan*, pp. 141-142; *Card, Cross & Jones*, p. 100; *Padfield*, p. 55; *Clerk & Lindsell*, para. 1-64.

[36] *Markesinis and Deakin*, p. 31; *Clerk & Lindsell*, para. 1-55.

[37] *Smith & Hogan*, p. 146.

[38] *Card, Cross & Jones*, p. 105. The Law Commission Consultation Paper No. 177 (2005), para. 3.55 makes also mention of gross negligence.

[39] *Prosser and Keeton*, pp. 209-211.

[40] For the definitions see *Prosser and Keeton*, pp. 211-212.

[41] *Prosser and Keeton*, p. 212.

3. Negligence and wilful misconduct

It is clear that what is called slight negligence is the lowest degree of fault and falls far from recklessness and wilful misconduct[42]. Nevertheless, negligence – or gross negligence – differs from recklessness since recklessness necessitates a conscious knowledge of an unjustifiable risk, whereas negligence does not necessitate actual knowledge[43]. Although a negligent person can also foresee the risk, he considers it one which is justifiably taken[44], unlike recklessness. More importantly, negligence is determined according to the objective standard of the reasonable person, whereas intention, recklessness and wilful misconduct necessitate an examination of the wrongdoer's actual state of mind[45].

B. Wilful Misconduct under Civil Law

The gravest part of wilful misconduct, *i.e.* causing specific damage with intent to cause it, does not pose any problems for civil lawyers. Nevertheless, the degree of fault to which it refers will be stated below[46]. However, the second part of wilful misconduct, *i.e.* recklessness with knowledge that damage would probably result, causes difficulties in determining the equivalent degree of fault. There have been a variety of views on the issue ranging from gross negligence to *dolus eventualis*. Some have even said that this second part of wilful misconduct cannot be classified under any degree of fault in civil law[47]. Whether this is really so will be examined in this section.

The main distinction between degrees of fault under civil law lies in negligence and intention. These forms are also subdivided. Negligence is divided into slight (ordinary) negligence and gross negligence. Intention is divided into direct intention and *dolus eventualis*. Nonetheless, all these subdivisions are not thoroughly explained under tort law, since both under Turkish (BK (1926) Art. 41, BK (2011) Art. 49) and German law (§ 823 BGB) slight negligence is sufficient for tort liability[48]. Therefore, the detailed explanations found in criminal law will also receive some attention during the comparison.

---

[42] *McNair*, p. 190.

[43] *Padfield*, p. 55; *Smith & Hogan*, p. 116; *Prosser and Keeton*, p. 212; *Clarke, CMR*, p. 320.

[44] *Smith & Hogan*, p. 116.

[45] *Card, Cross & Jones*, p. 105; *Smith & Hogan*, p. 141; *Dobbs*, p. 50.

[46] See *infra* II 1.

[47] *Çağa, Batider*, p. 301; explanations by Professor *Çağa*, in: discussions, *Kender, Atina Konvansiyonu*, pp. 123-124; OLG Frankfurt, 22.10.1980, VersR 1981, 164 (165); affirmed by BGH, 12.01.1982, TranspR 1982, 100 = VersR 1982, 369.

[48] On the question of fault under German tort law see Ulrich *Magnus*/Gerhard *Seher*, Fault under German Law, in: P. Widmer (Editor), Unification of Tort Law: Fault, The Hague 2005, pp. 101 *et seqq.*

I. Negligence (culpa, Fahrlässigkeit, ihmal)

Under civil law, negligence is not a specific type of tort, but only a degree of fault[49]. In this respect, there is no need to make a distinction between different usages of the same term, whereas there is such a need under common law.

Negligence necessitates a duty, whether arising out of a general duty of care or from a contract, and involves a harmful result which could have been avoided had the wrongdoer shown the necessary care[50]. Care is the ordinary care expected from an average ordinary person (*bonus pater familias*). Thus, negligence is determined according to this objective and abstract criterion[51]. The reason for having such an objective criterion is the idea of preserving the general reliance on every person having the necessary qualifications and skills to fulfil his duties[52].

Thus, in instances where an ordinary person would have foreseen and avoided the harmful result, an individual who fails to do so is negligent[53]. However, avoidance of every harmful result cannot be expected; the individual need only avoid what the ordinary person would have avoided under similar circumstances[54].

Negligent behaviour can be in the form of an act's commission or omission. Although an act or omission should be an intentional one, in cases of negligence the wrongdoer does not wish the harmful result to occur[55]. The facts of each case should be considered in order to determine whether the wrongdoer is negligent. Though the criterion is objective, the circumstances which affect the wrongdoer's conduct should also be taken into consideration. In this sense, for instance, com-

---

[49] *Palandt/Grüneberg*, § 276 Rn. 12.

[50] *Palandt/Grüneberg*, § 276 Rn. 12; *Tandoğan*, pp. 48-49; *Tekinay/et al.*, p. 494; *Oğuzman/Öz*, p. 529; *Karahasan*, p. 488; *Kılıçoğlu*, p. 255; *Eren*, p. 537; *Güven II*, p. 154; *Atamer, Nedensellik Bağı*, p. 31; *Schönke/Schröder*, § 15 Rn. 116; LeipKommStGB – *Vogel*, § 15 Rn. 212-213; *Demirbaş*, p. 347; *Artuk/Gökcen/Yenidünya*, pp. 508, 510; *Özgenç*, p. 250; *Kırman*, p. 156.

[51] *Palandt/Grüneberg*, § 276 Rn. 15, § 823 Rn. 43; *Larenz*, p. 284; *Staudinger/Löwisch* (2001), § 276 Rn. 25; MünchKommBGB – *Grundmann*, § 276 Rn. 55; Erman/*Westermann*, § 276 Rn. 10; *Tandoğan*, pp. 50-51; *Tekinay/et al.*, p. 494 fn. 3; *Güven II*, pp. 156-157; *Karahasan*, p. 489-490; *Kılıçoğlu*, pp. 255-256; *Eren*, p.537; *Kühl*, § 15 Rn. 37-38; *Dönmezer*, p. 210; *Toroslu*, p. 197.

[52] *Palandt/Grüneberg*, § 276 Rn. 15; *Larenz*, p. 286; Staudinger/*Löwisch* (2001), § 276 Rn. 25; MünchKommBGB – *Grundmann*, § 276 Rn. 54; *Tandoğan*, p. 51; *Atamer, Nedensellik Bağı*, p. 31; *Tekinay/et al.*, p. 494 fn. 3; *Eren*, pp. 531, 537-538; *Güven II*, pp. 157-158; *Roxin*, § 24 Rn. 21; *Schönke/Schröder*, § 15 Rn. 149; LeipKommStGB – *Vogel*, § 15 Rn. 225. See also *Dönmezer*, pp. 211-212.

[53] *Palandt/Grüneberg*, § 276 Rn. 12, 21; *Marsilius*, 297; *Schönke/Schröder*, § 15 Rn. 174; *Dönmezer*, p. 213.

[54] In criminal law, the criterion is the social adequacy, see *Schönke/Schröder*, § 15 Rn. 127; *Roxin*, § 24 Rn. 39; LeipKommStGB – *Vogel*, § 15 Rn. 214; *Toroslu*, p. 203.

[55] *Goldschmidt*, p. 104; LeipKommStGB – *Vogel*, § 15 Rn. 62; *Karahasan*, p. 488; *Kılıçoğlu*, p. 255; *Demirbaş*, pp. 347-348; *Dönmezer*, p. 212; *Artuk/Gökcen/Yenidünya*, pp. 495-496; *Toroslu*, p. 198.

mercial practices can be determinative[56]. The higher the probability of the harmful result happening, the higher the degree of care expected[57]. Nevertheless, the assessment should be made according to the situation present at the time of the examined wrongful conduct. If, under the circumstances, the conduct appears to be normal according to the objective criterion, the person in question is not negligent[58].

1. Slight negligence (*culpa levis, einfache Fahrlässigkeit, hafif ihmal*)

The lowest degree of fault is slight negligence. Under contract law principles, slight negligence is sufficient to hold the contracting party liable for the breach of contract[59]. The contracting party would be liable, if he (slightly) negligently breaches the contract. Negligent behaviour need not be related to the damages caused by it[60]. Slight negligence can be defined as the negligence where the wrongdoer did not show the necessary care which would have been shown by a reasonable person[61]. Nevertheless, the wrongdoer's conduct in violating the duty of care is not as grave as it would be in gross negligence[62].

Slight negligence is insufficient for fulfilling the prerequisites of wilful misconduct. The actual state of the wrongdoer's mind does not play any role in slight negligence. Liability for the slightly negligent conduct is based on whether the wrongdoer should have avoided the harmful result. Therefore, the carrier or shipowner will be liable for his (slightly) negligent conduct, however, within the limits adopted by the relevant international instrument[63].

2. Gross negligence (*culpa lata, grobe Fahrlässigkeit, ağır ihmal*)

a) Definition

Gross negligence under civil law is the negligent behaviour seen when a wrongdoer violates the duty of care expected from him in an unusually grave manner. In order to call conduct grossly negligent, it is necessary that the wrongdoer did not even consider the simplest precautions which would have been taken by anyone under the same or similar circumstances[64]. Where the wrongdoer fails to avoid a

---

[56]   *Larenz*, p. 283; Staudinger/*Löwisch* (2001), § 276 Rn. 47; Erman/*Westermann*, § 276 Rn. 11; *Tandoğan*, p. 53.
[57]   *Larenz*, p. 283; *Eren*, p. 539; *Güven II*, pp. 159-160. See also Staudinger/*Löwisch* (2001), § 276 Rn. 52; LeipKommStGB – *Vogel*, § 15 Rn. 264.
[58]   Erman/*Westermann*, § 276 Rn. 10; *Demirbaş*, pp. 350-351.
[59]   MünchKommBGB – *Grundmann*, § 276 Rn. 50.
[60]   MünchKommBGB – *Grundmann*, § 276 Rn. 52.
[61]   *Oğuzman/Öz*, p. 529; *Kılıçoğlu*, p. 256; *Eren*, p. 541; *Sözer, Taşıyıcının Sorumluluğu*, p. 796.
[62]   *Palandt/Grüneberg*, § 276 Rn. 14; *Tandoğan*, p. 55; *Eren*, p. 541; *Güven II*, p. 161.
[63]   *Schneider*, pp. 112-114.
[64]   *Palandt/Grüneberg*, § 277 Rn. 5; Erman/*Westermann*, § 276 Rn. 16; MünchKommBGB – *Grundmann*, § 276 Rn. 94; *Güven II*, p. 161; *Oğuzman/Öz*, p. 529; Staudinger/*Löwisch* (2001), § 276 Rn. 92; *Larenz*, pp. 291-292; *Tandoğan*, pp. 54-

harmful result which was easily foreseeable and avoidable, he is grossly negligent[65].

b) Gross negligence and wilful misconduct

Whether recklessness coupled with knowledge of the probable consequences is equal to gross negligence has been a matter of controversy. One view answers the question in the affirmative[66]. Another view asserts that the difference between wilful misconduct and gross negligence is exaggerated and that the borderline between two concepts is a vague one, which also causes difficulties in determining whether mischievous conduct amounts to wilful misconduct[67].

It has been rightfully stated that wilful misconduct does not cover cases of gross negligence[68]. Recklessness necessitates something more than gross negligence[69]. In a gross negligence analysis, what the wrongdoer had to do according to the criterion of the ordinary person is important; conversely, for a finding of recklessness actual knowledge is necessary[70]. Additionally, the actual knowledge must be related to the probable consequences, which means that the prerequisites adopted by the Hague Protocol of 1955 are more stringent than the requirements for a finding of gross negligence[71]. Therefore, it is not possible to agree with the view that the degree of fault adopted by the Hague Protocol is not significantly different than gross negligence and that its effect is more theoretical than it is practical[72]. It should also be remembered that under common law, mention is made of the degrees of negligence and gross negligence, referring to another degree of fault apart from recklessness, let alone recklessness coupled with subjective knowledge of the probable consequences.

c) Advertent and inadvertent gross negligence

Negligence (not only gross negligence) is also divided into two sub-categories, inadvertent negligence (*negligentia*) and advertent negligence (*luxuria*). In such a distinction, the gravity of the degree of fault does not play a role. The distinction takes into account whether the wrongdoer has foreseen that the harmful result would likely occur or not. Foresight of a harmful result is not a prerequisite of gross negligence. In this sense, a slightly negligent person could have foreseen the

---

55; *Kılıçoğlu*, p. 255; *Eren*, p. 540; *Sözer, Taşıyıcının Sorumluluğu*, p. 796; BGH, 11.05.1953, BGHZ 10, 14 (16).

[65] MünchKommBGB – *Grundmann*, § 276 Rn. 97.

[66] *Richter-Hannes*, pp. 79-80; *Matte*, p. 62; *Ülgen*, p. 203; *Kender, Atina Konvansiyonu*, pp. 118-119 fn. 18; *Göknil*, pp. 202-203; *Kırman*, pp. 162-163; *Sözer, TSHK*, p. 57-58; *Can*, p. 136.

[67] *Drion*, p. 216.

[68] *Ruhwedel*, p. 148; *Abraham*, Art. 25 Anm. 7-8.

[69] *Mankiewicz*, p. 124; *Thume, Vergleich*, 4; *Neumann*, 413. For the view that recklessness is equivalent to gross negligence see *Gran*, p. 848.

[70] *Gerber*, p. 87; *Stachow*, pp. 199-200.

[71] *Mankiewicz*, p. 124; *Çağa, Batider*, p. 301.

[72] *Thume, Vergleich*, 4.

possible consequences. In fact, someone can be grossly negligent, for the very reason that he has failed to foresee the harmful consequence which he ought to have foreseen. Consequently, gross negligence and advertent negligence are two different terms referring to different situations[73].

Nevertheless, the issue will be examined here in combination with gross negligence, since, as will be seen below, it has been asserted by many writers that wilful misconduct amounts to advertent gross negligence under civil law.

aa) Inadvertent gross negligence

If the wrongdoer does not foresee the possible consequences of his act or omission yet would have foreseen them had he shown the necessary care, the sort of negligence at issue is referred to as inadvertent negligence[74]. If the elements of inadvertent negligence and gross negligence are combined, inadvertent gross negligence can be defined as negligence where the wrongdoer violates his duty of care in a grave manner and does not foresee the possible consequences of his act or omission. It is clear that inadvertent gross negligence does not fulfil the prerequisites of recklessness coupled with foresight of the probable consequences[75]. Inadvertent gross negligence falls short on the requirement of foresight[76].

bb) Advertent gross negligence

If the wrongdoer foresees the possible consequences of his grossly negligent act or omission, his fault amounts to advertent gross negligence. Although the wrongdoer foresees the possible consequences, he, negligently, believes that the harmful result will not occur[77]. If the wrongdoer, recklessly, does not realise the foreseeable possible consequences, i.e. if there is negligence coupled with wilful blindness, this fault also amounts to advertent negligence[78]. However, it is not sufficient that the wrongdoer ought to have seen the possibility of the harmful result

---

[73] Staudinger/*Löwisch* (2001), § 276 Rn. 99; *Larenz*, p. 292; *Goldschmidt*, pp. 105-106; *Neumann*, 417; *Kühl*, § 15 Rn. 53.

[74] *Palandt/Grüneberg*, § 276 Rn. 13; *Goldschmidt*, pp. 105, 107-108; *Tandoğan*, p. 49; *Tekinay/et al.*, p. 495; *Karahasan*, p. 489; *Eren*, p. 541; *Güven II*, p. 155; *Sözer, Taşıyıcının Sorumluluğu*, p. 796; *Kırman*, p. 156; *Kühl*, § 15 Rn. 35, 53; *Schönke/Schröder*, § 15 Rn. 203; *Roxin*, § 24 Rn. 66; LeipKommStGB – *Vogel*, § 15 Rn. 148; *Demirbaş*, p. 357; *Artuk/Gökcen/Yenidünya*, pp. 479, 511.

[75] *Gerber*, p. 87; *Giemulla/Schmid*, WA Einleitung Rn. 4.

[76] *Çağa*, p. 202; *Guldimann*, p. 148.

[77] *Palandt/Grüneberg*, § 276 Rn. 13; *Goldschmidt*, p. 105; *Tandoğan*, p. 49; *Tekinay/et al.*, p. 495; *Karahasan*, p. 489; *Neumann*, 417; *Eren*, p. 541; *Güven II*, p. 155; *Modjaz*, p. 94; *Sözer, Taşıyıcının Sorumluluğu*, p. 796; *Kırman*, p. 156; *Kühl*, § 15 Rn. 35, 53; *Schönke/Schröder*, § 15 Rn. 203; *Roxin*, § 24 Rn. 66; LeipKommStGB – *Vogel*, § 15 Rn. 148, 287; *Demirbaş*, p. 357; *Artuk/Gökcen/Yenidünya*, pp. 479, 511; *Toroslu*, p. 207.

[78] *Palandt/Grüneberg*, § 277 Rn. 5; Erman/*Westermann*, § 276 Rn. 16; MünchKommBGB – *Grundmann*, § 276 Rn. 98; *Herber, Haftungsrecht*, pp. 215-216.

for a finding of advertent negligence[79]. In advertent negligence cases, the wrong-doer foresees the harmful result but does not wish it to occur. He even might have taken some insufficient precautions to avoid it[80].

Reference to *luxuria* as an equivalent to recklessness coupled with actual knowledge as to the probable consequences was made during the Hague Conference. There Mr. Riese, the German delegate, stated that the new definition covers both *dolus eventualis* and *luxuria*. He defined *luxuria* as "a form of negligence, but the most serious form" and gave an example of a pilot who foresees the possible danger but believes that he will avoid it since he trusts his skills[81].

Thereafter, it was argued that advertent negligence or advertent gross negligence is the degree of fault equivalent to recklessness coupled with subjective awareness of the probable consequences[82]. According to this view, grossly negligent behaviour is recklessness and advertence fulfils the requirement of subjective awareness of the probable consequences[83].

However, it was rightfully stated that advertent gross negligence is not covered by the definition of wilful misconduct[84]. The emphasis on advertent negligence is not on the foresight of the probable consequences; rather, it is on the wrongdoer's circumstance of being convinced that the possible result will not occur[85]. Moreover, the definition of the term wilful misconduct requires the foresight of probable consequences; in advertent negligence, it is only the possible consequences having been foreseen. Therefore, advertent negligence also falls short as to the requirement of the probability of the harmful result[86]. Moreover, in advertent gross negligence, the wrongdoer does not wish the harmful result to occur whereas

---

[79]   *Roxin*, § 24 Rn. 70.

[80]   *Güven II*, p. 155; *Demirbaş*, p. 349.

[81]   Mr. Riese (Germany), in: *Minutes, Hague*, p. 200.

[82]   *Giemulla/Schmid*, WA Art. 25 Rn. 10-11, 31, *Puttfarken*, Rn. 831; *Herber*, pp. 195, 215-216, 333; *Herber, Haftungsrecht*, pp. 14, 71; *Can*, p. 136; *Schubert*, p. 79; *Häußer*, p. 25; *Helm*, in: Großkomm. HGB Anh. VI nach § 452: CMR Art. 29 Rn. 7; *Beier*, p. 255; *Herber/Piper*, Art. 29 Rn. 5; *Herber, Anmerkung*, 176; BGH, 28.11.1978, VersR 1979, 188 (190); OLG Düsseldorf, 21.01.1993, TranspR 1993, 246 (247); Obergericht Zürich, 25.11.1969, ASDA-Bulletin 1970/2, 18 (20); Entwurf eines Gesetzes zur Neuregelung des Fracht-, Speditions- und Lagerrechts (Transportrechtsreformgesetz – TRG), Amtliche Begründung (zu den einzelnen Vorschriften), zu § 435, BT 13/8445, p. 72.

[83]   *Herber, Haftungsrecht*, p. 215; MünchKommHGB 2009 – *Herber*, § 435 Rn. 11-15; *Richter-Hannes, Multimodale Güterbeförderung*, p. 158; *Schneider*, pp. 118-120; *Bonelli*, p. 209; *Schobel*, p. 81-82; *Sözer, TSHK*, pp. 57-58; *Sözer, Taşıyıcının Sorumluluğu*, pp. 797-798.

[84]   *von Ziegler*, p. 203; *Harms*, in: *Thume, CMR-Kommentar*, Art. 29 Rn. 24; *Starck*, p. 131; *Richter-Hannes/Trotz*, p. 20; BGE 98 II 231 (241) (11.07.1972).

[85]   *Gerber*, p. 87; *Yazıcıoğlu*, p. 173.

[86]   MünchKommHGB 1997 – *Basedow*, CMR Art. 29 Rn. 4; *Guldimann*, p. 148; *Rabe, Vortrag*, p. 16; *Modjaz*, pp. 94-95; *Kienzle*, pp. 212-214; *Mankiewicz*, p. 124; *de la Motte*, pp. 302-303; *Stachow*, pp. 200-201; *Çağa*, *Batider*, p. 301; *Özdemir*, pp. 114, 119.

in recklessness with subjective knowledge of the probable consequences, the wrongdoer consciously risks the harmful result[87].

3. *Leichtfertigkeit*

Under German criminal law, some crimes do not require simple negligence, but reckless conduct (*Leichtfertigkeit*). It has been disputed what reckless conduct means in the sense of criminal law. However, in any case, it has been seen as a type of negligence unlike the recklessness known to common law. Under common law, recklessness is a separate degree of fault[88].

Nevertheless, under German criminal law, *Leichtfertigkeit* refers to a particularly high degree of negligence[89]. However, defining *Leichtfertigkeit* as a grave violation of a duty of care does not offer any clarity and does not show the difference between gross negligence and *Leichtfertigkeit*. Therefore, it has been said that attention should be paid to the knowledge of the wrongdoer: if he has foreseen or should have foreseen the possible results of his grave negligence, he should be guilty of *Leichtfertigkeit*[90]. However, such an interpretation has not been accepted by all criminal lawyers. It is argued that in *Leichtfertigkeit* cases focus should be on the unlawfulness of the negligent conduct, not on what the wrongdoer has foreseen or should have foreseen. If the wrongdoer's conduct creates an unjustifiable risk, he is guilty of *Leichtfertigkeit*; therefore, it is irrelevant whether he has foreseen the results or not[91]. From this perspective, an unjustifiable risk to human life is more critical than one to property and material assets[92].

Further, it has also been stated that both advertent and inadvertent negligence can amount to recklessness since there is no difference between advertent and inadvertent negligence in the sense of criminal liability[93]. Finally, the difference between *Leichtfertigkeit* and intention is that the criteria for *Leichtfertigkeit* remain objective, although subjective factors are also taken into account, whereas intention is determined according to subjective elements in respect of the wrongdoer[94].

It is clear that the *Leichtfertigkeit* in German criminal law and recklessness in common law are similar to the extent that both of them require conduct creating an unjustifiable risk. However, unlike in common law, *Leichtfertigkeit* in German criminal law does not necessitate subjective knowledge of the probable conse-

---

[87] *Çağa*, p. 202; *de la Motte*, pp. 302-303; *Çağa, Batider*, p. 301; *Özdemir*, pp. 114, 119.
[88] See *supra* A II.
[89] *Roxin*, § 24 Rn. 83; *Kühl*, § 15 Rn. 55.
[90] *Schönke/Schröder*, § 15 Rn. 205; LeipKommStGB – *Vogel*, § 15 Rn. 296-297. For more information see Herbert *Wegscheider*, Zum Begriff der Leichtfertigkeit, ZStW 98 (1986), 624.
[91] *Roxin*, § 24 Rn. 87.
[92] *Roxin*, § 24 Rn. 89.
[93] *Schönke/Schröder*, § 15 Rn. 205; *Roxin*, § 24 Rn. 90; *Kühl*, § 15 Rn. 55; LeipKommStGB – *Vogel*, § 15 Rn. 149, 295.
[94] *Schönke/Schröder*, § 15 Rn. 205.

quences. Even the view defining *Leichtfertigkeit* with foresight of probable consequences accepts that both advertent and inadvertent negligent conduct can constitute *Leichtfertigkeit*. Moreover, this view also encompasses under *Leichtfertigkeit* those situations where the wrongdoer *should have foreseen* the probable result. Therefore, *Leichtfertigkeit* under German criminal law does not satisfy the prerequisites of the recklessness coupled with subjective knowledge of probable consequences. It falls short on the subjective knowledge requirement.

II. Intentional Wrongdoing (dolus, Vorsatz, kasıt)

Intentional wrongdoing is a term which is not analysed in detail under private law since negligence is sufficient to hold someone liable under private law principles. However, contrary to private law, intentional wrongdoing is a very important concept in criminal law since, as a general rule, only intentionally unlawful conduct results in criminal liability. Consequently, the term is a well-studied and well-analysed areas of criminal law.

Intentional wrongdoing can simply be defined as "knowing and desiring the results of an unlawful conduct"[95]. In order to be guilty of intentional wrongdoing, the wrongdoer needs to have foreseen the results of his intentional unlawful conduct, and accepted them[96]. Whether or not a prerequisite for liability is the wrongdoer's also having wished to produce the harmful result is different under private and criminal law conceptions of intentional wrongdoing. Nonetheless, the motives behind the intentional wrongdoing are not important in determining whether the wrongdoer is guilty of intentional wrongdoing[97]. Moreover, intentional misconduct can be in the form of acts committed or omitted[98].

The differences between concepts of intentional wrongdoing in private and criminal law will be addressed below. However, a general difference between private and criminal law regarding the term should be emphasised here. In criminal law, ignorance of the law is not an excuse, whereas it is under private law when intentional wrongdoing is at issue. Therefore, if one does not know that he is violating a legal principle or a contract, he is not guilty of intentional wrongdoing under private law principles. Nevertheless, if one is not guilty of intentional

---

[95] *Palandt/Grüneberg*, § 276 Rn. 10; Erman/*Westermann*, § 276 Rn. 7; MünchKommBGB – *Grundmann*, § 276 Rn. 154; Staudinger/*Löwisch* (2001), § 276 Rn. 18; *Goldschmidt*, p. 80; *Tandoğan*, p. 46; *Tekinay/et al.*, p. 493; *Eren*, p. 535; *Kılıçoğlu*, p. 255; *Karahasan*, p. 487; *Atamer, Nedensellik Bağı*, p. 31; *Güven I*, p. 585; *Marsilius*, 296-297; *Sözer, Taşıyıcının Sorumluluğu*, p. 796; *Kühl*, § 15 Rn. 3; *Maurach/Zipf*, § 22 Rn. 1; *Schönke/Schröder*, § 15 Rn. 9; *Roxin*, § 12 Rn. 4; *Demirbaş*, p. 330; *Dönmezer*, p. 199.

[96] *Palandt/Grüneberg*, § 276 Rn. 10; Staudinger/*Löwisch* (2001), § 276 Rn. 18; *Larenz*, pp. 279-280.

[97] *Palandt/Grüneberg*, § 276 Rn. 10; Erman/*Westermann*, § 276 Rn. 7; *Tandoğan*, p. 48; *Tekinay/et al.*, p. 493; *Güven I*, p. 588; LeipKommStGB – *Vogel*, § 15 Rn. 40; *Demirbaş*, p. 332; *Dönmezer*, p. 203.

[98] LeipKommStGB – *Vogel*, § 15 Rn. 59.

wrongdoing, he may still be held liable under the negligence principles of private law[99].

Since intentional wrongdoing has been defined as knowing and desiring the results of unlawful conduct, it can be said that there are two elements in the concept: knowing the results of the unlawful conduct and desiring those results[100]. When should a person be regarded as "desiring a result"? The answer to this question forms the basis of different degrees of intentional wrongdoing. The wrongdoer can have the desire to produce a certain result; or he can foresee the occurrence of the result as being certain or virtually certain; or he can foresee the harmful result only as being possible, but he does not care whether it will occur or not and simply risks such an occurrence[101].

1. Direct intention (*dolus directus, Absicht/direkter Vorsatz, doğrudan kasıt*)

Direct intention is a term which refers to the highest level of intentional wrongdoing. In this respect, the wrongdoer is guilty of direct intention if he acted or failed to act with the purpose and desire of producing a certain unlawful result. In such an instance, the wrongdoer is conscious about the effects of his act or omission, and continues acting or failing to act with the desire of producing that effect. It can be said that the act or omission of the wrongdoer is designed to produce a certain result. Accomplishing the effect, *i.e.* the harmful unlawful result, is at the same time what the wrongdoer wants to achieve[102]. This degree of intentional wrongdoing can be labelled criminal intent or direct intention in the first degree (*dolus directus, Absicht, doğrudan kasıt*) since it involves the desire to achieve an unlawful result.

If the definition of the term wilful misconduct used in international transport conventions is recalled, the first part of that definition, *i.e.* "act or omission done with (the) intent to cause damage", necessitates the same prerequisites as criminal intent. Therefore, the first part of the definition of wilful misconduct is equivalent to criminal intent[103].

However, the term direct intention does not only refer to criminal intention. It also covers those cases where the wrongdoer has foreseen that the harmful result

---

[99]   *Palandt/Grüneberg*, § 276 Rn. 11; MünchKommBGB – *Grundmann*, § 276 Rn. 151; Staudinger/*Löwisch* (2001), § 276 Rn. 17, 21.

[100] *Tandoğan*, p. 46; *Eren*, p. 535; *Güven I*, p. 585; *Roxin*, § 12 Rn. 4. Similar *Goldschmidt*, p. 80.

[101] *Kühl*, § 15 Rn. 18-19.

[102] MünchKommBGB – *Grundmann*, § 276 Rn. 162; Staudinger/*Löwisch* (2001), § 276 Rn. 18; *Goldschmidt*, p. 81; *Tandoğan*, p. 47; *Eren*, p. 536; *Marsilius*, 296-297; *Oğuzman/Öz*, p. 528; *Karahasan*, p. 487; *Güven I*, p. 586; *Sözer, Taşıyıcının Sorumluluğu*, p. 796; *Kırman*, p. 156; *Roxin*, § 12 Rn. 2, 7; LeipKommStGB – *Vogel*, § 15 Rn. 79; *Maurach/Zipf*, § 22 Rn. 28; *Schönke/Schröder*, § 15 Rn. 66; *Taylor, Intention*, 106; *Artuk/Gökcen/Yenidünya*, p. 459; *Toroslu*, pp. 180-181, 187-188; *Özgenç*, p. 236.

[103] *Pohar*, p. 299.

will occur as a virtual certainty but has nevertheless accepted this fact and continues his act or omission[104] (*dolus directus, direkter Vorsatz, doğrudan kasıt*).
Where the wrongdoer has an intention as to a certain result, but also foresees the
occurrence of side effects inherent to this certain result, it is accepted that he also
produced those side effects with direct intention[105]. This fashion of intentional
wrongdoing is also referred to as the direct intention in the second degree. A classical example given to explain direct intention in the second degree would be
someone putting a time-bomb on an ocean liner in order to collect the insurance
money and, in so doing, foreseeing that the crew will not survive on the high
seas[106]. Thus, his intention covers the death of the crew as well[107], since any
unrealistic hopes of the wrongdoer that the inevitable result will not occur are not
taken into account[108].

If attention is again called to the definition of the term wilful misconduct
employed by the international transport conventions there should be no doubt that
the phrase "act or omission done with (the) intent to cause damage" also covers
direct intention in the second degree.

Here, an important difference between concepts of common and civil law
should be emphasised. As addressed before[109], only acts or omission done with
intent to produce a particular result are covered by the term direct intention,
whereas a wrongdoer's intention as to the inevitable results and side effects of an
act or omission is called oblique intention under common law. Therefore, the
scope of the term for direct intention is different under common law and civil law.
The common law term for direct intention correlates with the civil law term for
direct intention in the first degree; the common law term oblique intention correlates with the civil law term direct intention in the second degree. Therefore, the
term direct intention has a broader scope in civil law than the same term under
common law does, as it covers both direct and oblique intention of common law.

Another point to be addressed is that under both criminal law and private law,
intention and foresight as to the results of the act or omission are not always necessary for a conviction or liability in private law. Principally, the wrongdoer is
liable under private law if he acted or omitted to act intentionally; thus, foresight
and intention as to the harmful result is not a prerequisite. In criminal law, whether
direct intention in the first or second degree is necessary depends on the definition
of the crime in question. If the definition of the crime specifically stipulates that

---

[104] Staudinger/*Löwisch* (2001), § 276 Rn. 18; *Roxin*, § 12 Rn. 2, 18; *Maurach/Zipf*,
§ 22 Rn. 29; LeipKommStGB – *Vogel*, § 15 Rn. 91.

[105] *Roxin*, § 12 Rn. 18; LeipKommStGB – *Vogel*, § 15 Rn. 82; *Artuk/Gökcen/*
Yenidünya, p. 460; *Demirbaş*, p. 333; *Özgenç*, p. 236.

[106] This example is the same as the one given for oblique intention under common
law, see *supra* A I 2.

[107] *Roxin*, § 12 Rn. 18; *Maurach/Zipf*, § 22 Rn. 29; LeipKommStGB – *Vogel*, § 15
Rn. 82; *Taylor, Intention*, 107-108; *Artuk/Gökcen/Yenidünya*, pp. 460-461;
Demirbaş, p. 334; *Özgenç*, p. 236.

[108] LeipKommStGB – *Vogel*, § 15 Rn. 92; *Özgenç*, p. 236.

[109] See *supra* A I 1 and 2.

direct intention in the first degree is required, direct intention in the second degree would not be sufficient to fulfil the prerequisites of that crime[110].

2. Dolus eventualis (bedingter Vorsatz, dolaylı kasıt)

a) Definition

The general definition of intentional wrongdoing also covers *dolus eventualis*[111]. If the wrongdoer foresees the possible results of his act or omission, but nonetheless runs the risk of the occurrence of those results, his intention is called *dolus eventualis*[112]. Here, the wrongdoer has no special desire to produce the possible harmful result, nor does he have foresight of it on a level of virtual certainty. However, he foresees the possible occurrence, and accepts the risk of its occurrence (volitional element)[113]. The conduct of the wrongdoer in *dolus eventualis* is classified as intentional wrongdoing since there is a conscious decision as to the risk of possibly harmful results[114]. It is a conduct where the wrongdoer cannot be considered as "wishing to produce a certain result", but he cannot be considered as "not wishing" as well[115]. *Dolus eventualis* involves an "I do not care" attitude[116]. Wilful blindness, *i.e.* where the wrongdoer deliberately shuts his eyes to the possible occurrence of the harmful results, does not prevent a finding of *dolus eventualis*[117]. Similarly, unrealistic hopes of the wrongdoer as to the non-occurrence of the harmful result do not prevent a finding of *dolus eventualis*[118].

b) Difference from other fault concepts

The absence of a special desire to produce a certain result distinguishes *dolus eventualis* from direct intention in the first degree[119]. The foresight of the harmful result as possible distinguishes it from direct intention in the second degree, since

---

[110] *Roxin,* § 12 Rn. 3, 5; LeipKommStGB – *Vogel,* § 15 Rn. 86-90; *Schönke/Schröder,* § 15 Rn. 53, 69; *Kühl,* § 15 Rn. 20.

[111] The term can be translated into English as "conditional intention", but its Latin version is more accurate, see *Taylor, Intention,* 102.

[112] *Palandt/Grüneberg,* § 276 Rn. 10; Staudinger/*Löwisch* (2001), § 276 Rn. 18; *Marsilius,* 296-297; *Güven I,* p. 586; *Oğuzman/Öz,* p. 528; *Tekinay/et al.,* p. 493; *Kırman,* p. 156; *Kühl,* § 15 Rn. 23; *Schönke/Schröder,* § 15 Rn. 72, 84; *Artuk/ Gökcen/Yenidünya,* p. 461; *Demirbaş,* pp. 334, 342; *Dönmezer,* p. 206.

[113] Erman/*Westermann,* § 276 Rn. 7; MünchKommBGB – *Grundmann,* § 276 Rn. 161; *Goldschmidt,* p. 82; *Tandoğan,* p. 47; *Sözer, Taşıyıcının Sorumluluğu,* p. 796; *Roxin,* § 12 Rn. 2, 27; *Taylor, Intention,* 110.

[114] *Tandoğan,* p. 47; *Güven I,* p. 586; *Kühl,* § 15 Rn. 24; *Roxin,* § 12 Rn. 30, 72-73; *Özgenç,* p. 238.

[115] *Demirbaş,* p. 334.

[116] *Güven I,* p. 586; *Schönke/Schröder,* § 15 Rn. 84; *Artuk/Gökcen/Yenidünya,* p. 461.

[117] MünchKommBGB – *Grundmann,* § 276 Rn. 161.

[118] *Roxin,* § 12 Rn. 27.

[119] *Roxin,* § 12 Rn. 4; LeipKommStGB – *Vogel,* § 15 Rn. 97; *Artuk/Gökcen/ Yenidünya,* p. 462; *Özgenç,* p. 237.

for direct intention in the second degree the wrongdoer foresees the results of his act or omission as virtually certain or inevitable[120]. As direct intention in the second degree necessitates foresight of a virtual certainty, risking the foreseen *probable* results also falls within the limits of *dolus eventualis*[121].

The difference between advertent gross negligence and *dolus eventualis* is also important. As mentioned before[122], the wrongdoer's conduct amounts to advertent gross negligence in those instances where he has violated his duty of care in a grave manner with foresight of the possibly harmful results, but with the negligent, albeit earnest, belief that the harmful result will not occur or can be avoided. On the other hand, in *dolus eventualis*, the wrongdoer accepts and risks the occurrence of the harmful result[123]. It does not matter for him whether the harmful result will occur; he simply does not care[124]. The mental or emotional disposition of the wrongdoer towards the harmful result is positive in *dolus eventualis*, whereas it is negative in negligence. Therefore, the main difference between advertent gross negligence and *dolus eventualis* lies in the attitude of the wrongdoer[125]. In *dolus eventualis*, the wrongdoer chooses to continue his act or omission, since he prefers the occurrence of the harmful result to cessation of his act or omission[126], that is to say he "decides to accept the whole package"[127].

c) Wilful misconduct – a degree of fault between *dolus eventualis* and advertent (gross) negligence?

It has been said that recklessness coupled with subjective knowledge regarding the possible results is not equivalent to any of the degrees of fault under civil law. According to this view, considering the graveness of the necessary conduct for breaking the liability limits, the second part of the defined fault in the international transport conventions should be considered as somewhere between advertent gross negligence and *dolus eventualis*[128].

---

[120] *Goldschmidt*, p. 82; *Roxin*, § 12 Rn. 4, 20; LeipKommStGB – *Vogel*, § 15 Rn. 97.

[121] *Maurach/Zipf*, § 22 Rn. 30; *Toroslu*, p. 188.

[122] See *supra* I 2 c bb.

[123] *Palandt/Grüneberg*, § 276 Rn. 10, 13; Erman/*Westermann*, § 276 Rn. 7; Münch-KommBGB – *Grundmann*, § 276 Rn. 161; Staudinger/*Löwisch* (2001), § 276 Rn. 19; *Neumann*, 417; *Güven II*, p. 155; *Tekinay/et al.*, p. 495; *Tandoğan*, p. 49; *Eren*, p. 541; *Sözer, Taşıyıcının Sorumluluğu*, p. 796; *Kırman*, p. 156; *Yetiş Şamlı*, p. 40; *Maurach/Zipf*, § 22 Rn. 32; *Roxin*, § 12 Rn. 23, 27; LeipKommStGB – *Vogel*, § 15 Rn. 103; *Taylor, Intention*, 110; *Artuk/Gökcen/Yenidünya*, pp. 480, 497; *Demirbaş*, p. 336; *Toroslu*, pp. 207-208.

[124] *Maurach/Zipf*, § 22 Rn. 36; *Demirbaş*, p. 336; *Artuk/Gökcen/Yenidünya*, p. 513-513.

[125] *Marsilius*, 298. See also Ulrich *Schroth*, Die Differenz von dolus eventualis und bewusster Fahrlässigkeit, JuS 1992, 1.

[126] *Maurach/Zipf*, § 22 Rn. 36.

[127] *Taylor, Intention*, 111.

[128] *Giemulla/Schmid*, WA Art. 25 Rn. 32; *Starck*, p. 131; *Ilse*, p. 201; *Fremuth, Haftungsbegrenzungen*, 99; *Müller-Feldhammer*, p. 225; *Schneider*, p. 116;

However, it is rightfully stated that there is no other degree of fault between advertent gross negligence and *dolus eventualis*. With advertent gross negligence, the wrongdoer does not wish the harmful result to occur, whereas in *dolus eventualis* he is treated as if he had wished the harmful result to occur since he foresees and runs the risk. Thus, the wrongdoer either wishes the harmful result to happen or not. There is nothing to be found in between wishing and not wishing. Therefore, there is no other degree of fault between advertent gross negligence and *dolus eventualis*[129].

d) *Dolus eventualis* and wilful misconduct

It has already been mentioned that "intent to cause damage" refers to direct intention in the first and second degree[130] and that this is essentially undisputed. However, it is a matter of contention whether "recklessly and with knowledge that damage would probably occur" refers to advertent (gross) negligence or *dolus eventualis* or to a degree of fault in between. It has already been stressed that advertent (gross) negligence does not amount to recklessness coupled with subjective knowledge as to the probable consequences[131], and that there is no new degree of fault between advertent (gross) negligence and *dolus eventualis*[132]. Hence, does the second part of the definition adopted by the international transport conventions amount to *dolus eventualis*?

aa) Argument against

It has been said that reckless conduct coupled with subjective knowledge as to the probable consequences is not equivalent to *dolus eventualis*[133]. According to this view, the prerequisites of the defined conduct are milder than *dolus eventualis*[134]. It has even been said that in recklessness coupled with subjective knowledge as to probable consequences, the wrongdoer does not wish to produce the harmful result; therefore, it cannot be classified as *dolus eventualis*[135]. According to this view, acceptance and approval of the possible harmful results is missing in recklessness coupled with subjective knowledge as to the probable consequences[136]. The difference between foresight of possible as opposed to probable results has

---

Yazıcıoğlu, pp. 172-173; *Gürses*, p. 94; *Gençtürk*, pp. 247-248; OLG Frankfurt, 22.10.1980, VersR 1981, 164 (165).
[129] *Neumann*, 417; *Yetiş Şamlı*, pp. 95-96. See also *Taylor, Intention*, 108-109. It must be stated that ideas for a new degree of fault between negligence and intentional wrongdoing also failed to gain any support within criminal law doctrine, see *Roxin*, § 12 Rn. 74.
[130] See *supra* II 1.
[131] See *supra* I 2 c bb.
[132] See *supra* II 2 c.
[133] *von Ziegler*, p. 203.
[134] BGE 98 II 231 (241) (11.07.1972).
[135] *Giemulla/Schmid*, WA Art. 25 Rn. 32; *Özdemir*, p. 114.
[136] *Rabe, Vortrag*, p. 16.

been another reason for rejecting the equivalence of both degrees of fault[137]. It has also been suggested that *dolus eventualis* is covered by the first part of the definition "intent to cause damage", and, therefore, recklessness coupled with subjective knowledge of the probable consequences must refer to another degree of fault[138].

bb) Argument in favour

The term wilful misconduct has been translated into English as *dolus eventualis* by some authorities[139]. It has also been accepted that the term wilful misconduct covers *dol* and *dolus eventualis*[140]. Furthermore, it has even been said that recklessness coupled with subjective knowledge as to the probable results cannot be classified as negligence, but should be classified as intentional wrongdoing and, in fact, something more than *dolus eventualis*[141]. Thus, according to this view, the second part of the definition given in international transport conventions amounts at least to *dolus eventualis*.

cc) Result

If the prerequisites of recklessness coupled with subjective knowledge as to the probable consequences and the prerequisites of *dolus eventualis* are compared, it can be clearly seen that they overlap. Recklessness requires an act or omission in grave violation of law, so does *dolus eventualis*. Subjective knowledge requires awareness or advertence as to the results of the act or omission, so does *dolus eventualis*.

Under the recklessness concept of the international transport conventions, foresight must be related to the probable consequences of the act or omission. As was pointed out before[142], foresight of possible consequences is sufficient for a finding of *dolus eventualis*, and foresight of virtually certain or inevitable consequences results in a finding of *dolus directus*. Since the degree of likelihood "probable" lies between possible and certain, foresight of probable consequences will fall also within the sphere of *dolus eventualis*.

The view stating that there is no wish on the wrongdoer's side to produce the harmful result in recklessness coupled with subjective knowledge as to the probable consequences cannot be embraced. It must be remembered[143] that the recklessness of common law involves a conscious decision as to an unjustifiable risk,

---

[137] *Guldimann*, p. 147; *Stachow*, pp. 201-202; *Çağa, Batider*, p. 301; *Yazıcıoğlu*, pp. 172-173.

[138] *Modjaz*, pp. 95-96.

[139] Mr. Riese (German delegate) in: *Minutes, Hague*, p. 200.

[140] MünchKommHGB 1997 – *Basedow*, CMR Art. 29 Rn. 5; *Gerber*, p. 19 fn. 98. Bezirksgericht Zürich, 15.12.1964, ZLW 1965, 338 (344) (The Court stated that the definition of the degree of fault given in the Warsaw Convention is closely related to *dolus eventualis*).

[141] *Marsilius*, 305; *Çağa*, p. 202.

[142] See *supra* II 2 b.

[143] See *supra* A II.

as is the case in *dolus eventualis*. Although the volitional element is more pre-dominant in *dolus eventualis* than it is in recklessness, the attitude of the wrong-doer which is somewhere between "wishing" and "not wishing", that is to say the "I do not care" attitude in *dolus eventualis* is also the same as the attitude of the wrongdoer in the recklessness known to common law[144]. In both degrees of fault, the wrongdoer foresees the possible/probable consequences, yet he prefers to accept the risk of the occurrence of the harmful result rather than cease his act or omission[145]. Therefore, it can be said without any hesitation that acceptance and approval of the possible harmful results is not missing in the recklessness portion of the definition adopted by the international transport conventions and, therefore, that it overlaps with *dolus eventualis*.

For the sake of clarification, an example given in order to explain the difference between negligence and intentional wrongdoing should be repeated here[146]: a carrier agrees to perform a carriage starting punctually at 12 o'clock (the first contract). However, he agrees to perform another carriage starting at 11 o'clock (the second contract), from which he can hardly be back from the carriage sched-uled for 12 o'clock. He is intentionally in violation of the first carriage contract if he acts with the intention of missing the starting time of the first contract (direct intention), or if he accepts the risk of missing its starting time (*dolus eventualis*). However, reference to intentional wrongdoing cannot be made if he has forgotten about the first contract, or if his inability to start on time is due to a mistake in the calculation of the distances. In the latter two cases he is, of course, in breach of contract, but only negligently.

It is clear, that the first two cases given as examples of intentional wrongdoing refer to cases where the carrier acted "with intention to cause [a harmful result] or recklessly and with knowledge that [a harmful result] would probably occur".

The construction of the recklessness part of the definition under common law also supports such a conclusion. Reference has been made to "quasi intentional harm" or "almost intentional conduct"[147] or "a legitimate substitution for intent" or "a proxy for intent"[148]. The standard adopted by the international transport conventions have been found as being "very close to the intent end"[149]. Here, it must also be remembered that the term "direct intention" under civil law correlates to both degrees of intentional wrongdoing referred to as direct and oblique inten-tion under common law. Thus, in common law, there would be a gap between intention and negligence if there were no degree of fault known as recklessness[150].

---

[144] See also *Goldschmidt*, p. 83.
[145] See also *Neumann*, 417.
[146] *Larenz*, p. 280.
[147] *Gaskell, Breaking Limits*, p. 5.
[148] *Saba v. Compagnie Nationale Air France* (CA, 1996) 78 F.3d 664, 668 *per* Judge Silberman.
[149] *Bayer Corporation v. British Airways, Plc.* (CA, 2000) 210 F.3d 236, 238 *per* Judge Wilkinson.
[150] See also *Saba v. Compagnie Nationale Air France* (CA, 1996) 78 F.3d 664, 668 *per* Judge Silberman: "There is a continuum that runs from simple negligence

It can be stated that the same gap is filled with the term "*dolus eventualis*" under civil law.

The final point to be addressed is that according to the civil law understanding, the term "intentional wrongdoing" covers both direct intention and *dolus eventualis*. Therefore, it has been said that the phrase "intent to cause damage" in international transport conventions covers both direct intention and *dolus eventualis*[151]. However, from a common law point of view, "intent to cause damage" refers only to the direct and oblique intention of common law. If one recalls that the phrase "intent to cause damage and recklessly and with knowledge that damage would probably result" has been drafted to define wilful misconduct[152], a common law degree of fault, "intent to cause damage" must therefore refer only to the direct and oblique intention of common law, which do not cover the *dolus eventualis* of civil law. Therefore, the view that *dolus eventualis* is already covered by "intent to cause damage"; and that, therefore recklessness coupled with subjective knowledge of the probable consequences must refer to another degree of fault, cannot be accepted.

In this respect, the wording of the loss of the right to limit provisions in CIV 1980 and CIM 1980 should be emphasised. As addressed earlier[153], both provisions stipulate that a railway will lose the right to limit in case of wilful misconduct whereas in cases of gross negligence, the limitation amounts will be doubled. Thus, wilful misconduct (and therefore its definition) and gross negligence refer to different degrees of fault.

Accordingly, if all findings of this chapter are summarised in a table, it would appear as follows:

Civil Law		Common Law
Direct intention (*dolus directus*)		Intentional wrongdoing
Direct intention in the first degree		Direct intention
Direct intention in the second degree		Oblique intention
Dolus eventualis		Recklessness
Negligence		Negligence
Slight negligence	Gross negligence	
Advertent negligence	Inadvertent negligence	

Therefore, and due to all reasons given above, the phrase "intent to cause damage" refers to direct intention in the first and second degree of civil law, and "recklessly and with knowledge that damage would probably occur" refers to *dolus eventualis* of civil law.

---

through gross negligence to intentional misconduct. Recklessness, or reckless disregard, lies between gross negligence and intentional harm".

[151]   See *supra* § 4 B I 2 c aa and § 6 B I 1 a aa.
[152]   See *supra* § 4 B I 2 b.
[153]   See *supra* § 6 B I 3 a.

§ 9 Conclusion

International transport conventions which adopt a limited liability system also employ provisions regarding how and when those limits may be broken. The limited liability system has become, through its historical development, a common feature of international transport regimes; the same is true of the provisions regarding unlimited liability including the case of wilful misconduct[1]. Wilful misconduct is a common law term which has been used in carriage by rail and which was literally adopted in the MIA 1906. The function of the term in marine insurance law is to make reference to one of the situations where the insurer is not liable towards the assured for the loss occurred[2].

The term "wilful misconduct" has been defined in the Hague Protocol of 1955 as "intent to cause damage or recklessness with knowledge that damage would probably result"[3]. This definition has been employed, with small changes, by almost all international transport conventions. If it is also taken into consideration that an assured party will lose his insurance cover in cases of wilful misconduct, it is clear that if the carrier or shipowner loses his right to limit, he also loses his entire insurance cover on the grounds of wilful misconduct[4]. Thus, two important and interrelated concepts of international transport law: the limitation of liability and insurance, are in harmony in respect of the loss of the advantages provided by them.

When the limitation amounts are fixed by international instruments, those amounts may prove insufficient due to changes in the market. Although this problem has partly been overcome by reference to the Special Drawing Right in the international instruments, limitation amounts can be still insufficient due to changes in the economic capacity of the shipping market and the increase in the financial value of the goods carried. In case of carriage of passengers, any limitation to the amount of liability is, due to the nature of the issue, insufficient. This situation undoubtedly causes dissatisfaction on the part of the cargo interests as well as passengers and their relatives. The problem of low liability limits was, naturally, an important reason for initiating discussions as to when the carrier or shipowner is guilty of wilful misconduct[5]. Policy considerations for creating almost unbreakable liability limits, *i.e.* breaking the liability limits only in cases of personal misconduct of the carrier or shipowner, caused additional discussions as to the attribution of the fault of servants and agents to the relevant company[6]. There is no doubt that the scope of every legal provision is to be determined according to the general rules of interpretation. During the interpretation process, the outcome might be the result of a strict or liberal interpretation. Nevertheless, low liability limits should not be a reason for breaking the carrier's or shipowner's

---

[1] See *supra* § 2 C.
[2] See *supra* § 3 B II.
[3] For more information see *supra* § 4 B.
[4] *Gold/Chircop/Kindred*, p. 733. See also *supra* § 5 C II 2 b bb.
[5] See *supra* § 4 A II 3.
[6] See *supra* § 5 E.

liability limits, when his (sometimes personal) conduct does not amount to wilful misconduct[7].

The limitation of liability and the breaking of limits in case of wilful misconduct are two components of the regimes set by the international transport conventions. It is clear under which circumstances the right to limit is to be applied; this is also true even though it sometimes leads to "unjust" results due to "insufficient" or "inadequate" amounts of limitation. The most absurd example in this respect is the world most renowned maritime disaster. In accordance with the legal proceedings held in America, the owners of the *Titanic* were entitled to limit their liability to an amount equal to fourteen salvaged lifeboats and the pending freight[8]. Although today, it is quite unthinkable that any court would agree to such an unfair result, limitation of liability regimes for sea carriage have been, since the *Titanic* disaster, substantially changed to prevent unjust results. Similar developments can be followed in regimes for other means of transportation as well. Nevertheless, it is still by no means universally satisfactory, especially in carriage of passengers, that the carrier or shipowner can limit his liability. However, dissatisfaction with the low liability limits or the limited liability system should not result in forcing the limits of the relevant regime. If attempts were made to prevent unfair results or insufficient or inadequate amounts of limitation were to be avoided by holding the carrier or shipowner liable without any financial limits even when he is not guilty of wilful misconduct, the result would be nothing but legal ambiguity since it would be indiscernible just when a court would see the limitation as "unjust", or the limitation amounts as "insufficient" or "inadequate".

It must be remembered that the limited liability system was circumvented in the *Himalaya* case[9], which initiated relevant provisions in international transport conventions regarding the limitation rights of servants and agents of the carrier[10]. Unfortunately, the situation cannot be so easily clarified in cases of wilful misconduct, since consideration of the term or even the definition of the term depends on the interpretation of local courts. It has already been addressed in this work that both the term wilful misconduct and its definition do not refer to a low degree of fault, nor to gross negligence, nor even to advertent gross negligence, but to intentional wrongdoing, *i.e.* the *dolus directus* and *dolus eventualis* of continental law[11].

Additionally, breaking the liability limits only in circumscribed cases of personal conduct has been found unsatisfactory. It was feared that there would only be a few cases where the limits could be broken. However, the main reason for having unlimited liability provisions is not the desire for having unlimited liability

---

[7]   *Cheng*, pp. 96-99.
[8]   George E. *Duncan*, Limitation of Shipowners' Liability: Parties Entitled to Limit; the Vessel: the Fund, (1978-1979) 53 Tul. L. Rev. 1046, 1046-1049. See also *Ocean Steam Navigation Company, Limited v. William J. Mellor* (Supreme Court of the US, 1914) 233 U.S. 718.
[9]   *Adler v. Dickson* [1954] 2 Lloyd's Rep. 122 (QBD); affirmed by *Adler v. Dickson* [1954] 2 Lloyd's Rep. 267 (CA); see also *supra* § 5 D VI 2 a.
[10] For more information see *supra* § 5 D VI 2 b and § 6 B II 2.
[11] See *supra* § 8 B II.

cases from time to time. The main rationale of such provisions is that it would be immoral to let the carrier or shipowner limit his liability even when he is guilty of wilful misconduct[12]. It is contrary to public policy and also runs counter to the underlying motives for a limited liability system[13].

It is correct that change in the existing law has always been the result of the initiatives which are unhappy with it, and for the sake of advancement, such initiatives are needed. It would be, without any doubt, in the advantage of the passengers and cargo interests if the carriers or shipowners were to be held liable without any financial limits in cases of, for instance, grossly negligent conduct, or for the conduct of their servants and agents. However, the historical background and the development of the present regime regarding the breaking of limits in cases of wilful misconduct show that the drafters of the relevant international conventions wilfully created almost unbreakable limits, generally in exchange of higher liability limits[14] or strict liability regime[15]. Therefore, it is not possible to extend the scope of application of the relevant provisions.

Thus, instead of trying to circumvent the limited liability system by forcing the limits of the wilful misconduct provision, the underlying policy considerations of the "limitation of liability" should be discussed, and, if necessary, an initiative should be made to revise the whole system. Whatever the result may be of the discussions regarding the limitation of liability, it should never be forgotten that the motives for limitation of liability and the circumstances under which these limits should be broken are two distinct issues. Limitation of liability is a matter of policy, whereas breaking the limits is a matter of law under the relevant regimes, although it is true that they cannot always be easily disentangled[16]. Discussing whether the limitation of liability is still necessary is related to *lege ferenda*, whereas determining and interpreting the rule applicable is related to *lege lata*[17].

---

[12] *Drion*, pp. 47-48.
[13] See *supra* § 2 C. However see *supra* § 4 C II.
[14] See *supra* § 5 C II 2 b.
[15] See *supra* § 4 C II.
[16] *Gaskell, Hamburg Rules*, p. 161; *Gaskell, Breaking Limits*, p. 4.
[17] *Gaskell, Hamburg Rules*, pp. 162, 166-167; *Gaskell, Breaking Limits*, p. 4.

Bibliography

Abraham: Hans-Jürgen Abraham, Das Recht der Luftfahrt, Bd. 1, 3. Aufl., Berlin 1960

Abraham, Luftbeförderungsvertrag: Hans-Jürgen Abraham, Der Luftbeförderungsvertrag, Stuttgart 1955

Abraham, Rechtsprechung: Hans-Jürgen Abraham, Die internationale Rechtsprechung zum Warschauer Abkommen, ZLW 1953, 75

Abraham, Rechtsprechung 1952: Hans-Jürgen Abraham, Die internationale Rechtsprechung zum Warschauer Abkommen seit Sommer 1952, ZLW 1954, 71

Abraham, Grade des Verschuldens: Hans-Jürgen Abraham, Die Grade des Verschuldens des Luftfrachtführers in ihrer Auswirkung auf seine Ḣaftung aus Beförderungsverträgen, ZLW 1955, 255

Aikens/Lord/Bools: Richard Aikens/Richard Lord/Michael Bools, Bills of Lading, London 2006

Akıncı: Ziya Akıncı, Karayolu ile Milletlerarası Eşya Taşımacılığı ve CMR, Ankara 1999

Anderson: Philip Anderson, ISM Code: A Practical Guide to the Legal and Insurance Implications, 2nd Ed., London 2005

Angino: Richard C. Angino, Limitation of Liability in Admiralty: An Anachronism from the Days of Privity, (1965) 10 Vill. L. Rev. 721

Arkan: Sabih Arkan, Demiryoluyla Yapılan Uluslararası Eşya Taşımaları, Ankara 1987

Arkan, İnceleme: Sabih Arkan, 24.5.1980 tarihli "Eşyanın Değişik Tür Taşıtlarla Uluslararası Taşınmasına İlişkin Konvansiyon" Üzerinde Bir İnceleme, Batider 1982/2, p. 27

Arkan, Sempozyum: Demiryolu İşletmesinin Eşya Taşımalarından Doğan Sorumluluğu, in: Sorumluluk ve Sigorta Hukuku Bakımından İkinci Taşımacılık Sempozyumu (İstanbul, 24-25 Ocak 1985), Ankara 1985, p. 47

Arnould: Arnould's Law of Marine Insurance and Average, 17th Ed. by JONATHAN C. B. GILMAN and ROBERT MERKIN, London 2008

Artuk/Gökcen/Yenidünya: Mehmet Emin Artuk/Ahmet Gökcen/Caner Yenidünya, Ceza Hukuku, Genel Hükümler, 3. bası, Ankara 2007

Asariotis: Regina Asariotis, Haftungsbegrenzung und deren Durchbrechung im Seehandelsrecht: die englische Auffassung, TranspR 2004, 147

Atamer, Cebrî İcra: Kerim Atamer, Deniz Hukukunda Cebrî İcra, İstanbul 2006

Atamer, Yolcu Taşıma: Kerim Atamer, 2002 Atina Sözleşmesi'nde ve Türk Ticaret Kanunu Tasarısı'nda Deniz Yolu ile Yolcu Taşıma Sözleşmesi, Batider 2008/3, p. 101

Atamer, 1976 ve 1992 Sözleşmeleri: Kerim Atamer, "1976 Sınırlı Sorumluluk ve 1992 Petrol Kirliliği Sözleşmelerinin Tatbikatı"na Dair Yasal Düzenleme Taslağı ve Gerekçesi, in: Bilgi Toplumunda Hukuk: Ünal Tekinalp'e Armağan, c. I, 2003, p. 849

Atamer, Nedensellik Bağı: Yeşim Atamer, Haksız Fiillerden Doğan Sorumluluğun Sınırlandırılması, İstanbul 1996

Ataol: Hüseyin Ataol, Deniz Alacaklarına Karşı Sorumluluğun Sınırlandırılmasına İlişkin 1976 Londra Konvansiyonu'nda Öngörülen Sınırlı Sorumluluğun Kapsamı, in: Prof. Dr. Tahir Çağa'nın Anısına Armağan, İstanbul 2000, p. 57

Athanassopoulou: Victoria Athanassopoulou, Schiffsunternehmen und Schiffsüberlassungsverträge, Tübingen 2005 (Diss. Hamburg)

Aydın: Alihan Aydın, CMR'ye Göre Taşıyıcının Zıya, Hasar ve Gecikmeden Doğan Sorumluluğu, 2. bası, İstanbul 2006

Baatz/et al.: Yvonne Baatz/Charles Debattista/Filippo Lorenzon/Andrew Serdy/Hilton Staniland/Michael Tsimplis, The Rotterdam Rules: a Practical Annotation, London 2009

Basedow, Common Carriers: Jürgen Basedow, Common Carriers: Continuity and Disintegration in U.S. Transportation Law, ETL, 1983, 251

Basedow, Haftungshöchstsummen: Jürgen Basedow, Haftungshöchstsummen im internationalen Lufttransport: Gold von gestern und Grundrechte von heute, TranspR 1988, 353

Basedow, Hamburger Regeln: Jürgen Basedow, Seefrachtrecht: Die Hamburger Regeln sind in Kraft, ZEuP 1993, 100

Basedow, Passagier: Jürgen Basedow, Passagierschiffahrt, ZHR 148 (1984), 238

Basedow, Transportvertrag: Jürgen Basedow, Der Transportvertrag, Tübingen 1987

Baughen: Simon Baughen, Shipping Law, 4th Ed., London 2009

Baumbach/Lauterbach/Albers/Hartmann: Adolf Baumbach/Wolfgang Lauterbach/ Jan Albers/Peter Hartmann, Zivilprozessordnung mit FamFG, GVG und anderen Nebengesetzen, 68. Aufl., München 2010

Beaumont: K. M. Beaumont, Some Problems Involved in Revision of the Warsaw Convention, (1949) J. Air L. & Com. 14

Beaumont, Revision: K. M. Beaumont, Need for Revision and Amplification of the Warsaw Convention, (1949) J. Air L. & Com. 395

Beaumont, Hague Protocol: K. M. Beaumont, The Warsaw Convention of 1929, as amended by the Protocol signed at the Hague, on September 28, 1955, (1955) 22 J. Air L. & Com. 414

Becker: Dieter Becker, Die Haftung der Eisenbahn nach nationalem und internationalem Frachtrecht, Berlin 1968

Beier: Olaf Beier, Grundsätze eines europäischen transportmittelübergreifenden Schadensrechts für den Gütertransport, Frankfurt a.M. 1999 (Diss. Hamburg)

Bennett: Howard N. Bennett, The Law of Marine Insurance, Oxford 1996

Berlingieri, Comparative Analysis: Francesco Berlingieri, A Comparative Analysis of the Hague-Visby Rules, the Hamburg Rules and the Rotterdam Rules, accessible at <www.comitemaritime.org/Uploads/Rotterdam%20Rules/ Comparative_analysis.pdf> (03.04.2011)

Berlingieri, UNCITRAL: Francesco Berlingieri, Carrier's Obligations and Liabilities, CMI Yearbook 2007-2008, p. 279

Billah: Muhammad Masum Billah, Economic analysis of Limitation of Shipowners' Liability, (2006-2007) 19 U.S.F. Mar. L.J. 297

Bonelli: Franco Bonelli, Limitation of Liability of the Carrier, Present Regulation and Prospects of Reform, in: Francesco Berlingieri (Editor), Studies on the Revision of the Brussels Convention on Bills of Lading, Genoa 1974, p. 157

Brice: Geoffrey Brice, The Scope of Limitation Action, in: The Limitation of Shipowners' Liability: the New Law, London 1986, p. 18

Brinkmann: Moritz Brinkmann, Das Beweismaß im Zivilprozess aus rechtsvergleichender Sicht, Köln 2005

Brinkmann, Vergleich: Jan Brinkmann, Frachtgüterschaden im internationalen Straßen- und Lufttransportrecht: Ein Vergleich der Haftung nach dem Montrealer Übereinkommen und der CMR, TranspR 2006, 146

Buglass: Leslie J. Buglass, Limitation of Liability from a Marine Insurance Viewpoint, (1978-1979) 53 Tul. L. Rev. 1364

Burchard-Motz: Heinrich Burchard-Motz, Die Stockholmer Verhandlungen des Comité Maritime International über die Reform der Haager Regeln, in: Die

Stockholmer Konferenz des Comité Maritime International (vom 9. bis 15. Juni 1963) (zusammengestellt vom DVIS), Hamburg 1964, p. 5

von Caemmerer: Ernst von Caemmerer, Das Problem des Kausalzusammenhangs im Privatrecht, Freiburg 1956

Calkins: G. Nathan Calkins, Grand Canyon, Warsaw and the Hague Protocol, (1956) 23 J. Air L. & Com. 253

Can: Mertol Can, Türk Hukukunda ve Milletlerarası Hukukta Deniz Yolu ile Yolcu Taşıma Sözleşmesi, Ankara 2001

Carriage of Goods: David Yates (Editor-in-Chief), Contracts for the Carriage of Goods – by Land, Sea and Air, London 1993

Carver: Carver on Bills of Lading, 2nd Ed. (by GUENTER TREITEL/F.M.B. REYNOLDS), London 2005

Chalmers: Chalmers' Marine Insurance Act 1906, 10th Ed. (by E. R. HARDY IVAMY), London 1993

Cheka: C. N. Cheka, Conduct Barring Limitation, (1987) 18 J. Mar. L. & Com. 487

Chen: Liang Chen, To Limit Globally Sea Carriers' Liability under Bills of Lading towards Cargo Interests, ETL 2002, 167

Chen, Limitation: Xia Chen, Limitation of Liability for Maritime Claims, London 2001

Cheng: Bin Cheng, Wilful Misconduct: From Warsaw to the Hague and from Brussels to Paris, (1977) 2 Annals Air & Space 55

Christodoulou: Dimitrios Christodoulou, The International Safety Management (ISM) Code and the Rule of Attribution in Corporate Criminal Responsibility under English Law, Athens 2000

Clarke: Malcolm A. Clarke, The Law of Insurance Contracts, 6th Ed., London 2009

Clarke, Carriage by Air: Malcolm A. Clarke, Contracts of Carriage by Air, London 2002

Clarke, CIM: Malcolm A. Clarke, Article 36 of the New CIM, in: Transport – Wirtschaft – Recht: Gedächtnisschrift für Johann Georg Helm, Berlin 2001, p. 27

Clarke, CMR: Malcolm A. Clarke, International Carriage of Goods by Road: CMR, 5th Ed., London 2009

Clarke, Road Transport: Malcolm A. Clarke, Road Transport, [2006] J.B.L. 429

Clarke, Transport in Europe: Malcolm A. Clarke, The Transport of Goods in Europe: Patterns and Problems of Uniform Law, [1999] LMCLQ 36

Clarke/Yates: Malcolm A. Clarke/David Yates, Contracts of Carriage by Land and Air, 2nd Ed., London 2008

Clerk & Lindsell: Clerk & Lindsell on Torts, 20th Ed., London 2010

Cleton: Robert Cleton, Limitation of Liability for Maritime Claims, in: Essays on International & Comparative Law in Honour of Judge Erades: E Radice Arbor, The Hague 1983, p. 14

CMI Colloquium, Hamburg Rules: Report of Group 3: The Limits of Liability and the Loss of the Right to Limit (Group Chairman: F. Berlingieri), in: CMI Colloquium on the Hamburg Rules (Vienna, 8th – 10th January, 1979), p. 48

Coghlin: Terence Coghlin, The Convention on Limitation of Liability for Maritime Claims 1976, in: Samir Mankabady (Editor), The International Maritime Organisation, London 1984, p. 234

Coghlin/et al.: Terence Coghlin/*et al.*, Time Charters, 6th Ed., London 2008

Colinvaux: Colinvaux's Law of Insurance, 8th Ed. (by ROBERT MERKIN), London 2006

Cooke/et al.: Julian Cooke and *et al.*, Voyage Charters, 3rd Ed., London 2007

Card, Cross & Jones: Card, Cross and Jones, Criminal Law, 18th Ed., Oxford 2008

Cross & Tapper: Cross & Tapper on Evidence, 11th Ed., Oxford 2007

Czerwenka, Athener Übereinkommen: G. Beate Czerwenka, Das Protokoll von 2002 zum Athener Übereinkommen von 1974 über die Beförderung von Reisenden und ihrem Gepäck auf See, RRa 2003, 158

Czerwenka, CMNI: G. Beate Czerwenka, Das Budapester Übereinkommen über den Vertrag über die Güterbeförderung in der Binnenschiffahrt (CMNI), TranspR 2001, 277

Çağa: Tahir Çağa, Hava Taşıyıcısının Sınırlı ve Sınırsız Mesuliyetine Dair, Ticaret Hukuku ve Yargıtay Kararları Sempozyumu V (Ankara, 25-26 Mart 1988), Ankara 1989, pp. 173-211 (discussions: pp. 212-217)

Çağa, Batider: Tahir Çağa, Enternasyonal Deniz Hususi Hukukunda Yeni Bazı Gelişmeler, Batider 1977/2, p. 289

Çağa/Kender: Tahir Çağa/Rayegân Kender, Deniz Ticareti Hukuku, c. 2: Navlun Sözleşmesi, 8. bası, İstanbul 2006

Damar, Compulsory Insurance: Duygu Damar, Compulsory Insurance in International Maritime Conventions, (2009) 15 JIML 151

Davies, World's Airlines: R.E.G. Davies, A History of the World's Airlines, London 1964

Davies/Dickey: Martin Davies/Anthony Dickey, Shipping Law, 3ʳᵈ Ed., Sydney 2004

Demirbaş: Timur Demirbaş, Ceza Hukuku Genel Hükümler, 5. bası, Ankara 2007

Dettling-Ott: Regula Dettling-Ott, Internationales und schweizerisches Lufttransportrecht, Zürich 1993

Diamond: Anthony Diamond, The Hague-Visby Rules, [1978] LMCLQ 225

Diplock: Lord Diplock, Conventions and Morals – Limitation Clauses in International Maritime Conventions, (1969-1970) 1 J. Mar. L. & Com. 525

Dobbs: Dan B. Dobbs, The Law of Torts, Minnesota 2000

Dockray: Martin Dockray, Carriage of Goods by Sea, 3ʳᵈ Ed., London 2004

Documents, Hague: International Conference on Private Air Law (The Hague, September 1955), V. II: Documents, Montreal 1956

Donovan: James J. Donovan, The Origins and Development of Limitation of Shipowners' Liability, (1978-1979) 53 Tul. L. Rev. 999

Dönmezer: Sulhi Dönmezer, Genel Ceza Hukuku Dersleri, İstanbul 2003

Döring: Hermann Döring, Revision des Warschauer Abkommens: Grundsätzliche Fragen, ALR 1935, 1

Drion: H. Drion, Limitation of Liabilities in International Air Law, The Hague 1954

Driscoll/Larsen: William Driscoll/Paul B. Larsen, The Convention on International Multimodal Transport of Goods, (1982-1983) 57 Tul. L. Rev. 193

Ebenroth/Boujong/Joost/Strohn: C. Thomas Ebenroth/Karlheinz Boujong/Detlev Joost/Lutz Strohn, Handelsgesetzbuch, 2. Aufl., Bd. 2: §§ 343-475 h, Transportrecht, Bank- und Börsenrecht, München 2009

Eilenberger-Czwalinna: Maren Eilenberger-Czwalinna, Haftung des Verfrachters nach dem Zweiten Seerechtsänderungsgesetz, Hamburg 1998 (Diss. Hamburg)

Erdil: Engin Erdil, CMR Konvansiyonu Şerhi, İstanbul 2007

Eren: Fikret Eren, Borçlar Hukuku: Genel Hükümler, 12. bası, İstanbul 2010

Erman: Erman, Bürgerliches Gesetzbuch (Hrsg. HARM PETER WESTERMANN), 12. Aufl., Köln 2008

Eyer: Walter W. Eyer, Shipowners' Limitation of Liability – New Directions for an Old Doctrine, (1963-1964) 16 Stan. L. Rev. 370

Fremuth, Haftungsbegrenzungen: Fritz Fremuth, Haftungsbegrenzungen und deren Durchbrechung im allgemeinen deutschen Frachtrecht und nach der CMR, TranspR 2004, 99

Fremuth, Schwere Schuld: Fritz Fremuth, „Schwere Schuld" gem. Art. 29 CMR – Kritische Bestandsaufnahme der Rechtsprechung unter besonderer Berücksichtigung der Beweislast, in: Vertrieb, Versicherung, Transport: Karl-Heinz Thume zum 70. Geburtstag, Frankfurt a.M. 2008, p. 161

Fremuth/Thume: Fritz Fremuth/Karl-Heinz Thume, Kommentar zum Transportrecht, Heidelberg 2000

Gaskell, Athens 1974: Nicholas Gaskell, The Athens Convention 1974, NLJ 1987, 285 (Part I), 322 (Part II), 383 (Part III)

Gaskell, Hamburg Rules: Nicholas Gaskell, Damages, Delay and Limitation of Liability under the Hamburg Rules 1978, in: The Hamburg Rules: A Choice for the EEC? (International Colloquium held on 18 and 19 November 1993), Antwerp 1994

Gaskell, New Limits: Nicholas Gaskell, New Limits for Passengers and Others in the United Kingdom, [1998] LMCLQ 312

Gaskell, Breaking Limits: Nicholas Gaskell, Limitation: Introduction of Limitation of Liability, Breaking Limits, Paper presented to the 35th Maritime Law Short Course – Institute of Maritime Law (18th August – 5th September 2008)

Gaskell/Asariotis/Baatz: Nicholas Gaskell/Regina Asariotis/Yvonne Baatz, Bills of Lading: Law and Contracts, London 2000

Gauci, Limitation: Gotthard Gauci, Limitation of Liability in Maritime Law: an Anachronism?, Mar. Policy 19 (1995) No. 1, p. 65

Gauci, Oil Pollution: Gotthard Gauci, Oil Pollution at Sea, Chichester 1997

Gençtürk: Muharrem Gençtürk, Uluslararası Eşya Taşıma Hukuku (Gecikmeden Doğan Sorumluluk), İstanbul 2006

Georgiades: Euthymène Georgiades, Wie lässt sich gegenwärtig die Haftungsbeschränkung des Luftfrachtführers rechtfertigen?, ZLW 1970, 43

Gerber: Rudolf Gerber, Die Revision des Warschauer Abkommens, Zürich 1957 (Diss. Zürich)

Giefers: Patrick Giefers, Beweislast und Beweisführung bei der Haftung des Frachtführers nach der CMR, Frankfurt a.M. 1997 (Diss. Köln)

Giemulla: Elmar Giemulla, Lastenverteilung nach dem Warschauer Abkommen und Beweislastverteilung, in: Luftverkehrsrecht im Wandel: Festschrift für Werner Guldimann, Neuwied 1997, p. 115

Giemulla/Schmid: Elmar Giemulla/Ronald Schmid/*et al.*, Frankfurter Kommentar zum Luftverkehrsrecht, Bd. 4: Warschauer Abkommen, Neuwied 2004

Giemulla/Schmid, Montrealer Übereinkommen: Elmar Giemulla/Ronald Schmid/ *et al.*, Frankfurter Kommentar zum Luftverkehrsrecht, Bd. 3: Montrealer Übereinkommen, Neuwied 2004

Girvin: Stephen Girvin, Carriage of Goods by Sea, Oxford 2007

Glöckner: Herbert Glöckner, Leitfaden zur CMR, 7. Aufl., Berlin 1991

Glöckner, TranspR: Herbert Glöckner, Die Haftungsbeschränkungen und die Versicherung nach den Art. 3, 23-29 CMR, TranspR 1988, 327

Goedhuis: Daniel Goedhuis, National Airlegislations and the Warsaw Convention, The Hague 1937

Gold/Chircop/Kindred: Edgar Gold/Aldo Chircop/Hugh Kindred, Maritime Law, Toronto 2003

Goldhirsch: Lawrence B. Goldhirsch, The Warsaw Convention Annoted, 2nd Ed., The Hague 2000

Goldschmidt: Werner Goldschmidt, Die Schuld im Straf- und Zivilrecht, Breslau 1934

Gower & Davies: Gower and Davies' Principles of Modern Company Law, 8th Ed. (by PAUL L. DAVIES), London 2008

Göknil: Mazhar Nedim Göknil, Hava Hukuku, İstanbul 1951

Gran: Dieter Gran, Beweisführung und Einlassungsobliegenheit bei qualifiziertem Verschulden des Luftfrachtführers nach der Haftungsordnung des Warschauer Abkommens, in: Festschrift für Henning Piper, München 1996, p. 847

Griggs, Limitation: Patrick Griggs, Limitation of Liability for Maritime Claims: the Search for International Uniformity, [1997] LMCLQ 369

Griggs/Williams/Farr: Patrick Griggs/Richard Williams/Jeremy Farr, Limitation of Liability for Maritime Claims, 4th Ed., London 2005

Grime, Athens Convention: Robert Grime, The Carriage of Passengers and the Athens Convention in the United Kingdom, in: Samir Mankabady (Editor), The International Maritime Organisation, London 1984, p. 252

Grime, Loss of the Right: Robert Grime, The Loss of the Right to Limit, in: The Limitation of Shipowners' Liability: the New Law, London 1986, p. 102

Grime, 1976 Limitation Convention: R. P. Grime, Implementation and 1976 Limitation Convention, Mar. Policy 12 (1988) No. 3, p. 306

Grönfors: Kurt Grönfors, Die Harmonisierung des Transportrechts und die Hamburger Regeln, RablesZ 42 (1978), 696

Guerreri: Giuseppe Guerreri, American Jurisprudence on the Warsaw Convention, Montreal 1960

Guerreri, Wilful Misconduct: Giuseppe Guerreri, Wilful Misconduct in the Warsaw Convention: A Stumbling Block?, (1959-1960) 6 McGill L. J. 267

Guldimann: Werner Guldimann, Internationales Lufttransportrecht, Zürich 1965

Guldimann, Auslegung: Werner Guldimann, Zur Auslegung von Artikel 25 des Warschauer Abkommens, ZLW 1955, 270

Gürses: Özlem Gürses, Uluslararası Güvenli Yönetim Kodu'nun (ISM Code) Taşıyan ve Donatanın Sorumluluğuna Etkileri, İstanbul 2005

Güven: Osman Sabri Güven, Kusur Kavramı ve Çeşitleri, I: YD 1981, p. 570, II: YD 1982, p. 154

Haak: Krijn F. Haak, Haftung bei der Personenbeförderung: Rechtliche Entwicklungen im Bereich der internationalen Personenbeförderung, TranspR 2009, 162

Hacksteiner: Theresia K. Hacksteiner, Implementation des Budapester Übereinkommens über den Vertrag für die Güterbeförderung in der Binnenschifffahrt (CMNI), TranspR 2009, 145

Haddon-Cave: Charles Haddon-Cave, Limitation against Passenger Claims: Medieval, Unbreakable and Unconscionable, CMI Yearbook 2001, p. 234

Haenni: Joseph Haenni, International Encyclopedia of Comparative Law, V. XII: Law of Transport, Ch. 2: Carriage by Rail, Tübingen 1972

Häußer: Markus Häußer, Subunternehmer beim Seetransport: Haftungsfragen nach deutschem und englischem Recht im Spiegel der UNCITRAL draft convention on the carriage of goods [wholly or partly][by sea], Berlin 2006 (Diss. Mannheim)

Hart/Honoré: Herbert Lionel Adolphus Hart/ Tony Honoré, Causation in the Law, 2nd Ed., Oxford 1985

Heerey: Peter Heerey, Limitation of Maritime Claims, (1994) 10 MLAANZ Journal 1

Hellawell: Robert Hellawell, Allocation of Risks Between Cargo Owner and Carrier, (1979) 27 Am. J. Comp. L. 357

Helm: Johann Georg Helm, in: Großkommentar HGB, 4. Aufl. (Hrsg. von CANARIS/SCHILLING/ULMER), Bd. 7, Teilband 2, Anhang VI nach § 452: CMR, Berlin 2002

Herber: Rolf Herber, Seehandelsrecht, Berlin 1999

Herber, Anmerkung: Rolf Herber, Anmerkung zur Entscheidung des Griechischen Oberster Gerichtshof Athen (Urteil Nr. 2010/1990), TranspR 1992, 175

Herber, Athener Übereinkommen: Rolf Herber, Das Athener Übereinkommen vom 13. Dezember 1974 über die Beförderung von Reisenden und ihrem Gepäck auf See, ZIEV 1977, 2

Herber, Haftungsrecht: Rolf Herber, Das neue Haftungsrecht der Schiffahrt, Hamburg 1989

Herber, Überblick: Rolf Herber, Haftungsbegrenzungen und deren Durchbrechung im deutschen und internationalen Transportrecht: Überblick über die gesetzlichen Regelungen in Deutschland und in internationalen Übereinkommen, TranspR 2004, 93

Herber, VN-Übereinkommen: Rolf Herber, Einführung in das VN-Übereinkommen über den internationalen multimodalen Gütertransport, TranspR 1981, 37

Herber/Piper: Rolf Herber/Henning Piper, CMR: Internationales Straßentransportrecht, München 1996

Herber/Schmuck: Rolf Herber/Thomas Schmuck, Beweislast des Transportunternehmers für grobe Fahrlässigkeit, VersR 1991, 1209

Hickey: William J. Hickey Jr., Breaking the Limit-Liability for Wilful Misconduct under the Guatemala Protocol, (1976) 42 J. Air L. & Com. 603

Hill: Christopher Hill, Maritime Law, 6th Ed., London 2003

Hill & Messent: Doland J. Hill & Andrew Messent, CMR: Contracts for the International Carriage of Goods by Road, 3rd Ed., London 2000

Hodges, ISM Code: Susan Hodges, The Legal Implications of the ISM Code: Insurance and Limitation of Liability, (2000) 7 IJIL 39

Hodges/Hill: Susan Hodges/Christopher Hill, Principles of Maritime Law, London 2001

Hoffmann: Frank Hoffmann, Der Anscheinsbeweis und die Lehre von der res ipsa loquitur, Göttingen 1985 (Diss. Göttingen)

Hofmann/Grabherr: Max Hofmann/Edwin Grabherr, Luftverkehrsgesetz, München 2006

Honka: Hannu Honka, The Standard of the Vessel and the ISM Code, in: Johan *Schelin* (Editor), Modern Law of Charterparties, Stockholm 2003, p. 105

Huybrechts: Marc Huybrechts, Limitation of Liability and of Actions, [2002] LMCLQ 370

Ilse: Jan Hinnerk Ilse, Haftung des Seegüterbeförderers und Durchbrechung von Haftungsbeschränkungen bei qualifiziertem eigenem und Gehilfenverschulden, Hamburg 2005 (Diss. Hamburg)

Ivamy: E. R. Hardy Ivamy, Marine Insurance, 4th Ed., London 1985

Jacobson: Keith Jacobson, A Global Perspective on Airline Tort Liability: the Effect of Piamba Cortes v. American Airlines on American Airline Litigation, (2000-2001) 13 DePaul Bus. L. J. 273

Jefferies: Trevor R. Jefferies, Limiting Liability for Human Error: Is American Jurisprudence Steering U.S. Shipowners into the Rocks?, (1995) 7 U.S.F. Mar. L.J. 271

Jesser: Helga Jesser, Art. 29 CMR – Welches Verschulden steht dem Vorsatz gleich?, TranspR 1997, 169

Kadletz: Andreas Kadletz, Haftung und Versicherung im internationalen Lufttransportrecht, Frankfurt a.m. 1998 (Diss. Heidelberg)

Kahn-Freund: Otto Kahn-Freund, The Law of Carriage by Inland Transport, 4th Ed., London 1965

Kaner: İnci (Deniz) Kaner, Varşova Konvansiyonunda Taşıyıcının Sorumluluğu, İÜHFM 1984/1-4, p. 423

Karahasan: Mustafa Reşit Karahasan, Türk Borçlar Hukuku: Genel Hükümler, c. 1, İstanbul 2003

Kender, Atina Konvansiyonu: Rayegân Kender, Denizyolu ile Yolcu ve Bagaj Taşımasına Dair 1974 Atina Konvansiyonu ve Sigorta, in: Sorumluluk ve Sigorta Hukuku Bakımından İkinci Taşımacılık Sempozyumu (İstanbul, 24-25 Ocak 1985), Ankara 1985, p. 105

Keser Berber: Leyla Keser Berber, İlk Görünüş İspatı, (*prima facie* Beweis), in: Prof. Dr. Mahmut Tevfik Birsel'e Armağan, İzmir 2001, p. 231

Kılıçoğlu: Ahmet M. Kılıçoğlu, Borçlar Hukuku: Genel Hükümler, 13. bası, Ankara 2010

Kırman: Ahmet Kırman, Hava Yolu ile Yapılan Uluslararası Yolcu Taşımalarında Taşıyıcının Sorumluluğu, Ankara 1990

Kienzle: Jost Kienzle, Die Haftung des Carrier und des Actual Carrier nach den Hamburg-Regeln, Berlin 1993

Kierr: Raymond H. Kierr, The Effect of Direct Action Statutes on P & I Insurance, on Various Other Insurances of Maritime Liabilities, and on Limitation of Shipowners' Liability, (1968-1969) 43 Tul. L. Rev. 638

Kilbride: D.A. Kilbride, Six Decades of Insuring Liability under Warsaw, (1989) 14 AL 183

Killingbeck: Serge Killingbeck, Limitation of Liability for Maritime Claims and its Place in the Past, Present and Future – How Can it Survive?, (1999) 3 SCULR 1

Koffka/Bodenstein: Otto Koffka/Hans Georg Bodenstein, Luftverkehrsgesetz und Warschauer Abkommen, Berlin 1937

Koller: Ingo Koller, Transportrecht, 7. Aufl., München 2010

Koller, Aufklärung: Ingo Koller, Zur Aufklärung über die Schadensentstehung im Straßentransportrecht – Zugleich ein Beitrag zur Beweislast im Rahmen des Art. 29 CMR –, VersR 1990, 553

Koller, Leichtfertigkeit: Ingo Koller, Die Leichtfertigkeit im deutschen Transportrecht, VersR 2004, 1346

Koller, Unbeschränkte Haftung: Ingo Koller, Unbeschränkte Haftung des Luftbeförderers nach dem Montrealer Übereinkommen 1999?, TranspR 2005, 177

Koning: Ingrid Koning, Liability in Air Carriage: Carriage of Cargo under the Warsaw and Montreal Conventions, (2008) 4-5 Air & SL 318

Korioth: Werner Korioth, Haftung und Haftungsausschlüsse des Binnenschiffsfrachtführers im künftigen internationalen Binnenschiffahrtsfrachtrecht, in: Transport- und Vertriebsrecht 2000: Festgabe für Professor Dr. Rolf Herber, Neuwied 1999, p. 293

Kötz: Hein Kötz, Haftung für besondere Gefahr, AcP 170 (1970), 1

Krause & Krause: Charles F. Krause & Kent C. Krause, Aviation Tort and Regulatory Law, 2nd Ed., V. I, Eagan 2002

Kreindler: Lee S. Kreindler, Aviation Accident Law, V. 1, New York 2006

Kröger: Martin Kröger, Die Passagierbeförderung auf See, Berlin 2009 (Diss. Hamburg)

Kröger, Passengers: Bernd Kröger, Passengers Carried by Sea – Should They Be Granted the Same Rights as Airline Passengers?, CMI Yearbook 2001, p. 244

Kuhn: Robert Kuhn, Die Haftung für Schäden an Frachtgütern, Gepäck und Luftpostsendungen nach dem Warschauer Haftungssystem und den §§ 44-52 LuftVG, Köln 1987 (Diss. Köln)

Kühl: Kristian Kühl, Strafgesetzbuch Kommentar, 26., neu bearbeitete Auflage, München 2007

Lannan: Kate Lannan, Behind the Numbers: the Limitation on Carrier Liability in the Rotterdam Rules, ULR 2009, 901

Lacey: Frederick B. Lacey, Recent Developments in the Warsaw Convention, (1967) 33 J. Air L. & Com. 385

Larenz: Karl Larenz, Lehrbuch des Schuldrechts, Erster Bd.: Allgemeiner Teil, 14. Aufl., München 1987

Larsen/Sweeney/Gillick: Paul B. Larsen/Joseph C. Sweeney/John E Gillick, Aviation Law: Cases, Laws, and Related Sources, New York 2006

Leigh: Leonard Herschel Leigh, The Alter Ego of a Company, (1965) 28 MLR 584

LeipKommStGB: Leipziger Kommentar zum Strafgesetzbuch, 12., neu bearbeitete Auflage, Erster Bd.: Einleitung, §§ 1 bis 31, Berlin 2007

Liesecke: Rudolf Liesecke, Die neuere internationale Rechtsprechung zum Luftfrachtrecht des Warschauer Abkommens von 1929 nebst Haager Protokoll von 1955 (II), MDR 1968, 93

Loewe: Roland Loewe, Commentary on the Convention of 19 May 1956 on the Contract for the International Carriage of Goods by Road (CMR), ETL 1976, 311

Looks: Volker Looks, Rechtliche Auswirkungen des ISM Code (Vortrag gehalten vor dem DVIS am 25. Januar 2000), Hamburg 2000

Looks/Kraft: Volker Looks/Holger Kraft, Die zivilrechtlichen Auswirkungen des ISM Code, TranspR 1998, 221

Lopuski: Jan Lopuski, Liability for Damage in Maritime Shipping under the Aspect of Risk Allocation, (1979-1980) 10 Pol. Y.B. Int'l L.177

Lüddeke/Johnson: Christof Lüddeke/Andrew Johnson, The Hamburg Rules: From Hague to Hamburg via Visby, 2nd Ed., London 1995

Makins: Brian Makins, The Hamburg Rules: A Casualty?, 1994 Dir. Mar. 637

Mandaraka-Sheppard: Aleka Mandaraka-Sheppard, Modern Maritime Law, 2nd Ed., London 2007

Mankiewicz: René H. Mankiewicz, The Liability Regime of the International Air Carrier, London 1981

Mankiewicz, Hague Protocol: René H. Mankiewicz, Hague Protocol to Amend the Warsaw Convention, (1956) 5 Am. J. Comp. L. 78

Mankowski, Transportverträge: Peter Mankowski, Transportverträge, in: C. Reithmann/D. Martiny (Hrsg.), Internationales Vertragsrecht, 7. Aufl., Köln 2010

Markesinis and Deakin: Markesinis and Deakin's Tort Law, 6th Ed. (by SIMON DEAKIN, ANGUS JOHNSTON, BASIL MARKESINIS), Oxford 2008

Marsden: Marsden on Collisions at Sea (Editors: SIMON GAULT, STEVEN J. HAZELWOOD, ANDREW TETTENBORN), 13th Ed., London 2003

Marsilius: Georg Marsilius, Die Gleichstellung von Vorsatz und Fahrlässigkeit und die Haftungsbeschränkungen im Verkehrsrecht, ZIEV 1967, 295

Matte: Nicolas Mateesco Matte, International Encyclopedia of Comparative Law, V. XII: Law of Transport, Ch. 6: International Air Transport, Tübingen 1982

Matte, ETL: Nicolas Mateesco Matte, From Warsaw to Montreal, with Stop-Over at The Hague, ETL 1967, 877

Maurach/Zipf: Reinhart Maurach/Heinz Zipf, Strafrecht, Allgemeiner Teil, Teilband 1: Grundlehren des Strafrechts und Aufbau der Straftat, 8. Aufl., Heidelberg 1992

Mayson, French & Ryan: Mayson, French & Ryan on Company Law, 27th Ed., Oxford 2010

Mbiah: Kofi Mbiah, The Convention on Contracts for the International Carriage of Goods Wholly or Partly by Sea: the Liability and Limitation of Liability Regime, CMI Yearbook 2007-2008, p. 287

McGilchrist: Neil R. McGilchrist, Wilful Misconduct and the Warsaw Convention, [1977] LMCLQ 539

McGilchrist, Limitation: Neil R. McGilchrist, Limitation of Liability – at Sea and in the Air, [1975] LMCLQ 256

McNair: Lord McNair, The Law of the Air, 3rd Ed. (by MICHAEL R. E. KERR and ANTHONY H. M. EVANS), London 1964

Merkin: Robert Merkin, Marine Insurance Legislation, 4th Ed., London 2010

Meyer: Alex Meyer, Luftrecht in Fünf Jahrzehnten: Ausgewählte Schriften, Köln 1961

Meyer I: Alex Meyer, Internationale Luftfahrtabkommen, Bd. I, Köln & Berlin 1953

Milde: Michael Milde, The Problems of Liabilities in International Carriage by Air, Praha 1963

Miller: Georgette Miller, Liability in International Air Transport, Deventer 1977

Minutes, Hague: International Conference on Private Air Law (The Hague, September 1955), V. I: Minutes, Montreal 1956

Modjaz: Mohammed Ebrahim Modjaz, Die unbeschränkte Haftung des Beförderers bei schwerem Verschulden im internationalen Luft- und Strassentransport, Frankfurt a.M. 1967 (Diss. Frankfurt a.M.)

Moore: Micheal S. Moore, Causation and Responsibility, Oxford 2009

de la Motte: Thomas de la Motte, Die Auswirkungen des ISM-Codes auf das Seehaftungsrecht, Hamburg 1998 (Diss. Hamburg)

Mustill: Lord Mustill, Ships Are Different – or Are They?, [1993] LMCLQ 490

Mutz: Gerfried Mutz, Die Haftung der Eisenbahn für Tötung und Verletzung von Reisenden im internationalen Eisenbahnpersonenverkehr, Wien 1977

Mühlbauer: Thomas Mühlbauer, Der Haftungsanspruch wegen Verlustes von Reisegepäck und die Durchbrechung von Haftungslimits im Luftverkehr, TranspR 2003, 185

Müller, Inland Navigation: Walter Müller, International Encyclopedia of Comparative Law, V. XII: Law of Transport, Ch. 5: Inland Navigation, Tübingen 2003

Müller-Feldhammer: Ralf Müller-Feldhammer, Die Haftung des Unternehmers beim multimodalen Transport für Güterschäden und Güterverluste aus dem Beförderungsvertrag, Frankfurt a.m. 1996 (Diss. Leipzig)

Müller-Rostin: Wolf Müller-Rostin, Die Haftung des Luftfrachtführers bei der Beförderung von Luftfracht, TranspR 1989, 121

Müller-Rostin, Montrealer Übereinkommen: Wolf Müller-Rostin, Neuregelungen im internationalen Luftfrachtverkehr: Montrealer Protokoll Nr. 4 und Montrealer Übereinkommen, TranspR 2000, 234

Müller-Rostin, Unverbrüchlichkeit: Wolf Müller-Rostin, Die Unverbrüchlichkeit der Haftungsgrenzen bei Frachtschäden im Montrealer Protokoll Nr. 4 und im Montrealer Übereinkommen von 1999, in: Transport – Wirtschaft – Recht: Gedächtnisschrift für Johann Georg Helm, Berlin 2001, p. 227

MünchKommBGB: Münchener Kommentar zum Bürgerlichen Gesetzbuch, 5. Aufl. München 2003-2007

MünchKommHGB 1997: Münchener Kommentar zum Handelsgesetzbuch, Bd. 7: Viertes Buch: Handelsgeschäfte §§ 407-457 Transportrecht, München 1997

MünchKommHGB 2009: Münchener Kommentar zum Handelsgesetzbuch, Bd. 7: Viertes Buch: Handelsgeschäfte §§ 407-457 Transportrecht, München 2009

MünchKommZPO: Münchener Kommentar zur Zivilprozessordnung, 3. Aufl., Bd. 1: §§ 1-510c, München 2008

Neumann: Hilmar Neumann, Die unbeschränkte Haftung des Frachtführers nach § 435 HGB, TranspR 2002, 413

Notes: Notes and Comments: Transporting Goods by Air, (1959-1960) 69 Yale LJ 993

Official Records, London Conference: Official Records of the International Conference on the Limitation of Liability for Maritime Claims, 1976, London 1983

Ogg: Terry Ogg, IMO's International Safety Management Code (The ISM Code), (1996) 1 IJOSL 143

Oğuzman/Öz: M. Kemal Oğuzman/Turgut Öz, Borçlar Hukuku, 8. bası, İstanbul 2010

O'May: O'May on Marine Insurance (edited by JULIAN HILL), London 1993

Orr: George W. Orr, The Warsaw Convention, (1945) 31 Va. L. Rev. 423

Özçayır: Z. Oya Özçayır, Liability for Oil Pollution and Collisions, London 1998

Özdemir: Atalay Özdemir, Hava Taşıyıcısının Bagaj ve Yükün Kaybı, Hasarı ve Gecikmesinden Doğan Zararlar Nedeniyle Sorumluluğu, Ankara 1994

Özdemir, Eşya Taşıma: Turkay Özdemir, Uluslararası Eşya Taşıma Hukuku (Zıya ve/veya Hasar Sorumluluğu), İstanbul 2006

Özgenç: İzzet Özgenç, Türk Ceza Hukuku, Genel Hükümler, 3. bası, Ankara 2008

Padfield: Nicola Padfield, Criminal Law, 6th Ed., Oxford 2008

Palandt: Otto Palandt, Bürgerliches Gesetzbuch, 70. Aufl., München 2011

Pamborides: George P. Pamborides, The ISM Code: Potential Legal Implications, (1996) 2 Int.M.L. 56

Pekcanıtez/Atalay/Özekes: Hakan Pekcanıtez/Oğuz Atalay/Muhammet Özekes, Medenî Usûl Hukuku, 9. bası, Ankara 2010

Philipson/et al.: Trevor Philipson and *et al.*, Carriage by Air, London 2001

Pilley/Lorenzon: Richard Pilley/Filippo Lorenzon, International Regulations for Ship Operators, their Verification and Enforcement, in: Southampton on Shipping Law, London 2008, p. 227

Ping-fat: Sze Ping-fat, Carrier's Liability under the Hague, Hague-Visby and Hamburg Rules, The Hague 2002

Pohar: Mihael A. Pohar, Rechtsbeziehungen zwischen Fahrgast und Eisenbahn, Jena 2006

Porat/Stein: Ariel Porat/Alex Stein, Tort Liability under Uncertainty, Oxford 2001

Pöttinger: Franz Josef Pöttinger, Welches Verschulden steht im Rahmen des Art. 29 Abs 1 und 2 CMR dem Vorsatz gleich?, VersR 1986, 518

Prosser and Keeton: Prosser and Keeton on the Law of Torts, 5th Ed., Minnesota 1984

Puttfarken: Hans-Jürgen Puttfarken, Seehandelsrecht, Heidelberg 1997

Rabe: Dieter Rabe, Seehandelsrecht, 4. Aufl., München 2000

Rabe, Vortrag: Dieter Rabe, Das Zweite Seerechtsänderungsgesetz (Vortrag gehalten vor dem DVIS am 24. März 1987), Hamburg 1987

Rabe, TranspR: Dieter Rabe, Haftungsbegrenzungen und Haftungsdurchbrechung im Seerecht, TranspR 2004, 142

Ramming: Klaus Ramming, Von Kelsterbach nach Luanda – die neue PKW-Entscheidung des Bundesgerichtshofs: Anmerkung zu BGH, 18. Juni 2009 – I ZR 140/06, HmbSchRZ 2009, 295

Rein: Alex Rein, International Variations on Concepts of Limitation of Liability, (1978-1979) 53 Tul. L. Rev. 1259

Report on the Mental Element: The Law Commission No. 89, Criminal Law: Report on the Mental Element in Crime, London 1978

Report, Criminal Code: The Law Commission No. 218, Legislating the Criminal Code, Offences against the Person and General Principles, London 1993

Report, Warsaw: Association of the Bar of the City of New York, Committee on Aeronautics, Report on the Warsaw Convention as Amended by the Hague Protocol, (1959) 26 J. Air L. & Com. 255

Richter: Walther Richter, Die Konvention über die Beschränkung der Haftung für Seeforderungen, 1976 (Vortrag gehalten vor der Mitgliederversammlung des DVIS am 17. Februar 1977), Hamburg 1978

Richter-Hannes: Dolly Richter-Hannes, Die Hamburger Regeln 1978 – Neuregelung über die Beförderung zur See, Berlin 1982

Richter-Hannes, Multimodale Güterbeförderung: Dolly Richter-Hannes, Die UN-Konvention über die Internationale Multimodale Güterbeförderung, Wien 1982

Richter-Hannes, Vereinheitlichung: Dolly Richter-Hannes, Möglichkeit und Notwendigkeit der Vereinheitlichung des internationalen Transportrechts, Postdam-Babelsberg 1978

Richter-Hannes/Trotz: Dolly Richter-Hannes/Norbert Trotz, Die Änderung der Haager Regeln durch das Ergänzungsprotokoll von 1968, Rostock 1971

Riese: Otto Riese, Luftrecht, Stuttgart 1949

Risch: Paul Risch, Divergenzen in der Rechtsprechung zum Warschauer Abkommen und die Mittel zur Sicherung der einheitlichen Auslegung des vereinheitlichten Luftprivatrechts, München 1973 (Diss. Saarbrücken)

Røsæg: Erik Røsæg, Maritime Liabilities at the Crossroads, (2007) XXV Annuaire de Droit Maritime et Océanique 293

Rodopoulos: Georges Rodopoulos, Kritische Studie der Reflexwirkungen der Haftpflichtversicherung auf die Haftung, Frankfurt a.M. 1981 (Diss. Hamburg)

Rose: Francis D. Rose, Marine Insurance: Law and Practice, London 2004

Roxin: Claus Roxin, Strafrecht, Allgemeiner Teil, Bd. 1: Grundlagen, der Aufbau, der Verbrechenslehre, 4., vollständig neu bearbeitete Auflage, München 2006

Ruhwedel: Edgar Ruhwedel, Der Luftbeförderungsvertrag, 3. Aufl., Berlin 1998

Ruhwedel, Flugzeugkommandanten: Edgar Ruhwedel, Die Rechtsstellung des Flugzeugkommandanten im zivilen Luftverkehr, Bielefeld 1964

Ruhwedel, Montrealer Übereinkommen: Edgar Ruhwedel, Das Montrealer Übereinkommen zur Vereinheitlichung bestimmter Vorschriften über die Beförderung im internationalen Luftverkehr vom 28.5.1999, TranspR 2001, 189

Ruhwedel, Durchbrechung im Luftrecht: Edgar Ruhwedel, Haftungsbegrenzungen und deren Durchbrechung im Luftrecht, oder: Die absolute Beschränkung der Haftung bei Schäden an Luftfrachtgütern, TranspR 2004, 137

Schmid: Ronald Schmid, Die Arbeitsteiligkeit im modernen Luftverkehr und ihr Einfluß auf die Haftung des Luftfrachtführers (Der Begriff „Leute" im sog. Warschauer Abkommen), Frankfurt a.M. 1983 (Diss. Frankfurt a.M.)

Schmid, Zwei Motoren: Ronald Schmid, Mit nur zwei Motoren über den Atlantik, ZLW 1986, 283

Schmidt: Karsten Schmidt, Verfrachterkonossoment, Reederkonossement und Identity-of-Carrier-Klausel, Heidelberg 1980

Schneider: Laurenz Schneider, Haftung und Haftungsbeschränkung bei Personenschaden im internationalen Lufttransport, Basel 1999 (Diss. Basel)

Schobel: Beatrix Schobel, Die Haftungsbegrenzung des Luftfrachtführers nach dem Warschauer Abkommen, Frankfurt a.M. 1993 (Diss. Erlangen-Nürnberg)

Schoenbaum: Thomas J. Schoenbaum, Admiralty and Maritime Law, 4th Ed., V. I: Ch. 1-10, V. II: Ch. 11-End, Minnesota 2004

Schoner: Dieter Schoner, Art. 25 Hague Protocol – Theft of Bank Notes: German Federal Supreme Court (Bundesgerichtshof), Decision of 16 February 1979, (1981) 6 AL 97

Schoner, Rechtsprechung 1974-1976: Dieter Schoner, Die internationale Rechtsprechung zum Warschauer Abkommen in den Jahren 1974 bis 1976, Teil III, ZLW 1978, 259

Schönke/Schröder: Adolf Schönke/Horst Schröder, Strafgesezbuch Kommentar, 27., neu bearbeitete Auflage, München 2006

Schröder: Christian Schröder, Das Beweisrecht im englischen Zivilverfahren, München 2007

Schubert: Susan Schubert, Die Haftung für Reisende und ihr Gepäck auf Schiffen, Frankfurt a.M. 1981

Scrutton: Scrutton on Charterparties and Bills of Lading, 21st Ed. (by STEWART C. BOYD/STEVEN BERRY/ANDREW S. BURROWS/BERNARD EDER/DAVID FOXTON/ CRISTOPHER F. SMITH), London 2008

Selvig: Erling Selvig, The Hamburg Rules, the Hague Rules and Marine Insurance Practice, (1980-1981) 12 J. Mar. L. & Com. 299

Seven: Vural Seven, Taşıma Hukukunda Taşıyıcının Kusur Derecesine Bağlanan Sonuçlardan Kaynaklanan İspat Sorunları, Medeni Usul ve İcra İflas Hukuku Dergisi 2005/1, 51

Seward: R. C. Seward, The Insurance Viewpoint, in: The Limitation of Shipowners' Liability: the New Law, London 1986, p. 161

Shaw, ISM Code: Richard Shaw, The ISM Code and Limitation of Liability, (1998) 3 IJOSL 169

Shaw/Tsimplis: Richard Shaw/Michael Tsimplis, The Liabilities of the Vessel, in: Southampton on Shipping Law, London 2008, p. 155

Shawcross and Beaumont: Shawcross and Beaumont: Air Law, 4th Ed. by J. David McClean *et al.*, V. I: General Text, London 2006

Sheen: Barry Sheen, Limitation of Liability: The Law Gave and the Lords Have Taken Away, (1987) 18 J. Mar. L. & Com. 473

Silets: H. L. Silets, Something Special in the Air and on the Ground: The Potential for Unlimited Liability of International Air Carriers for Terrorist Attacks under the Warsaw Convention and its Revisions, (1987-1988) 53 J. Air L. & Com. 321

Smith & Hogan: John Smith & Brian Hogan, Criminal Law, 12th Ed. (by DAVID ORMEROD), Oxford 2008

Soyer, Athens Convention: Barış Soyer, Sundry Considerations on the Draft Protocol to the Athens Convention relating to the Carriage of Passengers and Their Luggage by Sea 1974, (2002) 33 J. Mar. L. & Com. 519

Soyer, ISM Code: Barış Soyer, Potential Legal Implications of the ISM Code for Marine Insurance, (1998) 5 IJIL 279

Sözer, Kurallar: Bülent Sözer, Milletlerarası Hava Taşımalarına İlişkin Kurallar ve Uygulanma Şartları, Batider 1977/2, p. 369

Sözer, Taşıyıcının Sorumluluğu: Bülent Sözer, Hava Yolu ile Yapılan Milletlerarası Taşımalarda Yolcunun Ölümü veya Yaralanması Sonucunda Doğan Zararlardan Taşıyıcının Sorumluluğu, Batider 1978/3, p. 765

Sözer, TSHK: Bülent Sözer, Türk Sivil Havacılık Kanunu'nun Hükümlerine Göre Taşıyanın ve İşletenin Sorumluluğu, Batider 1984/4, p. 3

Speiser: Stuart M. Speiser, The Negligence Case: Res Ipsa Loquitur, V. 1, New York 1972

Spera: Kurt Spera, Internationales Eisenbahnfrachtrecht, Wien 1986 (Looseleaf)

Sprague: George C. Sprague, Limitation of Ship Owners' Liability, (1934-1935) 12 N.Y.U.L.Q. Rev. 568

Stachow: Johann Christoph Stachow, Schweres Verschulden und Durchbrechung der beschränkten Haftung in modernen Transportrechtsabkommen, Hamburg 1998 (Diss. Hamburg)

Starck: Joachim Starck, Qualifiziertes Verschulden nach der Transportrechtsreform – Bemerkungen zu Begriff und Geltungsbereich, in: Transport- und Vertriebsrecht 2000: Festgabe für Professor Dr. Rolf Herber, Neuwied 1999, p. 128

Staring: Graydon S. Staring, The Roots and False Aspersions of Shipowner's Limitation of Liability, (2008) 39 J. Mar. L. & Com. 315

Staudinger: J. von Staudingers, Kommentar zum Bürgerlichen Gesetzbuch mit Einführungsgesetz und Nebengesetzen, Berlin 1995-2009

Steel: David Steel, Ships Are Different: the Case for Limitation of Liability, [1995] LMCLQ 77

Stein/Jonas: Friedrich Stein/Martin Jonas, Kommentar zur Zivilprozessordnung, 22. Aufl., Tübingen 2002-2008

Street: Street on Torts, 12ᵗʰ Ed. (by JOHN MURPHY), Oxford 2007

Strock: William C. Strock, Current Legislation and Decisions – Comments: Warsaw Convention – Article 25 – "Wilful Misconduct", (1966) 32 J. Air L. & Com. 291

Sturley: Michael F. Sturley, The History of COGSA and the Hague Rules, (1991) 22 J. Mar. L. & Com. 1

Sturley, UNCITRAL: Michael F. Sturley, The UNCITRAL Carriage of Goods Convention: Changes to Existing Law, CMI Yearbook 2007-2008, p. 254

Sturley/Fujita/van der Ziel: Michael F. Sturley/Tomotaka Fujita/Gertjan van der Ziel, The Rotterdam Rules, London 2010

Sullivan: George R. Sullivan, The Codification of Air Carrier Liability by International Convention, (1936) 7 J. Air L. 1

Sweeney: Joseph C. Sweeney, The Uncitral Draft Convention on Carriage of Goods by Sea, (1975-1976) 7 J. Mar. L. & Com. 327 (Part II), (1976-1977) 8 J. Mar. L. & Com. 167 (Part V)

Tandoğan: Haluk Tandoğan, Türk Mesuliyet Hukuku, Ankara 1961

Taschner: Hans Claudius Taschner, Begrenzung der Gefährdungshaftung durch Haftungshöchstsummen?, in: Peter Schlechtriem (Hrsg.), Zum deutschen und internationalen Schuldrecht: Kolloquium aus Anlaß des 75. Geburtstages von Ernst von Caemmerer, Tübingen 1983, p. 75

Taylor: Nigel P. Taylor, Limitation of Liability of Aircarriers to Aircrash Victims – Has the Warsaw Convention Reached its Retirement Age, 1994 JPIL 113

Taylor, Intention: Greg Taylor, Concepts of Intention in German Criminal Law, (2004) 24 Ox. J. Leg. Stud. 99

Tekil: Fahiman Tekil, Deniz Hukuku, 6. bası, İstanbul 2001

Tekinay/et al.: Selahattin Sulhi Tekinay/S. Akman/H. Burcuoğlu/A. Altop, Borçlar Hukuku: Genel Hükümler, 7. baskı, İstanbul 1993

Tetley: William Tetley, Marine Cargo Claims, 4ᵗʰ Ed., Québec 2008

Tetley, IoC: William Tetley, Whom to Sue – Identity of the Carrier, in: *Liber Amicorum* Lionel Tricot, Antwerpen 1988

Thomas: D. Rhidian Thomas, The Modern Law of Marine Insurance, V. 2, Ch. 7 by JULIAN HILL, London 2002

Thomas, British Concepts: Michael Thomas, British Concepts of Limitation of Liability, (1978-1979) 53 Tul. L. Rev. 1205

Thume, CMR-Kommentar: Karl-Heinz Thume (Hrsg.), Kommentar zur CMR, 2. Aufl., Frankfurt a.m. 2007

Thume, CMR-Frachtführer: Karl-Heinz Thume, Die unbeschränkte Haftung des CMR-Frachtführers, VersR 1993, 930

Thume, Vergleich: Karl-Heinz Thume, Durchbrechung der Haftungsbeschränkungen nach § 435 HGB im internationalen Vergleich, TranspR 2002, 1

Tobolweski: Aleksander Tobolewski, Monetary Limitations of Liability in Air Law, Montreal 1986

Toroslu: Nevzat Toroslu, Ceza Hukuku, Genel Kısım, Ankara 2008

Travaux Préparatoires, Hague-Visby Rules: Comité Maritime International, The Travaux Préparatoires of the Hague Rules and of the Hague – Visby Rules (edited by FRANCESCO BERLINGIERI), Antwerp 1997

Tsimplis, Bunker Pollution: Michael N. Tsimplis, The Bunker Pollution Convention 2001: Completing and Harmonizing the Liability Regime for Oil Pollution from Ships?, [2005] LMCLQ 83

Tsimplis, Marine Pollution: Michael Tsimplis, Marine Pollution from Shipping Activities, in: Southampton on Shipping Law, London 2008, p. 251

Tsimplis, Passenger Claims: M. N. Tsimplis, Liability in respect of Passenger Claims and its Limitation, (2009) 15 JIML 125

Tuma, ETL: Otmar J. Tuma, Art. 29 CMR: Bestandsaufnahme und Ausblick, ETL 1993, 649

Tuma, TranspR: Otmar J. Tuma, Der Verschuldensgrad des Artikel 29 CMR, TranspR 2007, 333

Ülgen: Hüseyin Ülgen, Hava Taşıma Sözleşmesi, Ankara 1987

Ülgener: Fehmi Ülgener, Çarter Sözleşmeleri, c. I: Genel Hükümler, Sefer Çarteri Sözleşmesi, İstanbul 2000

Ülgener, DenizHD: Fehmi Ülgener, Gemi İşletme Müteahhidi, Gemi Yöneteni ve Zaman Çartereri Kavramları, DenizHD 2001-2002/1-4, p. 9

Vlacic: Patrick Vlacic, Monetary Limitations of Liability – For How Long, 2006 Dir. Mar. 438

Waldron: A. J. Waldron, The Hamburg Rules – A Boondoggle for Lawyers, [1991] J.B.L. 305

Warsaw Conference Minutes: Second International Conference on Private Aeronautical Law (October 4-12, 1929, Warsaw) Minutes (translated by ROBERT C. HORNER/DIDIER LEGREZ), New Jersey 1975

Watson: Harold K. Watson, The 1976 IMCO Limitation Convention: A Comparative View, (1977-1978) 15 Hou. L. R. 249

Wieczorek/Schütze: Bernhard Wieczorek/Rolf A. Schütze, Zivilprozessordnung und Nebengesetze, 3. Aufl., Bd. 2: §§ 128 – 541, 1. Teilband: §§ 128 – 252, Berlin 2007

Wigmore, Evidence: Wigmore on Evidence, V. I, 3rd Ed., Boston 1940; V. II (revised by James H. Chadbourn), Boston 1979; V. IX (revised by James H. Chadbourn) Boston 1981

Williams, 1976 Limitation Convention: Richard Williams, What Limitation is There on the Right to Limit Liability under the 1976 Limitation Convention?, (1997) 2 IJOSL 117

Williams/Hepple: Glanville Williams/Bob A. Hepple, Foundations of the Law of Tort, 2nd Ed., London 1984

Wilson: John F. Wilson, Carriage of Goods by Sea, 7th Ed., London 2010

Winfield & Jolowicz: Winfield & Jolowicz on Tort, 17th Ed. (by W. V. H. ROGERS), London 2006

de Wit: Ralph de Wit, Multimodal Transport: Carrier liability and Documentation, London 1995

Yazıcıoğlu: Emine Yazıcıoğlu, Hamburg Kuralları'na Göre Taşıyanın Sorumluluğu – Lahey/Visby Kuralları ile Karşılaştırmalı Olarak –, İstanbul 2000

Yetiş Şamlı: Kübra Yetiş Şamlı, Taşıyıcının/Taşıyanın Sınırlı Sorumluluktan Yararlanma Hakkının Kaybı, İstanbul 2008

Zapp: Michael Zapp, Grobe Fahrlässigkeit und Artikel 29 CMR, TranspR 1994, 142

von Ziegler: Alexander von Ziegler, Schadenersatz im internationalen Seefrachtrecht, Baden-Baden 1990

Zöller: Richard Zöller, Zivilprozessordnung, 28. Aufl., Köln 2010

About the International Max Planck Research School for Maritime Affairs at the University of Hamburg

The International Max Planck Research School for Maritime Affairs at the University of Hamburg was established by the Max Planck Society for the Advancement of Science, in co-operation with the Max Planck Institute for Foreign Private Law and Private International Law (Hamburg), the Max Planck Institute for Comparative Foreign Public Law and International Law (Heidelberg), the Max Planck Institute for Meteorology (Hamburg) and the University of Hamburg. The School's research is focused on the legal, economic, and geophysical aspects of the use, protection, and organization of the oceans. Its researchers work in the fields of law, economics, and natural sciences. The School provides extensive research capacities as well as its own teaching curriculum. Currently, the School has 19 Directors who determine the general work of the School, act as supervisors for dissertations, elect applicants for the School's PhD-grants, and are the editors of this book series:

Prof. Dr. Dr. h.c. Jürgen Basedow is Director of the Max Planck Institute for Foreign Private Law and Private International Law; *Prof. Dr. Dr. h.c. Peter Ehlers* is the Director ret. of the German Federal Maritime and Hydrographic Agency; *Prof. Dr. Dr. h.c. Hartmut Graßl* is Director emeritus of the Max Planck Institute for Meteorology; Prof. *Florian Jeßberger* is Head of the International and Comparative Criminal Law Division at the University of Hamburg; *Prof. Dr. Lars Kaleschke* is Junior Professor at the Institute of Oceanography of the University of Hamburg; *Prof. Dr. Hans-Joachim Koch* is Managing Director of the Seminar of Environmental Law at the University of Hamburg; Prof. *Robert Koch* is Director of the Institute of Insurance Law at the University of Hamburg; *Prof. Dr. Doris König* is Professor at the Bucerius Law School; *Prof. Dr. Rainer Lagoni* is Director emeritus of the Institute of Maritime Law and the Law of the Sea at the University of Hamburg; *PD Dr. Gerhard Lammel* is Senior Scientist at the Max Planck Institute for Meteorology; *Prof. Dr. Ulrich Magnus* is Managing Director of the Seminar of Foreign Law and Private International Law at the University of Hamburg; *Prof. Dr. Peter Mankowski* is Director of the Seminar of Foreign and Private International Law at the University of Hamburg; Prof. *Stefan Oeter* is Managing Director of the Institute for International Affairs at the University of Hamburg; *Prof. Dr. Marian Paschke* is Managing Director of the Institute of Maritime Law and the Law of the Sea at the University of Hamburg; *PD Dr. Thomas Pohlmann* is Senior Scientist at the Centre for Marine and Climate Research and Member of the Institute of Oceanography at the University of Hamburg; *Dr. Uwe Schneider* is Assistant Professor at the Research Unit Sustainability and Global Change of the University of Hamburg; *Prof. Dr. Jürgen Sündermann* is Director emeritus of the Centre for Marine and Climate Research at the University of Hamburg; *Prof. Dr. Rüdiger Wolfrum* is Director at the Max Planck Institute for Comparative Foreign Public Law and International Law and a judge at the International Tribunal for the Law of the Sea; *Prof. Dr. Wilfried Zahel* is Professor emeritus at the Centre for Marine and Climate Research of the University of Hamburg.

At present, *Prof. Dr. Dr. h.c. Jürgen Basedow* and *Prof. Dr. Ulrich Magnus* serve as speakers of the Research School.